MARTHA GRAHAM

MARTHA GRAHAM

When Dance Became Modern

A LIFE

NEIL BALDWIN

ALFRED A. KNOPF | NEW YORK | 2022

THIS IS A BORZOI BOOK
PUBLISHED BY ALFRED A. KNOPF

www.aaknopf.com

Knopf, Borzoi Books, and the colophon
are registered trademarks of Penguin Random House LLC.

Page 553 constitutes an extension of this copyright page.

Library of Congress Cataloging-in-Publication Data
Names: Baldwin, Neil, [date] author.
Title: Martha Graham : when dance became modern : a life / Neil Baldwin.
Description: First edition. | New York : Alfred A. Knopf, 2022. | Includes bibliographical
references and index.
Identifiers: LCCN 2021047232 | ISBN 9780385352321 (hardcover) |
ISBN 9780385352338 (ebook)
Subjects: LCSH: Graham, Martha | Dancers—United States—Biography. |
Choreographers—United States—Biography. | Modern dance.
Classification: LCC GV1785.G7 B35 2022 | DDC 792.802/8092 [B]—dc23
LC record available at https://lccn.loc.gov/2021047232

Jacket photograph of Martha Graham by Edward Jean Steichen, 1931 © 2022
The Estate of Edward Steichen / Artists Rights Society (ARS), New York. Print:
National Portrait Gallery, Smithsonian Institution
Jacket design by Janet Hansen

Manufactured in the United States of America
First Edition

This book is for Levi, Shepard, August, and Hartley

You can't have art without resistance in the material.

—WILLIAM MORRIS

We forget too easily: woman as an intellectual has existed in appreciable numbers only for the last sixty or seventy years. We know stories of her and about her, but *her* history—a history of incredible exertion and courage, but also of incredible self-denial and renunciation of the claims of her nature—has still to be written.

—CHRISTA WOLF

The Muses get their name from a root that indicates ardor, the quick-tempered tension that leaps out in impatience, desire, or anger, the sort of tension that aches to know and to do.

—JEAN-LUC NANCY

Ambition is not enough; necessity is everything.

—MARTHA GRAHAM

Contents

INTRODUCTION The Legacy Begins xi

1. Pittsburgh 3

2. Santa Barbara 13

3. Ruth St. Denis and Ted Shawn—The Denishawn Dancers 23

4. Horst 44

5. Schopenhauer and Nietzsche 57

6. Kandinsky and Isadora Duncan 64

7. The Eastman School 80

8. From Mariarden to John Martin 101

9. Neighborhood Playhouse 115

10. *Heretic* 132

11. Dance Repertory Theatre and *Lamentation* 139

12. Introducing: Isamu Noguchi 154

13. League of Composers and *The Rite of Spring* in America 163

14. Northwest to Southwest 182

15. Know the Land 198

16. *Primitive Mysteries* 206

17. "We Will Never Understand One Another" 227

18. From *Ceremonials* to Radio City Music Hall   251

19. The American Rhythm   269

20. Airborne   279

21. Erick Hawkins and Lincoln Kirstein   291

22. Interlude—*Chronicle*   301

23. *American Document*   307

24. *Every Soul Is a Circus*   323

25. *Deaths and Entrances*—Ten Characters in Search of a Dance   331

26. Interlude—*Appalachian Spring*   341

27. *Dark Meadow*   346

28. *Serpent Heart*   355

29. The "Break-Up"   364

30. Horst Revisited   375

31. *Eye of Anguish*   380

32. The Choice   389

33. Coda   399

Acknowledgments   407

Notes   415

Bibliography   485

Index   529

The Legacy Begins

Martha Graham as "the one in red," in homage to Emily Dickinson.
Letter to the World, 1940. (Photograph by Barbara Morgan)

For me, growing up in the Manhattan neighborhood where Lincoln Center would someday be built, the name "Martha Graham" conjured a distant image: A goddess-like, athletic personage in a tight, shirred bodice extended at the hips into a flowing gown, her bare right foot weighted and planted as if holding to the floor, left leg poised aloft at an impossible angle revealing a long, muscular thigh emerging from the play of fabric in the eloquent garment. Her right arm is bent, her hand half-crooked at the wrist, fingers contracted and crowning a smooth brow while she gazes, angular-featured, luminous half-closed eyes fixed downward and focused inward, seeking an undefined, urgent answer.

Martha Graham made 180 theatrical dance pieces and invented, defined, sustained, shaped, and reshaped her dynamic movement style and breathing technique—contraction and release, a fluid, living organism that evolved and expanded in relation to her own body knowledge and the body types and personalities of the hundreds of dancers she taught, and the few she singled out, called upon, and summoned into her legendary company, founded in New York City in 1926.

Rugged individual and demanding collaborator, unique stylist and fierce standard-bearer, Graham worked with sculptor Isamu Noguchi, lighting designer Jean Rosenthal, costume designer Edythe Gilfond, and composers including Aaron Copland, Henry Cowell, Samuel Barber, Carlos Chávez, William Schuman—and Louis Horst. Married and ten years her senior, "Louie" was Graham's piano accompanist, music director and arranger, critic, and lover.

Martha Graham: When Dance Became Modern is about Martha Graham's small-town origins, dogged quest for artistic identity, vaudeville touring, anguished departure from show business, solitary seed-planting on untrodden ground, mysterious flowering, first taste of critical recognition, emergence into popular understanding, and her tumultuous marriage and tragic romance with a young dancer, Erick Hawkins, the first man to enter the company.

This is the story of how Martha Graham became *Martha Graham*.

THE EPIPHANY

"It takes about ten years to make a mature dancer," Graham declared in the mid-1930s and repeated often. "By ten years, if you're going to be a dancer at all, you will have mastered the instrument." For which I substitute "mastered the *subject*."

It was January 2008 when I began my sojourn as the distinguished visiting professor of theatre and dance in the College of the Arts at Montclair State University in New Jersey. *The thing itself* happened while I was sitting, notebook and pencil in hand, fifteen rows from the stage, in the orchestra of the cavernous Memorial Auditorium. I had been invited to observe a rehearsal of Graham's 1936 classic, "Steps in the Street (Devastation-Homelessness-

Exile)," the central section of her larger work, *Chronicle,* to be performed by student dance majors under the benevolent and unforgiving tutelage of the Martha Graham Dance Company senior artistic associate and *regisseur,* Denise Vale. This strong, outspoken woman had learned Steps thirty years prior, from Graham herself. Now a living embodiment, she was passing the legacy along, setting the piece on the students.

To the percussive, dissonant Wallingford Riegger score (praised by Henry Cowell as "the choiring of angels") Vale pushed the students through tight, torqued paces and jagged, measured steps. They arched their backs—voraciously seeking air as if through their navels—lifted and cupped their hands, and made staccato, linear Greek chorus processionals on- and off-stage, bare feet whisper-brushing the floor. Vale exhorted them with a litany of cries in the present tense—"Martha *says*—Either the foot is pointed or it is not!—keep that *beat* like a clock—*one! one! one!* . . . Martha *says*—It is all from the center of your body—*contract* the *center* of your body below the diaphragm! . . . Martha *says*—*hit* that floor with the ball of your foot!"

Palms flattened, the women compressed their spines, as, without pause, Vale commanded them to whip through a rapid-fire sequence of contractions—lower, middle torso, and upper—punctuated by simulta-neous, punched-out pushes of breath and voice (hovering between a grunt and a hiss), arms spread wide, hands flexing at the wrist, the core of the body delving back, back, and back.

She urged the girls deeper into Graham's "angular geometry of the body," down to the ground, accompanied by a contraction of the *hands*—flexed, then cupped and distorted fingers—and they spiraled, knees bent, into peni-tent position. The stage was the sought-for earth, springboard for action.

As I headed into the chilly evening, the realization hit me. Obsessed with exemplars of American cultural identity for my whole writing life, I had missed the connective tissue: modern dance.

Since that rehearsal, assured by colleagues in the dance department and the dance world at large about how salutary it is to bring another pair of eyes into the rehearsal space, I have become a passionate spectator, privileged to teach, critique, interview, and observe dancers, "athletes of God" who live so presently in their bodies, unlike those untrained in their art. John Donne wrote that "the body makes the mind"; dancers mind their bodies. In the moments after a performance that is never quite good enough, pac-ing backstage with hands on hips, chests heaving, not having caught their breath, they self-consciously self-admonish in waves of perspiring frustration about what they just did *wrong,* what needs to be *cleaned,* what slivers and imperceptible segments of the barely done six or eight or ten minutes need to be tightened and *fixed* for next time.

Supposedly at rest, taking a quick break, stretching, crooking their necks from side to side, sipping water, permitting themselves a spoonful of yogurt, a handful of nuts, or a few bites of an apple, the dancers I have come to know have jittery apprehensiveness fixated upon the coming class, rehearsal, or performance, no matter if it be later the same day, the next week, or on the season repertory pinned to the board outside the dressing room.

The readiness is all.

THE MODERNISTS

Unlike her contemporaries, E. E. Cummings, John Dos Passos, and Ernest Hemingway, Martha Graham did not dash off in 1917 to join the ambulance corps in search of adventure. Nor did she escape to Europe with the 1920s exiles—in F. Scott Fitzgerald's words, "the great years of the Cap d'Antibes"—save for one month of shows in London. Even while abroad, Graham's generation kept the sentimental compass turned westward, often returning to the States within a year or two, with the noteworthy exception of Isadora Duncan, Graham's predecessor-in-spirit, who spent most of her performing life in Europe until she died in 1927.

Gertrude Stein was a native daughter of Allegheny, Pennsylvania, where Graham was born. In *The Making of Americans,* Stein got to the point: "In the United States there is more space where nobody is than where anybody is. This is what makes America what it is . . . Beginning again and again is a natural thing."

The irascible Ezra Pound said: "Make it new. The artist is always beginning . . . any work of art which is not a beginning, an invention, a discovery, is of little worth . . . Let us remember that the very name *troubadour* means a 'finder,' one who discovers . . ."

T. S. Eliot, another Graham contemporary, loved and reviewed dance; Graham read his poetry, drama, and criticism. In his mature masterpiece, *Four Quartets,* Eliot observed that "each venture / Is a new beginning, a raid on the inarticulate . . ." For the poet, this meant setting forth across the empty page; for the dancer, it was the edge of the empty stage viewed from the wings.

The critic Waldo Frank shared this stylistic spirit in his 1919 book, *Our America*: "In this infancy of our adventure, America is a mystic Word. We go forth all to seek America. And in the seeking we create her."

Poems are printed on paper. Paintings are brushed on canvas. Like the fragmented, uneven lines of a constantly revised poem by Marianne Moore that begins with a blank page, and the scattered white patches traced in gray that painter Stuart Davis intentionally leaves raw, their contemporary, Martha Graham, inscribes her body through an empty, quiet room. Like the passages of dense modern poetry she copied longhand into her notebooks, the disruptive metric figures and off-rhythm steps of Graham's American dances reacted against the constraints of ballet. Breathing audibly, muscles straining, fabric rippling, she showed the materials of the work: *I am a person, and I am dancing.*

During Martha Graham's ascendancy, American music was also awakening to singularity and independence, exercising a pent-up desire to elevate the stature of homegrown composers to the level of European counterparts. In the early 1920s, for Manhattan concertgoers, Claude Debussy was *the* arch-modernist. But not for long. Graham believed that, like its "sister art," music, "the modern dance is an integrated art, in which the soul plays upon a disciplined body as a musician plays upon an instrument."

Martha Graham expressed her affinity with the aesthetic of American writers, painters, and composers, and with the no-frills, plainspoken work ethic of architect Frank Lloyd Wright, an economical modernist with whom she is allied: "We dancers, too, have stripped our medium of decorative unessentials. Just as fancy trimmings are no longer needed on Modern buildings, so dancing is no longer padded," Graham said.

THE EVASIVE SUBJECT

Martha Graham was proud of her physical and intellectual capacity to "contain multitudes," like another poetic hero, Walt Whitman. Working on this biography, breathing down my own neck, I incurred many psychic injuries struggling against my subject's steel-willed insistence that she should be arbiter of her own story and curator of her own body. Janet Eilber, one of Graham's premières danseuses, now artistic director of the Martha Graham Dance Company, sums it up, "I don't think she thought of a world without herself."

I have fixated upon an omnivorous artist who announced that "every act of creation bears within it the seeds of destruction," echoing Picasso's "Previously a picture was a sum of additions. With me, a picture is a sum of destructions." For four decades, from the time she left home, went away to school, hit the road as a Denishawn dancer, and launched and sustained her career, Martha Graham wrote to her mother once a week. Jennie Graham saved every letter, and, in 1958, when the matriarch died, Martha Graham went to Santa Barbara and burned them. In 1964, when Louis Horst died, leaving no written reminiscences, Graham destroyed their correspondence.

Graham "was not a friend of the dance collection" in its formative years at the New York Public Library, telling founding curator Genevieve Oswald, who sought her manuscripts and letters, "I don't want people snickering over me after I am dead." In the aftermath and cleanup of a 1999 Graham School basement flood, visual, audio, and written documentary material was lost and misplaced; while much remains at large, items are being returned incrementally to Martha Graham Resources. In the Music Division of the Library of Congress, in two gray Hollinger boxes, only eighteen of Martha Graham's dance composition stenographers' notebooks survive, tantalizingly jammed with her handwritten quotes from books; and ideas, sketches, steps, and sequences.

"We were friendly, but never *friendly* friendly," said Yuriko Kikuchi, who started with Graham in 1943. "Martha never confided anything to her dancers. We were like her different colors, for her to use as a painter." Another distinguished dancer, a true believer in her genius who saw himself as one of the loyal guardians of Martha Graham's mystique, Robert Cohan joined the company in 1946. Partnered at arm's length, he would never dream of prying into Martha's entanglements with Louis Horst or Erick Hawkins—"What they did privately, I don't know . . . It just was not our business," Cohan said. To Marian Horosko, author of *Martha Graham: The Evolution of Her Dance Theory and Training,* her mercurial subject was "approachable to the earnest but distant to the novice."

Fighting "against any dramatization of my peculiarities or my personality," Graham vigorously discouraged the *New York Times* dance critic Don McDonagh, who began work on his biography in the mid-1960s. She allowed him one eighty-nine-minute meeting of desultory conversation, telling him she refused to record any pedagogical technique films and wanted her choreographic notes discarded when she died. Graham telephoned others in her circle to dissuade them from meeting with the author. Edwin Denby's impassioned intercession saved the day; McDonagh's beautifully balanced, judicious, and sensitive *Martha Graham* was published in 1973.

Agnes de Mille said, "Martha always wanted to leave behind a legend, not a biography." More than any researcher before or since, she knew whereof she spoke. Labor on the monumental *Martha: The Life and Work of Martha Graham* started in February 1963; in June 1972, Graham told de Mille she would no longer be available to collaborate. De Mille finished writing in 1987 and waited to publish until Graham died four years later.

Martha Graham, the memoirist, did not go gentle into her good night. The impressionistic, disjointed *Blood Memory,* published in 1991, is by turns fascinating, funny, and impassioned. But its pieced-together opacity remains frustrating to the fact-seeker. The book that dance critic Marcia Siegel called "Marthology" took thirty-five years and the labor of many editorial hands to coalesce into a procrastinated mélange of taped interviews, reluctant and choppy dictation, fitful and contradictory journal jottings, and selectively recalled anecdotes by a conflicted author with no deadline. After all, Graham said, "Looking at the past is like lolling in a rocking chair . . . You can rock back and forth on the porch and never go forward. It is not for me."

THE LOVE IN DISCIPLINE

"Martha was her work, and came to life only in the theatre. She told the truth only on stage," wrote Helen McGehee, a principal dancer with Graham for more than twenty-five years. "Off stage she was really quite distant," said Sophie Maslow, who joined the company in 1931. "But on stage, performing, Martha was at her best, and we were very close. At the curtain call, when we came out for a bow, and Martha held my hand, she made me feel that we had really done something together."

Continuing to wrestle affectionately with my provocative angel, Martha Graham, I beg to differ with her warning that "the only justification for the pain & embarrassment of self-revealment is to point a way—perhaps to point a *way from*—rather than a way toward."

MARTHA GRAHAM

1

Pittsburgh

The serried ranks of the glacier-scarred Appalachian Mountain Divide rise up, a broad, thickly wooded and granite-faced north-south fault line of ridges penetrated by the Tuscarora, Kittatinny, Blue Mountain, and Lehigh tunnels, long stretches of darkness breaking open into early-spring light diffused upon "the soft chain of hills . . . their shoulders tightly-bound into a provocative embrace" around the "vast amphitheater" of the Allegheny Plateau, the confluence of the Monongahela, Allegheny, and Ohio Rivers—Pittsburgh.

Following in the footsteps of Alexis de Tocqueville, Mrs. Trollope, and Charles Dickens, popular biographer James Parton, on assignment from *The Atlantic Monthly*, visited the city in 1868, by which time it was known as a place where men carried "the obligatory extra white shirt" to work so "they [could] change around noon as the city's soot blackened their original attire." Parton's article concluded with a dark observation: "It is an unprofitable business, view-hunting, but if anyone would enjoy a spectacle as striking as Niagara," the author observed, "he may do so by simply walking up a long hill to Cliff Street in Pittsburg, and looking over into—hell with the lid taken off."

Local historian Charles W. Dahlinger wrote in his romantic saga, *Old Allegheny*, that rivalrous Pittsburgh "cast longing eyes across the river at her smaller [and prosperous] sister. Several times she stretched out her arms yearningly to take her to her bosom." However, these advances, in the form of the Consolidation Act of 1867, were rebuffed by majority vote of the citizens of Allegheny. Three more times over the next forty years, the proud "North Siders" rejected the Iron City's annexation resolutions, "to take [their residential suburb] in by the heels," demonstrating the stubborn independence and fierce pride of place for which Allegheny is still known.

New engine house, Fort Wayne and Chicago Railway Company, Pittsburgh. View downhill from Martha Graham's childhood home, 1531 Fremont Street, Allegheny City, 1905.

The Pittsburgh, Fort Wayne and Chicago Railway's sprawling, sunken depot in the northwestern Allegheny City Second Ward included a roundhouse, a constellation of repair shops, a brass foundry, and a powerhouse. The company sold the adjacent land uphill and to the east across Marquis Way and Fremont Street to business owners and real estate speculators who put up rows of homes "on tightly-adjacent plots [. . . not as attached 'party-wall'] row houses."

This enclave of two- and three-story, mansard-roofed long and narrow redbrick houses with modern conveniences, windows in front and back, close together with narrow alleys between them and with small patches of land as coveted yard space, sandwiched between earlier blue-collar Mexican War Streets further east (named for battles—Buena Vista and Palo Alto—and generals—Taylor, Sherman, and Jackson) and grander Victorian mansions of the Manchester region across the depot tracks to the west, evolved into a magnet for Allegheny's professional, independent wage-earning class.

Today the area is designated as the California-Kirkbride/Old Allegheny Rows Historic District. Fremont Street, renamed Brighton Place, eight lots long, runs on a gentle slope between Freedmore (formerly Fillmore/Franklin) Street to the north and Mero Way to the south. Halfway down Fremont/Brighton, a stone's throw from where the railroad depot used to be, a faded stretch of lawn covers the gap where number 1531, the birthplace of Martha Graham, once stood.

On Saturday, June 7, 2008, at ten in the morning, at the intersection of Brighton Road and California Avenue, the Allegheny City Society, in alliance with the Heinz History Center, the Pennsylvania Historical and Museum Commission, and the Pennsylvania Humanities Council dedicated a "Historical Marker Honoring the Memory of Martha Graham (May 11, 1894–April 1, 1991)."

In golden letters against a blue background, the plaque reads, "Born near here, dancer, choreographer and teacher Martha Graham created a modern and unique movement style. In 1927 [*sic*], she founded her School of Contemporary Dance, revolutionizing the art of modern dance with innovative works such as *Frontier* and *Appalachian Spring*."

Martha, age two, 1896.

The place-name comes from native Indian origins; according to sixteenth-century mapmakers, there once roamed an isolated, itinerant tribe called Apalatchi, meaning "the People on the Other Side," because they hunted in the Great Path terrain along the northern banks of the thousand-mile Ohio River, "where virgin forest met the rushing waters."

. . .

Named after her Irish paternal grandmother born in Newburgh, New York, Martha was the eldest of four children of George Greenfield Graham, MD, thirty-eight years old, and Jane ("Jennie") Beers, fourteen years her husband's junior. Jane came from the rural borough of Mars in Butler County along Breakneck Creek, north of Allegheny. She was "a compact, little wren of a woman," the middle daughter of three: sister Annie was the older, and sister Mary (called "Auntie Re") was the youngest.

Martha's sister, also named Mary (nicknamed "Mimi"), was born on May 15, 1896; followed by Georgia ("Geordie"), on March 1, 1900; and on

Jane ("Jennie") and George
Greenfield Graham, ca. early 1890s.

April 26, 1906, finally the precious "boy-child," William Henry arrived.

The who's who 1897 biography in *Life Sketches of Leading Citizens of Pittsburg and the Vicinity* (solemn frontispiece declaring that "biography is the home aspect of history"), claimed the "prominent and skilful physician . . . [as] a native of Allegheny," but Dr. Graham originally hailed from Washington County, Pennsylvania, center of the notorious 1791 Whiskey Rebellion. Dr. Graham's father, John Jr., of Pittsburgh, moved to a plantation outside Hannibal, Missouri, before the Civil War; afterward, he took the family back to Pennsylvania. Dr. Graham's paternal grandparents—John Sr. and Elizabeth—were Scottish. John Sr., beginning "in the hat trade," became president of the Bank of Pittsburgh and vice president of the board of Western Pennsylvania Hospital.

After attending the University of Pennsylvania, George Greenfield Graham followed family tradition and embarked upon a short-lived business career before matriculating at the Baltimore College of Physicians and Surgeons in the fall of 1880. He earned an MD in mental disorders and was hired as a resident in the department of medicine and surgery at West Penn Hospital in Pittsburgh's Polish Hill district, the first chartered public Civil War veterans' hospital in town. In the spring of 1883, he joined the staff of the Dixmont State Hospital for the Insane as assistant physician.

On a parklike hilltop overlooking the Ohio River in what is now suburban Kilbuck, eight miles northwest of Allegheny via the Pittsburgh, Fort Wayne and Chicago line, Dixmont Hospital opened its doors in 1862 responding to a plea from Dorothea Lynde Dix, the Maine-born nursing and lunacy reform movement pioneer: "I call your attention to the present state of Insane Persons confined within this [Pennsylvania] Commonwealth in cages, stalls, pens! Chained, naked, beaten with rods, lashed into obedience!" When "she closed her eyes in death—and awoke to joy forever" in the New Jersey state hospital in Morris Plains on July 19, 1887, Ms. Dix was eulogized by John Harper, president of the Dixmont Hospital Board, as having given up "the quietude of home, and . . . the fascinating pleasures of refined society . . . for the grand purpose of self-sacrifice on the altar of suffering humanity."

Dr. Graham spent ten years on the staff of Dixmont as—in the parlance of the day—an alienist, rising through the administration to become a member of the Committee on Lunacy and acting assistant superintendent of the facility, expanded to house more than thirteen hundred patients. Resigning from Dixmont on the brink of a crippling recession in the spring of 1893, Dr. Graham married the dark-haired, petite "Miss Jennie" Beers, daughter of John—a carpenter—and Mary (Hamilton), and hung up a shingle announcing his private practice from a surgery-cum-library in the parlor of their house on Fremont Street.

. . .

Martha Graham's father emerges from fragmentary and occasionally lyric passages in her discursive *Blood Memory* as an array of vignettes. Of one thing we may be certain: "My whole life started with my father," Graham said in her seventies; "I think I was my father's favorite," she wrote toward the end of her life. George Greenfield Graham was the tall, elegant, golden-haired, blue-eyed guardian of his daughter's hermetic girlhood. He insisted that, as his eldest, the young lady must be the diligent figurehead for her younger siblings, representing what was best about the close-knit Presbyterian family. She had to be impeccably attired and groomed at all times, especially on Sundays for churchgoing—white gloves, white skirt neatly pleated, hair pulled back and tied with a ribbon.

When in consultation with a patient, Dr. Graham expected quiet throughout the house and could not be disturbed; however, after visiting hours, or returning from house calls and rounds in the early-evening before dinner, he welcomed Martha into his lofty sanctum for Socratic conversation and introduced her to the enduring value of great books.

When spoken to by an adult, she was expected to be courteous in deportment and hide her impulses. "A bit Olympian," stern and demanding, on occasion, Dr. Graham would give his recalcitrant daughter a slap but never raised his voice to chastise Martha, preferring to murmur that she "disappointed" him.

Two incidents stand out from Martha's late-Victorian childhood—two of the physician's dicta—apocryphal or not. In the earlier memory, she was standing upon a pile of books next to her father's desk as he showed her a glass slide upon which he had placed a drop of water. Dr. Graham asked Martha what she saw, and she replied, "Pure water." He pulled down his microscope, placed the slide under the lens, beckoned Martha to peer through the viewfinder, and asked her to look more closely.

"There are wriggles in it!" she cried. "Yes. It is impure," Dr. Graham said. "Just remember this all your life, Martha. You must look for the truth." She wrote, "I have never forgotten the vividness of that moment, which has presided like a star over my life."

In the second episode, one of her father's patients, a teenaged girl, was invited to stay for supper with the family. Little Martha, "the small person of four or five, circled around her, looking, wondering, pondering, imitating . . ." Seated at table during the meal, Graham wrote, "[the girl] barely looked up from her plate, preferring to sit slightly slouched, bent into that awkwardness, as if folding herself into her own body." That night, after her father returned from escorting the girl home, Martha asked him "why she behaved this way . . . why she carrie[d] her head and mov[ed] her hands in a strange way." Dr. Graham replied that his patient was not well and her body was telling them so. Each of us, he said, speaks our story through our bodies. "Movement," he told Martha, "never lies."

"*Movement never lies*—at four or five that was an admonition," Graham wrote decades later. " 'Lie' in a Presbyterian household was and still is a clanging word which sets whispering all the little fluttering guilts which seek to become consumed in the flame of one's conscience."

The epiphany was reported by Martha Graham to Agnes de Mille as "Bodies never lie"; to Don McDonagh as "I can always tell from your movement if you lie"; and to an assembly of Juilliard students as "All that which you are comes out through movement . . . the body is a barometer of the soul's weather." Ernestine Stodelle transcribed Graham's recollection of the paternal incident thus: " 'Martha, you're not telling me the truth!' Wide-eyed, she stammered, 'How do you know?' 'I can tell by the way you are moving,' was [Dr. Graham's] candid retort."

Over the years, this clinical observation was melded into Martha Graham's technique, the body as the vessel containing unadulterated truth, the movement of the dancer manifesting that truth, and the dancer disciplined against involuntary revelations of emotion. This necessary tension leading to artifice was cited by Émile Zola in his essay on Manet: To be an artist in *any* medium, Zola wrote, "You must abandon yourself bravely to your nature and try not to lie to yourself."

. . .

At the turn of the century, the Graham household was crowded. Besides the peripatetic, professional father; his indulged and fragile wife; three girls ages six, four, and a newborn—and a floppy-eared mutt terrier—Jennie's parents, John and Mary Beers, had moved in. Holding the family together as nanny, cook, and housekeeper in the three-story home on the right side of the tracks was the spirited Irish maid Elizabeth Prendergast ("Lizzie," or "Sizzie," the little ones called her). A typical middle-class family in 1900 Allegheny would employ a single "live-in" for all work; stalwart Lizzie was up to the task. A grateful former patient of Dr. Graham's, at twenty-seven, she arrived on the doorstep of 1531 Fremont when Martha was still in her mother's arms, and stayed with the family for three decades. "[A] wonderful lapsed Catholic who could never understand why she had to go to confession . . . [s]he was wise and she was utterly dedicated and devoted," Martha Graham recalled. "She dominated the house."

In the second-floor nursery, Martha spent hours cross-legged on the floor "choreographing" complex cities out of building blocks. The sisters played dress-up, draping old veils and scarves, adorned themselves with "junky jewelry," put on improvised dramas, and sang songs, Lizzie doubling as audience and impresario. With Martha's father's encouragement—he was an accomplished piano player, favoring Gilbert and Sullivan and Strauss Viennese waltzes—she took lessons for a short time, although she never learned to read music fluently. When she tired of Lizzie's stories of "witches, wee folk, and the poetic mystery of things," and solitude beckoned, Martha withdrew into her bedroom, to read by the window in a "special wooden chair," an eclectic literary journey that began with stories from the Greek myths, moved on to Jules Verne's "fantastic voyages to the moon or under the sea," and alighted upon her constant favorite, poetry of all kinds, "and the imagination that poems inspired."

Alfred, Lord Tennyson's work was most appealing: "I had my own world," Graham remembered, "and my own world was *The Lady of Shalott*." It is bewitching to pry open the square blue covers embossed with decorative gold leaf, page through Howard Pyle's color-saturated art nouveau lithographs for *Shalott*, and imagine, through Martha's impressionable eyes, the "embowered" barefoot damsel by the window combing her thick auburn hair as it cascades around her shoulders, weaving "the shadows of a world" in her mind's fantasy-web, longing for Sir Lancelot's love, gazing into her magical circular mirror like a pre-Raphaelite Lady Lilith, and, "robed in snowy white . . . singing her own death dirge" afloat upon the river toward Camelot.

.   .   .

Weekdays, Martha and Mary attended the integrated Second Ward Elementary School on Sherman Avenue, later named the Mary [Junkin Buchanan] Cowley School. Beloved social activist and kindergarten advocate, "Our Mrs. Cowley" was founder and director of the Allegheny Playground Association.

"Each and every Sunday" morning, the Grahams prepared for the fifteen-minute walk to church, and Martha "smoothed out her dress, tying the sash just so, slipping into her best coat . . . putting on her most becoming bonnet, buttoning her gloves, lowering a little veil over her deep-set eyes." The route never varied. Stepping out the front door, backs to the railyard blacksmith shop and foundry, they descended the steps, turned right, and headed down Fremont, then one block east on Pennsylvania Avenue, and south one block along Irwin Avenue, bringing them to the northwest corner of the town commons, landscaped into Ober Park. From there they walked one more block south to Ohio Street, cutting through the park past St. Peter's Roman Catholic Church, to the four central blocks of Allegheny known as "the Diamond," where the cavernous Romanesque revival Civil War–era Market House with round-arched window openings—home to purveyors of "vegetables, meats, eggs, dairy products, flowers & etc"—sat on the southeast corner.

Across from the market loomed a spacious haven Martha visited often, the Carnegie Free Library with its four-sided peaked clock tower. The son of a weaver in Dunfermline, Scotland, Andrew Carnegie had arrived on these shores with his family and settled in Allegheny at the age of eleven in 1846. Forty years later, his fortune made as one of Allegheny's most famous and grateful sons, inspired by the philanthropy of Ezra Cornell in Ithaca and Enoch Pratt in Baltimore, Carnegie endowed the first of his many public libraries in America with a $331,000 gift to the city of Allegheny. "If ever there was a sight that makes my eyes glisten, it was this gem," he told his wife, Louise.

Three blocks farther south, where Sandusky Street met Stockton Avenue, stood the Second United Presbyterian Church of Allegheny, "a dark, rather sinister place, with just one little bunch of flowers on the pulpit." The Grahams' congregation, following Calvinist tradition, believed in the doctrine of *the elect*, individuals chosen by God "in his eternal and immutable counsel" to be "called and admitted into salvation." Governed by a Council of Elders, the church adhered to the Book of Order in worship, a text to which sprightly Martha did not pay much heed. She was so inspired by the "beauty and divinity" of the hymns that she wriggled off her mother's lap to scamper and dance up and down the aisles. On occasional Sunday evenings when she was a bit older, Martha was required by her parents to return to church for meetings of the Young People's Society of Christian Endeavor, founded "to promote an earnest Christian life among its members . . . to make them more useful in the service of God."

. . .

Daily life was not all study and rectitude. Dr. Graham was an active member of the American Medical Association, and on several summers between 1900 and 1905, he brought the family along to the society's annual meeting at the beach in Atlantic City, New Jersey, where they stayed in a hotel and toured about in a horse-drawn carriage. Martha waded in the surf close to shore under Lizzie's vigilant eye, crouched under the boardwalk to peer up at "slats of sun through the wooden planks," first set eyes on a wireless telegraph station, promenaded along Captain John Young's half-mile-long Million Dollar Pier, marveled at the aquarium, savored vanilla and honeycomb toffee "hokey pokey" ice cream treats, and "[sat] on a green velvet pouf" in the hotel lobby watching Punch and Judy puppets pummel each other.

At the end of April 1906, when Martha turned twelve, her brother, William Henry Graham, the first boy on the Beers side of the family, was born and baptized in a cut-glass crystal bowl that had belonged to Grandma Mary. "In her delight in having a son, Mrs. Graham used to carry the baby around the house all day long. 'Why don't you put that child down and let him walk?' her husband would ask; yet nothing could convince the doting mother to part with him." In chiaroscuro family photographs, Martha, Mary, and Geordie, beaming big sisters, take turns bathing the round-faced, serious infant; in another snapshot, as a toddler, he appears running, in a broad-brimmed straw hat and dusty overalls, intrepid and sturdy. But at

Proud big sister Martha (top) with (clockwise) Mary, baby William,
and Georgia ("Geordie"), 1906.

twenty months, Billy fell ill—measles, or scarlet fever, or meningitis—and
on January 24, 1908, he died. "My brother died in the winter," Graham told
Walter Terry half a century later, summoning up the emotional tonalities of
Appalachian Spring, and so, "when that season comes around every year, it is
a release from terror, snow, cold, and barrenness."

Jennie was distraught over the loss of her only son, and staying in the
house on Fremont Street became excruciating. And daughter Mary suffered
from chronic asthma. In harmony with the "health seeker movement," and
as remedy for their mourning, the Grahams decided to relocate to a salutary,
arid climate, "the magic of the sunshine" of the West Coast. It was time to
escape the din and clamor and "veils of soot" that rained down behind the
house by the Pittsburgh, Fort Wayne and Chicago Railway.

In the spring of 1908, the family entourage, Grandma Mary Beers and
maid Lizzie in tow, boarded the train in Pittsburgh and headed to Santa
Barbara. The place was considered "the pleasantest of all" towns out west,
"in which the tenderest invalid [could] pass the greater part of a day out of
doors with pleasure and benefit."

2

Santa Barbara

The rolling, clacketing, hot, and dusty journey from the world of darkness to the world of light took nine days, cutting across Ohio, Indiana, and Illinois on the Baltimore and Ohio Railroad to St. Louis and Topeka and Dodge City under an infinite azure sky sheltering golden fields, then angling southward on the Atchison, Topeka and Santa Fe line along the edge of Colorado and the burning, vivid deserts of Indian country to Albuquerque, before a final stretch across the rugged Zuni lands of Arizona. "When I would stand at the end of the last car," Graham wrote of her introspective fourteen-year-old self facing transcontinental space receding and advancing on railway time, "the East was the home I was leaving, though of course now hundreds if not thousands of miles away. And when I'd run to the front car I'd watch the West unroll before me. It really was a frontier."

. . .

Santa Barbara in 1908 was a mélange of comfortable frame houses and adobe bungalows, Spanish, Indian, Japanese, and Chinese (so-called Oriental) tongues, native Westerners and entrepreneurial Easterners, nestled between the chaparral-studded, grassy Sierra Madre mountains and the warm breezes and roaring surf of the Pacific Ocean. For newly arrived Martha, one of her first impressions—from among the ubiquitous crazy-quilt wildflowers, violets, tulips, poppies, irises, and lilies—was the pale, night-blooming cereus, Queen of the Night. Jennie Graham cultivated the exotic showpiece in the backyard of 1633 Garden Street, their stately, two-story yellow Charles Eastlake–style Victorian house with fanciful pillared open porch and bay

O, happy town beside the sea,
  Below the hills and near my heart,
  How few, who come and go, can tell!
The secret of thy witchery!
    But those who guess the heart of it
    Will stay to learn the art of it,
    And so, become a part of it!

Copyright 1912   Marguerite Wilkinson

The Mission Bells are ringing a Welcome for you

SANTA BARBARA
CALIFORNIA

"Where the mountains meet the sea."   A. R. EDMONDSON - SANTA BARBARA

Santa Barbara, 1912.

window at the corner of Valerio. When it was Martha's turn to go deep into the garden of an evening "carrying a shaded candle . . . and a bucket, [and] remove the snails from the calla lilies" by the wrought iron fence, she lingered barefoot in her nightgown among the old trees, leaning in to breathe the jasmine-vanilla fragrance from the saucer-like cereus, trumpeting white blooms deep as a wine goblet, flamboyant waxy petals glowing.

Once the family was settled into the Upper East neighborhood, as she had at Allegheny, Lizzie took Martha and her sisters on surreptitious church visits beginning with the nearby eighteenth-century Queen of the Missions, the colonnaded Old Mission Santa Barbara, a distinctive two-capilla chapel where the Franciscan Poor Sisters of St. Clare lived in cloistered silence, putting the gospel into practice, *sine glossa*, with simplicity and joy. Their vows meant permanent enclosure, obedience, poverty, perpetual fast, chastity, ora et labora, "prayer and work." The nuns recited the Divine Office after midnight, and, "in the dark stillness of the new day," watching quietly, Martha was seduced by the mysterious ritual of the Sisters "lying prone in prayer in front of the altar" in "loose-fitting garments of grey frieze bound [at the waist] by a linen rope having four knots representing their vows." Like Caravaggio's *Madonna of Loreto*, they were in sympathy with the common pilgrims who knelt to adore the barefoot Virgin.

To provide for "the Graham Girls"—as they were known around town—

in the manner to which they had become accustomed, Dr. Graham continued to reside in Allegheny, maintaining his medical practice there. During annual spring and summer returns to Santa Barbara, he visited his real estate investments in the Goleta Valley farmland, maintaining the tradition of excursions en famille. A favorite spot near home was Alameda Plaza, where the Grahams would stroll along gravel paths through a variety of lush plantings, palm trees, and cacti, pausing at the gazebo for a picnic lunch and a midafternoon concert of "selections from the best operas, overtures and light classics" presented by Caesar LaMonaca's Santa Barbara Band. On another outing farther afield, the family ventured to a seaside mesa near Punta del Castillo, former estate of ex–New York lawyer turned rancher Thomas Bloodgood Dibblee. Arms spread wide, Martha "charge[d] across the high plateau like a bareback circus rider leaping through hoop after hoop. 'Freedom!' she recalled years later, 'I ran. I fell down. I got up. I ran again.'"

. . .

In August 1909, Martha was enrolled at the sandstone-and-brick Santa Barbara High School (founded in 1875), close enough to her house that she could walk home for lunch. She was one of forty entering freshmen, the largest class ever. At fifteen years old, Martha Graham stood almost five feet two. She had a pale, oval-shaped, scrubbed face; unruly, thick brown hair parted in the middle, tied behind her ears with a grosgrain ribbon; wide, light brown eyes; and a thin, serious mouth. Describing herself compared to her two younger sisters, she was self-deprecating: "Mary was the beauty," blonde and blue-eyed, with "long, long legs," and "Geordie was pretty too," but Martha—preferring, as her mother said, to "follow [her] own inclinations"—was "part wild and part civilized . . . and very thin . . . in some ways, an outsider." Of those years, Martha said, "I was anything but timid and loving." Classmates agreed: "Dr. and Mrs. Graham were always very pleasant to [me] even if Martha remained cool and distant," Hazel Dewing, a frequent visitor to the Graham home and a friend of Martha's sister Mary recalled. "She was a dramatic girl . . . ," said Joyce Gardiner, another childhood pal. "I was always kind of scared of her."

Freshmen at SBHS were not permitted to engage in extracurricular activities. By Martha's second year, the standoffish "new girl" from the other side of the country revealed developing interests. She was sophomore editor of the school literary magazine-yearbook, *The Olive and Gold,* and chaired the

PHOTO BY BROCK-HIGGINS

(GIRLS' BASKETBALL TEAM).

1st Row--Miss Holt (Trainer), Edessa Arne, Anna Buck, Mr Ferguson (Coach), Anna Cardoza, Eva Stewart, Myrtle Fanning (Mgr.)
2nd Row--Martha Graham, Hilda Weston, Lilias Smith.

Martha, kneeling left, Santa Barbara High School girls' basketball team, winter 1911.

refreshment committee for her class dance at the Knights of Pythias Hall, with her mother as one of the chaperone "patronesses." Martha joined the girls' basketball team, providing inspiration for her first published story, "Just Girls!" The "time" of this piece was "Any time after basket ball [*sic*] practice," and the "place" was a "very disorderly room strewn with books, paper, tennis shoes, towels, basket ball suits, middies, etc.; room finally recognized as the dressing room of girls in S.B.H.S." The beleaguered coach-trainer, "Poor Miss Holt," addressed a dramatic-frenetic monologue to a gaggle of hyperactive girls, in particular the "Patient Myrtle [Martha]," whose final role, as the curtain descended, was to "faint *à la* Hero, with no gallant Benedick nor simple Friar at hand."

· · ·

One spring Saturday afternoon, the Grahams were promenading in downtown Santa Barbara, and Martha lingered to stare at a poster in a shop window advertising a week of eight dance performances by thirty-two-year-old Ruth St. Denis, protégée of David Belasco, at the Mason Opera House in Los Angeles on a coast-to-coast tour managed by New York producer Henry Birkhardt Harris. The woman in the photograph was lost in a spiritual trance, seated cross-legged, kohl-shaded eyelids lowered. Her hand-sewn, closely fitted, jewel-studded bodice set off the "frigid beauty" of her sinuous form. She was accessorized with pendant earrings and necklaces, glittery bracelets on her wrists and arms, and a crown perched above her pale forehead, and she cradled a bowl in her hands. Martha ran to catch up with the rest of the family and pleaded with her parents to buy tickets to the show. Mother demurred; but Father, home for a visit, agreed to escort Martha. Toward the end of April 1911, they took the ferry to Los Angeles.

Entering the opera house arm in arm through the majestic portico on Broadway between First and Second Streets, Dr. Graham and his daughter were quite the couple, he with trimmed goatee and tailored suit, she with a "matronly" gray dress and matching hat, and her father's special gift for the occasion, a corsage of fresh violets, pinned to her collar. They made their way through the long tiled lobby and the red-carpeted foyer and settled in the commodious red leather seats. St. Denis opened the show with three "'suppositious goddesses' of her own divising [*sic*]." The Tamboura entered in a red wig and transparent skirt spiraling like "quicksilver" to the beat of a tambourine. Waking from slumber upon a stone slab, in "The Dance of Day" she traced angular motions around a sundial representing "the life-cycle of Egypt's rise and fall." Most tellingly, St. Denis's "Veil of Isis"—a sequence of quivering, "luscious, seductive . . . hieroglyphic-type" movements dimin-

Ruth St. Denis when Martha and her father saw her in *Egypta*, spring 1911.

ishing to a stately pace—was Martha's first impression of the hawk-winged and cow-horned Queen of the Gods of Egypt, nurturing, divine mother of Horus, feared as the prophetess of magic.

For *Five East Indian Dances,* swathed in a diaphanous sari, bearing a tray of embers and smoldering incense above her head, neck tilted upward and chin jutting defiantly forward, hips thrusting from side to side, St. Denis glided on tiptoe among braziers, bare feet "tipped with henna," rippling arms imitating smoke lifting "wispily heavenward." Accompanied by the traditional Indian songs of Inayat Khan and his "native orchestra," her arms undulated "as if boneless," fingers curled around rings green as cobra eyes on her index and little fingers, "darting, shifting, posing and striking." Changing into a dhoti, a loose loincloth, the costume of a holy man "striding . . . through an imaginary forest," she balanced on one leg and tilted toward the north, south, east, and west; then prayed, seated in silence, breathing in and out. "Limber, pliant, and semi-nude . . . supple as a willow in the wind," she whirled through the "delirium" of the five senses—"bells for hearing, flowers for smelling, wine for tasting, jewels for seeing, and kisses of the palm for touching"—as Radha the "bronze-skinned and lithe-limbed" maiden, born a lowly cowherdess, who grew to capture the heart of Lord Krishna.

"My fate was sealed," Martha Graham said of that Los Angeles concert. Ruth St. Denis, "a goddess figure," became her "obsession . . . I knew at that moment I was going to be a dancer." Three months after being "transplanted [by St. Denis] through space and time to distant cultures and . . . occult dreams," Martha danced as a "Geisha Girl" at Santa Barbara's Potter Theatre in *A Night in Japan,* billed as "a tabloid version of *The Mikado.*" The show was the centerpiece of a "Kirmess Soiree" charity benefit for the new Santa Barbara Neighborhood House Association, "a social services center and gathering place to improve the lives of the less-privileged of our community," led by Superintendent Margaret Baylor, a Boston native descended from Henry Wadsworth Longfellow, who had come west from Chicago after training at Hull-House with Jane Addams.

·   ·   ·

Class Epithets.
Freshmen—Grassy.
Sophomores—Sassy.

Juniors—Brassy.
Seniors—Classy.

—*The Olive and Gold*, 1911–1912

Martha danced to the beat of a different drummer. Her class faculty adviser, the "extraordinary firebrand" . . . "red-haired and Irish" English and dramatic arts teacher, Mrs. Jane Carol Byrd, took the girl under a starched long-sleeved wing into her office, declaring: "You have a gift, Martha, there's no doubt about it. Where that gift will lead you, I cannot say. I think it will be along literary lines. But I do know you are destined to exercise power over people. You have something in you which will compel you to exert influence over people. See to it," Mrs. Byrd warned, waving a cautionary finger, "that you use this power for good." It was "the first of many such conferences," the prescient lady remembered, years later, "for although Martha was a 'natural' girl, entering into all school activities, she was always the leader . . . very unusual, full of strange contradictions, coldly intellectual, yet a mystic living in a world of dreams [and] fired with a personal drive."

In the fall of junior year, the basketball team, "a strong enrollment of thirty-five girls," elected Martha Graham to be their captain. "I wore my long hair in a single braid that swung across my back as I ran across the gymnasium floor . . . I took quite naturally to this sport because I wanted to *move*." She was also chosen as class representative to the student-body council, and served on the executive committee of the junior dance.

Martha's next literary alter ego was Ruth Ellis, the pent-up protagonist of her short story "Music and the Maid," four pages in *The Olive and Gold* and a quantum leap beyond the meek Myrtle of "Just Girls!" We meet Ruth at Hawthorne Hall, a girls' finishing school, sitting alone after dinner in a window seat, away from chattering others. "Hidden by the long draperies and dusty shadows . . . [her] . . . eyes full of wistful longing," Ruth eavesdrops upon shameful gossip and cruel "bursts of laughter" about "her social sins."

"Tears of vexation started into Ruth's eyes as she hurried to her room. . . . She went directly to her dressing-table, propped her elbows on the edge and gazed into the mirror. No, it was not a pretty face," Martha wrote of Ruth. "Her own steady grey eyes looked back at her, their clear depths darkened by pain. From the high brow the hair was drawn softly back. . . . The mouth was possessed of a firmness seldom seen in girlish faces; and the clear chin was like a boy's."

An aspiring singer, Ruth has been prevented from auditioning for the forthcoming school musical supervised by the visiting diva, Madame Schuman-Henk, because "Father thought [she] must get her other education first." Indeed, ever since the Ruth St. Denis incident, the parental refrain in the Graham household, when conversation turned to Martha's college future, went from her father's first and second rigorous choices, Vassar and Wellesley back east, to Mills College in the San Francisco Bay Area. The fictional Ruth was also tormented by guilt, exhorting herself to "try to repay daddy and mother for the sacrifices made to give me this [schooling]," within moments returning to the fantasy that one day she might perform, unfettered, before an appreciative audience.

The quandary of Ruth's uniqueness—is she condemned to perfection of life or art?—would be echoed in "The Soul Call," Martha's poem published in the spring of the following year, where "All Nature seems to beckon forth my soul, / And bind it to her by the fairy chains . . . ," but in the end, while "some in dreams have spanned this bridge," the lonely speaker must stand back and "rest content to have heard the call / To have enter'd in the Land of Heart's Desire."

At the conclusion of "Music and the Maid," on opening night, in a reversal of fortune, Madame Schuman-Henk deigns to listen to Ruth's tale of woe. "[H]er own eyes were wet when [the girl] had finished," and the directress springs into action, commanding Ruth to "Run along, *fräulein,* and get ready, quick." The curtain rises, Madame at the piano strikes a powerful chord, and "a slender, dark-haired girl glides" to the front of the ballroom: "Ruth Ellis stood beside the great singer! And the song welled forth [and] the audience sat spellbound [at] the wonderful golden music of the voice."

Martha's affinity for tales from antiquity continued when she was cast in the title role of the SBHS pre-Christmas theatre spectacular, the all-girls' Virgil class production of *Dido: The Phoenician Queen*, a verse translation by University of Chicago scholar Frank Justus Miller. Heralded by Aeneas's comparing her to Diana, Martha/Dido makes the grand entrance "with her band of chosen youths and maidens" moving "with stately tread" across the stage, ascending the temple steps like "a very goddess . . . among the lesser beings of her train." She is "dressed in white, the symbol of her widowhood . . . her dress . . . of light filmy stuff, draped in the Greek style, elaborately embroidered about the edges with a Greek pattern in gold thread. Her himation is a tender shade of rose pink."

The whole Graham family came out for Martha's star turn.

"There was something about her even then that made everyone stop and look," said Auntie Re, recently moved to Santa Barbara from Pennsylvania to live with her sister.

"I'll be your maid backstage when you become a famous actress," Lizzie assured Martha.

·   ·   ·

THE CLASS OF 1913
We are the class,
The Senior Class,
The jovial Senior Class!
We work with a will!
We never stand still!

—*The Olive and Gold*, spring 1913

Her sphere of influence continued to expand in senior year when Martha stepped up to the position of editor in chief of the yearbook, and gave a speech before the entire assembly on "the importance of '*Olive and Gold*' as a school paper." She was elected vice president of the student-body council, priding itself on "tak[ing] on . . . more and more power, until now there is practical self-government in every field." Martha also joined the Quorum, the popular "reading, recitation, and extemporaneous public speaking" society, established to "satisfy the many students [more than one hundred members], developing the mind along different branches." Among several public appearances during the school year, Martha served as a judge for a debate upon the matter, "Resolved: that the President of the United States should be elected by the direct vote of the people," and led the affirmative side of another "Discussion—Resolved: that under present conditions, country life is preferable to life in the city."

Martha had been dating "handsome and popular" John Newton, president of the senior class, when, in the spring term, John jilted Martha, asking Hazel Dewing to attend the senior dance with him, and the couple led the grand march processional together. Adding insult to injury, Hazel auditioned against Martha, and won, for the role of "the dainty, elusive, flowerlike heroine" of the senior class play, *Prunella, or, Love in a Dutch Garden,* "a fantasy in three acts" by Laurence Housman and Harley Granville-Barker. The story was "set in the present, but is true of all time." Against type, Martha was given a supporting role as the "timid, yet loving" Privacy, one of Prunella's three aunts (along with Aunt Prude, "dictatorial," and Aunt Prim, "most correct").

To choreograph "some very original [barefoot] dances . . . interpreting the motifs of Prunella, and some striking *tableaux*," Mrs. Jane Byrd, dramatic director, brought in as dancing director Miss Hope Weston, a Santa Barbara High School alumna on the staff of the Cumnock School of Expression in Los Angeles. The elaborate mise-en-scène—trellises of real irises and Lady Banksia roses—was acclaimed on opening night, April 5, 1913, by manager John Callis of the Potter Theatre to be "the most artistic yet" of the many student shows he had seen, praise echoed by the applause from a standing-room-only crowd.

The next morning, nineteen-year-old Martha Graham received the first published review of her work as a performer, a seal of critical approval from the Santa Barbara *Morning Press:* "The interpretation of 'Privacy,' the aunt who remains in the forlorn garden waiting for Prunella's return, was a fine bit of acting. Miss Martha Graham's voice exactly suited the part and she was careful not to overact when she discovers that the man who has bought her house [Pierrot, played in a clown suit by Robin Osborne, Martha's new boyfriend] is he who lured Prunella away. Sincerity and artistic appreciation of proportion marked every moment of Miss Graham's admirable work."

The valedictory judgment of her senior-year peers was that Martha Graham would become "the star . . . achiev[ing] signal success . . . in the literary field." For her part, Martha wanted to be remembered by her classmates for her activism and drive to raise the bar for others. Alongside her serious, calm graduation portrait in *The Olive and Gold,* the caption read: "Capable, generous, willing to do—To the noblest standards, faithful and true."

3

Ruth St. Denis and Ted Shawn—
The Denishawn Dancers

O ne thing Martha was *not* "willing to do," despite her parents' wish, was return east for college. After commencement, she remained close to home, continuing at Santa Barbara High School for a year of "postgraduate work" in psychology, advanced algebra, and chemistry to supplement the arts and literature on her transcript. Suddenly, in August 1914, came "the great tragedy that marked my teens, my childhood," Graham wrote. Her father died of heart failure. Martha "thought of William again . . . [her] young brother who died as an infant. Everything again seemed as dark as Pittsburgh."

George Greenfield Graham's speculative farming and ranching ventures had failed; however, his modest estate held sufficient funds to pay for Martha's continuing education. On October 1, 1914, the Personals column of the Santa Barbara *Daily News & Independent* noted that "Miss Martha Graham, daughter of Mrs. G. G. Graham of 1323 De la Vina Street, left for Los Angeles today where she will become a student at The Cumnock School of Expression," a private junior college for women, its mission "the belief that art and life are one and the same thing."

Cumnock was founded in 1894 by Mrs. Merrill Moore Grigg, a graduate of the Northwestern University School for Oratory in Chicago, where she had studied elocution and rhetoric under Robert McLean Cumnock, his declamatory gifts perfected at Chautauqua Institution Presbyterian Sunday School assemblies in upstate New York. Dr. Cumnock's students and fellow teachers at Northwestern "held him in high esteem, feeling that no one was more passionate about the importance of speech education."

Mrs. Grigg put admiration for her mentor into practice when in 1902 she opened the school's new building, a grand, three-gabled replica of Shakespeare's home at Stratford-upon-Avon. She created and taught a course called "Interpretative Readings . . . [T]hese classes for women," she announced, were "formed in response to a demand for post-[high school] graduate work . . . in Tennyson's *Idylls of the King* and Browning's *Saul,* and others in the new art form with musical setting."

Martha's studies in her first year included the Philosophy of Expression, literature and language, dramatic art, oratory, storytelling, and Voice Culture. Outside the literary-performance arena, Martha took health and movement classes in the Physical Culture Department (calisthenics, breathing, and stretching)—and thrice-weekly lessons in "aesthetic" and "interpretive" dancing.

. . .

> The poem, the musical composition, the statue, the painting, the building, are all projected works of the artist: they can go where he does not; they remain after he is gone. . . . But for the appreciation of these works which I call *the personal arts*—singing, dancing, and acting—we cannot wait, for our instruments are our very selves, and as interpreters, when we go, our works go with us.
> —RUTH ST. DENIS, "An Essay on the Future of the Dance," 1920

Daughter of common-law couple Tom Dennis and Ruth Emma Hull, Ruth St. Denis was born as Ruthie Dennis on January 20, 1879, at Eagleswood, an artists' colony on Raritan Bay near Perth Amboy, New Jersey. When she was five years old, the family moved to Pin Oaks Farm, on twenty acres outside Somerville. Mother Emma had been trained at the University of Michigan as a medical doctor, a career she had to give up when "nervous ailments" interfered. She converted the Dennis home into a "honeymoon hotel" and boardinghouse, raising her daughter single-handedly, while Tom, a machinist unable to hold a steady job, descended into drunkenness. To build Ruthie's intellect, Emma arranged daily delvings into the transcendental works of Emerson and Thoreau, debates on theosophy, and Bible reading.

These texts were leavened by supervised poetic recitations in tandem with "physical culture poses" based upon the teachings of François Delsarte, "a French professor of declamation." His "laws of gesture" and "science of applied aesthetics" determined that every bodily movement and vocal manifestation—in the three major realms of "oppositional, parallel, and successive"—must have meaning: "To each *spiritual* function responds a function of the *body*," Delsarte wrote. "To each grand function of the *body* corresponds a physical *act*."

Ruthie took avidly to the dances engendered by these exercises in poise and breath control. Her mother saw financial opportunity in her daughter's future and signed her up for professional dance lessons in New York City. On one such trip, when Ruthie was thirteen, they attended a matinee solo performance at the Madison Square Theatre by Genevieve Stebbins, actress and founding principal of the New York School of Expression and preeminent Delsartian popularizer in America.

Martha Graham's first vision of Ruth St. Denis in performance opened the door upon what dance could become in her life, just as Ruthie was enthralled by Stebbins's emotional honesty through a series of twelve "[*poses*] *plastiques*"—static and dynamic vignettes, pregnant moments abstracted from Greek and Egyptian themes, fixed in space like provisional marble statues on the stage for stylized pauses in time melting into slow, "successional" movement segues based upon the fluid verity of the eccentric "spiral line from head to toe." Watching Stebbins in her white sleeveless Greek tunic glide across the stage, Ruthie saw the expressive, living link between acting and dancing: "I glimpsed for the first time the individual possibilities of expression and the dignity and truth of the human body, moving in that atmosphere of grace and light."

"A talented girl is the product of a mother who has been repressed and into whom goes all that mother's ambition and culture," Ruth St. Denis told a dance class in the mid-1920s. Having relocated with her to Manhattan by the time Ruthie turned fifteen, Emma Dennis had become the classic stage mother. Her hyperactive entrepreneurial energies, an incessant stream of letters on behalf of her daughter to theatrical producers and agents, were driven by cash hunger; over the next five years, Ruth provided for her family in a succession of gigs at curio halls, dime museums, roof gardens, *tableaux vivants,* entertainment showplaces, skirt-dancing and vaudeville clubs—for which she managed to learn kicks, cartwheels, backbends, and splits. At the same time, "tall, loose-limbed," and adhering to her appetite for dance of all kinds, she became immersed in classical ballet study.

.   .   .

Ruthie's twenties continued in a whirlwind of "incongruous juxtapositions" at the Paris Exposition Universelle in 1900 where she was inspired by Loie

Fuller's "flamboyant, overblown" dances of multicolored lights and billowing garments in counterpoint to the "beautiful austerities" of Sada Yacco, the Japanese geisha turned dancer-actress. At home, Christian Science commandeered her spirit, and "the Wizard of Broadway," David Belasco (or "D.B.," as she came to call him) championed her as a performer. Mary Baker Eddy's advocacy of "God As Infinite Mind" in *Science and Health with Key to the Scriptures* threw Ruthie into "a condition of ecstasy," while Belasco's genius added mystique to Ruthie's persona by upgrading her to "Ruth St. Denis." He cast her as Adele, the café concert girl, in his production of *Zaza,* the saga of "an unconventional female . . . a popular singer in one of the gayest music halls of Paris who falls in love with a married man."

A succession of Belasco productions crossing the country culminated in an indelible moment in the spring of 1904. As Martha Graham would do, seven years later, when she saw St. Denis's bespangled image through the glass, St. Denis glimpsed a poster, this one in a Buffalo, New York, store window: A "modernized" Isis advertised Egyptian Deities cigarettes. St. Denis remembered that "[m]y destiny as a dancer sprung alive at that moment . . . I would become a rhythmic and impersonal instrument of spiritual revelation rather than a personal actress of comedy or tragedy."

The hiatus from theatrical touring was a time of introspective research into the mysterious "wisdom of the East." In her midtown Manhattan flat, St. Denis read The Egyptian Book of the Dead, the Bhagavad Gita on the material and the spiritual body, the *Natyashastra,* the classical Sanskrit play *Sakuntala,* and *The Light of Asia,* a rendition of the life of Gautama Buddha by the English poet Edwin Arnold.

It was time to make the break from Belasco and forge ahead on her own. St. Denis's independent showcase took shape as the intimate tale of *Radha: The Mystic Dance of the Five Senses,* the sensuous spectacle that would make such an indelible impression upon Martha Graham in Los Angeles. In January 1906, St. Denis began her *Radha* tour, amplified by the inclusion of selections from her *East Indian Cycle*—"The Nautch," "Incense," and "The Cobras."

After solo shows in New York City and Washington, accompanied by Mother Emma, St. Denis "sought the stamp of European approval," appearing at *variétés* ("theatres that demanded [that] a star be a popular one") in England and Scotland, France, Austria, Hungary, and Germany, for three and a half years. Being "intensely patriotic," she believed it was her destiny to return to America for the 1909–1910 season. Reuniting with her agent Henry

Birkhardt Harris to play 108 dates in seventeen cities, she promoted her farm girl goddess brands of "secular" and "religious" dances.

Thanks to Harris's deep pockets—production expenses exceeded $30,000—St. Denis launched a 1910–1911 national foray with the full-length version of her *Egypta*. "Thinking in pictures, linking image to image, pose to pose," she immersed herself in the scholarly literature, including exhibition catalogues from the British Museum. After sitting through four dense acts of the production featuring more than fifty dancers and musicians— "The Prayer to the Nile God," "The Tamboura," "The Mystery of Isis," and "The Festival of Ra"—New York critics expressed mixed emotions about the sprawling, ambiguous piece: Was it "dance," or was it "theatre"? Was *Egypta* a "spectacle" or was it "pantomime"?

St. Denis cut back to an assemblage of excerpts from *Egypta* for her tour, the rendition that nineteen-year-old Edwin ("Ted") Myers Shawn witnessed at the Broadway Theatre in Denver toward the end of March 1911, three weeks before the Los Angeles show attended by Martha Graham and her father. Shawn instantly declared himself an "ardent fan." In Ruth St. Denis onstage he beheld, from a reverential distance, ". . . always the glamour of the East, but without its menace and without its vice; the East exalted and austere. [Gustave] Moreau himself might have envied her those dreams of form and color made manifest."

Blindsided by the death of Henry Birkhardt Harris on the *Titanic* and desperate "to keep the wolf from the door," St. Denis cobbled together a string of private "command performances" in high-society homes and women's clubs, and vaudeville acts at Hammerstein's theatre in New York and Keith's Columbia in Boston, among others, and devised a double bill of new dance dramas. In the first offering, *Bakawali,* a dancing girl in the court of Lord Indra, has the ill fortune to fall in love with a mortal. In anger, "[t]he god summons her, and as she leaves her earthly lover, he clings to her celestial wind-chariot and is carried into the sky." Once returned to heaven, Bakawali must dance at the throne of the great Indra, "curving herself as flowers curve under a perfumed breeze."

The second work, in the Japanese mode, was *O-Mika*, the tale of a beautiful courtesan "whose outer robes fall away to reveal her as the life-giving presence of a deity . . . Miss St. Denis proved to be an interesting figure whenever she was seen," the *New York Times* observed. Her face an oval mask of white makeup, costumed in pantaloons and a series of five multicolored kimonos, she walked through a replica of the Yoshiwara "pleasure district" of

Ruth St. Denis.
(Photograph by Alvin Langdon Coburn)

old Edo, performed the "Flower Hat" and "Samurai Fight" dances, and "was most enthusiastically applauded."

The program was a critical success but a financial failure, and spring 1913 was bleak. Undaunted, she hit the road in the summer. On July 12, her first night in the open-air Ravinia Park Pavilion on Chicago's North Side, St. Denis concluded a string of familiar selections from her Oriental oeuvre with an impromptu, upbeat cakewalk to Victor Herbert's sprightly "Al Fresco." When the crowd went wild, St. Denis realized the missing link: She must latch on to "the modern dance" craze sweeping the land, the "turkey-trotting and bunny-hugging" and "grizzly-bearing." She needed to find a "reputable male dancer" to partner with her.

. . .

Ted Shawn, Martha Graham's first choreographic mentor, was born in Kansas City, Missouri, on October 21, 1891. His father, Ellsworth, an amateur short-story author and poet, worked as editorial writer for the *Kansas City Star*. His "good, but not exceptionally doting" mother, Mary (née Boothe), of Louisville, Kentucky, a former high school principal, was "a woman of education and culture . . . large, dark, very beautiful and also of fine mental attainments." She died when Ted was eleven. Her passing, and the death of his beloved older brother soon thereafter, left Ted, "an intense, inhibited, emotional child, . . . in a state of nervous collapse." A lover of the out-of-doors, he worked his way through Manual Training High School during the fall and spring terms as a newspaper delivery boy. In summer sojourns at the mountain resort town of Fraser, Colorado, Ted drove a butter-and-eggs grocery wagon, and the next year he was "cutting, snaking, pulling and running logs" at the sawmill.

His father remarried, and the family moved to Denver, where Ted, by then a strapping, broad-shouldered six feet tall, "possessed of a keen intellect and a highly poetic nature," enrolled in the university as a pre-theology major intending to enter the Methodist ministry. Three years into college, he was stricken with diphtheria; an overdose of medicine caused temporary paralysis of his feet, legs, and thighs. Doctors suggested dancing lessons as physical therapy. Despite the admonitions of "horror-stricken professors" and former fraternity brothers that "*men* don't dance," and religious taboos against social dancing, Ted dropped out of college, enrolled part-time at Barnes Commercial School, and began studies with Hazel Wallack, a ballet dancer retired from the Metropolitan Opera who "initiated [him] into the world of Classic Dance."

In March 1911, soon after Shawn started lessons, he attended his first Ruth St. Denis performance, "the turning point in his life." In a revelatory afterthought, he announced that, beyond being only "moved and thrilled" like the masses, "he left the theatre resolved to be a great dancer also, and to win the personal recognition of his Goddess." Shawn continued, "He became convinced that the dance was to be the means of transmitting his message of beauty and uplift to the world and he perused his studies in this new field with the same seriousness of purpose which had impelled him to train for the pulpit." Shawn's first public performance in Denver came later that year, a solo called "Harvest Dance," in a play of his own devising for an amateur theatre company.

As a consequence of aesthetic and romantic differences with "the willowy" Ms. Wallack—i.e., her "unyielding" resistance to her protégé's desire to experiment with "interpretive dancing," "pictorial," and "semi-jazzic" styles outside the strictures of formal ballroom and ballet; and her return of a diamond engagement ring—Shawn headed west to Los Angeles. The "unknown and obscure typist" worked days as an accountant and stenographer for the auditor of the city water department, and scrounged cash to rent practice time after-hours "in a deserted ball room" where he continued to try new steps and exercise his body. "To make money to further [his] art side," Shawn signed with twenty-four-year-old Norma Gould, proprietor of a children's ballet school, and standard-bearer for the American pageantry movement, outdoor community reenactments of local history portrayed through theatre, dance, and music.

In addition to teaching classes and choreographing, Shawn and Gould teamed up for afternoon thés dansants—tango teas—at the Angelus Hotel

Ted Shawn against a mural by Eduard Buk Ulreich in the Shawn dance studio
on Grand Avenue in Los Angeles, 1919–1920. (Photograph by Arthur Kales)

at Spring and Fourth Streets and were regulars at the Alexandria Hotel ballroom, touted as "one of the largest of its kind for social affairs of every
nature," where they "danced nightly for the after-theatre set." In the spring
of 1913, Shawn developed a "screenplay" for a black-and-white nine-minute
silent two-reeler, *The Dances of the Ages,* and successfully pitched it to J. Searle
Dawley, a director for the Edison Company in Long Beach, where it was
filmed during two weeks in May and released in June. Shawn and Gould
starred front and center in this dance-as-history romp through "snake-like
movements of the Dance of the Priest of Ra . . . a Grecian Bacchanalia . . .
the voluptuousness of the ancient Orient . . . and the minuet of 1760," concluding with "the cakewalk in America and then . . . the present era with
the modern rag."

. . .

In the new year, 1914, Shawn and Gould signed up with the Santa Fe Railroad to present "Dancing As an Interpretative Art," a series of shows at depot reading rooms along the three-week transcontinental route from Los Angeles to New York City. The promotional brochure announced, "Ted Shawn and Norma Gould [are] assisted by [dancers] Adelaide Munn and Otis Williams in the rendition of classical and historical works of the Masters, accompanied by a Virtuoso Pianiste and Violiniste [*sic*] and Soloist." During these fare-free "rough and ready one-night stands" across the Southwest, Shawn met and talked with Indian peoples who planted the seeds of his interest in their culture.

As soon as the entourage arrived in New York City, Shawn hopped a train to New Canaan, Connecticut, home of the Canadian poet Bliss Carman, and his soul mate and patron, Mary Perry King. In his pilgrimage toward spiritual fulfillment wedded with bodily well-being, Shawn had read Carman's book *The Making of Personality*. The author's "opinions about the dance" very much "excited" him, an exchange of letters ensued, and Shawn and his colleagues were invited to Sunshine House, Mrs. King's country estate, for a month of six-days-a-week fresh-air movement classes and immersion in "the musicalness of life."

There was a Delsartian tenor to Carman's advocacy of the "triune ideal of normal well-being and happiness, based upon a definite conception of symmetrical life and growth" recognizing "the growing popularity" of "physical education . . . Such work at its best cannot be merely a profession," Carman opined; rather, dance "is a subtle and comprehensive *art*."

Shawn delighted in Carman and King's belief that "dance awaken[s] in the personality latent primordial joy by making activity expressive, restor[ing] the soul to full possession and control of the body." In particular, "Greek dance . . . in the freedom of the sandalled foot and loosely-robed figure, [gives] opportunity for natural and expressive motion."

In the February 1914 issue of *Atlantic Monthly*, Shawn found another powerful work, "The Philosophy of Dancing," an essay by the English writer, social reformer, scholar of human sexuality—and editor of the works of Christopher Marlowe—Henry Havelock Ellis. "Our Bible has been written, and our Scriptures revealed, and we are grateful for the gift of the Gospel according to St. Havelock," Shawn enthused. "Our precious art has truly been the Cinderella among the arts for a long and weary time. . . . And now comes our liberator, who proclaims [dance] the first and most important among the arts! [In the second paragraph of his article, Havelock Ellis] says: 'If you have failed to recognize the importance of the art of dancing, you have failed to recognize not only the supreme manifestation of spiritual life, but also the supreme symbol of spiritual life.'"

"The Philosophy of Dancing" begins with the author's synthesis of "Dancing and architecture [as] the two primary and essential arts," two forms of expression that have always been "inevitable and basic." The former, through movement, shows what is "*in* the human person"; and the latter, through structural imperatives, says what is "*outside* the person." From the origins of dance in the ancient temples, Havelock Ellis goes on, the Mother of the Arts represented "the divine mystery of the world . . . the vital re-enactment of a sacred history." Dance, like architecture, is a reflection of spatial awareness, what the Germans call *Raum Kunst*—"the art of space."

Havelock Ellis traces the provenance of dance from the iconography of Egyptian monuments to the sides of Greek vases, seeing a primal impulse that transcends all cultures and nations. He draws together the three "metric" [his word] figures of poetry, dance, and the physical labor of man, aligning the practices of craft and art with the rhythms of quotidian life. After all, Havelock Ellis writes, it was Friedrich Nietzsche who, "from first to last, showed himself possessed by the conception of the art of life as a dance." Havelock Ellis concludes, "The dance lies at the beginning of art, and we find it also at the end . . . [with] the philosopher of today." The essay, its title revised to "The Art of Dancing," became chapter 2 of Havelock Ellis's 1923 book, *The Dance of Life*.

.   .   .

Ted Shawn "hurried with [the Havelock Ellis article] to the most understanding soul in the world, and I read it aloud to her. I cut it from the magazine and had it bound, and, in the years that [would] pass, read it to every class of students who [came] to our school," including Martha Graham. That "most understanding soul" was Ruth St. Denis. Shawn had heard that she was seeking a performance partner to broaden her commercial audience. He also came in adoring search of "lessons in her own spiritual approach to the dances of the Orient." They sat in the front room at her home on Eighty-Ninth Street and Riverside Drive, walls covered with photographs of her many roles. St. Denis was impressed with Shawn's beauty, noble carriage, and youthful self-possession. They "talked from tea-time to midnight."

The next morning, at St. Denis's request, Shawn returned with costumes and music, and performed a multicultural program of solo dances for her, "a pseudo-Greek number . . . a spirited Slavic dance . . . and the Dagger Dance . . . of a young Aztec," inspired by William H. Prescott's *History and Conquest of Mexico*. St. Denis was impressed and hired Shawn to join her company for a spring and summer tour of the southern United States. Twelve years Ruth St. Denis's junior, Ted Shawn was the devoted student and acolyte, the open ear who never tired of her pontifications and showered her with poems and flowers. And St. Denis ached for a consistent and trusting intimacy in her life, having suffered through the disintegration of her family, as her older brother, "Buzz," got married, and her mother gave up touring and retreated into depression.

Shawn needed a mentor he could love and an equal partner to share his ideal for new forms of dance. St. Denis, lonely priestess on a pedestal, needed a standard-bearer for her boundless ego and a lover she could rule. On August 13, 1914, the codependent duo were united in civil matrimony in New York City. She took to calling him "Boy" and would not wear a wedding ring. Six days later, the St. Denis-Shawn Company embarked upon a six-month Canadian and cross-country trek of one-night stands. The tour culminated in February 1915 in San Francisco, with the premiere of their first jointly choreographed dance, *The Garden of Kama,* inspired by the forbidden romance of the "East Indian Eros . . . in the guise of a poor fisher youth" and the worshipful, innocent "daughter of the house," the plot lifted from a tale purportedly translated from "a song of India" by the English author Adela Florence Nicolson under the pseudonym of Laurence Hope.

In Los Angeles, flush with cash, St. Denis's outstanding debts liquidated, the couple opened their own dance school, as Shawn put it, "in answer to the need for a freer and more flexible method of instruction," employing "a system that had no system" except the mandate to allow the student "to be one's self . . . to discover by every possible means the nature of the talent of each individual . . . and to which the whole personality of the pupil is best suited." The forceful, open-armed mission statement, declared that "[t]he art of the dance is too big to be encompassed by any one system. On the contrary, the dance includes all systems or schools of dance. Every way that any human being of any race or nationality, at any period of human history, has moved rhythmically to express himself, belongs to the dance."

The Ruth St. Denis School of Dancing and Its Related Arts matriculated its first class of teenagers in the summer of 1915, girls from Los Angeles, some of whose mothers wanted them to learn how to be graceful; others who dreamed of a life on the road; still others who fantasized about becoming Hollywood stars. The curriculum "admitting of freedom yet requiring hours of disciplined training" consisted of stretching and limbering exercises, classical ballet technique counterbalanced by "experimentation with free movement . . . contrapuntal dance . . . to widen style, range, and dance vocabulary," "dances without accompaniment of any sort," orchestral dance, lectures upon the various aspects of dance and "teaching relation of music to dance," "costume design and study of decorative backgrounds as well as making costume accessories."

St. Denis's outdoor class at sunset, "Oriental techniques," was held on a wooden platform covered with canvas shaded by eucalyptus trees and encircled by a terraced lawn, and began with an extended earthbound period of sitting with mindfulness of the vertical chakras and the natural act of in-and-out breathing control, pranayama, legs crossed in the Sukhasana, "easy pose," building up to the lotus position, its roots in young Ruthie's yoga lessons in Pin Oaks Farm, progressing to body configurations that found their way into "The Yogi," her 1908 solo. As Krishna says to Arjuna in the Bhagavad Gita's fourth discourse: "Some offer the in-breath / in the out-breath. / Others offer the out-breath / in the in-breath." Classes in the summer sun and the "house studio" were relieved with pauses for light lunches, fruit juices, and refreshing dips in a sheltered, grotto-like swimming pool.

Not forsaking the practical side of their enterprise, Shawn and St. Denis capitalized upon a growing market around the country among dance teachers hungering for career enrichment. A "normal course" for "dance masters" was offered through the school wherein, for a "special price [seven lessons for $15], including music and supervision of costumes," teachers obtained access to "Miss St. Denis' famous dances in their entirety."

The renamed Denishawn Company booked the thousand-seat Alcazar Theatre in San Francisco for two matinees in mid-October 1915. St. Denis had a row with her accompanist and fired him on the spot. Desperate for a replacement, she ran to the theatre manager, who said that one of the violinists in the house orchestra had a friend who might be interested in the job, a journeyman "Hessian stogie roller" pounding "a bit of this and a bit of that" on the piano for weddings around town, soft-shoe acts, and buck-and-wing hoofers. The fellow had a mellifluous voice and the tendency, while playing, to keep his heavy-lidded eyes half-shut "like an old Brahms."

. . .

Louis Horst, Martha Graham's first dedicated accompanist, was the son of German immigrants, Carolina "Lena" Nickell and Conrad Horst, who settled first in Belleville, Illinois, in 1882, then moved to Kansas City, where Louis was born, just after midnight, on January 13, 1884; not wanting the baby to be stigmatized by an unlucky birthday, Lena persuaded the doctor to put January 12 on his birth certificate. Younger sister May was the "tomboy." Louis grew up as "the quiet one," a reader and thinker. Conrad had played the cornet in the army; Horst family life in the new land was shaped by Father's career as an itinerant musician. When Louis was ten years old, Conrad got a job as an instructor for local bands around Bethlehem, Pennsylvania. At their next stop, San Francisco, Conrad joined the symphony orchestra as a trumpeter, with side jobs at the opera house and the Imperial Vienna Prater Band, and teaching at the local conservatory. "With no questions asked," his dexterous son, Louis, was going to become a chip off the old block but not via the brass route. Father handed him a violin and bow and told Louis that in addition to his avid reading, he had to practice the instrument several times a day. To this burden, by the time he graduated from Adams Cosmopolitan Public School at age fifteen, Louis added four hours of piano daily, favoring popular rags rather than classical modes.

The Wanderjahr continued. Louis as a young man "discovered the less-than-reputable side of San Francisco life," teaching himself the new jazz tunes and joining pickup bands wherever the work took him, to gambling clubs and whorehouses, the saloons of Nevada, gold mines in the Mojave Desert, and as far northward as Eureka. Ricocheting from one job to another, Louis added the oboe and the organ to his portfolio, edging away from the violin—as well as from his conservative Lutheran upbringing, neither of which suited his rambunctious lifestyle.

During this vaudeville boom time, Louis's affections for "the music of the people" coincided with a surge of theatres of all shapes and sizes up and down the California coast built to accommodate "circuit company" variety shows. Louis began a typical evening with an early "cocktails set" at a hotel. After the scheduled performance, he could be found across the street from a place such as the Van Ness Theatre at a rustic boîte, accompanying Ethel Barrymore until the predawn hour of the wolf approached, and it was time to call it a day.

His first official job as a musical conductor was for the farce-comedy *Don't Tell My Wife,* in the summer of 1908 at the Santa Cruz Casino, where he met and fell in love with the hotel's telephone operator, a high school student, Bessie "Betty" Myrle Cunningham. They were married the following year. Louis spent two years as a pit musician in the grand Columbia Theatre on Geary Street, San Francisco's premier venue "devoted to the leading dramatic and musical attractions." Then, the couple had to hit the road—to New York City, the first time for both, followed by gigs hip-hopping from Bronxville to Bermuda to Lakewood in New Jersey, a summer stint in the Maplewood Hotel in New Hampshire, then back to San Francisco for another two years at the Columbia. Although work in commercial theatre paid the rent, Louis toggled between accompanying silent films one week, performing classical concerts the next, and *The Ziegfeld Follies of 1914* the next. Cracks began to mar the facade of married life when Betty realized her nesting instincts would not harness her peripatetic husband's drive to make music.

So it transpired that when Louis Horst met Ruth St. Denis at the Alcazar Theatre and she told him she was looking for someone to "help out for a couple of weeks" while the troupe headed up the coast to Oregon and Washington, he jumped at the chance and packed his bags. Discovering they had a common interest in the precepts of Christian Science and the writings of Mary Baker Eddy, St. Denis took an instant liking to her new hire. And Horst, "a cut and paste music man" at heart and by habit, was unperturbed by St. Denis's mercurial spontaneity and the way the "priestess with a twinkle in one eye" changed routines from night to night, sometimes minutes before she went onstage.

Toward the end of October 1915, the company was preparing to leave Spokane for points east—North and South Dakota, Minneapolis, Bloomington, western Pennsylvania, and on to New York City. Horst was in the orchestra pit at eleven o'clock for morning warm-ups. St. Denis stepped off the stage and alighted upon the top of his upright piano. Looking down from her perch, and "kind of crooning [to Horst] in her Irish way," she said, "Ted and I were talking last night . . . and we just wondered whether you wouldn't stay on" for the rest of the journey. Horst agreed—and would remain for another decade, looking back upon the course of his career as BD and AD—Before Denishawn and After Denishawn.

. . .

In the early summer of 1916, the self-conscious twenty-two-year-old Martha Graham arrived for her private audition with "Miss Ruth" St. Denis in the sanctuary of the Denishawn School house studio, with its green-curtained windows and walls, "no bigger than a living room." Seated in readiness at a white grand piano in the corner was the third member of the inner circle triumvirate, a "bored-seeming" gentleman in shirtsleeves with a massive head, clear blue eyes, and bushy eyebrows, "Louie" Horst, poker-faced and smoking a cigar.

Graham was asked to change into a khaki-colored bathing ensemble, the uniform costume worn by all the students. Then Ruth St. Denis, in a billowing gown, swept in to begin the "diagnosis" study, saying to Graham, "Dance for me." In the presence of the priestess for the first time, the girl was transfixed, struggling to maintain her dignity. After an instant, turning to Horst, St. Denis called out, "Play a waltz." Graham "reacted beat by beat to the music . . . [and] moved about the room . . . furiously, spontaneously." When it was over, St. Denis said, "That will do, thank you." Horst muttered little more than "she has a special quality."

St. Denis took Shawn aside and told her colleague that the short, "exceed-

Martha Graham in the Cumnock School "Spirit of Spring" May Day Celebration, Los Angeles, 1915.

ingly shy," somewhat overweight girl with the "homely face," dark eyes, high cheekbones, angular jaw, and black hair tugged back was not the "Denishawn type." St. Denis added, disparagingly, that she did not know what she could "do" with Martha Graham, who was, quite frankly "too old to become a good dancer." The girl seemed ardent and conscientious and was welcome to take hatha yoga and other exercise sessions with Miss Ruth. Beyond that, Graham had one year remaining at the Cumnock School, and if Shawn was willing to supervise her, he could feel free.

Meeting privately with Graham, Shawn admitted she was "not the prima ballerina *assoluta*" by any stretch of his imagination and "certainly not your average northern European peaches and cream blonde" like the smiling Denishawn lovelies, eyelids fluttering, who paraded in and out of the dressing room, languidly shedding flimsy wraparound shantung gowns to reveal long limbs, sculpted torsos, and toned upper arms. That said, Shawn concurred with Horst: Martha Graham was . . . well . . . *different*. He sensed the "burning desire to dance" smoldering under her "unprepossessing" manner. She "had the fire" beneath that implacable visage.

Shawn decided to enroll the "untamed little black panther" in his morning ballet class and afternoon character dancing, ethnic dance, and Dalcroze eurythmics, encouraging bare feet and mobile arms. During breaks for notes, questions, and answers, Graham always sat in the back row, her gaze—"the great doelike orbs glowing and blazing and sparkling"—fixed in "smoldering watchfulness" at a distance, raising her hand when, and *only* when, she was sure she had something to say.

In their alone time when the day's final tension-relaxation exercises were over, Shawn told Graham, "You have a long row to hoe." The proprietary "papa" described magical, spell-conjuring Miss Ruth as the inspirer who encouraged the dancers, as in her beloved Gita, to be "like a lit lamp / that does not flicker." He, on the other hand, was the teacher, the pedagogue akin to a gardener "who does not create the seed or the bulb or the root; this, God has created. All the gardener can do is . . . everything possible so that the seed or the bulb or the root can become the finest example of what God put in to the beginnings of it."

Papa Shawn, only three years older than his novice, warned Martha Graham, "It will be a hard battle. It will not be easy. But," he reassured her, "I will stick by you."

·   ·   ·

At the end of June 1916, St. Denis received a note from Professor William Dallam Armes, director of music and drama at the University of California, Berkeley, praising her as "not only a dancer of marked individuality and ability, but as a creative artist, who has marked out many roads that others have followed," and inviting the Denishawn Company to perform at the university's William Randolph Hearst Greek Theatre. The outdoor amphitheater—accommodating more than ten thousand people when the surrounding hillsides were occupied—had opened on September 24, 1903, hailed as an architectural phenomenon "that has scarcely existed in the world since the memory days of Greece, one whose only roof was a perfect sky, azureous [*sic*] as that above Athens." The theatre had been limited to hosting "very few of the superlatively great" vocal, theatrical, and orchestral works. Denishawn would be the first dance company to grace its stage.

With less than a month to prepare, Miss Ruth and Papa Shawn concocted *A Dance Pageant of Egypt, Greece and India,* a two-hour extravaganza for 170 dancers melding three exotic cultures into one mammoth romanticized spectacle on the customs and concepts of the afterlife. The San Francisco Symphony Orchestra, more than sixty musicians, accompanied by the University of California Chorus, would be conducted by Louis Horst. The poster advertising the event depicted a Grecian urn decorated with a warrior sporting a shield emblazoned with the University of California logo standing contrapposto next to a maiden in a floor-length gown beside a group of shadowy, cloaked figures, one a seated snake charmer, swaying to unheard melodies.

The Greece segment of the show featured "Pyrrhic Dance," an all-male ballet, the robust, "tall athletic forms of young men [chosen] wherever possible to balance [Shawn's] own six feet." Shawn scorned Nijinsky's prancings as "feministic [*sic*] . . . America demands masculinity more than art." "Pyrrhic Dance" was meant to prove that modern dance could be "a respectable profession for brawny men." The tableaux consisted of a dance of youths training for the Olympic games, an offering to Bacchus, and Pluto brooding on his sable throne.

In the India section, ghat burns on the banks of the Ganges as the women of the village arrive, singly and in groups, to wash their saris and perform ablutions; the day passes through "the hot siesta period," and a widow performs the rite of suttee.

For *Egypt,* Shawn helped "dye the costumes Nile green." The pharaoh of the Lower land and the queen of the Upper land appear in "an Osirian ceremonial." The ensuing invasion is personified by Set, the god of evil; the soul of the divided land wends its way to the Hall of Judgment, where the crocodile god awaits; and, at last, the ceremonial dance of rebirth takes place. Martha Graham was one of the dancing girls in this friezelike portion of the show, hair clipped to chin length, bare feet pointed, parallel and firmly planted, right arm extended straight ahead, left arm in an angular crook above her head, bearing an ancient metallic triangle in each hand.

· · ·

In the fall of 1916, Martha returned to the Cumnock School for her final year. In anticipation of a visit to Los Angeles by the Bengali songwriter-poet Rabindranath Tagore, organized by Cumnock in alliance with the Drama League, Graham performed for her fellow students a selection from *Gitanjali,* Tagore's Nobel Prize–winning collection of verse lyrics. She was lauded as "a promising young reader [who] also excels in the art of dancing."

Over the spring holiday of her last semester, Graham was invited by Grace Chatfield-Taylor McGann to perform at a costume ball she and her husband, Robert, were hosting at their estate, the Peppers, on Hot Springs Road in fashionable Montecito. The March 9, 1917, gala was a charity benefit for the Queen Mary's Guild in aid of Allied soldiers' hospitals in Europe. Dinner was served in the grand ballroom, after which came "the artistic feature of the evening . . . a Santa Barbara girl, Martha Graham, [who] was a dancing pupil of Ruth St. Denis for a month last summer." Doing her bit for the war effort, Graham was praised by the *Santa Barbara News-Press* as a "clever little woman," quite "lithe and graceful" in a Javanese dance, her makeup "remarkably true to the type of the little brown women." For an encore, Graham performed "as a woman of the East with a water jar, doing very deft work with the handling of her drapery."

Following graduation, Graham returned posthaste to Denishawn, relocated in larger quarters vacated by the Westlake School for Girls, including dormitory space in the ivy-covered home building for the growing number of resident students. There was also a studio house; a craft house, where required classes in costume design and "decorative backgrounds" as well as French were taught (and Louis and Betty Horst lived); a costume house, with storage for "the extensive wardrobe of Miss St. Denis and Mr. Shawn's past productions"; and the idyllic open-air Denishawn dance theatre, an extended apron stage, walls adorned with jasmine and honeysuckle, where more than four hundred people could watch performances "protected from the night dews by a canopy."

Trim and slender "in a tweedy suit and toque," another out-of-town girl set down her suitcase on the doorstep of the home building of the Denishawn School. Twenty-two years old, well-mannered, "perfectly-proportioned, Titian-haired and barely five foot three," swan-necked, soft-spoken Doris Humphrey had come a long way from Oak Park, a suburb of Chicago where "there was no such thing as modern dance," to what she dreamed would be the "University of the Dance." Her father, Horace, was a photographer who sang in the Chicago Apollo Chorus, and her mother, Julia, was a concert pianist. As a child, music was Doris's first love; many nights she fell asleep listening to Julia's rippling, restless melodies drifting from the parlor into her bedroom—Edward MacDowell's *Hexentanz,* Christian Sinding's *Rustle of Spring.* Doris started ballet at the Francis W. Parker School, showing aptitude in pageants and interpretive dancing. She was possessed with

Doris Humphrey coached by Ruth St. Denis in "Soaring," 1920,
set to *Fantasiestücke,* op. 12 by Robert Schumann.

the uncanny ability to see a dance recital once, memorize all the pieces, then perform them, step for step, for friends and neighbors willing to drop a few pennies into her palm.

At seventeen, when she graduated from Parker, Doris founded a dancing school in partnership with her mother, offering classic, gymnastic, and ballroom for children. Doris's dance teacher in these growing-up years was Mary Wood Hinman. Through her association with Hull-House as a colleague of Jane Addams and John Dewey, Hinman inculcated in Doris the belief that "a wonderful teacher is someone you should cherish." Hinman urged her to seek greater challenges and study dance with Ruth St. Denis in California.

Arriving in Los Angeles, Doris auditioned for the "magnetic . . . magnificent" St. Denis, and, spellbound, "never look[ed] back." Meeting Miss Ruth was "the first time . . . [she] saw the dance as whole and complete." In contrast to her coolness toward Martha Graham, St. Denis took to Doris immediately, welcoming her affinity for "music visualizations" ranging from Bach through the Romantics and Debussy integral to the Denishawn repertory.

"If the music swells, the body swells," Miss Ruth told her, "and if the music grows quiet, the body comes to rest."

In the summer of 1917, Ted Shawn appointed Martha Graham, his "artist pupil," to take over some of the Denishawn children's classes, pleased to observe her patience keeping the little ones on task while encouraging them to use their imaginations. Shawn said that was the season when Graham broke out of her shell and "came to life." One afternoon, devising an exercise with the working title of "Bailarina Real," a hybrid Moorish-Spanish routine danced to Serenata, op. 13, by Italian composer Mario Tarenghi, Shawn wondered aloud with exasperation if any of the girls in the class would ever "get" what he was after.

Martha Graham, who had taken it all in silently, leapt up, threw on an ankle-length, circular pleated skirt, linked the hem to a bracelet on each wrist, and "tore across the room with a fervor" in a whirlwind of turns, flaring the heavy brocaded material "high and outward." Shawn, stunned and thrilled, cheered for Graham in front of the others. It would be another four years before she publicly performed the completely realized dance under its final title, "Serenata Morisca."

Before Christmas, Ted Shawn enlisted as a private in an army ambulance unit stationed at Camp Kearney near San Diego. He would commute back to Los Angeles and conduct classes on weekend leaves. During the week, expanding Graham's duties beyond the children's classes, he designated her as the junior director, responsible for teaching night dance classes to working girls. Between them, Shawn and Graham held the fort at Denishawn. Meanwhile, as "Ted found more pleasure in his own projects than in riding Ruth's coattails," St. Denis, with Horst and Humphrey in tow, set forth on the cross-country Orpheus and Pantages vaudeville circuits to raise money for Liberty Bonds.

This was not yet a permanent parting of the ways; Shawn and St. Denis would reunite for a national tour. However, power struggles over equal billing, and diverging artistic and commercial paths during and following the war foreshadowed the disintegration of their married-in-name-only relationship—and opened up a pathway into the spotlight for Martha Graham.

4

Horst

The *Saskatoon* (Saskatchewan) *Daily Star* theatre critic marveled at Ted Shawn's dance drama extravaganza *Julnar of the Sea*. "Better twenty minutes of this than half a century of 'leg shows,' of performing horses, of jugglers, cracked warblers and other junk commonly served under the name of vaudeville. . . . This [show] is music for a soul perishing in the desert of jazz." Based upon the tales between the 739th and 756th Arabian Nights, *Julnar* starred Lillian Powell, one of Shawn's star pupils, in the title role. She entered the Maxfield Parrish–like set as the virgin maiden coveted by King Shahriman, "wrapped in a veil of gold-purpled silk . . . her seven tresses hung down to her ankles like horses' tails. She had Nature kohl'd eyes, heavy lips and thighs and a waist of slenderest guise."

Powell led an ensemble of sixteen dancers through three acts with narration provided by Scheherazade, a languid apparition, wine goblet in hand, reclining on a chaise behind a transparent curtain. The sumptuous spectacle traveled under the supervision of Louis Horst as manager and musical director from the fall of 1919 to the spring of 1921, "more than twelve hundred continuous performances," Shawn wrote *("1,205* performances," according to Horst's meticulous notebooks).

Shawn did not accompany Horst and the Denishawns on their journey, preferring to remain in the Ted Shawn studio on Grand Avenue, creating and producing work for other dancers and singers, while his "accomplished terpsichoreans" enraptured audiences across the land with their "perfect tempo of bare feet . . . hit[ting] on all cylinders from the opening curtain . . . undeniable charm of facial features," and "gorgeous costumes." Ruth St. Denis, with pretensions toward high art rather than the big time, announced she was retiring from vaudeville to devise cultural evenings combining music

Louis Horst, founding editor of *Dance Observer* and self-described "Hessian stogie-roller," holding beloved dachshund, Max. (Line drawing by Aline Fruhauf, 1936)

and poetry, "express[ing] the finer quality of the soul-life." She would feature "all American girls from fine upper-middle class parentage who have had the advantage of a thorough education."

Martha Graham, however, was not at all snobbish when a welcome opportunity to perform came along to distract from the routine of teaching. In December 1919, Samuel Lionel "Roxy" Rothafel—back in Los Angeles after a half dozen years in New York City where he controlled four show business palaces—the Regent, Strand, Rialto, and Rivoli—knocked on Shawn's door. In Gotham, Roxy had built a reputation synchronizing orchestral music to silent films and presenting "ballet and special settings for soloists and overtures in connection with . . . the most progressive photoplays made."

Roxy and his business partner, Samuel L. Golden, had purchased a gilded LA venue, the California Theatre, at Main and Eighth Streets where, in the new year, they would present *The Cup of Fury*. Based upon the novel by Rupert Hughes, directed by T. Hayes Hunter, and starring Helene Chadwick and Rockliffe Fellowes, it was "the story of Marie-Louise, an American girl in England after the sinking of the *Lusitania,* left alone to face the charge of a crime—being in league with Germany and aiding the enemy."

Roxy told Shawn he needed "a bright youngster who would work cheap" at the top of the "footlight parade" prologue before the opening-night screening. Shawn wanted to know what kind of performance he had in mind. Roxy said he wanted a fire dance. Well, if it was *fire* he was looking for, Shawn had just the girl.

Martha Graham's performance on the night of January 4, 1920, the opening act on the program, was an "atmospheric prelude with scenic and lighting effects," inspired by Loie Fuller's 1896 pyrotechnical breakthrough, "La Danse du Feu "—red-gelled stereopticon flood lamps angled from the wings and through glass panels from below; dervish twists and turns; "a rushing pace with Wagnerian sonorities"; and yards of illuminated, billowing silk scarves. Whatever magic Graham pulled forth from her soul, Roxy asked her to stay on for the following week to present another "interpretative dance," the lead-in stage act for the premiere of *When the Clouds Roll By.* This romantic comedy, a silent film from United Artists, written by and starring Douglas Fairbanks Sr., was billed as a satirical send-up of "the innovational field of psychiatry" situated in bohemian Greenwich Village.

. . .

In an era that spanned the rapid rise and painful denouement of vaudeville, Ted Shawn strived to build a repertory that both entertained and elucidated. However, as he idealized the "pure cultures" of antiquity, he also conflated them. Reading depictions of "the Ancient Mysteries" in *Tertium Organum* (*The Third Canon of Thought—A Key to the Enigmas of the World*), by P. D. Ouspensky, he was drawn to "the special preparatory rituals in Egypt, in India, in Greece . . . actually leading the soul to the very doors of the new world." Intrigued by the remote otherness of this fantasized Orient, Shawn had to face the realities of present-day commerce to put on a show with "legs." His recipe of mixing up cultural appropriations was not going to result in dance works true to history: "The literal reproduction is the function of the scholar and the museum worker," he conceded, but "the function of the artist is to use authentic themes as seeds from which to produce an art creation of his own."

This spirit of inquiry moved Shawn to decide in the spring of 1920 that the time was right for a dance drama personifying the legend of the eleventh-century Toltec queen La Reina Xochitl, tailor-made for the physique and temperament of Martha Graham, his high-cheekboned protégée "with her gift for ferocity," now that she had begun to smell the greasepaint. From his creative palette, Shawn took a dab of "the vogue of things Mexican" in California, blended with tones of reverence for the "rituals . . . of the Indian celebrants" of the Great Plains and the Southwest, and threw in a Whitman-esque vision of the hemispheric unity of the Americas.

With the desire to "champion Indian dance" broadly defined, Shawn enlisted two collaborators for a two-act ballet that would stress "strong, close-to-the-ground movements . . . [and] direct and vigorous pantomime." For music, he turned to Homer Grunn, a native of Salem, Wisconsin, living and teaching in Los Angeles, who had studied piano and composition at the Stern Conservatory in Berlin. "An authority on American aboriginal melodies," Grunn's anthology of songs, *From Desert and Pueblo,* was the result of field trips to Indian reservations where he took "transcriptions and [made] settings" of the "primitive and picturesque music," adding into them "our chord structure, completing as it does the three basic principles of music: that is, melody, rhythm and harmony . . . result[ing] in an art product well worth preserving for all lovers of . . . American music."

In Homer Grunn, Shawn found a kindred spirit: "This, surely, is one great charge laid upon the American dancers," Shawn wrote, "to study, record and translate the dance art of the Indian to present and future generations."

For sets and costumes, Shawn approached Francisco Cornejo, a painter and archaeologist born in La Paz, Mexico, lecturing on pre-Columbian art at his Aztec Studio in San Francisco. "We talk about having an 'American' art," Cornejo declared, "but, sad to say, our architects, our sculptors, our painters, our craftsmen . . . neglect what we possess on our own continent . . . Maya and Aztec art bears no real resemblance to that of any other ancient nation, and is our heritage."

The curtain rises against a line of maguey (agave) cactus and a backdrop of the towering stepped facade of Chichén Itzá. Tending to the plants, with her seated maidens, feet in perfect parallel, is Martha Graham as Xochitl, her hair parted in the middle, Hopi style, a squash blossom tucked behind her ear. Her father, Papantzin, dressed in leopard skin, staggers in, intoxicated by pulque, liquor distilled from cactus honey. They will bring a gourd of the milky concoction as a gift to Emperor Tecpancaltzin. The second scene opens before a backdrop of the *piedra del sol,* the round calendar stone,

Martha Graham starring as Xochitl, June 1920. (Photograph by Nickolas Muray)

symbol of cyclical Aztec time in a sunburst of ochre and red. The emperor is seated upon his raised throne, six women grouped kneeling, crouching, and standing to his right and left. Their ritual dance "consists of flat-footed stampings and turns in various formations," handheld wooden fans waving.

Papantzin and Xochitl arrive. Graham is wearing a clinging, thin, scoop-necked half-sleeved dress adorned with jangling bells around the waist; the hem, raised above the knee, parts to reveal her bare thighs. From one shoulder trails a long scarf. As she offers the emperor a drink from the pulque gourd, he makes a show of appreciating her exotic beauty and orders her to dance for him. She manipulates the scarf "in a *plastique* solo" so alluring that the emperor removes his cloak and crown and signals to the attendant girls to distract Papantzin and usher him offstage.

Alone with Xochitl, the emperor forces himself upon her. Xochitl "resists with unexpected ferocity." Her screams bring her father back into the fray, knife in hand, threatening to kill the emperor. She steps away and begs Papantzin to have mercy. Moved by this gesture, Tecpancaltzin asks Xochitl to marry him, announcing to the court that henceforth she shall be known as empress of the Toltecs. After a dance of unity and celebration, the emperor gently enfolds Xochitl within his cloak of quetzal feathers and they ascend to the throne.

According to Toltec history, when civil strife enveloped their nation, the goddess Xochitl took on the trappings of a latter-day Amazon, leading a corps of woman warriors into battle. She was killed, alongside her husband, during a final courageous stand at Tultitlán.

The "native ballet" was promoted as the headliner on Alexander Pantages's vaudeville theatre circuit, *Xochitl*'s first phase of touring in the fall of 1920, from Vancouver in the Pacific Northwest through Tacoma, Washington, where the statuesque Robert Gorham, a favorite of Shawn's playing the emperor, broke a bone in his foot and was replaced by a Denishawn novice, Charles Weidman.

The nineteen-year-old who unexpectedly found himself partnering with Martha Graham was born in Lincoln, Nebraska, where his father, Charles Sr., was chief of the fire department. Charles's mother, Vesta Hoffman, hailed from Sioux City, Iowa. Weidman wrote with characteristic wit and whimsy that she "was, at one time, champion roller skater of the middle west." Like Martha Graham and Ted Shawn before him, Charles was galvanized into dance by a Ruth St. Denis performance. He went on to study with Eleanor Frampton, a Wellesley alumna who founded her dance school after receiving a BA in physical education from the University of Nebraska. Weidman's next teacher, when he arrived at Denishawn on a scholarship in the summer of 1920, was Doris Humphrey; the two would become colleagues and dance partners.

The Tacoma evening newspaper took note of the newcomer's "impressive stateliness" as the emperor. Weidman—who reminded Shawn of "a Charles Ray character then popular in the movies"—demurred, thinking of himself as anything but "stately"; he was "just a skinny kid, a lyric type of dancer . . . not strictly *à terre*." The next year, Shawn choreographed the role of Pierrot Forlorn for Weidman, and from that time, across his erratic career, bittersweet humor lingering beneath pathos, he became adept at "creating three-dimensional characters out of *clichés*."

Xochitl headed along the coast to Los Angeles, Long Beach, and Santa Barbara, Martha's hometown, where she made her first statement to the press, assuming the deliberate manner that would come to define her public persona, someone who "simply has intuitions of when and to whom she may speak and when and in whose presence to be silent." Graham told the *Santa*

Barbara News on October 2, 1920, "So far the only value of my work—if it has art value—is absolute sincerity . . . I would not do anything that I could not *feel*. A dance must dominate me, completely, until I lose sense of anything else. Later what I do may be called art, but not yet."

Of *Xochitl,* Graham said, "I love this dance-drama, and have every faith in it—it has brought the joy of life to me." Three weeks later, she caught the eye of a reporter for the *Santa Barbara News,* who recalled "discovering" Graham and filing "her first write-up" after seeing her Javanese dance at the McGanns' costume party in Montecito. "Since that evening," the unbylined critic wrote, bestowing a prophetic blessing, "Miss Graham has grown in grace and in the perfection of her art, and it is reasonable to believe she will attain the height, since sincerity of purpose and love of work such as here cannot fail to excel."

. . . .

Basking in the financial and artistic aura of *Julnar* and *Xochitl,* Ted Shawn knew that a carpe diem moment had arrived. He gathered the core studio team—musical director Louis Horst with starring dancers Martha Graham and Charles Weidman, supported by Betty May and Dorothea Bowen—and strung together a twenty-city cross-country "America's First Man Dancer" tour, outside the purview of the B. F. Keith, Orpheum, and Pantages organizations. They opened on September 8, 1921, at Frank C. Egan's Little Theatre on South Figueroa Street in Los Angeles and would conclude on December 2 at Edgar and Archie Selwyn's Apollo Theatre on Forty-Third Street in New York City.

Première danseuse Martha Graham, front and center, was imbued with fanatical energy. In Shawn's *Church Service in Dance,* modeled upon the Protestant rituals of Graham's childhood, she accompanied a recitation of Psalm 23, interpreting through her movement a sermon, an anthem, a hymn, and a benediction. "The Psalm loses none of its dignity or beauty when presented in this manner," Shawn said. "There is nothing either new or extraordinary in [my] suggestion that the church service be danced."

Drawing upon his readings in Havelock Ellis, Shawn reminded patrons that "[a]ll pagan religions relied upon the dance for their ritual, and Fra Angelico and others of the early Italians painted exquisitely lovely Sacred Ballets."

Graham made her debut in "Serenata Morisca" as "a strong, self-confident,

Martha Graham with Ted Shawn in "Malagueña," 1921.
(Photograph by Nickolas Muray)

arrogant, aristocratic woman who is very conscious of her physical attractiveness . . . the favorite of a king or Shah of some unspecified country . . . A large purple and red flower in her hair, arrayed in a pleated transparent skirt and shiny bodice with bells on her ankles, the figure who darts in with unabashed forwardness is obviously an entertainer."

She also performed several of St. Denis's "music visualizations" modified by Shawn, including "Capriccio," "Pastorale," and "Revolutionary Etude," set to Chopin's op. 10, no. 12 in C Minor, formally known as *Etude on the Bombardment of Warsaw*, in which Graham hurtled from the wings full-tilt onto the stage, "a ragged, wounded and terrified girl" dressed in red, "symbolic of flame and destruction . . . staring back at an imaginary assailant." The finale was a reprise of the second act of *Xochitl*, with Charles Weidman as the father and Shawn taking over as emperor. During the rape scene, Graham beat Shawn with her clenched fists severely, bruising his chest, and bit him so sharply on the lips that she drew blood.

After a night at the Potter Theatre in downtown Santa Barbara, and a stop in Riverside, the troupe headed north and east into Minnesota, where they spent a month in Rochester, Minneapolis–St. Paul, and Mankato; then on into Nebraska for a matinee and evening in Lincoln, where prodigal son Charles Weidman was applauded.

In Omaha, during a two-night stand on October 24 and 25, 1921, at the art deco Brandeis Theatre at Douglas and Seventeenth Streets, Martha Graham was singled out by Keene Abbott of the *World-Herald* as possessing "a quality of aloofness that is almost eerie in its fascination . . . something impalpable. She recalls the beautiful women Dante Gabriel Rossetti put on canvas." During one long afternoon, Louis Horst was in his hotel room making changes to an arrangement. Graham knocked at the door and asked to come in. She stretched out her arms to him, he came to her and kissed her, and the two began a liaison.

Betty Horst was already resentful of her husband's travels since she had become ill with tuberculosis and quit performing. Their relationship degenerated into what one friend described as "freestyle"; while Graham's featured roles in Shawn's programs meant she spent more time alone in the rehearsal room with her music director.

On the train between towns and cities, Charles Weidman noticed the twenty-seven-year-old dancer and her fatherly accompanist a decade older snuggling shoulder to shoulder, his prematurely white mane against her jet-black updo, sharing confidences by the hour, huddled in debate over the marginalia in Horst's volumes of Nietzsche and Schopenhauer. Sturdy as she was, "even Martha needed a wailing wall . . . ," Weidman said, "someone to back her up," a man to relieve the "tribulations" and "frustrations" that were necessary to her art but "wrecked her soul." Twenty years after Horst's death, in a reminiscent moment, Graham said, "He became my lover, yes . . . but it was like loving a child, because I was a child."

The group arrived in Austin for a performance at the Hancock Theatre in early November. The University of Texas had recently purchased the private library of Genaro García, the Mexican historian, translator, bibliophile, and director of the Museo Nacional de Historia, Arqueología y Etnología. Shawn, Horst, and Graham made a field trip to the forty-acre campus on a hill in the northern outskirts of the city and spent an unhurried day "poring over these . . . books, codices, pamphlets and prints dealing exclusively with the prehistoric civilizations of Mexico." The encyclopedic collection was housed in the university's Victorian Gothic main building, its outer walls adorned with ivy grown from cuttings imported from St. Giles' Church in Stoke Poges, Buckinghamshire, immortalized by Thomas Gray in his "Elegy Written in a Country Churchyard."

At the final tour date in the Apollo Theatre on Broadway, the *New York Times* deciphered *Xochitl* as "a Mexican *Rigoletto* in dances," Gilda as Xochitl, Rigoletto as her father, and the Duke of Mantua as the obsessed emperor. Stunned by the apparition of Martha Graham, Daniel Mayer, "the internationally-known impresario who managed Paderewski, Pavlova, [Caruso], and similarly shining stars," could not wait until the applause died down at the first intermission to meet the dancer. From the packed matinee house, all abuzz, he rushed backstage, barged into Shawn's dressing room, and said he wanted to manage the company, proposing two short trips—a foray into the southeastern United States in the spring, and overseas to London—and then a three-year concert tour.

Separated from Miss Ruth by an entire continent, Shawn established a New York Denishawn "studio" in the penthouse of the Hotel Chatsworth on Seventy-Second Street and Riverside Drive. He expected Graham to resume teaching, telling her one day over lunch at the C & L Restaurant on Broadway that she could start by going to the "smartest department stores downtown," Lord & Taylor, Wanamaker's, and Bonwit Teller, to recruit dance students from among career women and shopgirls by demonstrating movement techniques in the aisles. "I am an artist—*not* a saleswoman!" Graham shrieked. Rearing up "on her hind legs" in her "wildcat" manner, she continued, "Ted—*you* will do *anything* to make a living! You *cannot* talk to me that way!" She yanked the tablecloth, scattering silverware, dishes, and food, and stalked out.

The uneasy alliance between Graham and Shawn was further tested when Daniel Mayer said that to strengthen box office appeal his three-year producing commitment was contingent upon including performances by Ruth St. Denis, who demanded top billing, adding that she wanted Betty Horst, recovering from her sickbed, to rejoin the troupe, replacing Doris Humphrey, temporarily seduced into vaudeville. This irritated Graham, who had just moved out of the Chatsworth and into an apartment nearer to Horst after her squabble with Shawn. The ménage became messier when Horst—"guilt-ridden," but not quite enough to stop trying to have it both ways—agreed to his wife's reenlistment in the cast.

The April Mayer tour was brief, ten days in North and South Carolina. At the beginning of May 1922, the Denishawn dancers, with Horst as music director, sailed for London on Cunard's RMS *Samaria*. They were a "company" in name only: St. Denis told Shawn she felt increasingly "unmarried" to him. He retorted that he had "severed his umbilical cord."

. . .

The show went on in high style, two performances a day for a month, at the largest vaudeville venue in London, the 2,500-seat Coliseum Theatre of Varieties on St. Martin's Lane. St. Denis's bitterness was revealed in Graham's curtailed role on the program. Most angst-ridden was Miss Ruth's appropriation of the role of the princess in *Xochitl.* She permitted Graham one duet with Shawn, in "Spanish Suite," limiting her remaining stage appearances to ensemble work. Graham was one of "the three little sisters" bracketed between Betty May and Dorothea Bowen as part of the "East Indian Suite," a St. Denis confection whipped up for the May 15 matinee set to the music of American composer Bainbridge Crist. "The Dance of the Apsarases" featured a trio of Vedic water nymphs, favorites of the god-king Indra, "women who were the essence of innocence . . . flutter[ing] . . . brilliant as humming-birds," swiveling in saris "like diaphanous pastel tents" afloat over Punjabi pants, their "belled anklets" jingling with every step. Successions of ronds de jambe, backbends, and kicks were executed in unison, the piece beginning and ending with Graham and the other girls hand in hand and in single file.

Watching from the wings, waiting to join Graham in the next dance, set to Robert Schumann's *Soaring (Aufschwung)*, depicting the birth of Venus from the sea, Charles Weidman stood in awe of the "looseness" and "freedom" of her extensions. Even when accompanied by other dancers, Weidman saw that Martha Graham invariably stood out.

"The one man [Ted Shawn] most wanted to meet in England" was Havelock Ellis, author of "The Philosophy of Dancing," the 1914 essay that had so moved him. During the years since the first reading, having gone through all six volumes of Ellis's *Studies in the Psychology of Sex,* Shawn hoped "to touch the garment of Jesus." He made the pilgrimage to Ellis's home on Canterbury Road in Brixton. The two had an intimate talk, and Shawn gave Ellis a copy of his book on Ruth St. Denis, "poured out [his] suffering" and conflicted "agonies" about their moribund marriage, and listened, for the first time, to a candid discussion of homosexuality without shame by a "mature man, a philosopher who was both a scientist and a lover of the arts." Shawn confided to Ellis that he had not had homosexual experiences, "but he knew what was latent within him."

They parted company reluctantly. Ellis hoped Shawn would soon return, as "there seem so many subjects we left untouched . . . or only barely touched." He gave Shawn a letter of introduction to Edward Carpenter, author of *The Intermediate Sex*. Over drinks backstage in Shawn's dressing room between matinee and evening shows, Carpenter and Shawn spent an afternoon in shared affection for Walt Whitman. Traveling in America as a teenager in 1877, Carpenter had met the Good Gray Poet. That encounter, permitting himself "ground for the love of men," inspired Carpenter's book-length poem in homage to *Leaves of Grass,* entitled *Towards Democracy:* "Strange tender figure, full of grace and pity, / Yet outcast and misunderstood of men— / Thy Woman-soul within a Man's form dwelling. . . ." Shawn wrote thereafter that "it is my constant and sincere prayer that my own consciousness be expanded to the point that I may be 'a Whitman of the dance.'"

Martha Graham's offstage life in London was "a strange time" and "an emotional storm . . . of clashes and weeping" relieved by occasional sightseeing—*Madama Butterfly* at the Royal Opera House, and a boat trip up the Thames to Hampton Court. During commiserating walks through the labyrinthine West End streets, Shawn complained of his wife's wandering eye alighting upon one or another "callow youth." Graham despaired of Miss Ruth's antipathy to her ambitions in dance, and bemoaned Horst's feigned rectitude, the way he brushed aside Graham's pleadings and told her

Group of terra-cotta draped women from Tanagra. Greek, third century BC.

he would never divorce Betty, yet sharing a room with his wife at the Regent Palace Hotel.

During a weeklong June run of shows at the Hippodrome in Manchester, a rainy, somber northern town that reminded Graham of industrial Pittsburgh, Horst took advantage of his wife's remaining in London to take up again with Graham, escorting her to the City Art Gallery to survey its antiquities. They saw a collection of terra-cotta Tanagra figurines dating from the fourth to second centuries BC, named after the site in Boeotia, east of Thebes in central Greece, where they were discovered in the early 1870s. The statuettes, under six inches in height and originally multicolored— pale orange-pink skin, auburn hair, blue eyes, black eyebrows, red lips, gilt jewelry, and rose-madder purple garments—were of laughing, frolicking women and girls, singularly and in pairs, wrapped in togas, wearing hats or bearing fans, playing games, striking poses, and dancing.

5

Schopenhauer and Nietzsche

etween the publications of *Ulysses* and *The Waste Land*, the summer of 1922 was the season when Daisy Buchanan met Jay Gatsby in West Egg—and the time when "the modern dance" in America inhabited a postwar netherworld between Babbitts and bohemians. The moment was captured in the pages of *Modern Dance Magazine: A New Spirit in Art and Life*, filled with illustrated social dance steps, ballroom etiquette, listings of dance schools, and "serialized fiction on dance and dancers." *Modern* referred to "exhibition social dance" at the peak of popularity; and to the Delsartian style of Isadora Duncan and her pioneering generation, along with Ruth St. Denis's and Ted Shawn's "interpretative" presentations. *MDM*'s ideal reader was "the educated woman . . . of the new bourgeoisie," who leafed through *Ladies' Home Journal*, kept up with the latest household trends, and was just as interested in building self-confidence and showing "naturalness" in an active, "free" manner, sweeping across the ballroom floor with her husband or *beau*.

The useful applications for modern dance were proscribed in *Physical Culture*. This brainchild of fitness zealot Bernarr Macfadden reached its height of popularity in the early 1920s. As an outgrowth of his multimillion-dollar media empire in New York, Macfadden added *Dance Lovers Magazine*, which became *The Dance Magazine of the Stage and Screen*, the first dance periodical addressed to the general public. Although not a dancer himself, Macfadden extolled the virtues of a healthy, "liberated" body that shed "debilitating cultural constraints and prohibitions" when "modern, square, round and contra" dancing was combined with weight lifting, sleeping outdoors, and a regimented vegetarian diet.

The modern dance that endorsed poetic movement by middle-class bodies and "uplifted . . . the general tone" of theatrical dancing was disrupted by "the frantic jazzers" with soulless, subversive "modern dress and modern music and modern manners," insinuating themselves into dance halls and displaying "symptoms that indicate that somehow in this age we have lost our bearings . . . There is no longer an aura of mystery about the young woman today." Laurette Taylor summed up the scorn in her Broadway hit *The National Anthem*: "I'm sick of seeing young people dance around as though they couldn't help it," she declared. "It's not dancing but a series of collisions . . . the din and clamor, the tomtom music—no rhythm, no melody—just sex and bedlam!"

The chorus girl was a modern dancer, too, possessed with grit and determination borne of hours of rehearsals, her flimsy costume little more than "slender bits of chiffon." The chorine was praised as the soul of Ziegfeld, vaudeville, musical comedy, and Broadway, her nearly nude "human form divine" on display "exposed to the gaze of thousands, young and old," and vilified by moral crusaders as a ribald, degenerate vamp, a "gold-digger . . . essentially not a person but . . . a rollicking, laughing careless child of a day and a night."

As for the freewheeling flapper, F. Scott Fitzgerald, looking "back . . . with nostalgia," watched her "dance into the limelight" in 1920, flourish through the symbolic pinnacle of the Jazz Age, and flare out "by 1923 . . . [when] she had become *passé* . . . [and] the younger generation was starred no longer." *Vogue* portrayed her as "the extreme adolescence of America . . . pretty in the modern manner . . . a wild mixture of Paris, futurism, the primitives, and a little rouge."

⋅ ⋅ ⋅

One such homegrown girl, Louise Brooks, was training in the 1922 summer session of the Denishawn School in New York City following the company's tour of England. Among the sweltering group of barefoot men and women in black knit bathing attire crammed into a rented gym "with splintery pine floors" in the basement of the Presbyterian church next to the dusty din of a construction site at Seventy-Second Street and Broadway, a stretching fifteen-year-old with a firm grasp at the barre caught Ruth St. Denis's eye. Five feet two, holding poses without trembling, Louise showed strong thighs and a thickish torso; her stunning face was pale, with a firm jaw, and widely set, dark brown eyes framed by black hair "cropped just below the ears, the

Louise Brooks, right arm around Martha Graham's (center) waist,
rehearsing with the Denishawn Company at Coney Island, August 1922.

ends tapering forward on both sides as if forming arrows to her full lips . . .
a smooth curtain of thick bangs stop[ping] abruptly below her brows."

She was born Mary Louise Brooks in Cherryvale, southeastern Kansas,
and growing up a "high-spirited wisp" in Wichita, dancing was "all she cared
about"—and staggering into her bedroom after school with an armful of
leather-bound books from the family library. Since toddlerhood, she was
"always meant to be a dancer . . . doing funny steps around the house,"
attending ballet classes, "lap[ping] up everything [she] could learn." Louise
was a regular reader of *Vanity Fair* and *Harper's Bazaar,* accompanying her
mother, an accomplished pianist, to orchestral concerts and the theatre.

Seeing the Denishawn dancers when they stopped at Wichita for one
night at the Crawford Theatre the week before Thanksgiving in 1921, Louise was spellbound by Martha Graham, a streak of red in "Revolutionary
Etude," aflame as the tormented Xochitl. Mother and daughter went backstage afterward to meet Graham. Ted Shawn was impressed with the "lithe,
seductive" boyish-girl *garçonnet,* gave Louise a private audition, and asked if
she would like to attend the company's summer school. Louise was permitted to make the trip to Manhattan accompanied by a chaperone, Alice Mills.

"Together, we saw all the Broadway shows," Brooks recalled, "one of them being a favorite of mine, the *Ziegfeld Follies,*" which she would join as a "Cosmopolitan Girl." At the end of Denishawn's 1922 summer term, Louise joined the Mayer tour and stayed with the company for two years until she was fired by Ted Shawn for her indecorous tendency to become "very flirty in the hotels" and chat with businessmen in the elevators.

"That tour of the road was a great experience," Brooks said. "Jumping from town to town and from hotel to hotel. Ironing your own ballet costumes, miles and miles of them . . . always under direct discipline. No smoking, no drinking, no late hours—not with Ruth St. Denis!" The company had grown so large that they had a private railroad car where Brooks seized chances to chat with Martha Graham. "I identified with Louise as an outsider," Graham wrote in *Blood Memory.* "I befriended her, and she always seemed to be watching me perform, watching me in the dressing room. . . . I was utterly absorbed by her beauty. . . . [She] possessed a quality of strength, an inner power that one felt immediately in her presence."

Late in life, Brooks offered affectionate homage to her friend, attesting that she had "learned to act while watching Martha Graham dance"; she was so "compact, with her strong, straight back and neck."

.   .   .

Beyond sharing a dressing room mirror, pink and white makeup pots, and glycerin-and-powder body paint, Martha Graham and Louise Brooks enjoyed a mutual intellectual immersion in the works of Arthur Schopenhauer. During tête-à-tête train tutorials, emphasizing the philosopher's paean to music as the most platonic of the arts, the most "expressive of the inner being, the essence of phenomena, the will itself," Louis Horst "slipped one of his beloved editions of Schopenhauer . . . into Martha's hands." Seven years later, in Berlin, on the set of G. W. Pabst's *Pandora's Box,* film critic Lotte Eisner spotted "a very beautiful girl reading the *Aphorisms* of Schopenhauer in translation," underlining passages in the 1911 first English printing of the philosopher's *Essays.* The "remarkable actress endowed with uncommon intelligence" was Louise Brooks, between takes, in her role as Lulu, showing off the mannered plastique style she had acquired from Ted Shawn and Martha Graham.

"It was surprising to hear a dancer extol strength so passionately," W. Adolphe Roberts reported in *The Dance Magazine,* after meeting with Martha Graham during her early days in New York; and so, "I asked her to tell me the sources of her philosophy." She replied, "I owe all that I am to the study of Nietzsche and Schopenhauer." Graham said she had read the complete exposition of Schopenhauer's theories in *Die Welt als Wille und Vorstellung/The World as Will and Idea [or Representation]* (1818, first published in English in 1883), and his essays, dialogues, and aphorisms, *Parerga and Paralipomena/Secondary Works and Belated Observations* (1851).

Schopenhauer's appeal to Graham was his worldview—*self*-view—formulated in his late twenties when he encountered the Upanishads and the Bhagavad Gita: "*The world is my idea.*" This pronouncement, at the threshold of his philosophy, is "the real solution of the enigma of the world. . . . In this sense," Schopenhauer said, " 'the world is my idea' may be called a revelation." Louis Horst, Martha Graham, Louise Brooks, anyone crossing over into Schopenhauer territory, before proceeding another step, would need to accept this "given fact," the construct of "the life force, the *primum mobile.*" Self-knowledge, according to Schopenhauer, was founded upon being inside one's forward-moving body in the world. Embodied mindfulness generated the *will to live* that spoke to Martha Graham.

She read in Schopenhauer's essay "On Aesthetics" that "in the plastic arts . . . a single scene . . . from the endless confusion of ceaselessly active human life [can show] us what the life and nature of man is. . . . One single case stands for thousands." This force of will is driven through her unique body when the dancer constructs a piece of choreography.

"Art lies in setting the inner life into the most violent motion," Schopenhauer wrote; Martha Graham understood, and agreed, furthermore, that, as dancers, "Our existence has no foundation on which to rest except the transient present. Thus its form is essentially unceasing motion."

.   .   .

My friends, you who believe in Dionysiac music, you also know what tragedy means to us. In it, reborn from music, we have tragic myth.
　　　　　　　—FRIEDRICH NIETZSCHE, *The Birth of Tragedy*

Citations from Friedrich Nietzsche's works are scattered throughout Martha Graham's life. In addition to reading to her on the train—and "quizzing" Graham and Louise Brooks on their attentiveness—Louis Horst translated into his pocket journals aphorisms from Nietzsche's "Maxims and Interludes" in *Beyond Good and Evil,* a book emphasizing dance as a hard discipline, demanding hours, days, and years of training and practice. "Strong Free Joyous Action," a fragment from Nietzsche's *On the Genealogy of Morals,* was the introductory quote for Graham's solo, "Dance," to the music of Arthur Honegger at the Booth Theatre in New York on January 20, 1929; and in *The Twilight of the Idols* we find Nietzsche—who characterized himself as a composer, rather than a writer—advocating for "dancing in all its forms . . . dancing with the feet, with ideas, with words . . . and . . . one must also be able to dance with the *pen.*"

In *Thus Spake Zarathustra,* man's condition is compared to the rope-dancer balanced over the abyss, fighting to maintain his balance. Havelock Ellis concluded his seminal essay "The Art of Dancing"—Graham's favorite, thanks to Ted Shawn—with a quote from a letter by Nietzsche to his friend and fellow philology major Erwin Rohde: "My style is a dance. Every day I count wasted in which there has been no dancing." Graham reiterated that declaration when she cautioned a gathering of Juilliard dance students in the early fifties, "If you work today, and do not work tomorrow, you cannot make up that day! It's gone. You are one day behind what you can be. That day is gone forever out of your life. There is a curious inevitability about that." After Graham's death, a copy of Nietzsche's posthumous collection, *The Will to Power,* filled with marginalia, was found in her personal library.

Nietzsche was in his early twenties at the University of Leipzig, studying classical philology and the poetry and drama of the archaic Hellenic period, when he came upon a copy of *The World as Will and Idea* in a secondhand bookshop. The force that touched Nietzsche intimately was Schopenhauer's "*physiological* influence . . . [his] *breathing* testimony . . . to every little movement of the muscles."

How thrilling for Nietzsche to discover a philosopher who advocated radical individuality and freedom in spirit and body, glorifying the maenads' whirling Dionysian madness, and "intoxication" in "all musical and passionate arts." How inspiring to reaffirm that the dancer's necessary "aura of strangeness," the impulse to dive deeply into herself from "the lonely height of love and understanding," would lead to the wished-for "volcanic eruption." How pleasing to know that Schopenhauer, too, endorsed the artist's urge to take the *Untergangen,* the inward-diving gaze, to dare to "read [his] own life, and understand thence the hieroglyphs of the universal life!"

Among all his works, Nietzsche's first book, *The Birth of Tragedy,* with its visionary subtitle, *Out of the Spirit of Music,* exercised the firmest grasp upon Martha Graham's imagination from the time she first read it in 1922.

It was written in 1870–1871, published in English in New York City in 1910 to herald the birth of "Nietzsche-mania" in America, and Graham quoted passages to her dancers for decades. In this symphonic book, Nietzsche exalted dance as the supreme art form, claiming that gestures of theatre in "the first great culture" of the Greeks were spawned by music; lauded the physicality of the dancing chorus "floating . . . [upon] a ground lifted high above the paths of mortal men" and conjuring the "magic transformation" (*Verzauberung*) that gave drama its beating heart, and blessed the ten thousand spectators in the outdoor amphitheater of Athens with the "joy of becoming."

6

Kandinsky and Isadora Duncan

Sometimes . . . there is a ghostly rumble among the drums, an asthmatic whisper in the trombones [that] swings me back into the early twenties when . . . it seemed only a question of a few years before the older people would step aside and let the world be run by those who saw things as they were . . .

—F. SCOTT FITZGERALD, *Echoes of the Jazz Age*

On October 1, 1922, the Denishawn/Mayer train rumbled out of Penn Station, heading for the first venue of 180 performances, beginning at the Masonic Temple Theatre in Lewistown, Pennsylvania, northwest of Harrisburg, and coming full circle the following April with twelve shows at Town Hall in New York City. Ruth St. Denis, with her personal maid, and Ted Shawn, and Louis Horst as musical director, three additional musicians, a company treasurer, a stage manager, and a two-man backstage crew, were accompanied by dancers Martha Graham, Pearl Wheeler, Betty May, Lenore Scheffer, Julia Bennett, May Lynn, Louise Brooks, Peggy Taylor (later replaced by Betty Davis), Charles Weidman, and Paul Mathis (later replaced by Robert Gorham). But not Doris Humphrey; she would return as a guest artist for the New York season in the spring of 1923, just before Graham quit the company.

The tour program was a test of Graham's endurance. In the first part, *Music Visualizations,* she danced in "Revolutionary Etude" and "Soaring," among a succession of short pieces in the Dalcrozian mode, "illustrating [classical] musical forms" with "parallel movements" originating in the torso.

In the second section, Graham appeared in "Serenata Morisca," "Devidassi" (the ritual dancer in Indian temples possessed by divinity), and a new piece, "Betty's Music Box," "frothy as a strawberry ice-cream soda."

This confection starred Charles Weidman in the Pierrot costume from his preceding solo number, surrounded by three mincing, rosy-lipped maids spotlighted in pink, crowned with lavender muslin hats, wearing low-neck, calf-length ruffled pink gowns, and sharing pantomimed secrets and perky pliés—Martha Graham, Louise Brooks, and Betty May. In the third section, a reprise of *Xochitl,* Graham returned to her featured role. Finally, in *Orientalia,* conglomerating the cultures of China, Crete, India, Siam, Japan, Java, and Egypt, Graham was one of the three *apsarases,* choreographed by St. Denis, and then soloed in Shawn's Japanese "Lantern Dance."

After Pottsville and Newcastle and Pittsburgh and Altoona and Baltimore and Kalamazoo, and a triumphant night in Milwaukee concluding with a surprise thirty-first birthday party for Papa Ted beneath the towering gold-leaf proscenium of the Pabst Theatre, the Denishawn train steamed south along Lake Michigan and pulled into Chicago at midday on Sunday, October 22, to prepare for Monday and Tuesday night shows at Orchestra Hall. The next two days would be crammed with load-in and dress rehearsals.

Barely settled at the hotel, Horst and Graham dashed over to the Art Institute of Chicago, guarded by two vigilant bronze lions at the corner of Adams Street on Michigan Boulevard, where an exhibition of modern art from the collection of the late Arthur Jerome Eddy, on view since September 19, was in its final hours. When Graham attempted to reconstruct details of the visit half a century later, she said that "One of our stops when I toured the states with the *Follies* [in fact, Denishawn] was Chicago. I remember going into the Art Institute one afternoon. I entered a room where the first modern paintings I had ever seen were on display—Chagalls and Matisses—and something within me responded to those paintings." (In fact, neither Chagall nor Matisse was in the Eddy collection show; Derain, Duchamp, Gleizes, Franz Marc, Picabia, and Picasso, among many others' works, were there, including sculptures by Brancusi and Rodin.)

Suddenly, Graham said, "I saw across the room a beautiful painting, what was then called abstract art, a startling new idea. I nearly fainted because at that moment I knew I was not mad, that others saw the world, saw art, the way I did. It was by Wassily Kandinsky, and had a streak of red going from one end to the other. I said, 'I will do that someday. I will make a dance like that.'"

One of twenty works in the show by Kandinsky—whose work Eddy, a prosperous attorney, championed early on—the painting Martha Graham spotted was *Improvisation No. 30,* referred to by the artist as *Blauer Fleck*—

Kanonen (*Blue Spot—Cannons*). The four-foot square (111 × 111.3 cm) canvas, a vertiginous, impatient ode to scatter, wanted to blast out of the frame. It was illustrated and listed as "item No. 36" in the exhibition guidebook, accompanied by Eddy's parenthetical observation, "(This was not painted as an impression of war, but the atmosphere was so charged with war at the time it was painted [1913] that the artist must have unconsciously introduced the feeling.)"

The note paraphrased Kandinsky's statement about literal imagery in Eddy's book, *Cubists and Post-Impressionism,* published in 1914, following the New York Armory Show: "The presence of the cannons in the picture could probably be explained by the constant war talk that had been going on throughout the year," Kandinsky said. "But I did not intend to give a representation of war; to do so would have required different pictorial means."

Martha Graham in the fall of 1922 was a working dancer on a grueling tour at the borderline between rote reenactments of others' music visualizations and realizing her latent expressionist necessities—to borrow Kandinsky's term. Whether Graham actually said at the museum, "I will do that

Improvisation No. 30 (Cannons), by Wassily Kandinsky, oil on canvas, 1913;
pioneering abstraction and "inspiring vibrations in the soul."

someday. I will make a dance like that," to herself, or to Louis Horst, as they stood before the *Cannons* canvas on that Sunday afternoon in Chicago; or, in the spirit of self-fulfilling personal history, imagined she said it; or believed—attending to the call of her "blood memory"—that she should have said it, Martha Graham utterly apprehended Kandinsky's vision— "infusing painting with the power of music and theatre." From 1939 onward, most memorably the *Art of Tomorrow* show at Hilla Rebay and Solomon R. Guggenheim's Museum of Non-Objective Painting on East Fifty-Fourth Street, Graham never missed a Kandinsky exhibition in New York. Invoking his spirit, Graham told her students, "Dancing is a little closer sometimes to what is called non-representational painting . . . The whole adds up to an impression—to a sensation—to a feeling that [is not] a complete graph of meaning, except as you use meaning in an inner sense."

In his book, *Point and Line to Plane (Punkt und Linie zur Fläche),* Kandinsky defined a "composition" as a work in which "vital forces . . . in the form of tensions, are shut up within the elements." The artist's appeal to Graham is clear in Kandinsky's comment to his friend and patron Arthur Eddy about the elusiveness of explicit meaning, regardless of medium—the gap between *intentionality* in the making of a work of art and the viewers' *reception*: "The designation 'Cannons' selected by me *for my own use,* is not to be conceived as indicating the [non-objective] 'contents' of the picture. . . . These contents are indeed what the spectator *lives,* or *feels,* while under the effect of the *form and color combinations* of the picture. . . . So intensely did I feel the necessity of some of the forms, that I remember having given loud-voiced directions to myself, as for instance: 'But the corners must be heavy!'" [All italics here and below are Kandinsky's.]

Like Kandinsky, Graham was aware of the seesaw in her psyche between fulfillment and frustration, self-determination and fatalism: "The truth of the matter is," the painter further confided to Eddy "that every gifted artist, that is, an artist working under an impulse *from within,* must go in a way that in some mystical manner has been laid out for him from the very start. His life is nothing but the fulfillment of a task set for him *(for him, not by himself).* . . . [There] is a period of 'storm and stress' [*sturm und drang*], then follow desperate *searching,* pain, great pain—until *finally* his eyes open and he says to himself, '*There* is my way.'"

Kandinsky's interdisciplinary album, *Sounds (Klänge),* a hand-printed chromatic assemblage of fifty-six "not purely illustrative" woodcuts and thirty-eight "not purely verbal" prose poems, was published in 1912 by

F. Bruckmann in Munich. One of these "poems," "Sehen/Seeing," began with blue, then moved to red, the primary colors in *Cannons* that "spoke" to Martha Graham's eye.

"Sehen/Seeing"

Blue. Blue got up, got up and fell.
Sharp. Thin whistled and shoved, but didn't get through.
From every corner came a humming.
FatBrown got stuck—it seemed for all eternity.
It seemed. It seemed.
You must open your arms wider.
Wider. Wider.
And you must cover your face with a red cloth.
And maybe it hasn't shifted yet at all: it's just that you've
  shifted.
White leap after white leap.
And after this white leap another white leap.
And in this white leap a white leap, and every white leap a
  white leap.
But that's not good at all, that you don't see the gloom: in the
  gloom is
where it is.
That's where everything begins. . . . .
With a. . . . . Crash. . . . .

"[T]he juxtaposition of red and blue, these physically unrelated colors," Kandinsky wrote in *Über Das Geistige in Der Kunst/On the Spiritual in Art* (1911–1912), "is today chosen as one of the most strongly effective and most suitably harmonious because of the great spiritual contrast between them. . . . Our *harmony*," he emphasized, "is based upon the principle of *contrast*, the most important principle in art at all times."

. . .

Ruth St. Denis talked bluntly about what Chicagoans should—and should *not*—expect to see in the Denishawn Orchestra Hall performances:

"There is no dancing as the music makes the dancer feel," she said, "no aimless wandering about the stage picking imaginary daisies and drinking from invisible fountains. Rather, each eighth note, each arpeggio, each trill is conscientiously paralleled by an analogous movement of the dancer, with careful thought to the rendering of melodic themes, and the dancing of separate voices."

Maurice Rosenfeld of the *Daily News* gave special praise to the "stylistic and gorgeous" appearance of Martha Graham in full regalia as Xochitl. Edward Moore of the *Daily Tribune* observed that with respect to the "plastic possibilities of the human body," especially "its upper half, the arms, shoulders, and head, [St. Denis and Shawn have] added a pictorial character that American dancing sadly needed." And Karleton Hackett of the *Evening Post* was impressed with the dancers' physicality: "[F]or the complete demonstration of the feminine form divine, you have to see these Denishawn maidens."

Wednesday morning, October 25, on the road to a chain of one-night stands at Rockford, Ann Arbor, Elyria, and Sandusky, Martha Graham just missed crossing paths with Isadora Duncan, in Chicago for a weekend in her renunciatory American tour, visits to the United States having become fewer and fewer. In opposition to Denishawn's discipline, the forty-five-year-old Duncan promoted her "customary unrigid" intentions, saying her show would "follow no rules of a binding, artificial technique—it is natural, and follows only the laws of nature in giving rhythmic expression to music." Elaborate renditions of Wagner's *The Entrance of the Gods into Valhalla* and *The Ride of the Valkyries* and Tchaikovsky's *Pathétique Symphony* and *Marche Slave* were on the program.

In the wake of Duncan's diatribe at Boston Symphony Hall four days prior, no one could safely predict what would happen in Chicago. For the Boston performance, Duncan had been brightly lit, and her chiffon scarves, shifting as she gestured, revealed too much flesh. "Reiterated lifting of crossed arms" and idiosyncratic "crouches and writhings" left the Boston audience uncomfortable and critics disillusioned. She was "no longer a young woman . . . far from corybantic." Infrequent Isadora sightings over a span of merciless years called forth "her ancient prowess [rather] than her present powers." After the final curtain in Boston, Duncan strode downstage waving a red scarf, "vexed and irritated." Her bully pulpit rant rambled from appeals for money to discursive sermons on art and praise for Mother Russia.

Undaunted, Duncan pressed on, under Sol Hurok's sponsorship, from

Boston, into and out of Chicago, and a chain of Midwestern venues, plagued by declining health and the alcoholic and anti-Semitic rages of her husband, the poet Sergey Yesenin. Her final shows in the east were at the Brooklyn Academy of Music and Carnegie Hall at Christmas and the New Year; on February 3, 1923, she sailed to France—vowing never to return to the "philistine" land of her birth.

Martha Graham insisted she "never saw Isadora." Separated by a generation, their careers and itineraries were out of sync. Graham rose up as Duncan declined; Graham emerged with her all-female, all-American company in New York City in spring 1926, before Duncan's death as an expatriate in Nice, in autumn 1927. Graham did recall attending a concert of the Isadora Duncan dancers—Anna, Irma, Lisa, Theresa, Margot, and Erica—in 1920 when she was on the West Coast tour with *Xochitl* at the same time that these six "Isadorables," disciples sans their namesake-founder, were in Los Angeles. Graham conceded that there was "something [in Duncan] that was of a natural quality, yet had a certain formalism."

Louis Horst may have been present for the one time that "the famous barefoot dancer" performed "in sweeping black robes with touches of purple" in the Mason Opera House in Los Angeles on December 4, 1917. Regarding Duncan "as an isolated phenomenon," he "didn't particularly like her, because we [Denishawn] were more theatrical."

Isadora Duncan, ca. 1915–1923. (Photograph by Arnold Genthe)

Barely seeing, possibly seeing, or denying having witnessed the radiant Isadora—Martha Graham's disclaimers do not diminish her predecessor. Elizabeth Kendall notes that, Graham's protestations to the contrary, she "had learned . . . from a distant Isadora the idea of a mind behind the dance structures." Joan Acocella insists that "[a]fter [Duncan], it was taken for granted that female soloists were dealing with serious matters of the heart and soul. Martha Graham, though she was a pupil of St. Denis [and Shawn], is unimaginable without Duncan." Janet Eilber makes the distinction that "Isadora Duncan may have been the first modern dancer to connect emotion to movement, but Martha Graham gave this expression shape." And Graham attested in 1935 that Duncan was "the greatest individual stimulus to the dance of modern times."

The most profound connection of the two "talented loners" is their dedication to the empowerment of the soloist, in art generally, and dance particularly. Duncan, the pioneer, conceded credit to no prior dancer. Once Graham was established, she, too, resisted indebtedness. The evolution of her personal style and ideas moving forward made her look back with selective rejection. Graham said, "It is so intensely personal—I don't know what *other* dancers do—I don't know how *others* work—I only know how *I* work."

Both women were bookworms as children and grew up to become chronic autodidacts; Graham carried books of literature and art from her home library into the rehearsal room, laid them out on the floor for the dancers, frequently started class by reciting a line from a poem that had struck her, and posted obligatory reading lists to the bulletin board outside the studio. Duncan began her study of Nietzsche in 1903, testified that the philosopher "ravished my being," kept *Thus Spake Zarathustra* on her night table, and, like Graham, swore allegiance to *The Birth of Tragedy*.

As Graham had been in Manchester, Duncan in London was captivated by the terra-cotta Tanagra figurines on view in the British Museum in 1899, and revered the "universal Dionysiac movement" represented in Greek sculpture that infused Delsarte plastique aesthetic. For Duncan, the solar plexus was the "sacred home," the source wherein the soul awakened and surged upward to lift the chest. Graham, going to her omphalos, the diaphragm, birthed the *contraction*—an elaboration upon the natural act of breathing and the diastole and systole of the heartbeat crescendo and decrescendo, "the attack of the inhale or exhale, resonat[ing] throughout the entire body."

Pinpointing the distinctions between these two forces of nature, philosopher of dance Francis Sparshott said, "First come the expressivist individuals typified by Isadora Duncan. Then come the makers of expressivist systems, typified by Graham." Duncan draped herself with the necessary angel's mantle of bodily freedom, giving sway to excess; Graham was the teacher as taskmaster, "hard and disciplined as a diamond needle." Duncan said she was "an enemy of the Ballet, which [she] consider[ed] a false and preposterous art" contra nature's romantic ebb and flow. While Graham did not call for the erasure of ballet, she danced through and beyond the constraints of the "ballet box," into a modern discipline initiating movement centrally, in the lower spine, rather than distally, and giving in to the floor, rather than using it only as a springboard. Duncan's sublime goal was to achieve "multiple one-ness . . . a mystical vision on stage . . . ardently hop[ing] to create an orchestra of dancers"; Martha Graham excavated ancient mysteries in a gritty quest for groundedness.

"Strangely enough," Graham wrote, curating her words with care, "the America that produced Isadora Duncan . . . has been blinded for so long by the shining glory of an old culture . . . [creating] an impression of a culture foreign to us rather than an expression creatively from us." A California girl by birth, Duncan achieved renown in the capitals of Europe; Graham traversed the length and breadth of her own land to articulate a new dance language, staking out native terrain. So doing, she took a leaf from the pages of one of the classicists she loved, Cassius Longinus, rhetorician of the third century, advising that "emulative struggle with a predecessor engenders Sublime thought and expression."

. . . .

Graham received glowing notices in the final leg of the Denishawn-Mayer tour. In Baltimore, she was singled out as "conspicuously-accomplished and gifted"; in Raleigh, North Carolina, the critic found her possessing "gifts second only to her teachers"; and the Minneapolis–St. Paul *Pioneer Press* had no doubt that "the most interesting" of all the Denishawns was "Martha Graham, an exotic little [*sic*] dancer who should have unlimited future development before her."

When the company reached Town Hall, Ted Shawn treated New Yorkers to his "jewel in its setting," Martha Graham in "Serenata Morisca." "With tigerlike strides," glistening bracelets on bare arms, her purple silken skirt flaring into scalloped folds and blurs of silver and gold appliqués, Graham took possession of the stage with a chain of circular kicks and quick turns interspersed with coquettish, come-hither hip sways and undulating arms, gaze fixed upon an imaginary king on a raised throne downstage left. In the glare of a follow spot, pale limbs in relief against a black velvet cyclorama, Graham caught the attention of Shawn's friend, John Murray Anderson, songwriter, lighting director, former dancer, former antiques dealer, and founder of *The Greenwich Village Follies*. "Where have you been hiding *her*?" the astonished producer asked backstage. After Graham performed a private solo, Anderson quietly insisted she come work for him in the fall.

"*Comme ça*—a beautifully-dressed, finely mannered man of the theatre," Newfoundland-born, educated at boarding schools in England and Switzerland, apprenticing in stage production with Herbert Tree in London and Max Reinhardt at the Grosses Schauspielhaus in Berlin, dabbling in society entertainment summer stock at Bar Harbor, John Murray Anderson settled in New York City to advance his theatrical career. Under the aegis of producer Paul Salvin, who owned a cabaret-restaurant, the Palais Royal, on West Forty-Eighth Street, Anderson put together a series of patriotic benefits to raise funds for French troops during the war. His dream had long been to mount a musical of his own; Salvin and several "miscellaneous angels," impressed with the young fellow's energy and talents, created a new company for him, the Bohemians (Inc.), and raised $35,000 to bankroll the first *Greenwich Village Follies,* on the west side of Seventh Avenue South at Sheridan Square. The *Follies* moved to larger Midtown houses—the Nora Bayes Theatre, then the Shubert, and two years' running at the Winter Garden on the Great White Way—but Anderson kept *Greenwich Village* in the brand name. Florenz Ziegfeld complained that Salvin and friends had stolen his "Follies" concept (in fact, Ziegfeld had taken the name from a 1906 Broadway revue).

Anderson's moderne brainchild opened in the summer of 1919, original in every detail, from the perky song lyrics to the ornate overture curtain, painted by Reginald Marsh, depicting "street artists and musicians, poets, society folks slumming, famous and struggling writers, and other '*hobohemians.*'" Over the next three years, the *Follies* presented the vaudevillian Ted ("Is Everybody Happy?") Lewis and his Orchestra; the "Two Flaming Youths" comedy team of Bert Savoy and Jay Brennan; Bessie McCoy, the singing and dancing widow of Richard Harding Davis, making her comeback as the "Yama Yama Girl"; an experimental setting of Oscar Wilde's story "The Nightingale and the Rose," staged as a "ballet ballad" to an arrangement of Chopin nocturnes; and the risqué panoply of *The Naked Truth,* a "flash-act hoofer" spectacle "overflowing with scantily-clad models, art students and gawkers."

Martha Graham took Anderson's offer of employment at $1,400 a month over Denishawn's $40-a-week salary. With the funds willed to her from Dr. Graham's meager estate depleted, she could not look away from the jump in salary, income essential to helping her sisters support their mother. Graham had another reason for leaving the company where she had spent the past seven years, and the man who had given her the first break in show business, tearfully writing Ted Shawn she could no longer endure the stalemate of her triangular love life—"I *need* to take this job—Louis . . . is tearing me to pieces!" Horst "would not seek a formal dissolution" from Betty, an attitude that "touched a raw nerve."

In late April 1923, Shawn embarked upon a three-month working vacation to Spain and North Africa; Graham bade him an emotional farewell, alluding to the glimmers of fame: "I can't quite realize that so much of [my] recognition has come in little over a year. Oh, I am so proud of you—and of *myself,* because of your believing strength behind me. Don't say I've left the nest," she implored, "because Denishawn—in all—is my religion."

She worried how she would be able to distance herself from Shawn—and Miss Ruth—in the future: "Sometimes I believe you think I want to leave—am proud of it. Don't, Ted. No matter what I do my real heart is in 'the performance'—and to me there can never be any but Miss Ruth's and yours—no matter what 'show' I am in."

Years later, Graham told friend and confidant Walter Terry that separating herself from Denishawn was a rite of passage, "the time had come . . . to find her own way . . . and the *Follies* were a stepping stone to . . . independence."

To keep limber, and solvent, until her contract started at the *Follies,* Graham signed on for a second summer as an instructor at Mariarden, the two-hundred-acre theatrical camp near Peterborough, New Hampshire, founded by actress Marie Currier with the financial underwriting of her husband, Guy Currier. In "Marie's Arden" in the woods, Graham taught "[y]oga sitting with poses and gestures" and "modified ballet in bare feet." While she was in residence there, Shawn returned from his overseas holiday, mortified to find that Graham had taken over the classes he had conducted the previous year. At the peak of a "big fight," Graham "flared back," telling Shawn,

"I will create all of my own material from now on!" The two parted bitterly and would remain estranged for three decades.

. . .

Dancing night after night for two years—four numbers on some nights—Martha Graham's allure for John Murray Anderson was her glamorous exoticism. The fast-paced variety show had to have something—some*one*—on the bill to everybody's taste. The canny showman hired the versatile actress to provide a special kind of dance apart from "skits, travesties, and parodies," chorus numbers, quick takes of ragtime, the Charleston, and musical comedy "fancy dancing." Martha Graham possessed stamina; more important,

Graham, "nearly nude chorine," in John Murray Anderson's
The Greenwich Village Follies, June 1924.

Greenwich Village Follies girls mending toys for Christmas charity.
Martha Graham smiling, center, holding a horse; Louise Brooks to Graham's left
with a stuffed bunny. December 6, 1924.

she was the "classy *poesie*" ingredient in a recipe that the *Times* praised as
"lavish serial entertainment."

Lead-off comedian Joe E. Brown, at one harrowing moment in his *Follies*
act, "took a flying leap into the orchestra pit and bounced off a trampoline
onto the stage, missing the first violins by a hairs-breadth every time." Irene
Franklin, "the Redhead," sang the fanciful musical impressions for which she
was well-loved. Fresh from a yearlong run in London, the Dolly Sisters, identical twins Jenny and Rosie, "pouted and purred" through satirical excerpts
from their "inconsequential process of music, dance and dramatic interlude," *The League of Notions*. Brother and sister Eduardo and Elisa, polished
"two [shows]-a-day veterans" who called themselves the Royal Cansinos,
joined by Eduardo's wife, Volga Hayworth, by turns waltzed and stomped
around the stage; when five-year-old daughter Margarita (who would grow
up to be Rita Hayworth) cried in the wings, Anderson ordered that the child
be removed to the basement smoking room. With her Latin-spiced dance
experience, Martha Graham was often enlisted to open for the Cansinos.

Eventually, the time arrived in the course of every evening for what was known, in trade jargon, as "the art spot," when Martha Graham put on her crowd-pleasing solo, "Serenata Morisca," Anderson's favorite; followed by a star turn as a fairy girl to the prince in "The Garden of Kama," a tragedy of India repackaged by Anderson as a "ballet ballad" based upon the 1915 Denishawn original. The Japanese émigré Michio Ito choreographed the new arrangements of "Kama" for her. Festooned in layers of veils, "panting under an excess of clothing" as if trapped in a "lingerie salon—Dreadful— . . . I ran up a flight of stairs," Graham wrote, "oh, so *dramatic*—threw open the door and turned my back to the audience. I lifted the dagger and stabbed myself and then dropped the dagger and fell, I thought beautifully, to the floor."

Every time the curtain came down on another "Kama"—she had lost track of how many performances—Martha Graham realized with "divine dissatisfaction" that she "might as well still have been in Denishawn." Instead of spending money on bus fare, she hoarded nickels for a midnight snack at the flagship Horn and Hardart Automat, then walked downtown, alone, from Fiftieth Street and Broadway to the Village. Trying to fall asleep in her bare studio on an army surplus cot next to a coal stove, Graham knew, at thirty years old, there were more leaps to be made across stepping-stones on the journey to artistic freedom.

. . .

Louis Horst's decade with the Denishawn Company was weighing upon him, the show business grind made more lonely because Martha Graham was gone, replaced in *Xochitl* by her sister, the tall, blond Geordie. Still on board, Doris Humphrey and Charles Weidman saw their roles expand as lead soloists and faculty members of the school. The second (1923–1924) and third (1924–1925) Denishawn-Mayer circuits were successive six-month stretches from October to April to three hundred venues "all over the country, every little burg." The repertory embodied St. Denis's and Shawn's own work, reprising operatic epics featuring her "Spirit of the Sea," and his "Feather of the Dawn" among crowd-pleasing divertissements, visualizations, sketches, and suites.

The Denishawn domain was becoming an empire, according to the results of a survey, "Who Are America's Favorite Dancers?" conducted in *Dance Lovers Magazine*. Ted Shawn was the king, tied with Laurent Novikoff for the highest number of reader votes, and the queen, second to Anna Pavlova, was Ruth St. Denis. Denishawn School graduates and dancers had formed branch schools in Boston, Rochester, New York City, Minneapolis, Wichita, and San Francisco (run by Betty Horst). The goal was to become an educational presence furthering the American dance idea "in every important city in America and several European capitals."

In the summer of 1925, the company was asked to perform in Lewisohn Stadium, the first dance troupe so honored since the Bronx amphitheater had been built in 1915. Following that triumph, Shawn trumpeted, and "as a logical development of the three American [Mayer] tours," the company would sail in August for eighteen months on a global journey of terpsichorean diplomacy—Japan, China, Burma, India, Pakistan, Ceylon, Singapore, Java, and Indochina—"the first American ballet to serve as ambassador for the dance message of America to the old world."

"In going to the Orient," Shawn emphasized, "it is with the deepest loyalty and gratitude to America, and with the hope of bringing back greater gifts of beauty, and an art made richer and stronger by direct contact with the art forms of other nations."

.   .   .

Louis Horst had been a faithful contributor to the Denishawn legacy at the keyboard, from the orchestra pit, and financially, since the company's Technique Phonograph Records had been produced and marketed under his supervision. He prided himself upon being a loyal trouper, whose "innate sense of tempo" might have been "moderato, but [who] could move with extraordinary swiftness" in adverse theatrical weather.

Until now.

As the Denishawn train wended through the familiar hinterlands of Ohio and upstate New York toward Boston in the spring of 1925, Horst attended to the weary voice of his midlife quandary. Without Martha Graham by his side, Horst had no desire to drag his baggage across the world. He did not have the fortitude to turn another page in the massive book of Denishawn, which, according to its founding couple, had reached the chapter of its apotheosis.

"The Musician Comments," an essay for *The Denishawn Magazine* Horst worked on during his final road trip, begins as a frank rumination by a journeyman musician on his preference for "dance-playing" rather than "accompanying of singers . . . This wedding of music and dance," Horst reveals, "has been for years the greatest interest of my art life." However, the satisfactions—while many—had brought damaging consequences. Dance was still the handmaiden, and "yields to music" and, with commensurate regret, music must be "sacrificed . . . rushed, dragged, changed dynamically." The ideal should be for music *with* dance, establishing a union of complementary equals, as in the relationship of a man and a woman, where he is "egocentric" and she is "altrocentric."

"Dance [needs to] establish itself" as a primary art, Horst writes, built "upon a firm scientific basis, and prove to music that union with a partner as independent and scientific as itself will be a greater honor." Touching the heart of the matter, where the romance of the two arts fuses with that of their respective artists, Horst addresses his Martha, imagining a joyous future when "their very separateness will make them more at one than they are now; and composers will study the science of dance, and dancers study the science of music."

The Denishawn matinee at the Boston Opera House on April 4, 1925, featured a sprawling ballet of mystical "trance-dances," *The Vision of the Aissoua,* transposing *Cuadro Flamenco,* Shawn's 1922 work, from a café in a gypsy village in Spain to the Algerian desert. As soon as the curtain fell, Horst went backstage to tell Ted Shawn that the time had come to part ways: "These have been the happiest ten years," Horst said, "but I feel I just have to make a change."

Miss Ruth sobbed as the three comrades sat together and reminisced and argued into the early hours of the morning, but Horst's mind was made up. His plan was to spend the coming year studying music composition in Vienna.

7

The Eastman School

I left [the Follies] in 1925, when I wanted to create my own dances, on my own body.

—MARTHA GRAHAM

It takes about ten years to make a mature dancer. The training is two-fold: There is the study and practice of the craft in order to strengthen the muscular structure of the body . . . And then, there is the cultivation of the being. It is through this that the legends of the soul's journey are retold with all their gaiety and their tragedy and the bitterness and sweetness of living. . . . By ten years, if you are going to be a dancer at all, you will have mastered the instrument.

—MARTHA GRAHAM

In the midst of Martha Graham's "divine dissatisfaction," John Murray Anderson invited his friend, the Armenian-born, Paris-educated, Stanislavsky-trained Moscow Art Theatre veteran Rouben Mamoulian, to a *Greenwich Village Follies* performance. Kodak company founder, philanthropist, and performing arts devotee George Eastman had brought Mamoulian over from London, at the urging of émigré opera director Vladimir Rosing, to head, and expand, the Eastman School of Dance and Dramatic Action in Rochester, New York. Mamoulian had seen Graham once before, in May 1923, when Denishawn performed at Kilbourn Hall in Rochester and her luster remained undimmed. He found Graham's rendition of "Four Indian Love Lyrics" in Anderson's *The Garden of Kama* to be alluring.

Declaring his belief in "the supremacy of women in the art of the theatre," Mamoulian was in New York in the summer of 1925 to recruit the right *someone* to help him create the next department of Mr. Eastman's school,

Rouben Mamoulian (top) on the set of *Love Me Tonight*, Paramount Studios, 1932.

dedicated to dance choreography embracing "a much wider scope than just ballet . . . [and] employ[ing] the most modern ideas." New dance courses would focus upon "the adaptation of rhythmic bodily expression to dramatic expressiveness . . . [in] a project looking to a broader education than specific dance training affords."

"Pupils will not be accepted for dramatic instruction alone," Mamoulian said, "it will be given only in conjunction with dance training." Martha Graham was his ideal choice to lead the Eastman School transition. Her approach to "these twin arts . . . ruled by rhythm and grace" would be "intelligent and exciting!"

John Murray Anderson went into rehearsal for the seventh season of *The Greenwich Village Follies* with his own pedagogical plan. In July, in alliance with Broadway director and producer Robert Milton, Anderson had purchased the former home of the National Conservatory of Music, "a dilapidated collection of old bricks, stucco and steel" at 121–130 East Fifty-Eighth Street, "to be transformed into a place of great beauty," with twelve class and lecture rooms and a two-hundred-seat auditorium. "What you couldn't learn at John Murray Anderson–Robert Milton School of Theatre and Dance connected with the Theatre Arts wasn't worth knowing," they boasted. To prove that the teachers in his "national clearing-house for talent . . ." would be the crème de la crème drawn "from every form of dance instruction," Anderson wanted Martha Graham to help run the "character and interpretative" division of the new school.

To share—and mollify—the object of their affections and ambitions, Mamoulian and Anderson arrived at a compromise with "Miss Martha Graham, formerly featured artist with the Denishawn Dancers and for two seasons star of *The Greenwich Village Follies* . . . who has enjoyed a remarkably successful career for one so young in years." She would start at Eastman in mid-September, "remain[ing] for two months . . . devoting her entire time and attention to the new school," and, within six weeks, replace Ester Gustafson, a former student of Pavlova and a disciple of Isadora Duncan. From mid-November, in residence at the Sagamore Hotel in downtown Rochester for three working days every fortnight, Graham maintained her Manhattan lifeline, commuting by train to the Anderson-Milton School, to teach alongside Michio Ito.

.   .   .

The dance program at Eastman offered classes for children, senior classes, health education, and private instruction. Under Martha Graham's supervision, "[t]he word 'ballet' [was] being dropped," Mamoulian said, "because the new dance training will be of much broader scope, comprising all forms of the dance." The curriculum stressed the relationship of technical training to professional preparation—through pantomime, plastic movement, makeup, stage deportment, and diction, as well as attention to dance history. Every student was given the opportunity to perform before audiences in the Eastman Theatre and Kilbourn Hall and promised the experience of being filmed in their classes, "the motion pictures [then] thrown on the screen to illustrate the effects in technic."

To Mr. Eastman, "acting" and "theatre" were not isolated activities. He wanted the unity of dramatic action, with emphasis upon the cause and effect of events onstage. Mamoulian came up with the wording for the announcement bulletin published for the opening of the school, "to recognize anew the close kinship of the arts of the Dance and Drama, and to develop a new form of theatrical art in which drama and dance, linked with music, will combine into an inseparable unity." He strove to "revive the ideal of the Greeks"—*choros*—engendering theatre-as-dance/dance-as-theatre.

This was the milieu into which Martha Graham, at a salary of $260 per week, made a grand entrance on September 14, 1925. As she crossed the threshold of the Eastman Annex on Swan Street and mounted the stairs to Dance Studio B on the third floor, the solitary pilgrim hoped the day marked the beginning of a new adventure of seeking. Her teaching contract guaranteed that Graham would be given time in class to devise her own compositions. The Eastman School would become the setting for "that glory [she] had never touched." Graham recalled "the first morning [she] went into class," how she "wanted to begin, not with characters . . . but with movement—walking, running, skipping, leaping" across the room, no decorative presentation for its own sake. Through strength-building weight changes and deep stretches, Graham's students would awaken energies within and become aware of "inner meaning . . . something to dance *about!*"

The crowded class included several boys, but Graham singled out the three most promising girls. Seven months later, Evelyn Sabin, Betty Macdonald, and Thelma ("Teddy") Biracree would take the stage at the 48th Street Theatre to perform in the New York City premiere of Graham's dance group, where she shone like Venus enfolded in the angelic perfection of veiled handmaidens, "those gracious Virgins three."

The youngest of the sister goddesses, the "exquisite" Evelyn Sabin, was destined, Graham said, to "be a dreamer all her life." Seventeen when she came to Eastman, Sabin described the exercises instigated by Graham in a progressive sequence, "the floor work . . . walking, running, jumping, leaping . . . and the falls . . . The movement, to me, was always changing, developing and growing."

"The first day Martha walked in the door of the dance studio," eighteen-year-old Betty Macdonald said, she stood absolutely still, like a statue, facing the class, draped in an "East Indian sari *à la* Ruth St. Denis. . . . She hadn't even moved yet [but] she illuminated the whole place with her presence. . . . [She] was finding her own way of moving the body. . . . She wanted to move the body differently," initiating ideas in her center of gravity and carrying them over into her students. In Graham's classes, parts of the body other than the feet would come into contact with the floor, sculptural lines supporting one's earthbound weight. Spiraling around the back, torso twisting, "Graham falls . . . [were] percussive, as though someone hit you. . . . When

Graham (standing) and her diaphanous first dance group at the Eastman School,
(left to right) Evelyn Sabin, Betty Macdonald, and Thelma Biracree, 1925–1926.

you came [back] up, you came up with your entire body naturally," pressing
down with your weight *into* the floor to gather energy and rise upwards again
"not like a [ballet] toe-dancer who came up with prettiness and beauty."

Thelma Biracree agreed. "We learned how to kneel. . . . The floor was
a very important place for Martha." The oldest of the Eastman muses, at
twenty-one, and with a $25-per-week scholarship, Teddy became Graham's
rehearsal assistant and demonstrator. Teddy idolized her teacher, hoarding
stray "threads and little ravellings" that fell to the ground from the long
dress Graham wore over leotards. Graham demanded that Teddy sit cross-
legged, close her eyes, and visualize the Kundalini serpent power coiling up
her spine, from the sacral plexus to the many-petaled lotus crown at the
top of her head, and breathe deeply, "imagin[ing] a spiral going around
and around." Graham told the girls to "forget turn-outs. . . . She was an
incandescent teacher," Teddy said. "She set us on fire! . . . It was all quite
revolutionary for upstate New York!"

. . .

In Vienna, Louis Horst pursued his studies with Dr. Richard Stöhr, professor of music theory at the conservatory (Universität für Musik und darstellende Kunst Wien). Horst had ventured overseas "to get out of [his] system" the expectation that as a "serious" American artist it was de rigueur that he study in Europe; to put some distance between himself and Denishawn; and to see if foreign dislocation would help make sense of his preoccupation with Martha Graham, against "a pull he [said he] didn't want"—his married life. To refresh Horst's grasp of the rules of composition before making attempts to modify (or break) them, by reputation and specialty, Stöhr would seem to have been the ideal mentor. His *Praktischer Leitfaden*, the *Practical Manual on Harmony* (1909) and its companion volume on *Counterpoint* (1911) laid the groundwork for recent writings on "the relationship between dance and music."

Horst had prepared for this dual path through immersion in the works of the New Jersey–born pianist Percy Goetschius, protégé of Frank Damrosch at the Institute of Musical Art in New York. Goetschius's *Lessons in Music Form* (1904) and *The Homophonic Forms of Musical Composition* (1924), wherein the author noted the narrative parallels between the "linear . . . undulations . . . in our mind's eye" of a tune—"its rising, falling or resting"—and "the pencil of an artist trac[ing] the lines of an image on paper" spoke to Horst's love of modern painting and poetry.

A jovial student of the human condition, and an honest self-scrutinizer, Louis Horst was well aware of his musicianship range. If dancers wanted, or needed, to dance *to* something, Horst could slide his bench up to the piano—anytime, anywhere—and play pretty much anything thrust in front of him. But his current ideas about the interplay of music with dance reached for a more sophisticated plane: how to evolve music for dance initiated *by* the dancers' "germinal *idea* . . . the seed," shaped "in her torso" by her inward sense of time; and how to "compose" a musical structure for—and *with*—a dance, and its dancer. Horst's maturing goal for composition was that it be "a perfect blending of form and content," for, he said, "if the content dominates, then form suffers, and if the form dominates, the composition will suffer from dullness."

Outings to the horse races at Friedenau, the sulfur spa at Baden, and the Kunsthistorisches Museum, a twenty-minute stroll from his pension; several days of opera at the Festspielhaus in Salzburg; and perambulations into the open-air Volksgarten to hear the works of Mahler failed to distract Horst from the absence of Martha Graham. Nor did Professor Stöhr's weekly soirees in his rambling apartment, the living room table laden with cheese, sausages, salads, and cakes, a generous flow of wine animating lively debates "on what was new and exciting in music." Before a throng of students in the music parlor, the avuncular maestro sat down at his grand piano to play lieder, while his loving wife, Mitzi, stood behind him and massaged his head. Despite this cosmopolitan saturation of spirit and mind, in a matter of weeks, Horst, lurking alone in a corner, found Stöhr's manner to be "dry and pedagogical."

The explosion of *Freier Tanz* (free dance), during the "peak years for dance modernism" in cosmopolitan Vienna, eluded Horst's grasp. He attended only one dance recital, on June 5, an evening of solos by Lucy Kieselhausen, a student of Rudolf von Laban. He did not take the time to see the dramatic dance/spoken word shows at the Deutsches Volkstheater. He did not observe any of dancer-choreographer Gertrud Bodenwieser's *Künstlerischen Tanz* (artistic dance) or *Mimik und Tanz* (mime and dance) classes at the Academy of Music; nor did he visit the Dalcroze "Garden City of Helle-rau" School, recently moved from Dresden and presenting summer courses in *Tanzgymnastik* at Laxenburg Castle in suburban Vienna. Aimless and depressed, unable to arrange access to a dance practice studio, Horst man-aged to sketch one idea for a song cycle set to two favorite poems, "Mule Pack," by Kansas author William Haskell Simpson; and the mournful "Har-vest Dirge," by Alfred Kreymborg ("Why do you go away, cloud, like a hearse? / Remove your gold spectacles, stream, and weep?"), and a draft for a dance called "Scène Javanaise," dedicated to Graham.

Horst slogged on through the season. Only when he was in New York—"I *had* to have that contact with the City"—would he be able to find the right voice—and the right woman—to breathe life into his music. On Septem-ber 16, 1925, two days after Martha Graham began teaching at Eastman, Horst left Vienna, indulged in a brief Italian tour, then sailed on the *Mar-tha Washington* from Trieste via Lisbon to Manhattan. When he arrived on October 21, Graham was at the dock to meet her "fortress . . . [her] palisade of Teutonic determination"; and the couple returned to Rochester.

.   .   .

Louis Horst, the bibliophile, although disconnected from living dance cul-ture during the Vienna sojourn, did bring home several books with vivid photographs of Mary Wigman (born Karoline Sophie Marie Wiegmann in 1886) and her pupil, Gret Palucca, to introduce Graham to the style of *Ausdruckstanz*. Palucca never performed in America, although she toured widely in Europe. Graham would meet Wigman briefly when the dancer came to New York City in December 1930 to begin a transcontinental tour.

After a flirtation with ballet, Mary Wigman studied with Emile Jaques-Dalcroze, and learned through the measured sound-and-action of eurhythmics how to tighten and relax and move her body through space and time in dialogue with music. In 1913, Wigman encountered the pure motion and "admirable tenacity" of Rudolf von Laban, her "worshipped hero . . . the great discoverer and catalyst [who] opened the gates to the world of dance" at his arts collective in the wilds of Monte Verità. She was energized by the primal, colorful, angst-ridden style of her "passionately eloquent" friend, painter Emil Nolde, and after the Great War, electrified by the iconoclasm of Dada, she emerged from a Nietzschean nervous breakdown, weathered the critics' resistance, and founded her Dresden *Schule*. By 1925, Mary Wigman had reached the peak of popularity as the premier Weimar icon of expressionist, absolute dance—"hard, bitter and hungry."

In the pages of Rudolf von Delius's *Mary Wigman*, published in Dresden, Martha Graham saw a self-possessed woman with jet-black hair and a painted mouth who loved the camera—and, like Graham, had come late to dance. Arms akimbo, "acknowledging the pull of the earth" in defiance of three girls facing her, their chins lifted in pride; or draped in a shimmering, silvery gown, standing barefoot to enjoy "the play between the floor and the sole," her back impossibly arched, right arm raised perpendicular to the heavens; a woman

Mary Wigman aloft in *Hexentanz,* ca. 1914–1918. (Photograph by Hans Dursthoff)

in white at the center of a group of black-clad supplicants, feeling the vibration of flute, gong, and drumbeat in her bloodstream; dancing solo through silence, palm of the right hand pressed flat atop the left, elbows jutting to the side, energy accumulating in her body, breaking through at the surface, radiating into space.

Expressionist dance was a hyper-subjective *Tanzdrama* that created its own unsettling reality rather than replicate period pieces. In Wigman's 1925 manifesto published in Vienna, *We Are Standing at the Beginning,* Martha Graham read how, from the vanguard, Wigman challenged her students to hold the conviction that only emotion endured: "The shape of the dancing *Gestalt* must begin to take on a creative form," Wigman wrote, "must crystallize in the lasting process of the experiment . . . To experience an artistic dance creation means absorbing it through the eye and feeling it kinesthetically."

"Among my first students," Wigman recalled, "was a narrow-hipped, boyish-looking girl with a pert face framed by wild, reddish-blonde hair" cropped in a short, bobbed style. Munich-born "Gret Palucca . . . seemed without any inhibitions, almost as if possessed, the way she totally yielded to each challenge." Wigman was dark, immersive, brooding with willpower, the low dancing *Tieftanzerin*; Palucca, sixteen years younger, was the lunging, twisting *Hochtanzerin*, a fearless leaper, elevated by "merry confusion."

Teacher and student grew apart and became rivals. In March 1925, Palucca presented a recital at the Deutsches Nationaltheater in Weimar and visited the Bauhaus, where she found a receptive and "easy mingling and mixing between art and dance." She gaily danced for and with the students and faculty, including László Moholy-Nagy and Wassily Kandinsky. In *Painting, Photography, Film,* Moholy-Nagy had published a dramatic photograph by Charlotte Rudolph of Palucca airborne at an impossible altitude, accompanied by her looming shadow, feet tucked beneath her. Horst bought Moholy-Nagy's book to show to Graham and also picked up a copy of *Das Kunstblatt,* where Rudolph's photographs of Palucca were published. Kandinsky, intrigued by this ravishing *Physik-Kultur* exemplar of "the new woman," muscular legs and gymnast's figure on display, was working on a group of line drawings of Palucca inspired by four *Tanzbild* Dance Studies.

The drawings, in juxtaposition with Rudolph's photographs, became the focus for Kandinsky's essay "Dance Curves: On the Dances of Palucca," which he put together during the summer of 1925 while completing *Point and Line to Plane.* "Complete mastery is impossible without precision," Kandinsky insisted in "Dance Curves," a tribute to the discipline central to dance, and "[p]recision is the result of protracted effort . . . and is an extremely important precondition of outstanding talent." Distilling Palucca's sensuous, exuberant poses into his brand of linear music, Kandinsky explained in "Dance Curves" how his attention had been seized by the dancer's "gift of [her] large, simple form," applauding her dedication to "extraordinarily precise construction" in the disposition of her limber body.

. . .

Following Graham, Horst joined the teaching faculty at the Anderson–Milton School, which was expanding to courses in musical comedy, playwriting, and scenic and costume design. At Graham's classes there, and at Eastman, Horst was thrilled by her improvisational variety, how she "would work up percussion things, just standing still, and sharp, sculptured things, primitive-like, and kept working and finding . . . and, lying on the floor, contracting, she got early the idea . . . of tucking under." So that she could see her evolving methods embodied (although she did not, at this time, identify her technique by name), Graham prompted the students with exhortations surprising them into new forms of action: "Complete every gesture down to your very fingertips . . . take in space . . . reach out . . . [and] project beyond the perimeter." Experimentation was the theme. "Gradually, I was able to force out the old," she said, "and little new things began to grow."

During Graham's "period of searching," Horst was one of the select people she permitted herself to listen to; and he was one of the few who took time to listen to her. One other attendant ear was twenty-five-year-old Milwaukee-born flutist, percussionist, and composer, Otto Luening, recruited by Vladimir Rosing and George Eastman to become executive director of the Eastman School opera department and conductor of the Rochester American Opera Company. In his teens, Otto had trained at the Munich Academy of Fine Arts and the Zurich Conservatory, where, for a season, he was an actor and stage manager with James Joyce's English Players. Newly arrived in Rochester, Luening often shared a booth with Horst and Graham at the Fern Restaurant on North Union Street on evenings after classes and rehearsals. The three companions talked over dinner, Luening recalled, "very early in the [modern music] game . . . about how we ought to do things. . . . We were feeling around, about getting a different kind of unity for [dance, music, and theatre]. We wanted to make our own thing here [in America], to express things in simpler terms without always having a colossal orchestra or enormous stage sets."

In the studio, Luening found Graham's teaching style "daring and lyrical." In conversation, she was "warm, friendly and stimulating," struggling to articulate "her subconscious gropings and yearnings" in making dance. Horst was equally forthright in the after-hours chats with Luening about his developing partnership with Graham. Like Paul Hindemith, a composer he admired, Horst used "the term *Gebrauchsmusik* [functional music] for what he did" in support of her work, serving as "accompanying composer"—his words—"and let[ting] Martha be creative in her concept of what went on."

Luening was writing an organ score, "a fine period suite . . . suggestive of early Gregorian music" for a production of Maurice Maeterlinck's three-act morality-miracle play *Sister Beatrice,* scheduled to premiere in January 1926 at Kilbourn Hall. It was directed by Rouben Mamoulian in a contemporary English translation from the French by the writer Paul Horgan, Mamoulian's amanuensis and assistant. To liven up "the rhythmic structure" of the show with "the flow of bodies," Luening brought Martha Graham in during the rehearsal process to "improve the visual aspect . . . and choreograph the movement of the nuns." After run-throughs ended, and "we would fold because of fatigue," Luening remembered, "Martha would make us all scrambled eggs and coffee and then we would go back to work, because the show must go on."

Graham's performance schedule at Eastman followed the crammed pace of vaudeville. There were three shows a day, every day except Sunday, for the six-day run of a "deluxe" program. A typical Eastman Theatre show during the fall of 1925 took place during the week of October 25. The "opener" was Wagner's overture to *Rienzi*, performed by the Eastman Theatre orchestra under the baton of Guy Fraser Harrison. This was followed by a newsreel, "Eastman Theatre Current Events," then a presentation arranged for the students by Martha Graham, a Delsartian "Pompeian Afternoon" warmly welcomed by the *Democrat & Chronicle* as "an indication of delightful dance divertissements, including a series of exquisite stage pictures, set against a background of four Greek columns."

The misses Sabin, Macdonald, and Biracree were featured. After they departed into the wings, the lights came down for the feature film presentation, *Little Annie Rooney*, starring Mary Pickford, followed by a Mutt and Jeff comedy, *Mixing in Mexico*. "Now we're set to symphonic music and presented in natural color," the cartoon duo proclaimed. Two weeks later,

November 8–14, again with three performances a day (at "3:14, 7:14, and 9:14 p.m."), Graham arranged "A Serenade in Porcelain" that came on fifth in the lineup, preceded by an overture, the "current events," a comedy routine, and a vocal number by a student from the Eastman opera department; and followed by a dramatic "sketch" and the featured movie.

Leading up to *Sister Beatrice*, Martha Graham was credited as Eastman's "sole arranger of dance routines" such as "A Corner in Spain," accompanied by Claude Debussy's impressionist piece, *Danse Arabesque,* in which Sabin, Macdonald, and Biracree "are robed in flowing white; the stage light is dimmed and given a hint of color . . . The gesture of arm and body is made to flow down the line of figures and a group pose in the stage center is taken . . . This is a music that has grace and prismatic tone color [and] a rhythmic flow that travels through no set routine but moves fancy free with beauty as a goal."

.   .   .

I feel so strongly about Martha Graham because we date what we call the modern dance from Martha Graham's first New York recital in 1926.

—JOHN MARTIN

That was the start. That ends the Denishawn period. The beginning of Graham . . . April 18, 1926, Sunday at the 48th Street Theatre . . . a sacred concert.

—LOUIS HORST

The first independent recital by the Martha Graham Concert Group was presented in New York City. Al Jones and Morris Green, coproducers with John Murray Anderson of *The Greenwich Village Follies,* reserved one night "at cost" at William A. Brady's 48th Street Theatre, on the (mistaken) assumption that after the event Graham would return to their revue. With venue determined and date set, Louis Horst turned for financial help to his friend Ida Frances Steloff. The packed aisles of her Gotham Book Mart at 128 West Forty-Fifth Street, opposite the beaux arts Lyceum Theatre, had been for six years a haven for "the audience hankering for the new . . . the 'nuts,' " as Steloff affectionately called them, "who wanted [to read] T. S. Eliot, Ezra Pound, James Joyce and Gertrude Stein" and stopped in to satisfy their craving for literary modernism. Before founding the Gotham, Steloff had managed the drama books department at Brentano's on Fifth Avenue and knew her neighborhood clientele well. After eleven, when the curtains came down around Broadway and environs, Steloff kept the little "shop" (she never referred to the Gotham as a "store") open for the theatre crowd to browse through the extensive collection of oversize books on set decor and the visual arts, and "the artists nobody else had . . . Klimt, Rackham, Dulac."

Since the Denishawn days, Martha Graham and Louis Horst had been frequent Gotham visitors. Graham impressed Steloff as a curious reader, drawn to the shop's strengths in "Oriental teachings, mystical experiences, the Biblical prophets, and philosophers not connected with established Western churches." When Horst asked Steloff to guarantee a $1,000 high-interest loan from the Morris Plan to pay for the coming April show, Steloff agreed, although she had never seen Graham dance. As she knew it would be, "the concert was a great success," Steloff recalled, "and the loan was taken care of. That concert was the beginning of [Martha's] brilliant career."

Graham's dresses were integral to her performances—the ways they hung, swirled, and billowed, weighted hems grazing the floor in a perfect circle with the final note. "I went down to Orchard Street. I bought fabric for nineteen cents a yard," she said. "I draped them [on the dancers] myself. I fitted them all myself. I made my own costumes with my own two hands." It was a habit throughout her career. Graham sat on the floor, safety-pinned, cut, and stitched, or told the girls to do the basting themselves. She would watch them move about the studio while she assessed the need for alterations. If the dancer seemed self-conscious, the form of the fabric did not adapt to the body's sway, or the shift or the drape weren't right, Graham would rip it all apart and begin again until her fingers bled.

To the fashion editor of *The Bookman,* in the orchestra section of the 48th Street Theatre composing her "spring musings" on April 18, "tak[ing] interpretive dance these days to be in style," Martha Graham's design sense proved to be a triumph: "If there must be dancing in the streets, it should be done by Martha Graham. . . . Gray and blood-red and blue-lavender chiffon, molten silver cloth and cloth of gold come to life in her expert hands."

Also in the "large and distinguished" audience that night, despite the bad weather, were Rouben Mamoulian with a group of Eastman students in tow; Louise Groody, eponymous star of *No No Nanette*; lyricist and producer Charles Emerson Cook; S. Jay Kaufman, publicist, playwright, and friend of

Roxy Rothafel; and "other well-known authors and artists interested in the theatre generally and in the dance especially."

Among the "many aristocrats of the dance world," Troy and Margaret West Kinney were also at Graham's New York debut. The Kinneys were coauthors of *The Dance: Its Place in Art and Life*, published in 1914. An expanded second edition was published in 1924, adorned with Mr. Kinney's etchings and line drawings and more than two hundred photographs. Isadora Duncan and Ruth St. Denis (and, to a lesser extent, Ted Shawn) were acknowledged in the book; Martha Graham was not, her star not yet risen. The Kinneys, prominent among arbiters of the dance in all forms and cultures, were looking forward to what the former Denishawn danseuse and her Eastman students would demonstrate about "the future history of the art," going beyond the founding pillars of American modern dance: "Can they overcome the handicaps of their own experience in affairs of organization? Will they be wise in their selection of advisors and allies?"

. . .

Louis Horst's shaping mind and keyboard facility were present throughout the evening's narrative, his repertoire for piano sequenced to show off the dancers' facility—Graham's especially—from the nineteenth-century German Romantic tradition to the proto-modernists whose music was au courant in 1920s Europe. In the first half of the program, the numbers presenting Graham accompanied by Macdonald, Biracree, and Sabin included César Franck's late, flowing Prélude and Chorale for Solo Piano, with virtuosic runs and ripples and ruminative pauses and silences; and Debussy's "Clair de Lune," the third memorable movement of his *Suite Bergamasque,* the name taken from a poem by Verlaine in which the beloved's soul is a pastoral landscape populated by peasants reveling to the strains of a lute.

The three ladies without Graham performed Schubert's "Tänze," a short and stately waltz; Arabesque No. 1 in E Major by Debussy, done at Eastman the preceding fall, "three soft childish figures nude and silhouetted whitely against the black drop curtain [making] charming cameos"; and Alexander Scriabin's mysterious, "curving . . . sculptural . . . *legato,* simple but not stark" *Danse Languide,* in an evocative minor key, the fourth of his 1906 *Quatre Morceaux.*

Graham danced seven solos before the break: Schumann's 1839 Novelette,

Evelyn Sabin, Betty Macdonald, and Rosina Savelli (replacing Thelma Biracree) in Graham's *Danse Languide,* New York City, April 1927. (Photograph by Soichi Sunami)

Botticelli's *Primavera,* 1478.

op. 99, no. 9, with sprightly trills; an intermezzo by Brahms in C Major, under two minutes, featuring Horst's percussive left hand; Debussy's "The Maid with the Flaxen Hair," from the first book of his dreamy, wandering *Préludes,* Graham donning a two-braided, waist-length, Rapunzel-inspired wig; and Scriabin's *Désir*, dissonant, sparse, and minimalist, yet "made eloquent by Miss Graham's ability to make every muscle, every movement of arm and hand, count for emotional meaning." "Deux Valses" by Ravel came next, from his 1911 suite of *Valses Nobles et Sentimentales*—delicate, pensive, and airy: "You know my intense attraction to these wonderful rhythms," Ravel wrote of the piece, "and that I value the *joie de vivre* expressed in the dance much more deeply than [César] Franck's Puritanism." "Masques," a composition written for Graham by Horst, followed.

After a pause, a mahogany grand piano was wheeled to center stage, and Horst accompanied soprano Mabel Zoeller, picturesque in a sweeping blue gown, in four songs of his own. The first two were composed during his stay in Vienna. "Harvest Dirge" was to the poem by Alfred Kreymborg, New York writer, Gotham Book Mart habitué, and little magazine editor (*Others* and *Broom*). Horst had been thinking about the absent Martha when he chose the brief lyric of a mystery woman who "came / That wistful child— / On her way to red, / Deep red . . . Come sir, she's going, sir. / Come sir, she's gone." The second song, "Toys," was written to verse by Arthur Symons, the English poet, author of critical studies of Browning, Baudelaire, and the Symbolists. Horst's separation from Graham came to mind in lines such as "You know you are safe in my heart; / You know I have set you apart / In my heart, and hid you away, / Because joy that prattled and smiled / In the heart becomes grief to the heart."

Following intermission, Horst waved the avant-garde flag with *Trois Gnossiennes,* a piece by Erik Satie. The first, composed in 1890 and published in 1893, was a minimalist, delicate exercise in the mode of the composer's *Sarabandes* and *Trois Gymnopédies*. The absence of bar lines offered the pianist flexibility in execution. Adding to the mystique were Satie's idiosyncratic instructions in the score, "*Du bout de la pensée*" and "*postulez en vous meme*"—"at the tip of your mind" and "wonder about yourself." Horst and Graham had a shared history with *Gnossiennes*; Ted Shawn choreographed it as a floor plastique classroom exercise for her in 1917, and in 1919, performed the piece in concert as a "personal solo."

The story of *Gnossiennes* was born in the second millennium BC at the Minoan site of Knossos in Crete, five kilometers southeast of Herakalion, where, at the sprawling palace, processions of "wasp-waisted," blessed youths gamboled through the mazelike "architecture of twisting passageways" to perform ring dances on the massive holy temenos, a "dancing floor" in the shape of a squared circle. The dances were in tribute to Pótnia, the (Great

Mother) Goddess and all-powerful "mistress," depicted in seals and statuettes unearthed at the site as bare-breasted, wearing a ribbed, floor-length
A-line skirt, arms outstretched, palms cupped, or clenched around a ceremonial staff or double ax. The labyrinthine palace at Knossos had been
constructed in orientation to "the hilly landscape as the Goddess' body"; the
valley was Pótnia's "encircling arms, the conical hill her breast or nurturing
function, [and] the horned mountain her 'lap' or cleft vulva."

In "Frieze," the second of the *Trois Gnossiennes*, transplanted into the
48th Street Theatre from a Mycenaean tableau, the Eastman triple goddesses
carried the ancient idiom forward with the prancing steps of their white,
archaic feet, arms parallel, elbows crooked at right angles, hands flat with
palms displayed.

And "Tanagra," the third, was named after the Greek terra-cotta dancing female figurines "prized for their naturalness, vivacity and charm" that
Graham encountered on display in the Manchester art museum during her
1922 visit with Horst. In 1899, Isadora Duncan had created "Tanagra Figures," one of her popular solos, "a series of statue-poses, performed on each
foot, with fluid transitions . . . emphasizing the S curve of figures in Greek
sculptures . . . [and] the open angle of the hips and chest." Duncan had performed these wearing a classically draped toga, bare-headed or with a modest
crown set just above her forehead; miming, like Aphrodite, the adjustment
of an untied sandal, pinning a tunic to her shoulder, or stooping as if to "pick
up a handful of dirt." Ruth St. Denis danced her version of "Tanagra"—to
the music of Schumann—into the 1930s.

Martha Graham's "Tanagra" was different, a study in "abstraction and
essence" of barely three minutes, "in which she stood master over an equally
clear but infinitely tenuous, frail form." The loosely hanging long sleeves of
her himation (cloak) gathered into her clasped fingers were raised at intervals
above her head in homage to the clay statuettes constructed with articulated
limbs. A hood covered Graham's cropped and sculpted coiffure; in a later
iteration of the piece, she would wear a snugly fitting cap resembling Nike's,
the goddess of strength and victory. From her shoulders, Graham detached
a silken cape that billowed while she traveled fleet-footed across the stage.
She carried a fan in the shape of an aspen leaf that she set down upon a
soft, rounded ottoman, the dance evolving into sinuous spirals. The fan was
inspired by "a girl in a blue chiton [linen slip dress] and a pink mantle," one
of four Tanagra figurines in the room of Recent Accessions of the Classical
Department at the Metropolitan Museum of Art in the new wing of antiqui-

ties, opened to the public on April 5, two weeks before Graham's New York premiere. The curator of Greek and Roman art, Gisela Richter, continuing to build the museum's already rich collection of Tanagra statuettes, spoke of their "certain charm and daintiness that come from small scale and delicate workmanship."

Graham's next solos were Rachmaninoff's Romantic composition, *From a XII Century Tapestry,* retitled the following month as *A Florentine Madonna,* followed by *A Study in Lacquer* by Marcel Bernheim. She glided onto the stage in a kimono "of heavy gold cloth and pose[d]" casting angular shadows upon "a red Chinese screen, looking for all the world like one of the pleasant gilded ladies who wander so casually over ancient lacquered boxes." Garbed in "lovely draped batik of melting colors," the Eastman ladies returned, "their young faces brightened by the warm flowers in their shining hair," for "The Three Gopi Maidens," excerpted from *The Flute of Krishna,* a work in process choreographed by Graham to debut in Rochester.

After Graham reappeared for Ravel's impressionistic *Danse Rococo,* Macdonald, Sabin, and Biracree leaped forth for "The Marionette Show" by the English composer and conductor Eugene Goossens, a colleague from the Eastman School. The dancing of these "fey-like girls . . . who need only concert slips, bare limbs, and shoulder-length hair to delight the spectator" was "so frolicsome, so spontaneous, and unforced they were called back for an encore."

For the finale, Graham, "lithe and tigerish in a crisp silk gown of black and orange stripes" of her own design, and "with red poppies in her sleek black hair," presented Manuel de Falla's sultry *Portrait—After Beltran-Masses.* The painter and set designer Federico Beltran-Masses had become well-known in America for his daring, full-length naturalistic canvases of dancers and actors. *Portrait*—"a series of pictures that fire the imagination and make a hundred stories for every gesture"—received rapturous applause.

In her dressing room after the performance, Graham declared that she "itched" to gain more recruits for her classes, not from among artistes, but from the ranks of "overdomesticated" women: "It is my hope that they might come to life through an absorbing interest in the creative possibilities of the dance. To those who can become as open-minded and simple as little children," she said, "dance has a tremendous rejuvenating power; it is a spiritual touchstone, which puts us in tune with the beauty and truth of the universe." The dance, Martha Graham explained, was an ideal activity for "the woman whose mind is alert to the world happenings of the day, who responds to beauty in all forms, who finds time to read poetry and listen to good music."

. . .

"[T]he groupings, and the sense of movement, are being done with the knowledge that the camera is before us," Graham said, describing *The Flute of Krishna,* a six-and-a-half-minute silent film produced in experimental color by the Eastman Kodak Company. "I am relying upon this to carry over the thing I want to say, and there must be . . . nothing remotely resembling ballet, because it is a story, first of all, and as all life is danced and because all life is rhythm, it is so shown." The film ran for the week of May 9–15, 1926, at the Eastman Theatre. Robert Ross, one of Graham's students, starred as Krishna, accompanied by Evelyn Sabin as Radha, his affianced bride. Thelma Biracree and Betty Macdonald were joined by Constance Finkel as the three *apsarases,* Radha's Gopi attendants.

According to the Hindu story, Krishna in his youth was a cowherd whose seductive tunes attracted young women to dance with him; the god's flute was a musical instrument of singular appeal, a hollow reed open to breath's creative inspiration, permitting the sacred spirit to reach into the lowest part of the abdomen. The narrative flow of *The Flute of Krishna* was interrupted by plastique/freeze-frames, progressive shedding and swirling of veils, mid-riff contractions counterbalanced by backs arched toward the floor. "The Denishawn influence is obvious in the work's exoticism and in the use of elaborate costuming," notes Alice Helpern. "However, Graham's choreography treats the East Indian theme without replicating East Indian gesture, as a dance by [Shawn or] St. Denis would have done."

On Thursday evening, May 27, at Kilbourn Hall, Horst, Graham, and her students presented an encore of New York's April debut. One critic took the occasion to gently reprimand Graham, reminding the audience that "Rochester has seen less of her since she came here to teach than her eminent record should justify." Nevertheless, she was "a dancer of creative bent, who moulds music to her own concepts and fancies," even if "some of her numbers might pass as pantomime rather than dancing, to a spectator who failed to catch the constant and inevitable rhythm that permeates them." Accessible to the eye were "the three young women who flitted in and out, a trio of coryphées . . . These young dancers have gained [from Graham's teaching] the essentials of bodily grace and muscular control . . . they have been taught that even a motionless pose, or even a prostrate figure, may have beauty and meaning."

A new dance in the Rochester recital included an ensemble of men, for the first time in Graham's choreography: Harold Kolb, Harold Conkling, Henry Riebeselle—and Robert Ross, of *Krishna* fame, in the role of King Admeto (Admetos) to Graham's Queen Alceste (Alkestis) in a suite-saraband adapted from C. W. Gluck's 1767 opera, the libretto based upon Euripides's fifth-century BC play of a royal house roiling with self-sacrifice, rebirth, and transformation. "One cannot hope to reproduce a dance that is of another country or another age," Graham said; therefore, "it will not *be* a sarabande. It will be the shadow of the sarabande—the spirit that lies beneath the formal patterns of the old dance."

The male-female cast also presented Horst's *Scène Javanaise*, written in Vienna; an all-male bas-relief followed, with music by the English composer Cyril Scott, who had done the *Flute of Krishna* score. And Macdonald, Biracree, and Sabin were three angels in Ermanno Wolf-Ferrari's *Danza degli Angeli*.

Springtime at Eastman continued with an efflorescence of dances "produced by Rouben Mamoulian and arranged by Martha Graham"— "Gavotte," "A Corner in Spain," "Dream in a Wax Museum" (including "Dance of the French Dolls"), and "Forest Episode."

Rouben Mamoulian resigned on June 24, the cusp of summer 1926, and as meteoric as its rise nine months earlier, the Eastman School of Dance and Dramatic Action plummeted. Rumors of his discontent had been circulating since winter, fueled by clandestine trips to New York and public arguments with Vladimir Rosing. Mr. Eastman, expressing annoyance with the meager cash generated by the theatre and dance program, made it known that his pockets were not inexhaustible. Mamoulian's transition to the venerable Theatre Guild, and the directorship of its theatre school in New York, came as no surprise to his Rochester confrere, Paul Horgan, who had felt "it was only a question of time" until his mercurial supervisor, whom he nicknamed Dr. Faustus, "took flight for broader fields. . . . We had intimately watched his work . . . we knew the penetration, the ingenuity, and the superb taste he brought to every theatrical problem." A year later, Mamoulian would make his Broadway directorial debut at the helm of the Theatre Guild's triumphant production of Dorothy and DuBose Heyward's *Porgy*.

Although Martha Graham's brief tenure at Eastman had been a noble experiment, she remained troubled and restless. On June 26, after *Ave Maria*, her final performance of the season, she was called to an appointment with Howard Hanson, director of the Eastman School of Music, to renew her contract to teach and choreograph for a second year. Unable to bring herself to sign on the dotted line, Graham summarily "turned, walked out, packed [her] things, and returned to Manhattan."

8

From Mariarden to John Martin

It is a far cry from the "queen full of jewels"
. . . to the conjunction of the Monongahela and the
    Allegheny,
and the scholastic philosophy of the wilderness
to combat which one must stand outside and laugh
since to go in is to be lost . . .
it is not the plunder,
but "accessibility to experience."
           —MARIANNE MOORE, "New York," 1921

Twenty years before Martha Graham's arrival, Pennsylvania Station loomed large for Fred Astaire and his sister, Adele, in the drafty terminal "on a gray day" when there were "so many people, all in a hurry. The New York attitude as ever was to hurry," Astaire remembered, "whether you had to or not." Then as now, New York was an essential place for any dancer whose fate was to be in motion, day after day, bag slung over her shoulder, and shoulder to shoulder with others, jumping in and out of buses and subways and cabs in transit from one rehearsal or class or performance to another, shedding street clothes and slipping into leotards, tying back her hair, warming up, stretching . . . and . . . *go!*

On the world stage, Martha Graham's America was testing its voice as a soloist, after having fallen reluctantly, then deeply, into the disastrous and entangling alliances of the war. In the years rippling from the cataclysm and the Armistice, American artists expended prodigious energy flirting with, living with, and ultimately rebuffing Eurocentric ways. Home talents shifted slowly away from imitative envy of another tradition, and toward an invigorating revival.

Martha Graham's Manhattan in the 1920s was "a Roman candle hurtling into hyperborean space, its glitter and energy sparking a decade of creativity" between the traumas of war and the Depression. The *new* New York City, a teeming, hectic nexus of bustling crowds in gridded streets among soaring mansions in the sky and arching bridges, was a dense, unremitting place outsized enough to challenge Graham's personality.

The great metropolis, lit up, Duke Ellington said, with "the immediate excitement of starshine," became Martha Graham's home after two decades flitting between coasts like a hummingbird alighting upon and tasting assorted nectars, cross-pollinating bits and pieces: choreographing, teaching, reading (always reading), leaning against propped-up pillows in bed, a shawl around her shoulders against the chill, until the wee hours, scribbling in her journal, revisiting and revising, discarding, inventing, and perturbing her imagination.

Her lifestyle swinging between public performance and ascetic withdrawal, Graham had no off switch. She would complain of "a kind of 'inside' flu," of "nervous exhaustion," and immobilizing "fevers" brought on by overwork. "With modern art, there is no time to be a 'bohemian,'" she told Horst, "no time for parties where people sit around and talk about what they are going to do—but don't actually do anything."

For Graham, the jagged pulse and Brownian motion of Mayor Jimmy Walker's edgy cosmopolis—the pace of life and the proximity of artistic entrepreneurs—was "nervous, sharp, zigzag. It often stops in midair. It is what I am [looking] for in my dances." Like Georgia O'Keeffe's vertiginous skyscraper paintings—the black and gold, art deco American Radiator Building on West Fortieth Street, the multi-setbacked Shelton Hotel on Lexington and Forty-Ninth—tilted against the starry night, New York's angular, "alluring stage set," its "cyclopean drama of forms," infiltrated Graham's choreography.

.   .   .

Following a weekend of three recitals in August 1926 at Mrs. Currier's idyllic Mariarden colony in New Hampshire, reprising the 48th Street Theatre and Eastman repertories, with Louis Horst at the piano, Evelyn Sabin, Betty Macdonald, and Rosina Savelli, replacing Thelma Biracree—who remained in Rochester and opened a dance studio—Graham resumed classes at the John Murray Anderson–Robert Milton School.

One of her students, Bette Davis, was a "small, odd beauty . . . with an improbably boyish face sharply feminized by two huge, magnetic eyes" who had taken classes in interpretive nature dancing and "the art of bodily motion" at Mariarden during the summer of 1925. Davis had auditioned for Eva Le Gallienne's Civic Repertory Theatre and was rejected for what the founding diva critiqued as "a frivolous and insincere attitude." But Martha Graham saw the actress's potential. Her advice to the eighteen-year-old remained in Davis's memory long after she became a star: "Think of acting exactly like a ballet . . . To act is to dance," Graham told her, by which she meant, Davis said, that, like dancing, acting needed to be in the moment with "a continuity of movement in both voice and body—everything smoothly connected."

Graham's classes at Anderson–Milton were coed, twenty or more students, starting with rhythmic exercises at the barre, then divided into groups of four or five to dance for her. "It must be simple and clear," she would say. "I want to be able to look through your motions into you, as one can look into a child's eyes." She would not tolerate insincerity. "Let your movements be grotesque rather than weak," Martha Graham told them. She "was all tension—lightning!" Bette Davis said of her adored teacher, whose "burning dedication gave her spare body the power of ten men," liberating Davis's "emotion with [the] full body, as a dancer does."

Alternate evenings, Graham dashed to her other studio in Andrew Carnegie's Music Hall. To help pay for the concert programming he had put in motion, Carnegie brainstormed with architect Henry J. Hardenbergh—designer of the Plaza Hotel and the Dakota—and came up with the idea of generating rental income through offices, apartments, and studios built beside, behind, and on top of the performance hall. In 1894, the mansard roof of the main building was removed and skylit lofts were added, and a twelve-story building along West Fifty-Sixth Street east of Seventh Avenue was built. Two years later, a fifteen-story tower went up facing Fifty-Seventh Street, further east so as not to block the northern light bathing the Fifty-Sixth Street tower.

By the time Graham began teaching at Carnegie Hall, more than 170 studio spaces of all shapes and sizes linked by a warren of mismatched corridors, abbreviated staircases, and rickety elevators, created an urban arts colony for institutions and mavericks. From 1926–1928, among the dance community, Carnegie Hall was home to the Delsarte School, the Andalusian Academy of Dancing, the Cansinos, Alys Bentley, and the Denishawn School. The New

Graham teaching in her Carnegie Hall studio, 1927. (Sketch by Marion Greenwood)

York Philharmonic, the Authors Club, and the American Academy of Dramatic Arts had headquarters there. Painters at work in the Carnegie Studios included Everett Shinn of the Ashcan School; Edwin Blashfield, muralist and president of the American Academy of Design; graphic artist and creator of the Gibson girl, Charles Dana Gibson; and émigré abstractionist Hilla Rebay. Pianist Gustav Louis Becker gave theory classes in his studio, as did Pietro Yon, organist and music director for St. Patrick's Cathedral. On the ninth floor, Evangeline Adams, friend of Aleister Crowley and author of the 1927 bestselling *Astrology: Your Place in the Sun* ran a consultancy.

Louis Horst found a cozy practice room on the first floor in the South Tower for $75 a month, and paid the first year's rent, $150 a month, for Graham's almost bare studio, room 707, which had wide windows looking out onto Fifty-Sixth Street, and little else beyond a piano, a tall mirror, and a bookcase. The advertisement Horst took out for Graham offered "lessons [in] Oriental, Dramatic and Creative Dancing. Phone Circle 1350." More intimate than Anderson–Milton, her Carnegie Hall class began with six students. Graham favored young ladies "who have to work for their living. Stenographers and girls from millinery shops, for example. They come with all sorts of conventional notions of prettiness, graceful posturing, and whatnot," Graham said. "My first task is to teach them to admire strength—the virile gestures that are evocative of the only true beauty."

Floor work and a vigorous barre emphasized forward lunges and back falls. Graham was "friendly and informal with her pupils; she advised rather than instructed them. There were no sharp commands of one-two-three KICK . . . and if [the students] were sometimes uncertain of how to say what they wanted in their dances, they were helped [by Miss Graham] . . . discussing their defects or improvements."

In her closet-like anteroom after class, Graham would sit, think, and change costumes in solitude, a ritual she maintained for the next six decades. Cradling a cup of tea in her lap, she perched barefoot, "Buddha-fashion" on a low, elaborately upholstered velvet chaise longue. A snugly wrapped Mandarin silk dressing gown showed off her pale skin and muscular contours. Raven-black hair, parted at the center, pulled sternly into a tight coil, high cheekbones and ruby lips below deep-set kohl-adorned eyes, "she made one think of the East; she suggested it, not with theatrical devices of long earrings and exotic perfumes, but with the grace of the smallest movement and with the low rhythms of her voice that arose out of some deep spiritual calm."

. . .

I don't want to do the Broadway thing, you know. I want to have my own group and work out things in my own way.

—MARTHA GRAHAM, 1927

Familiar themes and innovative variations characterized Graham's concerts in late fall 1926 and midwinter 1927. The fall show was offered for one performance, Sunday, November 28, when the Klaw Theatre was dark and could be rented at a discount. Among the dances were Gluck's *Alceste*, which Betty Macdonald said "looked like a Botticelli painting," Mendelssohn's Scherzo, Debussy's "Clair de Lune," Goossens's "The Marionette Show," de Falla's "Gypsy Portrait," and Satie's *Gnossiennes,* Graham's signature "Tanagra," revealing "her marvelous . . . unsurpassed handling of drapery." She performed "in a tight skirt that flares at her ankles into a long ruffling train. She does not touch her hands to the train, only her feet control it, yet it dances, too."

A new offering was the Baal Shem Suite for violin and piano by Ernest Bloch, subtitled "Two Pictures of Chassidic Life." In the first "picture," "Simchas Torah (Rejoicing)," a sprightly, trilling tribute to Moses bringing the Ten Commandments to the Israelites, Graham, dressed in white, was accompanied by Sabin, Macdonald, and Savelli; the second, "Vidui (Contrition)," a "fervent lamentation" marking the penitential ritual of Yom Kippur, was a slow, meditative Graham solo in a minor key. Horst and Graham chose not to include the third, hastily added section, "Nigun (Improvisation)" because, Graham said, "spontaneity is not art. . . . The thing, once conceived, must be shaped and brought forth by the intelligence . . . A dancer must know what she is doing *every* moment."

Bloch wrote Baal Shem for his friend, the Swiss violinist, André de Ribaupierre, while teaching at the Cleveland Institute of Music in 1923. "It is the Jewish soul that interests me," Bloch said of the piece, "the complex, glowing, and agitated soul that I feel vibrating throughout the Bible . . . it is all this that I endeavour to hear in myself and to transcribe into my music." Accompanying Horst for the occasion, as well as in the Baal Shem offered at the Guild Theatre on Sunday evening, February 27, was a violinist from the New York Philharmonic Symphony Orchestra, Winthrop Sargeant, who would marry and divorce Graham's sister Georgia ("Geordie"), and become the music and dance critic for the *New Yorker.*

Another voice Horst introduced was Béla Bartók's. His feverish-folkish piano dance, "Allegro Barbaro," composed in 1911 and published in Vienna in 1918, was an ideal vehicle for Graham, barely two and a half minutes and crammed with abrupt shifts in tempo.

Toward the conclusion of the evening, Horst continued his literary explorations, setting *Three Poems of the East* performed by Graham and her "maidens" at the November concert, and by Graham solo in February. *On Listening to a Flute by Midnight,* or *Chinese Poem,* was played by flutist George Possell, a rising star of the New York Symphony Orchestra. The second poem, "She like a dancer puts her broidered garments on," variously entitled "East Indian Dance" or "Indian Poem," was taken from the *Rig Veda*: "as a cow yields her udder so she bares her breast. / Creating light for all the world of life, the Dawn hath laid the darkness open as the cows their stall. / We have beheld the brightness of her shining . . ." The third poem, "In measure while the gnats of music whirr, / The little amber-coloured dancers move," was set to a fragment of *Javanese Dancer,* by Arthur Symons, another writer Horst admired. The original poem began as if it were a portrait of Martha Graham: "Twitched strings, the clang of metal, beaten drums / Dull, shrill, continuous, disquieting; / And now the stealthy dancer comes, / Undulantly with cat-like steps that cling; / Smiling between her painted lids a smile/ Motionless, unintelligible . . ."

In the Guild Theatre audience was Martha Hill, a twenty-six-year-old dancer and dance instructor arrived in New York, by way of the Battle Creek Normal School of Physical Education and Kansas State Teachers College, to begin studies toward a BS at Columbia Teachers College. Frustrated by the constraints of ballet training, Hill was transfixed by Graham's original

Martha Hill at Kansas State Teachers College, 1924.

style and went through an epiphanic "instant conversion" that "just hit [her] amidships." The next day, she signed up for Graham's class at the Anderson–Milton School. Graham exercised such an influence that—according to Bessie Schonberg, a lifelong friend—thenceforth Hill "pruned her teaching into a very simple way of getting at the language of the body and the spine."

At the February 27 Guild Theatre recital, Robert Bell of the *Washington Post,* in the city to find out what the Graham commotion was all about, gave a powerful response: "[S]he is one of those artists who is not imitative, but who believes that within her own being are all the potential qualities of all emotions and characterizations. . . . She sees things clearly," Bell sensed, after one performance, "but in a rather detached manner as if she were watching from afar. . . . Moreover, about her there is a suggestion of the classical—so one does not get the quick passion of the moment. . . . And Miss Graham's interpretation of each dance is that somewhere beyond all the restless endeavor of this earth there is a calm peace, a beauty where the only struggle that remains is for the perfection and the betterment of self."

Graham's detachment was a self-conscious way to separate herself from belonging to anything, or anyone. Ted Shawn, Rouben Mamoulian, Howard Hanson, and John Murray Anderson had often heard Martha Graham's insistence upon autonomy. Eventually, she did become amenable to treating dancers in her company as willing accomplices from whom she could appropriate (or, as she unabashedly said, "steal") ideas for movement making; for now, Graham was the single choragus in the midst of every dance she made, creating on her own body.

.   .   .

"Several months ago," Bernarr Macfadden reminded readers in the June 1927 issue of *The Dance,* "these columns were filled with a plea for new dance ideas, motifs that reflected the life and literature of the times and the country." The call went out to disabuse dance aficionados of their lingering postwar "foreign fetishes . . . [the] strong inclination to ascribe art to Europe and machinery to America." The appeal was reminiscent of Ralph Waldo Emerson's cry complaining that "no poet ha[d] come" to birth an American language and idiom—a plea answered by the thirty-six-year-old Walt Whitman in his self-published *Leaves of Grass*.

At the conclusion of Isadora Duncan's fall 1927 memorial service in St. Mark's Church-in-the-Bowery, Eva Le Gallienne read aloud from Duncan's final essay, "I See America Dancing," where she prayed that some "young American composer" would "create the music for the dance . . . from the Solar Plexus, the temporal home for the soul . . . that shall express the America of Walt Whitman." Like that isolato of nineteenth-century Brooklyn who saw America singing, Martha Graham, denizen of Greenwich Village, was moved to respond, buoyed by the mid-1920s dance boom that transitioned American dance from the realm of social activity and physical culture into a native art.

Two months after Macfadden's essay, a special dance issue of *Theatre Arts Monthly* was published with a lead editorial, "The Great World Theatre—The Dearth of Dance Criticism in America." Look around you, the editors said, gathering every form of dance under an inclusive umbrella, seeing "the theatre of the dance in every corner of New York that is alive . . . [there are] folk-dancers in native costume . . . a hundred ball-rooms and cabarets . . . acrobatic and eccentric dancers . . . the choruses . . . the ballet . . . Dalcroze Eurythmics and its variants . . ."

But one venue was lacking, save for the rare Sunday or Monday experiment in a dark Broadway theatre: "the legitimate playhouse, where [dance] most belongs. . . ." Our "American dancers get large audiences and applause . . . There is no group of artists more sure of the rightness and the importance of what they are doing . . . But that is not enough if they are to realize their aims. What they need above everything is intelligent understanding of the dance itself."

Here was the unanswered question: "*What makes dance modern? Who knows?*" The editors continued, "Isn't there somebody who, when he reads the articles in this issue, and sees the pictures which make the pages themselves dance, will take it upon himself to rout out a man [*sic*] who knows the dance in all its forms well enough to evaluate it in criticism and impose him by force upon some newspaper office in America?" The art of dance required a legitimate critical voice to emerge from the entertainment wilderness.

The masterminds behind this "emphasis on dance as theatre art," advocating for the recognition of "indigenous concert dance," were *Theatre Arts Monthly* magazine's founding editor, Sheldon Cheney, and the colleague who succeeded him at the helm, Edith J. R. Isaacs. Cheney studied architecture at the University of California, Berkeley, and drama at Harvard. After attending the 1913 Armory Show in Boston, he moved to the Little Theatre of the Detroit Society of Arts and Crafts where, in November 1916, he started *Theatre Arts,* dedicated to "flaunting the word 'art' in the face of 'show business'" by providing "a forum for the young artist in revolt against the stale, the conventional, the stereotyped." The cover of the inaugural issue featured a drawing of a dancer and promoted an article by Ruth St. Denis, "The Dance As an Art Form." Cheney took the slim journal with him to New York and branched out to modernism in the visual arts and "the new movement in theatre."

In 1924, at thirty-eight, Cheney made an enduring contribution to mainstream art criticism with *A Primer of Modern Art.* The *New York Times* blessed the book as "effective and very much needed," praising the author for his broad vision of understanding that while "all valid art is part of the same mighty stream," modern art is distinguished from its predecessors by the "essential quality of emotionally expressive form . . . as a reflection of the intensity of contemporary life."

"The rhythm of mere life has quickened," Cheney said. "[L]ights are brighter and noises louder" and so, "art cannot remain as quiet as in the past."

These assertions, as well as Cheney's acknowledgment of the lineage between German expressionism and American modernism, brought his book to the attention of Louis Horst, who purchased it immediately. Horst likewise believed in the dynamic, active—musical—qualities of modernism; that "modern art is more personal, more mental than classical art." Cheney's stated equivalence that art is form, Horst agreed, resided "at the basis of [his own] theory of the dance," and he placed a finer point upon that statement: "Aesthetic existence needs a plan," Horst insisted. Unlike ballet, "modern dance is developed through the torso, and thus possesses inner harmonic texture, form that follows content."

After *A Primer of Modern Art,* Cheney passed the editorial and business reins of *Theatre Arts* to Mrs. Isaacs, who developed it into a monthly. Born in Milwaukee, Edith Juliet Rich was literary editor for the *Sentinel* and served as a critic for *Ainslee's,* a popular women's fiction magazine. She married Lewis Montefiore Isaacs of the prosperous New York Jewish family, a real estate lawyer, opera scholar, composer and musician, one of the founders of the MacDowell artists' colony in Peterborough, near Mariarden, and quiet benefactor of his wife's journal. Reflecting her "range of taste and knowledge," Mrs. Isaacs extended the purview of *Theatre Arts Monthly,* "from the written word through the fields of painting, music, poetry, and architecture." It was her idea to publish the special issue on modern dance.

Edith Juliet Rich Isaacs, editor of *Theatre Arts Monthly* magazine, ca. 1924.

Her town house on Central Park South was a short walk from Martha Graham's studio. Isaacs became an appreciative and frequent visitor to Graham's classes, took kindly to her, supported her with hospitality and financial patronage, and was her "spiritual mother" and "Darling Dear One" during volatile times. If angered, Graham was known to tear a pay phone from the wall or jump out of a moving cab. Just such an impulsive tantrum, when she crouched "outraged . . . as if possessed" on the floor of a Carnegie Hall elevator, prompted Isaacs to warn Louis Horst that "Martha needs to control herself and conquer these moods, or she will never become a true artist."

To Graham, controlling herself meant "finding essences, essences, essences," channeling and centering anxious energies into the next composition. At the Little Theatre recital on October 16, 1927, Graham performed Horst's rendition of Arthur Honegger's "Dance," excerpted from *Sept pièces pour piano* and pointedly retitled "Revolt." Eyes shut, fists raised skyward in a defiant boxing match with the gods, and her hair unloosed and hanging to her waist, black knee-length skirt slit to upper thigh—like a Käthe Kollwitz etching come to life—moving "to [the] mad music she was significant . . . as a downtrodden, agonized soul, trying in vain to free itself from the tremendous power that is crushing it to earth."

. . .

"What makes dance modern?"

The *New York World* responded to the *Theatre Arts Monthly* appeal, hiring Lucile Marsh as full-time dance critic. Born in Bridgeport, Connecticut, Marsh studied eurythmics after graduating from Barnard in 1920; taught dance at Smith College; published a pioneering book, *The Dance in Education,* in 1924; founded a dance troupe, the Marsh Concert Dancers, with her two sisters in 1925; and at NYU—contemporaneous with Margaret H'Doubler at the University of Wisconsin—created one of the earliest American college curricula on the dance.

"Martha Graham needs no introduction to devotees of dance art," Marsh wrote in anticipation of Graham's October 1927 show. "She is already known as one of its most sincere and idealistic priestesses. . . . However, what this dancer is most interested in is giving her audience a picture of certain great rhythms which she believes are inherent in all of us."

Her critique the next morning broached what the "problem" of Martha Graham would be for a contemporary audience at "a program after the modern rather than classic manner . . . [because] Miss Graham tends to begin far away from realism," Marsh began, "and some find it hard to follow her through the processes of refinement to which she subjects her themes."

It was the struggle, Marsh said, of "an artist . . . always admired for refusing to be a slave of her first success . . . Miss Graham proved last night that she was in no danger of becoming a rarified spectre of her former self." By adhering to strict principles of movement and theatricality, Marsh wondered, was Graham going to be able to accept that audiences might lag behind? It would seem not. In February and April 1928, the next times Graham performed Honegger's *Dance/Revolt,* it escalated in intensity and severity.

At the *Herald Tribune,* chief music critic Lawrence Gilman promoted his assistant, Mary F. Watkins, to the position of first official dance columnist. Serving as an ambulance driver in France during the Great War, Watkins became secretary and lover to the Wagnerian mezzo-soprano Olive Fremstad and then joined the *Tribune* in the spring of 1926. Unlike Marsh, Watkins did not have a dance background. "I had to judge [the dancers] from what I really thought rather than what I would have liked to have thought," she told Walter Terry.

What she "really thought" of Martha Graham, during the "transitional

Graham in *Dance/Revolt,* by Arthur Honegger, 1927.
(Photograph by Soichi Sunami)

period when Denishawn was on the way out," came in her review of the October 1927 Little Theatre evening. Graham was, Watkins wrote, "one of the most admirable of the rapidly multiplying clan of expressionistic dancers." Honegger's "Dance" affirmed that "Miss Graham has lost nothing of that grace and plastic facility of pose here previously admired." Over the coming five years, Watkins " 'got' more and more as [she] realized what [Martha Graham] was aiming at. . . . You can take her or leave her," Watkins wrote in 1931, "but you cannot divert that fixed gaze which looks so intently ahead into a world which is completely hers to explore."

.   .   .

At the end of October 1927, the newspaper of record stepped up, and John Joseph Martin was hired as the first dance columnist for the *New York Times.*

Martin was born in Louisville, Kentucky, where his father was a purchasing agent for the Louisville and Nashville Railroad, and his mother had been a professional singer. He studied classics, theatre, and ballroom dancing at the University of Louisville, violin at the Chicago Conservatory, and worked as an actor at Maurice Browne's Chicago Little Theatre. In 1915, he saw Isadora Duncan perform for the first time and crossed paths with Harriet Monroe, and the *Poetry* magazine crowd. After serving in the air force, Martin moved to New York City and became the vaudeville reviewer, then editor, of the *Dramatic Mirror,* a trade paper founded to rectify the impression of the theatrical profession "degraded by having its affairs treated in the professedly theatrical papers side by side with prize fights, cocking matches, baseball, and other sports."

After the *Mirror* folded, Martin worked as a press agent for producer-director Stuart Walker, then signed on as executive secretary and elocution instructor at the American Laboratory Theatre, founded by Richard Boleslavsky and Maria Ouspenskaya, émigré students of Stanislavsky at the Moscow Art Theatre. This job, too, was short-lived. Stopping by the music school of the Henry Street Settlement in search of other opportunities, Martin ran into the English dancer and Dalcroze instructor Elsa Findlay, who told him that Olin Downes, chief music critic at the *New York Times,* was looking to add a dance writer to the staff.

Seeing Martin's long and varied experience in theatre and despite protestations that he knew little about modern dance, after a quick interview, Downes took Martin on as a freelancer at $15 a week. "Well, fifteen dollars . . . even if it comes to that, is better than nothing," Martin said to his wife, Louise, "and it's interesting. I'll just stay for six months."

Martin's journalistic purview in 1927 was an emerging "dance movement whose immediate point of departure . . . was a sternly critical attitude toward existing dance." Modernist practitioners believed that "something was wrong which only this dance could right." Martha Graham was an acquired taste. Echoing Marsh and Watkins, Martin's approach to her style began with a few misfires. He perceived her as "going over whole-heartedly to the new German technique," found "her mask less plastic than her body," "her dramatic projection" to be "slight," and her "introspective quality [approaching] moroseness."

Dance historian George Beiswanger noted John Martin's incremental evolution—and education—from intrigued, at times mystified reviewer to nuanced critic over a span of thirty-five years at the *Times.* The power of his imprimatur grew in tandem with Graham's reputation. "As new waves of dance-making took shape, commanding [his] magisterial attention . . . [Martin] stretched the grids through which dance was observed," Beiswanger said, until at last Martin became an advocate for her work as unique to her generation: "[T]he passion of her dances . . . burns with the slow and deadly fire of the intellect," he wrote. "Martha Graham does the unforgivable thing for a dancer to do—she makes you think."

9

Neighborhood Playhouse

T he Denishawn Company returned from their fifteen-month tour of the Orient and began a cross-country circuit of concerts produced by Arthur Judson starting at Philharmonic Auditorium in Los Angeles. The concluding three days at Carnegie Hall in the spring of 1927 were the last Denishawn appearances by Doris Humphrey and Charles Weidman. "The minute they came back" to the States, Louis Horst said, "I attached myself to Doris like a leech and wouldn't let her go until she left. I said [to her], 'You have to. Martha is right and Denishawn is wrong.'"

For Humphrey, as for Graham, the breakup with Ruth St. Denis and Ted Shawn was painful. Humphrey confided to her parents, "The Shawns, I'm ashamed to say, are jealous of Martha. It's disgraceful, and as Louis knows the bitter things Ted has said about [Martha], he hasn't been near them." Regaining contact with Graham after the tour kindled Humphrey's conflicted emotions. The angular, "soul-wrecking" Graham and the float-ing, "cool" Humphrey had not been close in the early days, but "seeing her after such a long absence I get a fresh impression as of a new person." Humphrey imagined Graham as "a hot-house flower that grows best in a hot, moist climate, intensely feminine, not a flaming obvious flower—but a night-blooming thing with a faint exotic perfume" like the cereus in the Graham garden in Santa Barbara.

In the fall of 1927, to subsidize the construction of a permanent home, Denishawn signed for another tour with the traveling company of the Zieg-feld Follies. Humphrey decided to stay home, telling *Variety* she was taking a leave of absence, and "it's just wonderful to be in New York for a whole season attending everybody's recital but your own." Self-effacing and quietly ambitious, Humphrey was anxious to find her own way, "tired of darling little dances and long[ing] for a good thick juicy beef-dance-steak that I can chew on hard . . . I'm just at that in-between stage when . . . I'm struggling with phrases and continuity."

"Temperamentally," Humphrey mused, "I lean toward the flowing things." She intuited that "moving from the inside out . . . [is] the dominant expression of our generation, if not of our age." She would soon establish her fall and recovery technique, emphasizing the suspension of tension—equilibrium—in a dancing space, distinct from Martha Graham's ascetic contraction and release of tension.

Both "Martyr Martha" and "Doric Doris," as Horst teasingly nicknamed them, were edging away from Shawn's mimesis toward the borders of abstraction. "The modern artist," Humphrey wrote, "is adrift in a maelstrom of conflicting interpretations of life and must determine truths for himself by an individual analysis." Ruth St. Denis sensed her protégée's restless mood, dreading that yet another surrogate child might fly from the nest: "Doris feeling her freedom and wanting more of it, Teddy [Shawn] filled with fear and resentment."

Humphrey's dance program with Charles Weidman at the John Golden Theatre on April 15, 1928, exemplified her coalescing goals for modern dance. The evening began with *Color Harmony,* an abstract ballet based upon the scientific concept of the primary components of light: "Through the wild colors shoots a silver arrow—it separates the couples—it draws them one by one into form," Humphrey wrote, "all the flaming colors are laid down in rhythmic patterns—in a pyramidal form—up high steps to a climax, where a silver streak molds itself into a stream of light that goes up into infinity." Humphrey rehearsed the ensemble in silence, then commissioned Clifford Vaughan to write the score for chamber orchestra.

Color Harmony was followed by dances to the first movement of Grieg's Concerto for Piano and Orchestra, Bach's Air for the G String, and a surprise finale—"The Banshee," Humphrey's three-minute solo, the Scottish-Irish folkloric figure of a demon woman-spirit abducting a soul into the underworld. To begin, the composer, thirty-one-year-old Henry Cowell, "rose from his stool, and stepping resolutely behind the piano, thrust a hand into its open queue and started to pluck the wires. . . . Few members of the audience could help feeling that if they were the piano, they would certainly get up and sock the fellow."

An assistant held down the damper pedal while Cowell rubbed the lower strings up and down, counter to strumming crosswise, generating a dissonant medley of inhuman cries, wails, and bloodcurdling whines. Hidden behind a screen, Humphrey revealed then withdrew an arm, rippling fingers, a gesturing hand, and her upper body, at last emerged, garbed in tatters, her mouth open and wavy hair unbound, "a shaft of light as she sped across the stage" in a fury of motion before casting herself to the floor.

．．．

Martha Graham's springtime recital, Sunday, April 22, at the Little Theatre, consisted entirely of solos. She demonstrated her quick-change versatility in Louis Horst's *Fragments: Tragedy and Comedy* for gong and flute, "the result of Miss Graham's desire consciously to use vibration as a dramatic force." Horst claimed—notwithstanding Clifford Vaughan's *Color Harmony* for Doris Humphrey—that *Fragments* "was the first original musical score to be written for a dance after the dance had been composed." In other highlights during the evening, Graham reprised "Tanagra," "handling a chiffon drapery as few others can . . . [with] thrill and excitement [as] poor nouns to describe the effect . . ." She paid homage to an indigenous civilization with "Inca Suite—Harawi (Love Song)," "Huanaco Dance," and three other pieces Horst had extracted from *La Musique des Incas et ses survivances* by Raoul and Marguerite d'Harcourt.

Scriabin's *Fragilité*, a favorite for its "modernistic lyricism . . . was done in a stylized, transparent evening dress made of organdy, exposing enough of [Graham's] body to see its outline clearly." Ravel's *Valses Nobles*, received with thunderous applause, was "light and fresh," Graham wearing a "tight-fitting bodice and full skirt of cretonne with one slit on the left side."

"Immigrant," renamed by Horst and set in the disjunctive Kodály/Bartók mode from *Aus dem Balkan: Gesänge und Tänze*, was a stark pair of dances by Josip Stolcer-Slavenski, a Croatian-born composer who trained at the Belgrade conservatory. John Martin praised Graham for revealing "new vigor and animation" in these "highly-provocative newer dances," showing off "a full-bodied and almost maliciously-gay vitality." In "Steerage," Graham struck poses reminiscent of "Bavarian wood carvings of peasant figures with stiff black shawls and skirts that remained almost motionless." In "Strike," "one felt the surgings of all the revolutions of the world in that slender body" beneath a clingy, "drab one-piece dress." Charles Weidman came up with the mot juste for Graham's persona that night in "Strike." Her sinewy arms extended like arrows, "she looked," he said, "[as if] she picked up an imaginary rock and threw it!"

Two excerpts from Leo Ornstein's ten compositions for piano solo, *Poems of 1917* (op. 41, written 1918) stood out as studies in contrast by Graham and Horst. Born in Kremenchuk, Ukraine, in 1893, recognized as a prodigy, Leo immigrated with his family to New York City, where he enrolled to study piano in the Institute of Musical Art (the Juilliard School). His teacher, Bertha Fiering Tapper, took Ornstein on a world tour. By the late teens, he had created a furor with his own radical compositions and was considered equal to Stravinsky and Schoenberg.

The score for *Poems of 1917* had an antiwar prelude by Waldo Frank, the cultural historian and confidant of poet Hart Crane, whose "The Dance" section of his epic poem, *The Bridge,* would inspire Martha Graham and Aaron Copland's *Appalachian Spring.* A little more than one minute long, "Song Behind the Lines" (*andante con moto e malinconioso*—melancholy), the grim, initial offering from *Poems,* reinforced Ornstein's reputation for "repercussive ferocity." Horst's trilling right hand followed the dissonant, bleak message put forth by Graham's "nunlike figure" . . . "[her] open mouth and cupped, shaking hands . . . symboliz[ing] a sound, both a call and a scream." The second piece, "Dance of the Dead" (listed as "The Dance of Death"), at forty-four seconds in *vivo con fuoco,* with fire, was over before it began. Horst's left hand held sway with dervish-like rumblings as the inflammatory Ms. Graham brought "an acidic conclusion to these disquieting miniatures."

"I've had a year to get a perspective on a great many things," Doris Humphrey wrote in May 1928, "and the results have been—to me—revolutionary." In June, with Charles Weidman and another disaffected Denishawner, dancer and pianist Pauline Lawrence (future wife of José Limón), Humphrey opened a studio brimming with idealism for the future: "[The concert group] is my medium, just as marble is the sculptor's material, only, of course, that simile is not complete, because the group is made up of human beings who are able to add their own power of mind and body to the physical material that sculpture uses." Humphrey was thrilled to say that her "girls feel they are living a part of a vital art [and] they feel a spiritual release in the dance from the pressure of materialism in a machine-made age."

Billed at the top of the cast along with Michio Ito, Martha Graham signed on with Nahum Zemach, founder of Tel Aviv's Habima Players, and Leo Bulgakov, formerly of the Moscow Art Theatre, to an orchestral drama Gesamtkunstwerk set to Ernest Bloch's symphony *Israel.* The Cleveland Orchestra and a chorus "chanting passages from the Bible in the original

Hebrew," were under the baton of maestro Nikolai Sokoloff. The towering, craggy backdrop of the Wailing Wall in Jerusalem was sculptor Jo Davidson's first stage set.

Ted Shawn viewed this surge of collective creation through a dark lens. "Martha and Charles and Doris tried to fool the world," he recalled, bitterly. "They tried to act as if they had been born full-panoplied from the brow of Jove—no poppa, no mother, no antecedents. They acted like they had the revelation direct from God: this is dance!"

· · ·

The serious expressive dance choreography of *Israel* was envisioned, cast, produced, and directed by Irene Lewisohn, the "Our Crowd" doyenne whose belief in the "relationship of free movement to music" led her to Martha Graham. Irene, born 1886, and her elder sister, Alice, born 1883, were among the eight children of Rosalee (née Jacobs) and Leonard Lewisohn, an assimilated German Jew who made his fortune in copper and metals trading and, at his death in 1902, left an estate of $12 million. The sisters followed in their father's philanthropic footsteps, supporting, as he had, the social worker Lillian D. Wald—"the Leading Lady"—in residence at the Henry Street Settlement on the Lower East Side. In 1907, Alice and Irene founded the amateur Dramatic Club at Henry Street, to help brighten the lives of the children of eastern European immigrants and pogrom survivors, "respond[ing] in a natural way to a stirring of their emotional inheritance . . . [through] informal festivals of songs, dance and pageants . . . based upon customs and rituals . . . [inspired by] a desire to interpret ancient traditions that were once so full of meaning." Alice focused upon theatre and Irene, who had studied with Genevieve Stebbins, favored dance. When their popular shows outgrew the Henry Street gymnasium, the sisters constructed a prim, three-story, light red Flemish brick and stucco, marble-trimmed neo-Georgian Little Theatre building at 466 Grand Street on the corner of Pitt Street, where the 399-seat Neighborhood Playhouse opened its apple-green front doors on February 12, 1915.

In 1920, Alice and Irene formed a professional company at the Neighborhood Playhouse that grew to more than thirty actors and a corps of sixty festival dancers. Over the next half dozen years, they produced a series of plays including a six-week *Ibsen Season,* John Galsworthy's *The Mob, Harlequinade* by Harley Granville-Barker, Richard Brinsley Sheridan's *The Critic,*

Neighborhood Playhouse, ca. 1915–1917.

George Bernard Shaw's *Captain Brassbound's Conversion,* the New York City premieres of James Joyce's *Exile* and *The Player Queen* by William Butler Yeats, and the first performances in English of the Hasidic legend of *The Dybbuk* by S. Ansky ("Between two worlds, where spirits that are neither dead nor alive wander ceaselessly"); as well as a repertory of ballets and pantomimes, *Jephtha's Daughter, La Boutique Fantasque* with music by Rossini and Respighi, *Royal Fandango* by Gustavo Morales, a condensed version of Stravinsky's *Petrushka,* and *Le Tricorne* by Manuel de Falla.

One of several evenings in which the sisters joined theatre with dance was the five-scene *Salut au Monde,* on a stage dominated by a luminous globe—Walt Whitman's "great round wonder rolling through the air." Dramatic movement by the festival dancers was narrated by a chorus of men and women. This impressionistic work by Charles Tomlinson Griffes, based upon Whitman's poem and left unfinished at the composer's death, was completed by Edmond Rickett and presented at the playhouse over several weekends in April and May 1922. Stark Young, in the *New Republic,* hailed the collaborative celebration of the "theme of the brotherhood of the world and of all races and all centuries" as "one of the most important events of the year because . . . it is an experiment in terms of poetic idea interfused with and commented upon by light, music and dance forms." Critics took note of "its strange effect of austere leanness and authentic ritual of the spirit . . . and provocative arrangement of pauses and intervals of silence," and of the "wisdom" of the guiding spirits of the Neighborhood Playhouse.

By 1925, the Neighborhood Playhouse had become the only theatre in New York that designed and fabricated its own scenery, costumes, and properties—and the only performing arts producing organization run entirely by women. Working alongside the Lewisohn sisters were playwright and director Agnes Morgan, lawyer Helen Arthur, and costume and stage designers Esther Peck and Aline Bernstein. Unfortunately, the playhouse ran up a twelve-year accumulated operating deficit of half a million dollars "spent in fulfillment of an idea." In the spring of 1927, Alice and Irene announced, with regret, but not finality, that they would close up shop on the Lower East Side in recognition of "the steady march of residential New York to regions further and further north."

"We found our lives," Irene said, to be "a design of more or less disconnected patterns held together by the three walls of a stage and the fourth wall of an audience." All was not lost. The Lewisohns' patronage of the performing arts would prevail. "Our own growth demands that we now pause, to consider future development. . . . In 1915, as a small insurgent theatre with amateur actors, its location, its size, its endowment, and the kind and number of plays at its disposal were all adequate," said Alice. Now it was necessary to "step aside for a time, and find a new adjustment."

True to the sisters' words, the Neighborhood Playhouse lived on, flourishing in other venues around New York; Ernest Bloch's *Israel* opened on Saturday, May 4, 1928, at the Manhattan Opera House on West Thirty-Fourth Street. A half-hour symphony in three movements, with the second movement, "Yom Kippur," characterized by "wild dissonances and angular rhythms . . . reflecting . . . the lament of the sinner begging for forgiveness, strikingly portrayed by a plaintive oboe," was reminiscent of "Vidui (Contrition)," the excerpt from Bloch's Baal Shem Suite that Martha Graham had performed at the Klaw Theatre.

Contra Denishawn's music visualizations and with assent to Rouben Mamoulian's dramatic action at the Eastman School, Louis Horst shared Irene Lewisohn's belief that "the modern stage has too long remained in a state of representation. In performance it seldom seeks the underlying mood." He blessed the concept of "these orchestral dramas [like *Israel* that] gave [Martha Graham] the necessary push to express dramatic and emotional values." Responding to the challenge, Graham was bringing into form, from the core of her body, a spectrum of moods, impressions, and sensations. Orchestral drama was one such form, resting upon the musical score as the foundation for "gesture built on modern lines, vital, simple, direct and broad in phrasing . . . This was the task we set ourselves," Irene Lewisohn said.

Irene's effort continued at the Manhattan Opera House the following year with a production of *Ein Heldenleben* (*A Hero's Life*), Richard Strauss's tone poem starring Martha Graham and Charles Weidman. In the spring of 1930, at the Mecca Temple on Fifty-Fifth Street (now City Center), Graham—"an extremely busy person these days," John Martin remarked—again appeared with Weidman, and Blanche Talmud, in Martin Loeffler's *A Pagan Poem*, based upon Virgil's *Eighth Eclogue.* The work was Irene Lewisohn's "third [annual] experiment toward the creation of a synthetic dramatic form which shall go back to the origins of drama for its elements."

. . .

Partnered with Martha Graham in Claude Debussy's "Nuages" and "Fêtes," the duets that followed Bloch's *Israel,* was an "all-but-forgotten pioneer of American modern dance," the "oval-faced, expressive-eyed, totally mobile and nervous of limb" Michio Ito, his "panache of black hair toss[ing] to every motion of his body." Graham had known him since *The Greenwich Village Follies,* when Ito assisted her in choreographing "The Garden of Kama," and they were on the faculty at the Anderson–Milton School and in nearby studios at Carnegie Hall—she on the seventh floor, he on the sixth. In 1928, Ito was in the denouement of a hyperactive twelve-year tenure in New York. Before year's end, accompanied by his wife, Hazel Wright, and an ensemble of five dancers, he would leave Manhattan to live, teach, and perform in Los Angeles. One of Ito's first master class students would be Lester Horton, whose protégé, in turn, was Alvin Ailey.

The eldest of nine brothers and sisters, Michio Ito was born on April 13, 1892, into a wealthy, worldly-wise Tokyo family. His father, Tamekichi, an architect and a friend of Frank Lloyd Wright, was a graduate of the University of California. His mother, Kimiye, the daughter of a zoologist, encouraged Michio to take singing and dancing lessons. He studied at the Tokyo Academy of Music and the Mizuki Dance School, trained in Kabuki, and founded a performing group, the Toride Company. Joining the chorus of the Imperial Theatre, Japan's first Western-style theatre, he collected "as many

Victor Opera records" as he could, "construct[ing] castles in the sky listening to *Faust* and *Carmen.*" When Michio reached maturity, his parents agreed to subsidize his "dream . . . to go to Europe, to Paris, to learn Opera properly."

Ito was frustrated by traditional opera training because it did not allow him to take advantage of his aptitude for movement. An encounter with Isadora Duncan, and a performance by the Ballets Russes, were transformative. Only then, Ito recounted, "did I see total art, combining dance, singing, and music, for the first time. Nijinski [*sic*] was especially impressive. . . . I [was] completely drained after the performance and . . . spent the whole night walking the streets, my head afire with new ideas."

In the summer of 1913, moving to Berlin, Ito enrolled in the Dalcroze Institute at Hellerau, "five miles out of Dresden among red-pine woods at the top of a hill . . . my particular heaven," where he met Mary Wigman. Through the practice of kinesthetic response integral to eurythmics classes, after listening, "translating" what Jaques-Dalcroze played at the piano into "echoing" or "stepping" in measured patterns upon open, tiered platforms, Ito learned to emphasize "illusion rather than realistic representation." He stayed at Dalcroze until the outbreak of the Great War, when he left for The Hague and London.

Barely speaking English, conversant in French, and reluctant to try out his German in wartime, Ito arrived in London with a modest check from his tolerant father. He sought a like-minded community of proto-bohemians and heard that "a nest of artists" congregated over wine and coffee at the Café Royal, "a little way into [Regent Street] off Piccadilly Circus . . . where Oscar Wilde used to haunt." Here, Ito caught the attention of the lean and hungry American litterateur Ezra Pound "at a time when the poet was eagerly establishing a kind of cenacle." Pound was in possession of a cache of unpublished materials from the estate of Ernest Francisco Fenollosa, the Salem, Massachusetts–born historian of Japanese art and former professor of philosophy, political economy, and logic at Tokyo Imperial University. The manuscripts had been entrusted to Pound by Fenollosa's widow, Mary, who admired his verse, knew of his passion for all things Eastern, and, aware Pound was "pining for hieroglyphs and ideographs," believed he was the only person "who could deal as her late husband [would have] wished" with his notebooks, lecture drafts, line-by-line renditions of fourteenth-century Noh plays in the upper-class colloquial idiom, and Chinese poetry.

Among his literary and editorial activities, Pound was working as part-time secretary for the Irish poet William Butler Yeats, sharing a weekend cottage with him in the Sussex countryside. Disillusioned with Abbey Theatre and West End fare, Yeats was so demoralized that he had been thinking of giving up traditional playwriting. In "perfect and lonely" peace, in studios on separate floors, the men were engaged in a nascent effort to harness the beauty, stylized discipline, and "power of Noh," to create a new stripped-down, cross-disciplinary "non-exhibitionistic . . . poetic drama."

"I am very fond of [Ito]," Pound wrote to Harriet Monroe at *Poetry* magazine. "This man is a samurai, more like an American Indian to look at, the long face you see in some of the old prints. . . . His arm work is very interesting—better than the Russians . . . a fine fellow." Pound believed "Miscio Itow," as the poet spelled it, could provide a boost to an experiment integrating dance with theatre.

Yeats agreed: "My play is made possible by a Japanese dancer [whose] tragic image has stirred my imagination. . . . [H]e was able, as he rose from the floor, where he had been sitting cross-legged, or as he threw out his arm, to recede from us into a more powerful life." Pound and Yeats expressed indebtedness to Ito despite his protestations that, growing up in Tokyo, and finding Noh to be boring, he had studied the broader, more exaggerated form of Kabuki. But the two poets craved idealized *Japonaiserie*. (" 'Please help me with what I'm doing,' said Ezra.")

Ito began, modestly, to assist with the Fenollosa papers, and discovered that the scholar's analogies of Japanese drama with Greek theatre—two traditions that "resemble, but do not imitate" each other—were in tune with his belief in the relationship of dance with the other arts. Noh's restrained positions and movement, interspersed with stasis and silence, made use of masks, screens, chorus, and percussion: "The East can derive so much from the West. And the West, I am positive," Ito said, "is beginning to awaken to the fact that it has a great deal to learn from the East."

In Pound's next books, *Cathay: For the Most Part from the Chinese of Rihaku, from the Notes of the late Ernest Fenollosa, and the Decipherings of the Professors Mori and Ariga,* and *'Noh' or Accomplishment: A Study of the Classical Stage of Japan,* published in London in 1915 and 1916, he assembled Fenollosa's manuscripts on these subjects, crediting him as coauthor. *Cathay* and *Noh* enforced Pound's *dichten* = *condensare* ("To compose poetry is to condense")—"Use no superfluous word, no adjective which does not reveal something." The Chinese ideogram was the paradigm for "renovated poetry

Michio Ito in *At the Hawk's Well,* by W. B. Yeats, 1916.
(Photograph by Alvin Langdon Coburn)

in English" because it fulfilled Pound's demand for the unencumbered image. He also admired Noh chanting, like the spare recitative intonations in a church service; and the *mai*, or dance, integral to every Noh play, characterized by the barefoot punctuation of beats "as though walking in water."

The first of W. B. Yeats's newly imagined plays for dancers, *At the Hawk's Well,* infused the Noh vocabulary with "Mr. Itow's genius of movement" into ancient Irish folklore through the story of the god Cuchulain. Drafts were composed during the winter of 1915 and tried out at dress rehearsals during the spring 1916 social season in the Oxford drawing room of Lady Ottoline Morrell, and at Lady Islington's salon in London

Yeats insisted there must be "no studied lighting, no stage-pictures made in an artificial world." Music—drum and gong with flute, harp, or zither, reminiscent of Satie—as well as masks and costumes, were by Edmund Dulac, an artist and fairy-tale illustrator with a pre-Raphaelite palette. The backdrop was a sheet of silk, the well-water a rippling square of blue cloth. There were three main characters: an old man and a young man in full masks, and the guardian of the well, portrayed by Ito, bearing a "half-Greek, half-Asiatic" birdlike headdress and a feathered mantle. Dulac's rendition of the Hawk's persona "looked Egyptian. . . . As to the costume," Ito remembered, "I wore red tights, my front was cream and black, my head velvet and wings gold," extended outward by hidden sticks to create a swooping, gliding effect.

. . .

The Easter 1916 cataclysm in Dublin was an emotional and artistic distraction for Yeats, and he was unable to continue developing *At the Hawk's Well*. Ito accepted an invitation to New York City from producer Oliver Morosco. After a few variety shows, he engaged with more serious fare at the Washington Square Players, where he staged and designed *Bushido*, an eighteenth-century play by Takeda Izumo in which Katharine Cornell had a minor role. He performed in re-creations of the Noh drama *Tamura* at the Neighborhood Playhouse, and *Hawk's Well* at the Greenwich Village Theatre. He joined Diaghilev defector Adolph Bolm's Ballets Intime and created two works for the company. On tour with Bolm in 1917–1918, Ito's reputation grew. Boston dance critic. H. T. Parker noted the "short, abrupt motions, a procedure almost of graphic 'pointillage,' or dot upon dot and dash upon dash" that characterized Ito's polished technique.

In January 1919, after directing *The String of the Samisen* for the Provincetown Players—based upon the Bushido legend, and starring Edna St. Vincent Millay—Ito founded his school of dance on Fifty-Ninth Street and Madison Avenue. "Every one has his own feeling and his own expression; dance as you feel and as you want—that is a better dance for you than any other kind," he counseled students. Ito's pedagogy drew out the dancer's best possible movements, "to develop in my pupils the capacity of symbolism," he said, distilling the "gift of a poet who can express in twenty well-chosen words what a prose worker needs three thousand to express."

"I am a sculptor," Ito said, "for I work and I work over each pose until it means what I would have it mean. If you cry 'Stop!' in any place in my dance, you will find that it is a pose that means something." Ito's technique was built upon basic gestures imbued with the Japanese practice of "kata, or set forms." The knowledge of kata, required to achieve mastery in any art, was apt for dance, where striving was endless and perfection impossible. In Ito's modern dance classes, the hands, arms, head, and upper body were the prime movers, referencing the (Western) Greek idea that "these . . . were more expressive than legs and feet," while his two defined sequences of ten arm gestures, "A" and "B," reflected the (Eastern) yin and yang, with inhalation on the even-numbered movements and exhalation on the odd. The yogic breath-emphasis reversed, the off-balance body was in conflict with itself, extremities straining and pulling—torquing—against a torso "gratifyingly lack[ing] the soft center sometimes found in Denishawn and Isadora Duncan."

Michio Ito's impact upon Martha Graham was indelible. Long after the two parted ways, Graham "always said the Oriental body was perfect for her technique."

. . . .

In the fall of 1928, Irene and Alice Lewisohn opened the relocated Neighborhood Playhouse School of Theatre at 139 West Fifty-Sixth Street. They named their friend, Playhouse cofounder and board member Rita Wallach Morgenthau, as general director of the school. Daughter of Leopold Wallach, a prosperous railroad attorney, Rita had worked her way up on the staff of Henry Street Settlement, beginning as a "playground scupper," pushing children on the swings. She graduated from the Ethical Culture School in elementary education, and led the girls' drama club at the original playhouse. At the urging of Irene Lewisohn, Morgenthau's first two hires to teach at the School of Theatre were Louis Horst and Martha Graham.

Horst's Dance Composition course was his proving ground that the relationship to personal center of gravity and stage space did not belong exclusively to dancers. Rigorous exercises organized the kinesthetic components of the actors' bodies in connection with music principles such as rhythm, dynamics, and tempo, in the interest of establishing richer communication with the audience.

"Colloquial subjects are hard to sublimate into aesthetic expression," Horst said, pushing his actors toward self-scrutiny because, he told them, via the uncomfortable process of "being introspective, you become modern." The psychological ("Freudian") dimension tempered the historical perspective: "We can never throw off the past; rather, we do things in a new way" . . . "The moderns go to man's past reverently," Horst said. "They recognize the life of the ages as soil from which contemporary art takes nourishment." Once the student understands the underlying rules of tradition, he said, then, and only then, will the freedom to break rules be earned.

Horst's class at the Neighborhood Playhouse School was an analysis of what he designated "preclassic" (pre-ballet) dance forms, the court dances of the sixteenth through early eighteenth centuries, "when almost all the great music was written specifically for dance." In continued symbiosis with Martha Graham, "I teach dance *forms*, not dance," Horst said, stressing that operant word "with the precision of an etymologist." He sent his students over to the encyclopedic Circulating Music Collection of the New York Public Library at 121 East Fifty-Eighth Street and Lexington Avenue, supervised since its founding in 1920 by Dorothy Lawton. The assignment was to find scores for various dance designs, and research with fresh eyes the attributes of these dances as "reflecting the life of their period[s]"—the slow "dignity and grave pride" of the pavane, the bouncy "blitheness" of the galliard, the tense "quickness and hastiness" of the gigue, vivacity and "roughness" of the gavotte, tragic "sadness" of the saraband, and "refined magnificence" of the minuet.

Returning to the studio, students reconstructed the dances, bringing them to life, manipulating essential elements, and demonstrating for each other "miniature etudes . . . contemporaneous with the tempo of our times" . . . "[and] the uneven rhythms of all the modern arts." Louis Horst continued to teach and critique at the Neighborhood Playhouse School until his death in 1964. He dedicated *Pre-Classic Dance Forms,* the textbook compiled from these historicized dance classes, to Irene Lewisohn.

. . .

Martha Graham took many cues from Horst's pedagogy and applied them to her evolving dance practice; however, she was too strong-willed to become Galatea to his Pygmalion: "Any great art is the condensation of a strong feeling, a perfectly conscious thing," she said. Graham's class at the Neighborhood Playhouse School, often accompanied by Horst at the piano, emphasized moving in space on a stationary base. Within the still point of immobility hid the promise of further movement. For the first forty-five minutes of each two- to four-hour class, "[w]e were seated with our feet together" and knees out, "bouncing in the open fourth position until we almost died . . ." recalled Gertrude Shurr, one of Graham's most adoring students. A self-described "short, stocky muscle with a black ponytail who had too much energy," Shurr came up through Denishawn and briefly danced with the Humphrey-Weidman Concert Group. "Martha was an actress . . . dancing with her heart, and Doris was too cerebral" for Shurr, an effervescent vestal virgin with allegiance to one mistress. Graham told her to "feel

Gertrude Shurr (far left) in *Celebration,* with (left to right) Kathleen Slagle, unknown, May O'Donnell (high kicking), Marie Marchowsky, unknown, ca. 1934. (Photograph by Paul Hansen)

the space . . . encompass a place for yourself." Shurr "could see that Martha's inspiration for her dances came out of her innards." . . . "Nobody could describe the inner workings of the body better than Martha."

Graham was developing a movement system by "re-educating the body to its potential . . . I am trying to rediscover what the human body can do," she declared, taking pains to explain that her goal was not to utterly abandon classical ballet. In fact, "[h]er pliés were fabulous!" Shurr said. During the contraction, Graham encouraged Shurr and the others to be introspective while they "let the whole breath out" in a studio intentionally mirrorless, so there was nowhere to look but within. Graham told them to pay attention to the slightest transfers of weight, the workings of the "back, shoulders, spine, and pelvic bone," and to "see what the muscles do, what the flesh does, what the bones do." In tandem with their visceral expiring breaths, they should take an inventory of how breath-driven feelings could generate a new arrangement of limbs and torso. "Sometimes an ecstatic feeling" waited to be aroused, Shurr remembered, while in other instances, after such repetitive rhythmic breathing, it could be "a lamentation. . . . With Martha, we colored the movement with what we had in our minds."

At day's end, Graham sought refuge in her two-room second-floor apartment at 16 West Tenth Street, sparingly adorned with batiks on the wall,

Casual Meeting among the Fourteenth Street shopping crowd,
by Kenneth Hayes Miller, oil on canvas, 1928.

a grass rug, and oversize cushions. By the hour she arrived home from the
Neighborhood Playhouse to prepare for evening classes in her parquet parlor, the Greenwich Village jumble of tearooms, restaurants, and cabarets
had been claimed by an influx of nocturnal partiers. Graham avoided these
establishments; her after-hours students despaired of convincing her to go
out, even for a snack. "I never went in for those long [evenings] down in
the Village where people sat around and talked about things," Graham said.
"If you spend an evening talking with your friends and associates about the
dreams you have, those dreams will never go into manifestation. . . . You
have to deny yourself that privilege."

. . .

In the new year, on January 20 and March 3, 1929, Graham and Horst presented recitals at the Booth Theatre on West Forty-Fifth Street. She began
the first all-solo program with "Dance," prefaced by Nietzsche's "Strong Free
Joyous Action," taken from *On the Genealogy of Morals*, emphasizing the
philosopher's belief that "every table of [moral] values . . . requires first a
physiological investigation and interpretation." The journey to the "highest value, Love," Nietzsche wrote, will be enhanced by choosing the right
steps taken. Of the choreography for the Honegger piece, Bessie Schonberg

noted, Graham's "credo was that you moved between the shoulders and the knees, and that was it."

The entire *Dance* occurred on a small semicircular dais painted white, where Graham, in a tight, ankle-length red dress, "seek[ing] for beauty in sterner fashion . . . [with] stark symmetry," kept her stance anchored, "arresting, even aggressive, with the hard beauty of sculptured steel." To Martha Hill, that evening, Graham looked "as if she dared someone to come and move her feet."

At the other end of the spectrum was a series that Horst and Graham renamed *Four Insincerities* ("Petulance," "Remorse," "Politeness," and "Vivacity,") set to the 1911 piano score of *Four Pieces* by Sergei Prokofiev, op. 3, "reek[ing] with malevolent humor" and "provocativeness," danced "impudently" and—startlingly, for Graham—in high-heeled satin slippers.

The March 1929 performance reprised "Tanagra," so reassuringly familiar by now that its "lyrical calm made a happy oasis in a program bristling with cerebral provocation and emotional upheaval." For every such number known to their audiences—Scriabin's *Fragilité* and Milhaud's *Danza* were redone—Horst and Graham made sure to derail expectations. With *Adolescence (Prelude and Song),* originally called *Tanz-Stuck (Dance Piece)* from *Reihe kleiner Stücke (A Series of Short Pieces),* op. 37, by Paul Hindemith, Graham "wore her hair rolled under a long bob and was dressed in a simple dark smock like a French schoolgirl's pinafore" . . . "or the monkish oblate's frock . . . seated at the top of two steps on her round platform" where she reached out her arms making tentative incursions into the surrounding darkness, then returned to the encircling pool of the spotlight. Graham's movements exploring the space were "childishly frank and yet deft and penetrating" . . . "[with] pathos, wistfulness, and a definite hint of slowly groping, unleashed vigor."

Reflecting upon the concert a week later, John Martin posed "[t]he interesting question which arises out of this constant variation in style and content." He wondered if Martha Graham, "a veritable chameleon," was "passing through a period of unsettlement and will eventually find the ground upon which she wishes to stand, or whether"—as time would tell—"she has already found herself, and that self is one which must be incessantly in a state of change in order to create with vitality."

10

Heretic

Martha Graham and Dance Group in *Heretic,* 1929. (Photograph by Soichi Sunami)

Martha Graham exhibited her mercurial "state of change" to thrilling effect in the third recital of the spring 1929 season, Sunday evening, April 14, at Winthrop Ames's Booth Theatre. Louis Horst was accompanied by Hugo Bergamasco, flutist and theatre district restaurateur, and Dini de Remer, a pianist for Graham's classes at the Neighborhood Playhouse School. The curtain went up at eight forty-five. Graham, solitary and resolute, yet again reprised Honegger's Nietzschean *Dance/Revolt,* followed by glimmers of traditional music amid the dense discord of modern and contemporary fare, and the twelve-member, all-female dance group in *Heretic,* the disturbing final piece of the evening. "Couched exclusively in a modernist idiom," this work was applauded as "undoubtedly the crowning achievement of Miss Graham's career thus far."

The première danseuse, Graham's student Kitty Reese, would appear in Neighborhood Playhouse productions into the following year, before heading to Broadway. Ruth White stayed with Graham for a brief time, as did Hortense Bunsick and Sylvia Wasserstrom. Lillian Shapero came to the company recommended by Michio Ito; Ethel Rudy and Mary Rivoire had been students in Graham's classes at the Anderson–Milton School. Lillian Ray's career after Graham would be as a ballroom dancing instructor, and her friend Louise Creston was picked to appear as one of the peasant maidens encircling Graham's frenetic "Chosen One" in the spring 1930 American premiere of Stravinsky's *The Rite of Spring.* Virginia Briton would dance in *Primitive Mysteries* in 1931.

The April mini-retrospective was curated by Horst to show how far Martha Graham had come in the three years since her first New York concert. Betty Macdonald and Evelyn Sabin from Eastman School were welcomed, joined by Rosina Savelli. They danced to J. S. Bach, Hindemith, and Scriabin, after which, toward the end of the program, Graham soloed in Tibor Harsányi's sober "Resurrection," and the Eastman ladies returned in "Ronde," rearranged by Horst from former Ballets Russes conductor Rhené-Emmanuel Baton's 1922 tone poem, *Au pardon de Rumengol.* "[T]inged with a delicate impressionism," it honored the annual summertime pilgrimage to the Church of Notre Dame in Brittany, the composer's ancestral home.

The Dance Group without Graham made their appearance in the fourth composition on the program, "Fantasia Apocalypta—Erscheinungen zweier Chorale (Apocalyptic Fantasy—Apparitions: Two Chorales)," translated by Horst for the American audience as "Vision of the Apocalypse—(Theme and Variations)," a convoluted 1926 piece by Hermann Reutter, an associate of Hindemith. John Martin conceded that while it did "contain extraordinary moments," "Vision" came across as "a bit choppy," perhaps because Reutter had carved nine segments, each roughly two minutes, out of two very different songs: the magisterial *A Mighty Fortress Is Our God,* by Bach, and *O Sacred Head, Now Wounded,* a Middle Ages passion hymn. Kitty Reese, garbed in gray and black, "purported to project the emotional experience of a young monk contemplating the sorrows of the world." In contrast to the ensemble, she stood "elevated above the stage level and by means of plastic miming revealed his [*sic*] reactions to the significant designs of the 'chorus' below . . . casting sinister shadows . . . with amazing ease and an actual *elan*."

"[O]ne moving figure against a background of comparatively stationary ones," Reese took front and center "to achieve the very opposite in emotional effect" during the group's "puckish" and "piquant" rendition of Francis Poulenc's "Moment Rustica." This second section of his 1918 Sonata for Piano, *Four Hands*, executed with trilling syncopation by Horst and de Remer, was followed by three excerpts, nos. 2, 4, and 7, from *Huit Préludes* by Yulian Krein, renamed by Graham/Horst as *Sketches from the People*—"Monotony," "Supplication," and "Requiem." Krein was a student of his father, Russian composer Grigory Krein. In 1928, at fifteen, the boy was sent for violin composition classes at the Paris Conservatory with Paul Dukas, under whose tutelage he wrote the *Huit Préludes*.

.   .   .

The artist [Graham] had been "building soil," planting seed, tending the early, tentative shoots, testing and cutting away the unfruitful. But with *Heretic* the harvest was at hand.

—GEORGE BEISWANGER, *Martha Graham: A Perspective*, 1941

The last dance on the program was also a jumping-off place—the chiaroscuro uncompromising *Heretic*, the work Gertrude Shurr attested was Graham's "dividing line between old and new." It was arranged by Horst as the end-to-end cycling of ten measures lifted from a late-eighteenth-century folk song, "Breton[s] têtus" ("The Stubborn Breton[s]"), discovered in an anthology of sheet music published in 1899 by Plon, *Chansons de la Fleur-de-Lys*, a collaboration between the French poet, singer, and playwright Theodore Botrel, known as "the Bard of Brittany," and Charles de Sivry, his piano accompanist from Le Chat Noir cabaret in Montmartre.

"Economy of instrumentation, functional relationship to the [piece], harmonic appropriateness to the emotional scheme of the work, rhythmic integration"—*Heretic* is a living model for Louis Horst's ideal of music for modern dance, a Spartan surface and a roiling core. "These ten measures," Horst explained, "are divided into eight of allegro feroce and two of andante religioso. Most of the [dance] movement takes place during the silent pause after each section. It is repeated without change of tempo or dynamics, thereby heightening the dramatic intensity and climax of the movement." Horst's use of repetition in *Heretic* echoes Kandinsky's enthusiasm in his own poetry for "the apt use of a word . . . to intensify the internal structure but also bring out unsuspected spiritual properties."

The piece begins with the twelve members of the group, dressed in ankle-length, tubelike black-jersey dresses, hair under snug black turbans, positioned onstage in an hermetic world, tight-lipped, facing front, arms crossed, shoulder to shoulder, in a flattened "tight-knit semi-circle." Martha Graham, in a long, white gown with snug sleeves, hair brushed back and cut to a bit below shoulder-blade length, darts in front in a shaft of light, and embarks upon a succession of approach and avoidance movements parallel with and in opposition to the others', attempting to break the wall of their posturing. She is a precisionist study in contrasts of appearance and manner who "querie[s] and argue[s]" against "the obdurate responses" of the group. At one moment, she is supplicant, arms extended, palms cupped, head tilted back and upward; at another, she is trapped, hunched into a contraction of submission and inhibited despair, hair swinging forward, shrouding her face.

She steps forth and skims across the lined-up group, oblivious; then, in the suspended silence before the next percussive measures, swerves around their backs. The women part ranks, stalking and lunging into alliances of four and six, seeming to permit her incursion. But once the heretic has gained a downstage haven, they press in upon her, lockstepping, pincer-like and impassive, breathing as one organism, fists raised, looking upon her "in stiff-necked recrimination." Rising in unison on their toes, dropping with a "stubborn thump of their heels," the "black phalanx of intransigents" set themselves to watch gravely, waiting out the heretic's accentuated tilts to and fro while she shifts stance and direction.

She gazes backward over her shoulder with a wistful glimmer that the others might follow. But the dark, stone-faced cadre reveals no sign of pity, and—energy waning, knees bending—the heretic twists into a back fall. She spirals and crumples to the floor. The light fades, and she releases her weight into the ground, all passion spent, with "the tiniest ripple of that prone body."

· · ·

When asked, "What are you trying to 'say'? What do you 'mean' by this dance?" Martha Graham would have agreed with another artist who chose words carefully, her contemporary Marianne Moore, in the poem "To a Snail" (1924): "Contractility is a virtue" because "the principle . . . is hid." To Graham, whether the spectator grasped her (so-called) intention was immaterial. The choreographer did not manufacture a chain of significances to be loosed like a flock of pigeons into the audience; kinesthetic empathy was the desired outcome. The viewer, "in a state of motor preparedness," as John Martin put it, "watches, not at all through his mind, but through his eyes and hears through his ears," moved by movement. "Though he sits there motionlessly," Martin said, "he translates automatically into his own motor experience the movement he is seeing . . . which effects in him a similar emotional experience to that which has prompted the dancer to make [her] dance in the first place."

In Martha Graham's studio, students and company members were pushed to generate movement, not seek refuge in imitation. Her practice was to work eye to eye, with the Stanislavskian given circumstances. She drove the female bodies in the room in front of her to be open and vulnerable, follow Walt Whitman's example, and contain multitudes.

Writing *Heretic*, Louis Horst jotted in his notebook, "There is no beauty without an element of strangeness," mistakenly attributing the quote to the poet John Keats. The sentiment belongs to another romantic soul who adored antiquity, Francis Bacon, and his 1625 essay, "Of Beauty": "There is no excellent beauty that hath not some strangeness in the proportion." Walter Pater took up Bacon's baton in the postscript to his essay "Appreciation" (1889) when he declared, "It is the addition of strangeness to beauty that constitutes the romantic character in art."

As for the origin for the title of the work, Graham recollected that "I felt at the time that I was a heretic. I was outside the realm of women. I did not dance the way other people danced. I had what I called a contraction and a release. I used the floor. I used the flexed foot. I showed effort." In archaic Greek, *heretic*, αἵρεσις meant "choice" or "thing chosen," alluding to the path of temptation. In *Beyond Good and Evil*, Nietzsche sang of this risk-taking, the addictive desire to hurtle "like a rider on a forward-flying steed . . . we moderns, we half-barbarians . . . are in the midst of our bliss only when we are most in danger." Graham had also read deeply in the works of the British classics scholar, Jane Ellen Harrison, author of *Prolegomena to the Study of Greek Religion*, who proudly announced to her colleagues at

Cambridge University in 1909 that "to be a heretic today is almost a human obligation."

This was how Graham wanted to appear when she sped through *Heretic*—looking for something as essential as the end of the dance itself. *Heretic* was a harbinger of her roles as l'Élue, the dervish maiden who dances to death in *The Rite of Spring,* and as the One Who Seeks in the 1946 work, *Dark Meadow.*

In *The Painter of Modern Life* (1863), Charles Baudelaire describes modernity in dance terms, as "the fleeting, the transitory, the contingent." He says that for "any 'modernity' to be worthy [it must] one day take its place as 'antiquity,'" that modernism will always be "locked together with the Greek ideal." The role of the Greek chorus, crossing and recrossing the stage, dancing in strophe and antistrophe, was to reflect upon—in a collective voice blended from a dozen individuals—the actions and thoughts of the protagonist.

Keen-eyed choreographer Elizabeth Selden, present for the advent of *Heretic,* recognized Martha Graham's enactment of "the age-old tragedy of the solitary struggle, no matter what one sees in the main figure: the pioneer, or the unheard prophet, or the radical pitting himself [*sic*] against the forces of conservatism, or the individualist appealing in vain to the mass mind." She concluded that "Martha Graham is a master in such uncompromising economy."

Composer Dane Rudhyar, an early admirer of Graham, saw *Heretic* in 1929 as signaling "the second act of a great artistic birth-drama in America." During the Great War, after publishing a study of Debussy under his birth name, Daniel Chennevière, he had emigrated from Paris to New York. In the spirit of self-renewal, reading in Buddhism and Baha'i, he chose to call himself "Rudhyar," rooted in *rudra,* Sanskrit for "dynamic action." Remade, he set out for California in 1920 and joined Halcyon, a theosophical community on the coast, near San Luis Obispo. In search of re-creating the mystical "Tone . . . a living entity" to be found in Asian music, Rudhyar befriended Henry Cowell, immersed, through his New Music Society, in the allure of "Oriental civilization, art and science." Rudhyar was certain that "the Great American culture-to-be" would be unleashed by an infusion of "dissonant harmony." His crusade to draw upon the regenerative powers of the energies of Eastern music led him to the haven of Denishawn, where he met and befriended Graham, and on occasion substituted for Louis Horst at the piano.

"Martha Graham is a personality of strangely compelling power and vitality," Rudhyar wrote, "entirely unlike Isadora Duncan, her erratic and inspired predecessor . . . [Graham] is a dancer, essentially, instinctively, in her blood and nerves, in her strange diaphanous body. She is vitality streaming in dance-rhythm; powerful, emotional, magical rhythms. . . . She has brought forth a new type of dance-motions, a new sense of body rhythm, of body utterance.

"Her gestures," Rudhyar rhapsodized, "are utterances."

11

Dance Repertory Theatre and *Lamentation*

The new Dance Repertory Theatre is scheduled for a week's performances this month. . . . The program will include joint recitals with
Martha Graham, [Helen Becker] Tamiris, Doris Humphrey, Charles
Weidman, as well as solo concerts by each of them. It will give these
talented dancers a chance to measure both their achievements and
their experiment by the tests of union and of comparison."
                                     —*Theatre Arts Monthly,* January 1930

An enterprise in "mutual independence," the Dance Repertory Theatre was led by a flame-haired, "theatrically outrageous" ex-showgirl
who "swept across the dancing horizon" to the brazen syncopation
of *Rhapsody in Blue* in her first New York recital. Helen Becker was born into
poverty on the Lower East Side in 1902, the daughter of Russian Jews who
had fled the pogroms. Her mother died when Helen was three. The irrepressible child shared a crowded walk-up with her father, who was a tailor, and
four brothers. She resorted to dancing in the streets until the family scraped
together enough money to enroll her in Irene Lewisohn's interpretive dance
forms classes at the Henry Street Settlement. At fifteen, Helen joined the
Metropolitan Opera Ballet, and stayed for three seasons at a salary of twelve
dollars a week, then toured South America for two years with the Adolfo
Bracale Opera Company.

In her early twenties, Becker began to call herself Tamiris, after the warrior
queen of the Scythian Massagetae peoples who defeated Cyrus the Great.
After a restless stint in Hassard Short and Irving Berlin's *Music Box Revue,*
classes at the Isadora Duncan School, and studies with Michel Fokine,
Tamiris wondered, in her uncompleted autobiography, "What more can

Tamiris sets the stage on fire, April 1929. (Caricaturist unknown)

I learn—in schools? Each school develops its own type of dancer—I don't want to be a Duncan dancer—or a ballet dancer—I want to be *myself*— But what was myself?" she wrote, realizing that "I *was* all the things I had learned—I would make some dances—my very own."

She did just that on October 9, 1927, in a program of dance moods at the Little Theatre. Assisted by Louis Horst at the piano, "she presented a lovely picture" in pieces ranging from Debussy to Cyril Scott to Gershwin. In January 1928, she returned to Broadway, with *Bull Ring, Prize Fight Studies*—Horst beating upon the keyboard—and a spirited *Maple Leaf Rag*. The "evenly-flowing movement . . . of her strongly-responsive body . . . paint[ing] with broad sweeps rather than delicate lines," her interpretations of *Negro Spirituals* at this concert began a nine-dance anthology that would take fourteen years to complete. In a "Manifest[o]" accompanying the program, Tamiris wrote that "[t]he dance of today must have a dynamic tempo and be valid, precise, spontaneous, free, normal, natural and human."

Then she was off for eight months, to dance in Salzburg, at the invitation of the Mozarteum Society, and in Paris and Berlin. The tour abroad further enlivened Tamiris's curiosity about Americana during the Harlem Renaissance. When she returned to New York for the spring 1929 season, her exultant recital included more *Negro Spirituals*—"vivacious to the point of being rompish"—and *Dance of the City* accompanied by an offstage wailing siren. A *Jazz Sonata and Sonatina for Radio* by George Antheil rounded out her program. Antheil was the neoclassical bad boy of contemporary music, whose 1926 *Ballet Mécanique* score called for pianos, percussion, electric buzzers, and airplane propellers.

Tamiris was younger than Graham, Humphrey, and Weidman, and did not come out of the Denishawn tradition. In this maverick spirit, she was the catalyst for the Dance Repertory Theatre during the spring and summer of 1929. When Tamiris came up with the idea for the coalition, Horst agreed to serve as musical director. As accompanist to all of them at one time or another, he said he was "the tail to their kites." Enticed by the possibility of economic relief from "their lonely, scattered, expensive, single one-night concerts," the charter members negotiated conditions for participation, stating that although, for the purpose of the project they were hiring one manager, Helen Arthur of the Actor-Managers, Inc., they were "uniting so that we can stay separate." A board of sponsors—Mrs. William K. Vanderbilt; Anne Morgan, daughter of J.P.; Mrs. John White Alexander, widow of the artist; and Mrs. Ralph Jonas, wife of the lawyer and philanthropist—raised $5,000 to underwrite the first season.

"In spite of all misgivings," Doris Humphrey admitted, reflecting the others' reservations and resolutions, the Dance Repertory Theatre "is the best thing to do." Maxine Elliott's Theatre, on Thirty-Ninth Street east of Broadway and south of the Metropolitan Opera House, was booked for nine shows, Sunday through Sunday, January 5–12, 1930 (there were two performances on Saturday).

Tamiris plunged onstage and into her opening-night solos with *Three Negro Spirituals:* "Nobody Knows the Trouble I've Seen," "Swing Low, Sweet Chariot," and "Joshua Fit the Battle of Jericho." "In these dances," she said, "I wanted to express the spirit of the Negro people—in the first, his sense of oppression—in the [third], his fight—and struggle and remembrance when the walls came tumbling down." Huge arcs of dynamic variety enlisting her whole body, bursts of swoops, arms like waving pistons and thighs pumping like a sprinter's alternated with meticulous shuffling steps, sinuous hip sways and shuffling half slides. As she moved in a diagonal from upstage left to downstage right, Tamiris acted out sequential roles, going along with the words measure by measure, allowing a smile to play across her lips. "Cheers of enthusiasm" echoed through the hall.

In the coming days she reprised "Twentieth Century Bacchante" ("with its frank voluptuousness"), adapted by Horst from Louis Gruenberg's Waltz, three selections from *Dance of the City:* "Peasant Rhythms," "Play Dance," and "Romantic," to music by Stravinsky, and two American Serenades by George Antheil. In "Triangle Dance," true to the name, her ensemble of three dancers rang out rhythms on instruments of different sizes and tones. By week's end, Tamiris's excursion revealed "the warm, vigorous delicacy of her movement, as well as the subtle and sometimes penetrating viewpoint of her art."

. . .

Doris Humphrey, Charles Weidman, and ensemble, assisted by Pauline Lawrence, presented many modes for the Dance Repertory Theatre. The featured piece was *Water Study,* originally staged October 28, 1928, at the Civic Repertory Theatre. When the work was born, Humphrey jotted in her notebook, "Nature moves usually in an unfolding succession to a climax and a more sudden succession to cessation or death . . . All natural movement must follow that law of nature—of which water is the best example to follow."

She elaborated in a letter to Mary F. Watkins at the *Herald Tribune* "that I think the ensemble is the only medium which is impersonal—a quality which the dance sadly lacks . . . [I]n looking at the ensemble, one is conscious first of the movement and its quality, because the bodies all merge into one moving mass." In contrast to the metric figure of *Negro Spirituals, Water Study* coalesces in darkness and continues for seven minutes "in the absence of sound," with a tucked, kneeling line of fourteen women in nude-colored unitards, palms not pressing but resting flat against the floor, passing a muscular ripple along their backs from right to left and left to right, making their way toward breathing and moving as one.

Kneeling with arms curved forward together, as if about to dive, they elevate to standing, and thence to *sautés,* toes pointed downward and arms arrowed upward. The group divides and regroups, circles and gambols, then slides floorward, casting like waves brushing an imagined shore, "clear, transparent and forever renewed, as unpredictable as it is refreshing." They rise, recede into a common mass, divide, and come together. The ebb and flow of elongated bodies peak and diminish, and the cycle regains its shadowy origin: Blue lights fade, backs bend, and all is calm and still, receding "into that perfect rest which knows nothing of what has gone before nor of what will come after."

Charles Weidman, the pantomiming Pierrot, continued "his own brand of humorous ragging" for the Dance Repertory Theatre with vignettes and character work, "Japanese Actor," "Minstrels" ("Chaplinesque . . . bits of comedy" in doublets and a peaked cap), "Once Upon a Time" ("a parody of a Marionette Theatre"), "Passion and Compassion" ("a double portrait of Savonarola and St. Francis of Assisi"), "The Conspirator" ("tell[ing] without the aid of music a plan of convicts ostensibly to break prison"), and "Three Studies (Diffidence, Annoyance, Rage.)" On his own or, in "The Conspirator," with John Glenn and Eugene LeSueur, members of his all-male group, Weidman was a crowd-pleaser who did not take himself too seriously or—in the critics' judgment, and to his eventual detriment—not seriously enough.

Weidman presented a more grounded personality partnered with Humphrey in Dane Rudhyar's "Salutation to the Depths," the composer at the key-

Charles Weidman and Doris Humphrey, ca. 1928–1930.

board. The Varèse-like piece was excerpted from *Enfoldment (The Enfolding)* (1924), the second book of Rudhyar's epic mystical collection, *Pentagrams*.

Humphrey and Weidman's subsequent duets in the Dance Repertory Theatre week, including Henry Purcell's *Air on a Ground Bass,* costumed in dramatic red and black, and Scriabin's Etude no. 12 ("with fine spirit and beauty of line"), were well received. Her dignity and stately grace balanced his vigor and gravitas in a harmonic collaboration that would be burnished over the next fifteen years, and was palpable during their debut in Boston in March 1930, at the storied Opera House. "Doris Humphrey and Charles Weidman . . . are young, earnest, ambitious, unspoiled," wrote H. T. Parker in the *Evening Transcript*. "They believe in what they do; work at it with mind and imagination . . . They minister to no decaying art," Parker added, but rather, mindful of the modern dance trend, "to one that is rising in American regard and understanding."

.   .   .

Toward the conclusion of her opening performance for the Dance Repertory Theatre, Martha Graham, solo and brightly lit, performed Paul Hindemith's *Adolescence* on a platform, center stage, while "behind the wings could be seen the rounded back, flying fingers and white shock of hair of Louis Horst playing the piano; [and] in some remote corner backstage, crowded together in semidarkness, ten girls, clad in long black rayon-jersey dresses with kerchiefs tightly wound around their heads, were silently 'warming up.'" Among them, ascended to Dance Group status, were Graham's students Martha Hill, Bessie Schonberg, Anna Sokolow, and Gertrude Shurr, preparing for "the transcendent" . . . "inevitable and indispensable" *Heretic*. When the curtain came down, the crowd in Maxine Elliott's Theatre—standing room only for Graham's shows—erupted with shouts of *bravo!* and a deafening applause "that had [a] hysterical quality which expresses both wonder and awe . . . [for] these extraordinary pupils, whose work is keyed to the pulse of their teacher."

Graham and Horst began with Satie's "Tanagra," Ravel's *Valses,* Stolcer-Slavenski's "Immigrant," Prokofiev's *Four Insincerities,* and Poulenc's "Moment Rustica." These familiar pieces reassured those who came to the theatre with predisposed admiration for "this dancer's tense and acid art . . . [that] she has evolved for herself and for her Group a plastic speech so stylized, so completely original and incisive that were one to meet a Graham

"[W]oeful, joyful . . . subtly ironic"—Martha Graham in *Harlequinade,* 1930.
(Photograph, 1940, by Barbara Morgan)

pupil in the desert wastes or the Arctic wilderness," Mary Watkins wrote, "she would be as recognizable as if placarded." Graham's technique was crystallizing, gesture by idiomatic gesture, with each new season.

Martha Graham injected an element of surprise into her Wednesday concert—"a neurotic, grim, sardonic sort of grotesquerie . . . and a stabbing wit which enliven her most beguiling masterpieces." Two solos, with music by Austrian composers discovered by Horst, were predicated upon one of Graham's favorite themes: the conflict of opposites. The first, to Ernst

Krenek's Piano Sonata op. 59, no. 2, retitled *Two Chants: Futility and Ecstatic Song*, did not create much of a stir.

The second, *Harlequinade: Pessimist and Optimist*, was adapted from Ernest Toch's *Der Jongleur (The Juggler)*, one of his *Drei Burlesken*—Three [Burlesque] Piano Pieces, op. 31–33 (1924–1925). John Martin praised it as "the most finished of [Graham's] new compositions." Mary Watkins said it was "a work designed to her measure and fitting her most brilliant talents like a glove." Elizabeth Selden adored its "sheer heaping up of disconnected details . . . leaping from climax to climax." Graham continued to perform *Harlequinade* on tour well into the 1930s, selecting it as one of the sixteen dances for Barbara Morgan's monumental anthology of black-and-white photographs. Graham's program note in Morgan's anthology returned to Kandinsky's insistence upon the nonrepresentational nature of his *Improvisation No. 30*. She warned readers that "[w]hat I may add in the way of words is in no way an explanation of [*Harlequinade*] but is to be considered as a dancer's attitude toward the art in which she works."

Two pieces for the group were also new. Honegger's Contrepoint no. 1 for oboe and cello (1926) was adapted by Horst as "Prelude to a Dance." The second group work was "Portals," by Carl Ruggles, the prolific, prickly Vermonter (by way of Minnesota) who made "dissonant counterpoint" diatonic music in the morning and primal oil paintings in the afternoon. "Portals," the composer noted, was a severe, "new slow movement for cello solo and [twelve] strings coming in . . . It's a new scheme of composition and eminates [*sic*] from not repeating any note until the 10th [measure]." The title was from the two-line poem by Walt Whitman, "What are those of the known, but to ascend and enter the Unknown? / And what are those of life, but for Death?"

Graham had seen the piece at Carnegie Hall on October 26, 1929, performed by an ensemble called the Conductorless Symphony Orchestra. In December, she met Ruggles at a musicale by pianist-composer Ruth Crawford, hosted by Blanche Wetherill Walton, a former student of Edward MacDowell, in her Central Park West apartment. Over "ice cream and prohibition wine," Graham gave Ruggles her phone number, saying she wanted to talk about dancing to "Portals" in her imminent Dance Repertory Theatre concert. At the eleventh hour, the performance fell through. Bessie Schonberg remembered that "[w]hen we got together, [the Ruggles piece] didn't work. It was too late. The only thing to do was to let the dance go on in silence."

Horst's quick plan B for the absent "Portals" was called "Project in Movement for a Divine Comedy." Packaged as "Miss Graham's first adventure in the field of dancing without music," "Project" was a heroic concept for soloist and ensemble cast in the mold of Blake's 1826 watercolors and sketches for Dante. In front of two silent lines of dancers, Graham "moved through the design with lofty and detached absorption . . . [in] an otherwise obscure passage toward life and inference." No one dared surmise that Graham's experiment was in response to Doris Humphrey's soundless *Water Study*.

. . .

Alas for my face, alas for my forehead
and my ribs, how I long
to twist and turn my back and my spine
now to one side of my body, now to the other
as I endlessly weep and lament . . .
Alas, look where I sit here in degradation
near the tents of Agamemnon . . .
Just as the mother-bird raises the cry
for its nestlings, so shall I begin the chant . . .
—Hecuba mourning for fallen Troy in Euripides's *The Trojan Women*

Lamentation, Martha Graham's sensational solo, premiered at Maxine Elliott's Theatre on Wednesday, January 8, 1930, when Louis Horst, offstage, launched into Zoltán Kodály's op. 3 no. 2 (*Andante poco rubato*) from *Nine Pieces for Piano* (1905–1909).

The lights come up to reveal Graham perched ramrod-straight, "reared up—way up" on the edge of a low rectangular bench, her legs spread wide, feet riveted to the floor in second position, her body sheathed, from head-hugging hood to ankles, in a seamless purple tricot tube over a gray long-sleeved leotard. Elbows resting upon her knees, her fists at her abdomen, fingers collecting bunched-up fabric curled around an imagined rod. The ensuing three and one half minutes commence with Graham, a metronome with a rigid spine, rocking from side to side, weight on one hip then the other "like the stem of a lotus flower rooted in the mud responding to the water of the flowing stream," shaking her head in a spate of no's. She arches her neck forward and tilts it back, and pursues accelerating and decelerating segues of wide, then constrained diagonal swayings that stiffen into angu-

"The personification of grief itself . . .": Martha Graham in *Lamentation,* 1930.
(Photograph, 1935, by Barbara Morgan)

lar tilts. Feet tilt in response, the right heel, then the left, pressing into the ground.

Graham rises slightly, knees bent, thrusts her joined fists down to plumb the space of her open thighs, then brings fists upward, crooking one leg up and out. Pushing her angled torso against the garment embracing and tugging her, she attempts to escape from fabric skin against body skin, as if to break handcuffs that bind proffered wrists.

She separates and raises her arms, cloth and skin synchronous. She pulls her arms apart, palms supplicating upward, her pale, masklike face and kohl-lidded eyes slowly revealed to the spectator. But there is no solace. She twists to the right in fear, averted face shielded with the back of her hand, to seek an impossible way out somewhere behind her. The hood at its apex and her spread arms make a triangle of purple cloth that pivots upward into an hourglass. She spasms from the waist and, hunchbacked, sweeps the ground in front of her.

She departs from the bench into a half crouch, weight on thighs, and stands, in the waning half minute, to collect the sacred garment over a tent of extended fingers, and brings cupped hands together—in prayer, shame, resignation—to conceal her red lips. Baring her head to the heavens before curving into herself and carving a series of contractions, Graham returns to the seated posture held when she began, her burrowing, headless shape subsumed by taut folds of enveloping purple while the light fades.

Martha Graham was taciturn about the origin of *Lamentation*. In 1941, she sanctioned a perfunctory description of the dance as "not the sorrow of a specific person, time or place, but the personification of grief itself." In the summer of 1942, *Lamentation* was filmed at Bennington College by sculptor in residence Simon Moselsio and his wife, Herta. They wanted to shoot footage of Graham delivering a three-minute introduction to the piece, but after an awkward conversation with her, attempting to discern what she had in mind, the plan was abandoned. Instead, John Martin, attired in white shirt, suit, and tie, was enlisted to read a scripted preface. Graham did tell the Moselsios during their fitful talk that "[w]hen I [first] did it I wanted to do something that was basic and fairly eternal, that is the language that is in everybody whether or not you can understand each other in words. Grief is one of the basic things that is in everyone."

Louis Horst said, "We tend in real life to sway when we grieve—to bend low and close in—just as when we feel joyous we tend to expand and lift our bodies," he said. "[But] to do *Lamentation* you don't have to feel sad emotionally. You know the movements which communicate sadness just as I can go to the piano and play a combination of notes that will sound like a funeral march, even though I don't feel it . . . A dance has to restrain emotion." Agnes de Mille wrote that, early on, Graham recounted to her how a woman came backstage after seeing *Lamentation,* and told the dancer that witnessing it had freed her to weep for the recent death of her nine-year-old son in a traffic accident. "And she mourned in Martha's arms," de Mille continued, and "Martha related that this dance had on several occasions worked the same kind of catharsis."

Graham also alluded to having found momentary inspiration for *Lamentation* in the fall of 1926 during a break while devising her solo, "Contrition," to the music of Ernest Bloch in celebration of Yom Kippur, the

Jewish Day of Atonement. "[I was sitting] against the wall of my studio in Carnegie Hall . . . and I had a shawl over my head. Evidently, I identified so strongly with it that I fainted." Winthrop Sargeant gave credence to Graham's remembrance: "*Contrition* was important as being the forerunner of *Lamentation*."

Heretic had explored motifs of confinement and liberation. In *Lamentation,* there was no adversarial group chorus; Graham was at odds with herself. She designed the costume with the express purpose of working against it, drawing from a sculptural sense rooted in her Delsarte/Denishawn tableaux and plastique training.

"Sculpture and the dance are very linked or interrelated," Martha Graham told Simon Moselsio during their Bennington conversation, "because they both use form in space and they both have the sense of dynamic that keeps them from being decorative only." She said, "I used the costume—a straight tube of material—because I felt that [when] one presses from the center of the body, you carve in space . . . I used the simple material so that I could give a sense of volume, weight, mass, three dimensions, rather than a sense of line."

During her many visits to the Metropolitan Museum of Art, Martha Graham had seen the dignified, calm, enthroned terra-cotta statue in the Greek Archaic Period Room on the ground floor. The primordial, holy Great Mother "unattached to a man . . . worshipped from Egypt to India, from Greece and Asia Minor to darkest Africa" lives at the depths of *Lamentation.* Eyes closed, arms stiffly at her sides, wearing a close-fitting, long-sleeved dress, the seated goddess with splayed legs is the revered object of austere devotion and the feared agent of terrible passion. Queen of the life cycle, her essential blood magic births fruitfulness, and presides over decay and death. Preexisting the separation of the world parents that engendered the Titans, Zeus and the entire pantheon, she is Gaia, the sole deity who embodies earth's spirit.

She was venerated on the island of Crete in the second millennium BC, Erik Satie's source for *Gnossiennes.* By the seventh century, the cult of the mother was established on the slope of mainland Eleusis, where the story was told of poor Demeter, her head shrouded by a mourning veil, sitting on a fleece-covered stool by the circular stone Kallichoron, "Wellspring of Fair Dances," chanting the threnos for her abducted daughter, Kore. In the *Iliad,* the wrecking of Troy's "crown of towers" is likened to a lamenting woman tearing a gleaming veil from her brow. The epic poem concludes with the

Terra-cotta statuette of a seated woman. Greek, late archaic/early fifth century BC.

"cry for all cries"—*aiai! aiai!*—of the anxious women who will become slaves of the victorious Greeks.

"Why does tragedy exist?" Anne Carson asks, in the preface to her Euripides. "Because you are full of rage. And why are you full of rage?" The answer comes, "Because you are full of grief."

Whether it was widowed Hecuba, echoed by Andromache, "accompanying herself by rocking back and forth" in grief for her husband, Priam, and for the dearest of all her sons, Hector, and for her city, "smouldering Ilium"; or the defiant chorus of "suppliants, mothers, young brides, [and] virgins" for their endangered Thebes; or Antigone for Polynices; Clytemnestra for Iphigeneia; Elektra for her beloved father, Agamemnon, as he wandered the Underworld; or the prophetess Cassandra's "dirge" for herself "against her own ill-starred fortune"—*lamentation* came to life through the questions, solos, and refrains of the powerful female characters commanding the emotional core of Greek tragedy.

Women were not permitted to traverse the *orkhestra* of the theatre at the great Dionysia at Athens. However, in the world of ancient Greek society at large, lamentation for the dead—*moirologia*—was one of women's important and sanctioned roles, continuing in the rural villages of the present day. At funerals, memorial services, and cemetery visits, the women of modern Greece are expected, through ritual movements of their bodies and songs of their voices, to inhabit the connection between dead and living, to bear witness, testify, and suffer.

The myth tells of the sixth-born Muse, Terpsichore ("delight in dancing"), paragon of choral movement and song. Her son, fathered by divine Apollo, was the clear-voiced Linos, who taught the arts of music to his younger brother, Orpheus. When Linos was killed by his student Herakles, it was the sad duty of honey-tongued Terpsichore—seated, plucking a lyre—to "lull her beloved son to rest."

Praising him through her tears, she sang the original lament.

. . .

We forget what a strange and complex idea it is to re-enact private anguish on a public stage. This idea and the vision of man which it implies are Greek.

—GEORGE STEINER

Walter Terry, a college student of eighteen, was in the audience at Maxine Elliott's Theatre for the *Lamentation* premiere; its "indelible images" stuck in his mind. "This was all so different from the conventions of ballet," he realized. "In *Giselle,* for example, when Giselle dies, her young suitor holds her in his arms and weeps. But what was happening to him *inside*? . . . Whatever the hero felt inside you never saw, only the surface conventions of sorrow. Martha in *Lamentation* showed you the total, agonized lamenting of that young suitor plus all those lovers . . . all humans who had experienced loss and with it, unbearable anguish."

Also in the theatre for a first look at *Lamentation* was twenty-six-year-old photographer Walker Evans, whose three photographs of the Brooklyn Bridge would appear in his friend and neighbor Hart Crane's long poem *The Bridge,* to be published in February by Caresse Crosby's Black Sun Press. Evans was already a Martha Graham fan, having spotted her gliding quietly among rows of books in the Fifty-Seventh Street store where he worked as a clerk. The morning after Graham's concert, in bed at home in Columbia Heights and suffering from tonsillitis as a consequence of bravoing himself hoarse, Evans declared that her dancing was "better than ever."

Mary Watkins anointed Graham "the only authentic genius of the Dance Repertory Theatre . . . a unique and essentially solitary figure, for which the frame must be most prudently and specially designed." As in her childhood, Martha Graham was "the different one," giving definition to the modern dance with every movement outside the borders that contained the "others"—Doris Humphrey, Charles Weidman, and Tamiris.

John Martin, still a partisan, came away ambivalent. New York had, indeed, been treated to "a new band of liberators" this winter, and the Dance Repertory Theatre was an important step for the art form. Martin cautioned "this is not the final word. . . . The one thing that the modern dance can be relied on *not* to possess is a fixed standard of any sort. Every dancer is to some extent an inventor, an innovator, a pioneer . . . in the modern scheme of things." For the coming year—there was talk of a 1931 reprise—Martin warned that Dance Repertory Theatre must reappear "less as a miniature war between the holders of disparate theories and more as a unified whole made up of disparate parts."

"What is 'modernism' in the American art of the dance?" Edith Isaacs assigned Margaret Gage to address the question under the aegis of *Theatre Arts Monthly,* by spending a week at the Dance Repertory Theatre. Gage was on the dance and drama faculty of the Bennett School, an all-girls' institution "of liberal and applied arts" in the Duchess County hamlet of Millbrook, New York, east of Poughkeepsie, where she founded an outdoor theatre, set dances for Shakespeare's plays, and choreographed an annual festival of Greek drama, favoring Euripides's *Iphigeneia, Medea,* and *The Trojan Women.*

At Gage's invitation, in colleagueship with Elizabeth Selden, also teaching at Bennett, Martha Graham had performed at the school in January 1929. On March 29, 1930, Graham returned to Bennett with Louis Horst and the twelve members of her group for an evening that ran from "Tanagra" to *Adolescence* to the notorious and silent *Project in Movement for a Divine Comedy*—renamed *Chorus Movement for a Dance Drama.*

Margaret Gage's "Study in American Modernism" was published in the March 1930 issue of *Theatre Arts Monthly.* "'Modernism' in the American dance means unswerving and unsentimental directness of idea presented in a style dictated wholly by that idea," she wrote, "with everything ruthlessly whittled away that is non-essential to the main structural lines."

Held to that exacting standard, despite "broad creative flashes in the work of all four artists that thrilled" her, Gage determined that Tamiris was "not so mature in her art. One feels that she is still in the experimental stages . . . [and] Doris Humphrey and Charles Weidman cover a wide field in the dance, resulting sometimes in confusion and mixture of styles and periods."

Gage made no attempt to conceal the object of her admiration: Among the four dance artists, she wrote, Martha Graham was "the most consistent 'modernist.' She cleaves straight to her point with no apologies and no concessions—she expresses her ideas utterly and simply, and you may like them or not as you please!"

12

Introducing: Isamu Noguchi

I'm curious about how you related what you were doing in your studio to the problems that were set by the dance as [Martha Graham] envisioned it.

Well, the theatre stage for me was a very challenging and basic concept. The whole volume of the theatre stage and how things related within it and to the people moving, was, for me, a sculptural problem.

—ISAMU NOGUCHI in conversation with Paul Cummings, 1973

Two bronzes of his friend, Martha Graham, were among fifteen portrait busts by the sculptor Isamu Noguchi at his one-man show from February 1–14, 1930, in Marie Wertheim Sterner's gallery on East Fifty-Seventh Street. The works were mounted upon cubes at eye height atop widely spaced marble cylinders. There was a quality of Rodin and Lachaise in the pieces. Slightly larger than life-size yet speaking of monumentality, their nervous energy conjured up Giacometti. There was assurance and introspection in the tilt of Graham's head and her heavy-lidded downward gaze; and evidence of the artist's facile hand through modelling, impression, and final casting, pinches and gouges where he had left rough-edged bits of clay on her cheekbones and incised ridges across her forehead. At the opening reception, art critic Edward Alden Jewell chatted with the cordial, puckish, tousle-haired twenty-six-year-old sculptor. "He has illuminating theories about 'realism,'" Jewell wrote, "illuminating, and yet deep, very deep. . . . In these heads, you read a thesis that has been brilliantly pursued. . . . Isamu Noguchi is decidedly a young man with a future."

From the mid-1930s until his death in 1988, sculptor, architect, and landscape artist Isamu Noguchi was Martha Graham's set designer and kindred

Graham disliked this 1929 bronze portrait head by Noguchi . . .

. . . preferring this version; both on view at the Marie Sterner Gallery, New York, February 1930.

collaborator. His father, writer Yonejiro (Yone) Noguchi, who emigrated from Tokyo to San Francisco while in his teens, became established as the first "poet of the Flowery Kingdom . . . who writes in the English tongue." In New York City in 1901, seeking editorial assistance, Yone met Leonie Gilmour, a Bryn Mawr graduate, high school teacher, and freelance fiction writer, and hired her to work on his manuscripts. Before Yone deserted her to return to Japan, Leonie became pregnant, and went to stay with her mother in Los Angeles's Boyle Heights neighborhood. The baby boy born there was "perfectly brown as any other Japanese child . . . with velvety dark eyes."

It took more than two years for Yone, who had taken up with another woman, to persuade Leonie to bring their son to Tokyo, where Yone called him Isamu ("valor" in Japanese). The child's earliest memory was of his mother reading Greek mythology tales aloud. "He is a worshipper of Apollo," Leonie observed. In the spring of 1911, she took a lover, and on January 27, 1912, Isamu's half sister was born in the seaside village of Chigasaki; Leonie named her Ailes, after the "girl that stepped on two bare feet" in an Irish poem she liked, "Beauty's a Flower," by Moira O'Neill.

At thirteen, after commuting to St. Joseph's College, a Jesuit school (which he hated), and apprenticing with a cabinetmaker (which he loved), Isamu was sent stateside, to Interlaken, a preparatory boarding school in Indiana. When the school was converted to an army training camp, the founder, Dr. Edward A. Rumely, a wealthy physician and inventor, shepherded Isamu through high school in La Porte. Recognizing the boy's artistic talents, after graduation, Rumely arranged for him to apprentice with a disciple of Rodin, the sculptor Gutzon Borglum, who would become renowned as the creator of the Mount Rushmore presidential heads. Noguchi lived in a shack on the grounds of Borglum's estate outside Stamford, Connecticut. An unwilling instructor, Borglum was "an irascible fellow" who told Noguchi he "would never be a sculptor."

At eighteen, Noguchi decamped to New York City. Under the continuing patronage of Dr. Rumely, who came east to take over as editor and publisher of the New York *Evening Mail,* Noguchi, "adaptable almost to a fault, landing always like a cat upon his feet," regained the path of art after an unenthusiastic diversion into the premedical program at Columbia University. At the Leonardo Da Vinci Art School on the Lower East Side, he learned the essentials of stonecutting; the director, Onorio Ruotolo, also trained the young man in working with clay. By this time, Noguchi's husbandless mother and fatherless sister had arrived in New York; Ailes Gilmour (nicknamed "Ai-Chan") was enrolled in the Ethical Culture School, where Leonie had gone as a child.

In the summer of 1924, in the Da Vinci Art School lobby, Isamu Noguchi presented his first show and soon thereafter took a studio on University Place. Notwithstanding his disparagement of "the academic thing," Noguchi knew he could earn money as a sculpture portraitist in the naturalistic mode, with help from Dr. Rumely, who encouraged him, "You have the real stuff in you! . . . It is that quality which will carry you far in life."

Wanting to make connections, Noguchi sought out his father's friend, Michio Ito, and fashioned a polished-bronze portrait of the dancer with a high brow, cut-out eyes, and pugnacious lower lip, the classic Noh persona. Ito hired Noguchi to fabricate the masks for his *Hawk's Well* production. Theatrical appetite whetted, Noguchi sat in on Ito's classes at the Anderson–Milton School, and caught his first glimpse of Martha Graham, also teaching there, "evolving her new and fundamental approach." Watching the evolution of Graham's work, Noguchi had the feeling he was witnessing the "inception of modern dance."

. . .

When he could seize spare time between sittings, Noguchi did not need to venture far to immerse himself in the modern art movement. He frequented exhibitions at Alfred Stieglitz's Intimate Gallery, J. B. Neumann's New Art Circle, and the Whitney Studio Club. One perambulating day, in the winter of 1926, Noguchi happened into a retrospective of the works of Constantin Brancusi at Joseph and Ernest Brummer's gallery. Crowding the room were twenty-seven paintings and works on paper, and forty-two sculptures honed to sublime abstraction, among them the towering, tapered, gleaming bronze curve, *Bird in Space*; *Le premier cri,* a smooth egg resting on its side, jagged notched mouth open; and the lovingly intertwined white marble *Three Penguins.* The Brancusi show had been

Isamu Noguchi, *Michio Ito,* bronze, 1926.

organized by the Romanian sculptor's "American dealer and advocate," Marcel Duchamp.

On the premises that day, Duchamp offered Noguchi a personal tour. "Out of the limitations of matter and the working of it came the essence of [Brancusi's] sculpture," Noguchi recalled. "The images [were] nestled within the medium."

"Transfixed by [Brancusi's] vision," communicating artistic truth not by accretion but by refinement through deliberate and direct carving, Noguchi turned away from the built-up medium of clay. "The interpretation of the human figure will always remain [sculpture's] chief objective," Noguchi said. "I am nevertheless of the opinion that nature offers many another subject which would lend itself to some strange and exquisite sculptural treatment."

Noguchi applied for a three-year John Simon Guggenheim Memorial Foundation Fellowship, first to be spent in Paris "acquir[ing] proficiency in stone and wood cutting," and then two years "in Asia, going first to India, then through China to Japan . . . I have selected the Orient as the location

Isamu Noguchi in his University Place studio, with plaster sculpture in progress, *Undine (Nadja),* 1926.

for my productive activities," he told the selection committee, "for the reason that I feel great attachment for it, having spent half my life there. My father, Yone Noguchi, is Japanese and has long been an interpreter of the East to the West, through poetry. I wish to fulfill my heritage." Dr. Rumely, Michio Ito, Irene Lewisohn of the Neighborhood Playhouse, critic Paul Rosenfeld, and photographer and gallerist Alfred Stieglitz wrote letters endorsing Noguchi's application, and it was unanimously approved.

The day following his springtime 1927 arrival in Paris, Noguchi met writer Robert McAlmon, the American publisher of Contact Editions, who escorted him from the Café de Flore to Constantin Brancusi's whitewashed atelier on the Impasse Ronsin, a mazelike cul-de-sac off rue de Vaugirard near the Gare Montparnasse. Huge, slanted windows let light down into a "private jungle" of handmade sculptures, Cycladic and streamlined, rough-hewn and smooth, casting what Brancusi called "friendly shadows" on the cement floor littered with dust, shavings, and stone chips, evidence that "every inch of the surface" of the artist's work had "been won at the point of the chisel."

Brancusi agreed to let Noguchi "hang around and help him a bit." Neither could speak the other's language, so "communication was through the eyes, through gesture, and through materials and tools to be used . . . precisely how a chisel should be held and how to true a plane of limestone. He would show me by doing it himself," Noguchi said, "indicating that I should do the same." Mornings, to the scratchy rhythms of African tribal music on an old Victrola, master and student labored side by side. Noguchi learned how to cut bases out of limestone, "dress and finish marble . . . determine contours" of stone, and sharpen tools. In the afternoons, he went to classes in drawing from life—"a different girl every day"—at Académie de la Grande Chaumière.

After several months with Brancusi, Noguchi needed to get away from his teacher and make new art. He took a studio in Gentilly, near Montrouge, and produced a series of constructivist-edged, tactile black-and-white gouaches. The flattened, geometric works on paper became prototypes for a series of stone, wood, and metal sculptures. Noguchi admitted that some of these—*Sphere Section, Globular,* and *Foot Tree*—were Brancusi-esque studies in living volume. Others, such as *Sail Shape, Positional Shape,* and *Leda,* in bent and folded sheet metal and reflective brass, sliced into space rather than curvaceously embracing it.

．　　．　　．

Seduced by friendships in café society with Stuart Davis and Alexander Calder, Noguchi lingered in Paris's street life and never got around to his proposed Asian journey.

He returned to New York City in early 1929, and showed *Paris Abstractions* at an out-of-the-way gallery-shop run by architect and interior designer Eugene Schoen. The *Times* thought the work "surpassingly good," but nothing sold. Noguchi was crestfallen. "I was too poor and could not afford [abstract sculpture]," he remembered; and, tellingly, "too poor inside myself to insist upon it . . . All my dreams were left in Paris." Dr. Rumely paid for a studio for Noguchi in Carnegie Hall so he could return to the practical realm of clay portraiture. "Making heads," he said, "was a matter of eating . . . [and] a means of earning money to have friends."

Noguchi's sister, Ailes, went from Ethical Culture to Cherry Lawn, a progressive open-air school, in Darien, Connecticut. Taking after her mother, she distinguished herself as literary editor of the student magazine, *The Cherry Pit*. "The girl who stepped on two bare feet" began dance studies, and when she graduated was granted a fifteen-dollar-a-week "living scholarship . . . for food, lodging and free tuition" at the Neighborhood Playhouse School on West Fifty-Sixth Street, down the block from her brother's studio.

Ailes Gilmour, age twenty, in the Martha Graham Dance Group, 1932.

Gilmour was admitted into contraction and release classes with "the brilliant and blazing" Martha Graham, whom she had seen in *Heretic* and *Adolescence*; and studied "music and dance forms" with Louis Horst. Noguchi observed his sister's classes as well as the children's lessons Graham continued to teach at the school.

Ailes Gilmour knew coming into Martha Graham's presence that "the starkness and simplicity of movement in her work . . . was not pretty . . . People unused to the bare bones of dance were often repelled . . . [but] I loved it!" she said. "There, it seemed, was *truth*." When day classes concluded, Gilmour followed Graham downtown to her apartment, "where we would rehearse until one or two in the morning . . . and Martha would give us rye bread and cheese." Thus did Gilmour earn her spot in "Martha Graham's special Group," her "pleased as Punch" mother reported to Isamu, for the premiere of *Primitive Mysteries* on February 2, 1931.

.   .   .

You are among these heads for scarcely three minutes before you begin calling them by their first names.

—C. J. BULLIET, "Of Picasso, Noguchi, and the Chinese," *Chicago Evening Post*, April 1, 1930

Marie Sterner, wife of portraitist Albert Sterner, was the first woman to work as a dealer-curator at the prestigious Knoedler Gallery, where her career began in 1915. Her gallery show revealed the expansion of Isamu Noguchi's social and artistic circles in New York and his manic pace of production since returning from Paris. Here were portrait heads of photographer Berenice Abbott, Dymaxion House inventor R. Buckminster Fuller (plated in chrome), composer George Gershwin (polished bronze), Rockefeller Center consulting architect Harvey Wiley Corbett, actress Edla Frankau, artist—and Noguchi's current lover—Marion Greenwood (cast iron), painter Lajos Tihanyi, and modern dancer Martha Graham.

Graham criticized the first bronze Noguchi made of her as "too serious. . . . It had shown a side of my face, my left side, which changes only when I work. . . . He had seen too deeply." To oblige her, he made a second version, more benign. Among the portraits the artist showed at Sterner, Graham's was the only one with two variants. Noguchi never destroyed the first, his usual practice with other unsatisfactory heads, because, in Graham, he sensed energies divided like his. She was a heretic singled out as different. He was the Japanese American (or American Japanese) hybrid, typecast in the stereotype of *gaijin*—"outside person." As in dance, Noguchi wrote, "We [artists] breathe in, we breathe out, inward turning, alone, or outgoing."

Graham's recurrent inner argument was between teaching and performing; Noguchi toggled between art for a living and art for life. Graham faced up to—and denied—Isadora Duncan, and Noguchi needed to break from the anxieties stirred by Brancusi's tutelage. Like the moody dancer, ecstatic and introspective, Noguchi knew that "after the elation and effort that go with preparing an exhibition, comes a depression."

Insisting as a teacher that "shape shapes meaning," Graham sought to free the potential in her students' torsioned bodies. Noguchi's ideal for sculpture, in any form—academic figuration, or the less-is-more abstraction of the handmade stage sets he would put together for Graham—was to coax forth and build "projections of the imagination into environmental space . . . on the stage in its own world of timeless time, [where] form plays its integral part in the re-enactment of a ritual."

When Marie Sterner's show closed, "Bucky" Fuller lent Noguchi his station wagon, and the friends packed the busts and drove to a little gallery, the Harvard Society for Contemporary Art, upstairs from the Coop in Cambridge, founded by undergraduates Lincoln Kirstein, John Walker III, and Edward M. Warburg. The portraits were on view until mid-March, when

Noguchi and Fuller drove with a station wagon full of art works to Chicago, where the heads and several figure studies were shown at the Arts Club from the end of March to early April.

On April 16, 1930, saving money for a steamer ticket from the sales of his work, Isamu Noguchi sailed from New York Harbor for Calais, then headed to Paris; from there, he would travel to Berlin, Moscow, Beijing, and, at last, Tokyo and Kyoto.

"Tell Martha," Noguchi wrote from the Continent to sister Ailes, "I hope we may be able to do something together next year."

13

League of Composers and
The Rite of Spring in America

The centre of the world has shifted. Paris is no longer the capitol of Cosmopolis. All the intelligence of the world is focused on New York; it has become the battleground of modern civilization; all the roads now lead in this direction.

— HENRY MCBRIDE, *The Dial*, April 1929

American vocabularies for dance, sculpture, painting, and poetry were finding new expression. And typical of the refreshed spirit in music was the League of Composers, founded in New York City in March 1923. "The day of the unknown American composer is over," the league's manifesto declared, its goal "to encourage, support and make possible the production of music representative of the present time . . . the entire range of modern works which are important and in need of a hearing" . . . "by 'the musical youngsters' of America" and beyond—to "England, the Continent," and "composers of all nations."

Among the participants in the ardent group "fostering new musical works of a radical hue" were Marion Eugénie Bauer, Marc Blitzstein, Aaron Copland, Henry Cowell, Louis Gruenberg, Leo Ornstein, Wallingford Riegger, Dane Rudhyar, Carl Ruggles, and Carlos Salzedo; joined by set and costume designers Norman Bel Geddes, Donald Oenslager, Robert Edmond Jones, and Nicholas Roerich.

After she formed the Dance Group, Martha Graham joined venturesome collaborators and supporters on the league's auxiliary committee, vice chaired by Adelaide (Mrs. Otto H.) Kahn.

The founding spirit and executive director of the League of Composers was Claire Reis, a petite, dynamic mother of two, imbued with volunteer spirit. Louise Varèse, the poet and wife of the composer, said Reis had

Claire Reis with child prodigy violinist Max Rosen,
whom she accompanied on piano, New York City, ca. early 1910s.

"enough energy to split atoms." She was born Claire Raphael in Browns-
ville, Texas, on August 4, 1888, and raised in a well-to-do musical family.
Claire's mother advised her that playing the piano for charity—rather than
concerts—was the nobler path to artistry.

In her teens, she studied with Bertha Fiering Tapper at the New York
Institute of Musical Art, forerunner of the Juilliard School. In the winter of
1912, Claire's formal training concluded. Fulfilling her mother's wishes and
in the feminist footsteps of Jane Addams and Lillian Wald, she created the
People's Music League, a division of the People's Institute at Cooper Union.
The league's volunteer musicians presented free concerts for immigrant children and their families in public school auditoriums throughout the city.

In alliance with Margaret Naumburg, a protégée of John Dewey at
Columbia University, Reis helped launch the Children's School, later the

Walden School; and worked as a kindergarten and Montessori music teacher and eurythmics instructor. She was active in the suffragist Women's City Club of New York and the International Composers' Guild, from which she resigned in protest against its elitism, prior to founding the populist League of Composers.

Her husband, Arthur M. Reis, president of his family's men's sportswear manufacturing company, provided funds for his wife's cultural causes, made his car and driver available to pick up visiting conductors and musicians at the train station and chauffeur them around town, and ceded the first-floor parlor of their Upper West Side town house for teatime meetings, recitals, and soirees. The Reises' third-floor playroom "that had been used chiefly for toy trains and ping-pong," became the league's administrative office and the editorial headquarters for the *League of Composers' Review* that in its second year changed to *Modern Music.* Over twenty-three volumes, Virgil Thomson said, the journal "told the musical story of its time so completely, so authoritatively, so straight-from-the-field-of-battle and from the creative laboratory."

According to one dour New York critic, the league's first two seasons were exercises in "unmitigated tonal asperity." Undaunted, Reis forged ahead with premieres of Ernest Bloch's Piano Quintet, Igor Stravinsky's Three Pieces for Clarinet, Louis Gruenberg's *Daniel Jazz,* and early segments of George Antheil's *Ballet Mécanique.* In the summer of 1924, twenty-three-year-old Aaron Copland returned to New York City from Paris, where his composition teacher, Nadia Boulanger, had introduced him to Serge Koussevitzky, recently signed to take up the baton at the Boston Symphony Orchestra. Reis commissioned Copland to write a new work for chamber orchestra, and reached out to Koussevitzky to ask if he would conduct the premiere. The maestro, an admirer of the young fellow from Brooklyn, responded "that he was willing to play anything [Copland] gave him for the next season."

The result was *Music for the Theatre: Suite in Five Parts for Small Orchestra,* originally entitled *Incidental Music for an Imaginary Drama.* After a perfor-

Aaron Copland, ca. 1920s.

mance in Boston, the bluesy/bouncy work with brash and piercing music-hall brass, chugging hurry-up rhythms, and snappy snare drums offset with sly, perky minor-key oboe and clarinet was presented in Town Hall under the sponsorship of the League of Composers, on November 28, 1925.

"Some of us will and some of us will not agree with the League's estimate of Mr. Copland's talent," equivocated Olin Downes in the *New York Times*. Copland and Reis became close friends for half a century and he remained indebted to "this intensely-loyal . . . energetic champion of living composers" for believing in his work early in his career "in the turbulent world of the developing contemporary arts."

. . .

In its first four years, from 1923 to 1927, the league produced sixty-four premier performances; twenty-five were works by Americans. In 1928, the league presented Igor Stravinsky's sprightly, Faustian *L'Histoire du Soldat (The Soldier's Tale)*, at Jolson's 59th Street Theatre with drama and pantomime arranged by Michio Ito. For the spring 1929 season, Claire Reis set her sights on the first American staged version of Stravinsky's *Les Noces (Svadebka/ The Wedding)* with a corps de ballet of men and women, powerful chorale, passionate soloists, and four pianos, played by Marc Blitzstein, Aaron Copland, Frederick Jacobi, and Louis Gruenberg. Through the good graces of Adelaide Kahn's husband, Otto, chairman of the Metropolitan Opera House board of directors, the league reserved, at cost, the ultimate venue.

Reis knew of Leopold Stokowski's obsession with bringing as much Stravinsky to America as possible. She arranged an audience—with harpsichordist Wanda Landowska as go-between—at the golden-haired maestro's apartment. He made an entrance in a silk kimono and sandals. "I know all the musical geniuses," Stokowski told Reis with a laugh, "but I have never met the theatre people."

Reis brought in Serge Soudeikine to design the lighting, rough-hewn stage decor, and rustic costumes for the tableaux of *Les Noces*, the blessings of the bride and bridegroom, the departure of the bride from the parental home, and the final wedding feast. A concoction of ritualistic, whirling gambols and Russian liturgical chants, sorrowful wedding laments, joyous folk songs, and fragmentary typical sayings knitted together with repetitive, driving cadences, *Les Noces* was a spectacle.

At the helm of the Philadelphia Orchestra in March 1922, Stokowski had led a concert version of *The Rite of Spring: Pictures of Pagan Russia.* Now, "Stoki" went to Paris to meet with the composer and receive his imprimatur for a fully staged American premiere of the ballet. *The Rite of Spring* was still in the throes of revision. For another four decades, Stravinsky would return with further slicings and rebarrings, tighten tempos and limit pitch ranges. Pierre Monteux—veteran of the Folies-Bergère and conductor of the original 1913 *Rite*—made a new, abridged recording with the Grand Orchestre Symphonique in January 1929, against which the chronically dissatisfied Stravinsky conducted the Walther Straram Concerts Orchestra in a corrective recording in May.

From Paris, Stokowski reported that Stravinsky "has [continued to make] important changes in rhythm and orchestration." Most hands-on were seventeen pages of the "Danse Sacrale" score in part II of the *Rite,* redrawn to intensify the primitive drama and accelerate the already merciless pace compressed into and through the four minutes and fifty-eight seconds' duration of the brutal, demanding dance of the chosen maiden, "the Chosen One" ("l'Élue"). Stravinsky's efforts, concentrated predominantly upon this dance of sacrifice, were published in 1929 by Editions Russes de Musique/Russischer Musikverlag as the revised first edition of *The Rite of Spring,* "the completely re-engraved version . . . in which the *Rite* first achieves its 'standard' form."

In an account of how *The Rite of Spring*—most accurately translated, *Holy Spring*—was engendered, Stravinsky did not credit the scenario to his collaborator, Nicholas Roerich. He claimed that the theme—or "embryo"— was hatched during the finishing touches on *The Firebird* (*L'Oiseau de Feu*) in 1910. A "vision . . . from the Russian prehistoric epoch" came to him, Stravinsky wrote, of a circle of seated elders, spectators at the final *agon* of a girl given up "in propitiation of the gods." It was a two-part drama, beginning with "secret night games of the young virgins on the sacred hill. One of the women is consecrated for the sacrificial offering . . . [This] Great Offering, which is the title of the Second Part, ends with the spectacular death of the Chosen One, witnessed by the old wise men."

In the spring of 1929, Stravinsky was still embroiled in an arduous chromatic wrestling match—Pieter C. van den Toorn calls it a "metrical tug-of-war"—with the "Danse Sacrale." In the American *Rite of Spring,* this conflict with the given material of the work, "holding [to] the rules, or acting beyond them," would be brought to life in dance by a new Chosen Maiden, blessed with disciplined intelligence and evocative bravado.

. . .

Armed with Stravinsky's revisions, under the auspices of RCA Victor Records, on September 24–25, 1929, a week before the October 3 opening of the concert season, Stokowski led the Philadelphia Orchestra at the Academy of Music in the American recording of *The Rite of Spring*. One more session would follow on March 12, 1930, to complete eight 78-rpm sides, "the earliest documentation we have of how the work sounded when played by a first-rate ensemble under its own musical director."

From the solitary opening bassoon, a high, poignant folk song at dawn in "The Adoration of the Earth/Introduction," to the truncated grinding collapse of "The Sacrifice," the score "slashed the fabric of the music" with disconcerting, unpredictable metric reversals unfamiliar to players and listeners accustomed to transitional phrases between contrasting sections. The awakening menagerie of stirrings and celebratory clarion calls in the "Augurs/Harbingers of Spring" gives in to the driving strings' emphases in the "Dances of the Adolescents/Adolescentes" [boys and girls] punctuated and overridden by distant horns, tensions building to the frenetic stop-and-start stamping, single-file whirlwind "Ritual of Abduction." A plaintive, wave-like minor melody threads through a deep-throated labyrinth of pulsating undercurrents in "Spring Rounds (Khorovod)." The "Rival Tribes" clamor against one another, jazzed-up, brisk folk tunes fighting to be recognized.

The "Wise Elders," led by their patriarch, slowly gather in an ominous lull before the bursts and hard stops of hurried strings marking the "Dance of the Earth." Like magical clouds drifting to veil the moon, a melancholy woodwind theme introduces the "Pagan Night of Part II," and carries through as an insinuating, meandering pastorale for the "Mystic Circles of the Young Girls" that shifts into a sinister, hard-counted pizzicato, setting the scene for the "Glorification of the Chosen One—L'Élue."

The roiling rhythm of trumpets herald her presence. Out of the jumble of voices she emerges before "The Summoned Ancients." The momentum is cut to imperious breathtaking before her "Sacrificial Dance"—a harsh, disjunctive path beaten through sardonic instrumentation building from accelerated off-centered tympanic pulses into a rude, shrieking march toward the inevitable climax.

. . .

Despite his background as a concert violinist and teacher, and as critic for *Musical America* and *The Musician* before he took over as manager of the Philadelphia Orchestra, Arthur Judson recoiled when Claire Reis came to him with her proposal for another producing alliance with the League of Composers. "Why, Mrs. Reis," he muttered in dismay, "you cannot *possibly* think that you could fill the Metropolitan Opera House with [*The Rite of Spring*]! . . . You really have all my sympathy if you insist on carrying out this program."

Judson had begun discussions with David Sarnoff about providing concert artists for NBC, America's radio network. However, he balked at Stokowski's request to present *The Rite of Spring* during the orchestra's series of broadcasts scheduled for November and December as publicity for the April 1930 performances in New York and Philadelphia. "I am frankly afraid of the Stravinsky number on the . . . program," Judson wrote. "Millions of people who have never heard an orchestra are going to 'listen in.' They are going to be greatly pleased with the first number ["Dances of the Polovetzi Maidens" from Borodin's *Prince Igor*, that had followed the *Rite* at its 1913 premiere], but after about five minutes of the Stravinsky they are going to say 'Oh, hell!' and turn off the radio . . . [and] you will probably lose about ninety per cent." Judson also feared jeopardizing the sponsorship of the Philco Corporation, makers of the new "Balanced-Unit" radio, advertised as "unique in trueness and clearness of tone."

Stokowski stood his ground, firing back that "the *Sacre* of Stravinsky . . . is the greatest work of our time . . . [I]f I cannot radio the best music at present I will wait until I can, because I am not willing to lower my flag."

On the day and time—5:30 to 6:30 p.m., Sunday, November 3, 1929—to his surprise, a correspondent for the *Musical Leader* who had written to Stokowski inveighing against broadcasting *Rite* was won over by the conductor's introductory speech and the fidelity of the sound: "The amazing thing was the clear transmission of the 'Sacre du Printemps' . . . From every point of view this was actually the best bit of broadcasting we have ever heard!" The critic praised Stokowski's teachable moments in his concert talk, "ask[ing] listeners [at home] to 'make an effort' to understand and enjoy the Stravinsky composition. His verbal notes were amazingly clear and concise . . . and [did] not wander off into verbal fugues or variations."

·   ·   ·

Mrs. Reis's next move in her quest to assemble the team for the rebirth of *The Rite of Spring* was to track down the "prime mover," Nicholas Konstantinovich Roerich, author of *The Great Sacrifice*, the origin story, and designer of the first stage settings and costumes. Roerich grew up in a well-to-do St. Petersburg family where, despite a brew of cultural interests—archaeology and ethnology, art history and painting, poetry, Eastern mysticism, music and opera—his lawyer father insisted Nicholas attend the Karl von May gymnasium and the Faculty of Law at the University of St. Petersburg. There, he met Sergei Diaghilev.

An impassioned "Slavophil," Roerich was drawn to the pre-Christian history of Russia. He traveled widely in the countryside, assisting at archaeological digs ("with each swing of the shovel, each stroke of the spade, an alluring kingdom emerges"), making plein air sketches of castles, monasteries, churches, and other landmarks, and colorful canvases that captured the gilded Byzantine spirit of ancient days. When he took commissions to design sets and paint backdrops for theatrical productions such as Rimsky-Korsakov's *Snegourotchka* and Borodin's *Prince Igor* drawn from "the old *byliny*"—traditional peasant tales and folk myths—Roerich likened his process to the composer who "chooses a certain key to write in, so I paint in a certain key of color, or perhaps I might say a leitmotif of color, on which I base my entire scheme."

After the raucous 1913 *Rite* in Paris, Roerich and his pianist-Theosophist wife, Helena, spent several years in exile in Scandinavia and England during the Russian Revolution and the Great War, then moved to America. In the summer of 1921 they visited the Grand Canyon and the craggy terrain of New Mexico and Arizona; Roerich's paintings reflected "the intensity of the blue endless sky, crimson sunsets, fiery red mountains, and endless open landscapes." The sacred dances of the Jemez Pueblo peoples and "their linen-bound feet, embroidered shirts, and the headdresses of the women" recalled for him the ceremonial costumes of the indigenous peoples of Siberia.

Provisionally settled for two years in New York City, Roerich founded the Master Institute of United Arts, a creative collegium modeled upon the salons of his youth. Following the allure of spiritual enlightenment, from 1923 to 1929 the Roerichs, accompanied by their sons, George and Svetoslav, traveled from Egypt to Turkestan to Tibet to Mongolia to India, and built a home in the idyllic Kulu Valley on the banks of the Beas River at the edge of the Himalayas before returning to New York.

On October 17, 1929, the Master Institute of the Roerich Museum, the

Corona Mundi International Art Center, the Urusvati Himalayan Research Institute, and the Roerich Art Cinema and Library opened the doors to their twenty-seven-story art deco Master Building. The terraced residential apartment hotel/studio complex/urban commune at 310 Riverside Drive and 103rd Street was dedicated "to the creative efforts of . . . this mighty and all-embracing country . . . [whose] prosperity is turning towards the gathering and cherishing of the creations of art and science."

"Great and young are America's aspirations," Roerich declared. "Here Emerson and Whitman, Edison and Carnegie [*sic*] were born." In tribute to such heroic origins, The Master Building was a prepossessing citadel of steel, graced with a deep purple brick base "to give the effect of a growing thing" and create "a beautiful spectacle of changing colors under the play of sunlight" crowned by a "gleaming, pure-white summit."

Here Claire Reis was ushered, "confused but challenged," into the presence of an "esoteric personality . . . seated behind a large, empty desk in an enormous empty room. . . . His domed skull, the waxen color of his skin, the slanting eyes and pointed beard, suggested a world very foreign to our western hemisphere. . . . 'Thank you for bringing me Mr. Stokowski's greetings,' were Nicholas Roerich's opening words after a long silence following [her] remarks. Then, weighing each word, he added, 'Yes, I will be glad to do the stage *décor* for this production.'"

Le Sacre continued to occupy a place of "eternal novelty" in Roerich's heart. As he wrote in his 1931 book, *Realm of Light*, "[S]pring is eternal, and love is eternal, and sacrifice is eternal. Thus, in this new [1930] conception, Stravinsky touches the eternal in music. He [is] modern because he evoked the future."

.   .   .

Who should choreograph the American premiere of *The Rite of Spring*?

Roerich and Stokowski insisted upon Léonide Massine. In December 1920, following a string of successes including *Parade*, *La Boutique Fantasque*, *Tricorne*, and *Pulcinella*, Massine, with Stravinsky's blessing, had successfully finessed the first rechoreographing of Vaslav Nijinsky's 1913 lost—essentially forgotten—eight-performance *Sacre*. In 1921, after too many arguments with Diaghilev, Massine quit the Ballets Russes, and opened his own school under the patronage of Count Etienne de Beaumont's *Les Soirées de Paris*. Four years later, accepting Diaghilev's plea to return, he mounted several experimental dances, including *Flore et Zéphire,* with sets by Georges Braque; *Les Matelots,* with music by Georges Auric, a member of "Les Six"; and Sergei Prokofiev's *Le Pas d'Acier.* Following the spring 1928 Ballets Russes season, Massine split from Diaghilev again, and in Paris, staged two melodramas for Les Ballets of Ida Rubinstein, the wealthy former Ballets Russes dancer.

In November, accompanied by his seventeen-year-old bride, Folies-Bergère danseuse Eugenia Delarova, Massine departed for America. He had been hired by "Roxy" Rothafel's "entertainment manufactory" to assist at presenting dances during movie intermissions in the six-thousand-seat Roxy Theatre on Fiftieth Street. Massine and Delarova arrived in New York "without so much as a word of warning, with no fanfare of trumpets and no committees of welcome at the pier . . . Why import a distinguished maître de ballet," wondered John Martin, "to do what can be done better by any number of native routine devisers? . . . The next few months will bear close watching to see just how he fares and why."

Massine did not fare well. Over a thunderous organ at the grand opening of the Roxy, the master of ceremonies intoned, "Ye Portals bright, high and majestic, open to our gaze the path to wonderland, and show us the realm where fantasy reigns . . . oh glorious, mighty hall, [may] thy magic and charm unite us all to worship at beauty's throne." Massine's daily reality was quite the opposite. His job was to feed the insatiable maw of Roxy's "vaudevillian, razzle-dazzle" assembly line of "interminable rows of sequined and high-kicking chorus girls," devising a stage revue every Thursday, as well as special "Spring Ballets, Easter Ballets, Christmas Ballets . . . St. Valentine's Day, Halloween and Thanksgiving [dances]." On top of this burden, he, too, was required to dance four times a day.

This middlebrow misery was exacerbated by the news in August 1929 that Diaghilev had died in Venice. The shock waves from this loss released Massine's romanticized indebtedness. Grief transformed Massine's former lover into a saint whose legacy cried out to be sustained. In a fit of panic, and for two years, Massine tried to raise money to revive the Ballets Russes in America—to no avail. By the time Claire Reis "asked [Massine] to join [the] group of artists and to undertake the choreography for this ballet he knew so well," two successful performances of *Le Sacre* at Covent Garden in London had already been wildly hailed.

. . .

Le Sacre du Printemps team, American premiere, (top to bottom, right) Leopold Stokowski, Léonide Massine, and Nicholas Roerich, 1930. (Line drawing by Aline Fruhauf)

One star remained to be discovered for *The Rite of Spring* in America: the principal dancer, "l'Élue," whose "stupendous Danse Sacrale at the climax of the work" awakened the earth from winter slumber.

Under Nicholas Roerich's approving eye, Martha Graham was teaching her modern technique at the Master Institute. Stopping by the studio one afternoon, another passionate spectator, Evangeline Love Brewster Johnson—the second Mrs. Stokowski—was so captivated that she signed up to take class with Graham, attesting to her teacher's "power to portray the universal through the particular." Her husband agreed: "Graham is unique in her expression of the fundamentals of life through dance. She is one of the world's great artists." Bessie Schonberg, who rehearsed for *Le Sacre* but did not perform, saw that "[i]t was Stokowski, really, who was responsible for the whole thing. He fell in love with Martha. . . . He was extremely devoted to her." Stokowski told Massine: Martha Graham was the Chosen One.

Martha Graham was "the ideal choice," John Martin chimed in. "Excellent as Maria Piltz may have been in the [original] Nijinsky production, and

Lydia Sokolova in the previous Massine version," Martin said, "neither of them could have been fitting by temperament, training or inclination more exactly than Miss Graham to the creation of a role of this character in an idiom of movement to match Stravinsky's particular musical idiom."

"I was chosen for a certain passion," Graham said, "a passionate, destructive, ruthless quality which I had at that time, and also for a body that had animal strength." She had a history of being singled out. In January 1920, before Ted Shawn lifted Graham from the Denishawn ensemble for her break as Xochitl, the Mesoamerican princess possessed of black panther ferocity, Roxy Rothafel had cast her as the sultry, whirlwind "Fire Dancer" in his *Footlight Parade* at the California Movie Theatre.

Fast-forward ten years. The program for *The Rite of Spring* noted that Léonide Massine, director of choreography, was participating through the courtesy of S. L. Rothafel, employer of record. Roxy also stepped up to aid the ballet's charity beneficiary, the National Music League and Composers' Fund, providing scholarships for young artists on the verge of professional careers. The fundraising effort for *Le Sacre* was undertaken by the League of Composers' auxiliary committee. "Recently returned from Paris" to assume the chairmanship was Claire Reis's well-connected friend, the Countess Mercati, née Marie Manice, of Belmont Park, Long Island. The countess, a perennial patron of modern music, had supported the league's presentations of *L'Histoire du Soldat* and *Les Noces*. With her vice chair, Mrs. Otto Kahn, she "enlisted the cooperation of many women in society and the musical world," including Mrs. Vincent Astor, Mrs. George F. Baker Jr., Mrs. Charles S. Guggenheim, Mrs. Winthrop Aldrich, Mrs. Henry Morgenthau, Mrs. Oliver Gould Jennings, and Mrs. M. Orme Wilson.

. . .

[I]t is obvious that a specifically personal and twentieth-century feeling is expressed by the gestures of Martha Graham's choreography. Her celebrated "contraction" is not simply a "device." In the same way, there is a new world of feeling in the works of Arnold Schoenberg from 1910 to 1913.

—ALLEN SHAWN, *Arnold Schoenberg's Journey*

For the companion piece to *The Rite of Spring*, Stokowski chose Arnold Schoenberg's opera-ballet *Die glückliche Hand* (*The Lucky Hand* or *The Hand of Fate*). Stokowski's crusade to bring Stravinsky to American audiences was equaled only by his commitment to Schoenberg's difficult oeuvre. The maestro had premiered Variations for Orchestra in Philadelphia in 1929, and would present the magisterial *Gurre-Lieder* cantata in 1932, the year before the composer, fleeing Nazism, emigrated from Berlin through Paris to the United States.

Die glückliche Hand was written to be what the composer described as "a major drama compressed into about twenty minutes as if photographed with a time-exposure." At one time Schoenberg had considered making the four-scene monodrama into a movie. His passion as a painter of self-portraits—he called them "gazes" (*Blicke*)—and as an "abstract visionary" in oils, drew enthusiasm from his confidant, Wassily Kandinsky.

"We must be conscious that there are puzzles around us," Schoenberg wrote to Kandinsky in 1912 while in the grip of *Die glückliche Hand.* "And we must find the courage to look these puzzles in the eye without timidly asking about the 'solution.'" The "independent progress through their own destinies, the independent life of the individual voices" Kandinsky admired about Schoenberg's musical compositions reflected the composer's ambivalence between "heart and brain."

The protagonist, known only as "the Man," is a poet ("maker") artisan, capable of forging "a perfect gem [in some variants, a crown] with a single blow of a hammer." The poet's genius—or conscience—is represented at the beginning and end of the drama by a phantasmagorical, bat-winged, bloodsucking "Chimera," talons clinging to the Man's neck and back. Clambering upon a perilous, rocky landscape in a fruitless journey, the Man is hounded by a lamenting, masked and speech-singing (*Sprechstimme*), "Chorus," reproaching him for his blindness to the object of his affections, the lissome "Woman" with a circlet of roses in her hair, who runs from the Man into the arms of an elegantly cloaked "Gentleman/Stranger."

Emerging from primal silence, *Die glückliche Hand* brings a thick, hallucinatory air of expectation, a ghost story layered into a dream, Schoenberg's "unrest or imbalance inherent in the very material of the music." Like a snapshot emerging into view in the chemical bath of a darkroom developing tray, a haunting montage of otherworldly, invisible voices in the gloom vie for attention, brass and woodwinds approaching in surge-like waves while stealthy violins tremble beneath. As the nightmare wanes, threats take on contours, and the musical dynamics become excruciating. The orchestra pushes deafening crescendos to the perimeters of the sonic envelope, and the listener cannot help but feel repulsed; while, at the same time, the mixed, and, in this production, unseen choral voices, never in unison with the recitative baritone of "the Man," tempt our voyeuristic impulses and we lack the will to turn away.

Schoenberg did not want his art music to be categorized as atonal. Rather, he wrote, dissonance and consonance must be understood as gradations on a continuum, not contradictions. Finding a new form (for which he used the word *Gestalt*), the modern artist was obligated to gaze down the corridor of prior ideas (*Gedanken*) that "can never perish," coming to terms with the styles preceding his own.

When the score of *Die glückliche Hand* was ready to be performed in October 1924 at the Vienna Volksoper, Schoenberg was adamant about how it should be played. Bar by bar, "nothing about the music is to be changed." Similar instructions for the stage-lighting color schemes and hues to be deployed during the production were conditioned by his painterly eye, cues tied to the music. He stipulated that "gestures, colors and light are treated here similarly to the way tones are usually treated—figures and shapes, so to speak, are formed from individual light values and shades of color."

To direct the American premiere of *Die glückliche Hand*, Claire Reis hired Rouben Mamoulian of the Theatre Guild and the American Opera Company. Since leaving the Eastman School, Martha Graham's former supervisor had made his mark on Broadway with DuBose and Dorothy Heyward's *Porgy*, and, in 1929, in the early days of sound films, he directed *Applause*, starring Helen Morgan as a burlesque queen who had seen better days. Mamoulian was undaunted by the Schoenberg piece. "It's not going to beat me," he told Reis during rehearsals, "even if we have to work on it every night, all night."

For sets, costumes, and lighting, Reis turned to a "close friend ever since his Harvard days," Robert Edmond "Bobby" Jones. Proponent of the new stagecraft in American theatre integrating production values with action and mood, he was gifted with the erudite perspective to bring to life Schoenberg's brooding mise-en-scène of "jutting forms and menacing shadows." As Jones wrote in *The Dramatic Imagination*, "A good scene design should be not a picture, but an image . . . It echoes, it enhances, it animates. It is an expectancy, a foreboding, a tension."

Singing the Man would be Ivan Ivantzoff, former opera star of the Imperial Theatre of Petrograd. The artist-chorus, seventeen men and women students handpicked from the Curtis Institute of Music, was rehearsed by Stokowski's protégé, the wunderkind Sylvan Levin, twenty-six-year-old concert pianist and assistant conductor of the Philadelphia Grand Opera Company.

The Chimera would be played by the character actor Olin Howland, who had been seen as "the Soldier" in *L'Histoire du Soldat*. And cast in the roles of the Woman and the Gentleman/Stranger, fresh from their triumph in the Dance Repertory Theatre, were the professional partners, Doris Humphrey and Charles Weidman.

. . .

MARTHA GRAHAM—headlined in boldface, all capital letters—led the huge corps de ballet of *The Rite of Spring,* composed of nineteen men, featuring Gould Stevens as "the Sage" (the oldest of the elders), and twenty women, led by Anita Bay as "the Witch" (the twig-bearing matriarch). Three of the dancers, Rose Yasgour, Helen Strumlauf, and Eleanor King, came from the Humphrey-Weidman Company. At Graham's insistence, eleven of the women were from the ranks of her Dance Group: Hortense Bunsick, Irene Emery, Lily Mehlman, Louise Gotto Creston (misspelled "Preston" in the program), Lillian Ray, Kitty Reese, Mary Rivoire, Ethel Rudy, Anna Sokolow, Lillian Shapero, and Sylvia Wasserstrom.

From the first day of rehearsal to a piano reduction of the score played by Louis Horst in the cork-floored gymnasium of the Dalton School in Manhattan, there were creative differences between the hotheaded première danseuse who, "when she did move, it was with condescension," and the slender, mathematically precise ballet master giving prompts in heavily accented English and preferring to direct in French and Russian. "Miss *Grah*-ham, I will teach you your dance," Massine began, addressing "Martha, frozen to her little spot."

"She loved to sit against the wall," Bessie Schonberg recalled, "with that famous chin right down on her chest. And she sat there" at the periphery of the room and sulked for what seemed like an eternity, the small of her back wedged against the baseboard, "as if she had been petrified. And then she shot up straight and walked out and threw the door shut."

Massine escalated their "tug of war," turning his back on Graham while she danced, warning her that she must monitor her exertions; her predecessor in the role, Lydia Sokolova, had fainted after every performance. Massine threatened to replace Graham with Anita Bay ("I think the part is too difficult for you, Miss Gra'm. Perhaps you are not well"). She snapped back, "Did *Mr. Stokowski* say that?"

When Massine half murmured yes, Graham ran straight to the maestro, who, denying the assertion, interceded on her behalf, as he often did outside the studio and within. "Oh, but I was angry . . . !" Graham said. "I strode up and down and lashed my tail!"

Stokowski reassured her, "You must dance for *me.*"

A frequent visitor to the rehearsal hall, Stokowski did not hesitate to rise from his seat next to Claire Reis and her lady board members, stride to the center of the floor, and, with Massine looking on, demonstrate different movements.

At the eleventh hour, Graham protested that under no circumstances would she be forced to perform in Roerich's "eternal garment," a brocaded peasant tunic with clunky, tie-up moccasin boots on her feet, heavy wooden beads around her neck, and fake blond plaits beating against her back— "These are not costumes for dancing!" Graham, the Fire Dancer with an inner-mounting flame, would perform barefoot, in a calf-length red rehearsal dress made with her own hands, brow encircled with a diadem of fresh flowers, raven hair loosened to her waist.

Such soap-operatic machinations were the stuff of Graham's life as a dancer in extremis in her mid-thirties. Her threats during *Le Sacre* rehearsals were no different from the dramas ignited when she quit Denishawn, Eastman, and the Greenwich Village Follies. "Quitting" was never an end, but the gateway to start anew. At every juncture, finding her own way as an artist in the Nietzschean spirit, she would be the tightrope-walking risk-taker.

Martha Graham held to the continuous task of chasing or creating challenges. Her self-generated disequilibrium kept alive the drive to stay in the game. "Hellcat tantrums" and vague "sicknesses," inkwell throwing, tablecloth yanking, phone slamming and other choleric fits of pique were expulsions of psychic breath to relieve the pressure cooker in her skull.

The flow of years dulled the jagged edges of eyewitness stories and gossip about the "hissingly difficult collaboration" between Massine and Graham. The choreographer reflected in his memoirs that "[a]s rehearsals progressed . . . I found the ballet again taking shape in my mind. Martha Graham's powerful performance as the Chosen Maiden added considerable strength to the production. I found her a most subtle and responsive dancer to work with . . ."

Questioned about her notorious histrionics by Oliver Daniel, Graham put Stokowski's biographer off the trail: "I'm sorry to disappoint you on that. . . . There were certain things balletically that I changed a little bit. But my style was beginning to develop at that time, and I would do the thing the way I would do it, you see, and usually Massine was very generous and he said, 'We'll keep that.'"

In late February 1930, Graham took the time to attend a performance at the 49th Street Theatre by the Peking Opera, on their first visit to America. Mei Lanfang, the company's iconic leading actor, knowing of Graham's interest in Eastern culture, offered her complimentary tickets. She took in the sparse decor, the elaborate costuming, and the dissonant, percussive music, "watching carefully just how far the slender, graceful and perfectly-proportioned Mei raises his foot, how his toes are pointed, his knees bent, the swaying of his body, the tilt of his head, the precise tempo of his move-ment . . . executed at a well-defined rhythm and tempo."

. . .

To have a body is to be looked at.

—MAURICE MERLEAU-PONTY

The Rite of Spring, preceded by *Die glückliche Hand,* premiered in the Phila-delphia Metropolitan Opera House at Broad and Poplar Streets on April 11, 12, and 14, and at the Metropolitan Opera House on Broadway between Thirty-Ninth and Fortieth Streets in New York City on April 22–23, 1930. Three weeks before opening night, the Met's 3,625 gilded, plush red seats, with an additional 224 standing-room places, were sold out.

At the slow, quiet advent of part II of *The Rite,* Mary Watkins sought the figure of Martha Graham, "lost in the crowd of dancing maidens" and seem-ing to "stagger" with "a slight irregularity of tempo." Following Graham's angularity against Nicholas Roerich's menacing backcloth of steppes under a black and yellow sky, Watkins realized Graham's off-rhythms signaled she "already [felt] set apart" from the group. Before her solo began, she moved to downstage center, "almost onto the apron . . . while the other dancers were going tutti, all full force" in large jumps, "a kind of pitched-forward grand jeté."

Standing immobile, a staring plastique, Graham waited for the moment when, "opening up like a concertina wire and closing in again," the men

Graham with Kitty Reese and Lillian Shapero (left to right), in *Le Sacre du Printemps,* 1930. (Photograph by Goluth Studio, New York City)

and women of the chorus would reclaim her, like the dance of the celestial bodies, the holy chain of stars, the Muses hand in hand around the summit of Mount Helicon, the *choreia* ring dance of the angels. Along with the rapt spectators in the Metropolitan Opera House that night, Bessie Schonberg "couldn't take [her] eyes off" Martha Graham's heretical body, "even before she danced. She was magnetic."

Graham had held back during group rehearsals for the "Danse Sacrale." Anna Sokolow believed her teacher was conserving energy for the times when, in the morning behind closed doors, before anyone arrived in the studio, Graham made the dance her own, determined to keep her arms around the role, as well as private authority over its choreographer. Hundreds of practice leaps were preludes to the ones that truly mattered—in the performance itself, when Graham planned to reveal the definitive gesture: She would not become the maiden until the instant of enacting her.

Graham's unleashed athleticism was a shock onstage to the dancers in her group who thought they knew her best. Lily Mehlman was stunned at Graham's "attitude and power . . . her hair flying, her legs way in the air . . . We'd never seen Martha do anything like that before." When she rebounded, springing off the floor as if it were a drumhead, her splits were "fully extended things," with "flexed feet" and hands at an angle, "like little screams," Bessie Schonberg said, and her "arms and legs windmill[ed] in front of her like a prehistoric bird whose wings try to raise the body . . . then into a delirious spin, the feet almost on the points striking the ground like daggers . . . with uncontrollable centrifugal acceleration."

The audience gasped at Graham's victory over the stage, and stood and cheered when she took her bows, standing between Massine and Stokowski.

Before the crowd dispersed into the night, the maestro gave an impassioned valedictory in front of the curtain, telling the audience they were privileged to have just witnessed a "theatre of synthesis . . . [in] a new rhythm," a style of dance prefiguring a new, unique "American art form."

Martha Graham's "dance of propitiation in *The Rite of Spring* was not only a triumph of execution but of composition, a primordial paroxysm of untutored lethal rhapsody," Mary Watkins raved. H. T. Parker of the *Boston Evening Transcript* was bewitched by the "mistress of the mentality of the dance . . . Miss Graham's . . . vertiginous, multirhythmed finale, the sacrificial ecstasy that shall drain body and soul away." John Martin swept aside customary decorum. "It was a performance of the first magnitude, compelling, poignant [and] sure-footed." With *Le Sacre,* Martin avowed, Graham had attained "the pinnacle of her powers."

By the time she restaged *Rite* on her company, Martha Graham had long since stopped dancing. At eighty-three, in a dispassionate voice, she conceded that, as a woman, her hunger for artistic freedom had come at great cost. "Somehow or another one identifies oneself with a central figure," she said. "You perform a sacrifice, whatever it is, and whether it's your life or whether it's giving up the extraneous things of your life for a purpose—for the necessity—it's a sacrificial act."

14

Northwest to Southwest

There is existing in America today what many call the "Left-Wing" of the Dance—a group that has brought to the dance an added freedom as to technique, thematic material, and choreography. It symbolizes the trend of the times in its revolt from old forms and, when necessary or desirable, its free use of old forms . . . Today dance exists for itself, and ignores entertainment for a purpose.

> —Excerpt from program *Foreword,* "Martha Graham in Recital,"
> June 2, 1930, Metropolitan Theatre, Seattle, Washington

Louis Horst was offstage at the piano, dachshund Max curled at his feet next to the pedals. Fresh from her *Le Sacre* triumph, for the Seattle audience new to her, Graham offered a spectrum of solos beginning with Honegger's "Salutation," "Static in character, angular in line . . . more suited to a modern age than the fulsome sweep of the more conventional dance forms." She made social commentary with *Immigrant,* by Stolcer-Slavenski, and "Songs Behind the Lines" by Ornstein, "crying against the useless conventions of war." She showed flamboyant dexterity in "Tanagra," throwing her "glove-silk shawl . . . into space so that it went out into a right angle to her body and then, with the speed of lightning, she pulled it back before it fell so that it lay across her hand." The spare power of *Lamentation* received an ovation.

"The art [of dance] is coming into its own," Graham said after the show, "and an American style is being perfected." Everhardt Armstrong of the *Post-Intelligencer* viewed her American style through the lens of European modernism. He invoked Rodin, "of whom, it was said, [he] shivered the syntax of stone. . . . Likewise," Armstrong observed, "Martha Graham has shivered the syntax of dance" in "Tanagra." He aligned Graham's movement vocabulary with "some of the wilder flights of James Joyce."

Richard E. Hays of the *Seattle Times,* transfixed by Martha Graham, "every minute . . . she was on stage," had last seen her perform a decade prior, touring through the Pacific Northwest on the Pantages vaudeville theatre circuit in *Xochitl.* Back then, she was "a beautiful dancer . . . well-trained, graceful," but "routine." Now, however, Hays noticed, "somewhere in the last ten years, [of] hard, serious, intelligent study," Martha Graham had sought and found within herself "the courage to be different," evolving into "a disciple of modernism—ultra-modernism, if you please . . . bearing a significant message."

During that Seattle autumn of 1920, Graham also caught the attention of an admirer who had known her since Denishawn: Nellie Centennial Cornish (the middle name commemorated her 1876 birth). Raised in Spokane, descendant of three generations of pioneers, Nellie was blessed with a cultured father, a banker in love with books and writing. She worked as a governess, pursued piano, and, after studies in the Montessori method and the newly established field of music education, in 1914 she opened her school dedicated to integration of all the arts.

Seven years later, bursting with more than a thousand students, the Cornish School moved into a Spanish-baroque building on East Roy Street in downtown Seattle, where budding artists of all ages took workshops in music, drama, voice, and painting. Next to the dance studio, "there were dressing rooms, staffed with matrons, who handed students beautiful white towels for use after showering." Known to all as Miss Aunt Nellie, the matronly director was a benevolent lady of quick wit and boundless energy, a "little whirlwind." The upstairs apartment she shared with an adopted Russian daughter, Elena Miranova, was a home away from home for lonely youngsters, the welcoming scene of coffee-and-cookies receptions where the school community gathered to chat with visiting artists and teachers.

On a recruiting trip to New York City, Cornish visited the Neighborhood Playhouse, sat in on Graham's and Horst's lessons in "historical, folk and interpretive dance," and felt "the fresh wind blowing" through their classes. At the end of the fall 1928 term at Cornish, she "called the dance students into her office one by one to tell each of them personally that she had decided to abolish classical ballet and replace it with modern dance."

Early in the spring 1929 term, stopping at Cornish on the way from New

Nellie Cornish (center) with school faculty, ca. early 1930s.

York to Los Angeles to set up his company and school, Michio Ito conducted a four-week course. Dance enrollments continued to grow, and Cornish was able to interest Martha Graham and Louis Horst in joining the school . . . to teach "the dance of the future."

.   .   .

The poised, diminutive, perfectly groomed woman stepped into the Cornish dance studio, accompanied by a portly, white-haired man, who took a seat at the Steinway. "I want you to call me *Martha*," she said in a low voice to the group of girls standing in a half circle, "and this is Mr. Horst, my musical director; you may call him *Louie*." Her head tilted imperiously, intimations of tension humming beneath her cool exterior, she continued, slowly, enunciative: "We have a lot of work to do together this summer. There must be total, concentrated focus. I will accept nothing less than clarity and precision. No improvisation. We have no time for trivialities. No dreaming. No sentimentality; no 'tip-toe through the raindrops.' No 'marking.' And no resting; you may rest *after* class."

Graham paused. The students waited in silence. Her lips trembled in what could have been a smile. "I have something very exciting to share with you," she said. "I have just come from dancing the Chosen One, l'Élue, in Léonide Massine's *Le Sacre du Printemps* at the Metropolitan Opera House in New York. Before the finale of the ballet, I had to stand absolutely still, for a very long time. And I discovered something—how to command the stage and make the audience long for me to move. I realized that I could 'steal the audience' away from the other dancers. In the coming weeks, I am going to teach you how to do that; but, in order to succeed, you will need to forget everything you have learned before."

To begin, she told the girls to take off their ballet shoes and sit on the floor in the open fourth position, "not only for the purpose of loosening up the muscles around the hip hinge, but also to develop a centered spine." To feel the vertebrae stacked one atop the other in alignment, Graham said to imagine "a flood-light focused on the spinal column." One behind the other, "rocking slightly on [their] sitting-bones," each dancer observed her partner's back, as Graham told them to "press the vertebra that need to be straightened." They worked on rising straight up and lowering themselves into the floor at her command—"You have to rebound! Push down to come up, it's like a spring!"—striving for fluid motion, "moving through the hips first and then the torso" without the aid of the hands, balanced like "a scale of justice" with equal weight on both sides of the center line; then, hands on waists, elbows out, twisting the torso right and left.

Standing, Graham told the girls to place their feet three inches apart in parallel, flat against the floorboards "like a Grecian frieze . . . You are courageous pioneer women in 'the land of the free,'" Graham exhorted them. "This is your earth. Close your eyes, feel the ground, the pebbles, the rocks. Imagine your toe-nails turned into talons, penetrating, retracting . . . Open your eyes, cup your hands to either side of your face, like the blinders on the carriage-horses in New York City; now . . . peer down the tracks as the 'choo-choo train' fades into the distance over mountains, rivers, and prairies."

They moved their legs farther apart, to take a position. "Live within the pose," Graham said, "feel yourselves rising, out of the hips, like smoke . . . Feel the shoulders, balancing like a crossbar on the spine, moving in opposition to the crossbar in your hips, like skyscrapers swaying in the wind." Heads balanced on the top vertebrae—Graham called it "the axis"—her pupils "tried to find [their] center, lose it, then recover it."

She wanted them "to value and enjoy the smallest changes as they occur[red]" in their bodies during pliés and battements, to be alert and thoughtful, observe subtleties of breathing, tremors in bones and muscles and between joints when they drew in breath and exhaled, sensing "as if with cat's whiskers" the skin of the dancers on either side.

When they walked, it must be "with quality," the weight of the body shifting on each step, "with presence . . . pushing off, through deep water, and then shallow . . . Press the toes and the ball and the arch of the foot down, as if into wet sand," Graham said.

She pointed below the navel. "This is your center of vitality," from which "to push your way. And now—imagine how it would feel to bring the weight forward of the four people behind you: Lift your chest and surge, a figure-head at the prow, cutting through the waves," she said.

"Prime the pump," Graham told her students.

"Spit!" she commanded. "You are fishwives at the marketplace . . . Cry out in unison—*No!*" she said, and they yelled at the top of their lungs. "I want you to sob . . . show me those great Greek emotions . . . Now *hiss* . . . like a cat, like a snake . . . Now—tickle your partner and laugh, like country folk in a tavern. I want you to explode, reel with laughter, until you are rolling on the floor and can't stand up . . ." Every cleansing breath forcibly expelled—especially, she told them, by laughing through their teeth—drove the women toward the nirvana of the contraction.

Finally: They were not onstage to please the audience. "Smiling is absolutely out. . . . You are proud, aloof, mask-like. . . . Don't just hand them everything on a platter. Don't give it away. Give them little leads. Entice them!" Graham said.

. . .

What a pitiful sorrow it would be to hurl this primordial city down to Hades, the slave and quarry of the spear in the crumbling ash, destroyed and losing its honor at the hands of Achaean men and through the will of the gods, with its women overcome and taken into slavery—*oh! oh!*—young and old women alike, pulled by the locks of their hair, as if they were horses held by the mane, their veils all ripped and torn. The city, emptied, wails in many different voices of lament for its lost population.

—AESCHYLUS, *Seven Against Thebes*

The Swiss director Jean Mercier arrived in Seattle in the summer of 1930. Colleague of Jacques Copeau and Adolphe Appia at the Théâtre du Vieux-

Colombier in Paris, he was at the Cornish School on a three-year work visa to head the drama department, and subsequently would take up residence at the University of Michigan in Ann Arbor. Mercier's inaugural project, running for three nights beginning July 29, was to be a production by the Cornish Players of *Seven Against Thebes* by Aeschylus.

Hailing from Eleusis, origin of the Mysteries, site of "the wisdom-bringing waters of the depths, the murmuring springs and fountains," and a veteran of the Battle of Marathon, Aeschylus was the first and most experimental of the three Athenian tragic poets. *Seven Against Thebes*, presented at the Great Dionysia in 467 BC, was the final work of a trilogy based upon the story of Oedipus; the first two dramas, *Laios* and *Oedipus*, are lost. In the course of the play, the inevitable curse of Oedipus, son of Laios and Jocasta, is played out against his incest-bred brother-sons, doomed to kill each other. The elder, Polynices ("full of strife"), exiled to Argos from Thebes, has returned with an army "led by seven attacking champions" to fight his usurping brother, Eteocles ("justly famed" and "truly bewept"), defender of his kingship of the motherland. The walled city is saved from violation and destruction. However, in hand-to-hand combat at the Gate of Apollo, Eteocles kills and is killed by Polynices, thus "Each, by murdering his brother, sheds his father's blood."

Miss Aunt Nellie's hope in hiring Jean Mercier was that "he and Martha Graham, by combined effort," would bring "experimental forces" into this dramatic arena of antiquity. The headstrong Mercier "was not inclined to cooperate," and Cornish had to step into the fray with a backup plan. She noted that some editions of *Thebes* included "a semi-chorus of mourning women [and] attendants" performing as a subset of the full chorus. Cornish offered Graham the opportunity to invent "entr'acte/Dance Interludes" for this group. From among her students, Graham selected Nelle Fisher, Bethene Miller, Grace Cornell, Dorothy Bird, and Bonnie Bird.

The latter three of Martha Graham's five chosen ones went on to dance with her professionally in New York. Chicago-born Grace Cornell appeared in the February 1931 premieres of *Primitive Mysteries* and *Bacchanale* before sailing to Berlin to train with Rudolf von Laban. Returning to New York the following year, Cornell joined José Limón in a "Spring Festival" of duets at the Roxy Theatre.

Bonnie Bird, originally from Portland, Oregon, grew up on a ranch outside Seattle, and began Cornish classes in her freshman year. Granted a scholarship to the Neighborhood Playhouse School, she would follow

Graham eastward. Bonnie worked as one of Graham's seamstresses; before performances, it was her responsibility to display the costumes in progress under the theatre spotlight for Graham to preview how they would look in situ. Bonnie also substituted for Gertrude Shurr as a studio and teaching assistant. On November 19, 1933, at the Guild Theatre, Bonnie made her debut as a Dance Group member in *Primitive Mysteries*.

Dorothy Bird, from Vancouver Island, although no relation to Bonnie, was joined to her "like a Siamese twin" as a friend and roommate. Her ambition to be a dancer began outside the stage door after a concert in Victoria when Anna Pavlova placed her hand on Dorothy's shoulder and kissed her. At eighteen, she left her native Canada for the Cornish School "down in the U.S.A." One of Graham's confidantes, Dorothy treasured their talks walking to class in the mornings from her teacher's apartment, when Graham regaled

Dorothy Bird in a restaging of *Heretic,* ca. mid-1930s.
(Photograph by Paul Hansen)

her with fond tales of her New York dancers. Dorothy made the journey to join the group, and served as a class demonstrator. After six years, "it dawned on [Dorothy] that there was a big world outside of Martha's studio" and she quit for the Great White Way, incurring her mentor's bitter wrath. In later years, "the wayward child" returned to the embrace of "her second mother" and taught the Graham technique.

. . .

In addition to the cast of characters of *Thebes*—the two warring brothers; their sisters, Ismene and Antigone; and two messengers—were thirteen actors comprising the chorus in Mercier's production (twelve chorus members and the choragus), distinguished from Martha Graham's five students, simply called the dancers. Aeschylus rehearsed and directed his choruses, wrote the music for their songs, and invented many dance steps. For *Thebes,* he was said to have hired the original pantomime actor in Western theatre, Telestes (or Telesis). According to first-century philosopher Aristocles of Messene, Telestes "depicted events with his hands in a most skillful manner . . . detach[ing] himself from the chorus to interpret, through rhythmic steps and gestures, the action that the chorus sang or recited."

Costumes were a priority, as in all Graham productions. Bonnie Bird helped dye and construct the garments out of multicolored cheesecloth, hand-stitched, held together with safety pins, and wound around the dancers' bodies. Makeup for the masklike "face-front face" was white greasepaint foundation smeared over necks, cheeks, and brows, black lines applied above and below eyes, liquified candle wax brushed into eyelashes, and "bold, gash-like" red lipstick slashed on mouths.

At the start of the show, Dorothy was "roughly pushed" into line at the back of the theatre, "flattened against the side wall" awaiting the cue for the "ominous" processional to begin, a walk down the raked side aisle of the 250-seat space. "You should resemble the figure of Mercury," Graham told them, mimicking the image painted on a Greek vase, "and you must flatten and twist to retain the two-dimensional quality."

Down in front, the five dancers mounted a short flight of steps to the stage and, hands locked together, formed a "Circle of Pain" leading into a "Dance of Grief." Shared voices lamented "the destruction of their city and the capture and rape of its women . . . paeans of death"—*iakkhe*—to the implacable heavens. They leaned in and downward, then, jumping with feet together, "rose up high as if in protest," fists aloft, arms swinging in whip-lashes, opened out like eagles' wings.

The Thebans withstood the invasion, and it was the women's lot to express anxiety for misfortunes that might transpire and the fear that if the gods willed, their voices could be silenced. Before Polynices and Eteocles fight to the death, the attendant women try to make peace between the broth-ers. Resisting Eteocles's accusations that their complaints are weakening his martial resolve, the will of the Theban women remains strong: They declaim grieving poems and sing piercing songs.

Martha Graham's students danced "in a most uneven, unsettled rhythm . . . in connection with the terror which their words express," writes H. D. F. Kitto in his scansion of the off-beat parados of *Seven Against Thebes,* "picturing . . . a swirling, tumultuous movement designed by Aeschylus to make visible the idea of panic."

. . . .   .

At the conclusion of the Cornish residency, Graham took the train south to Santa Barbara for a restorative sojourn with her mother. After thirteen years as a widow, Jennie Graham had married Homer N. Duffy, an executive in the Bekins Moving & Storage Company. Following nostalgic early-morning chats with nanny Lizzie Prendergast, Graham languished for "breathless . . . golden days" on the back porch shaded by eucalyptus trees, "awake and asleep at the same time," savoring Edith Hamilton's *The Greek Way,* a gift from painter Mark Tobey, with whom she had had a brief affair at Cornish. On "[m]agical nights," she strolled through familiar neighborhoods, peer-ing into candlelit parlors, and revisited the Old Mission of the Sisters of St. Clare.

The composer Henry Cowell came from the Bay Area to see her. A native of rural Menlo Park, the gifted teenager had studied piano, violin, and the-ory with Charles Seeger, chair of the music department at UC Berkeley. Graham had met Cowell in the late 1920s in New York City, where he helped found the Pan-American Association of Composers, edited and published the "ultramodern" *New Music Quarterly,* and created a multicultural course, "Music of the World's Peoples," at the New School for Social Research. In February 1928, Louis Horst had played the earliest version of Cowell's piano composition *Steel and Stone* for Charles Weidman's dance ensemble; two

Henry Cowell playing tone-clusters, ca. 1924–1926.

months following, Cowell was at the keyboard for his outrageous "Banshee" to Doris Humphrey's wild gesticulations.

Now it was Graham's turn. Cowell believed her to be the most inventive native dancer of his—or any—American era, and that they were destined to collaborate. He envisioned a thirteen-minute tone poem scored for full orchestra. To emphasize the primacy of percussive sounds for dance, Cowell embellished the score with gongs, tam-tam, cymbals, castanets, wood blocks, bells, and piano strings struck with a padded gong-stick. *Synchrony of Dance—Music—Light* commenced with a bright trumpet solo showcasing the minor theme. The trumpet continued behind string-driven pulses expanding outward through five seamless phases (allegretto, allegro molto, molto lento, moderate, larghetto). Piccolo, percussion, and cymbal-driven cacophonies became punchy, swirling into a gathering storm. The pastoral decrescendo was interlaced with silences Graham likened to ripples in a pool, before rising to a thunderous climax she called a "triumphant march of peace."

Their goal in *Synchrony* was to remedy a defect in the relationship between music and the dance choreographed to match it, an imbalance Louis Horst had bemoaned for years. When the spectator focused upon interpreting the dance, his attention to "musical values" waned; conversely, when attentions shifted to what the music was doing, understanding of the dance diminished. In response, Cowell sought an "elastic," flexible, "contrapuntal relation between the high points of interest" such that "neither one of the arts relied on the other, and neither is servant of the other" . . . "Just as in a three-part polyphonic musical work one will find very often one of the three parts stationary while the other two move in contrary motion," Cowell and Graham cowrote in an (unpublished) program note, "one finds in 'Synchrony' that, if the music is at its climax the dance is quiescent and vice-versa."

Cowell completed Synchrony on September 22, 1930, and began to copy parts; but the title did not live up to its name, and Graham's initial enthusiasm waned. The "murky timbre" experiment was never performed as a dance, only in a concert version. There were no hard feelings; Cowell went on to write the music for Graham's Heroic Dance the following year; Four Casual Developments in 1934; and Sarabande, Deep Song, and Immediate Tragedy in 1937.

Norman Lloyd, who also composed for Graham, paid tribute to Cowell as a "sound-companion" engaged in a forty-year "romance" with dancers. "I suspect that the American dancer felt that Cowell was one of them, too," Lloyd said. "He, too, was an explorer of new resources . . . His music reverberated, suspended itself, cut capers, was thoughtful—and never overcame the dancer with pretentious complexity."

.   .   .

We have lived upon this land from days beyond history's records, far past any living memory, deep into the time of legend. The story of my people and the story of this place are one single story.

—TAOS PUEBLO MAN

From Santa Barbara, Graham traveled to Albuquerque, where she met Louis Horst to begin their trek into the land of the Tiwa, Keresan, and Northern Tewa Pueblos. They would drive north and east along the Rio Grande River through Isleta ("Little Island"), San Felipe, Santo Domingo, Santa Fe, and onward to Taos and the foothills of the rose-hued Sangre de Cristo Mountains. Graham's interest in native cultures had begun with childhood wanderings in the vestiges of Indian trails among the Allegheny County and Western Appalachian hills, and continued in her youth close to the California deserts and woodlands. During Denishawn tours, she shared in Horst's artifact-sleuthing and museum-going, and heard Ted Shawn reverently invoke the "full-blooded masculine vigor" of American [North as well as Central] Indian dances populated with hunters and warriors. "Indian dance art," Shawn believed, was the surest foundation for "the future of a serious national dance."

In 1924, Shawn had witnessed the daylong Isleta Pueblo Winter Solstice Dance, sixty performers amid "white adobe houses around an open square, blue New Mexico sky, bluer than the Mediterranean at its best." That spring *Xochitl* collaborator Homer Grunn sent Shawn a musical setting adapting the San Ildefonso Pueblo Eagle Dance, "for two dancers, feathered wings, body Indigo blue, legs yellow, one white one pink head dress [*sic*] with bill of the eagle in front." Mixing Mexican and Pueblo themes, Shawn dreamed of a (never-realized) scenario for a future master work devoted to "the Indians of the far Northwest, the Esquimaux of Vancouver Island."

Martha Graham came to the spiritual places of New Mexico for a different kind of fieldwork. She needed to breathe the rarified mountain air, clean emptiness punctuated by the clink of distant mule bells, lose her pallor, and feel the rejuvenating sun-heat on her upturned face, pace on unpaved clay letting her enlivened nerve endings absorb rhythms and rituals to catalyze her choreography, and embrace and carry earthborn beats and pulses back east, for the dearly missed women in her company.

·   ·   ·

After the primitivisms of *Le Sacre* and *Seven Against Thebes,* Graham arrived in the Southwest to stand among the pueblos as a frame for the religious duty of ceremonial dance. In her student days in Los Angeles, Martha Graham read Havelock Ellis's *The Dance of Life,* and never forgot that "[d]ancing and building are the two primary and essential arts. The art of dancing stands at the source of all the arts that express themselves first in the human person," Havelock Ellis had written, and "the art of building, or architecture, is the beginning of all the arts that lie outside the person; and in the end they unite." Rudolf von Laban wrote in *Choreutics* that "[m]ovement is, so to speak, living architecture . . . living in the sense of changing emplacements as well as changing cohesion. This architecture is created by human movements."

Pueblo architecture was born out of the spirit of the Corn Mother emerging from belowground realms "where men and animals lived together and spoke the same language," into harmony with the earthly world. The brown-gray adobe and wood buildings are organized according to the four cardinal points of the compass; the fifth and sixth directions are sky and earth. Unlike

Greek architecture, set apart from the surrounding landscape, the pueblo "conform[s] to the land in which it is built." The communal plaza—the human place—is oriented, in turn, toward the surrounding mountains—the natural place. The pueblo plaza, the sacred center, "connot[es] the mystery of spirit . . . only when [the Pueblo begin to] dance is the plaza transformed into a place of worship."

One of the warnings outsiders are given when prohibited from taking photographs is that they are not there to watch something called a performance. A dance, for the Pueblo, is not a show or an art form—it is a prayer, integral to the ebb and flow of daily life. "Tribal communities do not use the clock to determine when it is 'time' to conduct activities," the Pueblo say. "Acts of nature, as well as the sequence of events that must take place . . . determine start and finish times for ceremonies."

Thanking the rising sun for another day, ceremonial participants meet in the kiva, a cloistered, secluded circular chamber, for a rehearsal round of prayer and dance, and final adjustments to traditional regalia and facial adornment: on the women, black or white heavy cotton or woolen sleeveless dresses called mantas, red circles on their cheeks, and hands whitened; for the men, white kilts with strings of bells or shells and knee-high moccasins. Along with the male singers, the dancers move to the Plaza in a slow, "musically-accented walk . . . step[ping] down and then bounc[ing] up with the rhythm of the weight" to the "clatter of deer-hoof rattles" and the solemn beat of a double-headed cowhide barrel drum.

"I observed that the dance-step of the Pueblo Indians consisted in a *calcare terram*," C. G. Jung wrote after his transformative Taos visit, "a persistent, pounding of the earth with the heels. . . . The foot and treading movement are invested with that of re-entry into the womb" when Mother Earth is trampled, and planted with seed. To show how high the fruits of their labor will grow, the dancers rise with joy. Arms held at right angles to the body, fragrant evergreen branches gathered in wrist-cuffs, palms lifted and turned skyward welcoming rain, they arrange in parallel lines and circulate, feet "cleaving to earth softly, and softly lifting away" around the periphery of the plaza, while singers and musicians remain in the middle. When the song cycle is complete, the group, in silence save for tinkling knee-bells, returns to the kiva for a brief rest, then reemerges, to carry on until dusk.

At the dancing ground, there is no distinction between reverent dancers and rapt observers. All present are immersed in prayer, to "seek, find, regain and renew life"; all are members of the community alongside the ghosts of *okhua,* vigilant spirits of departed ancestors.

. . .

At mid-September, via a dirt road seventy windswept miles from Santa Fe, "a pale, uneven parched world, where a motor-car lurches and churns in sand," Graham and Horst reached Taos, most isolated of the eastern pueblos, a plateau village of seven hundred people, seven thousand feet above sea level. As life had ever been by the banks of the Rio Grande, at Taos the spiritualism of the native people was a combination of faiths. Across the plaza from the Catholic mission of San Geronimo, the two visitors saw the northside kivas "Knife," "Day," and "Big Earring."

A century earlier, in rural Hispano New Mexico, Christian practices had been different. The Penitent Brothers, Los Hermanos Penitentes, formally known as La Cofradía de Nuestro Padre Jesús Nazareno (the Brotherhood of Our Father Jesus the Nazarene), was a lay society founded in grassroots response to the 1821 crisis precipitated when the regional Mexican government expelled all Franciscan, Dominican, and Jesuit missionaries. Bereft of

Taos Pueblo with kiva in foreground, n.d.

access to the sacraments and religious leaders who had ministered to colonists and Indians alike, the Penitentes emerged, in service to the sick and the poor. They presided over burials, brought in the harvest, and "kept watch over village morals."

The Penitentes originated in three places in the upper Rio Grande region of New Mexico, "throughout the tumultuous nineteenth century"—Santa Cruz de la Cañada, twenty-five miles northwest of Santa Fe; Nuestra Señora de Dolores del Alto, at Abiquiu, twenty-five miles farther north; and Nuestra Señora de Guadalupe in Taos. In the early 1880s, condemned as heretics by the Catholic establishment and forced into seclusion, the Penitentes were excommunicated.

By the time of Graham and Horst's arrival, the Taos Penitentes were reborn as "the largest major stronghold . . . the single overarching authority for the Brotherhood." During Holy Week, in addition to springtime pastoral duties—gathering the people together on saints' days for hymns and songs of worship (alabados), sharing food, teaching the catechism, and praying the rosary—the Penitentes bared the dark side of their name. They lived the Passion of Christ, through fasting, suffering, and ritual mortification. Initiates were stripped to the waist, crosses incised into their backs with flints. Children carrying figures of the Holy Virgin led processionals imitating the Way of the Cross on stony, winding roads through villages and into hilly scrubland, accompanied by the sorrowful, "unearthly whistle of the *pitero*," the native flute player.

To murmurous chants, Hermanos bore splintery pinewood crosses upon their naked, bloodied backs and marched to mock crucifixions, dragged logs tied to their ankles, and fell to their knees every fifty feet to pray; others, heads bowed beneath black hoods, lashed themselves across rounded shoulders with braided ropes of yucca and cactus scourges. At the end of the worshippers' line, dragged by a penitent in bloodstained white pants, came the *carreta del muerto*, the death wagon.

For Good Friday evening, everyone returned to the morada. The meeting house "at the symbolic heart" of the Penitente community was a single-story stone and adobe structure with a solitary window and a large cross leaning outside. Inside the shadowy dirt floor sanctuary, pew-like benches abutted whitewashed walls decorated with wood carvings and paintings on animal skin, and an "altar bright with *Chromas* of the Patron Saints . . . [displayed] the holy family, and the Virgin of Guadalupe."

After midnight, the last candle snuffed in the cramped room, celebrants performed the ritual of *Las Tinieblas*, "rattling chains, clashing cymbals, [with] muffled blows, shrieks and chants" and hymns recounting Christ's final moments on the cross.

During their summer 1930 excursion in and around the pueblos, Martha Graham and Louis Horst did not visit the Penitentes. They read immersively about the harsh Lenten synthesis of Los Hermanos and Indian cultures in ethnographic works by denizens of the region, Mary Hunter Austin, Alice Corbin Henderson, and Mabel Dodge Luhan. In the coming decade, Martha Graham pursued the hybrid mysteries of the Southwest in sojourns and conversations with this trio of "windblown women." In August 1940, inhabiting the "Virgin-Magdalen-Mother" role in *El Penitente,* Graham cautioned that while her work "reflects many of the sect practices in both Old and New Mexico today . . . *El Penitente* bears no factual resemblance to the sects."

"I have never taken literally from Indian cultures. . . . It is much more fundamental than that," she insisted. "The Indians taught me the absolute sacredness of the land, the use of the body as reiteration of the sound of the earth."

15

Know the Land

So the answer to the problem of the American dance on the part of the individualists who point the way is, "Know the land"—its exciting strange contrasts of barrenness and futility—its great sweep of distances—its monstrous architecture—and the divine machinery of its invention.

—MARTHA GRAHAM, "Seeking an American Art of the Dance"

In October 1930, Brentano's Company of New York published *Revolt in the Arts: A Survey of the Creation, Distribution and Appreciation of Art in America*. The art deco jacket of the anthology displayed, in black and red sans serif type, the marquee contributors, "nationally known workers in every field of art" marshalling their collective wisdom to explore "the inextricable relations of art and life" in the modern era.

Alongside the essays of producer David Belasco, columnist Heywood Broun, poet Hart Crane, composers George Gershwin and Oscar Hammerstein, stage designer Robert Edmond Jones, actresses Lillian Gish and Eva Le Gallienne, actor Alfred Lunt, artist John Sloan, architect Frank Lloyd Wright, and twenty-five other luminaries—including Isadora Duncan's older sister, Elizabeth, from her Schloss Klessheim school near Salzburg—stood the manifesto "Seeking an American Art of the Dance," by Martha Graham.

Graham had been chosen by the volume's editor, Oliver Martin Sayler. Born in Huntington, Indiana, in 1887, a graduate of Oberlin College, Sayler began his journalistic career as drama critic for the Indianapolis *Evening News*. He visited Moscow in the treacherous winter of 1917 to begin research on *The Russian Theatre under the Revolution*. "If there is in our country a critic as fitted as Mr. Sayler to discuss this art, I know him not," wrote Norman Hapgood. "The book is worthy to present to our people the most energetic and intense stage that, in over a century, mankind has anywhere produced."

In the pages of *The North American Review, Theatre Arts Monthly,* and other magazines, Sayler was outspoken on the avant-garde importance of Russian theatre; as press agent for producers Morris Gest and F. Ray Comstock, he helped bring Konstantin Stanislavsky and the Moscow Art Theatre to New York City for eight weeks in the winter of 1922–1923. Shifting his advocacy closer to home, Sayler praised the Provincetown Players, incubator for "the fierce white light" of Eugene O'Neill, and the large-spirited Lewisohn sisters. Sayler hoped their Neighborhood Playhouse School would become "a laboratory built securely on the ground floor of an ultimate National Theatre."

With *Revolt in the Arts,* Sayler extended his "prodigious erudition" beyond drama, taking on "all the contents of the [arts] storehouse, from the talkies to the skyscrapers." John Martin acknowledged in the *Times* that, while the author "knows the theatre from a practical as well as a theoretical viewpoint, and can be listened to with respect," he now "does the dance the unusual honor of including it without apology among the other arts and on equal terms."

It was the reprise of a theme Martin had sounded six months prior, in "The Modern Dance in America," his essay in the premiere issue of advertising art director Vaughn Flannery and Philadelphia architect George Howe's *USA: A Quarterly Magazine of the American Scene* ("frankly a magazine of opinion," Flannery and Howe wrote. "Its contents often are controversial and, we hope, stimulating"). Martin concluded the piece asserting "there is now a concerted movement toward a dance art that is valid as an expression of American life and thought . . . developing along lines that are not paralleled anywhere else in the world . . . proving to be at best an objectification of the simple, direct, outspoken and vigorous honesty which underlies our habit of life. . . . Something exists in the flesh today, which yesterday was only a dream." In the next issue of *USA,* Summer 1930, under the headline "Rhythmic Heresy—Old and New," were two stunning Soichi Sunami photographs of Martha Graham: fists against cheekbones, mid-stride, in "Strike," and kneeling in supplication before the Dance Group in *Heretic.*

Sayler set the stage for Graham by evaluating the impact of her two predecessors, Isadora Duncan and Ted Shawn. "America [is] dancing, but not as Isadora envisioned!" Sayler wrote. "So much smoke, but so little fire!" We did not possess a vital national theatre, nor did we enjoy a unified American ballet. Instead, he continued, the current culture was faced "with a score of isolated concert dancers and their pupils." To rectify the decentered state of American dance, Sayler called for a latter-day "Maecenas" to step forward, following the example of the wealthy Roman who supported Horace and Virgil, a modern philanthropist who would dedicate his or her patronage to "contemporary Terpsichore."

Sayler reminded the reader that "Ted Shawn [had] beckoned us down a path toward which it would appear we were temporarily predisposed, when he" attested in *The American Ballet* (1926) that "[w]e need never borrow material from any nation, for we are full to abundance with undeveloped ideas and themes."

. . .

Martha Graham's affection for language is brought to bear in the verbal choreography of her first published essay, "Seeking an American Art of the Dance," filled with insights into her journey as an artist to 1930, and offering guidance toward where she means to travel next. Beginning with the title word, "Seeking," she leaps ahead sixteen years to her dense, sexual *Dark Meadow*; Empedocles's pre-Socratic "dark meadow" of Ate, through which flows the River Lethe, where the soul fell from the region of light. In *Dark Meadow,* Graham, portraying the "One Who Seeks," moves through that daunting place according to her reading of the Gospel of Matthew, 7:8: "For everyone who asks receives; the one who seeks finds; and to the one who knocks, the door will be opened."

In "Seeking an American Art of the Dance," Graham likens herself to a monecious flower, containing the generative force essential to "cradling an art" as well as an "urge" that is "masculine." The contraction exposes her body to the whole world as material for her work; and the ensuing expressive release births a thing of originality and beauty, as, "when a painting is finished," said John Dewey, in one of his 1931 William James Lectures at Harvard, and "it is like a newborn child the artist himself must have time for understanding. . . ."

Another big theme for Graham is that American dance, "gradually assuming a form" to achieve legitimacy, must overcome "the shining glory of old cultures . . . transplanted" to our shores. Graham enumerates the Spanish, Oriental, and German cultures, as well as the Russian ballet of Diaghilev.

She had performed these traditions at Denishawn, Eastman, and Greenwich Village Follies. However, looking forward, she says, we must move beyond the "imperialism . . . and weakling exoticism" of other nationalities, and shed Isadora Duncan's misplaced expression of indebtedness, "[after] coming to Europe," to her "three great Masters . . . precursors of the Dance in our century—Beethoven, Nietzsche and Wagner." The time has come, in Martha Graham's opinion, to put forth an art made "*in* this country and *of* this country."

"To arrive at the starting point for . . . the American gesture," Graham continues, "I avoid using the term American 'ballet.' " To ensure the future of American dance, there needs to be a stylistic turn away from the "crystalline cold technique" of balletic "decadence" toward an embrace of "what is for us the Primitive [*sic*]," unearthed in the "psyche" of "the intense individualist," the "visionary" girded for the perilous journey through her inner landscape.

Graham cites just such a group of artists who came together in 1929–1930, the Dance Repertory Theatre. Commending the collective spirit, Graham anticipates the fragmentation of "strongly conflicting types, interesting and vital in their dissimilarity." Distinguishing between "the group of Doris Humphrey and in another sense my own," Graham nevertheless confers credit upon the Dance Repertory Theatre for elevating the profile of the concert dance and stimulating "the public into protest and curiosity."

Toward the end, completing the circle, Graham returns, as Louis Horst always did, "to form, which is at the heart" of dance. She enumerates the qualities for which her choreography has become known: "economy of gesture, an intensity and integrity of mood, a simplified external means, and above all a concentration on 'the stuff' of the dance, which is—movement divinely significant." She identifies the "two primitive sources" providing inspiration to the American dance form, "the Indian and the Negro," the former through "ritualistic tribal drama" and the latter through "rhythms of disintegration."

Inner and outer "spirit of place" pervades Martha Graham's "Seeking an American Art of the Dance." There is a Romantic tenor to her parting appeal—addressed as much to herself as others—that "the problem of . . . the great mass drama that is American dance" will only be resolved when dancers come to know the land in two ways: within the somatic borders of their creative imaginations, and imprinting weighted footsteps upon indigenous soil.

. . .

"Form!" was Louis Horst's familiar hue and cry. . . . [He] demanded form and content in a work, the ingredients to be found in good painting, sculpture, music, literature, drama, poetry.

—ERNESTINE STODELLE

After the Southwestern journey, returning to Manhattan in late September 1930, Martha Graham and Louis Horst settled down, she to a brownstone at 46 East Ninth Street between Broadway and University Place, and he to an apartment graced with a grand piano at 153 West Fifty-Seventh Street. The pair resumed work at the Neighborhood Playhouse School. She taught movement for dancers and actors, while, across the hall, he introduced a new class, Modern Dance Forms, the sequel to Pre-Classic Dance Forms. Horst described this more adventurous course as "lessons based on his own analysis of the idioms, isms [sic] and sources of modern expression in all the arts."

For three decades at the playhouse, as well as at the Perry-Mansfield school, Sarah Lawrence, Barnard, Mills College, Connecticut College, Bennington, and Juilliard, Horst revised and expanded the curriculum for Modern and Pre-Classic Dance Forms and published serialized essays drawn from his course exercises in *Dance Magazine,* and *Dance Observer,* the journal he

Horst and Graham sharing a happy moment with the camp dog,
Socrates, and unidentified cat, at Perry-Mansfield Women's Camp,
Steamboat Springs, Colorado, ca. early 1930s.

founded. In 1961, critic and dancer-choreographer Marian Van Tuyl prevailed upon Horst, "the pianistic saint of dance," three years before his death, to collaborate with Carroll Russell and collate these syllabi into a proper book, and, through her Impulse Publications in San Francisco, Van Tuyl finally brought out *Modern Dance Forms in Relation to the Other Modern Arts.*

Since the seminal "Musician Comments" essay for *Denishawn Magazine* and his mid-1920s Vienna summer, Horst had advocated that the dance must stand on its own within the modern movement. His erudite narrative for the 1930 Neighborhood Playhouse course was the armature upon which the 1961 book would be sculpted.

The Modern Dance Forms course was in three sections: "Understanding by Contrast"; "Backgrounds of Modern Art"; and "Immediacies of Modern Art" [changed to "Modern Life" in the published book]. "Contrast" is about the conflict common to all dramatic expression, with focus upon the three temporal arts, poetry, music, and dance. Modern poetry, in proximity to dance, Horst writes, employs vers libre and enjambment; modern music is characterized by rhythmic restlessness and unresolved dissonance; and modern dance reveals asymmetry in space. *Danse de la Brouette (La Femme et le Danseur),* by Erik Satie, and several *Dissonanzen* studies by the German organist Lothar Windsperger serve as prompts for the student to devise studies for modern space.

The next section, "Backgrounds of Modern Art," reasserts another theme of eternal importance to Horst and Graham. He repeats her conviction that "[w]e can never throw off the past. We do things in a new way." He quotes Sheldon Cheney—*A Primer of Modern Art* (1924), a clear resource for *Modern Dance Forms*—that "[t]he surest way to understand modern art is to know the period preceding your own and compare."

"Backgrounds" is subdivided into roughly historic categories. "Earth primitive" challenges the student, in Graham's familiar command, to "[w]alk—as if for the first time" to the "lean and taut . . . mysteries" and music of Béla Bartók's *Bagatelle,* and Zoltán Kodály's op. 11, no. 3 (accompanying Paul Verlaine's poem, "Il pleure dans mon coeur"). "Air primitive," the art of "uncanny things . . . omens, apparitions and enchantments," presents *Cants Màgics* and *Charmes,* by the Catalan Federico Mompou, both danced by Graham. "Archaic" art, "stark, planal and powerful," draws from two Graham/Satie pieces, *Gymnopédie* and *Trois Gnossiennes.* "Religious medieval," referencing art that is "attenuated or twisted out of natural postures to the point of torture" and ecstatic penitence, points to the compositions of the Belgian Paul de Maleingreau, including *Introits, Salve Sancta Parens,* and *St. Thomas, Martyr.* And "secular medieval" depicts daily life outside the church, scenes of "grotesque humor, pastorals, plaints of love," as in Charles Koechlin's *Douze Petites Pièces* (*Retour de Printemps, Rosée au Jardin,* and others).

Laurence Louppe, in her landmark *Poetics of Contemporary Dance,* credits Louis Horst for pushing Martha Graham to cross boundaries and "look elsewhere [among the arts] for structures capable of providing openings to choreographic composition" that remained "an important trait of American dance and its continuous relations with other modernities." Louppe also gives tribute to Horst's persistence "in proposing the cubists or pictorial primitives as examples of expressivity or of construction, in making Brancusi or Picasso known to the dancers"—as well as, among others, Isamu Noguchi, Henry Moore, Edvard Munch, Stuart Davis, and Reginald Marsh: "[Louis Horst] established the first link of resonance and correspondence between *avant-garde* practices and dance."

In the chapter "The Immediacies of Modern Art [Life]," Horst acknowledges "Freud's revelations concerning the subconscious" in *Civilization and Its Discontents,* published in 1930. One "immediacy" is the "turned in" physical gestures of the modern dance body, calling forth the "uniqueness of each individual . . . impatient with shallowness" in the same manner that Graham evoked her pupils' singularities. The musical examples by Alexander Scriabin, including *Danse Languide, Prélude, Etude,* and *Désir,* were all danced by Graham.

The "Cerebral" section discusses modernism's volte-face from nineteenth-century chromatic excessiveness and "overindulgence" to geometric strictures of "ordered, calculated unsentimentality." Ernst Toch's *Tanz- und Spielstücke* and the harmonic language of Arnold Schoenberg's early atonal "little piano pieces," such as op. 19, no. 2, are invoked to prove Horst's point. "Impressionism," while "not strictly an immediacy of *modern* life," Horst concedes, remains important to the modern dancer, conveying emotion and mood through color, lyricism, and sophistication. As an example, he proposes Maurice Ravel's *Valses Nobles et Sentimentales.*

"Jazz" and "Americana" complete the curriculum of Modern Dance Forms. The compositions of Blair Fairchild, Louis Gruenberg, George Gershwin, Aaron Copland, Wendell Keeney, Paul Nordoff—and Louis Horst's jocular arrangement of "She'll Be Coming 'Round the Mountain"—sound the finale with a flourish. "Modern American dance . . . expresses the extension, the out-going, expanded movement typical of the American . . . It was born of our land," Horst writes, "our kind of people, and our early history . . ."

Like Martha Graham, "the typical American has a lust to move, to go, to look for new frontiers."

16

Primitive Mysteries

The whole flowering of concert dance had its seed in this period . . .
of the originators. But from the first, Martha Graham was the most
startling inventor, and by all odds the greatest performer that trod our
native stage.

—AGNES DE MILLE

When Charles Weidman invited Agnes George de Mille to join the
Dance Repertory Theatre, the feisty, unblushingly "spoiled egocentric [and] wealthy girl" was already a show business veteran.
Fifteen years earlier, at the age of ten, Agnes made her Hollywood debut as
Jenny in *The Ragamuffin*, playing a "waif of the streets." The silent film, produced by Jesse Lasky, was written and directed by Agnes's father, William,
older brother of Cecil B. DeMille.

Agnes and her younger sister, Margaret, were born in New York City.
"Pop" DeMille, a playwright disillusioned with Belasco and Broadway,
dreamed of joining forces with "Uncle Ce," and so, in 1914, he had taken the
girls, and their mother, Anna—daughter of Henry George, single-tax proponent and author of the mega-selling *Progress and Poverty*—out west. Once
the "family of compulsive achievers" was settled, Agnes was enrolled in the
Hollywood School for Girls. Her favorite sport was tennis, her favorite class
was pantomime, and she fell in love with ballet after the "bright, unworldly
experience" of seeing Anna Pavlova perform "with the stunning sweetness
of a hummingbird in action." During her early teens, Agnes studied with
the former Ballets Russes star Theodore Kosloff. Graduating cum laude in
English from the University of California in 1926, "all [she] longed for was
to dance the mazurka in *Sylphides*. . . ."

Agnes's wish almost became true when her parents divorced. The sisters received trust funds and, mother Anna in tow, made a whirlwind tour of Europe, then moved with her to New York City. Margaret attended Barnard, while Agnes, with her mother's supervision and her father's blessing, rented a rehearsal hall, hired a pianist, and began to make "character sketch" dances. One piece, "'49," to the music of the "cowboy-composer" David Wendel Guion—popularizer of "Home on the Range" and "Turkey in the Straw"— mimed the tribulations of a stalwart pioneer girl heading to California during the gold rush.

Another, "Stage Fright," a "satire of the harried child . . . petrified backstage as she is about to go on for her performance," came about after a visit to the Metropolitan Museum of Art, where de Mille said she had identified with "the wax statuette of [Degas's] twisted ballet child and thought she looked like [her]. The aching knees, the strained back, the dirty, smudgy face, the pride." The first bronze cast of the wax and clay *Little Fourteen-Year-Old Dancer* (*Petite Danseuse de Quatorze Ans*), with cotton skirt and satin hair ribbon, was made in 1922 but did not enter the Met collections until 1929, with Louisine Havemeyer's Degas bequest; de Mille must have seen a photograph in *Vanity Fair,* or was recalling one of Degas's decadent "Paris Opera rats" paintings.

In the new year of 1927, "a young dancer fresh and pink as . . . tropical lilies . . . on dewy mornings," de Mille landed her first break as Columbine, a role created for her by music director Macklin Marrow in *La Finta Giardiniera* (*The Pretend Gardener*), a two-act operetta by Mozart. De Mille flitted about as a ghostly spirit materializing in the finale to reunite three pairs of separated lovers. In the jewel-box Mayfair Theatre, she "dance-pantomimed" gaily in a "garden of clipped box-trees, fruit-laden limes and flowering camellias [providing] just the touch of artifice needed . . . for Mozart's gossamer music, like a butterfly for lightness and iridescent flashing color."

After another year of auditions in music halls and nightclubs, and a summer excursion to Santa Fe for a hastily arranged solo concert, de Mille tried out for the former Ziegfeld and Greenwich Village Follies showman Jacques Cartier, putting together a recital and sharing the program and expenses for two concerts at the Republic Theatre. John Martin gave short shrift to the veteran Cartier as "more or less familiar hereabouts" but took an instant liking to "Miss De Mille," the colloquial novice. In her professional debut, presenting, among others, "'49" and "Stage Fright," updated and retitled as "Ballet Study No. 2," de Mille "showed an ebullient humor that intensified the underlying tragedy of the ballet dancer's technical slavery," Martin wrote,

Agnes de Mille, 1932. (Photograph by Paul Tanqueray)

"an exquisite appreciation of Degas's angle on the subject, and the ability to make the number a technical tour de force. . . ."

Another Ballets Russes émigré, Adolph Bolm, was regisseur and choreographer for the Chicago Civic Opera Ballet and Chicago Allied Arts, and led his touring company, Ballet Intime. Bolm's première danseuse, the Indianapolis-born Ruth Page, had danced with Pavlova on her tour of South America in 1918. Agnes de Mille wrote admiringly to Bolm and Page, asking to be considered for a role. An opportunity arose after Page starred as Terpsichore in Bolm's setting of the premiere of Stravinsky's *Apollon Musagète,* commissioned by Elizabeth Sprague Coolidge at the Library of Congress, and in September 1928, accepted an invitation to perform in Japan at the coronation of Emperor Hirohito. For what was billed as his last annual tour, an embittered Bolm chose de Mille to succeed the defecting Page.

Bolm's music director was Louis Horst. While the dance company and small orchestra made their way by train through Chicago, Des Moines, Louisville, Montgomery, Hollins, Macon, and Pittsburgh, as he had done with

Graham during Denishawn, Horst, clad in a bulky overcoat, his thick neck enveloped by a flowing scarf, squeezed his frame into the worn leather seat, side by side with de Mille. "Trying to reinforce [her] aesthetics," his speech-ifying worked "like yeast on [her] creative thought." Hour after hour, he bent her ear on the verities of Nietzsche, the latest pulp-fiction sensation, the best restaurants and hotels to be found in the cities en route, the relative merits and shortcomings of Isadora Duncan and Mary Wigman, Harald Kreutzberg and Tamiris—and the glories of his favored dancer and life force, Martha Graham.

Continuing his paternalism after the Ballet Intime tour, Horst took it upon himself to put old wine in new bottles, making two compositions for de Mille. In reverence for preclassic dance forms, Horst's *Spring Song* was a setting for voice, bugle, trumpet, and piano of the early-thirteenth-century round: "Sumer is icumen in," attributed to John of Fornsete, monk of Read-ing Abbey. Horst also set to voice and piano a cycle of *Civil War Songs* based upon the classic *Jenny Loved a Soldier* originally presented in 1863 at Niblo's Garden in lower Manhattan, birthplace of the first "book musical."

For a special February 17, 1929, Sunday matinee at the Martin Beck The-atre starring de Mille, Horst in shirtsleeves played from his spot in the wings and brought in the puckish Charles Weidman, with his "natural gift for sat-ire [and] rare genius of the clown," to partner with de Mille. In addition to Horst's pieces, the program included the overheated, Algerian-infused *Café Dancer (Ouled Nail)*, in which a jinglingly accessorized, garishly made-up de Mille accompanied herself with a handheld frame drum; *May Day,* "a picnic scene to Beethoven" where she danced Tyrolean-style in a voluminous skirt and garlanded brow, with Weidman, "the unresponsive swain," sporting a rakish feathered cap and lederhosen; and *Tryout,* a "graphic portrait of a Broadway chorus girl showing what she can do with jazz on her toes."

.   .   .

Including newcomer Agnes de Mille, the second—and final—season of the Dance Repertory Theatre ran for nine performances, from Sunday through Sunday, February 1 through 8, 1931, at the Craig Theatre on West Fifty-Fourth Street. Each of the five artists took over the marquee in turn. Fol-lowing in the footsteps of Charles Weidman was de Mille's new partner, Warren Leonard, who worked with her for the next five years. The athletic, ex-vaudevillian tapper, "a street kid from Washington Heights [and] the son of a Christian Science practitioner" came to her "with two ballet slippers stuck in his pockets, one on either side of his great coat," bearing an effusive letter of recommendation from his former teacher at the Stanislavsky American Laboratory School, John Martin, pre–*New York Times*.

De Mille and Leonard's debut week at Dance Repertory Theatre of "light, undemanding tasteful dances . . . won over the public" in contrast to the stern, "uncompromising concert work" of the other principals. Louis Horst played up de Mille's strengths as "a comedienne in serious times," reprising solos from prior seasons—while showcasing ornate, period-piece duets, including a spirited cancan to Offenbach's 1858 overture to *Orpheus in the Underworld (Orphée aux Enfers); Burgomaster's Branle,* inspired by Jan Van Eyck's iconic *The Arnolfini Portrait* and set to the 1927 *Dutch Songs (Holländisches Volksleben)* for piano by Julius Röntgen; and *Parvenues*, a suite of late-nineteenth-century waltzes by Johann Strauss II and Emil Waldteufel in which de Mille and Leonard were "an overdressed nouveau-riche couple trying to appear sophisticated at their first great ball."

"[B]y turns Amazon, earth mother, devotee of Walt Whitman, celebrant of the Negro's joys and miseries," Tamiris returned to the Dance Repertory Theatre stage, accompanied by Genevieve Pitot on piano, with an ensemble reprise of "Triangle Dance," three of her eight *Negro Spirituals*, and a stark new solo, "Crucifixion" ("They crucified my Lord / An' he never said a mumblin' word / They crucified my Lord / An' he never said a mumblin' word / Not a word, not a word, not a word"), stepping away upstage, eyes closed, arms straight, torso twisted, edging her cupped hands toward her hips, then sliding her hands up and down, "her body rigid, as if 'nailed to the tree,' as the lyrics wailed."

The most ambitious addition to Tamiris's repertory was Aaron Copland's *Olympus Americanus (A Twentieth-Century Ballet)*, for small orchestra, inspired by Copland's lean, six-minute, angular 1921–1922 *Passacaglia for Piano,* and dedicated to his teacher in harmony, counterpoint, and composition, Nadia Boulanger. "I am told that it is not an easy piece to play," Copland said laconically, due to its "emphasis on architectural structure." Nor was it an easy piece to dance. Choreographed for an ensemble of twelve, there were five sections: "Basking in the Sun," "Dance on an Ancient Theme (Priapic Ritual)," "Dance to Hermes and Aphrodite," "The Races," and "Triumphant." Critical response was muted; when Tamiris attempted to coordinate the movements of other dancers, she sacrificed narrative clarity. The choreographer's strength resided in her individual charisma—what José

Limón, watching "this superb creature" from the wings, called her "élan, openness and compassion."

Charles Weidman and Doris Humphrey continued their partnership in three pieces seen the prior year, *Air on a Ground Bass*, with music by Henry Purcell, Dane Rudhyar's "Salutation to the Depths," and Ravel's *La Valse/Choreographic Waltz*. The surprise of the Wednesday evening, February 4 program was the first performance of "Steel and Stone," with music by Henry Cowell. "Modern architecture and modern dance were recognized as the new arts in America," Humphrey-Weidman dancer Eleanor King, performing that night, recalled, "and their conjunction was inevitable in dance . . . Most of ['Steel and Stone'] was designed from floor level, balancing on one hand and one or both feet, striving upward."

Accompanying Weidman were Charles Laskey, a former weightlifter from Staten Island, who would go on to dance for George Balanchine; and José Limón, an aspiring painter from Mexico possessed of "pantherine grace," recruited two years previously from the ranks of Weidman's students to make his New York concert debut in *Rhythmic Dances of Java*.

The "pantherine grace" of José Limón, Mills College Amphitheatre, summer 1939.
(Photograph by Imogen Cunningham)

The week's most substantial Charles Weidman work was based upon the 1896 short story "The Happy Hypocrite: A Fairy Tale for Tired Men," by Max Beerbohm. The accompanying two-piano arrangement was by Minneapolis-born Herbert Elwell, who, like Copland, had studied with Boulanger. "Mr. Weidman has broken new ground in this venture," John Martin was pleased to report, "for it is thus far the first 'ballet d'action' to be devised by any of the modern dancers in this country." Beerbohm, who gave his imprimatur to Weidman's production, wrote "Hypocrite" during his dandyish flaneur days in fin de siècle London while his friend Oscar Wilde was in prison. It is the saga of the vain, aging (at thirty-five) Regency lecher and womanizer Lord George Hell, whose decadent sights are set upon a penniless sixteen-year-old dancer-actress, Jenny Mere, an idealist seeking a spiritual soul mate. Lord Hell dons a waxen mask of "saintly" handsomeness and rectitude, and fools Jenny into marriage, moving into a country cottage for a simple life of domesticity. His degenerate past is revealed when Lord Hell's former mistress, Signora la Gambogi, tracks him down and tears off the false visage. Whereupon Lord Hell discovers that his flesh and bone face beneath the persona has become miraculously pure, "line for line, feature for feature." He begs forgiveness for his duplicity, and Jenny takes him back into her arms.

With gusto, and a "delectable" sense of playfulness and "high comedy," Charles Weidman took on the flamboyant title role; Letitia Ide, "who looked like a young goddess and moved like one as well," was Jenny; Eleanor King played the mask-maker; and la Gambogi was danced by Denishawn alumna Cleo Atheneos. "To watch [Weidman and Ide] picking invisible daisies together in a field that wasn't there, to witness his conversion as the countenance of Lord Heaven becomes a permanent fixture and Jenny acquires 'the husband with the face of a saint' she had always wanted" made for a panto-mimic parable shaped to whimsical perfection by Weidman and his group.

．　．　．

Doris Humphrey is more impersonal and mental [than Martha Graham]. She organizes masses and lines of bodies; she sees gestures as entities in themselves; she *composes* dances.

—DANE RUDHYAR

The picture of equanimity, Doris Humphrey gathered her dancers in the rehearsal room, her bearing calm and cool, speaking in subdued tones, insisting that the soloist suppress her ego, remain mindful of the group surrounding her, and resist being the étoile—until she came to life and "leapt across the studio . . . the mass of red-gold hair flying behind her like a trail of fire . . ." transformed into "the radiant creature with the body of Botticelli's *Primavera* . . . mov[ing] like a gazelle . . . a creature enamored of the air."

The collision of grace with drama epitomized Doris Humphrey's choreography. Advocating for the "impersonal," she allied that concept with another formative theme of modern dance: "composition." Looking back upon the period up to 1930, Humphrey accentuated the "notoriously unintellectual" character of the dancer to explain why, unlike Martha Graham, she did not believe in "a set vocabulary of movements hardened into technical sequences." Rather, to Doris Humphrey's way of thinking, the dancer was motivated by "the [natural] life forces that move all persons" . . . "fall and recovery, climaxed by that moment of suspension when the person asserted his freedom."

Humphrey considered *Dances for Women* [entitled *Study of Women* in the Dance Repertory Theatre program], performed twice during the week, her most serious new work, although it would soon fade from her repertory. The music was composed and played by Dane Rudhyar "beat[ing] on exposed piano strings and gongs." The first part, "the abstraction of birth," was filled with generative imagery of plant life: twelve dancers aligned "in contracting positions . . . like the stem and branches of a tree form." Fingers curled and gradually unfolded "like tendrils," fingertips pitter-pattered on palms like raindrops. Toward the end of the segment, Katharine Manning and Letitia Ide lifted Humphrey onto a platform upstage center (in support, beneath and out of sight, crouched José Limón), where she did a "solo of flowering."

One by one, the dancers rose, forming index fingers and thumbs into pelvic triangles, hips thrusting forward and back and from side to side. The second part was "a tiny mincing dance for a quartet dressed in pink, up on their toes . . . moving in boxlike space to tinkling music," the women as objects of male regard in "formalized triviality." In the final part, after a costume change, the dancers' arms thrust up through black expanses of billowing fabric, "representing woman as militant."

Humphrey's other new work for her ensemble, *Dance of the Chosen* (retitled *The Shakers*), had been presented informally at Hunter College in December 1930. Revised and restaged over the decades, *The Shakers* remains a mainstay of her canon.

The United Society of Believers in Christ's Second Appearance, a dissenting charismatic separatist sect of the Quakers, was founded in northern England, at Bolton, near Manchester. The first settlers came to colonial America prior to the revolution, establishing communities in rural Niskayuna, New York, throughout New England, and as far south as Georgia and Florida. The leadership was female, the dawn-to-dusk farming life utilitarian, the hand-spun and -sewn apparel drably modest and rustic, the architectural aesthetic symmetrical and unadorned, the Puritan morality celibate (adding to the ranks only by taking in orphans or converts)—and the spiritual songs and dances repetitive and aphoristic, accelerating from measured dignity to frenetic Pentecostal whirling. Thus did "Shaking Quakers" become known as "Shakers."

One of the popular Shaker hymns praised King David dancing before God as he brought the Ark of the Covenant to Jerusalem: "Come, life, Shaker life, come, life eternal, Shake, shake out of me all that is carnal." Ernestine Henoch Stodelle, a member of Doris Humphrey's ensemble from 1930 to 1934, wondered forty years later, "Did we, as the 'original' Shakers, sense the 'immortality' of [her] inspired work when we started rehearsals [for *Dance of the Chosen*]? . . . The historical fact that the Shaker clan would gather in their immaculate Meeting Houses to pray together and then to dance out their creed, 'Ye shall be saved when ye are shaken free of sin,' was as stimulating to us as it was to Miss Humphrey."

Shaker "believers" shunned the vanities of instrumentation and vocal harmonizing when they "sang in gift . . . forcible, clear & plain to the Heavenly Host," marched heel-and-toe, "took nimble steps," waved their arms skyward, and stooped, beckoned, "motioned and pantomimed." For the music of *Dance of the Chosen,* Humphrey opted for a single drum and the offstage soprano of Pauline Lawrence accompanying herself with an accordion (later a harmonium).

All the performers were women: six Brethren attired in long, black coats and flat, wide-brimmed black hats, and six Sisters in starched bonnets and brown burlap dresses with white collars. "Down the center between the sexes," Stodelle recalled, "was an invisible line, which no sister or brother crossed, no matter how fervent their dancing would become." (In Doris Humphrey's staging for her repertory class at the Connecticut College School of Dance in August 1955, a chalk center line was drawn on the floor).

Humphrey was the presiding "Eldress," silent and seated. As the piece progressed, she awakened into motion to weave among the women until she paused to clap and call out an incantational, jubilant exhortation.

Doris Humphrey (center) and ensemble in *The Shakers*.
(Photograph, 1938, by Barbara Morgan)

"There was a center figure, yes," Humphrey wrote, referring to herself in the third person, "but by far the strongest and most important movement was given to the group, and it was their collective strength which gave power to the dance."

Doris Humphrey was fascinated by the "compulsions" of the Shakers, "a group of people who are united as individuals in their efforts to reach what they feel is salvation" . . . "they are creating a world . . . where the spirit can soar." Before Sabbath-day meetings, the brothers and sisters retired in their separate rooms "in silence for the space of half an hour," to seek within themselves "a sense of the Gospel" before being summoned forth to dance— "Let us *labor*!"

The *Dance of the Chosen* unfolds quietly, the divided men and women kneeling in an upstage-facing "three-sided square," hands clasped in prayer, gazing heavenward. With the introduction of the heartbeat-drumbeat, an austere tribalism pervades the group. The Eldress points at an angle upward, and heavy stomping begins, alternating with prancing on toes, and hops, leaps, and skips accompanied by clapping in unison, heads tilted up and down to the airy, soaring voice of the soprano and with "the wheeling of ranks . . . strait [*sic*], not only to the right and left, but also forward and back."

After a pause, a hoarse cry emerges from the ensemble—Eleanor King, in the role of "Man 1" in the original production—"My life! My carnal life! I shall lay it down—because it is depraved!" This is the cue for the Eldress, mounting a box upstage center, to issue her impassioned declamation: "It hath been revealed—ye shall be saved when ye are shaken free of sin!" Bending at the waist, hands dangling from wrists, she delves into paroxysms. Brothers and sisters follow her lead, hands flopping as if sprinkling water from fingertips; they lunge, crouch, and pound on the floor with their hands.

The two facing groups approach the edge of the barrier line in bounding hops and deafening percussion, thrusting forward and writhing back with effortful expulsions of breath. They lean in, then out, in a tug-of-war. The singer's chants welling up again, the Eldress reaches a dizzy ecstasy of twirling, pivoting on her planted left foot as her right foot propels her. The ensemble falls to the ground. She alone remains upright, exhaling a final "*Amen!*"

. . .

I have seen few things ever in the theatre more beautiful than the first number in the *Mysteries* as it went this year, the Indian forms, solid in drawing and in composition as Diego Rivera at his best, the figure in white of the chief dancer, the motives of those groups and salutations, the foot above the shielding hands, the motives of worship and celebration.

—STARK YOUNG

Primitive Mysteries, Martha Graham's newborn masterpiece, premiered on the evening of February 2, 1931, and was repeated on February 6. In service to Louis Horst's ideal of music aspiring to purity—"the dance comes *first*!"—twelve women, including Martha Hill, under the name "Martha Todd . . . because stage dancing was still not seen [in some circles] as a 'proper' activity," and Georgia "Geordie" Graham, Martha's younger sister, had been rehearsing with Graham, in silence, every night for three months. When the "rhythmic patterns and tempos [had been] set, [and] before the

Martha Graham Dance Composition, with impressions of *Primitive Mysteries,*
by Lucy Brown L'Engle, oil on board, 1931.

music [was] written," Graham allowed Horst into the studio in January to
see what they had made: "You must not fit what you are doing to the music,"
she warned the dancers, "but let the music show what you are doing." Ever
the mischievous accompanist who loved to keep the women on their toes,
Horst would divert into Bach chorales or "hints of Gregorian chants" during
Graham's warm-up exercises.

To the counts Graham had laid down, Horst brought a score with silences
between phrases, so that, he said, it would "have the transparency of primitive music, so you can look through it and see the dance . . . The music is the
frame to the picture." His chord-driven piano conjured the pounding feet of
the Taos Pueblo, above which floated in unison Hugo Bergamasco's flute and
William Sargeant's oboe, as if wafting through mountain air. Horst insisted
that, while the evocative framework of *Primitive Mysteries* "welded . . . tone
and movement," he was not aiming to replicate native melodies. "Martha
didn't like music that had a melodic line," said Sophie Maslow. "It had to be
percussive and bare."

Observing from a discreet distance, and en passant—defying the gospel
that "Miss Graham would not tolerate being watched from the wings"—José
Limón "was struck by the sacerdotal authority with which she rehearsed"
Primitive Mysteries, "and by the hushed, almost religious atmosphere" in

the room. May O'Donnell, cast in the piece the following year, said that Graham—in order to listen properly, waiting to formulate new sensations— "needed a lot of quietness . . . You could sense by the movement the direction she was going in. She wasn't a person who talked much."

The dancers were aware that Graham had recently made a trip with Horst to the New Mexico desert, where "he stimulated Martha into trying to capture some of that feeling," and that "the Indian rituals . . . had had a deep effect on her whole vision." Bessie Schonberg, a company member in 1930–1931, was asked over the years if Graham "ever told [her] what she had seen out there [in New Mexico]. . . . Well," came Schonberg's vague reply, "she saw people in her own country living in ways which I think she had had no conception of. She was seeing them in many ways through Louis's eyes." Sophie Maslow was ambiguous about the roots for the dance when she recalled decades later that "Martha didn't say very much about the source of [Primitive Mysteries]. . . . She never did much explaining. . . . It was a combination of American Indian life and rituals [and] the Catholicism that the Spaniards had brought to the United States . . . That was about the only thing she spoke about." A brief program note for a performance at Bennington College in the spring of 1933 reenforced Graham's Neoplatonic perspective, framing it as a work of religious fusion, "embodying in dance form the Aboriginal [sic] and Christian rituals."

"The work is echt Graham," Anna Kisselgoff wrote, when Primitive Mysteries, dormant since the Louis Horst Memorial Concert at the American Dance Festival in 1964, was revived in New York in the spring of 1977, despite the reluctance of the octogenarian creator, who stayed away from rehearsals—led by Sophie Maslow, assisted by Yuriko and by Takako Asakawa—until the last sessions. "Some people make a cocoon and weave a web of the past around themselves," Graham said coolly. "I've never wanted to do that." She did resuscitate a few oblique observations. The piece "was taken from the feeling the Southwest had about the Virgin," she said. "She is very concrete to the people, a part of their lives." The voluminously layered, pure-white organdy dress with petal-like shoulders Graham wore for her role as "the Virgin" was prompted by memories of "the white night-blooming Cereus flowers . . . by [her] window in Santa Barbara, when 'it was very still . . . You could hear the leaves opening. . . .'"

Rather than waste time in the studio belaboring the meaning of Primitive Mysteries, Martha Graham spoke of actions—what was to be done. In rehearsal, during quiet stretches, she would drape a shawl over her shoulders and survey the room, eagle eyes catching every detail, without taking notes. She saw into her dancers' emotions, and induced them to reveal movements to her, appropriating their capabilities, quirks, and characteristics for the work in process. When she spotted something she liked during these exercises, Graham would shout, "We'll *keep* that!"

A zen master, at one instant Graham singled out the smoothly coiffed Mary Rivoire, her hair concealed under a net and immobile, her masklike face exotically made up, as an example of the implacable persona she wanted. She praised the incremental qualities of Ailes Gilmour, now a full member of the group. Her "elongated throat," the muscular neck viewed from the side, was so "eloquent," Graham told the dancers. "See how Ailes presses the air down with her hands as she rises," Graham said to the others. "It is as if she carves her own body's shape out of the air, like a Rodin figure emerging from marble."

Repeated "deep stretch" exercises were meant to build power for the "strength on the back leg" necessary to support the unsupported, gradual back fall and instigate the forward thrust so important to "the Walk," weighted and unhurried, taken on a contraction, with "a step, a pause, and then a step again on the same foot." At the Cornish School, Graham had likened this movement to the resistance one felt wading through surf; according to Dorothy Bird, in New York, although Graham could not swim, they had gone out to Jones Beach and she made the women practice in the chilly Atlantic.

During her mid- to late thirties, Graham wanted to create and set new work on a loyal cadre of dancers while continuing to maintain a dependable repertory. She came up against the irritations and exigencies of production— scarce stage time in the theatre to run music, adapt spacing, and fix tech cues, and trying on and rejecting lighting schemes in the same way she draped costumes, only to rip up and refashion them. The day before *Primitive Mysteries* opened, "Martha's mood [was] like a bowstring drawn tight" and "she had developed the most frightful headache."

Cluttered with props and scenery from the current play, the Craig Theatre set was not struck until midnight. When the group finally began a run-through, the dancers were "anxious [and] unsure," trying harder than usual to do what they were told—to do their best for Martha. At one point, Graham as the Virgin, lifted by weary and fearful "Attendants," slipped and stumbled. "Her nerves shattered. 'That will do!' she erupted, incensed. 'That's enough. . . . You don't care. . . . Get out of the theatre. Get out of my sight. Go home!'" In disbelief, the women "dressed in silence." Horst pursued Graham to her dressing room, where he sat with her, cajoled and calmed her, and eventually the two returned, whereupon rehearsal resumed, lasting until 3:00 a.m.

In the work of Martha Graham, impelled toward receding perfection, more was *always* expected. The only way for a dancer to conquer the anxiety that came with not-dancing (not-sculpting, not-writing, not-painting . . .) was to take class every day, then take class again; to rehearse, and rehearse again; to perform, and perform again.

. . .

[E]ach member of the [*Primitive Mysteries*] group seems to take the first step because it is timed to a beat, whereas Graham seems to step because the beat has forced her to move.

—ROY HARGRAVE

Behold yourself in me as I speak, and seeing what I do, keep silent about my mysteries. You who are dancing, know that this human suffering which I am about to bear is yours.

—ANONYMOUS, the Acts of John

From the opening instant of "Hymn to the Virgin," the first part of the *Primitive Mysteries* triptych, the dancers emerge onto a soundless tabula rasa, a "phalanx" of maidens in dark wool jersey dresses of grayish blue, "the sacred color, celestial blue, the color of heaven." With the white-clad Virgin in their midst, the sisterhood makes a solemn entrance from stage left with hushed, meted-out, glide-and-pause steps, summoned from some distant, secret place, out of sight and mind: called from the Pueblo kiva into the central square, to face awaiting villagers and visitors, or processing along the sacred way from the wellspring of dance's origins at Eleusis. The three lines of "players" arrive at the public sphere and halt briefly, dresses swaying forward against the backs of their thighs. Only then does the music for the "ritual of adoration" begin.

Interrupting the primal silence come a mournful oboe and a flittering

Martha Graham as "the Virgin," and ensemble, in *Primitive Mysteries,* 1931.
(Photograph by Paul Hansen)

flute, the instrument borne by humpbacked Kokopelli, Pueblo deity of storytelling, agriculture, and childbirth. The dancers divide, two groups circling downstage and one group humbly seated "like carved stone figures of the ancestors" upstage, never taking their enraptured eyes off Martha Graham, chosen by God for the Annunciation. Hair loose and feet bare, with exuberant grand battements, she darts back and forth like a pollinating bee between two foregrounded clusters of dancers.

The devotees encircle her in stilled obeisance. In response, she gestures with gentle, seductive benedictions, they embrace her delicately, haloing her head with bent arms and pyramided hands imitating the *mandorla* rays of grace framing the Virgin of Guadeloupe, and cherishingly envelop her, "catch her, and send her off." In counterpoint, the seated back row of tall ladies rises to life, light leaps with heavy footfalls pounding silence into submission. Bodies are reconfigured into threes and fours before regaining the floor. Two kneeling rows form a passageway of laid-down cupped hands, an impression of water, as, "benign[ly] calm," the Virgin weightlessly treads upon its surface, inclining with courtliness left and right, making her way forward.

The group convenes into a tribal circle, a living organism within which Mary, motionless, at the center, alone of all her sex, does not move. The *choreia* ring dance rotates one way, then the opposite, reversing and spinning, inside out and outside in. The Virgin sits, earthbound, arms akimbo over raised knees. The repressed energy she contains surpasses the energy expended by the group. They coalesce into silent lines around her and proceed offstage the way they came in, toward a timeless time, a placeless place.

After a pause, the quiet lines of dancers return for part two: "Crucifixus." The "Handmaidens" arranged downstage left, the Virgin is upstage with two Attendants, one on either side. They arch over her, arms angled spear-like, pointing at the distant cross on the hill of Golgotha. The Mater Dolorosa covers her eyes, "knuckles bulging like carbuncles," weeping before the agon of her only Son. Her steps maintain a flexed, tenacious grip on the earth, inching ahead, back indented, stomach flattened. Palms and extended fingers pressed to face and forehead in a crown of pain depict the Eleusinian rite of the *mystai,* "the initiates made worthy through suffering," and *myein,* "closing the eyes or the mouth," under a secret spell, sorrow and suffering engendering strength and power.

With an annunciatory piano chord, the Virgin flings her arms parallel to the floor and steps forward, unleashing the ensemble into animalistic action. They spring into a circle around Mary and her Attendants, and, half-crouching, prance clockwise, quick-footed, "stomping like bison," arms extended straight behind their backs, hands locked together, scapulae protruding like angels' wings, as "flintlike, the movement runs dangerously near the thin borderline where faith becomes fanaticism, and religion, madness."

At first slow motion, their crashing lunges accelerate to a frenzy of "pitched-forward grands jetés," the tempo of "the suspended bodies . . . cutting through space" accelerating to a vertiginous pace, before slowing down as prelude to the recessional that marked the conclusion of part one—in silence but for the heaving inhalations and exhalations of the dancers transformed by their cathartic "experience of a great rhythm."

In part three, "Hosannah!" the dance shifts from circular to sprightly. Like Louis Horst's distinctions between "earth primitive" and "air primitive," the piece becomes asymmetrical, piccolo and oboe keeping a birdsong rhythm, with "brooding" piano chords between. Arranged in parallel lines again, the dancers calibrate into a tableau of two arcs framing Martha Graham and her single acolyte ("Disciple") in a succession of slow plastiques. Legs splayed, feet flat, arms wide, the seated Virgin assumes the wide-open pose of the Great Mother. She supports the disciple's backbend and fall, accepting her into her lap as a cradled pietà, and there is a suspended moment of eye contact.

The circle of dancers narrows and kneels in "concluding obeisance," and the fallen Disciple, gathering her energy, returns, reborn, to a standing position. Making a halo with her "spread and shining fingers," she forms a tribute-crown behind the Virgin Mother, who lies on her back, arms up and extended, "hands meeting in a spired point." Rising again, Mary assumes the Vitruvian stance, arms and legs outstretched across an imaginary squared circle, straining to find the limits of her kinesphere. Akin to the Magna Mater of Piero della Francesca, her scapular (the cloak, Graham's "sacred garment") spread in a final beneficent and protective gesture, the Virgin departs into the whirling "celestial dance of Heaven" escorted by her faithful "throng of exulting angels."

.   .   .

In addition to *Primitive Mysteries,* Martha Graham, accompanied by six dancers, premiered another group work for the Dance Repertory Theatre. *Bacchanale,* true to the name, was a "Dionysiac," "wildly abandoned . . . and rhapsodic" piece, by Wallingford Riegger displaying "moments of such technical virtuosity that the audience gasped in its seats." Born in Albany, Georgia, Riegger grew up in New York City, studying at the Institute of Musical Arts with Percy Goetschius, one of Louis Horst's teachers, and in Berlin at the Hochschule für Musik with Robert Hausmann, Max Bruch, and Edgar Stillman-Kelley. *Bacchanale* was Riegger's first foray into writing for Graham, who had asked him to collaborate with her after seeing him conduct his *Caprice/Study in Sonority.*

Riegger was subjected to Graham's "dance first, music second" rite of passage. She balked at a composition that must "fit such design as this: five bars of four-quarter time, two bars of three-quarter time with the accent on the second beat of the measure, four bars of quarter time with a hold over the last note, ten bars of three-quarter time with an accelerando, etc." Rather, Graham lectured him on the virtues of sparseness and leanness and, following Horst's lead, Riegger pared down strings in deference to oboe, piccolo, and percussion. Their alliance deepened, and he went on to write *Frenetic Rhythms* in 1933 and the propulsive *Chronicle* in 1936.

After the spectacle of *Primitive Mysteries,* Graham presented three *Rhapsodics—Song—Interlude—Dance,* with music by Béla Bartók; and offered *Two Primitive Canticles (Ave and Salve)* and *Dolorosa,* written in the mid- and late 1920s in Paris by Heitor Villa-Lobos, the preeminent Brazilian modernist. Graham would later include these *poemas indigenas* as part of her "Primitive Cycle."

Witnessing *Dolorosa* on November 1, 1932, at Clark University in Worcester, Massachusetts, one of Graham's most insightful critics, Stark Young of the *New Republic,* was moved to comment that her "first idea [for a dance] will be more like that of a designer of patterns, lines, angles, rugs, tiles, fabrics, what you will, or like the basic outlay of what will later be a painting. From this pattern or single form there will develop other forms; which in their turn may suggest an idea less visually abstract and more a subject, more a literary or psychological meaning."

．　．　．

Taking a retrospective view of *Heretic* through the lens of *Primitive Mysteries*—considering the earlier ensemble work as a prototype for the latter—does not do justice to Martha Graham's choreographic ingenuity. Drawing a connection from one work to a subsequent one may help establish provenance in the visual and poetic arts; in dance, however, narrative progress is not dependably definitive. *Primitive Mysteries* is more open-formed, more *up and out* than the linear *Heretic.* In the earlier piece, the dancers were constrained to begin and end in the same space; now, they have their exits and their entrances from and to a limitless world. The foregrounded "Heretic" is constantly opposed to and struggling with her sisters; in *Primitive Mysteries,* rather than rebuff and detain the Virgin, the others welcome and protect her. The "Outsider" in *Heretic* who tested herself against the stolid uniformity of the group has become in *Primitive Mysteries* the Chosen One, empowering and sanctioning the group.

Heretic ended with prostration and exhaustion. *Primitive Mysteries* concluded with dignity and decorum, and then—as soon as the curtain came down—"the house burst into cheers . . . not just a scattering of 'bravos,' but the expression of a mass of people whose emotional tension found spontaneous release . . . paying memorable tribute to a native artist." Gertrude Shurr was present at the creation when "the new formations, the subject-matter [of *Primitive Mysteries*], took New York by storm." After all the tearful rehearsals and sleepless nights haunted by existential panic attacks, "Martha was just dumbfounded" at the repeated cries of "*encore!*" All the women of the group crowded around her "backstage . . . [and] there was much crying and hugging."

Stark Young wrote, "Of this composition I can say that it is one of the few things I have ever seen in dancing where the idea, its origin, the source from which it grew, the development of its excitement and sanctity, gave me a sense of baffled awe and surprise . . ." Mary Watkins was also seized by the magic that evening. *Primitive Mysteries* "is, in our opinion, the most significant choreography which has yet come out of America," she wrote. "It is not only a masterpiece of construction, but it achieves a mood which actually lifts both spectators and dancers to the rarified heights of spiritual ecstasy . . . Miss Graham [is] the leader of the moderns in our wide and varied field of plastic aestheticism."

Elizabeth Selden, musing upon the aesthetic of "the dancer's quest" singled out Martha Graham as the most advanced of her contemporaries through her mastery of "distortion." There was distortion, Selden explained, when Graham excised the connective tissue from a story line; in the disconcerting "spatial order" of the arrangement and deployment of women's bodies; and in the discordant "intensity" of her visual imagery, using idiosyncratic costuming and dramatic, angular lighting.

Following Martha Graham to the outermost frontier where "stark realism" bordered upon "expressionism," Selden decided that "she is the modern dancer *par excellence*."

Approached by the Shubert Organization with an offer to syndicate the collective repertory and take it on the road, the disparate members of the Dance Repertory Theatre could not find it within themselves to rise to the occasion. De Mille complained that the box office revenues were disproportionately allocated among the others, and blamed Graham and Humphrey for not abiding by Tamiris as titular leader. Humphrey, despite the fine reception for *The Shakers,* was resentful that she had been hemmed in by the constraints of the program and continued to harbor cool mistrust toward Graham, who did not stand in the way of the critics' chorus singing that she had stolen the show. As for Louis Horst, he tried to take the moderate higher road and keep the peace, but to no avail. *Synergy*—coined by

Isamu Noguchi's friend Bucky Fuller, as a magnificent whole greater than the sum of its parts—was absent. On March 8, 1931, the Dance Repertory Theatre announced "that it has suspended its activities for the season."

Nevertheless, the new American dance by these diverging practitioners had shown qualities "in common with modern painting and sculpture" . . . "and the public . . . could see [now] that there was something called 'the modern dance,' something strong and contemporary and determinedly independent of superficial beguilements."

17

"We Will Never Understand One Another"

What was to come in the nineteen-thirties?
Only one thing could one be sure of.
It would not be repetition.
The stream of time often doubles on its course,
but it always makes for itself a new channel.

—FREDERICK LEWIS ALLEN,
Only Yesterday: An Informal History of the 1920's

Despite her pique in the discordant aftermath of the Dance Repertory Theatre, Agnes de Mille remained in awe of Martha Graham and ached to join her company. "Martha, let me work with you," de Mille pleaded.

"Certainly not," Graham replied. "Find your own way. I won't let you lean on me."

"Martha, you have genius," was the rejoinder. "You know where you are going."

To which Graham irritably snapped, "I don't know where I'm going. None of us know that," and, for good measure, "And someday I'm going to give you a good smack."

Embittered by the difficulties of her artistic journey, de Mille published a long essay in *Theatre Arts Monthly* called "The New Ballerina," a conflicted depiction of the noble art, beginning with her nostalgia for the faded era of "the great romantic solo dancer." The beloved "Pavlowa" of the author's rose-tinted childhood was no more; the graceful "Camargo, Taglioni . . . Genée . . . and Barbarini" were gone, and, with their passing, went the sophisticated balletomanes, audiences, and critics alike.

The sad fact that "there are no endowed dancing schools in America" exacerbates the dilemma for the young woman trying to make her way as a concert dancer. "In the struggle for bread," de Mille writes, she must take odd jobs, posing for painters and photographers, waiting tables, clerking in a dismal Midtown office, or selling hosiery behind a department store counter, in order to pay for after-hours classes that distract her loyalty away from the gracious formalism of ballet in subservience to the ascetic discipline of "a new kind of dancing." And, in the end, all she will have to show might be "to appear three or four times a year on the stage."

De Mille adds a personal caveat borne of her own experience that "[a] knowledge of various techniques does not always enrich the student." On the contrary, "[i]t frequently renders her uncertain, hesitant, without defined style or reliable craftsmanship." For example, she continues, Martha Graham is "an . . . artist on the New York stage danc[ing] the problems and hungers and convictions of the people among whom she lives." Pulling the tradition of her art away from the refined prettiness of the ballerina and toward that of "the unconscious folk dancer . . . in the public square," in Graham, "[t]he dance and not the dancer predominates," de Mille writes. The "abstract beauty" of ballets de Mille grew up with, *The Dying Swan*, *The Dragonfly*, *Carneval*, has been supplanted by the earthy primacy of "social forces" in *Steerage*, *Heretic*, and *Primitive Mysteries*.

In search of that beauty, de Mille, accompanied by her mother, and endorsed with a loan from her brother-in-law, left New York for Paris, Brussels, and London, where she found shelter and support at the Mercury Theatre and Ballet Club in Notting Hill Gate, under the nurturing wings of Marie Rambert and her husband, producer Ashley Dukes.

.　.　.

On January 4, 1931, the League of Composers introduced a concert at the Art Center on East Fifty-Sixth Street with a talk on "some aspects of modern music" by Eugene Goossens, formerly of Eastman, now conductor and music director of the Cincinnati Symphony Orchestra. "In addition to the technical problems confronting the present-day composer," he said, "the preconceived prejudices of many hearers make the lot of the writer of new music a difficult one." The program included the first American appearance of the Budapest String Quartet, offering convoluted works by Hindemith (op. 16) and Kodály (op. 10).

The centerpiece, between Goossens's talk and the quartet, was *Piano Variations* by Aaron Copland, dedicated to his lover, the Canadian writer Gerald Sykes. Copland's severe solo showed he was disinclined to accommodate to his "auditors," who gave the bespectacled young man with spindly flying fingers "courteous attention and some applause." An underwhelmed critic observed that "more than one 'stream of consciousness' passage recalled similar essays in words by Gertrude Stein."

There was one empathic pair of ears in the room that day; Martha Graham, present to support her friend, was attracted to the "strange, hard beauty" of Copland's eleven-measure theme followed by twenty of his *Variations* and a coda. The "bare, brutal motif . . . [was] hammered out" on the keyboard, "steely colors and incisive attacks" twisting and turning, "assaultive, whimsical, ironic, frenzied and more." Calling upon Copland at his apartment the next day, suspending her "choreography before music" rule, Graham told him she wanted to make a dance to the piece. Copland was "utterly astonished that anyone would consider this kind of music suitable for dance." He told Graham she was free to proceed, with the stipulation that the thirteen-minute length not be cut. She agreed, and the two spent the afternoon chatting about how delightful it would be to collaborate on a full-length ballet. It would take another year before Graham was ready to perform her dance to Copland's *Variations,* and a dozen more years for *Appalachian Spring* to flower.

. . .

With fanfare, the New School for Social Research, founded in 1919 and led since 1922 by economist Alvin Johnson, opened its "gleaming, streamlined" new seven-story headquarters at 66 West Twelfth Street in Manhattan on New Year's Day 1931. The building, designed in the international style by Viennese architect Joseph Urban, rose head and shoulders above the neighboring brick row houses, "its severely blocked façade alternating bands of patterned brick and infenestrated glass . . . standing for . . . something wide-awake and freshly-minted." A ground-floor art gallery featured avant-garde works from Katherine Dreier's Société Anonyme; the third-floor boardroom was the setting for Thomas Hart Benton's monumental, ten-panel melting-pot mural, *America Today*, populated with a lively hinterlands-to-metropolis "panoply of pre-Depression American types, from flappers to farmers, steel workers to stock market tycoons"; and the walls of the seventh-floor cafeteria were graced with Mexican artist José Clemente Orozco's dynamic earth-toned frescoes, *Call to Revolution and Table of Universal Brotherhood.*

Weekday evenings, in sessions at 5:20 and 8:20 p.m., for the convenience of students arriving after work, New School classrooms were abuzz with intellectual éminences grises. Horace M. Kallen lectured on Western civilization and contemporary politics; Sidney Hook and Roswell Barnes tackled sociopolitical issues; Freda Kirchwey, Robert Frost, Waldo Frank, Gorham B. Munson, and Francis Fergusson took up poetic and literary banners; Meyer Levin, twenty years before *Anne Frank,* taught marionette design; Julian Huxley expounded on heredity and the environment; and Frank Lloyd Wright "preached" (his word) the virtues of "a truly organic American architecture that grows out of the inherent characteristics of materials and 'unfolds' from within its own cultural and natural conditions."

The performing arts enjoyed two different forums. On the first floor, drawing upon his background in theatre and set design, Joseph Urban created an oval auditorium with a lofty, arched proscenium; and in the basement was a hexagonal room, each wall painted a different color, fitted at the center with a circular, sunken dance stage surrounded by a raised seating area. For this underground haven, Henry Cowell, who taught twentieth-century music at the New School, and Louis Horst, serving on the dance committee, asked critic John Martin to create and moderate a course: "Dance Forms and Their Development . . . from folk and ritual dances" through "contemporary American modernism." Doris Humphrey presided as lecture-demonstrator for the first class in the series.

On Tuesday evening, February 20, it was Martha Graham's turn to be guest speaker. After directing the Dance Group to "move on a breath" as an example of her technique, Graham introduced three dances, *Heretic, Bacchanale,* and *Primitive Mysteries,* in which she did not perform, deeming Urban's round platform not "a proper stage." The twelve dancers "clad in sweaters," arranged themselves in two rows on the floor behind her, and, with no effort to conceal her reluctance, Graham, "wearing a long tunic, and her hair . . . tied back from her forehead," asked if there were any questions.

Unbeknownst to Graham, choreographer Michel Fokine, the émigré former Mariinsky Theatre and Ballets Russes dancer, was in the audience. Living in New York City for the past decade, in 1921 he had opened a ballet school on Riverside Drive, and three years later founded his American Ballet Company, a successful enterprise with performances at the Metropolitan Opera House, Carnegie Hall, Lewisohn Stadium, and tours around the country, recently at the Hollywood Bowl.

To Fokine, Martha Graham's body language that night—posture stiff, wrists tight, fists clenched—resembled "a fanatical prophetess," and her "girls [*sic*] . . . flying and walking on flat feet . . . arms either hanging limply or raised with elbows turned outward . . . chest[s] . . . extended forward in a decided manner or caved inward . . . expressions sad, and even cross, all the time" were "ugly in form and hateful in spirit . . . [expressing] a somewhat 'barking' movement of the torso and the head."

Michel Fokine, ca. 1930s.

As the talk-back proceeded, Fokine sat quietly, keeping sentiments about "those barking girls!" to himself, until "one of the ladies [in the audience] asked Miss Graham, 'What is your opinion of ballet?'"

She answered flatly, "I accept the ballet as one form of dancing. I like, for instance, Pavlowa; especially where Pavlowa bows after her dances. She bows very well." At this shocking stab of condescension to the beloved woman who had been his first partner, and for whom he choreographed *The Dying Swan* to the music of Saint-Saëns in 1907, Michel Fokine's heart was seized with the anguished memory of "the greatest dancer of this age, who had just died [three weeks prior, on January 31], so dear to all of us."

The diminutive, balding man in a business suit—Fokine looked to Martha Graham like a banker—was compelled to speak up, and raised his hand. "It seems, sir, that you have a question?" she said.

"Yes," he replied. "In working with your girls, do you have in mind the development of natural movement, or do you disregard naturalness in your art?" Silence shrouded the room. Graham stood still as a statue. Fokine repeated the question, pantomiming the movements: "In order to lift the arms, your girls lift first their shoulders, then their elbows, and only after that, the entire arm. In life it happens differently," he said. "If I want to take my hat off the hanger . . . I simply lift my entire arm and take the object desired."

"But still, you lift your shoulder to lift your arm," Graham said. "Your movement should come from *here.*" She touched the center of her body, between her chest and her stomach. Mimicking her gesture, Fokine shook his head and countered that "nothing unusual happens 'here.'" After another palpable pause, Graham scoffed, "You know nothing about the movement of the body!"

How dare this "young dancer" address him thus, Fokine thought—he, who had spent "over forty years" blending Duncanesque movement into the "old ballet" to dissolve inhibitions and fixity of form, and inculcate ebullience, freedom, and comedic irreverence. "Why is the ballet *terrible?*" he pressed on, returning to Graham's earlier statement.

She took the fifth position in defiance. "How can one dance a Grecian dance from *this* position?"

To which Fokine invoked his adaptations from antiquity. "I myself have choreographed *Daphnis and Chloe,* and *Narcisse,* and *Echo,*" he said, "the kinds of ballets composed of natural movements and on the lines of the purest Grecian art. You criticize the ballet without knowing anything about it." The uneasy moderator, John Martin, looking at his watch, intervened. "Mr. Fokine," he said, "you cannot continue this argument. The ballet has its own field, and modern dancing its own, also. Ballet has had its chance to express itself during three centuries, so the modern dancing has a right to express itself in three weeks."

Hearing her interlocutor's name invoked, "I did not know that I was speaking with Mr. Fokine," Martha Graham said. "How she would have spoken with me if I had disclosed my identity, I do not know," Fokine mused. As far as Graham was concerned, the discussion was over. "We will never understand one another," she said, insofar as what "ballet" meant or should mean.

Based upon the beliefs Fokine laid out in his *Five Principles* (1914), the two dancers should not have been arguing that night. In the book, he "admits [into what he called the *New Ballet*] the conventional use of gesture," advancing "from the expressiveness of the individual body to the expressiveness of a group of bodies," and "refusing [that ballet should] be a slave either of music or of scenic decoration." With twenty-twenty hindsight, during the coincidence of a spring 1977 weeklong Fokine Festival at the Metropolitan Opera House with a new season of the Martha Graham Dance Company at the Lunt-Fontanne Theatre, Clive Barnes pointed out the irony of that 1931 confrontation. The New School sparring match was "a triumph of misunderstanding"; rather, he wrote, "Miss Graham, more than any other contemporary choreographer, is [Massine's] spiritual godchild."

. . .

Actor-producer Robert Henderson joined forces with actress Blanche Yurka in Sophocles's *Electra,* and Yurka turned to Martha Graham and Louis Horst to create three solo interludes for the play. Graham leaped at the opportunity to participate because the tragedy held familial meaning. A childless, unmarried woman (*alektra* is Greek for "unbedded"), one of three sisters, yearns for the return of her adored brother, Orestes, sent abroad for

Blanche Yurka, 1931.

his safety since infancy, and "refuses to put [her] father's death to rest," vowing "never / will I leave off lamenting, / never." In Electra's unrequited grief for Agamemnon, she identifies with the nightingale, a bird that was once a woman, and she no longer gives birth to children, but "to wars in [her] melancholy soul," stubborn mourning songs—*aien*—with breast-beating refrains.

Coming off an extended run in Gilbert Seldes's adaptation of Aristophanes's *Lysistrata,* to take on *Electra,* Blanche Yurka had earned a reputation as "one of the foremost *artistes* of the American stage" with a talent for playing "iron-willed women." Born of Czech parents in 1887, and growing up in St. Paul, Minnesota, Blanche moved with her family to New York City to study voice and ballet, and, at sixteen, debuted as a flower girl and "Grail Bearer" in the American premiere of *Parsifal* at the Metropolitan Opera. Under the aegis of David Belasco, she shifted to stage acting, starting as an understudy in William C. (Agnes's father) de Mille's play, *The Warrens of Virginia* in 1907. She appeared in numerous shows on Broadway, creating a sensation at the age of thirty-five in 1922 as Queen Gertrude opposite John Barrymore's forty-two-year-old Hamlet, directed by Arthur Hopkins. Yurka also tackled demanding Ibsen roles, directing and starring as Hedda in *Hedda Gabler*; Gina Ekdahl in *The Wild Duck,* which she also directed; and Ellida Wangel in *The Lady from the Sea.*

"Blanche Yurka plunges this correspondent into adjectival poverty by the richness and surety of her performances," wrote John Anderson in the *New York Post.* "She renders me further destitute with the slow tension of building a character before your eyes."

For the text of her *Electra,* Yurka chose the 1927 translation by the King's College Classics lecturer and scholar, John Tressider Sheppard, premiered at Cambridge University. At the top of the title page of her typescript, Yurka wrote, "All Chorus speeches spoken by 'Woman,'" reattributing every passage throughout the fifty-six pages calling for the Chorus—either speaking in unison, or its five members declaiming singly—into a dominant female voice. Sophocles's Electra, unlike her counterparts in Aeschylus's and Euripides's versions, calls her female companions "citizenesses"—a community of women—"employing *polites,* the surprising feminine form of the noun, in Greek, so rare, so improbable in fifth-century texts."

As "the Dancer" in *Electra,* Martha Graham set three solos on herself. The first, "Prelude [or Invocation]," signaled the appearance at Mycenae of Orestes, accompanied by his silent friend Pylades of Phocis, and Paedagogus (the old man) onto the plaza before the palace of stepfather-usurper Aegisthus; the second, "Entrance [of Clytemnestra]," Graham's "fury dance," heralded the imperious "Queen," with a warning from the "Chorus" that "Vengeance is coming—her hands like an army / her feet like a host"; and the third was a "Lamentation for Electra [Over the Urn]" "supposedly containing the ashes of Orestes," his ploy, feigning death, to return for revenge.

Virginia Woolf might as well have been referring to Martha Graham when she wrote, in her tribute to "the Greek tongue" that "[Sophocles's] Electra stands before us like a figure so tightly bound that she can only move an inch this way, an inch that . . . Every ounce of fat has been pared off, leaving the flesh firm . . . spare and bare as it is . . . dancing, shaking, all alive, but controlled." When the play began a three-city college tour on May 18, 1931, at Jordan Hall in Boston sponsored by the Harvard Dramatic Club, H. T. Parker of the *Evening Transcript* noticed Martha Graham's "extra-illustration [through] taut stylization of movement [in] trying contrast to the rest of the play."

At the McCarter Theatre in Princeton the following night, an unbylined writer for *Theatre Guild Magazine* also observed "the peculiar stylizations of Miss Graham," her disjunctive movements reminiscent of *Primitive Mysteries.* "Her clear percussion seemed a world apart" from the measured verbal pace of the play. The dance interludes came across, to this critic, like "separate thing[s] entirely. Set like an alien in the midst of naturalism," Graham, "with her devastatingly obvious attempt at counterpoint," distracted the audience from "the poetic choral passages."

Perhaps, the writer speculated, Graham identified so strongly with the heroine that she "chose the clear path and *herself* became Electra," raising the possibility that in a coming season she would mount her own production of the play, with herself in the starring role.

Electra completed its out-of-town run with a weeklong engagement at the Lydia Mendelssohn Theatre at the University of Michigan at Ann Arbor. When Yurka and Henderson arrived at the Selwyn Theatre on Broadway for four matinees of *Electra* over ten days in January 1932, Graham had long since quit the show, replaced by a former "Isadorable," Anna Duncan.

Twenty-six years later, presenting the evening-length epic ballet *Clytemnestra*, Martha Graham insisted to Agnes de Mille that "she didn't know where [it] came from. 'It has no antecedents, no roots,'" the choreographer said bluntly. "'It is like an orchid blooming in the air, a parasite on my own life.'"

. . .

Composer and harpist Carlos Salzedo encouraged Martha Graham to apply for a grant from the John Simon Guggenheim Memorial Foundation, established in 1925 by Senator and Mrs. Simon Guggenheim in memory of their elder son, who had died at seventeen. The mission of the foundation was to "add to the educational, literary, artistic, and scientific power of this country, and also to provide for the cause of better international understanding." True to this stipulation, Fellows were required to spend their terms outside of the United States.

Salzedo had been drawn to the dance through his friendship with Vaslav Nijinsky, whose physicality inspired the composer to develop ways to liberate the dynamic potential of his demanding instrument—"which part of the fingertip to use, how to attack the note, what speed should the finger close into the palm after sounding." A founding member of Claire Reis's League of Composers, Salzedo first met Graham there, and also knew her through their mutual patron, Irene Lewisohn of the Neighborhood Playhouse. During the twenties and thirties—accompanied by his wife, Lucile Lawrence, also a harpist—Salzedo was often present at Graham's recitals.

Sympathetic to Graham's financial difficulties, Salzedo appealed on her behalf to the impresario and producer of the Metropolitan Opera Musical

Bureau, F. C. Coppicus: Would he be willing to manage Graham and her Dance Group for a national tour? Coppicus's reply was that she would first have to test her box office viability on a European junket, an enterprise the American *danseuse* had never attempted. Salzedo then turned to another friend, Henry Allen Moe, director of the Guggenheim Foundation, only to discover that the institution's commitment to "the artistic power of this country" did not, as yet, extend to financial support for the dance.

However, Moe consented to consider an application from Martha Graham in May 1931, requesting that she "please give [him] a list of persons who know your work in the field of creative dancing? I want to consult with them." The door was opened for testimonial letters from Graham's sprawling network of collaborators, sponsors, critics, and admirers. Leopold Stokowski, Alexander Smallens, Henry Cowell, Wallingford Riegger, Otto Luening, Nellie Cornish, Irene Lewisohn, Rita Wallach Morgenthau, Blanche Walton, Alvin Johnson, Edith Isaacs, Dorothy Lawton, John Martin, Mary F. Watkins, and Mary Hunter Austin attested to Graham's standing among American modern artists as the living, breathing rationale for the field of the dance to become the next initiative in the culture of philanthropy—and the philanthropy of culture.

. . .

In her annual summer custom, Martha Graham went west for a month to her mother's. At a dinner in Santa Barbara, Graham met the photographer Imogen Cunningham, visiting from Oakland. Born in Portland, Oregon, the fifth of ten children, named by her father after the cross-dressing daughter of King Cymbeline, and growing up in Port Angeles, Washington, Imogen graduated from the University of Washington in Seattle, apprenticed with photographer Edward S. Curtis—platinum-print chronicler of the monumental *The North American Indian*—and studied chemical photographic lab technique in Dresden. Married, and the mother of three, at forty-eight she was on the brink of a career retrospective at the M. H. de Young Memorial Museum in San Francisco.

Just as Martha Graham professed that Denishawn and the Greenwich Village Follies were faded from her memory, Imogen Cunningham had moved beyond gauzy, soft-focus pictorialism and was obsessed with close-in, clinical detail. Both artists favored the purity of straight, unmanipulated images; Cunningham's affinity with *Neue Sachlichkeit* paralleled Graham's "stoic descriptiveness" in choreography. "She uses her medium . . . with honesty," said photographer Edward Weston, in praise of Cunningham, "no tricks, no evasion; a clean cut presentation of the thing itself."

Imogen Cunningham was no stranger to the dance; in the early 1920s, for her first commercial assignment, she photographed a tableau by Adolf Bolm's Ballet Intime; in 1929, she documented dance students leaping outdoors at Mills College in Oakland; and her current work explored what she believed to be the most expressive components of the human body—the hands and the feet.

Graham agreed to pose for a private portrait session at her family's old farm in Goleta Valley against a backdrop of rough-hewn, open barn doors. The sun was bright, "the [day] was hot, the smell unpleasant and the flies bothersome." Cunningham used her trusty Graflex, a 4x5 single-lens reflex with a focusing hood. Encased in Honduras mahogany and black Moroccan leather, the "RB" (rotating back) model allowing her to shoot vertically or horizontally without having to turn the camera on its side.

Two of Cunningham's modest Graham portraits were published in the December 1931 issue of *Vanity Fair*. In a pose from *Primitive Mysteries,* shaded eyelids and sculpted lips are set into a pale oval face, heels of palms impressed against temples, extended fingertips like a ten-pointed crown. In the other picture, eyes are downcast, hands cupped tentatively around the neckline of a demure frock. The magazine called Martha Graham "the leading exponent of modern choreographic art . . . [who] has worked to evolve a dance of integrity of movement and idea."

Cunningham took nearly one hundred pictures of Martha Graham that day, harsh sunlight bringing out planes and contours as the restless camera roamed from head to toes. Graham never looks into the lens, her expressions flickering from meditative and prayerful to ecstatic and pained. Her neck is arched to show bulging vessels and straining muscles. The viewer's gaze is led downward to a bare shoulder, lifted arms, an unclothed bust and torso. The knitted garment falls away to reveal rounded, raised breasts dappled by daylight. Knees apart beneath the tented folds of a summer frock, hands cup or clasp into the concave fabric. In the floor exercise that began her classes, Graham's feet, soles nearly touching, rest upon a black cloth or on the ground. Or the skirt is pulled above bended knees to show relaxed, bare legs, the dancer's head cropped from the frame.

It was one thing for Martha Graham to allow herself to be *seen,* another to be seen *into.* After reviewing the contact sheets with Graham from their

Three of ninety-one poses Martha Graham made for Imogen Cunningham during
their daylong outdoor shoot at Goleta, near Santa Barbara, late summer 1931.
The "crown of fingers" (top right) is reminiscent of the Virgin's stance in *Primitive Mysteries*.
(Photographs by Imogen Cunningham)

day en plein air, Imogen Cunningham "suspected the choreographer's disapproval," and never heard from her again.

. . .

Tanned and healthy from gardening, sunbathing, and meditating on her mother's lawn; and obsessed with planning her next dance piece, toward the end of August, Graham joined Horst for their second tour through the New Mexico pueblos. Attuned to solstices and seasons, Graham was fascinated by Indian rituals that attached communal dances to feast days year-round, marking the start of buffalo and antelope hunting, the change of pastures, first planting, the appearance of fruits, and the harvest. Anthony Dorame, a member of the Tesuque Pueblo, has written, "Cycles are circles that travel in straight lines. The seasons come in cycles, yet each season marks the passage of another year. We receive our names, plant, harvest, marry, dance, sing, and are buried in concert with the cycles."

Sixty miles west of Albuquerque, atop the Great Mesa of the Acoma (in Keresan language, Haak'u, "the place prepared"), the old stories said that the people had lived there for eternity. Unlike kivas, Acoma structures were rectangular, and set within residential areas. Horst and Graham witnessed the Acoma Corn Dance, filled with poetic songs. Their next stop, heading north and east, was the pastoral Laguna (K'awaika) village, nestled into a

Mesa Encantada from Acoma Pueblo, 1899. (Photograph by William Henry Jackson)

sandstone slope above the San Jose River. A few blocks from the kiva, the visitors entered the eighteenth-century St. Joseph's Church. Near an abandoned walled reservoir they saw faint imprints "where the feet of women once wore deep trails into the rock."

Further north lay the Zia Pueblo, on the banks of the Jemez River, built upon the "four stratified worlds" underground. At the deepest foundation, the Yellow World, lived Tsityostinako, the original mother, accompanied by her two barefoot daughters, Uchtsiti and Naotsiti. Endowed with the "powers of creation," they invented the sacred dances for the society: "We are the best dancers," the Zia say. "Our people raise their knees higher and stamp harder than any Pueblo." The two sisters led their people upward over time through the intervening Blue-Green and Red Worlds to emerge onto the surface of the White World, an Amazonian place of feminine power, where "the women boasted that they could do without men."

Heading north from Zia, at the south end of the Cañon de Don Diego, was Jemez (in Towa language, Walatowa, "this is the place"), a people known as "the highlanders of New Mexico, constructing their pueblos on lofty mesas among the yellow pine." The Jemez were fort-builders with a long history of resistance to the Spanish occupation. By the time of Graham's visit, the insular community was refusing Anglo admittance during traditional religious ceremonies.

The next "bead upon a crooked string" of towns on the east side of the Rio Grande was Santo Domingo. Horst and Graham came to observe the Pine Dance. Imbued with "tribal pride and élan," columns of men leaped, faces darkened, bunches of evergreen symbolizing everlasting life strapped to their torsos, wrists, and ankles. The male Santo Domingo ceremonial leader was called *yaya*, "mother," in tribute to the Corn Mother Iyatiko.

The mile-high pueblo south of the convergence of the Rio Grande and the Rio Chama was called San Juan; its pre-Spanish name, Xuocute'i Owingeh, in Tewa means, "village of the dew-bedecked corn structure." In the Christian-Indian culture of San Juan, "a standard admonition to Tewa of all ages was to 'listen to the women, for they are of the home.'" Of special interest to Horst and Graham, across the plaza from the kiva and facing the San Juan Bautista Church, stood the Shrine of Our Lady of Lourdes, built in 1889–1890 of lava rock in French Gothic style, and containing a replica of the grotto where the Virgin Mary was said to have appeared to St. Bernadette in the Pyrenees of southern France.

South of San Juan, in the shadow of the Sangre de Cristo Mountains, was Santa Clara, third largest of the six northern Tewa-speaking pueblos, whose storied ancestors came from "The Village Under the Lake," *Po-quin-owin-geh.* In the sixteenth century, in search of sustenance, these people had journeyed from the drought-plagued cave region ten miles to the west, called Puye ("where the rabbits assemble"). Spending a day at Puye, Horst and Graham marveled at stair steps and finger grips incised into the two-hundred-foot-high rock-face leading to abandoned dwellings carved out of pumice. Crowning the rugged mesa, they found the two-story community house adorned with fading petroglyphs.

At their last stop, neighboring Pueblo de San Ildefonso, they watched the Butterfly Dance, couples in sequenced competition making "small jumps, as the man and the woman moved toward or away from each other." The men carried immense shields made of radiating feathers and the women wore shin-length white dresses, white moccasins, tufted headgear, and winglike feather fans.

.   .   .

Did you think, then, that it was only on MacDougal Street that art renews itself?

—MARY HUNTER AUSTIN, *The Land of Journeys' Ending,* 1924

Disillusioned with the crowded cacophony of Greenwich Village—where she met Martha Graham—Mary Hunter Austin put down roots out west for the last decade of a prolific and restless literary life during which she produced twenty-seven books of stories, novels, nonfiction, drama, and poetry. In 1925, she renounced the intrusive "little whorls of success that kept appearing on the surface of affairs" in New York's concrete canyons, and began life anew in Santa Fe, building Casa Querida, the tidy, "beloved house" on Camino del Monte Sol, nucleus of a budding artists' colony, and welcomed Graham and Horst in the summer of 1931.

Mary Hunter was born in Carlinville, Illinois, in 1868, and, after graduating from Blackburn College, moved with her widowed mother and siblings to a homestead in the San Joaquin Valley near Bakersfield, California. At twenty-three, she married land developer Stafford Wallace Austin, and they settled in the Owens Valley town of Lone Pine. She gave birth to a developmentally disabled daughter, tried to maintain a career as a schoolteacher, and pursued the dream of being a freelance writer.

Mary Austin (second from left) on the Carmel Bay Beach, with Carmel Arts and Crafts Club members (left to right) George Sterling, Jack London, and James "Jimmie" Hooper, ca. 1905. (Photograph by Arnold Genthe)

Two spirit-of-place sketches published in *The Overland Monthly* conveyed Austin's affection for the untamed Great Basin deserts and hardscrabble towns of the eastern Sierra Nevada and its Amerind peoples, and paved the way for her first book, *The Land of Little Rain,* published by Houghton Mifflin in 1903. Her beloved landscape was feminine: "If the desert were a woman, I know well what she would be," she imagined, in *Stories from the Country of Lost Borders,* "deep-breasted, broad in the hips, tawny, with tawny hair, great masses of it, lying smooth along her perfect curves."

Literary success emboldened Mary to abandon her failed marriage. She left Stafford Austin, placed daughter Ruth into a sanatorium (and never saw her again), and set off for Carmel-by-the-Sea, where she built a writing platform in the branches of an oak tree. Trips abroad to Florence, Paris, and London followed. In 1909, she moved to New York, took a pied-à-terre at the National Arts Club in Gramercy Park, suffered through a long affair with Lincoln Steffens, and fell into the company of writers Charlotte Perkins Gilman, Emma Goldman, Willa Cather, and Mabel Dodge. "Sick for the color of the sea and the smell of wild lilac," Austin continued her nostalgic annual journeys to California, Arizona, and New Mexico.

Mary Austin's customary attire was a lace shawl around her shoulders, her thick, wavy gray-brown hair coiled into a tortoise-shell comb, under a black mantilla. "Imagine a woman," Carey McWilliams, social historian of California and editor of *The Nation* from 1955 to 1975, wrote in homage, "with the stout mental courage of [Aldous] Huxley and a streak of ineradicable mysticism, and you will have a fair understanding of the incongruous traits [within her] that were dominant." Despite ill health, she carried herself with a vigorous "blend of brass and innocence," said Sinclair Lewis; she was "feminine, damnably feminine, and not ashamed of it." Photographer Ansel Adams observed that she "worked within a shell of intense concentration," whether writing, gardening, or baking bread.

Fifteen years before she made the dance *El Penitente*, Martha Graham had read *The Land of Journeys' Ending*, Austin's vivid ethnography of the peoples of the Southwest, including a lengthy, graphic paean to the rituals of the Penitente flagellants. Graham was also moved by "A Bridge Between Cultures," a seminal essay in the May 1925 *Theatre Arts Monthly*, by Mabel Dodge, the patron saint of Taos, living there with her Pueblo Indian husband, Tony Luhan. Dodge agreed with her dear friend, Mary Austin, that artists back east, "lost in the never-never land, are ignorant of the sublimities of a world beyond Broadway."

The Land of Journeys' Ending was prophetic because, Luhan wrote, Austin saw the territory along the Rio Grande as "the land of the new birth of the synthetic American culture we have all desired."

Of all Mary Austin's works, Martha Graham found *The American Rhythm* (1923) most in harmony with her poetic imagination. From the beginning, Austin wants the reader to connect with the inner artistic impulse: "What is the familiar *trochee*," Austin asks, "but the *lub* dub, *lub* dub of the heart?" Here is the source of the blood memory Martha Graham would mythologize in her late-life memoir.

And we will "find [this rhythm] in the dance," Austin says, "the pattern by which men and women . . . welded themselves into societies and became reconciled to the Allness." She recalls Ralph Waldo Emerson, who tapped into that same diastole and systole when he "stumbled" upon "the American trail about Monadnoc," entitling this long, raggedly iambic poem after the peak in southern New Hampshire with the Abenaki Indian name meaning "the mountain that stands alone."

At the visceral core of *The American Rhythm* Austin glorifies "what the Indian describes as his sacred middle," where, like Graham's contraction, "something [takes] place as authentic as anger, tears or laughter," she writes, "the 'purr' of the homeland in the midriff of his being." She explains that "when the thing that went on in him reached the explosive point, [the Indian] gave vent to more or less patterned noises, patterned by the path of emotion through his own instrument, a pattern which became rememberable [*sic*] for the relief it afforded."

When she stood in the plaza of Santo Domingo for the Corn Dance, Austin "knew the land," and sensed the vibration in the clay ground: "The natural rhythm of timing feet will run from the pound of the men's thick soles, through the softer shuffle of the women, to the patter of the children tailing out the procession . . . rising and falling and overlapping like a musical round . . . steady and quick like the heart of the sun beating."

.   .   .

In September, Horst and Graham resumed instruction at the Neighborhood Playhouse School in its new quarters at 441 Madison Avenue. Actors in "voice production and stagecraft" workshops mingled with the dance students in Graham's classes. With funding from Sol Hurok, a few blocks uptown, at Steinway Hall, the Mary Wigman School opened its doors, attracting zealots eager to encounter "the new thought" of *Ausdruckstanz*. Wigman entrusted the school's leadership to her "only official representative" in America, Hanya Holm, one of her first students and Concert Dance Group members.

Petite, doll-like, and witty, with honey-blond hair and "wide, china blue eyes," Hanya Holm was born Johanna Josepha Eckert at Worms am Rhein, in 1893. Like Graham, Holm came late to dance, learning a rhythmic approach through Dalcroze and Laban. At twenty-eight, Holm began training at Mary Wigman's Central School in Dresden. She moved up quickly to assistant instructor and assumed the role of co-director when her mentor was on the road. Over the following decade, Holm assisted in devising Wigman's choreography, supervising rehearsals for *Der Feier* (*Celebration*) in 1928 and *Totenmal* (*Call of the Dead*). Dedicated to the fallen soldiers of the Great War, this ritualistic multimedia spectacle by Swiss poet Albert Talhoff for spoken word and song, a swaying, masked movement choir, light altars, color organ, and percussion overwhelmed the Third Dancers' Congress in Munich—and John Martin, in the audience, was transfixed.

Holm systematized Wigman's teaching methods "from the inside out," reminding her students that, to "discover the eloquent body," one must begin by doing away with the mirror. "Today's girl . . . long[ed] for self-

Hanya Holm, 1938. (Photograph by Barbara Morgan)

expression," Wigman said, but a superficial urge to "emote . . . was not enough."

Hanya Holm agreed: "To me, dancing is a way of thinking." True understanding would arrive only when the dancer broke away from the conception of her physical self as a mere vehicle. During *Übungsstunde*, the training hour at the beginning of every class, repetitions "as hard to describe as the swoop of a wing" drilled the students into "the dark vistas and blinding horizons" of the studio space, until, exhausted, they tottered at the precipice.

Voyages of discovery to inspire the dancers also took the form of field trips—to the library, to seek out philosophy and history for group discussion; and museums, to linger in contemplation of painting and sculpture. Holm's purist philosophy and kindly, other-directed manner were well received in her adopted city. Her classes were booked to capacity. Three years after her arrival in New York, Holm observed that "with this awakening of the American consciousness to its own inherent and unexplored fields, the artist is given that help and freedom so necessary in the building of a foundation for a true American art."

"Mary Wigman *is* the German dance," John Martin reported upon his return from meeting her in Munich. Martin's admiration convinced Sol Hurok to bring Wigman to New York in the fall of 1930 for the first of three triumphant transcontinental tours. The "Teutonic Amazon . . . with a warm smile" disembarked at the West Side piers accompanied by her costume mistress (and sometime percussionist), Meta Menz, and Hans Hasting, her accompanist. On December 26, the day before Wigman's concert at Chanin's 46th Street Theatre, Hurok threw a lavish tea party for her in the grand ballroom of the Plaza Hotel.

Doris Humphrey, Charles Weidman, Louis Horst, and Martha Graham (singled out by Hurok as "that great pioneer of our native contemporary dance") showed up at the affair out of curiosity, but with "little enthusiasm for an artist they considered an interloper" and newcomer, competing for the still small modern dance audience. Graham maintained a facade of indifference, saying that inferences about the relationship of her style to Wigman's should be "left to others. The modern dance in America," Graham pointed out, "was firmly grounded in its own way—*before* Mary Wigman came to this country."

John Martin knew it was fruitless to make comparisons between Mary Wigman, Hanya Holm, and Martha Graham. They converged "in the method of militancy, which has characterized nearly all the great art which makes up the heritage of the average man [*sic*] . . . Miss Graham," Martin wrote, "has said that until recently when she went upon the stage with a new composition, she went . . . with the whip in her hand. [And] Frau Wigman has for years accepted the resistance of hostile audiences as a challenge: 'You will like this dance before I have finished with you,' she has in effect said."

. . .

"There may be pictures here that you do not like, but they are here to stay, so you may as well get used to them," the director of the Whitney Museum, Juliana Force, declared at opening day, November 17, 1931, "marking the end of one epoch and the beginning of a new one" for the visual arts in America. Curator Hermon More concurred: "Our chief concern will be with the present and the future. In short, it is our desire to help create rather than conserve a tradition."

Seventeen years earlier, from a lofty, "sun-washed former stable" on Mac-Dougal Alley, sculptor and arts patron Gertrude Vanderbilt Whitney had established the Studio Club as "a haven for native talent" to show the work of "liberal, non-partisan" Americans ignored by the academies. By 1929, her Studio Galleries had grown from twenty artist members to more than four hundred. It was time for a museum. Four adjoining nineteenth-century row houses on West Eighth Street in Greenwich Village, numbers 8, 10, 12, and 14, were remade into a single facade of "old brick walls faced with yellowish pink stucco." The main entrance at number 10 was crowned by a chromium bald eagle. Ten rooms by interior designer Bruce Butterfield were arranged "to achieve the most harmonious effect, each picture isolated from its neighbor by generous wall space, to give the effect of a residence rather than a crowded public institution."

Strolling through Shaker furniture, folk art, and reading rooms, before reaching the cavernous Sculpture Gallery, one arrived in Gallery III on the first floor of 12 West Eighth Street, the Yellow Room, with works by, among others, painters Rockwell Kent, George Luks, Marsden Hartley, Charles Sheeler, Charles Burchfield, and Yasuo Kuniyoshi. Among this starry constellation stood two busts: *Head of a Woman*, by Elizabeth Chase, and *Head*, a newly acquired bronze of modern dancer Ruth Page, with oval, Modigliani-like face, smooth cheeks, upturned nose, pouting lips, and a tidy hair bun.

The sculptor was Page's former lover, Isamu Noguchi. After a year and a half abroad, he had "returned to the excitements of New York" by way of Tokyo, where he endured a strained reunion with his father; and Kyoto, where he lived in a ditch digger's hut and made multicolored glazed terracotta pots. As he had promised, Noguchi regained contact with Martha Graham, proposing they collaborate on a dance choreographed among Lev Theremin's electronic rods generating otherworldly music. Nothing came of the notion. Four years later Noguchi and Graham began their collaboration; for her solo, *Frontier*, he made a minimalist set, a fence post and two stretched ropes.

* * *

I believe that the "quality" of an artist derives from the quantity of the past that he carries within him—from his artistic atavism.
—JUAN GRIS, Letter to Daniel-Henry Kahnweiler, 1921

Martha Graham's dance to Aaron Copland's *Piano Variations* was on the program for her fifteenth concert in New York, December 6, 1931, at the Martin Beck Theatre, with two other new dances, "Serenade," also a solo, with music by Arnold Schoenberg; and "Incantation," for the Dance Group, with music by Heitor Villa-Lobos.

"It was one of the first works where I felt that 'This is me,'" Copland said of *Variations*. "In my mind, the piece had a certain 'rightness' about it." When a composer found a "nugget of expressivity" in a musical idea, Copland believed, he should "hold onto [it] for dear life." Graham struggled mightily with the piece, withdrawing into the studio to build the solo in rigidly enforced privacy, tying a red grosgrain ribbon around the doorknob to signal that there could be no eyewitnesses except for Louis Horst at the piano.

The stated theme is followed by twenty variations concluding with a Coda. Segues can barely be discerned because the separations are not pronounced. Each variation, Copland said, should appear "to develop organically from the previous one and all contribute to a carefully-constructed whole." In the composition, he "worked on the variations individually, not knowing exactly where or how they would eventually fit together."

One reviewer made an apt analogy between the *Variations* and a circularly repetitive prose poem by Gertrude Stein. For both modernists, a work of art was constructed like a geared machine of well-oiled, interdependent yet unique components. Stein distributed identical word sequences upon the printed page; Copland positioned initially non-sequential variations to create the appearance of a narrative. Their contemporary, the painter Stuart Davis, repositioned blocks of color and words-as-signs in his flattened streetscapes, calling them "mental collages."

"Strike each note sharply," Copland's score commands. The four-note establishing theme, *deliberamente*, with assertiveness, is grave, somber, and, in a halting pace, proceeds in martial call and response. Trying to flow, attempting to detach from proscribed notation, it is pulled back. This "straining-against-itself" jagged advancement and retraction, favoring tightly woven, conflicting patterns, is quintessential Graham.

Once the thematic premise is entrenched in the middle *Variations*, Copland's piece vacillates, jumping from percussive boldness to *marcato* to blurred *cantabile*, a decorous dream on the road to a nightmare. The meandering becomes straightforward and up-tempo, until a melancholy tenor intrudes, reaching downward to trip over itself in the lower registers. To emphasize the stubborn tension, the thirteenth *Variation* transitions from "threatening" to "heavy staccato." In the final, angry moments, the approach-avoidance dynamic leaps to the forefront, attacks becoming vehement, withdrawals halting, silences hanging off-kilter. The endgame, discursive and truncated, stumbles down a darkening echo chamber.

Martha Graham devised her thirteen-minute solo in a hermetic atmosphere and delivered a shock to the Martin Beck Theatre audience. What she looked like in performance must be stitched together from ad hoc fragments. John Martin bemoaned the ephemerality of the piece. It was "written in sand . . . depend[ing] entirely upon her memory and a stray marking here and there on the musical scores." Here, he said, was an opaque, reductive dance that marks "the beginning of a new period in Miss Graham's ever-changing art, a period in which she abstracts her material to such a degree that it becomes scarcely more than a single richly etched line . . . extend[ing] the theories of modernism to lengths heretofore unknown on the concert stage . . . It defies analysis."

Stark Young could only say that *Variations* was "sometimes fine and astonishing, sometimes confusing, and of an uncertain fluency and accent." Lincoln Kirstein left the concert of two minds, "irritated to the point of exasperation and physically worn out . . . unequipped for her simplicity and self-blinded to her genuinely primitive expression," but admitting that "the force of the personality of the woman magnetized [him] continually."

To Bessie Schonberg, "[*Variations*] was very repetitive. [Martha] used a relatively small vocabulary for such a long piece . . . she fell and picked herself up, and then fell and moved on. . . .'"

Jane Dudley remembered a "series of back-falls which she kept repeating over and over and over again." In the Graham lexicon, the fall was an affirmation, not a sign of defeat or closure; the floor was used, she would say, as "something to hit against and *rise* from, a way of saying '*Yes.*'" Agnes de Mille watched "Martha perform the astonishing feat of squatting on one foot, the heel on the floor, the other foot extended in the air straight before her, and in one count rise to a standing position on the strength of the single supporting thigh and leg." Graham added one convoluted clue: It was "a series of ecstatic variations on a ritualistic theme . . . A barbaric crescendo expressing the dionysiac passion of the ancient dithyramb."

Dithyrambic was the title Graham and Horst substituted—at the last moment—for Copland's *Piano Variations.* Dating from the origin of tragedy, dithyrambs were ecstatic songs danced at the beginning of the annual competitive dramatic festival in Athens by a chorus whose "wits had been blitzed with wine . . . accompanied by the double-pipe and lyre." *Strophe* and *antistrophe*, backwards and forwards, clockwise and counterclockwise, dithyrambs expressed the joy that surged among the people every spring-time with "the resurrection of the earth" at Dionysus's return, "the cardinal essence of the mysteries."

Copland confided to the poet Lola Ridge, "There is a certain essence of contemporary reality . . . expressed in the *Variations* . . . To live on—to develop—means," he said, "to enter always more and more deeply into the very essence of tragic reality." In *The Republic,* another text known to Graham, Plato names the dithyramb as the quintessential verse form, because "the poet is the only speaker."

Martha Graham, solitary poet of the body, was reborn in *Dithyrambic.*

18

From *Ceremonials* to Radio City Music Hall

Leading dancers are said to be playing to satisfactory grosses throughout the country, compared to a time not so far back when few, other
than the friends of the artist, were concerned in the recitals. Noticeable
point is that, with one possible exception, none of those doing the best
business are Americans. The one breaking the rule is supposed to be
Martha Graham.

—*Variety*, March 8, 1932

D iaghilev, Pavlova, and Duncan were gone. Fokine and St. Denis were
marginalized. And Martha Graham was in rehearsal for her longest
dance to date, the thirty-minute *Ceremonials,* coming to the Guild
Theatre on February 28, 1932. "Engendered by the primitive idiom" of the
Pueblo, the piece was made up of three main segments; "Vigil," "Song of
Vengeance," and "Sacred Formula" and featured the sixteen-member Dance
Group including Ailes Gilmour, Lillian Shapero, Anna Sokolow, and Sophie
Maslow. Two *Intervals,* variously entitled *Fun Dance, Joy Dance,* or *Dance of
the Delight-Makers,* were performed by Graham, Mary Rivoire, and Ger-
trude Shurr.

The composer was Lehman Engel. Born and raised in Jackson, Mississippi, the son of Juliette Lehman and Ellis Engel, a shoe salesman, Lehman
graduated from Central High School the year after Eudora Welty. He pursued piano at the Cincinnati College of Music, where he wrote his first
opera, *The Pierrot of the Minuet,* based upon the 1897 one-act "dramatic
phantasy" by Ernest Dowson. Engel then received a scholarship to Juilliard
to study composition under Rubin Goldmark, and subsequently was tutored
by Roger Sessions.

In 1930, at the age of twenty, Engel accompanied John Martin to a Martha

Graham concert. Bewitched by "the high priestess," he emerged "wrapped in a magical mood of her making" and resolved to write a piece for her. Armed with a letter of introduction from Martin, after months of appeals, rebuffs, and reschedulings, Engel met with Graham at Louis Horst's apartment. The pair "listened intently to [his] music" and decided to collaborate with the ardent, energetic fellow Horst nicknamed "Noisy Sunshine."

Graham made the steps for *Ceremonials* counting out loud while her dancers paced in silence, unaccompanied. From time to time she paused to call out impressionistic imagery for the soundscape—"the stillness of the sunrise," or "the sound of a forest at night," and Engel dutifully jotted down her words. At the conclusion of the studio sessions, he went home to "compose to [her] framework of moods," then returned the following day to play for Graham what he had come up with. She sat huddled against the wall, a shawl around her shoulders (she often "felt chilly" during dance-making), knees up, hands covering her eyes in order "to hear better," responding with interjections—"too many notes," or "here the music should sustain . . . here it should move rapidly." When Graham stood up to "try it on" her body, Engel, at the piano, was poised to make more cuts.

The amenable composer supported this reciprocity in tandem between music and movement, guided by the epiphany that when music precedes choreography, "from the contemporary dancer's point of view, [the] manner of creation is not the ideal one." The piece evolved smoothly—until the waning hours before showtime, when, sleepless, Graham "decided that the girls' costumes were not 'right.'" In a frightening Sturm und Drang familiar to many, she ripped the garments to shreds, pinning and refitting them on the dancers while the seamstress stood by trembling and the clock ticked. To Engel, Graham was convinced that the "work in progress might not turn out well, but she had to complete it and perform it before she could discard it and proceed clearly to the next work, whatever it might finally be."

Graham fled to her apartment, gripped with dread and saying she suffered from a head cold, and withdrew "into her little sleeping cell." Louis Horst, sitting by the bed in the only armchair, "droned on through his nose, 'Now Martha, you've got to pull yourself together . . . You're a big enough artist to indulge yourself this way, to fall apart the week before and still deliver on the night. But the girls are not experienced enough. You destroy their morale. You tear them down . . . You cannot work them this hard and then depress them. They will not be able to perform.'"

"*Ceremonials* is no good," she moaned.

"It *is* good, Martha," said Louis, enlisting his most persuasively wise timbre.

"It is not good. I know whether it's good or not. It is not good."

"It may not be so successful as [*Primitive*] *Mysteries*," Horst conceded tactfully, "but it has its own merits. . . . One cannot always create on the same level. . . . Transitions are as important as achievements."

Opening night, "the performance was jittery," Engel said. "The girls were still visibly counting their steps: one and two, turn, walk, two, three, four, stop," traveling barefoot across the splintery wood stage of the Guild Theatre laid over cement and punctuated with cracks and screw holes. John Martin praised Engel's score for woodwind, piano, and male voices, and commended Graham for welcoming the young "newcomer with such an important commission," but felt that *Ceremonials* was presented "in a tentative and unfinished state." A month later, close to dropping the piece from the repertoire, Graham took a deep breath and gave it one more try, in an abridged version, deleting the "Song of Vengeance" and recasting the *Intervals.* Despite these edits, Martin could not resist comparing the discursiveness and longueurs of the piece to the "simplicity and inevitability" of *Primitive Mysteries.*

Like *Ceremonials*, many of Graham's works were a hair's breadth from disintegration until the moment the dancers walked on from the wings. Daily studio exercises, the spawning ground for "final" (so-called) compositions, were structured to keep the dancers right where she wanted them, vulnerable and off-balance. Change, the only certainty, could come at any instant in the life span of a Martha Graham dance.

. . .

In mid-winter, Agnes R. Wayman, chair of the physical education department at Barnard College, convened a symposium of modern dance teachers from Barnard, Vassar, Wellesley, Smith, and NYU. Dance instructor Don Oscar Becque, a protégé of Mabel Elsworth Todd, was in attendance; as were Hanya Holm, representing the Mary Wigman School, and Martha Graham. Also present as an observer was Robert Devore Leigh, president-elect of Bennington College, a progressive institution in Vermont that, come September, would open the doors to its first class of eighty-five young women. Leigh was impressed with performance demonstrations during the conference by the NYU Dance Club under the supervision of Martha Hill, Graham's former student and company member. Looking to hire a director of physical education and dance at Bennington, at the strong recommendations of Graham and John Martin, Leigh offered Hill the job, to "take dance . . . from a sport to an art form." She kept her position at NYU and commuted by train from New York City. Thus the seeds were planted for what became, two summers later, the Bennington School of the Dance.

In April, Martha Graham and Dance Group debuted at the one-thousand-seat Jordan Hall, home of the Boston Symphony Orchestra. The program of thirteen numbers ranged from the "grave, stripped and penetrating" *Lamentation,* to the "potent illusion" of *Primitive Mysteries, Serenade* "à la Pierrot," the "denotement [*sic*] of pessimist and optimist" in *Harlequinade,* ending with *Dithyrambic,* "an abstraction of the dance," and the "Fun Dance" excerpt from *Ceremonials.*

H. T. Parker, following Graham's oeuvre since Massine's *Rite of Spring,* considered the show a "revelation . . . modernist in the use of short, sharp, bare and direct movement; in the breaking of a curve so that for the instant it seems an angular motion; in the energizing of every stroke, in the preference for impinging over modulated line; for significance over beauty in the discarding of every superfluity; in a sense of the body as an instrument of percussion and repercussion."

Parker observed that in Graham's "curiously and meaningfully blended" combination of "modernist technique and primitive suggestion," she performed "as though she were thinking and groping toward the evolution of a dance that should have its roots in a primitive America, yet in ultimate development be expressive of her modernistic mind and time."

Graham foregrounds this spirit of inquiry in her second published essay, "The Dance in America," appearing in the premiere issue of *Trend: A Quarterly of the Seven Arts,* an elegant letterpress magazine adorned with tipped-in photographs and woodblock prints. Picking up where she left off in "Seeking an American Art of the Dance"—"Know the land"—Graham advances her case, opening "The Dance in America" with a plea to the "dancer as creator," that she turn "[to] the land itself . . . look up and down and not abroad," for the "rhythms" that will energize her. She warns audiences, "beholder[s]" of the art, against becoming distracted by "personalities" coming and going on the stage. To avoid misreading a modern dance, Graham insists, spectators must focus their collective eye upon its "potentialities" and unachieved truths, because, invoking her father's adage, "movement is the one speech which cannot lie. . . . We are weaving a new fabric . . . from the threads

Hart Crane, ca. late 1920s.

of many old cultures, [but] the whole cloth will be entirely indigenous," a swaddling blanket that embraces "dance today . . . the unspanked baby of the American theatre."

The editor of *Trend* who endorsed Graham's resolve in "The Dance in America" that "from a cognizance of old forms we shall build a new order" was the Cleveland-born poet and playwright Samuel Loveman. Following his hometown companion Hart Crane to New York City, their "darling Babylon," in 1924, settling eventually in Brooklyn, Loveman eked out a living as an accountant and bookstore clerk, translated Baudelaire, Verlaine, and Heine, and ran the Society of Teachers and Composers out of his flat on St. Mark's Avenue in Crown Heights. He was a member of the all-volunteer, "band of brothers" (and one sister, Martha Hill), including Louis Horst's old friend, Ralph Taylor; composer Lehman Engel; Paul Love, dance editor for *Theatre Guild Magazine* and the *World-Telegram*; and Graham's brother-in-law, Winthrop Sargeant, gathering at Horst's apartment to found *The Dance Observer* monthly magazine "advocate sheet" in December 1933. In 1947, after Hart Crane's mother, Grace, died, Sam Loveman became his friend's literary executor.

At noon on April 27, 1932, three months before his thirty-third birthday, returning from a year's sojourn in Mexico at the conclusion of a Guggenheim Fellowship in creative writing, Hart Crane jumped from the stern of the SS *Orizaba* three hundred miles north of Havana, and drowned. Two words from "The Dance" section of Crane's poem, *The Bridge*—the epic he began in 1923 and published in 1930, with photographs by Walker Evans—would become the title of Martha Graham's collaboration with Aaron Copland in remembrance of her girlhood landscape: "O *Appalachian Spring*! I gained the ledge; / Steep, inaccessible smile that eastward bends / And northward reaches in that violet wedge / Of Adirondacks!—wisped of azure wands . . ."

Along with their goal, in the poet's words, "to attempt a mystical synthesis of 'America,'" another idealized urge connected Graham and Crane: the desire to "unlatch the door to the pure Indian world," so that "one is on the pure mythical and smoky soil at last!" In the layered intensity of *The Bridge,* Crane's voice demands that "history and fact, location, etc. all have to be transfigured into abstract form."

In "The Dance," Pocahontas, ecstatic Chosen One and the favorite of her father, Powhatan, "ran the neighboring canyons all the spring; / She spouted arms; she rose with maize—to die. . . ." Her body scape was transformed into the Virgin Land, to be "stirred again, / She is the torrent and the singing tree; / And she is virgin to the last of men . . . / And winds across the llano grass resume / Her hair's warm sibilance. Her breasts are fanned / O stream by slope and vineyard—into bloom!"

Hart Crane's plan, while living in Mexico after *The Bridge,* was to compose a "blank verse tragedy . . . featuring Montezuma and Cortez [*sic*]" that he had "dream[ed] about for years." That vision died with his suicide.

"I am unraveled, umbilical anew," Crane wrote in "Purgatorio," one of his last poems. "So ring the church bells here in Mexico— / (They ring too obdurately here to need my call)."

·   ·   ·

Martha Graham's application for a Latin American Exchange Fellowship from the Guggenheim Foundation to pursue four months of "studies of the native dances of Mexico and Yucatan" was approved in early 1932 by the Trustees upon nomination by the Committee of Selection, in the amount of eight hundred dollars (prorated from the $2,500 full-year stipend). Recipient of the first Guggenheim awarded to a dancer, and thrilled at the precedent, Graham was grateful to accept relief from borderline poverty and aware of the incumbent responsibility. She was tremulous with anticipation at the prospect of expanding her knowledge of indigenous cultures farther afield. "It is hardly a surprise that she has elected to go to Mexico and Yucatan rather than to Europe," the *New York Times* reported, because "for the last two years she has been turning more and more to the actual soil of the Western world for her inspiration."

Arriving at Graham's "long, narrow, gray-walled and barren studio" to interview the "new woman banner-carrier of the art of movement" about her forthcoming trip, Ben Washer of the New York *World-Telegram* found himself in the presence of "a taut, slim, curiously positive but not particularly pretty black-haired girl," who "sits on the floor" of her front parlor with "no draperies at the windows" to speak plainly of her early "years of mental turmoil . . . absorb[ing] the rhythm of New York." Graham had come to understand, she told Washer, that "the dancer's method of statement must change as the centuries change." Ultimately, "[Graham] looks upon herself more as an instrument than a woman . . . continuing to make America a seat of dancing progress and the American woman its generating power."

Martha Graham and Louis Horst arrived aboard the *Morro Castle* in the port of Veracruz in late June 1932. Many American artists before them had explored "not only the main roads but also the detours and byways" south of the border to make new work during the "Mexican craze" that peaked in the 1920s and '30s—photographer Edward Weston; painters Andrew Dasburg and Marsden Hartley; writers Anita Brenner, Malcolm Cowley, Katherine Anne Porter, and Mary Austin; critic and editor Waldo Frank; conductor Leopold Stokowski; and poet-translator Witter Bynner.

Despite awareness of that tradition, Graham could not insulate herself against the jarring emotional impact of the real thing. Setting foot on Mexican soil for the first time, she was knocked off-balance by the high-altitude heat, dusty street-level exoticism, and crowded novelty. An unsettled, alienated malaise hung on for the four weeks that she and Horst managed to remain.

Their first stop was the Zapotec-Mixtec site of Monte Albán, the White Mountain, venerated to the worship of Cocijo, the rain god. Fifteen hundred feet above the Oaxaca Valley, protected by the Sierra Madre Oriental range, Monte Albán was the largest urban center in the region during its peak of power five hundred years before Christ. At the time of Graham's visit, archaeologist Alfonso Caso and his team from the Instituto Nacional de Antropología e Historia (INAH) had begun to unearth an underground network of tombs at Monte Albán. Twenty-four miles southeast, the couple stopped at Mitla, the deserted "place of the dead . . . where the soul comes to rest." Low-slung, bleached buildings were huddled in groups, patio walls adorned with ornamental moldings fabricated from tiny volcanic stone pieces fitted together without mortar and set into red stucco in a variety of incised and protruding stepped-spiral designs.

After Cuernavaca, Acolman, Tenayuca, Texcoco, Cholula, and Puebla, they headed for Teotihuacán (in Nahuatl, "the place where men become gods"), the sprawling complex thirty miles northeast of Mexico City. Graham and Horst were enthralled by the monumental dignity of the place. The visitors paused at the Temple of Quetzalcoatl, the Feathered Serpent, excavated a decade earlier by Miguel Gamio, director of archaeology at the

Graham triumphant at the summit of the Pyramid of the Sun,
Teotihuacán, Mexico, summer 1932. (Photographs by Louis Horst)

Museo Nacional. Stone heads tenoned into the facade, snouts square and
open, jaws fanged in rictus grins, protruded from roseate collars sculpted
like maize leaves.

At the northernmost end of the site, beyond the Pyramid of the Moon,
loomed the dun-colored Cerro Gordo, the Big Mountain, its ancient name
Tenan, Mother of Waters. To the southeast, across a tan field dotted with
scrubby trees, rose the Pyramid of the Sun, its base decorated with frescoes of green-feathered, red- and orange-tinted jaguars, jaws agape spewing
forth stylized puffy clouds between tusklike teeth. Graham mounted the

facade, two hundred forty-two narrow steps, to reach the top of the pyramid, and stood at the gently rounded ceremonial altar, raising clenched fists in triumph.

During a cocktail party in the Mexico City home of caricaturist and pan-ethnographer Miguel Covarrubias, and his wife, dancer, and painter Rosa Rolando, Graham and Horst were drawn into conversation with the minister of public education, Narciso Bassols. Anthropologist Frances Toor, American-born founder-editor of *Mexican Folkways,* was the interpreter. Bassols told Graham that he had set up a school of the dance with emphasis upon preserving the traditions of the Maya peoples, and offered to select a few talented students to study with Graham in New York, inviting her to return during the winter to give lecture-demonstrations.

At the end of the tour, thanks to a letter of introduction from Claire Reis, Graham and Horst met composer Carlos Chávez, founding director of the Mexican National Symphony Orchestra and director of the Mexican National Conservatory of Music. Chávez had visited New York in 1923–1924, returning to share a loft on Fourteenth Street from 1926–1928 with a fellow Mexican, the surrealist painter and muralist Rufino Tamayo. Diving into the contemporary American music scene, Chávez befriended Aaron Copland, Henry Cowell, and Edgard Varèse. His "colorful, densely-scored" sonatinas and ensemble compositions were presented under the auspices of the League of Composers; and his "chaotic reimagining of Indianist folk tunes," *H.P. (Horsepower/Caballos de Vapor)*, a symphony for ballet, with scenery and costumes by Diego Rivera, had been performed by the Philadelphia Grand Opera Company Ballet and the Philadelphia Orchestra under the baton of Leopold Stokowski. Chávez offered to provide Graham and Horst with a piano piece for the fall season.

· · ·

The beat of the Corn Dance is life, repetitive as the heart-beat, interminably insistent as the pulse of the sun in the corn.
　　　　　　　　—VINCENT SCULLY, *Pueblo: Mountain, Village, Dance*

Louis Horst, settled into a cabin in the mountains near Steamboat Springs, Colorado, at the women's summer theatre and dance camp founded in 1913 by Smith College graduates Charlotte Perry and Portia Mansfield,

Great Corn Dance at Santo Domingo (Kewa) Pueblo, New Mexico.
(Photograph by National Museum of the American Indian Photo Services)

resumed outdoor classes in music appreciation and movement technique.
Martha Graham, back in Santa Fe, was welcomed at afternoon tea hosted
by Mary Hunter Austin on her patio overlooking a front garden of corn
plantings. The purpose of Graham's visit this time was to return to the Santo
Domingo Pueblo for the celebrated all-day Great Corn Dance on August 4.
Two weeks with her mother would follow, then Horst would rejoin her in
Santa Fe for visits to the Laguna, Acoma, and Isleta pueblos.

On the east bank of "the crawling brown waters of the Rio Grande"
between Santa Fe and Albuquerque, known for its "tribal pride and elan,"
Santo Domingo was the largest (seventy-five thousand acres of range and
grazing lands, giant cottonwoods, and piñon mesas) and "most fiercely
conservative" of the Northeast Keresan pueblos. Santo Domingo lore says
that, like the revered corn, the people were birthed underground, and arose
into life, to be taught the sedentary lifeways of agriculture by rain-bearing
kachina spirits.

With the Spanish invasion came the overlay of Roman Catholicism
engendering a calendar of rituals and events that blended traditions: October harvest time brought the Feast of the Dead in conjunction with All
Souls' Day in November; New Year's Day mass in the church was followed
by kiva clans' public dances; the Mexican matachin dance arrived in February; the four-day Green (New) Corn Festival marked Easter time; and San

Juan's and San Pedro's feast days in June meant "grab day," adapting the Spanish custom of *gallo* "present-throwing" from the rooftops.

Martha Graham and Mary Hunter Austin, along with hundreds of visitors and villagers—mothers and toddlers on rooftops, elders with blankets around their shoulders—gather in silence by the side of a canal on the town's eastern edge to await the drumbeat pulses from the kivas where dancers have been sequestered for days of fasting and meditation.

With a deep-throated "chant . . . halfway between wail and moan," the white-clad chorus of fifty men, the leader bearing a twenty-foot-high pole topped with a multicolored feathered banner, appears, "intoning . . . the deep, rich call for clouds and rain." The first kiva group of men dancers enter, in double file, heads down, elbows pumping, bells around their waists, thick-soled moccasins on their feet. These are the Squash People, "a little forest of trees in motion." From the second kiva, the Turquoise People emerge, bodies painted blue-gray, breasts adorned with rattling seashells and silver pendants, parrot feathers tied to the tops of their heads, spruce and pine evergreen branches strapped to upper arms and grasped in left hands, shaking seed-filled dry gourds crackling like rattlesnakes.

Then come the "mud-priest" clowns, *koshari*, bones and fetish-bags and rags around their waists, heads crowned with rustling tufted corncob stalks. Painted blue and ocher, speckled with black and white, they whoop, yell, and leap, court jesters "with the air of wizards on a binge," stooping to toss pebbles out of the dancers' path, joking with each other and the audience. The women dancers, last to arrive, breathe measuredly, eyes downcast, shuffling, barefoot, black hair flowing. Dressed in red-belted black cotton dresses embroidered with red and green thread, one shoulder bare, they bear tablita headdresses—thin panels of wood and cardboard carved into stately, gaily painted silhouettes of jagged mountains, terraced mesas, and scalloped clouds.

Over seven hours, long lines facing each other break and segue into triangular figurations—one man slightly ahead of two women flanking him, hands placed lightly on his shoulders, and then into a huge counterclockwise circle. The Great Corn Dance rhythms change when drummers halt and "reverse in a splendid split-second . . . The weights of the legs and thorax are pulled together in the pelvis." Knees flexed, not straightened, "send the beat upward." The torso is tilted frontward, spine lengthened; foot soles, horizontal, are "alive to the earth" like the "pawing" of deer and bison.

Martha Graham said explicitly and often that she did not make these recurring pilgrimages to New Mexico in hallucinatory midsummer heat to "steal the power" of Indian choreography: "In any art you see a vision, but that vision must be disciplined and poured into a mold for interpretation to the public," she would tell a fine arts class at Clark University in November. "That is why dancing is a *form,* something you learn as form . . . I have danced beset with fever, with the influenza, with strained ligaments in my feet. I would have been lost had I depended upon emotion."

.   .   .

Substitute teaching Graham classes during the summer of 1932, Gertrude Shurr befriended Marie Daphne O'Donnell, a long-limbed twenty-six-year-old nicknamed "May" because her birthday was the first of that month. May's journey to East Ninth Street began the year prior, studying with Michio Ito at UCLA. An observer in Ito's studio suggested that with O'Donnell's capacity for concentration, she would do well to seek out Martha Graham.

O'Donnell took the Canadian Pacific northern route to New York, rented a room at the YWCA on Fifty-Third Street and Lexington Avenue, and went to Hanya Holm's dance class at the Wigman School since it was close by. Finding it overcrowded and impersonal, she switched to Graham's, where Martha knew everyone's name. In the cramped front parlor, O'Donnell sat between Jane Dudley and Sophie Maslow. At the end of the first session, Graham called her aside, praising the newcomer's rapport with seated bends, "back falls, long stretches in the thighs . . . and brushes" with the feet. "You do this work very well. You should study with one of my teachers," she told O'Donnell. The result was that "Gert [Shurr] turned [her] inside out . . . Even when Martha wasn't to be loved," O'Donnell said—as when Graham refused to explicate a movement, lost her temper, or chastised the two pals for "sneaking off" to take in a ballet—Shurr assuaged May's fears, saying, " 'Oh, I understand Martha. That is the way she has to be.' " The two became apartment-mates and lifelong friends.

O'Donnell's Graham Company debut came in the fall recital, Sunday afternoon, November 20, at the Guild Theatre. The featured ensemble piece was *Chorus of Youth—Companions,* with a score by Louis Horst for piano, flute, oboe, clarinet, and cello. Delicate and well-wrought, it benefited from Graham's relinquishing a modicum of authority: "She watched us very carefully" during rehearsals, O'Donnell said, "even if it was a walk, and you made something out of it, she was sensitive to that. . . . She was very astute. Knowing Anna [Sokolow] had a passion for raw movement, Martha would say, 'Let's do that the way Anna does.'"

Graham partnered Ailes Gilmour, "the exotic, dark-haired Oriental One," with Dorothy Bird, "the sunny, fair-haired Blue-eyed One," walking and running, "softly, side by side, like a team of horses, [their] long hair loose, brushed out like manes." Bright costumes added to the sprightly dance, "white skirts with solid red or blue tops with kerchiefs . . . like middy tops."

Another premiere in the matinee, *Dance Songs*, was a four-part solo for Graham clad in a short-sleeved, horizontally striped, body-hugging, ankle-length knitted sheath. The composer was Imre Weisshaus, a former student of Béla Bartók and Antal Molnár at the Academy of Franz Liszt in Budapest. Each song carried a different musical line and title. "Sometimes a baritone voice sings alone [Simon Rady, in 'Ceremonial'], sometimes a drum punctuates his song ['Morning Song'] and sometimes a flute carries the burden of the music [Hugo Bergamasco, in 'Satiric Festival Song' and 'Song of Rapture']." Lehman Engel, donning his critic's hat, noted Graham's deepening explorations. "Consider these four *Dance Songs*," he wrote. "They contained the essence of all of Martha Graham's achievements for a long and important period. . . . In them, a very ancient past (a past beyond remembrance) breathes again—perhaps breathes for the first time."

In *Prelude,* with Horst at the keyboard playing Carlos Chávez's score, Bonnie Bird watched "Martha move . . . quickly, lightly, almost unconcernedly catching the changing tempi in amazingly dextrous [*sic*] foot-rhythms." Stark Young saw "certain reiterations [as] manifest" in Graham's performance, and welcomed "the return of a form, a tone, or rhythm. This seems a very wise tendency," he wrote, because "the lack of reiteration is one of the things that send so much modern art off into nothing."

In "Repetition in Music," one of a series of Charles Eliot Norton lectures he delivered at Harvard in 1958–1959 at the invitation of Archibald MacLeish, Chávez reflected upon the "supreme art" of Stravinsky's *Rite of Spring,* noting that "the idea of repetition and variation can be replaced by the notion of constant rebirth, of true derivation: a stream that never comes back to its source; a stream in eternal development, like a spiral."

Graham, who told her students that the only preparation for one grand jeté onstage was hundreds of practice leaps in the studio, echoed Chávez's insistence in another lecture-essay, "Art as Communication," that the creative artist "has to concentrate, concentrate thoroughly, so that in this light inspiration is sheer concentration . . . We provoke inspiration when we set ourselves to work."

Carlos Chávez further reflected Graham's conviction that to make modern music, be it Mexican or American, required "a knowledge of our history and of our country [that] will make us really feel ourselves . . . *musica culta*—art music—the 'national style.'" To inject that "fertilizing force" into his astringent modern idiom, Chávez practiced what he preached, traveling rural provinces to recover anonymous Indian chants and folk tunes, observe dances, and collect handmade instruments—*teponaztli* (drums), *caracoles marinos* (conch shells), *sonaja* (clay and bone rattles), and *vihuela* (guitars).

The moment the curtain came down at the Guild, Graham rushed to her apartment, and Bonnie Bird helped her pack for the overnight train to the Woman's College of the University at Greensboro, North Carolina, where the director of physical education, Mary Channing Coleman, was active in the movement to give creative dance its own identity in higher education. On Monday, Graham met with a group of dance students to discuss "her theory of dancing, and contrasted dancing of other countries with that of America." That evening, in Graham's recital at the Aycock Auditorium, Chávez's *Prelude* was renamed *Salutation*. On Wednesday, November 23, when Graham performed the work again at Randolph-Macon College for Women in Lynchburg, Virginia, the "dark-haired . . . graceful creature . . . of grave and penetrating beauty" was praised for bringing "a buoyancy, an exuberance, a freshness . . . unlike any of the other dances on the program."

*   *   *

Graham completed her frantic southern swing and at the end of November dashed out of town again, this time to the Playhouse Square theatre in Cleveland, summoned to action by actress Katharine Cornell and her husband, the director Guthrie McClintic. They offered $500 for Graham's assistance at rehearsals for *Lucrece*, translated by Thornton Wilder from the French (*Le Viol de Lucrèce*) of André Obey, costarring Blanche Yurka, with whom Graham had worked on *Electra*, and designed by Robert Edmond Jones. The show was scheduled to move by Christmas to the Belasco Theatre on Broadway. At the eleventh hour, Cornell realized that her elaborate pantomime movement sequences in act I were not ready.

Katharine Cornell's first sight of Martha Graham's virtuosity had been the opening of *Primitive Mysteries* in February 1931, the week before Cornell stepped into her most successful and longest-running role, as Elizabeth Barrett, opposite Brian Ahearne as Robert Browning, in Rudolf Besier's *The Barretts of Wimpole Street*. Posed by Edward Steichen at her soignée, aloof best, in a black dress, her pale neck graced with a strand of miniature pearls, anointed by *Vanity Fair* as "Ethereal Kit . . . the Garbo of the stage," Katharine Cornell was born in Berlin in 1893 and grew up in a wealthy family in Buffalo, New

Katharine Cornell as Lucrece, 1933. (Photograph by Carl Van Vechten)

York. Her father, Peter, was a physician and theatre entrepreneur. Katharine studied drama in boarding school. At twenty-two, she joined the Washington Square Players and the Jessie Bonstelle Company, and toured to London where she played Jo March in *Little Women*. Soon thereafter, she met and married Guthrie McClintic, casting director and stage manager for Winthrop Ames. Through four decades, McClintic was Cornell's artistic champion and strategist.

Her ingénue Broadway role was as the rebellious Sydney Fairfield, in *A Bill of Divorcement*. In the mid-twenties, Cornell was the "languorous" seductress Iris March swanning through Michael Arlen's *The Green Hat*, and she infused new life into *Candida*, by George Bernard Shaw, "mov[ing] across the stage with a long, slow stride, so that her full skirt broke into folds at the back below her knee in a way that was lyric with beauty and womanliness," enthused Mabel Dodge Luhan, reveling in the radiance of the actress's "antique *ampleur* of character . . . This girl is built for speed and endurance like a race horse or a doe." In 1927, hungry to portray strong women "from lusty to romantic," Cornell starred in *The Letter*, by W. Somerset Maugham, as Leslie Crosby, the wife of a plantation owner, who kills her lover. "If you're too accustomed to using your head instead of your feelings" onstage, Cornell warned the next generation of actresses, "you won't be able to call on your feelings when you want them."

André Obey derived his Lucrece from Shakespeare's *The Rape of Lucrece,* taken, in turn, from Ovid's retelling of Livy's doomed romantic triangle: the Roman general, Collatine; and Tarquin, his friend, who, enthralled by Lucrece's beauty, steals away from the battlefield at Ardea and, failing to seduce her, ravishes her. Summoning Collatine to return, Lucrece is consumed by anguish and remorse, confesses to her husband, and kills herself.

The action moves from bravado byplay among the encamped soldiers bantering about whose lady is most faithful, to Lucrece's hearth and home, where she endures her husband's absence and sits, biding time "surrounded by the women of her household, weaving, as she does every evening, as she did last night, and the night before." From the moment Lucrece is introduced, and for the entirety of act I, scene 2, she sews, spins, and walks about in silence to the accompaniment of spoken commentary by two golden-masked narrators enthroned on both sides of the stage. Martha Graham's guidance of Cornell as Lucrece through these establishing sequences was praised by Gervaise Butler as "poetry in action."

.   .   .

From this maelstrom of manic activity, Graham carved out two days and nights for the Dance Group's dress rehearsal of *Choric Dance for an Antique Greek Tragedy*—including "Chorus for Furies," to be performed at the December 27 gala opening of Radio City Music Hall. "Roxy" Rothafel's cavernous entertainment temple on Fiftieth Street and Sixth Avenue (Where the Fun Never Sets) was consecrated "the greatest theatrical adventure the World has ever known." Film exhibitor, stage producer, radio broadcaster, music arranger, theatre manager, war propagandist, and international celebrity, Roxy had been infatuated by Graham since 1920, when he hired her on Ted Shawn's recommendation as the Flame Dancer to lend a spark to the prelude for *The Cup of Fury.*

In gleeful anticipation of the "pageant of the entire theatre" to be deployed in his pleasure dome in the middle of Manhattan, Roxy chauvinistically hyped "the dance in America . . . to be far in advance of any European country he visited" and "Miss Martha Graham he frankly pronounces [as] the greatest dancer in the world." Roxy pledged that Graham would "belong to the official family" of Radio City Music Hall. He was going to give her oversight for all the "modern dancing" pieces presented there; moreover, he boasted, she would have "complete freedom to pursue her concert work as she sees fit, outside the boundaries of Radio City." For Graham, the guaranteed paycheck was a godsend.

Opening night it was pouring rain. The doors to Radio City opened at seven thirty, guarded by 250 of New York's Finest, and twenty-five plainclothes detectives from the pickpocket and bomb squads. Lining up in the marble lobby, proceeding through the sixty-foot-high mirrored grand foyer and up the curved staircase, were businessmen, high-society matrons, and "almost every bigwig in show biz" (according to *Variety*) including the Rockefellers, Morgans, Gimbels, Chryslers, Hearsts, Sarnoffs, Wanamakers, and Morgenthaus; as well as Gene Tunney, Al Jolson, Ruby Keeler, Amelia Earhart Putnam, Leopold Stokowski, Noel Coward, Paul Muni, Irving Berlin, Adolph Zukor, Morris Gest, Lee Shubert, and Max Gordon. "The Sixth Ave L never thought it would look down on so many high-class celebrities," Ed Sullivan gushed. "Millionaires to the right, ex-millionaires to the left volleyed and thundered."

Patrons entered the auditorium while twin pipe organs boomed. Designed to Roxy's vision of an art deco sunburst, the cornucopia-shaped theatre was constructed with eight semicircular plaster gilded arches diminishing in size from the back as they approached a proscenium wide as a city block. Two hundred multicolored spotlights powered by enough electricity, Roxy said, "to supply a city the size of Minneapolis" bathed the 6,200 red-velvet chairs in an otherworldly glow.

When all had found their places, trumpeters in red satin heralded the entrance of the ushers, who started the show with a snappy salute. The golden curtain rose at eight forty-five with a guaranteed crowd-pleaser, the wildly popular Wigman-trained German expressionist Harald Kreutzberg, as "the Angel of Fate." "We all watched him when he came down the stairs swinging his cape," Gertrude Shurr, waiting in the wings, remembered. "Martha just adored him." Martha Hill was enthralled by Kreutzberg's "dramatic quality . . . onstage, he appeared seven feet tall." Singers Jan Peerce, and Vera Schwartz, the German contralto, followed; then W. C. Fields, Amos 'n' Andy, and the Flying Wallendas.

Intermission came at midnight. The second portion of the show lapped over into the wee hours, beginning with excerpts from *Carmen,* directed by former Metropolitan Opera baritone Desire Defrere, starring Coe Glade, Titta Ruffo, and Arnoldo Lindi, and embellished by the Radio City Music Hall Roxyette precision dancers, doubled from twenty-four to forty-eight.

By the time the exhaustive display was done, half the audience had gone home. They missed the fast-talking George Lovejoy "Doc" Rockwell ("Quack! Quack! Quack!") holding a stethoscope in one hand and a five-foot banana stalk in the other for his crowd-pleasing "piccolo bit." They missed a *Minstrelsy* medley, starring Ray Bolger, the Tuskegee Choir, and the Berry Brothers—and they missed Martha Graham and her Dance Group.

19

The American Rhythm

Mr. Rothafel's is the much simpler theory . . . [to have] Martha Grahams for the highbrows and Dr. Rockwells for the lowbrows. But he may yet live to learn that congruity is not only an artistic canon, but a commercial one.

—"MORE MOUNTAINS, MORE MICE," *The Nation*, January 11, 1933

We ran backward, taking huge steps, with head flung up and torso arched high," recalled Dorothy Bird of *Choric Dance*. "We thought of ourselves as members of a Greek chorus, screaming out in protest against the Fates. Our costumes were made of dark brown and off-white woolen material. The skirts were huge, and the bodices were tightly-fitted. . . ." John Martin, loyally hanging on until the bitter end of the show, wrote that Graham's Radio City debut was "extraordinarily fine. . . . There is nothing that devours space so ravenously as movement does [and] Miss Graham supplied movement to a degree that has been heretofore rare for her. She ran furiously, she leaped, she extended herself to fit the space with a composition worthy of its dimensions." Mary Watkins was gripped by the bravery with which "this uncompromising Cenobite of the dance [took] a turn on the vaudeville stage."

Ed Sullivan, the vox populi, found the entertainment in Graham's art. "It was a positive pleasure," he said, "to see Martha Graham go sprinting across the large stage with pure archaic force and savage splendor . . . with a flowing stride that reminded me of Paavo Nurmi," the long-distance running Olympic world record–holder known as "The Flying Finn."

Choric Dance for an Antique Greek Tragedy was one of Graham's most athletic pieces, but evidence of what transpired that night is sparse because, unlike Harald Kreutzberg, who provided a program note to his Angel of

Samuel "Roxy" Rothafel,
the Radio City mogul, ca. early 1930s.

Fate, Graham gave "no descriptive matter, with the result," complained *Variety*, that "the Einstein theory is easier to understand."

Salaries for the Radio City backstage mechanics and engineers were three times as much as performers' fees. Within a week, an operating deficit was mounting, Graham's Dance Group, along with fourteen other acts, was summarily "expelled . . . on the toe of [Roxy's] boot," and her photograph removed from the lobby showcases.

Vaudeville's "gurgling death rattle" had begun in the late twenties with the advent of talking pictures, Vitaphone shorts, cartoons, newsreels, and radio. On January 11, without consulting Roxy—out of town, depressed, and recovering from surgery—the music hall reopened, showcasing first-run movies preceded by a much-streamlined, one-hour stage show. "They're all wolves, this Broadway crowd!" Roxy fumed. "What did they think I was, a miracle man, a demi-god?" Within the year, he resigned. "Never again will the two-a-day [movie] addict witness big-time Vaudeville," warned critic Sarah Addington in *Theatre Arts*.

Martha Graham disappeared from Radio City, as did *Spirit of the Dance,* a monumental cast aluminum sculpture in the main lounge. The nude dancer gazes to her right. Her relaxed arms hanging, she holds the suggestion of a garment just removed and takes a lunge in fourth position onto her left knee. There is dynamism in the torqued upper torso. Her reserved,

Spirit of the Dance, by William Zorach, bronze with brown patina, inspired by Martha Graham, 1932.

inward bearing contrasts with the metallic sheen of open nakedness. William Zorach, the sculptor, had been interested in dance since his days painting scenery and acting with the Provincetown Players. Born in Lithuania, he grew up in Ohio, studied at the Cleveland Art School and the American Academy of Design, and showed his paintings at the landmark 1913 Armory Show. "I remember Martha Graham telling me that she used to study my sculpture for the expressive gestures she found in it," Zorach wrote. "And I used to study her dance for the same reason."

Coming up through the ranks through years and miles of sweat and tears on the coast-to-coast circuit with Denishawn, and night after night in New York City with the Greenwich Village Follies, Martha Graham's *Rite of Spring* at the Metropolitan Opera House was meant to be her highbrow big-time moment—and Radio City, for the masses, her star-making breakthrough. Graham accepted Roxy's embrace on behalf of the culture industry with no intention of relinquishing her foothold in concert dance. He signed her up with the understanding that, while he paid her handsomely, she could continue the serious projects of the Dance Group. But at the level of inviolate truth Martha Graham demanded of herself, she could not simultaneously tolerate job security as a subsidized entertainer and protect the purity of her work as a modern dance-maker.

What next?

.   .   .

Habituated to regaining her equilibrium, Graham had sprung up after the brutal choreographic and critical falls in *Dithyrambic,* and, at this point in her trajectory, the former varsity basketball player focused now upon rebounding from the cruel Radio City setback. From hearthside evenings in Allegheny when Dr. Graham looked into his daughter's eyes, spoke of spiritual honesty, and read from Greek mythology, to Santa Barbara mission visits with her Catholic nanny, Martha had always loved the ritual actions of goddesses from antiquity, proto-Christianity, and the primitive Americas—the power of ceremony across the epochs.

In Louis Horst's home library was a well-thumbed copy of William Hone's *Ancient Mysteries Described: Especially the English Miracle Plays, founded on Apocryphal New Testament Story* (1823). Miracle plays flourished in France from the eleventh to the fourteenth centuries, all-male dramas about the lives and martyrdom of the saints, in vernacular or Latin, originally acted

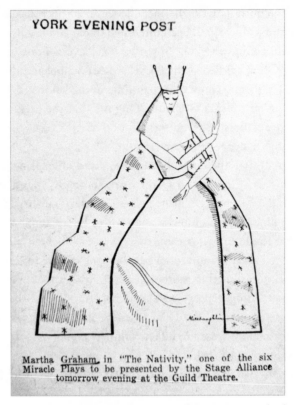

YORK EVENING POST

Martha Graham, in "The Nativity," one of the six Miracle Plays to be presented by the Stage Alliance tomorrow evening at the Guild Theatre.

Martha Graham, again incarnate as the crowned Virgin, in *Miracle Plays,* 1933.
(Drawing by Alice Laughlin; costume by Natalie Hays Hammond)

outside the church. A subgenre dealt with falsely accused women, "innocent persecuted heroines" who maintained an heretical stoicism. The mystery plays, from the Latin *mysterium*—secret truth—in the fourteenth to the sixteenth centuries, were dramatized processional tableaux and episodes from the Bible from the Creation and the Fall to the Annunciation and the Last Judgment. Mystery plays had a narrator and chorus, and were performed by amateur actors and guild members—men only—often over a cycle of several feast days, supervised by a pageant master.

Miracle or mystery, money was no object for bluestocking producer-companions, Natalie Hays Hammond and Alice Denniston Laughlin, founders of the Stage Alliance "to bring fresh and unusual patterns to the theatre." They had one woman in mind to join their sisterhood. Martha Graham would direct and star in *Six Miracle Plays* at the Guild Theatre, planned for February 5 and 12, 1933. They asked Louis Horst to arrange accompaniment for a woodwind quartet and an all-male choir. Hammond, a painter and textile artist, was the heiress-daughter of mining speculator John Hays Hammond. During World War II, she would build a compound in Glouces-ter, Massachusetts, for resourceful "single women [to] live their lives sur-rounded by other professional women." Laughlin, born in Pittsburgh and a graduate of the Art Students League, was an engraver, stained-glass window craftswoman, member of the Mural Artists Guild, and a descendant of James Laughlin, founder of the steel corporation.

Graham responded to Hammond and Laughlin that she wanted to unleash the "terribly stirring" dramatic potential in medieval dramatiza-tions of Bible stories. The women set to work. Alice Laughlin designed the "sparse, pure, admirable" set representing hell, earth, and heaven. Natalie Hammond designed costumes in a "magenta, vermillion and puce" palette, hand-painted by Ailes Gilmour. Hammond also selected and edited the manuscripts, three French plays narrated by Danish-born actor Paul Leyssac: *Les Trois Rois* (originally entitled *Le Drame des Mages*); Christmas Eve, *La Nativité* (thirteenth century); and *Les Trois Maries* (an eleventh-century Eas-ter drama); three English plays narrated by American Shakespearean actress Alma Kruger, excerpted from the Coventry mystery: *The Miraculous Birth and the Midwives*, a song from the Chester Plays called *The Lamentation of the Virgin Mary*. Graham's sister Geordie played the title role in *The Magda-len*, tempted by the devil and his supporting cast of deadly sins.

The *Miracle Plays*, Martha Graham's *Tanztheater*, revisited her persona as the chosen handmaid of the Lord, the Virgin Mother at the crux of the action "wearing a sovereign crown [and] robed as the Queen of Heaven"; and "laying her cheek on St. Joseph's palm," displaying "the right tragic knowledge for this woman in whose heart all man's pain was prophesied for-ever." Using pantomime and plastique to follow the spoken text, Graham's stage presence was "danced drama rather than dramatic dance."

Her incarnations of Mary for the Stage Alliance inspired eloquent critical responses. Her modernist movement laminated upon a medieval framework struck home with Brooks Atkinson: "This is the perfect medium for Miss Graham," he wrote. "Her Gothic poses and angular gestures and the spiri-tual aura of her beauty recreate the sacred impulse of medieval art . . . When this pantomimic motive is translated into the rhythms of a group of dancers, it looks modern."

Mary Watkins's admiration bloomed: "Miss Graham is, in every fiber of her artistic nature, eminently equipped for such work," she said. "Her physical presence, which is at once human and wooden, intimate and remote, spare and beautiful, might have served as the model for any of the saints on the cathedral porticos; her personality, alternately ardent and withdrawn, flowers in grotesqueries such as Villon and his contemporaries might have recognized as their own conceits. Her style and her art, ceremonial, shorn of superfluities, angular, rigid, recollected and humble, relate her congenially to those elder artists who worked unwittingly, even as she now works in the supremest sophistication."

Lehman Engel was transported to past eras and forward into the contemporary realm: "Martha Graham threw away the entire weight of eight hundred years and with the force of her genius she imbued [the plays] with life." A recent Graham convert, Museum of Modern Art curator James Johnson Sweeney, identified her hybrid power in the *Miracle Plays* as akin to "the new archaism" in modern painting released when "the surface soil" of the medium becomes "exhausted" and has to be "turned [over] deeply and completely to produce anything young in vigor or sap."

. . .

In a new apartment at 29 West Twelfth Street, no longer living above or in the store (as it were), and teaching around the corner in a fourth-floor loft studio at 66 Fifth Avenue, with the advent of the spring dance season, Graham set off for the Green Mountains of Vermont with her fourteen-member Dance Group. Martha Hill at Bennington had reached out to an audience beyond college students and faculty, opening a special evening with "the foremost American concert dancer" to members of the general public. "Miss Graham's work is built on a pulse through the body—a tension and release—which is her dramatization of the breath impulse," readers of the *Bennington Banner* were told in anticipation of Graham's first recital at the college on March 13, 1933. "[She aims] for economy of expression," Hill said, "for simplification and for directness . . . to find a quality of movement which is American and rises from the land itself."

The program was a Graham primer, from Chávez's *Prelude*, subtitled *Dance of Greeting*, and Lehman Engel's "Fun Dance," excerpted from *Ceremonials*; to the classics *Primitive Mysteries* and *Lamentation*, subtitled *Dance of Sorrow*; to the essential *Heretic* (summarized by Graham with six words as "[a] dance dramatizing the forces of intolerance").

The following month, the American Alliance for Health, Physical Education, Recreation, and Dance recognized Martha Graham's commitment to the necessity that modern dance transition out of the college gymnasium and into the concert hall. Mary Josephine Shelly, instructor in dance and physical education at Columbia Teacher's College, and soon to become Martha Hill's administrative colleague at Bennington, invited Graham to present a talk on "The American Dance" for the "Dancing Section" of the Alliance's Eastern District Convention at the Hotel Kimball in Springfield, Massachusetts. In what was, according to Shelly, "a most stimulating address," delivered on April 7, Graham invoked Mary Austin's "typically American rhythm . . . A dark soul, one of the New York critics has called her," wrote a listener in the hall that morning, "Miss Graham seems puritanical in her devotion to the dance, [and] in her seriousness as she expounds her belief . . . [that] America must produce its own dance in consonance with its own inherent rhythm . . . in the sense that artists are realizing (after a long period of dilettantism) that they cannot flower or indeed even survive unless they are rooted in their own time and place."

. . .

Those who seek their worship *out there* do not understand at all. Turn inward, and *there* you will find the footprints of the mystery of being.
—JOSEPH CAMPBELL, *Classical Mysteries of the Great Goddess*

The repertory for Martha Graham's final concert of the spring 1933 season on May 4, at the Guild Theatre began with Chávez's *Prelude*, and went on to Paul Hindemith's *Elegiac* (not the composer's original title; many names for Graham pieces leaped into her mind at the last moment). With Luigi Cancellieri on clarinet, the work was likely transcribed from an unaccompanied viola sonata. At Horst's instigation, in 1927, Graham had performed Hindemith's jaunty, rollicking *Tanzstücke/Five Dance Pieces* (op. 19) composed for piano in 1920. Horst appreciated the technique that the self-taught Hindemith endorsed when introducing his 1922 *Ragtime Suite*, op. 26: "Play this piece ferociously, but always very strict in rhythm, like a machine . . . Consider the piano as an interesting kind of percussion instrument and treat it accordingly." In 1929, Graham presented Hindemith's *Adolescence (Prelude and Song)*; and in 1944, Elizabeth Sprague Coolidge commissioned Hindemith's somber *Mirror Before Me/Herodiade* for Graham.

Graham in *Ekstasis,* 1933, "reveal[ing] the exquisite awareness of the body in
motion: shifting balances, alternating tensions, delight issuing from inevitabilities."
(Photograph, 1935, by Barbara Morgan)

Reprises of Copland's *Dithyrambic* and Imre Weisshaus's *Dance Songs* followed *Elegaic.* Then *Ekstasis,* a solo in two lyric fragments by Lehman Engel,
was unveiled. As the title implied, Graham was enraptured, her "feet barely
moving on the floor," wrote Dorothy Bird, like the seated, swaying *Lamentation,* then "one foot would float up, as first one arm and then the other lifted
and turned like a tendril reaching out. Her rib cage turned and twisted and
moved to the side away from her hips and legs. Her neck opened first on one
side, then the other, and her cheek pressed against the air."

Graham made the costume for *Ekstasis* from "one particular length of
roughly woven, clay-colored jersey tubing . . . perhaps silk or linen. Martha climbed into it. The material conformed . . . to the changing shapes of
her body," resisting and encouraging opposite movements with what Engel

called "rest-impulses . . . [that] set the *musical* fabric in motion." For Graham, the pelvic thrusts of *Ekstasis* were the locus for "the *beginning* of a cycle of distortion, not for distortion's sake, but for *deeper* meaning and feeling." Her ecstasy was not loss of sense—delirium—but a deliberate meshing of "intellect, emotion and action in a climax where no one power is limited by another."

The concert ended with *Tragic Patterns*, by Louis Horst. The original score is interrupted throughout with slashed pencil cuts and elisions. Expository measures that are slow, majestic, lyrical, or melodic are pared to bones and sinew—percussive, military, repetitive, nimble, accelerating without warning. Following the melancholy, contrapuntal "Chorus for Supplicants," the second, "Chorus for Maenads," is rapturous. The Maenads," "wild white

Terra-cotta statuette of a dancing woman. Greek, South Italian, Tarentine, third century BC. "The bare breast of the figure suggests she is a maenad, a follower of Dionysus."

women-worshipers . . . whose fleet limbs darted arrow-like" beneath long, whirling chitons draped with fawnskins, danced "divinely-veiled" to clashing cymbals, pounded tympanon drums, and piped aulos flutes in honor of the festival-god Dionysus, possessed with such raw, manic energy it was said that with bare hands they dismembered goats and tore up trees by the roots.

Martha Graham's Maenads "paraded against a startling blue cyclorama, an absorbing study in ceremonial mood, to which much was contributed by the white-clad accuracy and abnegation of the devoted young priestesses" of the Dance Group—Dorothy Bird, Louise Creston, Ailes Gilmour, Sophie Maslow, Lily Mehlman, May O'Donnell, Lillian Ray, Mary Rivoire, Lillian Shapero, Gertrude Shurr, and Anna Sokolow. The young votaries bound by love to their *choragos,* the leading dancer, clasped hands and encircled Martha Graham—*didaskousa,* their teacher—who executed her part with frenzied inspiration, "reminiscent of her spectacular 'Dance of Death' in the *Sacre du Printemps.*"

"Chorus for Furies," the final segment of *Tragic Patterns*, had a convoluted provenance, traced to Horst's second work entitled *Lamentation* (as distinguished from the iconic 1930 solo) written in May 1931, for Graham's performance in Blanche Yurka's *Electra*; elements of that composition were, in turn, transposed into Graham's "Dance for Furies" at the ill-fated Radio City Music Hall debut in December 1932, and reworked for the current *Tragic Patterns* with a drum added for emphasis. At the end of Graham's "marvelously supple," vindictive—and vindicating—solo, dramatizing the storied power of the three Erinyes, the audience broke out of "absorbed silence" to stand as one and cheer "another new Martha Graham to replace all the other new Martha Grahams of the past."

The wheel had come full circle from those hours on the Denishawn train when Louis Horst read to Martha Graham from Nietzsche's *The Birth of Tragedy: Out of the Spirit of Music*, the writer's voice singing from the depths of his "mystical and almost maenadic soul." Animating the ancient theatre, the Dionysiac deep-breathing chorus paraded across the *orkestra* on the terraced southern slope of the Acropolis while tens of thousands of spectators at the outdoor festival embarked upon their own psychic journeys. According to Nietzsche, as Graham understood well, the goal of the *Untergangen*—the voyage to the core of body and mind—was to realize that the conduct of one's life was justified only by courageous embrace of art's truth: "Movement never lies."

At the end of *The Birth of Tragedy*, Nietzsche beckons to the reader—"the friend who has been sympathetically following"—taking her by the hand for a few more steps along the wilderness trail "to a high and lonely vantage point where [s]he will have few companions." Pausing up there to reflect upon the implications for a culture that forsakes the legacy of its myths, Nietzsche appeals to his generation to maintain "the ambition always to be worthy of our sublime predecessors."

The principle held for Martha Graham's world, in *The American Rhythm*, when Mary Austin declared, "In Elizabethan verse, there was pomp [and] lute notes," but "in America, it was back to the foot pace of the new earth, ax stroke and paddle stroke."

20

Airborne

The Pueblos beckoned.

Mary Austin introduced Graham and Horst to Mabel Dodge Luhan, who opened her Santa Fe home to them. In a whirlwind, they headed from there to Jemez, Santo Domingo, Picuris, Las Tampas, Las Truchas, Chimayo, Santa Clara, and Zia; and crossed the border to the Walpi Pueblo in Arizona, mother village of the Hopi, perched on the rim of the First Mesa. In the small plaza offering a limitless vista across the desert, they witnessed the Snake Dance, anticipating the harvest, praying for rain and celebrating the return of the Kachina spirits to their underworld abode— "Behold! The Men of the Antelope—The Men of the Snake—Brothers!— Behold!—The unseen ones have heard our prayers—Black clouds gather over distant hills." Hopi ceremonies were reminiscent of the Tewa, but knees jutted higher and beats came quicker, Antelope priests' humming voices rising above chattering rattles. The eternal rhythms and circular choruses penetrated Graham's limbs and brain.

Returning to the stage of the Guild Theatre in November 1933, she lusted for space. Leaps hung in the air, extensions were sustained, turns more frequent. *Frenetic Rhythms: Three Dances of Possession,* to the music of Wallingford Riegger, ran the gamut from "atavism [and] grotesque animality" to "auto-intoxication" to "extraversion [and] arrant vulgarity," causing John Martin, drowning in a sea of superlatives, to say that "[w]henever [Martha Graham] changes she proves herself right."

For the last show of the run, Graham stipulated that balcony seats be sold in advance at reduced price to students and to dancers from other companies. The crowd reached such an extreme that the Guild fire department representative had to shut down the box office.

She drove the ensemble to greater heights, showing confidence in the veterans—the Birds (Dorothy and Bonnie), Sophie Maslow, May O'Donnell, Gertrude Shurr, Anna Sokolow—while exploiting the energies of the younger members. "To the American dancer," Graham wrote fervently, "I say: Know our *country* . . . When its vitality, its freshness, its exuberance, its overabundant youth and vigor, its contrasts of plenitude and barrenness are made manifest in movement on the stage, we begin to see the American dance. . . . We look to the dance to impart the sensation of living in an affirmation of life."

Louis Horst captured Graham's sentiments with the sensational *Celebration,* scored for piercing trumpet, winsomely muted for slower interludes, and snappy, martial snare drum. Graham did not perform, stepping aside to showcase twelve women in tight bodices and flared, slit skirts swirling at mid-calf, insisting they shrug off exhaustion with four hundred leaps executed in seven minutes.

Celebration was a dance glorifying dance, backstroke-windmilling arms, air-swimming with calisthenic ardor to show, as Graham liked to say, what the human body can do, seated, traveling, and in the air. Some leaps sprung straight, arms wide, toes pointed down; in others, legs were bent, arms thrown upward, hands cupped. Circles and *sautés,* the breakup of the ensemble into trios and dispersed shuffling sub-groups explored different movements, bringing forward motifs from *Primitive Mysteries.*

The lights, also devised by Graham, faded at an end that was not really the end; music and dance continued on while the curtain fell.

To newer company recruits Marie Marchowsky and Ethel Butler, *Celebration* encompassed the spectrum of Graham technique up to the mid-thirties: Floor work demanded the dancers stretch and push themselves up from below, spine-driven, thigh-powered rebounds without pause transitioning into lateral "low- and mid-body" maneuvers that invaded space horizontally, "going out on a limb . . . against the stream . . . pulsing" to "real *American* tempos—sharp and quick," with a dash of balleticism.

By the end of the year, Martha Graham had created and choreographed eighty-six works in her career.

·   ·   ·

Since 1925, one of Graham's anecdotal standards for historical storytelling had been the magical-realist, populist *In the American Grain* by William

Carlos Williams. Her interest in homestead poetical voices embraced Emily Dickinson, Walt Whitman, and Hart Crane. Identifying with American "spirit of place," she had pledged allegiance to this literary chorus in her "Know the Land" essay.

Since the publication of *Poems, 1924–1933,* she had similarly been drawn to the erudite work of Archibald MacLeish, like Martha Graham a child of the heartland, born in Glencoe, Illinois, in 1892, growing up on the shores of Lake Michigan. Mindful of Yankee ancestry and tracing forebears to the *Mayflower,* he, too, read deeply in classical antiquity, medieval romance, and pre-Columbian Mesoamerica. After graduating from Yale, where he swam and played football, MacLeish served as an ambulance driver and artillery officer in France during the Great War and practiced law in Boston for three years. "A special speech is born," wrote Karl Shapiro of MacLeish's verse in the thirties. "Out of this searching, [comes] something absolute . . . a linguistic dream."

In 1934, MacLeish asked Henry Luce for a six-month leave of absence from his job as a traveling correspondent for *Fortune* magazine to write his first stage play in verse. *Panic* was a critique of capitalism set against the background of the Depression and modeled upon Sophocles's *Oedipus,* produced at the Phoenix Theatre by John Houseman, directed by James Light, with costumes and lighting by Jo Mielziner. Nineteen-year-old Orson Welles, a student of Graham's at the Neighborhood Playhouse, starred in the role of McGafferty, a banker victimized by hubris who fails to heed the doom-laden economic prophesies of the oracular "Blind Man."

A friend since Paris in the early twenties when MacLeish's wife, Ada Hitchcock, was studying piano and composition with Nadia Boulanger, Aaron Copland approached "Archie" in the fall of 1933 about developing a libretto for an unnamed Martha Graham work about "the conflict of the individual vs. the mass." There would be a radical change from past custom; the piece might "include a man also." The project never got off the ground, but MacLeish had seen Graham perform, and was thrilled when he showed her the *Panic* script and "she was crazy about [it] . . . She thought, 'that's the way you ought to write a play.'" He enlisted Graham to "represent the emotions of the [economic panic] in symbols of the dance" and she choreographed the histrionic "Chorus of the Unemployed"—"Run with the Marching Men; with the thunder of a Thousand heels in the earth—" they cried. "Making of mortal burden a / Banner to shout and to break in the / Blazing of sunlight!"

. . .

Graham struck a chord of continuity in her next work, *American Provincials—Act of Piety; Act of Judgment*. She described it as an "excoriation of early New England religious intolerance," having for "its background the world of Hawthorne's *Scarlet Letter*." Its origins can partially be attributed to her teaching residency four months prior at the inaugural season of Martha Hill's Bennington School of the Dance where, "like the burning lightning, she made the scene alive with interest."

American Provincials was Graham at her most self-referential and unsentimental. In a solo of *Piety*, she gazed at some impossibly distant star; then, squatting to earth, taut hands in contraction shadowed closed eyes; and the tortured Puritan struggled with personal demons inflamed by visions of an angry God. In *Judgment*, Graham was harbored, then cast out, by a black-clad Group, referencing *Heretic*; however, this time around, the enlightened dancer showed ineffable elegance, her perfectly gathered bun nestled above a pale neck, nuances of maturity clothed in sculpted muted gray and creamy white and a startling, fresh fluidity.

The stage was set for *Frontier: American Perspective of the Plains* at the Guild Theatre on April 18, 1935.

Graham in *Frontier*, 1935. (Photograph, December 19, 1937, by Robert Fraser)

After five years of inconclusive intentions, Isamu Noguchi connected with Martha Graham on *Frontier,* with the first of more than twenty sets (or, as Graham preferred, "decor") he would design for—and with—her over a half-century partnership of "curious intimacy [and] distant closeness." Upstage center was a simple, rustic section of two-railed fence, the kind one would see bordering a pasture; harnessed to the floor, directly behind the fence at midpoint, two lengths of rope ascended diagonally upward, a gentle V shape "like cables looping off" into the fly space and "regions unknown" beyond. Recalling the train tracks Graham watched unspool during her girlhood trip westward from Pittsburgh to Santa Barbara, "It's not the rope that is the sculpture," Noguchi said. "It is the space which it creates that is the sculpture."

To begin: Louis Horst's trumpet-clarinet-oboe fusillade heralds the dawn. Composed and ready, Martha Graham, in a floor-length, homespun, pinkish-brown jumper worn over a white blouse with dolman sleeves, faces the audience. Arms spread wide, palms resting upon the top rail, she leans right and left, swings to sit atop the fence, swivels to look right, straight ahead, then left, lowering and raising her body, pridefully surveying the domain. In a contraction, smiling, she arches back, a gymnast, or horseback rider. Upon the fence-barre, one knee, propped up, mirrors the angled rope. Snare-drum, piano, and piccolo join in a Yankee Doodle–like parade. She begins a series of exultant high kicks to the side, right arm curved to nearly touch her extended left leg, *sautés* and kicks to the side and back, hands clasped behind her. Coquettish, hips swiveling, square-dancing, she advances, exploring wider spaces downstage. She rocks and weight-shifts: one heel, then the other, presses the ground; one palm, then the other, slaps the ground.

Two "long sets of bourrées" to piano and flute demarcate imagined plots of land; arms cradle and rock an imagined baby. Skirt brushing the earth, feet hidden, along invisible lines she float-glides downstage right, then upstage, advancing to claim her territory, abruptly changing to wild leaps before once more sketching out borders. Coming to rest with a level stare, anchored at her fence post home, an extended arm in slow semicircle traces the horizon. She descends into a back fall. Legs spread in fourth position sweep the surface of the earth, and arms aimed ahead pull in, hands clasped in prayer. Smiling broadly now, she rests one foot on the lower bar and gazes outward into the distance with wonderment, welcoming the freedom of isolation, perched atop the vantage point she calls her own.

"That girl, who was myself, is seeing a great landscape—untrammeled," Martha Graham said of *Frontier*, "and I felt it when I danced . . . flinging myself against the sky." The dance, she continued, "is very different from anything that is Puritan—it's not puritanical at all!" It enacts "the great appetite for space that made us pioneers."

.   .   .

Introducing her next polemical work, Graham wrote, "In every country there are basic themes of thought and action . . . These themes are part of the national consciousness and form an inheritance that contributes to the present." Where *Frontier* had a singular focus, *Panorama,* populated with thirty-six dancers, arrived bearing a vast prospectus.

The dance, she announced, "endeavors to present three themes which are basically American. No. I—*Theme of Dedication . . .* based on that early intensity of fanaticism with which our Puritan fathers sang their hymns of dedication of a new nation; No. II—*Imperial Theme . . .* a southern locale was chosen since here was to be found the most striking expression of a people in bondage ridden by superstition and strange fears; No. III—*Popular Theme . . .* of the people and their awakening social consciousness in the contemporary scene."

Graham's goals outstripped the production's practicalities. The premiere was set for the Bennington summer repertory, on Wednesday, August 14, 1935, at 9:00 p.m., in the Vermont State Armory. Graham began rehearsals on July 15, casting twenty-four workshop students from the School of the Dance (chosen by audition out of seventy applicants) in addition to the Concert Group. Louis Horst had planned to write the militant, forty-minutes-plus score for woodwinds and percussion with strings. Exhausted, he stepped away with one month to go, asking (actually telling) a college accompanist, Norman Lloyd, to take it on. Startling the young composer with obligatory homework, Graham thrust an armload of "source material . . . books, sermons and such" at him. Lloyd quickly "learned from her how you soak up material and background—not that you ever used any of it directly. . . . It was a mad scramble." Just before the curtain, at Graham's urging, he was still polishing the score for her final solo.

Panorama was the first of Graham's partnerships with Arch Lauterer, technical director and professor of scenic design at Bennington College by way of the Cleveland Playhouse. Lauterer believed that "[t]he purpose of design for the dance is *to show the movement*," taking into consideration "the point of sight from which the audience will see" the show. Allied with Horst's philosophy on the relationship of music to dance, lighting must "proceed from the base rhythms of the dance as a whole" . . . "The theatre planning problem" particular to dance, Lauterer said, "is to create a plastic stage space that can serve all the media. . . ." He welcomed Graham's carte blanche challenge to invent a new "space language," "completely re-creat[ing] the interior . . . of the Armory" into a three-level performance space, building platforms in a palette of black and silver, bleachers with folding chairs, a thrust extending the curtainless small stage, and widely separated, fanlike wings to accommodate the rapid flow of bare-midriffed dancers in "pongee skirts over trunks and bra tops with short sleeves."

Lauterer's layered vision put up logistical obstacles for Alexander "Sandy" Calder's first mobiles for theatre, explicated by John Martin as, "it seems, bits of decor capable of mechanical movement." Five red-and-white-striped discs, six feet in diameter, "recalling the days of Dadaism," were laboriously made to dip and rise via lengths of rope tied to the dancers' wrists and draped over pulleys high above the stage. Calder also built a jointed, accordion-like wooden contraption that at the press of a button was supposed to extend across the scene like a bolt of lightning. It had to be discarded. In *Horizons*, a four-part dance suite six months later at the Guild Theatre, "built on the theme of Exploration and Discovery," Graham made one last attempt to experiment with mobiles as "notes of bravado . . . visual preludes" into the mise-en-scène.

Critical response to *Panorama* was sparse and superficial, with the jarring exception of John Martin, who concluded that—circumventing its socially minded intent, and resentful at Graham's naive veering away from her pared-down aesthetic and toward a more Baroque style—the piece was "not Miss Graham's finest work by any means . . . It is too long, in some places gives evidence of the haste with which it has been composed," and "contains occasional extravagances of movement." In the end, he admitted to the hope that, with the hard work of revision, "by the time Miss Graham is ready to present it in New York," *Panorama* might rise to the occasion.

The morning following the *Panorama* premiere, a friend in New York phoned and read Graham the *Times* critique before she went for breakfast with Norman and Ruth Lloyd at the Hotel Putnam on Main Street in downtown Bennington. John Martin was already seated in the restaurant. Unwilling to suppress the fury of a woman wronged, Graham leaped up and strode across the room to his table, shouting bitterly—as she had accused Michel Fokine from the New School stage—"You have never understood me!"

Martin was mortified by her gauche behavior. Through the vicissitudes of their uneasy friendship, his admiration, tempered by buttoned-up professionalism, was undermined by Graham's guerrilla tactics.

The piece was not performed again until 1992, a twelve-minute reconstruction, sans mobiles, led by Graham veteran Yuriko based upon six and a half minutes of a 1935 silent, black-and-white documentary, fragments of *Part III—Popular Theme*. In the updated version, dozens of dancers gowned in flowing crimson run in place, leap with angled port de bras, spring like gazelles, disperse, and regroup into circles, amidst much planting of archaic feet. Midway, in a contemplative adagio, a quintet of tall ladies take, hold, and release a sequence of decorous plastique poses.

. . .

Edna Ocko, dance editor for the left-wing monthly *New Theatre*—pianist, student of Hanya Holm, and cofounder of the New Dance Group and the Workers Dance League—brought fresh appreciation to Graham's current work: "The most delicate moments . . . of her technic . . . are fraught with latent power. When the body stands, it seems immovable," she said, falling under the spell of *Frontier*, and "the body in motion is belligerent and defiant. . . . In training, the [Graham] pupil is told to be strong, 'strong enough to destroy barriers,'" Ocko continued, after visiting one of Graham's classes, and "that her body must surmount all physical difficulties and be 'energy on the move,' creating and recreating strength and change within itself."

Another proponent of the rightness of Martha Graham's "new departures, spiritual and material" was Elizabeth McCausland. Born in Wichita, Kansas, in 1899, after earning a master's degree in English from Smith College in 1922, she joined the Springfield (Massachusetts) *Union and Republican* as a general feature writer and, armed with a social conscience, evolved into a versatile cultural critic. In the late twenties and early thirties, her journalistic attention turned to personal interviews with empowered women, from social work pioneer Jane Addams to peace activist Rosika Schwimmer to painter Georgia O'Keeffe, who became McCausland's friend and entrée into the arts. Trenchant essays on Käthe Kollwitz and Gertrude Stein followed. In 1933, after a journey to the Great Corn Dance at Santo Domingo Pueblo, McCausland met and interviewed Martha Graham.

"The ideal of the dance today," McCausland wrote, in the first of a succession of articles about Graham over the coming decade, "not as an escape from life but as a means of putting one close to life, takes on added importance in Martha Graham's eyes." Impressed with the piece, and touched by a sheaf of poems McCausland gave her, Graham invited her to lunch and tea, and Louis Horst enlisted her as a contributor to his *Dance Observer*.

Elizabeth McCausland left Springfield for New York City in the winter of 1935. She moved in with Berenice Abbott at 50 Commerce Street—a vast loft with space to accommodate Abbott's platen printing press—and collaborated with the photographer on *Changing New York,* the WPA book that became an urban classic. McCausland branched out into *Parnassus, Magazine of Art, The New Republic,* and other journals, maintaining her Sunday arts page at the *Republican,* where, in February 1936, she weighed in on Martha Graham's "definite change . . . The direction of her growth is a centrifugal one, a movement outward into space.

"Instead of a static preoccupation with abstract considerations of form and medium . . . now the dancer may be thought of as looking outward into the world." McCausland wrote, "Martha Graham has added the dimension of action to the former dimensions of space and time, only it is now necessary for her to go even farther."

And she did.

Leaving New York City on her first solo transcontinental tour, Graham made a point of publicly rejecting an invitation from Joseph Goebbels, *Reichsminister* of Public Enlightenment and Propaganda, and Rudolf von Laban, president of the Deutsche Neue Tanzbuehne, to participate in the International Dance Festival in conjunction with the eleventh Olympic Games in Berlin. "I would find it impossible to dance in Germany at the present time," Graham responded. "So many artists whom I respect and admire have been persecuted, have been deprived of their right to work, and for such unsatisfactory and ridiculous reasons, that I should consider it impossible to identify myself, by accepting the invitation, with the regime that has made such things possible."

After Cleveland, Chicago, Boise, and Portland, Graham performed thirteen times along the West Coast between March 20 and April 10. The California trip was a geographical "movement outward"; the repertory, however, was an inward journey of solos, a retrospective through six years, from the *Homesteading Song* in *Horizons* rewinding through *Frontier, American Provincials, Frenetic Rhythms, Ekstasis* (retitled *Ekstasie*), and *Lamentation.* The selection was punishing for the dancer as well as for audiences new to her work expecting romanticism and receiving angularity: "She is given to cold grotesquerie. . . . Mood is too often absent from what she does . . . arty and self-conscious . . . motivated by cerebration with little apparent sincerity . . . arid of deep feeling . . . immersed in idiosyncrasies . . . a little vulgar and almost cruel."

One sophisticated exception, Alfred Frankenstein of the *San Francisco Chronicle*, came to Graham's style versed in modernist vocabularies of visual arts and music. A graduate of the University of Chicago who started his professional career as a clarinetist, Frankenstein made the effort to push through his "occasional momentary bewilderment" and plunge beneath the jarring surface of Graham's dances. To his way of seeing, her coldness was crystalline, her intellectualism passionate. In the presence of Martha Graham, he wrote, "one felt a wealth of ideas, a conviction and strength and positiveness of purpose, and a sureness of direction on new paths."

· · ·

The dance is no easy solution to light entertainment. The American dance is not an effeminate art form. This wrong conditioning has gone on too long. We look to America to bring forth an art as powerful as this country.

—MARTHA GRAHAM, "The American Dance"

In the third summer session at the Bennington School of the Dance, Doris Humphrey and Charles Weidman conducted Women's and Men's Workshops, and took center stage for premieres of Weidman's hourlong opus, *Quest,* featuring lead dancer José Limón, with music by Norman Lloyd; and Humphrey's epic "With My Red Fires," the final, "powerful, matriarchal" section of her *Trilogy,* with music by Wallingford Riegger. Hanya Holm came with a group from the New York Wigman School for her first concert in the east. John Martin returned and conducted a seminar on dance history and criticism; his wife, Louise, taught exercises in dramatic movement from pantomime. Louis Horst, as always "witty and caustic," enlisted Lloyd for their Program in Music Composition for the Dance, based upon "the old classic forms from which movement sprang," and Irmgard Dombois-Bartenieff lectured on labanotation.

"Martha Graham is here, but would you believe it, she won't come out and show herself," Sybil Shearer wrote to her lover, the playwright and dancer Gerald Davidson. "It gives the whole place a tense expectancy." Keeping a low profile, Graham presented two evenings of solos reprising her national tour, and presided over one workshop from her chaise longue, with Dorothy Bird as demonstrator.

On July 6, 1936, in the surprise of the season, Martha Hill, over the dissenting voice of Mary Jo Shelly, announced that Lincoln Kirstein and his Ballet Caravan would be coming to Bennington for a two-performance premiere. "That high green hill of learning . . . like all growing organisms, is constantly presenting new phases, new problems, taking on new shapes," Margaret Lloyd reported, on campus for the *Christian Science Monitor*. "There are no stereotypes at Bennington . . . It is alive with oppositions. It is a discussion place as well as a dancing place."

Kirstein described Ballet Caravan as a democratic laboratory affiliated with the American Ballet Company he had founded in partnership with Edward Warburg and *maître* George Balanchine. A group of twelve School of American Ballet students would present choreography by William Dollar, Eugene Loring, and Lew Christensen, troupe members "dominantly interested in classic ballet . . . applied to native themes . . . never dulled by a veneer of Russian glamor [or] post-Imperial ballet style." They would tour New England in the summer, "more of a hard vacation than work," Kirstein said, earning a living for six months until their contract resumed with the Metropolitan Opera. Martha Hill—approached by Kirstein despite the trepidation of his dancers, prepared for "heckling"—claimed that the Caravan's "hastily arranged" engagement, their first opportunity to be seen by the public, was a "*rapprochement*" between classical and modern dance factions, consonant with Bennington's progressive philosophy to "ferret out choreography that championed a healthier American spirit."

The College Theatre was packed for the Ballet Caravan performance on July 17, beginning with "Encounters," set to Mozart's "Haffner" Serenade, featuring Annabelle Lyon, Ruby Asquith, Harold Christensen; and Harold's brother, Lew, the Adonis-like dancer-choreographer from Brigham City, Utah, whom Kirstein praised as a "divinity [with] Praxitelian head and body, imperceptibly musculated but firmly and largely proportioned, blond hair and bland air recall[ing] Greek marbles." The second number, "Harlequin for President," "a satire on life, love and politics" in commedia dell'arte style, with music selections from Domenico Scarlatti, was choreographed by Milwaukee-born Le Roy Kerpestein—stage name, Eugene Loring—an athletic and fine-featured Michel Fokine protégé.

The third part of the program was a series of six unattributed *Divertissements* in which all twelve Caravan members were cast. Walter Terry, in the house for the *Boston Herald,* charitably observed, "The audience kindly overlooked the flaws in technique, and heartily applauded the group of young men and women for their sincerity of purpose." To eighteen-year-old Ruthanna Boris of the Caravan corps, "when Bennington applauded us, we felt more than ever that we were headed in the right direction" . . . "American ballet dancers dancing America!" Kirstein was relieved when the curtain came down: "Everyone was extremely generous," including the "charming and demonstrative" Martha Graham, who swept into the dressing room and told Kirstein that, despite their differences over the years, "she firmly believed in [Ballet Caravan's] destiny and in the vitality of the classic form."

One of the ensemble "kids" (as Kirstein was fond of calling them) milling about at the fringes of the room was Erick Hawkins, a tall, "powerfully-sinewed" twenty-seven-year-old with a hawklike, "craggy visage, broad brow, beaked nose, and strong jaw line" who looked part Indian, "as if he had been carved from granite." He had admired Martha Graham for a long time, always from afar. "Nervous as a kitten," Hawkins, blushing, was shocked, when—brushing past Eugene Loring and Lew Christensen—she "singled [him] out" backstage.

21

Erick Hawkins and Lincoln Kirstein

Frederick Hawkins was born at the cusp of the Rockies and the Great Plains in the Colorado frontier town of Trinidad, thirteen miles north of the New Mexico border on the Santa Fe Trail overlooking the banks of the Purgatoire River. He cherished memories of watching a Penitente procession at Easter when he was five years old, and recalled Indian dances in the Sangre de Cristo Mountains near his home at the base of Fishers Peak. Frederick's father, Eugene, an itinerant machinist from rural Bucklin, Missouri, and his mother, Myrtle, labored to keep the wolf from the door in support of the boy and his four sisters. After two years in Redondo, California, the family settled in Kansas City, where, in September 1921, twelve-year-old Frederick enrolled in Northeast High School.

Frederick was a serious youngster, and music was his first passion, but the family could barely afford once-a-week piano lessons. By his teens, the Chopin-obsessed lad was scraping together pennies running errands around the neighborhood so he could buy a ticket to hear the St. Louis Symphony (Kansas City did not yet have its own orchestra) at Convention Hall. Reading followed music in Frederick's pursuits. Inspired by the "loving kindness" of an English teacher, Frances Spencer, he kept a checklist of books, within moments of completing a volume from the public library picking up a new one—from Scott's *Ivanhoe* to *Quentin Durward*, from Dickens's *A Tale of Two Cities* to *David Copperfield*, and, eclectically, from Tennyson's *Idylls of the King* to Melville's *Moby-Dick*. Spencer mentored Frederick's interest in classical literature, and cast him as Tiresias in the junior class production of Sophocles's *Antigone*; he was proud of his rendition of the blind prophet's warning speech to Creon. He also joined the debate team, and served as business manager of the student newspaper and yearbook.

Graduating from high school sixth in his class of 459 students in June 1925, with honors in history, Frederick harbored only "one most compelling ambition" for college: Harvard. He took jobs at a haberdashery store and as a messenger boy for an advertising agency to make enough money to attend the only institution "unsurpassed in her professors and equipment . . . I could aspire to go to no greater university . . . at my present stage of life," he wrote. In the spring of 1926, Frederick submitted his application, accompanied by an essay labored upon for months about his moral and intellectual idol, Thomas Jefferson.

Erick Hawkins in front of his house on Harvard Street in Cambridge, August 1930.

On July 7, he received a letter of admission, supported by a $300 scholarship from the Harvard Club of Kansas City. The next day, kissing his mother and leaving a farewell note for his father, Frederick Hawkins boarded the train to Chicago, with stops at Washington, DC, Philadelphia, and New York City before arriving at Boston. He was the first student to check into the freshman dormitory, Standish Hall, and given a room on the fifth floor overlooking the Charles River. Bags unpacked, Frederick made his way into Cambridge to seek part-time work waiting on tables and housecleaning.

Bearing an ever-present knapsack, taking long, bouncing strides across the yard past cliques of Brahmin trust fund boys, Frederick held his head high although self-conscious about his threadbare appearance. In high school, swimming had been his sole sport; now, hopeful of meeting others, he tried squash, tennis, cross-country running, and rowing. With the intention of majoring in music, he spent most evenings in his room listening to gramophone records, except on Saturdays, when the Boston Symphony was in town. First-semester courses in Latin and Greek, and rereading Aeschylus's *Prometheus Bound,* rekindled an old fire. "The Greeks probably show us all the fundamental ideas and issues that occur in modern times," he decided in his journal. Initial grades in Greek were at the gentleman's C level; by the final senior term, when he and Robert Fitzgerald were in the same class, Frederick was earning A's.

During his second year, self-discipline became fanatical. "I must have *no* lost time," he resolved, joining a weekly scripture and prayer group of fellows devoted to "living a Christian life . . . in search of purity and truth." He immersed himself in Aquinas's doctrines, and considered a career in the ministry, resolving to find spiritual satisfaction through service to others and doing good works.

A perfect storm descended in the winter of junior year when word came from St. Louis that Eugene Hawkins, struggling under a burden of debt and property defaults, could no longer help with his son's tuition. The financial blow was compounded by an artistic epiphany in New York City. Frederick attended his first dance concert, at the Hudson Theatre on Sunday evening, January 20, 1929, featuring the return, after a year's absence, of Harald Kreutzberg, partnered with the smoldering Yvonne Georgi, "dark-eyed, free-limbed . . . with flesh like ivory melted."

Accompanist Louis Horst played Friedrich Wilckens's score for *The Angel of the Last Judgment* (the title appropriated from Kandinsky's 1911 painting), "great sweeps of stride and gesture like the rolling sentences of The Book of Revelation." It might have been the witty dancer's mercurial, angular intensity; or the elegant spectacle of Kreutzberg's "beautiful hands, his exquisite profile," with shaven head glistening; or the streamlined, athletic "way he ran . . . express[ing] nuances of emotion with the greatest economy of movement." In the front row of the orchestra, Frederick "came under [Kreutzberg's] spell" and said to himself at intermission, "That's what *I'm* going to do!"

On the basis of the family's near insolvency, an aversion to borrowing more money, and a pledge to save funds and rematriculate under his own steam, Frederick was granted a leave of absence from Harvard until the fall term. He left Cambridge in February and relocated to New York City to work as a College Board preparation tutor and companion for the son of Chase Manhattan Bank vice president Lyman Rhoades, receiving a respectably self-supporting salary of $200 a month.

       . . .

Existentially mindful of the occasion, on his twentieth birthday, April 20, 1929, Hawkins began to write a bildungsroman of his worldly journey thus far. The conscientious, stock-taking memoir dissolved within half a year into a swirl of options. Resolved to follow the artistic path, for the first time he tasted financial independence. Tutoring for a succession of wealthy families on the Upper East Side, far less risky career possibilities interfered, revealing ambivalence about the future: "psychologist, educator, physiologist . . ." Things were going so well with the prep school clientele—monthly stipends increased to $240—that Hawkins requested and was permitted an extension of the Harvard hiatus.

He returned to Cambridge from New York in the late summer of 1930, continued private tutoring in West Roxbury, and pared down his academic concentrations to Greek and world history. A more amenable attitude vis-à-vis dance ensued. Seeing Harald Kreutzberg had made a vivid impression; the tide truly turned when Hawkins witnessed Martha Graham three times within the space of a year—her "ecstatic . . . deep physical intensity and courage" in the February 1931 *Primitive Mysteries,* which he would remember, step by measured step, for the rest of his life; her stunning performance in Blanche Yurka's *Elektra* in May; and her landmark *Dithyrambic* to Aaron Copland's *Piano Variations* in December.

In his final semesters at Harvard, Hawkins dropped Latin and fine arts. His preoccupations were confined to classical studies reminiscent of "a time when the naked human body was truly beautiful," and ballet lessons in the studio of Edwin Strawbridge, a former actor and mime, and founder of

Harald Kreutzberg leading a master class at Salzburg Mozarteum, ca. early 1930s.

a group of male dancers. With designer Lee Simonson and the League of Composers, Strawbridge had choreographed the restaging of Prokofiev's constructivist spectacle, *Le Pas d'Acier*.

Harald Kreutzberg endured as "a finely-muscled, deep-chested figure of darksome splendors" in Hawkins's fervid imagination; drawn to the charismatic performer, he attended several recitals in New York and Boston. With a new partner, Ruth Page, Kreutzberg showed a flair for surprises, running the "gamut of intensities and shadings . . . short, sharp phrases . . . broken, contrasted, interwoven rhythms . . . plays of linear fancy," and a facility at intermingling song and spoken word with movement.

In the spring of 1932, Hawkins finished the required coursework and received his bachelor's degree from Harvard. On May 21, 1933, he announced with pride, "I am studying to be a dancer and actor," and, one month later, sailed from New York for a summer's sojourn in Harald Kreutzberg's class at the Salzburg Mozarteum.

.   .   .

A boy called Erick Hawkins, Harvard ex-1930 [*sic*], whom I remembered seeing in the Yard, having studied with Edwin Strawbridge and Harald Kreutzberg, now wishes to study with Balanchine. Nice serious kid.

—LINCOLN KIRSTEIN, diary entry, October 24, 1933

It is not surprising that Erick (as he had taken to calling himself) Hawkins never met Lincoln Kirstein at college. Although they were in the same entering class, Kirstein arrived on campus from a different world. He was born in Rochester, New York, in 1907, of privileged German-Jewish descent, the firstborn son of Rose (née Stein) and Louis Kirstein, investor and rising executive in the Filene department store company. Lincoln's sister, Mina, ten years older, doted upon him. After the family moved to Boston, he attended the Edward Devotion School in upscale Brookline, confiding to his diary, at the ripe age of twelve, "Not that I am any better than the [other] boys, just that I have a more questioning imagination." At thirteen, he saw Pavlova, and two years later, after his sight of the Diaghilev Ballets Russes, became permanently "infected with the 'red and gold disease.'"

At Exeter Academy, Lincoln's interests extended into playwriting, stamp collecting, classical music, Romantic poetry, and the decadent verses of

Wilde and Swinburne. Unable to tolerate the rigors of coursework, Lincoln was transferred to the Berkshire School, at the foot of Mount Everett in rural Sheffield, Massachusetts, where, rather than study, he preferred long walks in the countryside. A passion for painting, drawing, and stained glass was birthed when Lincoln discovered William Blake. During a summer trip to London with his mother and younger brother, George, he was introduced to John Maynard Keynes; on the Continent, Lincoln attended the Bayreuth Festival. Back home, he was intensively tutored to sit

Lincoln Kirstein, early 1930s.
(Photograph by George Platt Lynes)

for the Harvard entrance exam. On the third attempt, in 1926, "through the mindless strategy of memorizing the first five books of Euclid," he got in.

Harvard proved fertile ground for Kirstein to advance his extracurricular cultural agenda. Along with Varian Fry, a freshman "bull session" neighbor in Gore Hall, and advised by R. P. ("Dick") Blackmur, a nonmatriculated poet working in a Cambridge bookstore, he started a literary quarterly, *Hound & Horn*, intended as a modernist alternative to the entrenched *Advocate*. The young literati published Ezra Pound, T. S. Eliot, James Agee, Glenway Wescott, and E. E. Cummings, among many Americans and others. The following year, in alliance with Edward ("Eddie") M. M. Warburg, dormitory buddy and Our Crowd scion of the investment banking family, and John Walker III, heir to a Pittsburgh iron and steel fortune, Kirstein founded the Harvard Society of Contemporary Art. The gallery was nestled in two rented rooms upstairs from the Coop in Cambridge, where the friends would do homework and wait for "all the lorgnetted ladies from Back Bay [to] come . . . and say, 'Young men, tell me about this [painting], what is this meant to mean?'" Kirstein's emphasis, again, was on indigenous (an oft-used adjective) voices—Alexander Calder, Edward Hopper, Georgia O'Keeffe, Ben Shahn, and Isamu Noguchi.

Another art percolated among Kirstein's attentions: the dance. Eddie

Warburg sensed early on, emerging from late-night, booze-laden, some-times "snarling" residence hall conversations, that "Lincoln always had the latest news" and was "miles ahead of [the rest of] us mentally . . . Like a highly-sensitized film . . . [he was] exposed to tremendous forces in the creative fields." Warburg remembered "The real basis of all our discussions was what could be done on the *American* scene to enable artists . . . to be self-supporting? Lincoln had been going over that one with a fine-tooth comb, and the interesting thing he found from following what Diaghilev had accomplished in Europe [with the Ballets Russes] was having a common goal of musicians doing the composing of the music, painters doing lots of the scenery and decor and costume design and things, and the dancers doing the dancing. And all of this would be a joint effort centered around the earn-ings of [an American] ballet company . . ."

On summer vacation, Kirstein spent several weeks in Paris and London, treating himself to a Ballets Russes marathon. He laid eyes upon the work of the brilliant twenty-five-year-old George Balanchine (born Balanchivadze), Diaghilev's chief resident choreographer. *Le Fils Prodigue/ The Prodigal Son*, performed by Serge Lifar and Felia Dubrovska, was Balanchine's last Diaghi-lev premiere. Kirstein was entranced: "Gestures flowed smoothly, richly into one another like honey into a jar." He took note of Balanchine's "isolated genius . . . [his] sparseness, the lack of decoration which is by no means a lack of refinement . . . leading into a revivified, purer, cleaner classicism" . . . "He is the most ingenious technician in ballet I have ever seen."

Diaghilev was gone at the end of August. The dissolution of his company followed. But Kirstein's undying "idea of ballet as . . . a mode of expression at once traditional but also modern, classical but open to experiment" remained, with the ambitious Diaghilev as his paradigm, "a Napoleonic man of action with the soul of an artist and the taste of a connoisseur."

In February of his final semester, Kirstein saw Massine's staging of *The Rite of Spring* at the Metropolitan Opera House. "It was better than one would have dared to hope," he reported in *Hound & Horn*, "which, when all was considered, was not much." *Le Sacre* was his initial sighting of Martha Graham, who, frankly, "was not a success" as the Chosen Maiden. The "nec-essary waste" of the whole experience drove Kirstein to reassert that "America had no good school for theatrical dancing . . ."

Lincoln Kirstein inevitably moved to New York City after Harvard. He had an autobiographical first novel to complete; spent time with his wid-owed sister, Mina Curtiss, a teacher of English language and literature at her alma mater, Smith College; met and partied with "high bohemia" artists, left-leaning literati, and "carnal indispensibles" of both sexes; took documentary picture-taking field trips with Walker Evans; immersed himself in the mystic teachings of George Gurdjieff; brought westerner Yvor Winters and southerner Allen Tate onto the editorial masthead of *Hound & Horn*; was present at the creation of the Museum of Modern Art; and, in the fall and winter of 1932–1933, took ballet classes with the very formal Michel Fokine, and "finally realized" while at the barre—Kirstein's biographer, Martin Duberman writes—"that what he wanted to do more than anything else in his life 'with enormous excitement . . . [was] something connected with dancing.'"

Back to Paris in the summer of 1933: Virgil Thomson took Kirstein to the Théâtre des Champs-Elysées to catch Boris Kochno and George Balanchine's short-lived company, Les Ballets 1933. On July 16, in London, backstage after Les Ballets' performance at the Savoy, Kirstein and "the little sprig" Balanchine met at last. Kirstein found the "dark, very slight" dancer to be "totally charming" and "socially adorable," and asked him about his next career move. "It had become increasingly apparent," Kirstein observed,

George Balanchine, 1935.
"He always objected to being photographed. . . . He would screw up his face or say something funny— but he was good-natured."
(Photograph by Paul Hansen)

"that Western Europe had less and less to offer a young choreographer . . . Italy and Germany were hopeless . . . France, or rather, Paris," in his blunt opinion, "was a home for left-overs, intrigue, and dregs from the days of Diaghileff . . . [and] England was also (even posthumously) a Diaghileff province."

How about coming to America? Kirstein posed the question, and became "frightfully worked-up . . . frightfully excited" when Balanchine replied that he could well envision "the possibility of an American ballet." There would need to be "first, a School," Balanchine stipulated, to find and nurture talent; and then a Company could follow. "My pen burns in my hand as I write. . . . We have a real chance to have an American ballet . . . ," Kirstein wrote in a white heat to his friend Arthur Everett "Chick" Austin Jr., director of the Wadsworth Atheneum in Hartford, Connecticut. Appealing to good-natured Eddie Warburg, who had been teaching art history at Bryn Mawr and was now a Museum of Modern Art trustee, for funds to help bring Balanchine and his business manager, Vladimir Dmitriev, to the States, Kirstein said, "There's only one man who has any future—and that's Balanchine!" Warburg agreed, "and the next thing we knew we were in for the damndest buggy ride I've ever gone through."

On September 1, 1933, after farewell coffee in Salzburg with Harald Kreutzberg, and receiving his blessing, Erick Hawkins left for Copenhagen. On October 7, by way of Hamburg and Southampton, he arrived in New York. Ten days later, Balanchine and Dmitriev disembarked from the SS

George Balanchine with two American Ballet Company beauties, 1935.
(Photograph by Paul Hansen)

Olympic, and were met at the dock by Kirstein, Warburg, and Austin. In the cab to the Barbizon-Plaza, Balanchine declared that he aimed to open their school "with at least one hundred students," and expected "to produce [a show] by April."

The week following, on October 24, galvanized to attention after reading John Martin's article about Balanchine in the *New York Times,* Hawkins resolved that "[y]ou couldn't just regurgitate what they did in Europe . . . I wanted to be with the best—to go with the Master!" He went straight to Kirstein's East Fifty-Third Street apartment and signed on for the School of American Ballet. Its home would be on the spacious fifth floor of the Tuxedo Building on Madison Avenue at Fifty-Ninth Street, where "instruction will be given," Martin reported, "in classic technique, character dancing, *plastique* and adagio, and there will be lectures on art, architecture, costume [and] music."

Then Erick Hawkins treated himself to a new pair of $3.00 ballet shoes.

22

Interlude—*Chronicle*

You do not realize how the headlines that make daily history affect the muscles of the human body.

—MARTHA GRAHAM

During the week in July 1936 that Martha Graham met Erick Hawkins backstage at Bennington, the Spanish Civil War broke out in Seville, Barcelona, and Madrid. Wallingford Riegger (*Bacchanale*, 1930; *Frenetic Rhythms*, 1931) was composer in residence at the college, working with Hanya Holm and Doris Humphrey. While "it was not until the fall that [Martha] was ready to call on me," Riegger wrote, "for her first large dance creation based upon a social theme, war," she began that summer to prepare for what would become the epic *Chronicle,* over seventy-five minutes in three parts, scored colorfully for flute, trumpets, oboe, clarinets, and percussion.

"She choreographed a lot of whipping and lashing movements," Dorothy Bird recalled of long hours in the studio. "In places . . . where I had to bow my head or tip forward, I interpreted these movements as symbolizing submission." Two newer company members encountered challenges adjusting to twists and jolts in Graham's vocabulary.

"She would just improvise and we would have to 'keep it,'" said Jane Dudley, one of the "tall ladies" who had danced in the student workshop for *Panorama.* Graham wanted "a peasant rhythm . . . but *not* a 'dance for the people,'" Dudley remembered. "'I do not believe in relaxation during dance,' she would tell us, 'the body must always be used *in extremis,* even on the floor.'" For "Steps in the Street," the second segment of *Chronicle,* Graham was looking for "the kind of hoof-marks the camel makes in desert sands."

"Martha kept experimenting, all the time," said Marie Marchowsky, who had also debuted in *Panorama*. You could never dig deeply enough; there was always another layer rooted below. Graham would "give" the dancers a step, a brief gesture, but they would have to find a personal source for the energy to realize the movement. "She would grit her teeth [and say] that if you wanted to make dance into a valid modern art form, you had to be a fanatic," Marchowsky said. "Her dances were vital and large, and she expected enormous intensity. . . . She wanted us to think about every single thing we did, [to seek] extravagance—and ecstasy, get rid of sophistication, get rid of 'chicness.'" For "Steps in the Street," Graham said, "you were supposed to stretch your spine [and] stand 'placed' above your feet."

There were no explanatory notes in the printed programs for the December 20 and 27, 1936, runs of *Chronicle*, taking the stage of the Guild Theatre in New York as Americans of the vanguard International Brigade on the SS *Normandie* left to join the popular front against the rise of fascism in Spain. The new composition was "based upon the advent and consequences of war," and "concerns itself with the contemporary situation."

Graham bore down upon these general remarks a year later, when, she disclaimed, à la Kandinsky for his *Cannons,* that the work "does not attempt to show the actualities of war; rather does it, by evoking war's images, set forth the fateful prelude to war, portray the devastation of spirit which it leaves in its wake, [and] suggest an answer."

By 1941, World War II had taken over the globe, Graham's premonitions were subsumed by events, and she advanced several degrees further: "*Chronicle* traces the ugly logic of imperialism," Graham wrote then, "the need for conquest, the unavoidable unmasking of the rooted evil, and the approach of the masses to a logical conclusion. It shows the brutalization of conquest, the hypocrisy of imperialism, the marching of men without cause, without direction."

In "Spectre—1914," the first part of *Chronicle*, a backdrop red, white, and black banner stretches across the stage. The lights come up on Martha Graham, spirit-shadow embodiment of the conflict, seated sideways on two tiered Noguchi cylinders, arms resting on knees hidden beneath the draped expanse of a billowing crimson-lined black gown. She slowly stands, elongating her back with crippling ardor, her spine wanting to burst from the black leotard; not once—for this entire solo—will she be uncoupled from earth's grip. She manages to raise a fist in tortured defiance. The rest of her remains pent-up, leaden. Under duress, she shoves in all directions, a whirling dervish, hair whipping unbound. The dress takes on a life of its own, shrouding her head, bursting up and out spasmodically like broken wings of a fallen angel; extended, the garment is a rippling barrier she steps through haltingly, taunted by snare drum clatter. Prostrate at the center of the encircling gown, hopes discarded, she extends an open hand skyward in operatic supplication.

There is no response. She retreats to the silvery platform. It has become an altar, and she reclines there, back curved to the breaking point, sternum upward to receive the sacrificial obsidian knife. Her arms wheel in counterpoint to penetrant contractions. Nothing is resolved, and she comes to rest in the seated pose with which she began.

In part two, "Steps in the Street: Devastation-Homelessness-Exile," over the eternal expanse of two minutes, silent save for expelled breaths and floor-brushed barefoot whisperings, the dancers enter, dispersed and backwards, looking over shoulders to a gone world. In twisted unison they stride, converging and dispersing, variant poses on a theme, one arm crooked to cheek or neck, the other wrapped around waist or hip. A cymbal-clash—and they array across the stage, a group of five and a group of four, with a Chosen One (May O'Donnell in the premiere) at the center praying for the slim chance of a new day. They begin a clocklike *beat-beat-beat*, "one, one, one" in place. The reverse walk—arms extended, wrists crossed as if cuffed—seeks eman-

Graham (seated, center, with veil) and Concert Group in *Chronicle*, December 19, 1937. (Photograph by Robert Fraser)

cipation from chains of bondage. Even bent double, down-gazing, through the power of will the dancers discover ways to stand firm, thrusting up and forward.

Feet flutter balletically, toes implanted to the floor offset against the weighted hem of ankle-length dark dresses parting to reveal the power of alabaster thighs when surging bison leaps return, detonated by trumpet blasts, kept aloft by exuberant songs of xylophone and oboe. A final quick circle of airborne joy is tempered by the recessional, two parallel lines of dancers marching to stage left on either side of the Chosen One. She steps against their tide, pleading for a glimmer of surcease from above, before she, too, recedes from view.

In "Prelude to Action," light comes up again. The gloomy, recessive figure of "Spectre—1914" has become an aroused, white-clad prophetess. The martial pace quickens. From her command post atop the highest of Noguchi's three staircase-like tiers, Martha Graham incites her women—first seven, then eight, then nine, then the full complement of ten—to embrace all corners of the scene, "as if you are making your way around a room full of furniture," she told them in rehearsal, "don't jostle anything!"

Springing down to be with and among them, Graham encourages with exultant motion, pointing arms and dazzling, purpose-driven darts. Her precipitant, lurching steps slice the air. The dancers are determined to leave the earth below; stag-leaps morph into circles, cartwheels, shooting stars.

Graham dominates time; holding and sustaining poses for microseconds beyond assumed conclusions, snaring and enthralling the dancers who engage the spectators beyond the footlights. Multiple gazes break the fourth wall: Our ritual is a prelude calling for your action, they say, as, with one body, they step-pause, step-pause to the downstage edge, and halt, arms outstretched, palms upward: Here we are; we have displayed our selves. We are ready—are *you*?

In the headlong waning hours before the first performance, backstage became "a madhouse," Bonnie Bird remembered. The day prior to opening, Ethel Butler tore a muscle in her right calf; the rest of the troupe had to readjust placements, "which made me frightfully nervous," Bird wrote, "as I had rehearsed my own place for months and suddenly I had to appear for someone else with only one rehearsal." Striking the Noguchi sculpture at the end of part one and installing the elements of his three-level stairsteps before the beginning of part three extended the intervals between the segments, "which caused the audience to shout to the rafters."

The reviews were impatient. *Chronicle* was "aspiring, if not much else," the *New York Post* opined; there were too few lucid "green isles in a gloomy, turbid sea of unintelligibility." *Dance* magazine reported "with sorrow that *Chronicle* is not a successful production. . . . It is a massive work but lacks the power to arouse the feeling that Miss Graham must have put into it." Jerome D. Bohm of the *New York Herald Tribune* agreed that "the suite . . . would profit greatly by radical pruning." In the aftermath of his distaste for *Panorama,* John Martin could not define a route to the new work. *Chronicle* "abounds in striking phrases and develops them with great ingenuity into a kind of neo-classic formality," he wrote, "but its success in this direction makes it at once a subject for the admiration of the intellect rather than for a release of the emotions."

The premiere of *Chronicle* occasioned the publication of the first review of Martha Graham by an aspiring thirty-three-year-old critic, Edwin Denby, whose friends Aaron Copland and Virgil Thomson suggested to *Modern Music* editor Minna Lederman at the League of Composers that she give the "broken-down dancer and would-be writer" a chance to show his mettle. Rising to the assignment with the perceptual brilliance that would inform his signature lyric style, Denby, too, came away from the December 20 performance yearning for Graham's linear form to show fluid feeling. "It seems to me her courage could go even further," he wrote. "She seems to watch over her integrity with too jealous an eye. She allows her dance to unfold only on a dictatorially determined level. But a dance unfolds of its own accord on a great many contradictory levels."

Graham summoned the troupe back into the studio the next day, and they "rehearsed furiously all Christmas week," until three or four every morning, cutting and editing. Stripping *Chronicle* "to the bone," Graham and Horst wrangled the resistant dance; the audience at the December 27 revision rose at the conclusion, in full-throated approval.

John Martin found it hard to believe that a mere seven days earlier, *Chronicle* seemed so "serious, intellectual and undeniably dry." Martha Graham had worked her welcome magic, "breathing life and passion" into the dance, so that, now, miraculously, "a kind of heroic elevation of spirit . . . diffused itself through the whole work . . . illuminating its underlying intentions."

Martha Graham's benign rival, Doris Humphrey, said that "[a]ll dances are too long," a worthy adage—unless the choreographer is making a calculated decision to challenge temporality. Over time, like other vintage dances returning to focus with Graham's (reluctant) approval after having faded from the repertory for decades, *Chronicle* divulges a lineage through *Heretic* and *Primitive Mysteries* that would not have been apparent to its original viewers. The current—contemporary—version of *Chronicle* faithfully maintains the three-part unfurling, and comes in at thirty gripping minutes, a marker of progress along the journey of Martha Graham's forceful motifs—the group set against, and with, the shunned outcast and chosen leader; the studied disposition of bodies in space with contained and released energies; and the unimpeded, glorified authority of female physical power.

For a roster of this cosmopolitan downtown-modern power, one only need turn to the directory of studios advertised on the back cover of the January 1937 *Dance Observer*:

Martha Graham—66 5th Avenue, Room 404
Hanya Holm—215 West 11th Street
Louis Horst—63 East 11th Street
Doris Humphrey—151 West 18th Street
Eleanor King—51 West 12th Street
Lillian Shapero—79 West 12th Street
Gertrude Shurr—66 5th Avenue
Anna Sokolow—19 West 16th Street
Tamiris—52 West 8th Street
Charles Weidman—151 West 18th Street

23

American Document

It is difficult
to get the news from poems
yet men die miserably every day
for lack
of what is found there.

—WILLIAM CARLOS WILLIAMS, "Asphodel, That Greeny Flower"

M artha Graham, the revolutionary with a sense of history, said spectators should not assume she was creating art ahead of their time. Rather, *she* was of her time. It was *they* who lagged behind, "unwilling to desert nostalgic memories of an earlier day and face the present." She kept her own counsel until the end of an hour and a half of private warm-up sessions from floor work to jumps, when her body might—or might not—possess what she would—or would not—be ready to share with company members gathered, hovering, outside the studio door. "You could see the transitions from her Denishawn-like solos, to protest works, political statements, pure movement pieces, Americana, and then the myths," observed May O'Donnell, who danced with Graham from 1932 to 1938. "But at the same time, no one, probably not even Martha, knew where she was going except to make her feelings concrete."

May O'Donnell and Anna Sokolow were featured soloists in Graham's *American Lyric* at the Guild Theatre on December 26, 1937. Subtitled *Dance of Assembly*, the music was composed by twenty-seven-year-old Alex North, trained at the Curtis Institute, Juilliard, and the Moscow Conservatory, teacher at Bennington, and one of Graham's select rehearsal pianists. Hoping for a choreographic cri de coeur in support of endangered Depression-era civil liberties, Blanche Evan, dance writer for the proletarian-leftist *New*

Masses, came away disappointed. The subtitle, she acknowledged, "boasts a fine base for a dance script . . . But again the movement symbols employed in the dance are not symbols expressive of the theme. They are the movements from the composer's [*sic*] pre-determined category of pure 'kinesthetic,' detached and abstract and purely physical. The audience seems to remain emotionally unmoved and intellectually unsatisfied." Evan pointed, instead, to *Frontier* as an example of the equivalence she expected from Martha Graham: "When the curtain opens, one sees what appears to be an impression of a pioneer woman, dressed accordingly—not some vague generality of womanhood. . . . And she has her hand above her eyes, as if she's looking across wide horizons."

"If she wishes to deal with ideas," Evan scolded, Graham "cannot simply turn her back on this element of recognizability. She must find and build a new technique, not of abstract movement, but of a means of communicating her ideas through movement." But if Martha Graham wanted to efface depiction in one dance, then spin around in pursuit of blatant imagery in the next; and if she wanted to combine, or alternate, representation with inference, these were her stubborn, willful prerogatives, and always would be: to establish story lines, then derail them; react to headlines, then lunge beyond them.

May O'Donnell played a mediating role in the genesis of Martha Graham's next composition. During the summer of 1937, on a tour of the West Coast, the Graham troupe stopped in San Francisco, where O'Donnell and Gertrude Shurr were invited to teach a Graham technique workshop at Betty Horst's Studio of the Dance. There, O'Donnell met the composer Ray Burns Green, a San Francisco native, returned from two years' study abroad, supported by the George Ladd Prix de Paris, with Nadia Boulanger, Darius Milhaud, and Pierre Monteux.

Taken by O'Donnell's elegance and grace, Green wrote a maestoso "folklorish" dance for her. The original title was *Western Scenes*, and there were three parts: "Hiyah!" "Along the Trail," and "Round Up." "Crack these chords!" Green wrote in the margins, "Rip a gut! . . . go to town!"

When she returned to New York, O'Donnell shared Green's score—now called *Of Pioneer Women*, the sections renamed "Sarah Goes a Courtin','" "Markers on the Trail," and "Jubilation for a Frontier"—with Louis Horst. Always looking and listening for new voices, Horst showed the work to Martha Graham, who was so impressed that when Ray Green arrived in pursuit of his lady love, Graham called upon him to make a new piano arrangement for *Celebration*. One more lyrical layer would come seven years later, when Graham created the far-seeing "Pioneer Woman" part for May O'Donnell in *Appalachian Spring*, "looking out over the world, watching the springtime come" to rural Pennsylvania, "helping to bring it alive."

During *American Lyric* rehearsals, Graham had been rereading her bed-side copy of *In the American Grain*, the collection of story-essays by the poet-physician William Carlos Williams, exploring the textures of American history ranging from the voyage of the *Mayflower*, to the tragic life of the Abenaki Indian maiden Jacataqua, to "the Advent of the Slaves," to "Cotton Mather's wonders of the invisible world." The book, Williams wrote, "sought to re-name the things seen . . . under which the true character lies hid . . . to separate out from the original records some flavor of an actual peculiarity. . . ." Williams, who thought of himself as Graham's friend in "constant devotion," had been recently told—by whom he did not say—that "it was [his] duty to write her biography." He was tempted, but never undertook the project. Graham, in turn, asked Williams if she could borrow *In the American Grain* as the title for her nascent dance; he readily gave permission, but she decided otherwise.

Ray Green was a willing, apprehensive listener as Graham telegraphed her plans, never writing anything down, telling him with "fiendish . . . ruthless concentration" that "[s]he wanted me to do a panoramic piece," taking on "the whole American epic" with the sweep of heartland vistas she had long admired in the canvases of Thomas Hart Benton and Grant Wood. It seemed to Green that the prelude to the dance's action already existed in Graham's head when she spoke rapidly to him of wanting certain "beats" rather than melodic lines, "percussions" fabricated from "Indian rhythmic motifs . . . African folk-song [infused] Negro spirituals . . . [and] hymns from Puritan times."

Thus were the seeds planted for what bloomed into *American Document*, the variegated Green-Graham bouquet springing forth in the Bennington summer of 1938.

*   *   *

The doors of the School of American Ballet had opened in the new year, 1934, and Erick Hawkins, among the first students to sign up, jumped in with a boundless zeal his comrades came to see as akin to a bull in a china shop. Fellow dancers resented his hunger for the spotlight and instant conviction that he was destined for greatness. His tenure with the school and the company was further muddled by his inner conflict between wanting to perform and yearning to teach. Affectionate and acerbic, the fickle Lincoln Kirstein complimented Hawkins, writing on March 5 of "a good rehearsal of [Balanchine's] *Mozartiana* . . . even big Erick Hawkins bouncing along" in his Christian Bérard costume; mocked him two months later, during Balanchine's *Songes (Dreams),* as "the galumphing King [Knave] . . . awkward old Erick socked Jack [Heilig] by mistake with a stick he was using as a sword"; then praised him as "better than [Harold] Laskey" in the "demonstration debut" of the school's producing company on the lawn of the Warburg family estate in White Plains, New York, in June.

With instinctive *maître* Balanchine pushing him to be lighter on his feet, Hawkins endured a different kind of emotional turmoil during the first seasons of the American Ballet Company, on tour, then in residence at the Metropolitan Opera House. Hawkins longed "to have Balanchine's creative flow," insofar as that quality would "give me the proper foundation to build my own career and make a work of art of the ballet in America." Kirstein, subsidizing Hawkins with spontaneous tuition scholarships, encouraged him to show his evolving choreographic work to Balanchine, whose terse, equivocating critiques in halting English were along the lines of "You must continue." Hawkins's abrupt temper resulted in his being voted off the company for several months in 1935 and 1936.

When Hawkins met Martha Graham at the Ballet Caravan premiere at Bennington, he had completed making *Spring Round (Rondo),* on Balanchine's advice set to Carl Maria Von Weber's first (C Major) and third (D Minor) piano sonatas, and he sounded as if one foot were already out the door. "As soon as I have a fair mastery of ballet," Hawkins confided impatiently to his diary, "I shall have to begin a style of my own which will make an attempt to bridge the gap."

What this "gap" was, Erick Hawkins did not divulge—it lay between large-gestured impulses he had difficulty restraining within the ballet mode, and the allure of individualistic modern dance.

A sign that Hawkins might be finding a voice came with his full-length *Show Piece,* presented by Ballet Caravan's *corps* and ensemble, and "designed to exhibit the virtuosity of the Company" at their second Bennington summer. The group's music director was "a young American, Elliott Carter Jr." The score was self-awarely—with good reason—subtitled *Ballet Workout in One Act* by the twenty-six-year-old clarinettist-oboist-composer, Tucson-born Robert McBride, student of Otto Luening and devotee of Benny Goodman and Teddy Wilson. *Show Piece* took the dancers through a jazz-inflected, "care-free session of musical exercise . . . restless and exuberant rhythms, acrid harmonies, good humor, [and] speed" in a strenuous gamut running from "Bolero," "Heroic Air," and "Jig" to "Pantomime," "Imitation," "Parade," and "Strut." Balanchine approved ("Bravo, Erick!"), telling Hawkins *Show Piece* "is the best of Caravan" . . . "That's the piece of choreography that's been *done.*" Edwin Denby liked the snappy, spirited, "good-humored inventiveness . . . American straightforwardness" and "unspoiled . . . rather athletic quality of movement."

And "at present," Denby could not help noticing, "the boys steal the show."

· · ·

To construct *American Document* during midwinter and spring of 1938, Martha Graham brought her dogmatic imagination to bear upon a core group of iron-limbed, determined goddesses "passionate in [their] allegiance" and esprit de corps. Anita Alvarez, Thelma Babitz, Ethel Butler, Jane Dudley, Nina Fonaroff, Natalie Harris, Marie Marchowsky, Sophie Maslow, Marjorie Mazia—and the inseparables, May O'Donnell and Gertrude Shurr—believed in their heart of hearts that they were present at the creation of an ensemble-driven choral work for the greatest dance company of women in the world.

Meanwhile, between Caravan performances, Erick Hawkins, studying at the School of American Ballet with English-born, Pavlova-trained Muriel Stuart, was intransigently vocal, "sick of arabesques . . . needing a wider range, another vocabulary," and not afraid to tell Kirstein. Hawkins was "feeling [his] way" through the labyrinthine labor of making a ballet based upon the legend of the Minotaur that would meld his return to Greek antiquity with anti-fascist rumblings. Three years prior, Stuart had taken an indelible workshop with Martha Graham. Her own movement style "less-stringent than ballet but not quite modern," Stuart planted the idea in Hawkins's restive mind that exposure to Graham's radical ways might help him find the way out of his choreographic maze.

Graham and Horst were about to start their annual June course in the 66 Fifth Avenue studio—advertised as an "Intensive Four Weeks of Dance Techniques and Composition." Lincoln Kirstein loaned Hawkins the tuition.

With Erick Hawkins, rehearsing *American Document* at Bennington College en plein air, summer 1938. (Photograph by Barbara Morgan)

The first thing Hawkins noticed when he walked into Martha Graham's class was a Pueblo icon of the Virgin Mary on the wall. Standing as close as he dared to Graham, he sensed "radio-like waves" emanating from her taut body. "She was different" than any instructor he ever had, just the way Van Gogh, he thought, was different than any modern painter—those vivid, skewed canvases accosting him. "Martha got me going," Hawkins said. "She made me question my most basic ballet premises." Hearing about *American Document,* a work in progress, Hawkins quietly asked if he might linger after class to observe rehearsals.

He sat on the floor in the corner, because there were no chairs. Graham proceeded as she always did, showing, not telling, trying new phrases "dreamed up" by Ray Green, pacing out his "counts by sequences" to snare drum and piano. She was ruthless, "cutting entire movements and replacing them with less, or boiling them down to almost nothing." Nina Fonaroff moaned that "[d]ance history could have been made out of what Martha threw in the garbage" during the evolution of *American Document.* From time to time, Graham conferred with Hawkins. He was intellectual, and curious, posing "detailed questions" about the piece; to the dancers' amazement, Graham—and Horst—actually answered.

Toward the end of the month, the company prepared to move to Bennington College, where, accompanied by Green and Horst, they would flesh out *American Document* in anticipation of the August premiere. On one of the last late nights in the New York studio, during a pause between the wide-ranging floor patterns for Ray Green's "Indian Episode" and "Emancipation Episode," with Sophie Maslow leading the ensemble, Graham was expected to enter for a transitional solo. Instead, she suddenly "announced . . . out of the blue . . . "*Erick and I* will come in here,' to everyone's shock."

To Jane Dudley, the interloper "Hero-Prince" had crossed the forbidden threshold into the temple of the "Queen-Goddess"; Hawkins, she complained, "took 'our Martha' from us . . . Into our sacred circle came a foreign element."

Marie Marchowsky was put off by his unsubtle "posturing." Hawkins, she believed, did not understand the foundational principles of modern theatre-dance. It was not as if Martha Graham had never danced with a man before; there had been Ted Shawn, and Charles Weidman, and Robert Gorham, and Michio Ito. And yet, May O'Donnell mused, "in some ways it was easier just to work with the girls. . . . The minute you get a man and a female there's a different kind of insinuation."

Erick Hawkins—at twenty-nine, fifteen years younger than Martha Graham—was boisterous and fit, perfectly toned—"full of beans . . . I looked like a million dollars," he pronounced of himself that summer, proud of his suntanned body and sculpted legs set against trim white tennis shorts. "We called him 'the torso,'" Otto Luening said. Anyone watching their entangled, caressing rehearsals could see Graham had fallen hard. When she swatted Hawkins on his damp, shirtless chest it was with a playful smile. After her "euphoric" second day in the Bennington studio, "all aflutter" . . . "flirtatiously . . . girlish and coy . . . prancing around with Erick" in the sacred and profane "Song of Songs" episode taking shape for *American Document,* Graham told Ray Green, cutting and pasting and scribbling notes, that from now on, the lovers "would work out the details [of the duet] . . . privately."

Of an evening, at the kitchen table in Cricket Hill House on campus, where Graham, her mother, Mrs. Duffy, visiting from Santa Barbara, and the poet Ben Belitt were staying, Martha Hill would stop in for a cup of tea and a chat with Hawkins. The affair was "common knowledge," around the school, Hill recalled, and "Martha was also in love with the idea of Erick as a beautiful male figure who could carry out [her] ideas in a way that she had not been able to do with the woman's group."

Although Hawkins was assumed to be "on loan" from Ballet Caravan, Graham ceded authority to him during rehearsals, making it clear to the ensemble that whatever missteps he made along the way were above reproach.

Graham's music director, merciless coach, and wailing wall, Louis Horst, for several months had been sleeping with twenty-four-year-old Nina Fonaroff, a member of the Dance Group; but at the keyboard, whether within the four walls of the carriage barn, or beneath Arch Lauterer's striped tent pitched next to the library, Horst remained the professional grouchy, cigar-smoking Papa Bear. To complicate the ménage, his wife, Betty, decided to come east from San Francisco for the Bennington summer.

. . .

When we worked together, and I'd be setting up my lights, and she'd be doing her performance makeup, [Martha and I] wouldn't talk. When both of us were ready, we'd lift a hand and then we'd go and sit on the floor at quite a distance while we were "becoming."

—BARBARA MORGAN, dance photographer,
reminiscing about summer 1938 at Bennington

Barbara Morgan, self-portrait with her "good old standby" 4×5 Graflex Speed Graphic, ca. 1940. (Photograph by Barbara Morgan)

Barbara Morgan, on ladder, photographing Martha Graham (on floor, center, light dress) and company in *American Provincials,* "part sex, part pride, all demoniacal," at the Guild Theatre, New York City, ca. 1934. (Photograph by Barbara Morgan)

My first glimpse of the world of the Modern Dance was at a technique demonstration at the Bennington Summer School [in 1938]. With an affirmation that came throbbing from a zone of inexhaustible life-abundance, those young students made visible, through the form and sweep of the human body, something of the potency of the pulsation of the blood and the all-generating throb of time.

—JOSEPH CAMPBELL, philosopher and mythologist, observing his wife, Jean Erdman, a member of Martha Graham's assistant group

Besides the burnished, graphic omnipresence of Barbara Morgan's camera eye—her "net and channel to trap the latent images" of Martha Graham's vision, onstage and in rehearsal—the dance-theatre piece *American Document* has come down the years with sparse and scattered documentation. Ray Green's score does survive, dated August–October 1938, with a scrawled cover sheet laying out the sequence of the episodes; however, no full-scale recording was made, and a cassette of Green's solo piano rendition for a 1989 revival was lost. The accompanying *Dance Libretto,* the first time Graham used spoken word as dance narrative, was partially researched by Francis Fergusson, who had worked as regisseur to Richard Boleslavsky at the American Repertory Theatre, and editor at Lincoln Kirstein's *Hound & Horn,* before joining the Bennington faculty as professor of humanities and theatre in 1934. Fergusson, "naturally intimidated" in Graham's presence, downplayed his role, saying he merely helped her with "a little scenario."

On moving picture film, all that remains are seven and a half minutes of fragmentary black-and-white excerpts taken at a rehearsal in the Bennington Armory for the August 6, 1938, premiere, and two grainy, cloudy minutes shot by Ann Barzel from the balcony of the Chicago Opera House in the spring of 1939 when the Graham Dance Company was on tour. A kaleidoscopic clutch of newspaper clippings trace the critical spectrum from exalted reverence to embarrassed perplexity. Martha Graham's exposition helps, somewhat: "The dance is supposed to bring back to its full meaning what has largely become meaningless in America through familiarity. I refer to such a word as democracy that reminds us of the rights we have but may not avail ourselves of," she admonished an interviewer, Marcia Minor, arts and culture critic for the *Daily Worker.* "As the line goes in the script of the dance, 'We forget too much.'"

. . .

Ladies and Gentlemen, good evening.
This is a theatre.
The place is here in the United States of America.
The time is now—tonight.
The characters are:
    The dance group, led by Sophie,
    You, the audience,
    The Interlocutor—I am the Interlocutor,
    And Erick and Martha.

With these words from center stage, Houseley Stevens Jr., a tall, rangy graduate of the Neighborhood Playhouse, dressed in workman's khaki overalls, arms hanging loosely at his sides, introduces the players, the moment, and the locale of *American Document.* His folksy manner recalls the stage manager's monologue in Thornton Wilder's *Our Town,* premiered seven months earlier. The company enters single file, slow-motion brush-stepping

Erick Hawkins (center left), Sophie Maslow (center), and ensemble in "The Dance of
Declaration" from *American Document,* "an adventure in theatre made necessary
by the broad scope of the choreographer's idea," 1938. (Photograph by Barbara Morgan)

and flexed feet, trancelike, to a drumroll; in the tradition of the minstrel show
walk-around parade, they face the audience and bow in canon. As Stevens
concludes, the dancers joyously cartwheel, and then, with what were buffalo
leaps in *Primitive Mysteries,* cross the stage, strut-prancing like high-stepping
horses or "a troupe of erect peacocks driving a chariot," backs straight, hips
lifted, making way for the annunciatory "First Episode: Declaration."

"An American—What is an American? / 1776— / Five men wrote a
document. / Its name rings like a bell. / Here it comes: Declaration!" The
preamble ("In CONGRESS, July 4th, 1776 . . .") is recited, and the two
confident "End Figures," Anita Alvarez and Thelma Babitz, keep a steady
beat. Four doors upstage swing open and four dancers, dressed in blue, "like
visual trumpets" prefigure the "Dance of Declaration" foregrounded by
Erick Hawkins and Sophie Maslow, poised in salute before two groups, one
in angelic arabesques, the other twisted on the spiral, backs aslant, *Chronicle*-
style. The Interlocutor crosses stage right to left, asking "America?—what is
America?" It is time for the elegaic "Second [Indian] Episode," a title Graham changed to "Occupation" when the "Libretto" was published during
wartime four years later.

"I do not remember, / You do not remember / The flock of pigeons in
the virgin forests / Between the bayous and the Great Lakes / . . . / But my
blood remembers, / My heart remembers. / It beats like a drum sometimes,

to words— / Listen, / Here they come: / Mississippi, Susquehanna, Allegheny, Monongahela, Pottawatomie . . .'"

With this roll call of converging rivers from her Pittsburgh childhood,
Martha Graham, in bright red, enters upstage center, walking slowly forward, measured and mournful, to present a constrained solo—"forceful,
direct, undecorated"—of the "Native Figure," "the soul, the Psyche of the
Indian nations . . . ruler of a horizonless domain, as grave and imposing as
one of [her] own gods." Hands cupped, feet planted, she kneels in resignation. The close-in vocabulary of Graham's solo expands, "spread as the land
spreads and close to the land, built on the earth." One by one, the ensemble
returns for "Lament for the Land," led by May O'Donnell, to the words of
Red Jacket of the Senecas: "Listen to what we say. / There was a time when
our forefathers owned this great Island—Their seats extended from the Rising to the Setting Sun. / But an evil day came upon us. / Your forefathers
crossed the Great Water and landed on this Island—."

For the enactment of the "Third Episode: The Puritan," "Martha and
Erick enter upstage left," hand in hand—she is in a form-fitting ankle-length
white gown, he wears white shorts. The Interlocutor's recited text intersperses incantatory passages from the harsh sermons of Jonathan Edwards,
the eighteenth-century Great Awakening revivalist, with amorous paeans
from the biblical Song of Songs: "Death comes hissing like a fiery dragon
with the sting on the mouth of it / Let him kiss me with the kisses of his
mouth, / For thy love is better than wine / Then shall God surrender thy
forsaken soul into the hands of devils . . . / I am my beloved's / And his
desire is toward me."

The "tender gesture," Hawkins would write one distant day, "is the only
real relationship of people to one another on stage." He gazes at Graham
solicitously, solemnly, gentle-heartedly, while she twirls around him. Facing her, he cradles the backs of her upper arms; she slips liquidly through
his tender grip and swoons at his feet. He moves to stand behind her. His
arms encircle her waist, and, lifting, he presents her to the world; she gives
in, rising weightless. Her visage tranquil, like Shiva, the "unmoved mover,"
snakelike, she thrusts and twists her pelvis; and Hawkins's spread-eagle star-
jumps want to go on forever.

Choreographing her partner's support, Graham does not concede wom-
anly power; willing to be vulnerable, she seduces him. Body to body, yin to
yang, there is no quarrel for dominance in the *American Document* duet.
Orchestrated eros defeats the specter of sinfulness. As they entered, the two

dancers leave together, upstage center. The Interlocutor exits downstage. Six dancers enter in the walk-around and exit. The Interlocutor enters alone and introduces "Emancipation."

The "Fourth Episode" brings forward Martha Graham's 1930 appeal to "know the land," as the Interlocutor poses the question, "A state—what is it?" The dancers enter singly. "One state has mountains, / One state has no mountains. / One state has sea, / One state has no sea. / One state has corn, / One state has gold, / One state has cotton. / Once, more than one state had slaves. / Now, no state has slaves. / Now, every state has one deep word. / Here it comes: / Emancipation!" While Lincoln's proclamation of January 1, 1863, is recited, the group on their knees enacts a passionate dance, "in contrapuntal rows, their hands to their throats," then "com[e] up in ranks . . . shaken with ecstasy," to form a semicircle, arms spread, gazing upward.

In this early iteration, before *American Document* expanded with the advent of World War II, the piece moves into the denouement with an explicit "glimpse of 1938," a poignant trio called "After Piece." "Listen to what we say. / We are three women. / We are three million women. / We are the mothers of the hungry dead. / We are the mothers of the hungry living. / We are the mothers of those to be born."

Marie Marchowsky, Jane Dudley, and Sophie Maslow "walk off in silence [and] Erick enters from the opposite side, seeming to be about to follow them. Instead, he turns in center stage," and "dances to [a] small, dry drum beat and to the words of the Interlocutor . . . This is one man / This is one million men. / This man has a faith. / It is you."

The singular person of Erick Hawkins, head high, marching fearlessly toward the future, fulfills Ralph Waldo Emerson's promise of the American "Representative Man."

"Democracy!" the Interlocutor cries, and there follows a dance by the entire company similar to the "Dance of Declaration" . . . The company exits except for Martha and Erick, who are in opposite corners of the stage. As they exit, the Interlocutor speaks. "*That government of the people, by the people, and for the people shall not perish from the earth.*"

.   .   .

Experiencing *American Document* at Bennington, Lincoln Kirstein raved, "[Erick Hawkins's] strong, solid angry human dancing provided a splendid support, a positive male presence. [Martha Graham's] use of a dancer trained

Erick Hawkins (far left) in the ballet *Billy the Kid*, by Aaron Copland, on commission from Lincoln Kirstein, and choreographed by Eugene Loring for Ballet Caravan, 1938. (Photograph by George Platt Lynes)

in another classicism showed that elasticity which makes her unique in an experimental field." Kirstein had no doubt that he was privileged to witness "the most important extended dance creation by a living American . . . so nobly framed, so flawlessly executed, that every other work, new or old, offered at the Festival seemed by comparison puerile, unprofessional, or academic."

His critical tune had certainly mellowed since "[he] first began to see Graham" eight years prior, denouncing the anarchic "stark hysteria" of her *Rite of Spring* debacle; went on to ask, "What does she wish to convey . . . What is Miss Graham's subject matter?" and to scorn her "chronic ambiguity"; then professed to be "blind to [her] aesthetic," inquiring why she could not "set herself to the perhaps irksome task of forcing herself to fit . . . a story even, [or] a literary idea . . . [which] would do wonders for her." *American Document* halted Kirstein's skeptical questions and laid his misgivings to rest. He was convinced that Martha Graham was a genius who, like William Blake, had "to create her 'own system or be enslaved by another man's.'" Martha

Graham, he decided, had drawn forth a major theatrical-literary idea from the poetic texts of the nation.

Kirstein's proprietary attachment to Erick Hawkins ran deep; he said proudly that, in Hawkins, Graham had chosen "an instinctive, clean, conscious . . . well-trained classic dancer," a partner whose role was to elicit from her "a purer and frequently deeper repository of essential classicism," so that she was no longer as "inimical to the developed classic dance" or professedly "independent of *any* tradition whatsoever."

"By communication [it] is not meant to tell a story or to project an idea," Graham wrote in the fall, "but to communicate experience by means of *action*." One attends to her drawled stress on the final word. "This is the reason for the appearance of modern dance," Graham continued. "[t]he departure of the dance from the classical and romantic delineations was not an end in itself, but a *means* to an end. . . . The old forms . . . had to undergo metamorphosis—in some cases destruction, to serve a medium for a time differently organized."

"All of this has nothing to do with propaganda as known and practiced," she declared, above the patriotic cheers that greeted *American Document*. Rather than acquiesce to demands for meaning, Graham said, "The reality of the dance is its truth to our inner life. . . . Dance need not change—it has only to stand revealed."

Unlike Loie Fuller, Isadora Duncan, Ruth St. Denis, and the artists and writers of the storied "Lost Generation," Martha Graham turned her back on Europe, connecting to the local terrain as the proving ground for her art. Twelve years after leaving Denishawn, Graham demonstrated, through her protean body, that she was possessed with pride of place, a woman of pilgrim ancestry born in the rustic Appalachians on the edge of the Midwest who had traveled across the length and breadth of the nation, and its neighbors to the north and south, and had lived on both coasts, in the rugged countryside and the crowded city.

When Martha Graham gazed upon mythic antiquity, contracted the core of her body, and, like the pioneers, ventured outward toward unknown spaces, dance became modern. Her supple, compact, conditioned physique drew energy through the toes and soles of her bare feet, into her pelvic center, spiraling up her spine and along her sinewy arms, out to tensile fingertips—energy breathed through a tenacious, brooding intellect into a mercurial movement style that took risks and sought new paths.

Jean Erdman wrote to Joseph Campbell while the company was on tour with *American Document* that while Graham "knew that 'document' [*sic*] was a 'good show,' . . . it was too conscious [in] the use of historical incident, & of folk material . . . [Martha hoped] that someday there would be a dance which would not depend upon incident at all—but which would arise of its own accord & spontaneously from the land."

24

Every Soul Is a Circus

The creative process . . . consists in the unconscious activation of an archetypal image . . . By giving [the image] shape, the artist translates it into the language of the present, and so makes it possible for us to find our way back to the deepest springs of life . . . Art is constantly at work educating the spirit of the age, conjuring up the forms in which the age is most lacking.

— C. G. JUNG, *The Spirit in Man, Art and Literature*, May 1922

The so-called "modern dance" is not a contemporary phenomenon. . . . Always there has been some dancer who was dissatisfied with the existing forms [and] for whom the traditional style became too sterile and who broke it open . . . In this constant reorientation and revaluation, in this repeated returning to original sources, lies not only the future but the power of the dance.

— MARTHA GRAHAM, "The Future of the Dance,"
Dance Magazine, April 1939

Bounded in time for a certain number of minutes and seconds, *American Document* would end—if any of Martha Graham's dances can be said to "end"—when the stage lights went down; out of reversion to darkness, the next work would find a path to the surface of her mind. Hinting at this engendering-place during on-the-road confidences to Jean Erdman, Graham cited "the depths of man's inner nature, the unconscious, where memory dwells," awakening to help "the more vitally-organized instrument, the body . . . prepare for a deep, stirring, creative communication."

Martha Graham met the comparative literature professor Joseph Campbell when they were both teaching at Sarah Lawrence College, where Graham had been hired by Marian Knighton, director of the dance department in the mid-thirties. Jean Erdman enrolled as a freshman drama major, but, after her first dance class, "smitten with adoration," she realized Martha Graham had "determined [her] for dance." Erdman married Campbell in 1938, after she graduated. At Bennington to observe his wife perform as a member of the Graham company, Campbell was hit with a "Dionysos-dance" epiphany: His "spirit was transported beyond the reach of words," he wrote. "Movement, meaning and feeling were identical. . . . I was beholding bodies hurled about by the volcano-fires of the throbbing abyss. . . . I tell you, it was something. It was immense."

At Bennington, Campbell was befriended by Erick Hawkins, another classics scholar, also conversant with the works of C. G. Jung from Harvard days. He had recently read Jung's tribute to Richard Wilhelm, translator of the seventeenth-century hybrid "Buddhist-Taoist . . . Chinese yoga . . . alchemical" *The Secret of the Golden Flower.* Hawkins joined Campbell in helping Martha Graham navigate the Master's writings. In Greenwich Village, Campbell and Erdman lived nearby, and "Martha called up Joe all the time, whenever she had a question," be it about the archetype, the Shadows, or the psyches and symbols she encountered during netherworldly, nighttime reading odysseys. Campbell found Graham's approach to Jung's psychology of myth refreshing because "it wasn't so much with the goal of replicating the [primordial] stories" as wanting to develop "her own take, [and] let the enactment" find form in dance "as a human, emotional journey," seeking "certain vital connections with the lost arts of the ancients" so that the theatrical stage became "the new *temenos.*"

The lovers' journey for Martha Graham and Erick Hawkins had diverted from sheer heat to degrees of difference. Reflecting upon the sensational beginning of their affair, Graham emphasized that, at Bennington, the crucible of modern dance, holding her freedom closely, she had sought to value Hawkins's singularity, and was not trying to "make [him] dance well, *with me.*" She invoked her bard gods, D. H. Lawrence and Walt Whitman, speaking with reverence for "spirit of place" in Indian country, urging Hawkins to cultivate his "body electric." In the tough love of early partnership, subverting the balletic hierarchy, Graham viewed herself as the emotional and physical weight-bearer. "Do not think of choreography," she told him, "just *dance.*" In her eyes, Hawkins's ongoing labors making sketches for pieces to set upon himself were tolerable, but transient. Unable (or unwilling) to drop the mythic oracle's mantle from her shoulders, Graham admonished her Promethean lover to "enjoy life now . . . because your time to be chained to the rock will come."

Accompanied by Mercier Philip Cunningham, her assistant and nineteen-year-old star pupil, Bonnie Bird came from the Cornish School in Seattle in the summer of 1938 to teach a two-week Graham technique course at Mills College in Oakland, California. Mercier hailed from small-town Centralia, Washington, and, unlike his two brothers, who followed their straitlaced father into the practice of law, his artistic fate was determined when, as a child, he fell in love with tap dance. For the 1939 Bennington Dance summer term, Martha Hill and Mary Josephine Shelly, with the blessing of Mills president Aurelia Reinhardt, took the Festival three thousand miles westward. Martha Graham was in residence, too. As soon as she espied the wiry, "lean and muscular" fellow with his "long back, tiny waist and narrow pelvis," she knew Mercier should become the second male dancer in her company, ideal foil to powerhouse Erick Hawkins. Snatching aside the lanky boy with "the head of a satyr"—he jumped like a satyr as well—"outdoors under the eucalyptus trees" and out of sight from the other teachers—Hanya Holm, Doris Humphrey, and Charles Weidman—Graham convinced Mercier to move to New York City for her winter season. The young man sought Bonnie Bird's approval for the big step. "She knew she could not refuse him," but, she teasingly said, " 'You're just not finished. I haven't finished [training] your *arms*!' "

.   .   .

Vachel Lindsay's epic *Every Soul Is a Circus* occupied the first ten pages of *Poetry: A Magazine of Verse,* published in Chicago in October 1928. "Direct, steady-gazed" Harriet Monroe, philanthropic founder-publisher of the journal, put forth a bold "Open Door" editorial call: "May the great poet we are looking for never find it shut, or half-shut, against his ample genius!" Fifteen years prior, she had discovered Lindsay's work, featuring in the magazine's opening pages his "General William Booth Enters into Heaven," "a rousing description and chant based upon the life and death of the founder of the Salvation Army," set to music by Charles Ives, and launching the poet's reputation as a writer "of athletic exuberance, community pride and evangelism."

The height of Vachel Lindsay's renown as "a modern knight-errant, the Don Quixote of [his] so-called unbelieving, unromantic age" was long past. By the time *Every Soul Is a Circus* appeared, he was in the weary, bankrupt, suicidal final act of an ecstatic troubadour drama spent chanting rhythmic, vernacular song poems and peddling signed broadsheets and pamphlets on the streets of America's cities and towns in exchange for meals and lodging. He had traveled, camping and tramping and *Preaching the Gospel of Beauty* (an early travel journal) from his village birthplace in Springfield, Illinois, to Chicago, New York, Jacksonville, Los Angeles, Seattle, St. Louis, Santa Fe, and countless points between and beyond.

At the halfway mark in the long text of *Every Soul Is a Circus,* four lines appear that would become—appropriated and slightly edited by Martha Graham—the epigraph for her dance (subtitled "A Satire") premiering on December 27, 1939, in the St. James Theatre. Her comic piece traces the ins and outs of a flirtatious woman threading between competing men: "For every soul is a circus, / And every mind is a tent, / And every heart is a sawdust ring / Where the circling race is spent."

Vachel Lindsay's exhortation to his "brothers of the poet trade" to "leave [their] ivory towers," gave impetus to the first dance featuring Merce Cunningham and Erick Hawkins in pursuit of an ambivalent, elusive Martha Graham. The piece covers wider territory than the metaphorical "circus of life" the choreographer alludes to in her flimsy program note.

The locale for the poem is Chicago, on Michigan Avenue, by "the dark Art Institute" where Lindsay studied painting in 1900, taking on an hallucinatory, Blakean style; where, on tour in 1922, Graham encountered Kandinsky's *Improvisation No. 30 (Cannons),* and resolved, someday, to make a dance like that; and where, in February 1940, when the landmark exhibition *Picasso: Forty Years of His Art* opened, dance critics would invoke "Miss Graham" as "greatest among the living in her sphere as is Picasso in his . . . ," amid "the controversies of 'modern' art, whether it be two or three dimensional."

The poem goes on to conjure the songs of "prophets old," and "mastodons trumpeting" and lions' roars "ten thousand years before your jazz"; invokes the "marble Gods" and "Athenian violets" of antiquity; praises "stark-naked Indians, painted in stripes"; and looks heavenward to "the planets" like "trapezes, / High, high above the grave."

Beyond these connections, the unacknowledged affinity with Martha Graham is the incandescent woman at the heart of Lindsay's *Every Soul Is a Circus,* soprano Jenny Lind, the "Swedish Nightingale." She parades through the poem on the arm of P. T. Barnum, the flamboyant impresario who brought "the cultured, delicate opera star" to these shores for a concert tour in 1850–1851 that grossed more than $700,000, her share of the proceeds going toward the establishment of a school for indigent girls in Stockholm.

Thirty-year-old Jenny Lind, according to reporters' impressions, was "of medium height . . . not what some would call handsome . . . the plainest of commonplace girls . . . however, in her eye and brow there is the best part of beauty—its intelligence." Her wardrobe was the essence of simplicity. "Becomingly dressed in white satin," she appeared barely accessorized "save [for] diamonds on her bodice and a brilliant bracelet on her arms." There was "a frankness about her manner, a freshness about her opinions." Her bearing was like "the flame of a great soul in a dark lantern," her gestures of hand and arm, "crisp and intelligent," accompanied a voice that surged "entirely at her will" from "murmurous . . . and refined" to "gushing forth . . . with astonishing power."

Jenny Lind's demure appearance belied the stamina of a workhorse plowing through ninety-five solo concerts in ten months, many exceeding two hours, with repertory ranging from Rossini and Bellini to Meyerbeer and Verdi. She carried off this feat with a mystique-like discipline that began by not announcing the precise time and place of her arrival in a city; and, following the applause, continued with her disappearance from view, withdrawing from dressing room to hotel, to rest, guarding her privacy in silence and solitude.

·   ·   ·

The poem *Every Soul Is a Circus* is a brazen tour de force of fantasized Americana: P. T. Barnum's Jenny Lind caravan actually never set foot in Chicago. When Martha Graham's dance reached the stage, she introduced her rendition, in a disclaimer replete with irony, "This is not the literal circus of canvas and sawdust ring," reconceiving Lindsay's setting, "but a circus of ridiculous situations and silly behavior. In every woman there is the desire to be featured in a 'Star Turn,' as the apex of a triangle and as the beloved of a duet. In the life of every woman there is some focus which, however temporarily, holds the whip hand. Throughout the circus of life every woman is her own most appreciative spectator. In this circus of the silly woman's life, the sum total of episodes, of interludes, does not add up to dignity but to an addled confusion."

She was prompting reviewers and audiences to delve beneath her "delight in irony," and dare to laugh—not only with her, but even at her. And it worked. After opening night on Broadway, George Beiswanger commented that *Every Soul Is a Circus* marked Martha Graham's "release" into a "new feeling of the right to breathe art's own free air." To John Martin, "a more perfect example of the power of movement per se to evoke laughter would be hard to find." Walter Terry anointed Graham "the Beatrice Lillie of the modern dance," who "has been hiding it from us all these years." Audiences in New York and during the four-month transcontinental tour "rewarded Graham with bursts of helpless laughter . . . [and] shouts of surprise," appreciating her "fun-poking" accompanied by "splendid miming" and various "Chaplinesques" that were downright "belly-laugh provoking . . . with quite a few cheers and whistles thrown in for good measure."

The show begins under a peaked big top tent fancifully suggested by long, curving ribbons, in the style of *Frontier,* suspended over a toy theatre. The set and decor designer, Philip Stapp, was a colleague of Graham's at Bennington. The characters of this Arenic World were costumed by Edythe Gilfond, who had worked with Graham on *American Document.* The "neo-Romantic" accompaniment for eleven instruments "brim[med] with energetic force," including "parades, fanfares, interludes and jazz dances . . . balanced between fast-moving themes and lyrical melodies." It was by Philadelphia-born Paul Nordoff, whom Graham had met in 1934 when, as a graduate fellow in piano and composition at Juilliard, he had been asked by Katharine Cornell to provide incidental music for voice, harp, violin, and cello for her production of *Romeo and Juliet,* co-starring Brian Aherne as Mercutio, Edith Evans as the Nurse, Basil Rathbone as Romeo—and Orson Welles as Tybalt. Nordoff's idiom of "lively precision" was well suited to Graham's needs; as were the severe, epigrammatic poems by his friend E. E. Cummings that Nordoff made into exquisite art songs.

First sighted, to the pound of a bass drum and the roll of a snare, Martha Graham, "Empress of the Arena," is languid and bored, a damsel in despair "actively lolling" on a black couch, stage left. "The Ringmaster," Erick Hawkins, brandishing a whip and resplendent in red bolero jacket, struts in and mounts a circular platform. His promenades and postures, broad arm-swings and whistling whip-snaps, are exercises in futility with no impact upon the Empress. Askance, she "stands by," deaf to his commands, keeping her distance. When he "sweeps her off her feet" it is only because she has decided, for that moment, to "let him have his way."

Here comes Nelle Fisher, the "First Arenic Performer," followed by a parade of four jeunes filles en fleurs, the "Other Arenic Performers," Sophie

Graham (Empress of the Arena) and Erick Hawkins (Ringmaster)
in *Every Soul Is a Circus,* 1940. (Photograph by Barbara Morgan)

Maslow, Ethel Butler, Frieda Flier, and Marjorie Mazia. And the "Ideal Spectator," Jean Erdman, has "a little entrance . . . walked in . . . bounced around . . . and did a few turns, not really dancing," disappointed that for her debut solo with the company she was made to perch in a small observation enclosure, upstage right, and bide her time as the surrogate-audience/doppelgänger.

Martha Graham's vaunted star turn is melodramatic, as if in a silent movie, piano trilling to her clichéd, self-mocking gestures of distress and yearning. At last, Mercier Cunningham, the "faun-like" company newcomer, springs in, "the Acrobat" attempting to lure the Empress away. She tilts toward this beguiling saltimbanco for a few beats, retreats, spins into the Ringmaster's embrace, and is borne about the stage by both, going along for the ride, enacting the triangle of affections.

For Arenic World, part 2, the Ringmaster and the Empress, counterpoised at the opposite ends of a seesaw and accompanied by a "jazz duet . . . written in 12/8," with "a lilting quality . . . simple chords of strings and piano . . . and [a] syncopated theme (woodwinds) balanced with a chromatic melody in sixths (flute and strings)," demonstrate courtly harmony; but once they dismount, the playground illusion of balance dissipates, supplanted by mock patty-cake, thigh-slapping, trite arm-in-arm excursions, and an exaggerated tango.

The tables turn—she leads, he follows; she turns her back—he grasps her waist and reins her in. The Empress plants her bare feet atop the Ringmaster's boots, their steps coupled, before he stalks out, ceding to the Acrobat, more at ease among the coterie of Arenic performers than with the Empress. She returns, wearing a black over-cloak, hair undone, bearing a long-stemmed white flower with which she fans and caresses the noncommittal men.

Incessant pushes and pulls have taken a toll on the Empress's spirit. She retreats to her sanctuary, the divan, "a whole theatre of woe" where the bittersweet, "silly" circus began. The Ringmaster follows, to sit by her side. To no avail. She wants to be alone. He leaves for the last time.

She dives into a collapse on the chaise—and the Arenic World goes dark.

25

Deaths and Entrances—Ten Characters in Search of a Dance

In reality you could get along beautifully without me but please think you can't darling.

—MARTHA GRAHAM, letter to Erick Hawkins, summer 1941

The Martha Graham Dance Company headed for Richmond, Virginia; Charleston, South Carolina; Baton Rouge, Louisiana, and points south and west, across Texas to Arizona and Los Angeles, with a redblooded program of *Frontier*, *American Document*, *Columbiad*, and *Every Soul Is a Circus* guaranteed to please the heartland.

Erick Hawkins, a notebook tucked in his valise, stole moments on trains and in hotel rooms to continue sketching plans for his own brand of repertory. He began on an upbeat with *Primer for Action*, a list of conventional balletic movements, in no set sequence, illustrated by inked stick-figures— "[arm] extension . . . arabesque . . . second position . . . leg extension." Insinuated among these terms were hybrids with penciled variants, such as "control on one foot—single pir[ouette] . . . slide." At the next level— in modified Graham vocabulary, although floor work was conspicuous by its absence—were "Contraction—with head . . . Surprising rhythm . . . Prance—try with hop."

Hawkins had come up through ballet and would continue to teach in his large-gestured, methodical style at Bennington and at 66 Fifth Avenue; Graham prohibited the next wave of dancers to seek ballet instruction elsewhere (they secretly disobeyed) but begrudgingly allowed her archaic foot to soften into a turnout. Hawkins's *Primer for Action*—to a score by pianist and Bennington composer in residence Ralph Gilbert, with decor by WPA artist and fellow Missourian Carlos Dyer—was a quick graph of the kind of modern dance evolving in Hawkins's airborne body, out of ballet classicism and toward Graham technique, while clinging to partially articulated pretensions for new work.

In a draft for a program note accompanied by a big question mark in the margin, Hawkins spoke of "[?] The movements of the parts of the body, and the elemental kinds of motion that combine [to . . . into . . .] *for* dance action." In spring 1941, Martha Graham published an essay, "A Modern Dancer's Primer for Action," in Boston University professor Frederick Rand Rogers's textbook, *Dance: A Basic Educational Technique*. Whereas Hawkins's *Primer* had been eclectic, Graham specified that "throughout the performance of these technical exercises, a woman remains a woman, and a man a man, because power means to become what one *is,* to the highest degree of realization."

After the Empress's radiant despair in *Every Soul Is a Circus* came flagellation, transfiguration, and the suffering of the Virgin Mary in Graham's *El Penitente*; the embraces and estrangement of a red-clad Emily Dickinson, another kind of heretic, in her *Letter to the World* ("That never wrote to Me"); and the dalliances, "dilemmas," and "squabble and scuffle" in *Punch and the Judy,* a quintessential battle of the sexes. Thus did Martha Graham's signature works continue—with herself at the center.

Erick Hawkins kept to the territory he was given—relative to her, on her stage—while furthering his choreographic projects in a parallel universe populated by strong foregrounded men. Bennington College, on July 13, 1940, was the venue for the premiere of his *Liberty Tree*, a solo inspired by the "stately elm" at Washington and Essex Streets in Boston "whose lofty branches seem'd to touch the skies," scene of the raucous celebration where the "colonist mob worshipped" following the repeal of the Stamp Act. Again accompanied by Ralph Gilbert, Hawkins marched through the four-part, forty-minute suite as the Massachusetts Patriot; the Kentucky Trail Breaker, bare-chested and bearing a menacing flintlock; a Kansas Free-Stater, reminiscent of John Brown; and a Nomad Harvester from California.

The vintage portraits were followed by "a Green Mountain's Dance," *Yankee Blue Breeches*, who, "whenever he is, surprised by enemies and is drowned, comes to life again, as a hero always does." The piece was introduced with a rustic saying Hawkins scrounged up, "I wasn't brot [*sic*] up in the woods to be scared by owls." In summer 1941, Hawkins premiered two more new works, a lyric duet with Jean Erdman, *In Time of Armament*, based upon a sonnet sequence from *The Five-Fold Mesh*, a collection of poems by

Ben Belitt of the Bennington literature and language faculty; and the ambitious *Trickster Coyote*, memorializing the dancer's childhood in the Penitente country of the Colorado mountain foothills, a "wryly astringent" piece to Henry Cowell's pounding, squawking score for percussion and wind, featuring the exotic redwood and brass Chinese oboe (*suona*), "with a sting like chili in its raw sounds." To "evoke the moodily-moping" Coyote title figure, "clearly the outsider, unruly and never at home," who, the legend says, comes back to life when killed by his own foolishness, Hawkins wore a hairy, grinning ceremonial mask fabricated by James W. Harker.

The surge of Americana was sustained into the following spring with *Land Be Bright*, produced by Austin Wilder under the auspices of radio station WGN's Concert Division, at the Civic Opera House in Chicago. A paragraph by Vachel Lindsay introducing the program, excerpted from his last prose work, *The Litany of Washington Street*, published in March 1929, five months after *Every Soul Is a Circus*, avowed that "[t]his is a work of the imagination, somewhat in the spirit of statehouse and courthouse and dollar bill mural painting. It is somewhat in the spirit of the best Fourth of July decorations and speeches . . ." Martha Graham cast herself as Betsy Ross, stitching the first flag of the Republic, and Erick Hawkins was Chingachgook, Washington Irving's Mohican chief.

Emboldened to free Graham from her hand-to-mouth existence, Hawkins wrote a solicitation to the pianist, composer, and philanthropist, Elizabeth Sprague Coolidge, proposing that she bestow an overdue imprimatur upon "one of the great creative artists of America." Hawkins suggested a partnership with Aaron Copland, a "first-rank composer" who had worked with Graham in the past, implying that such enlightened generosity would also serve as "a patriotic act."

During the ensuing months—between Mrs. Coolidge's approval of the commission, and the fall of 1942, "when the collaboration between Graham and Copland," which would, after much back-and-forthing, evolve over the ensuing two years into *Appalachian Spring* "began in earnest"—Erick Hawkins devised a quirky marriage-fantasy duet on his own. It began as *Uncle Sam and His Best Girl*, later subtitled, variously, *Mr. and Mrs. John America*; *Us: or, The Happy Couple*; and *His Better Half*. Hawkins was Uncle Sam; his "Best Girl . . . Lady Liberty," would be Martha Graham, at her happiest when "drunk with . . . freedom."

The curtain rises on Uncle Sam preparing to call upon his love, jauntily gathering a fresh bouquet, "shining shoes, brushing then putting on vest and cutaway coat, then hat." She waits behind a screen, and he "walks around as if to tease her, then invites her to descend and take his arm . . ." In a subsequent draft, "let[ting] the identification come to a head gradually . . . building up costumes by ingenious additions," Uncle Sam becomes "a man with overalls and white shirt with long sleeves [and] a Farmer's straw hat upon his head"; and Lady Liberty, no longer attired like the statue in New York Harbor, wears, with Hawkins's eye for fashion, "a dress with a tight waist band. Square neck slightly *directoire* [neoclassical]. Gray in several shades of layers and petticoats then top skirt pulled up and snapped." But—lo and behold—in the spirit of their concealed selves, "he might put on a coat, then have her pull it off him which would turn it inside out, revealing the stripes, red and white," and "She would prop up her dress then put on Liberty's tiara [and] He hands her the torch- [doubling as a] bouquet. They walk off to a barn dance, arm in arm . . . in a gentle-easy *schottische*."

When they drift into other dance styles, the couple's harmony breaks. "There are awkward moments before a dance begins" and "Uncle Sam steps on her toe—they quarrel—[a] spat in movement . . . The cause of their quarrel," Hawkins concedes, "is that Uncle Sam won't dance the right steps properly. Liberty weeps." Art imitates life; she "Slaps him once for his perverseness. . . . They make up and go into wild polka around in circles to exhaustion. Work up to a frenzy til exhausted & have to stop for breath—shuffle step interlude." Further disruptions occur when Sam makes advances to Liberty, "starts to make love to her & that leads into a waltz" from which he spins away and "steps aside to watch her waltz alone & then rejoins her for [the] climax" that concludes when habit dictates that "he lifts her up onto a pedestal. . . . She wants [her torch] but he won't bring it to her 'til she wafts him a kiss" and, a wish within a dream, the Lady applauds Sam's "dextrous [*sic*] tricks . . . while [his] jig accelerates to wildness."

Uncle Sam dances exhibitionistically into another "spirited climax," then "grabs her [down from the pedestal] and they make a whirlwind finish. Might work into 'Stars and Stripes Forever' and then postlude of 'Good Night Ladies' as they dance simply together. . . . They walk home—relax—take off clothes—formally—and he [lies] down on floor as tho [*sic*] going to bed." In two fragmentary sentences, Hawkins succumbs to the couple-characters' "sorrow and comforting of each other." He mourns "their passing on and becoming the ghosts they show they are in the opening mvts [*sic*]."

. . .

The piece I am working on here . . . You may be shocked by the subject-matter. It is about the Brontë[s]. I am not trying to do another Emily [Dickinson—*Letter to the World*], however. It is so very different in approach as well as in nature . . . I have lived in excitement while doing it.

—MARTHA GRAHAM, at Bennington,
to Edith J. R. Isaacs, August 26, 1942

If, by chance, some word, some phrase, or sentence from a book, should move [the dancer's] imagination, then she must retire to her own quietness and brood the mysterious gift. The seed requires time to stir to life the contents of her own silence.

—JOSEPH CAMPBELL, "Text, or Idea?," *Dance Observer*, June–July 1944

At summer's end 1942, for one glorious week before Labor Day, alone in an apartment on the edge of campus, Martha Graham cherished the quietness, "feel[ing] no time sense" in the pastoral serenity of Bennington College. After a ruminative walk over the field to the Commons for breakfast, her daily routine was spent in "delicious" solitude—an hour and a half of "technic," followed by "milk and a bath and rest and read[ing] . . . on the couch under the window [to] watch the clouds and the wild sky," working on the "script" for her nascent dance project, pausing for a light dinner, then, perhaps, a visit to the college library before settling down "in front of the fire at night" for continued labor on a long piece she hoped to have ready for Christmas in New York.

The working title was "Doom-eager," a phrase Graham seized upon after hearing Robert Edmond Jones speak it—during a lecture in 1941 at the Neighborhood Playhouse on "The Art of the Theatre"—in misattributed praise of the daring, "passionate protagonist" of a nameless Icelandic saga who brushes aside all fears of mortality. The true source of the term was deeper and more potent: Ezra Pound invoked the emboldened hero in Book I of his 1916 translation of *The Wanderer*, an early Anglo-Saxon poem, as determinedly "doom eager" [*domgeorne*] . . . "meagre of speech . . . ready to pay the price . . . [who] bindeth fast his blood-bedraggled heart in his breast," no matter what perils loom in the distance.

The setting for the piece was inspired by Haworth Parsonage, "redolent with ghosts" on the bleak Yorkshire moors where the Brontë sisters lived and wrote—Anne, Charlotte, and Graham's fantasized alter ego, Emily, author of *Wuthering Heights,* her only novel, a tortuous tale of misconstrued love and embittered revenge; imbued, Graham said, with "the strange wild thing that obsession brings. . . . The only way I can explain it is that it is the legend of genius," Graham confessed to her friend Edith Isaacs, editor of *Theatre Arts Monthly.*

"I know I am crazy," she wrote Isaacs, "but I like to be that way because that is the way things someday get done."

The "Doom-eager" dance was not completed for the winter season; nor did it enter the repertory when announced, tentatively, for the following spring. Graham continued to refer vaguely to "the thing I am working on . . . an experience of the emotions involving that part of us that is responsible for the creative dream." At long last, in workshop mode, with plain black jersey dresses stitched by Charlotte Trowbridge assisted by the women of the company, and trousers for the men that Erick Hawkins picked up at an army surplus store, *Deaths and Entrances*—it was, finally, named—reached the Bennington College attic theatre stage on Sunday, July 18, 1943, "a preview rather than . . . a performance." The score was by Hunter Johnson, with Louis Horst as music director; and the decor (set, lighting, and props) by Arch Lauterer. The title was from a Dylan Thomas poem Graham came upon in *Horizon* magazine, written during the fall 1940 Blitz. "On almost the incendiary eve / Of deaths and entrances / When near and strange wounded on London's waves / Have sought your single grave."

The provenance was rooted in Thomas's affection for *Deaths Duell,* John Donne's final sermon as Dean of St. Paul's Cathedral, delivered in February 1631. The metaphysical poet nearing the end of his life was fixated upon man's cyclical journey, "Deliverance from that Death, the death of the *wombe,* is an *entrance,* a delivery over to *another death.*" Donne's meditation touched a nerve in Martha Graham's propensity for exegesis. "There are so many little deaths, those moments of doubt, loneliness, fear . . . moments when one ceases to be for a short time," she wrote to David Zellmer—serving in the air force in the South Pacific, he had danced in *Letter to the World* and *Punch and the Judy*—and "then there is the entrance again into the real world of energy that is the source of life, that is the immortality."

On that rainy summer night at Bennington, after a drawn-out gestation, *Deaths and Entrances* could no longer be assumed to be a story "about" the Brontës. The three sisters, notably without proper names, played by Graham, Sophie Maslow, and Jane Dudley, had become "abstracted for [Graham's] use." Entering *Deaths and Entrances* from a past life were three—likewise

Martha Graham Dance Company in *Deaths and Entrances,* with (left to right) Sophie Maslow, Erick Hawkins, Merce Cunningham, Graham, John Butler, Jane Dudley, Pearl Lang, Ethel Butler, and Nina Fonaroff, ca. 1943. (Photograph by Arnold Eagle)

unnamed—remembered children, danced by Pearl Lang, Ethel Butler, and Nina Fonaroff, recalling Martha Graham and her two sisters, Geordie and Mary, who, all-too-briefly, treasured the company of their little brother William Henry, like Branwell Brontë the only boy among girls. Playing the semblance of a proud, self-assertive woman, Martha Graham was doubly shadowed by "the Dark Beloved," Erick Hawkins, and "the Poetic Beloved," Merce Cunningham, themselves, in turn, mirrored by two "young men/ cavaliers" new to the company, Robert Horan and John Butler.

This mélange of ten characters in search of childhood memories, "dreams of romance," and "hatreds bred of longings" was layered into "Doom-eager"/ *Deaths and Entrances*—Graham wrote, without attribution—by her "imagination kindled at antique fires," appropriating a nineteenth-century critic's phrase referring to "the imperfect genius," William Blake. Accustomed by now to Graham's literary machinations, critic Margaret Lloyd alertly understood that "the work . . . uses the Brontës and their milieu as a *flying-field,* a starting-off place into the land of common experience in the heart of man . . . This is the secret of Martha Graham's greatness."

•   •   •

Reality and imagination are no longer two distinct experiences.

—EDWIN DENBY, reviewing *Deaths and Entrances*
in *The New York Herald Tribune*, December 27, 1943

That was the operant distinction when *Deaths and Entrances* opened at the Forty-Sixth Street Theatre, a house "packed . . . to the last inch of standing room," on Sunday, December 26, 1943. It was *re*-presented—after Martha Graham heard the audience applaud and overcame her apprehensions—on January 9. Four decades later, Erick Hawkins spoke uneasily about his part. " 'The Dark Beloved'—that was me," he told David Sears. "I was pretty tempestuous and stormy" at the time, Hawkins continued, with a tinge of bitterness, calling himself Heathcliff to latch on to a fleshly identity because Graham had over-choreographed his puppet-role and it "had no resolution." Hawkins, standing like a marionette with cut strings, arms limply at his sides, and Merce Cunningham, identically attired and expressionless, often seemed to be attendants rather than suitors, assuming a succession of formalized poses, one critic observed, "more in the nature of abstractions than people."

The *Deaths and Entrances* set—suggesting the interior of an old house with three dark, blocky pieces of furniture and "a huge curtained window with the curtains permanently drawn"—maneuvers the viewer into anticipating a traditional theatrical narrative; but within minutes the picture devolves into an impressionistic dreamscape of suspended time and boundless space. Martha Graham anticipates this desired effect in her program note reference to "the secret life of the heart." Like the heart, the dance keeps beating according to its biological imperative. And, like the endangered heart, there will be arrhythmic instances from which it will need to recover.

Strings and woodwinds, familiar adversaries in Graham dances, with brass grace notes, battle for dominance, the whole knit together by Helen Lanfer's thunderous, chord-driven piano, starting in knotty menace, hopping and segueing into slowed-down clarinet and oboe, while the "Emily" figure, in black, separated from her sisters in gray, defines her solitude, "thronged with memories of love's disappointments and rivalries." The sisters' "flame burns fiercely," George Beiswanger wrote, "but the heat is turned within, where hopes and fears, longings and rages continually re-create an inner, almost mythological world."

When the Dark Beloved, Erick Hawkins, appears, it is more intrusion than arrival; "Emily's" expression is pained, unwelcoming. The Poetic Beloved, Merce Cunningham, a distraction, not a respite, draws reluctant "Emily" out of her introspection. The men plead; she agonizes. Following a stylized fistfight, they await her next move, squaring off close to her on either side yet projecting vast distances. She breaks the symmetry, turns her back, shuns them, and sallies forth. Duets, when they occur, are initiated by perfunctory handoffs from one so-called beloved to the other, Graham exorcising emotions from "adolescently tender" to "terrifying and horrible."

At the opposite extreme, the three remembered sisters, in flouncy pinafores and skirts and gay headbands, flow in and flit out like woodland sprites. Their light-footed entrances, vestiges of a simpler past, disturb Emily rather than inspire her. In the time of the present, Martha Graham degenerates into an anguished, trapped maenad, careening this way and that, facing an indeterminate future. She dances parallel to, rather than with, her sisters, unable to accept solace, "giv[ing] animation and rhythm to the ebbing of energy" with liquid variations in speed and emphasis, meticulously calculated and reading as spontaneous.

When the Dark Beloved and the Poetic Beloved return, Graham is drawn to one, pulled by the other; neither man satisfies. Finding no refuge in human love, at wit's end, she arrives alone at stillness.

She grasps in uplifted hands a glass chalice, grail of art and nurturing vessel of the Divine Feminine.

.   .   .

Deaths and Entrances barely launched, Martha Graham's agitated attention alighted upon another dark story about three sisters' rivalries and divided affections. "I am reading some about and in King Lear," she told Erick Hawkins. "I think I will have to do something that stems from that some day." In the Bennington library, she also found "Freud and the Future," Thomas Mann's tribute essay concluding that "the analytic revelation is a revolutionary force . . . Once roused and on the alert, it cannot be put to sleep again."

Hawkins's choreographic enterprises continued to pursue romantic ends, his planning notes and sketches glorifying a certain type of ardent, demonstrative fellow who shrugged off control of his feelings to chase the object of his affection. Graham, on the other hand, preferred to examine the fickle forces dividing women from men, the most potent of these, in her view, being the allure of art-making: "I wish I could tell you in some way that you could never be a stone around my neck as you say. I am afraid I might be around yours," she warned her lover, "and that is I think a deep cause of trouble between us."

26

Interlude—*Appalachian Spring*

If the *Mona Lisa* is in the Louvre, where are *Hamlet* and *Lycidas*?
—JAMES MCLAVERTY, *Studies in Biography* (1984),
citing F. W. Bateson, *Essays in Critical Dissent* (1972)

. . . to which we add, in the spirit of dance becoming modern, "and where (furthermore, *when*) is *Appalachian Spring*?"

To aficionados and devotees, *Appalachian Spring* has become familiar, over the past eight decades, by holding steadfast in the repertory of the Martha Graham Dance Company. The musical score by Aaron Copland, its "harmonic treatment, based chiefly on open fourths and fifths" infused with Shaker and folk tunes, "evok[ing] our sparse and dissonant rural tradition rather than the thick suavities of our urban manner," sets the comforting, beloved tone. When the piece was born at the Library of Congress on October 30, 1944, during wartime, it staked a claim in the culture at large with a potent mixture of sepia American nostalgia and future-facing hope—real or imagined—to keep the dance in the *Zeitgeist*. As our current tortured age, like every age, seeks definition through art, the work's arms remain open.

Martha Graham imposed her unchanging will to change upon *Appalachian Spring*. To select two black-and-white filmed versions of the piece with Graham starring in both—to sit as a spectator before the premiere in the Elizabeth Sprague Coolidge Auditorium, and the orchestrated *Dance on Film* of 1958 directed by Peter Glushanok—and oscillate between them, is to realize, and gratefully accept, that her classic is defined by layers of impermanence.

Onto Isamu Noguchi's quiet, deftly framed set, bare wood outlines of a peak-roofed house, a porch with narrow rocking chair, a wall with a bench that is also a church pew, a stylized tree stump doubling as a pulpit platform,

Martha Graham (center) and Erick Hawkins (right) in *Appalachian Spring*, with May O'Donnell (left, seated) and Marjorie Mazia, Yuriko, and Nina Fonaroff, ca. 1944. (Photograph by Arnold Eagle)

and, across the yard, a fence, the dramatis personae come in "Very Slowly," as Copland demands. The processional, like "Steps in the Street," presages a lull before the storm. Erick Hawkins, at thirty-six, in tie and black jacket, is the original 1944 "Husbandman." Stuart Hodes, at thirty-four, would become the more informal "Husband" in 1958. This distinction is key to the origin of the dance, because the former name meant householder and tiller of the soil, not necessarily a married man. Martha Graham is, of course, the "Bride," also dressed in somber black; fourteen years later, having married Hawkins in 1948, she would be the beige-garbed "Wife."

Merce Cunningham created the role of the "Revivalist"; Bertram Ross took on the long dark coat and wide-brimmed hat for the later iteration, "The Preacher." Elegant May O'Donnell embodied the wise, mature "Pioneering Woman," succeeded, as the "Pioneer Woman," by Matt Turney. The four maiden "Followers"—Nina Fonaroff, Pearl Lang, Marjorie Mazia, and Yuriko—became known as "Worshippers." In 1958, Yuriko remained, joined by Helen McGehee, Ethel Winter, and Miriam Cole.

There is eye contact, but an absence of intimacy, while the paths of "Bride" and "Husbandman" diverge, she to sit within the home, back tensely turned, guarded by the Pioneering Woman. The Bride will sneak an occasional glance over her right shoulder toward the downstage fence that feels miles away, where her man stands, crooked arm resting upon the top rail, appearing composed, gazing with the intimation of a smile over the expanse of plains.

The Followers awaken, into a round of deep planting and reaped harvest, reminiscent of the *Rite* from a long ago *Spring*. The Revivalist's flock inspires the Husbandman to burst from reverie, demonstrating to his reclusive lady—with slides into near-splits, kicks that arrow upward, hands on hips, arms akimbo, and knees practically touching his chin—that he is 'rarin' to go." Yet, when he lays claim to the Bride, takes her arm, pulls her from shelter, descends the home steps, and they hit the ground together, they are met by a huge minor chord. She heads over to the fence before the couple retreats to make way for the Revivalist instigating his Followers into a square dance manic with primitive pageantry.

Twelve minutes have passed. It is time for the maenad, Martha Graham. She enters the hurricane she has made and, spiraling toward its dark heart, becomes lost, out of sync with the resolved Husbandman standing by the fence, protection against the wilderness and gateway to the rest of life. A jarring move, the Bride cradles an imagined newborn, only to hand it off to the Pioneering Woman who joins with the Revivalist to greet and embrace Bride and groom in courtly fashion. The men shake hands solemnly, bowing in obeisance.

With Copland's rousing rendering of "Simple Gifts," first performed and sung (or "received") in 1848 by Elder Joseph Brackette of Alfred, Maine, "turning about with his coat-tails a-flying" in a Shaker worship service "Quick Dance," the clouds of decorum lift, allowing the couple to proclaim and advertise their love, in equal measure, for each other and to the world. Graham permits herself a wide smile in the premiere version of the pas de deux; fourteen years later, a reserve brought by age has taken over. In both performances, the lyrics of uplift, reverence, and instruction return us to the bedrock of Martha Graham's purposeful choreography:

> *'Tis the gift to be simple, 'tis the gift to be free,*
> *'Tis the gift to come down, where we ought to be,*
> *And when we find ourselves in the place just right,*

'Twill be in the valley of love and delight.
When true simplicity is gain'd,
To bow and to bend we shan't be ashamed,
To turn, turn will be our delight
Till by turning, turning we come round right.

The palette darkens. The Revivalist lurches about, falling to his knees, flailing. His "wedding sermon segues into fire-and-brimstone threats that have more than an edge of hysteria to them." He points at the couple, warning against temptations of the flesh. "The Pioneering Woman . . . remembers and sympathizes with [their] dreams," and, arms around the Husbandman, she presages the "disappointments and harsh demands and dangers to be found in the still-untamed land. The horizon may be wide and endless," her gestures say, "but it also is empty [and] the encroaching night is not necessarily beneficent."

Her message lingers in the Husbandman's thoughts; tempted, he looks longingly beyond the fence. Will the homestead be a refuge from the nec-

Erick Hawkins (left) and Martha Graham (right) are greeted by Elizabeth Sprague Coolidge (center), following the debut performance of *Appalachian Spring* at the Library of Congress, October 30, 1944.

essary storm of their coming lives, or an inhibiting haven? The reprise of "Simple Gifts" provides a clue; he goes to the Bride, encourages her to revisit her twisting, omnidirectional steps, heartened by her doom-eagerness.

In the waning moments of *Appalachian Spring*, desire and reticence are writ large in the body of the Wife/Bride. Will today's amorous promises become satisfied in tomorrow's "promised land"? The decisive Husbandman/ Husband, mounting the few stairs to the home, crosses the threshold, and stands behind the rocking chair, waiting.

Martha Graham pauses, immobile, inhabiting the stillness she always loves, and runs her palms down the front and sides of her dress, smoothing anxieties of wonderment and anticipation. She is the Chosen One chosen by him; what will the choice be for herself?

She spins rightward and enters the house.

In the 1944 premiere of *Appalachian Spring*, she sits deliberately, Erick Hawkins places his right palm gently on her chest, just below her shoulder, and the lights fade.

Fourteen years later, Stuart Hodes places his hand upon her shoulder, their eyes meet, she lays her right hand atop his, and, with her left arm extended, gestures, up—and away.

27

Dark Meadow

Martha Graham's succinct program note, a premise for the action to come, tells the spectator that *Dark Meadow* "is concerned with the adventure of seeking. This dance is the reenactment of the Mysteries which attend that adventure." Four tributary themes to be traversed in the journey, named separately, she says, will converge: "Remembrance of the ancestral footsteps . . . Terror of loss . . . Ceaselessness of love . . ." and "Recurring ecstasy of the flowering branch." The music is a double quartet for strings and winds by Carlos Chávez; artistic collaboration by Isamu Noguchi; costumes are by Edythe Gilfond, and lighting by Jean Rosenthal. The dramatic figures—designated as "She of the Ground" (May O'Donnell), "He Who Summons" (Erick Hawkins), "They Who Dance Together" (Pearl Lang, Natanya Neumann, Marjorie Mazia, David Zellmer, Yuriko, Mark Ryder, Ethel Winter, and Douglas Watson)—are led by the choreographer-protagonist, "One Who Seeks" (Martha Graham).

In the pre-Socratic poet Empedocles's *Fragments* 119-20-21, Graham found an image of "the Soul having fallen from the region of light into the roofed-in Cave, the Dark Meadow of Até." Here and now, we are seated in a theatre, in the thrall of Martha Graham sweeping us to a barren realm where the red-robed One Who Seeks has spent an eternity. Voices of oboe, bassoon, clarinet, and flute vacillate from harmonious to dire; processional, sadly dissonant, they push and pull her among a quartet of anthropomorphic plinths.

He Who Summons makes an entrance, after minutes that could be days or eons, into the space around him. During the summoner's sprawling-limbed, tribal display-dance, prideful breastbone uplifted, the seeker recedes, eyes downcast, maintaining an estranged demeanor while the festive, ecstatic ensemble performs a rustic *zarabanda*. We who have become

Erick Hawkins (He Who Summons) and Graham (One Who Seeks),
in *Dark Meadow,* 1946. (Photograph, 1948, by Philippe Halsman)

attuned to Graham's postures of passivity know she may appear distanced
but remains empowered.

The string-driven duet of summoner and seeker is a struggle of opposites
rather than a pas de deux. She faces away from him. He tugs and restrains
rather than embraces her, lifts a plastique-statue rather than a pliant body.
After strained irresolution come retreats to separate terrains; she spins downstage left, he hurtles upstage right.

The lithe, statuesque She of the Ground, the couple's green-caped foil, is a
mediating force across the landscape, head held high, arms extended parallel
to the earth, archaic feet planted, high-stepping decorously. At intervals, she
will kneel in prayer to the originating soil, and defer to the frenetic solilo-
quies of the wandering One Who Seeks, taking tremulous turns, trapped in
an exorcism.

One of the four obelisk-stelae is a heightened triangle, at its peak a skeletal cross, inverted dagger-like armatures draped with black cloth. The impassive summoner hides there, invisible to the seeker. A compassless soul, trembling and blinded, she arrives at the altar of his temple and begins to pull down the fabric. It unspools from the tombstone. He is revealed—to us, not her.

She teases the material out, unrolling it on the ground. In a reprise of *Lamentation*, the One Who Seeks gathers the cloth Lethe into thick folds, and, prostrate, eagerly shrouding herself in the garment she has fashioned, assumes monstrous, inchoate shapes.

Accustomed to Graham's conventions of exposition, development, and recapitulation, we lived in hopes that "They Who Dance Together," the four couples, would do justice to their typecasting. Alas, we are compelled to witness a masque dance of death, men lifting women pietà-like. We anticipated that the attractive She of the Ground would claim her magnetic role; instead, she becomes the summoner's second woman, inciting the seeker's jealous tension.

In their final encounters, we watch He Who Summons and One Who Seeks partnered in a "Postludio" of rough strife entwined in the weeds of the *Dark Meadow*. The score has darkened. Brief triumphs succumb to reluctant defeats. The two lovers reprise unresolved conflicts and subverted expectations: Holding on to each other for dear life, then letting go—embrace or bondage? His palms, fingertips joined, meet upon the flesh of her brow—permitting sight, or predicting blindness? His hand laid on her hip provides then relinquishes support when she twists away—freedom or abandonment? When her body is crouched below his, is he protector—or dominator? When she turns her head and gazes out and to the right during his ardent embrace, is she imagining their intimate future—or, ever the soloist, rebuffing his seductions?

. . .

"Only twenty stenographic notebooks survive her eternal career," we think. "She must have saved these for a reason." White-gloved, lifting the lid of the first of two gray Hollinger boxes, inhaling deeply and reaching within to open Martha Graham's Notebook for *Dark Meadow*, before we read her written words, the kinetic map of her ideas takes form. Often, the blurred handwriting is a spiky, florid, feverish electrocardiogram; or, worn to a stub necessitating changes to ink, the pencil slows down, meanders, lingers. Some entries are signposts, one-word insights (targeted with hand-drawn spears, arrows, or asterisks), itemized aperçus, underlined aide-mémoire. Graham flits, a thieving magpie (her beloved folktale bird, *die fachtiger ekster*) from subject to subject, branch to branch, pausing to steal a choice nibble before springing away. For other stretches, when she writes discursively to find out what she is thinking, in the style of the modern poets, lines detached from the left margin interrupt themselves with hyphens and dashes, and, widely spaced, jaggedly reach toward but shy away from the right-hand verge of the sheet. Other passages scan as if tossed into the stone soup to spark a synapse, or awaken a latent thought.

Martha Graham's notebook pages overflow with the dense labors— intuitive and free-associative here, closely reasoned there—of an excited autodidact: transcriptions from library books—authors, titles, call numbers, and page numbers cited—lengthy passages copied verbatim and meticulously recopied a few pages later, word for word.

And so, as One Who Seeks Martha Graham, our archaeological dig begins, spade thrust into the fecund earth of the *Dark Meadow* notebook to uncover and extract relics, dust and polish and align them, one by one, in a well-lit mental vitrine, a multifaceted exhibition that will attempt to elucidate Graham's errand of inquiry—but does not interpret ("perish the thought!" we imagine her, recoiling, eyebrows raised).

C. G. Jung's idea of the "animus" catches our eye, archetype of male reason and spirit in woman corresponding to the female "soul image"/"anima" embedded in man. Believing Jung's insistence that the unconscious soul, "irreducible to conscious intelligence . . . allows opposites to happen together"—Erick Hawkins claims to have introduced Graham to Jung's corpus. Jean Erdman recalls that, in 1938, Joseph Campbell, guided Graham to Jung's 1921 *Psychological Types* and his 1928 *Essays in Analytical Psychology*. In any case, years before she encountered Jung's magisterial works, Martha Graham had already weathered countless storms of the psyche.

Set into motion by this yin-yang catalyst is a staggering anthology of passages Graham transcribes from a scholarly trio-sisterhood of immense significance to her: Jessie Laidlaw Weston's *From Ritual to Romance: An Exploration of the Gnostic Roots of the Grail Myth* (1920); Jane Ellen Harrison's *Themis: A Study of the Social Origins of Greek Religion* (1927); and Maud Bodkin's *Archetypal Patterns in Poetry: Psychological Studies of Imagination* (1934). Graham also cites Virginia Woolf's escape from "the proper stuff of fiction" into the stream of consciousness of *Mrs. Dalloway*, insisting upon the primacy of "the writer's visions" in a room (or dance studio) of her own; Wallace Fowlie on the "hero as Quester" in the poetry of T. S. Eliot; J. A. Stewart's *Myths of Plato,* invoking the ancients' emphasis upon the stages of madness, from the Prophet's, to the Initiated's, to the Poet's, to the True Lover's derangement; onward to another prime exemplar of hallucinatory lunacy, William Blake's *The Marriage of Heaven and Hell*; and thence to Coleridge's "willing suspension of disbelief" in the *Lyrical Ballads*. At the end of this ecstatic literary parade, Graham circles back to coalescing personae for the *Dark Meadow* dance: "she of the ground . . . he who guides . . . the wandering one . . . [and] one who seeks . . ."

There was to be no curtain or blackout between the four components of the danced *Dark Meadow,* and Graham does not enumerate in the pages of her notebook a step-by-step transition from armloads of books to formal choreography. She drifts into a series of seamless scenic fragments, intimating, for example, that the idea for at least one of Noguchi's erect stelae was hatched in her mind as the kind of rock upon which Jacob, pausing in flight from his brother Esau, lay his head, and dreamed of a stairway resting upon the earth and reaching into the heavens.

Timing the projected work, she adds up the movements. A rough draft of the thing itself comes in at just over thirty-five minutes (early concert versions will vary between forty-three and fifty minutes). It is preemptive to assume that, as many of her mystified dancers used to say—and still do—pointing to their foreheads, "Martha had the whole thing 'up here,'" because there are countless decisions and revisions in her notes. Key elements of "Sarabande," "Quest," "Eternal/Poet Woman," and "Labyrinth" that have come in early will remain in place, while other conceptual spaces extracted from myth and mystery drop away from the evolving dance: the Haunted Castle with its "inner rooms and sanctuaries," the Ceremonial Hill, the Dolorous Tower, the stepped Pyramid of the Sun she mounted at Teotihuacán; and "Riverrun," James Joyce's Anna Livia Plurabelle–Liffey River coursing through his native Dublin. At the mouth of the cornucopia, Graham pivots to a cherished figure, the Virgin, asking herself, "Who is this Woman . . . could there be anything of the Dark Madonna in all this?"

Answering her own question, if tentatively, "Perhaps a kind of invoking from within oneself the Powers of the Spirit to bring about a better condition—" before resolving to press onward, she strides into a storied landscape populated by empowered women. The spirit of Hecate dances here, nocturnal huntress, enchantress of the crossroads—she will be invoked as Medea's ally in the next Graham ballet; and here, too, are Hagar, the bondwoman; the sleeping beauty; Isis, Graham's first featured Denishawn role; Hera, jealous beloved of Zeus, beside his enticing nightmare, Lamia; the "dreadful [Tooth] Mothers of the voracious jaws of death"; a procession of "Heroines" and "Fées," gossamer maidens emerging from Celtic mists; and here, too, is Lilith, Adam's long-haired first wife, not born of him, but made from the same clay, and "longing for rebirth." After mingling with and incorporating this cadre of sisters, Graham stops to breathe for a moment in the lush *Dark Meadow* poesis, footnoting Jung's 1921 *Psychology of the Unconscious*, wherein he marked the "Place of transformation—The place of discipline [as] really the place of the uterus."

Emerging from the stony depths of the womb-cave at the aperture of life obscured by Druidic fog, the denouement of the *Dark Meadow* notebook traces an arc to the end of striving, "the power of choice belonging to the Grail." Reading alongside Martha Graham, we follow her sautés, airborne, the wind in our faces, obeying Nietzsche's command to "dance with the pen." The end of the *Dark Meadow* dance is unconsummated; but when Graham names the pale Triple Goddess, patroness of fertility, poetry, and smithcraft, "Three Brigits in One"—we recall the ceremonial goblet carried from the Brontë sisters' mansion palace of *Deaths and Entrances*.

Penetrating the layers of Martha Graham's thought process enacted in the notebooks, we have glimpsed sampled memories of dances she *has* made— yes, that was indeed "the Perilous couch" from *Every Soul Is a Circus* appearing in and then receding from *Dark Meadow*—mingled with an array of raw ideas and imminent possibilities, prompted by readings, into works she *intends* to make. Once she is satisfied, if only momentarily, that she can apprehend an array of raw ideas in front of her (with her own two eyes, as she often said), Graham permits herself to take a position, and decide what to do with, how to arrange, the multitudinous words and excerpts of differing shapes and sizes, like gazing at her apprehensive dancers sitting on the floor of the studio, soles together, hands on hips, swaying, awaiting her unannounced entrance, in order that they be told to begin anew, at her enunciation, "*And—*"

The fifty-two-year-old doom-eager dancer dares herself to lay bare the Truth of art. Poised stage left, between two rows of velvet wings, upon the threshold of uncharted territory, Martha Graham stands, withholding the as-yet-unrevealed dance, the as-yet-unleashed "power of the Footstep to startle us—to send us into other areas—until music begins & she is swept into ancient time . . ." Thus do her notebook passages unwrap her obsession, "the oldest & strongest emotion of mankind . . . fear, & the oldest & strongest kind of fear . . . fear of the unknown."

She has no choice, she writes, but to summon her strength for the battle, "begin everything in silence—Alone," and step into the spotlight, bearing the only weapon available—her body, because the wordless syntax of dance action will supersede pages upon pages inscribed with "ancestral stratifications of thought."

The time has come to *move,* and serve as prime mover for others. Martha Graham plants the word-signs for *Dark Meadow* in succession, incarnating the near-readied piece—"the Wild Huntsman (Dionysus zagneus)" whose mother, Semele, was the earth, will be Erick Hawkins, in the spirit of the prancing, preening muscular entity he represents, He Who Summons; the "Spectral army [of] ecstatic mad women . . . They Who Dance Together," will be company members Lang, Mazia, Yuriko, and Winter; "the Phallic Demons of Fertility"; will be Isamu Noguchi's smooth-edged, quiet edifices; and "The Sibyl of Cumae . . . the Prophetess," the "Oracle of Dreams," She of the Ground: will be May O'Donnell, lighting the way forward, bearing a multibranched "Golden Bough."

.   .   .

Sets vanish, costumes drop away, eyeshadow and rouge are scrubbed, and hair is unbound. Martha Graham has accounted for all dramatis personae but one, the first person, barefoot and off script: "I will not be released from this bondage until I have released myself," she writes in her notebook. "No man can do it for me." She adored and feared her dear, all-powerful father, the physician-king, George Greenfield Graham. She embraced, bit, clawed, and slapped "Papa" Ted Shawn, the teacher to whom she actually listened. She leaned and cried on Charles Weidman's brotherly platonic shoulder. Louis Horst sat by Graham's side and loved her through innumerable dressing room lamentations.

Years before she laid eyes on Erick Hawkins, Martha Graham had been One Who Seeks. From antiquity, "a goddess with a young subordinate god [was] known . . . on every coast of the Mediterranean which looks toward [Knossos] in Crete," Isis with Horus, Cybele with Attis, Rhea with Zeus. To find and make changes in her work, her company, and her body, Graham needed an Adonis to her Aphrodite.

That was then; but this was now. The public facade Graham and Hawkins had maintained over the past eight years was crumbling from the wear and tear of sacrifice—Martha Graham's requirement for art-making. Incumbent upon her as it was to imitate surrender on the stage of performance, as a woman, she could not tolerate it in everyday life.

Partnering on the bright stage demanded that daily emotions be left in the wings. "When you were in Dark Meadow," Hawkins remembered, "you were in a mythic place." When Graham set a role on Hawkins, it was, de facto, an intimate time in their lives, be it violent or tender, dissonant or concordant. Graham lost, destroyed, or misplaced most of Hawkins's letters and notes to her; our archival dig has uncovered only three shards contemporaneous with *Dark Meadow*. From these fragments we must extrapolate contours.

Our first item is a parenthetical sentence, verging upon afterthought, toward the end of a review of the premiere of *Dark Meadow* at the Plymouth Theatre in New York, January 21, 1946, that appeared in the March issue of *Dance Observer*. "Erick Hawkins did the best dancing of his career in *Dark Meadow*," the sentence began, "and thereby helped to make up for the wordy and almost motionless sermonizing of his solo work, *John Brown*." The critical rubric maintained that when directed by Graham in any of her signature pieces, Hawkins was a dependable, stalwart figure; however, when she gave him a spot on her program for a dance of his own making, he lacked panache and originality. More than three decades later, through a glass darkly, Hawkins recalled that when his dances were presented among Graham's, she never gave him notes or feedback. And, despite its lingering opacity, Graham was adamant that *Dark Meadow* remain in her repertory.

The second fragment we have discovered is a contorted, frantic note from Graham to Hawkins, scribbled after she had been awake all night following a performance of *Punch and the Judy* during the Plymouth Theatre run. The final curtain had barely brushed the floor when, in a rage, Hawkins blew the lid of the pressure-cooker, exploded out of the theatre, and vanished into the night, under the impression (mistaken, she insists) that Graham had allowed Merce Cunningham to take a solo bow—but not him. Explaining that Cunningham had not heard her command for an ensemble curtain call, Graham refrains from an outright apology. Rather, upon reflection, she "understands [Hawkins] a little better" and "is sorry for both of us." She extends the offer of a bow at the next performance of *Punch and the Judy* later that week, after which they will return to "entire company bows."

Our third retrieved specimen is disconcerting. The extravagant twelve-day display of Martha Graham's genius brought to Broadway by S. Hurok was over—*Dark Meadow, Salem Shore, Herodiade, Punch and the Judy, Appalachian Spring, Deaths and Entrances,* and *Letter to the World,* with the addition of Erick Hawkins's *John Brown.* The lovers' debate continued in the aftermath.

"Your statement worries me," she writes in a March note, pleading fatigue, deflecting Hawkins's emotional assertions, and calling his manner "offended . . . possessed." He tells her he remains unfulfilled in the roles she makes for him. "They may not be what you desire," Graham presses on, "I suppose no one's ever is," countering that Hawkins's roles are "strong," and that she is not trying to "use" him, or "hold [him] back in the shadow."

Here as elsewhere in their self-conscious twists of dialogue, it is difficult to tease out the disciplined dance of art from the uneven vernacular of everyday life. By "roles," are they talking about the heroic, smitten Husbandman of *Appalachian Spring*; or the moody fellow puttering around the West Twelfth Street apartment? Does relegating Hawkins to "the shadow" refer to his offstage longueurs sulking while young men newer to the company strut through *Letter to the World*; or following up on her reminder that the floor of the 66 Fifth Avenue studio must be properly waxed and buffed by the time she returns from her August and September refuge at her mother's, thousands of miles away?

.   .   .

It is springtime, 1946.

Another ambitious work taking shape, Martha Graham pledges in the last line of the *Dark Meadow* notebook that before the inevitable recurrence of dissatisfaction on the far horizon she will conjure faith in dance's present moment, right now: "For there is no hope—there is only what we do—."

28

Serpent Heart

Martha Graham, poised and self-assured in her ninetieth year, spine straight, lips set and eyes agleam, "her noble tininess clothed in robes that she makes regal," stares into the camera and introduces her reconceived story of Euripides's heretic Medea, as if May 10, 1946, were only last night, and she, Erick Hawkins, Yuriko (in her debut lead performance), and May O'Donnell (returned to the company) had just seized possession of the Columbia University McMillin Theatre stage.

"Medea was more than human," Graham tells us, no words wasted. "And when the laws of heart and body are interfered with," she continues, "there arises within her a passion we all understand, an envy, a covetousness, a maliciousness—an untamable thing of fire." Her gaze of insight widens. "She lived on an island. When Jason, the first man to sail the seas, came to this island," Graham concludes, he lit the flame of "the powerful, never-ending curse of jealousy . . . in this dangerous, beautiful, implacable woman."

Imagine the new South Wing of Antiquities in the Metropolitan Museum of Art, Manhattan, late 1920s. A diminutive young lady, well-put-together in a calf-length pleated skirt and bodice-hugging woolen sweater, hair swept up beneath a chic beret, indulges herself in a weekend field trip. Walking through the halls, deep in thought, she comes upon a glass-enclosed "marble relief fragment from the Roman Imperial period, first and second century AD, a copy of a Greek marble relief of about 420–410 BC." It is a likeness, she reads, of "the witch Medea . . . that probably decorated the parapet surrounding the Altar of the Twelve Gods in the Athenian Agora." The implacable head in profile arrests Martha Graham's attention. There is something ominous about Medea's benign expression, bearing no hint of demons concealed within.

In Euripides's primordial drama, the goddess-princess Medea, granddaughter of the Sun and niece of Circe, grows up on the island of Colchis. From distant Iolkos, Jason's surrogate father, King Peleas, dispatches him to Colchis aboard the *Argo,* an enchanted ship, to steal the Golden Fleece. Skilled in potion-making *pharmaka,* the sorceress Medea falls in love with Jason and casts a deadly spell upon the Fleece's fire-breathing guardian serpent dragon. The triumphant couple returns to Iolkos. After instigating Peleas's assassination, they flee to Corinth, where Jason, in exile, betrays his wife in the arms of King Creon's daughter, Glauce. She is drugged and burnt to death by Medea who, redoubling the tragedy, kills her own golden-haired sons.

The gestures of "quick-tempered" Medea spoke to Martha Graham: the way Medea "turns away her pale, pale neck and bemoans . . . her dear father," regretful that her "first mistake [was] when [she] left King Aeetes' house"; her bouts of bitter "sufferings and laments" on women's fate as "the most wretched creatures" condemned "to take a master for our body . . ."; her disillusionment with Jason as "an unjust man who is a clever speaker . . . confident that his tongue can gloss over injustice"; and her sweet emancipation when, wronged and wrongful, she survives unpunished, and by Zeus's fortuitous grace "[flies] off in her golden chariot."

In the third-century BCE version of Medea's tale, a lyrical flashback called *The Voyage of Argo,* Apollonius of Rhodes romanticizes the giddy moment when Eros, "unobserved . . . crouched low at Jason's feet . . . [drew] his bow and shot at Medea . . . leaving his shaft deep in the girl's breast, hot as fire. Time and again she darted a bright glance at Jason . . . And her heart stood still, [overflowing] with the sweetness of her pain . . . In the turmoil of her soul, her soft cheeks turned from rose to white and white to rose." This incarnation, "Medea of the many wiles," like Martha Graham visiting Erick Hawkins in the Bennington dressing room after the Ballet Caravan premiere, is "prey to all the inquietude that Love awakens . . . how Jason looked; the clothes he wore, the things he said, the way he sat, and how he walked to the door. . . . But she feared for him."

He was "brilliant and beautiful, like Sirius rising from Ocean . . . like a warhorse eager for battle, pawing the ground . . . he exulted in the strength of his limbs." In Medea's ensuing, fitful dreams, premonitions of her reversal of fortune, Jason is darkly transformed, "full of menace . . . splendid to look at but fraught with trouble for the lovesick girl . . . and the pair of them stood face to face without a word or sound."

Five years before *Serpent Heart* was realized onstage, Martha Graham had birthed a scenario predicated upon readings in antiquity ("I have used the form of a Greek play as an outline"), characteristically contradicting herself in drafts sent to Aaron Copland for his review and consideration in February 1941 and July 1942. Once more, she began with denial as rationale for her artistic choices. It was "in no sense a Greek play . . . [but, rather,]" she told Copland, "the real conflict tak[ing] place not between the man [Jason] and her [Medea], but between the Woman and her Fury, herself." She uprooted the locale from the Black Sea to "the halls of some [nineteenth-century] New England house," home of Graham's oft-claimed tenth-generation Puritan ancestry on her mother's side, where lived an heretical, exotic woman "monstrous as the dark female force . . . a daughter of Colchis in her secret heart. A strangely passionate outward chastity often cloaked [her] fury whose madness was the fanatical domination of desire."

The music not yet composed, Graham mused to Copland that if percussion such as the *tympanum* borne by maenads were to be woven in, they "should not be used as primitive instruments[,] but rather as delicate instruments of the nerves . . . to make hidden areas of feeling objective, rather than as excitements, or accents." Likewise, the *Daughter of Colchis* was not yet choreographed. Graham's "Action . . . Parados . . . Ode . . . Paean . . . Exodos" laid out a narrative path for what Erick Hawkins called her affinity for "poetic creatures . . . in mythic places." This desperate Woman of Colchis, in a dark cloak concealing a glittering dress, was "at times queenly, at times like a wounded animal"; the Man in her life was "the poet, the dreamer, the free masculine spirit . . . [like] Poe to his Ligeia." The human duo interplayed with three conjured spirit-beings: [His] Muse and [Her] Fury, battling for emotional supremacy, joined by the Passer-by, an empathic Chorus figure.

Despite these ongoing revisions, in late summer 1942 Copland broke the news to the waiting Martha that he found her overheated saga of a spurned sorceress "too severe." With no hard feelings, and buoyed by funds from Elizabeth Sprague Coolidge, Graham gave her "Daughter" away to another trusted suitor-collaborator, Carlos Chávez. Aaron Copland went on to other projects, including *Appalachian Spring*. Chávez welcomed the *Medea* commission. But a haphazard convergence of lost manuscript scores, procrastination, and missed deadlines pushed the hoped-for unveiling of *La Hija de*

Samuel Barber, ca. mid-1940s.

Cólquide to the indefinite future; Chávez's completed work did not arrive in Graham's mailbox at Bennington until the summer of 1945. Recycling instincts in play, she decided to reserve Chávez's double quartet for winds and strings as accompaniment for the percolating *Dark Meadow,* because, in the interim, Graham had met a gifted ally to breathe life into Medea: Samuel Barber.

Born in West Chester, Pennsylvania, in 1910 and, like Martha Graham, the child of a physician, Samuel Barber was raised in a genteel, cosmopolitan family steeped in Presbyterian-Quaker propriety. His mother was an accomplished pianist, and her sister, Louise Homer, was a soprano at the Metropolitan Opera. Sam, solitary and "unduly pampered," encouraged to start piano lessons at age six, wrote his first opera, *The Rose Tree,* at twelve, and was, as a teenager, "a triple threat prodigy in composition, voice and piano," enrolled at the Curtis Institute of Music, where he befriended his future life partner, Gian Carlo Menotti. Barber's compositional career took off with his first major works, *Overture to the School for Scandal* and *Music for a Scene from Shelley.* At twenty-five, he received the Prix de Rome. His stately, elegiac *Adagio for Strings* was premiered by the NBC Symphony Orchestra under the baton of Arturo Toscanini. Barber wrote a second symphony while in the army air corps during World War II.

In the early to mid-forties, Samuel Barber was introduced to Martha Graham by a friend in her company, the poet Robert Horan. At 66 Fifth Avenue, the visiting composer was allowed to remain in the studio after the end of class, and watched Graham "improvise . . . alone," "while Louis Horst played . . . his jacket covered with ashes, his white hair combed back only by his fingers, wheezing and blinking . . ." These special moments in the city led to Graham's occasional trips to "Capricorn," the elegant country house that Barber shared with Menotti on seventy hilly acres in Mount Kisco. "It was a red-letter day whenever she visited me," Barber remembered.

On the shady porch, composer and choreographer indulged in their shared relish for gossip, after a few hearty laughs moving to common interests ranging from a passion for literature, to witty stories of Scotch-Irish ancestors, to strategies of form in James Joyce ("She had an underlined copy of *Ulysses"*), to the ceremonial rituals of Pueblo and Navajo Indians. At one of these autumnal tea-times, in "her *very* seductive . . . and *so* convincing . . . way of speaking," having been invited by the Alice M. Ditson Fund of Columbia University to devise a new work for the Second Annual Festival of Contemporary Music coming up in the spring of 1946, Graham broached her gestating idea for Medea. "It was very hard to say 'no' to Martha," Barber recalled. She gave him the *Daughter of Colchis* script, soon followed by a rapid-fire barrage of dense, epigrammatic story sketches. At the end of November, "as soon as he finished orchestrating his *Concerto for Violoncello,"* Barber set to work on the Medea in earnest, writing agitatedly to his friend Henry-Louis de la Grange, "She is our greatest dancer . . . but it must be ready by February!"

. . .

Martha Graham's gift of "complete freedom" during the composition process became Samuel Barber's burden. When it came to the soundscape, resolutely not dictating that he must "adhere to a beat," she exuded an uncanny "sense of music without being musical, perhaps." Her posture of tentative, disciplined inquiry meant that in the one month between the time Barber's first draft score in nine sections for fourteen-piece chamber orchestra was ready, and the opening night at Columbia University, the piece went through two more versions. And in the studio, as Medea took "trembling" shape and "every eye was upon her . . . like Maria Callas in opera," Barber appreciated the paradoxical behavior of Martha Graham that made her, in his view, "one of the great artists[:] the way she gives you the freedom to decide what you are looking at—maybe too much."

Until the day before the premiere, Graham and Barber's piece bore the title, "Pain and Wrath Are the Sinners," the last line of an invocation offered to the "shining sky" and the "divine earth" by the First Corinthian Woman on behalf of the aggrieved Medea, whose "mind is not here. / She does not know what she prays for." An incantatory program note advised the audience that they were about to become complicit in a graphic conflict of the sexes, because "within the cave of the heart is a place of darkness . . . peopled with shadows of acts of violence, terror and magic. Try as we might to escape this monstrous heritage, we are caught up into its surge, and the past is alive." In an eleventh-hour anxiety attack, "Graham changed the name of the ballet from 'Pain and Wrath . . .' to 'Serpent Heart,'" placing more stress upon "one like Medea [who] destroys that which she has been unable to

Martha Graham (One Like Medea) in *Cave of the Heart,* ca. 1946.
(Photograph by Cris Alexander)

possess . . ." The elusive "beloved" object of her passion was danced by Erick Hawkins, whom she called "one like Jason."

The fabrication of the stage setting for "Serpent Heart" was also embattled. Martha Graham got into some "terrible fights" with Isamu Noguchi; Samuel Barber was shocked to see her slap the sculptor across the face during one rehearsal. In the end, true to form and habit, the artist achieved the dancer's metaphorical intentions. "A group of flat-topped stones . . . on the left side of the stage" invoked the island origins of the tale. Toward the center of the space was a massive, gray, textured heart-like "chair-table sculpture" on its back, "with stubby protrusions that became known as 'Aorta.'" To the right downstage rested a greenish "flat, U-shaped stone" recalling the rough-hewn Aztec serpent in the Templo Mayor of Mexico City—with alert head and stubby tail—serving double duty as the "stand" for the bronze-gold "skeletal-frame-vest . . . with spidery, protruding wires" that Graham harnessed to herself and inhabited for her quivery, clicking, peripatetic solo.

. . .

Playing more often to larger houses, Martha Graham's formidable histrionic power projected Medea's pain; her heavily made-up, mask face was set in an enraptured expression, and, shoulders square to the hips, her body devoured space. Even from the balcony of the McMillan Theatre, each discrete, taut instant of the dancer's sweeps and curves, calibrated like the cross-hatches of an etching, was discernible.

A foreboding theme, woodwinds rising and falling in dialogue with strings, heralds the parados and Medea's entrance, and stalks her, threading through the entire piece. Jason's martial poses, large and proud, demonstrate "Here I am!" A stomping mannequin of crooked elbows, clenched fists, and feet in profile, he completes the expository solo by reaching for the Princess's sculpted, tender hand. Petite, gentle, accompanied by flute and clarinet trills, she is a flighty woodland sprite, clambering weightless up the tree limbs of Jason's taut thighs and sinewed arms to ride upon his shoulder. Warrior hero and complaisant bride, in floating harmony, are oblivious while Medea languishes, clawing the earth. The tender lyricism of their duet lends a peaceful air; yet, if we close our eyes, we detect minor tones lurking. The "Chorus" figure paces to and fro, with gestures of benign inclination rather than touch, the colors in her establishing theme applied with light strokes. She participates in the drama through shifts in attention, from powerless to aloof to engaged, tilting toward and between the other three dramatis personae.

In the *Dance of Vengeance*, at the peak of the work's cruelest arc, we grasp what Samuel Barber witnessed in the rehearsal studio when Martha Graham gasped into the stops and starts, shrieks and blasts of his energetic score. "Like the swing of a pendulum, between relaxed lyrical flow and tense angularity," electricity lances through Medea's body; in pained ripples, contractions emanate below her midriff, then dissipate with the illusion of spreading in spasms against her will. Following upon the muffled horn's frantic pulses, double bass and cello carve Medea's descent, impelled down a spiral staircase—Martha Graham's *Untergangen*.

On three pages buried in a stenographic notebook, "Fragments for Solo Dances," Graham lays out a plan for this four and one-half minute solo. She pushes off the floor into a "Warrior stance," to disgorge her bitter story in a torrent of bourrées, knee-crawls, back-shoulder falls, and front and back "Bali turns . . . Facing Jason . . . crawling to Jason . . . darting to Jason . . . banking upstage to Jason . . ." She extracts a red ribbon from her bodice, stretching it elongated above her head, coiling it around her waist and arm, crushing it into her palm, casting it away then scooping it from the ground. For the outrageous finale, Medea shoves the vengeance-soaked snake-ribbon into her mouth, "eats" it, "spits" it out, and thrusts it between her breasts.

In Graham's written notes, the "Vengeance" solo is framed for an audience of one: Jason, he who spurned Medea. However, onstage, the man has departed, while the Chorus remains, prostrate and blind, eyes shielded from the spectacle of repression, consumption, and regurgitation. Medea dashes away and offstage, and the Chorus awakens, entering what Barber calls a *Kantikos Agonias*, a chant of dawning anxiety and impotence. Medea returns; having done the grisly deed, as was foretold, she drags Princess Glauce's corpse across the ground in a purple cloak, and exposes the body to Jason and the Chorus.

Heralded by "music of mixed triumph and lamentation," bringing to mind a flock of birds frightened by a sudden thunderclap bursting thickly from a bare tree and dissipating into a pallid sky, and webbed in a spidery guise of sun-burnished gold as befits her celestial ancestry, Medea, "a woman, a foreigner, alone . . . go[es] forth / Under the cold eyes of the weakness-despising stars—"

Ambivalent critical responses spelled trouble. While Martha Graham,

One Like Medea, was "daring . . . profound . . . rich and powerful . . . [and] danced magnificently . . . in high-voltage theatricality," Erick Hawkins, One Like Jason, was "heroic, but the emotional contacts with [Medea were] not yet clearly-established . . . [and he] did not quite escape an effect of strain . . . His role . . . needs variety and a closer integration with the rest of the work."

29

The "Break-Up"

What pattern do I want of my life until I am in the grave? Here I am 37 and have the choice of at least knowing what I would like to aim at. . . . Is it not possible to plan my work and life as I plan at dance [?]
—ERICK HAWKINS, Notebook, August 1946

I t was the summer of his existential discontent. Erick Hawkins's well-meaning attempts to use the solitary time and inventory his progress while Martha Graham had removed herself to Santa Barbara were disrupted by overthinking. One haunted dream would not relinquish the past: He was in the elevator at the School of American Ballet "where [he] went up and down for four years." The operator was out on a break, so Hawkins took the lever in hand "and started up," but when he got to the top floor, it kept going higher, he lost control, the cable snapped, the elevator went into free fall, and he woke up. Did this mean he was "trying to go too high in attempting to get a studio of [his] own," and would "fall with a bang . . . holding [himself] in too high estimation? . . . However difficult though my way will be," he wondered, "how can I live except by being independent?"

In another ambivalent dream, Hawkins floated upon the maternal sea, one hand "holding onto a pier or a pile," the other to "a buoyant object that kept bobbing up and down." The surging tide forced him to loosen his grip on the dock. He drifted out into the ocean, "aware of the dilemma [he] had to face, as it got worse, whether to let go of the object, swim back to the safety of the pier, and <u>save</u> [him]self . . . from submergence . . ."

In a third nocturnal trance, a familiar voice—his own, disembodied—called to Hawkins, "You must not be afraid and not murmur against God," not the supreme deity, he sensed, but "that 'imaginative' aspect of myself which I must release completely; 'use' completely, [the] God in that inner man, the 'kingdom' within you, your better self, creative self"; in the same way that Ralph Waldo Emerson, whose works Hawkins had devoured in college, exhorted classmates at the Harvard Divinity School that the only path to freedom was to write their own Bibles.

Other trepidations were let loose by Hawkins's urge to reread *Psychology of the Unconscious: A Study of the Transformations and Symbolisms of the Libido*, Jung's work begun in 1909 that signaled the rupture from Freud when "it struck [Jung] what it means to live with a myth, and what it means to live without one . . . the man who thinks he can live without myth, or outside it, is an exception . . . The psyche is not of today . . . individual consciousness is only the flower and the fruit of a season," Jung came to understand, "writing at top speed," digging out from under "a landslide that cannot be stopped" of ritual stories from "Egyptian to Babylonian to Hindu and Gnostic and American Indian." Ultimately, Jung posed the question to himself, "What is the myth *you* are living? . . . and regarded this as [his] task of tasks." Hawkins responded by underlining this passage in his copy of the book: "By sacrifice, man ransoms himself from the fear of death and reconciles the destroying mother," an insight arising from the loneliness in Graham's absence that "this summer . . . I had an inkling of the meaning of sacrifice— the 'letting go.' I think that is the next step," Hawkins observed, "not literally 'the fear of death,' but of 'failure,' the fear that everything will not be ideal."

As an antidote to these obstacles, Hawkins made a checklist of abiding goals, a dutiful exercise since adolescence. "I want to be a fine artist, a dancer and an actor," he announced, a lofty place to start. Furthermore, "I want to create a form which will combine dance, glory of poetry, music, beauty of costume and set," consistent with his characterization of modern dance as all-embracing and multifaceted, "a complete synthesis . . . a unifying architecture." Predicated upon this foundation, "I want to say in my art the great living experiences of man's living-process, to show people the symbols of their salvation, to coalesce for them as they saw [*sic*] my work the great affirmations that give wholeness to the human psyche."

So far, so good—until Hawkins became frustrated trying to pin down, from the same stance, his mercurial, longing feelings about beloved "M," fearing the sacrilege of inscribing Graham's full name. "I want to be able to perform completely on my own and as an equal in M's company," he wrote, veering away from uncomfortably specific to distanced general. "I want to overcome all sense of comparison with any other dancer and choreographer."

As soon as the plan was mapped out, it collapsed under the weight of yearning: "I want to love without fear, with compassion, without separation from others, to be a part of the Big Self without causing suffering to another being . . . to deserve affection and enjoy the warmth of being loved."

Get-togethers with a few acquaintances in the city during Hawkins's monastic dog days in hopes of some emotional relief were not satisfying. Leonard Robinson, a *New Yorker* staffer and short-story writer, told Hawkins unhelpfully over lunch that if he ever got married, to Martha Graham, or anyone for that matter, "sticking to dancing" would not bring the financial emancipation he sought. Teaching, especially younger students, continued to be Hawkins's professional passion. Two six-week technique classes at the Adelphi College Center of Creative Arts founded by Ruth St. Denis helped subsidize visits to a therapist. Dr. Ruth Foster guided Hawkins Socratically through a maze of troubles, pointing out his fixation upon "'conflicting images' . . . Yes, that seems very good," Hawkins conceded. "One wants one thing but some other ideal is also attractive due to the patterns of life. . . . Say I was independent, and yet want to lean on M's security and so I have conflict, resentment, anxiety, and guilt."

.   .   .

Despite such self-diagnosed ambivalence, Hawkins's work ethic held secure. Several text-based pieces—from barely conceived to achieved but not quite finished—occupied him simultaneously. Hawkins admonished himself with a pep talk, remembering "the days I worked well on *John Brown* at Bennington." He needed to "start with new intensity to tackle [and] compose and find an expressive new ending" for this dance "passion play" of the defiant Abolitionist leader who led the Harper's Ferry uprising and "came to recognize the power of the spirit within." In dialogue with an interlocutor played by West Virginian Will Hare, a cofounder of the Actors Studio, Erick Hawkins starring as *John Brown* had premiered at the National Theatre in New York on May 16, 1945. The conversational script by poet Robert Richman, founder of the Institute for Contemporary Arts in Washington, DC, was "distilled and refined" from Brown's letters and journals, mingled with the writings of Emerson, Henry David Thoreau, George Mason, and Frederick Douglass. The percussion-driven score was by Charles Borromeo Mills, a former student of Aaron Copland and Roger Sessions whom Hawkins liked for his "severe but eloquent contrapuntal style." Isamu Noguchi's "construction simultaneously suggested a tree, a clothes rack, and a gallows . . . [and] the

Erick Hawkins (Stephen), holding apple (left), and Stuart Hodes (Trainer/Guardian Angel), perched upon Isamu Noguchi's thirteen-foot jungle gym, in *Stephen Acrobat,* 1946. (Photograph by Philippe Halsman)

choreography emphasized clenched fists, determined strides and kicks, defiant pacings, and reachings of the arms to high heaven."

John Martin, a continuing thorn in Hawkins's side, and besotted with Graham's *Appalachian Spring* and *Every Soul Is a Circus* presented on the same program with *John Brown*, condescended that while the dancer was "unquestionably sincere and has his heart in the right place," the work "comes close to the point of being embarrassing." Stark Young took the high ground, assessing the man dancer on his merits, and presciently: "Mr. Erick

Hawkins grows steadily," he wrote. "His is an art beginning with character and manliness, a deep, ascetic, rigorous fineness of understanding and a constant search for what is clean and final."

"I want to vivify every bar of movement that doesn't now enhance the inner emotional heart life . . . ," Hawkins said, with convoluted intentions. For his next invented persona, he was going to revive the high-wire movement quality from *Every Soul Is a Circus,* with "an innocent hardiness of self-preservation [and] equilibration under impetus," wrote Parker Tyler with an unerring eye upon his friend's body. "I see how I want to make the [new] role into Stephen," Hawkins wrote, "not leaving it at 'Acrobat' in abstract but making [it] into Stephen—a living Stephen the acrobat." The first name referred to James Joyce's *ur*-novel, *Stephen Hero,* drafted in 1904 when the author was twenty-two years old; and revised, by 1916, into *Portrait of the Artist as a Young Man.*

Joyce's work reminded Hawkins of the attendant perils in his life-journey from desert to metropolis. Joyce christened his protagonist Stephen Dedalus, after the master craftsman who made the Labyrinth at Knossos for King Minos of Crete, only to be imprisoned in that maze with his son, Icarus. Dedalus fabricated wings of osier-wood sticks, wax, and feathers to help them fly to Sicily. But the boy came too close to the sun, the wings melted, and he plummeted into the sea. Erick Hawkins's nightmarish fears of pride going before a dreaded fall from the heights of his own love and art were realized in Isamu Noguchi's spindly, thirteen-foot framework tower for the *Stephen Acrobat* set, a fragile, latticed ladder to the stars.

Stephen Acrobat would premiere six months later at the Ziegfeld Theatre. "[S]winging in the golden air" in the role of "Trainer," beside, above, and below Erick Hawkins on Noguchi's hybrid jungle gym, and intermittently declaiming verse by Robert Richman, was twenty-three-year-old Brooklyn-born Stuart Hodes. Among "the number of men returning from service in the armed forces . . . on the eve of choice . . . who [were] unafraid to face the arts as participants—some for the first time," Hodes was an ex–bomber pilot bringing raw energy and doom-eager airborne experience, who had "burst, like a football player . . . moving really fast, out of nowhere" into the Martha Graham studio in December 1946. He considered himself a "classicist," like Hawkins having gravitated to Graham from Muriel Stuart's tutelage at the School of American Ballet. Hodes took pride in his strength and endurance, and was unfazed by the required one-hour warm-ups before every class and rehearsal at 66 Fifth Avenue, after which Graham would inquire with a wry smile if he "had a good *suffer* today."

During the *Stephen Acrobat* performance, when Hawkins took a bite from a shiny red apple, it became evident that he had invented a "male Eve" who "eats of the Tree of Knowledge" and suffers the consequences. Rolling in agony on the floor, Stephen is ridiculed "sepulchrally" by the Trainer/Guardian Angel as "a fool."

. . .

Another book Hawkins reopened in search of new ideas was Géza Róheim's *The Riddle of the Sphinx, or Human Origins,* a meditation upon "ancestral spirits . . . the eternal ones of the dream." The expatriate Hungarian anthropologist was in residence at the New York Psychoanalytic Institute on East Eighty-Second Street. Hawkins paid him a visit, and their conversation about the Sphinx of archaic Greek thought, and the wandering, phallic Mother of Animals in Hopi mythology, moved him to "write out the first sketch of meanings for [a dance to be entitled] 'The Strangler.'" In "M's" absence, Hawkins's thoughts turned to half-recalled childhood moments of separation from his mother and father, rites of passage, and the lived consequences of paths taken—and not. He conjured the monstrous, "half lion, half woman," winged Sphinx, sent by the goddess Hera, "represent[ing] father and mother in the primal scene," face-to-face with "Oidipous," the Corinthian riddle-solver, "at the moment of his initiation into manhood." Hawkins situated their fateful encounter at "the ritual dancing-place in a stony pass on the road from Delphi as it approaches Thebes." With a script by poet Robert Fitzgerald, *The Strangler* took two years to bring to the stage.

On the heels of John Brown, Stephen Acrobat, and Oedipus ("realiz[ing] with astonishment that he is still alive for us"), came Erick Hawkins's most inflammatory character of the summer, "Ahab," "the story of a man who is irreconcilably determined on self-destruction." Hawkins resolved that the nascent work—planned to be an eighteen- to twenty-minute choreographic dialogue between the monomaniacal captain of the *Pequod* and his interlocutor, Ishmael, the only surviving crewmember—would be completed "by May [1947]." However, it had to wait another year to be crafted into "A Dance in Four Parts for Two Men," devised in partnership with poet Charles Olson—larger-than-life champion of sprung-rhythmed, breath-caesura-driven projective verse, and author of *Call Me Ishmael,* a study of Melville. "If I can execute this idea," Hawkins wrote to his collaborator, in a state of agitation, "it could be a terrific dance of madness—like the explosion of a star."

Despite Hawkins's best efforts, the Manichaean product of the alliance between the two broad-shouldered colleagues could not find a theatrical home. "I am glad I did not proceed to do the work when I first envisaged it thirty-five years ago," Hawkins averred—mistakenly, or revisionistically—at a performance on September 4, 1986, of the expanded, reimagined *Ahab* by Erick Hawkins Dance Company and Theatre Orchestra at Cambridge, on the occasion of Harvard's 350th anniversary. "Having lived a while now," Hawkins admitted, "perhaps I can, a little, understand Ahab."

The labored and dense scenarios, prompts, and suggested lines for "paraphrasing or weaving into the script" for *The Fiery Hunt* laid bare the dancer's demons. Peering through the eyes of Jung, whom the poet had not (yet) read, Hawkins told Olson that "the Whale [was] not the true antagonist" of Ahab; rather, "the conflict [was] within [his] psyche . . . between Ahab's sanity and the area of his psyche that broke off as it were thru [*sic*] his will and formed an autonomous complex."

Ahab's "tragic flaw . . . militates against an acceptance of reality, of life as it is and is possible for the individual," such that "the only path open is madness . . . It is like Faust or Macbeth." Ahab has become "overwhelmed by feelings" erupting from his unconscious to the surface, Hawkins said, identifying transparently with the crippled captain's "struggle to maintain his humanness" as a damaged pilgrim, unable to shed "unsleeping, ever-passing thought[s]," possessed by an "image of himself as grand, some god-child wronged. He dances the course he'll follow as though he will be triumphant . . . as though his abstract dance leads Ahab to the pondering of the nature of himself . . . Ahab rises from the bed and rushes headlong into the NIGHTMARE DANCE . . . ," pivoting to "a quiet, tender dance . . . as though he were brushing his charges back to sleep. It is the godlike man to offset the mad . . ." a delusion that, Hawkins wrote, "when you think [it] is fled may merely have transfigured itself."

When Ahab's traumatized body is torn with discord, "the torso throughout should be firm as though he were a ruler," but "the arms, however, and occasionally, the legs should convey a demanding, grasping quality." And the harpoon, the heavy weapon-burden Ahab carries against Moby-Dick, should become, Hawkins tells Olson—overlaying Martha Graham upon

Herman Melville—"a caliper to the choreography . . . an inverted equivalent of the Cross in [her] *Penitente . . .*"

.   .   .

Hawkins's mind was crammed and his heart ached. The analysand's fears of "disentanglement" and "libido displacement" warred with the Husband-man's hunger to join hands with his faraway Bride, "to write Mr. and Mrs., and to walk down the street and back into a house and show everyone this is where we sleep together." Due to arrive in New York by mid-September, Graham wrote Hawkins, that she, too, had taken time to reflect. "I hope you are not angry with me and feel that I am short-sighted," she said; he must think of himself, she insisted, as "completely free from me in every way. I think I am clear about what I did and what I want to do." Her mixture of instruction and equivocation ratcheted up his perplexity about their status as partners in business, onstage, and in the bedroom.

In the journal, Hawkins talked open-endedly to himself; but when he tried to elucidate his feelings for Graham in the pages of a letter, the default position was to waver and concede. "I think we still have not worked out our relation," he replied, falling back into the self-blame she triggered. "If we are to work together we shall still have to iron out things . . . Maybe I just don't know how to work with others in a give and take . . . ," he continued, further undermining himself. "Perhaps it is that you want to give me the lead and let me do it . . . Whenever it gets to the point that you think it would be better for me to disassociate myself from the running of things," he went on, referring to the day-to-day operation and management of the studio and school, "please for my sake as well as your own say so."

Within days after Graham stepped off the train from California, Hawkins seized Saturday, September 21, 1946, face-to-face, distances dissolved, conjectures and hypotheses discarded, as the moment of his "complete break with Martha . . . when I told her I must separate completely." It had come down to self-preservation. He had to be first to cut the cord.

Graham gritted her teeth and vowed to "get through" the "difficult . . . terrible days" and quell her "chattering devils," reminding Hawkins that she required, reciprocally, "the same privilege [of] freedom" he claimed by taking the initiative. At the apartment, they no longer shared a bed, came and went at different times, and, to avoid speaking, left notes for each other on the kitchen table. They both continued to teach at the school, setting up alternating class schedules so their paths would not cross. "Freedom" remained Graham's mantra, "from this compulsion—obsession—whatever it may be," but, counterintuitively, she wondered, with what boundaries? She sought advice from the psychoanalyst and social philosopher Erich Fromm, chairman of the faculty at the William Alanson White Institute of Psychiatry, Psychoanalysis and Psychology, whom she had met at Bennington three years before. His *Escape from Freedom* (1941) espoused "the particular kind of relatedness of the individual toward the world, not that of satisfaction or frustration of single instinctual desires." Fromm counseled Graham that she needed to concentrate upon herself, the soloist, and set aside an unfeasible course toward emancipation that would pull Hawkins along.

Graham's conceptualization of "marriage in the real sense" was discordant with Hawkins's. He had long fantasized that their union would be formally sanctified. Not so, she told him. "It is you as my companion, my spiritual husband that I miss rather than as my lover," reiterating that "I still regard myself as your wife . . . of the past seven and a half years."

.   .   .

Martha Graham emerged from autumn's crucible and revised and retitled *Serpent Heart* for rebirth as *Cave of the Heart* on February 27, 1947, at the Ziegfeld Theatre, downplaying the Jason and Medea myth. Now the characters were generic: "Sorceress" (Graham), "Adventurer" (Hawkins), "Victim" (Yuriko), and "Chorus" (O'Donnell). What had been welcomed, qualifiedly, the year before as "a daring but wayward and uncoordinated experiment in high-voltage theatricality" was hailed as a clarified work, "ambiguities and obscurities eliminated . . . and its action mov[ing] in a straight line to a truly awesome denouement." Cecil Smith, the dance critic of *Theatre Arts Monthly*, saw new qualities of "idealization and aesthetic detachment, and . . . a certain moral force" in the stripped-down choreography, intuiting the principals' resolve to exploit their offstage alienation, rather than abandon adversity in the wings. "As the tension and conflict between [Sorceress and Adventurer] increases, they step out of their legendary roles from time to time," Graham's program note, written with Samuel Barber, said, "and become the modern man and woman, caught in the nets of jealousy and destructive love . . ."

For the next evening's program—although she knew quite well how proud Hawkins, the Greek and Latin scholar, was of his translation of Catullus's miniature epic (*epyllion*), *Poem 64*, Ariadne's tale of the faithless Theseus who deserted her at Naxos—Graham did not cast her estranged lover in *Errand into the Maze*. Her costar in the duet, with music by Gian Carlo Menotti, was Mark Ryder, returning to the company after army service. The title was from the first line of a Ben Belitt poem, "Dance Piece," written in homage to Graham. Her "errand" was into the mind and heart of Ariadne, King Minos's daughter, who had helped Theseus find a way through the Labyrinth and slay the Minotaur. In her subversive, contraction-convulsed version, Graham, "frozen in frenzy" and, like Ariadne, no longer needing a mate, screws up the courage to battle and flatten into submission Ryder's horned and yoked "Creature of Fear." Having choreographed a route out of the relationship, she concludes, "There is the accomplishment of the errand, the instant of triumph, and the emergence from the dark."

Three months later, in *Night Journey*, moving from the white, folded ridges of Ariadne's labyrinthine brain and reversing another legend of recognition, Graham took a trip into the twisted black chambers of Queen Jocasta's incestuous "heart at the instant when she recognizes the ultimate terms of her destiny." Hawkins incarnated her cursed "son-husband . . . lover-child." Unlike the Oedipus of *The Strangler*, Graham directed him inescapably bound to her by a thick umbilical rope that she could loose and tighten in unpredictable rhythms.

·   ·   ·

"I want to find a way to dance that will be truly to 'dance Him,'" Hawkins wrote, claiming a heroic self with a capital "H" in his spring 1947 journal. "I want to find the deep core of myself so as to let the rhythm, sensitivity, perception, clarity, [and] excitement come out and project."

Beyond this adventuresome premise, drafting notes in June for "What Is Modern Dance?," a speech to be given at the annual convention of the National Theatre Conference in November, Hawkins responded to the question, "Technically: An attempt to use the body in movement with the torso as the motivating source as compared with the European 19 [*sic*] century ballet use of torso as corseted upright with arabesques of arms and hips," and, he added, Graham-like, "Use of body in more than rigid uprightness, and so use of falling and the floors. Use of *volume*." He went on, "I believe that today building on what so far has been accomplished in the modern dance in America it is possible for the art to reach a comparable maturity."

He concluded with a rhetorical flourish, "How can one call it anything *but* modern dance, since it is the dance of those who . . . dance what they have to say and work to find the means to say it in their own native tongue."

Surveying Martha Graham's career heading into the late forties, Baird Hastings—Paris Conservatory diplomate in conducting, friend and unofficial assistant editor to Louis Horst for *Dance Observer,* founding editor of Lincoln Kirstein's *Dance Index,* and veteran ballet columnist for *American Dancer* and *Dance Magazine*—emphasized her sheer physicality: "In order to understand her," Hastings wrote, "one must remember that even in her most theatrical works," such as those of recent seasons, "she is but little literary or symbolic."

Rather, Hastings said, setting aside Graham's reading lists, "[s]he is," and has always been, about "*'movement'* . . . even if one understands her [narratives] but partially . . . As Isadora Duncan before her, Martha Graham performed numerous experiments in order to find her 'body' [by saying], 'What next,' instead of 'That's that.' One must never be satisfied with oneself."

30

Horst Revisited

What you call a classicist is someone who knows how to hang on to true values. Classicism is that directness by which any art is formed without fat, and which I feel when I say my choreography is chiseled in granite . . .

—DAVID SEARS, "Erick Hawkins Speaks His Mind on Dance,"
New York Times, October 7, 1984

. . . and for Martha Graham and Erick Hawkins, adherence to the verities of dance meant testing classic stories in their minds and on their bodies. Their take on the modern mode in dance was to be skeptical of iconoclasm; to stretch—rather than break—the form, in the same way that, as lovers, they were separated, yet still in love.

After the perilous *Night Journey,* Graham withdrew into her heart's hurtfulness and did not make a new work for more than a year. She meted out Hawkins's rope, permitting him to sally forth without her on a pared-down tour of "Theatre Dance Pieces" costarring Stuart Hodes and Ethel Winter, accompanied by Hazel Johnson, a Bennington College colleague and 66 Fifth Avenue studio pianist. A typical program was Hawkins's *John Brown, Yankee Blue Breeches,* and *Stephen Acrobat,* interspersed with Graham's *El Penitente* and *Salem Shore.*

For the summer of 1948, Martha Hill, guiding light for the glorious Bennington years, and, since 1930, director of dance at New York University, joined with Rosemary Park, newly installed president of Connecticut College, to present the inaugural season of the American Dance Festival at the New London campus by the Thames River where it would remain for the next three decades. Hill invited José Limón, who had taken up Doris Humphrey's mantle; the trio of Jane Dudley, Sophie Maslow, and William Bales;

Martha Graham, emerging with *Wilderness Stair: Diversion of Angels*; and Erick Hawkins's *The Strangler*.

The Strangler: A Rite of Passage (expanded title) had come a long way since Hawkins's meeting with Géza Róheim, including a dense score by the Czech émigré composer Bohuslav Martinů. Hawkins had remembered a performance by the Boston Symphony Orchestra of Martinů's vivid Symphony No. 1, and commissioned him, stipulating that, to thicken the primitivist consistency of the piece, there should be indigenous Mexican instrumentation such as found in Carlos Chávez's music for dance. Disparate voices of *teponaztli* (slitted-log drum), *cochiti* (double-headed drum), *sonasum* (Yaqui deer-dance metal disc rattle), and *tenenboim* (ankle-rattles made from moth larvae, shells, and pebbles) hover above and dive among a Western-style wind ensemble of flute, piccolo, oboe, clarinet, and bassoon; piano, gong, and cymbals chime in for a cacophonic conglomeration of "diatonic harmonies . . . and short rhythmic and melodic cells, seasoned with periodic minor 2nds and tritons."

Two supporting players accompanied Hawkins as Oidipous. For the Sphinx, "her wings a symbol of the physical ecstasy of the parents . . . her name refer[ring] to the danger of parental domination," Hawkins chose a fresh face, the young Chicago-born actress-dancer Anne Meacham, a Yale School of Drama graduate he had met at the Neighborhood Playhouse. The role of the interlocutor Chorus, declaiming Robert Fitzgerald's text, "a single figure [who] speaks as the eternal everpresent witness . . . for Oidipous at this moment of his initiation into manhood," was given to Joseph Wiseman, a thirty-year-old rising star from Montreal who had made a name on Broadway in Robert E. Sherwood's *Abe Lincoln in Illinois,* three Maxwell Anderson plays, and a production of *Antony and Cleopatra* directed by and starring Katharine "Kit" Cornell, Martha Graham's generous friend. Graham did not dance in Hawkins's piece, and he did not dance in hers.

After the first performance of *Wilderness Stair: Diversion of Angels,* Graham, the change agent, abandoned the first two words in the title and Isamu Noguchi's billowing burlap backdrop evoking the sandy peaks and valleys of the American Southwest. As with *Errand into the Maze,* Graham turned to a Ben Belitt poem, "The Habits of Angels," about another journey, one that began with Jacob's dream: "Contest, the habit of angels, / Tempted the man from the wilderness stair." Regarding the choreography to an exuberant score by Norman Dello Joio, critic Frances Herridge noted, "Out of a group of four men and six girls, three are individualized. One, Natanya Neumann,

Robert Cohan and Pearl Lang in *Wilderness Stair: Diversion of Angels,* ca. 1948.
(Photograph by Cris Alexander)

in a long blue costume, is often the center figure, dominant, static, mature. Pearl Lang in a shorter red costume, cuts through the group frantically, passionately, in sharp off-balances."

Lang was the surrogate for Graham, who did not cast herself. The Triple Goddess would be brought to life by others. "All are aspects of the same woman," Graham wrote, decades later; in particular, "[i]t's very hard to dance the woman in red. She has to have a curious vulnerability, almost like a breathlessness and a deep eroticism." The third featured woman was Helen McGehee, "in an even shorter yellow costume [that] adds the sparkle of sunlight on water. The contrasts," Herridge continued, "suggest three stages of growth: childhood, adolescence, and maturity."

Diversion of Angels, remaining in the Graham repertory, has "[won] audiences for itself all over the world" as a "purely lyric abstraction dealing with youth and love" . . . "practically everything opponents of modern dance say

Louis Horst, American Dance Festival,
Connecticut College, summer 1948.
(Photograph by Nina Fonaroff)

modern dance cannot be . . . light, bright and virtuosic" and "full of the enthusiasm and rapid vigor of youth [with] a compelling sense of amorous play."

The tempo of lighthearted lovers cavorting on the Palmer Auditorium stage did not carry over into the orchestra, where Louis Horst soldiered ahead, conducting interminable run-throughs by intimidated student musicians from Juilliard struggling with Dello Joio's complex score, and irritated by Hawkins's constant presence hovering at Graham's side. Poor Louis, put-upon, "felt useless," he told Beth Osgood, his assistant: "He rattled on about Martha. She didn't need him anymore, he said. She wasn't showing him things anymore. She could be abusive in front of others." At the dress rehearsal, enduring a "cantankerous tirade," by Horst, "Martha conferred with Erick and then turned to the pit and said 'Look Louis, this has got to stop!" He carried on, ignoring her, and she "stormed up the aisle" and out the door, seething, "I could kill him."

It was not the first time Martha Graham had locked horns with Louis Horst over the quarter century they had been a team—but it was the last. Erick Hawkins's interposition ten years prior marked the beginning of the deterioration of Horst's alliance with Graham. The younger man disparaged Graham's affair with her avuncular music director as "incidental . . . aborted . . . over a small period of time . . . When people work together so closely like this" in the hothouse of show business, Hawkins told Don McDonagh, "you might go to bed together, but not very seriously." Hawkins respected Horst's artistic affinities with and moderating influence upon Graham. However, that precious rapport fell away as she opened her practice to a wider range of composers.

Despite the pressures climaxing at the American Dance Festival, Louis Horst hung on until summer's bitter end, when he "couldn't take it anymore . . . I went into [Martha's] dressing room. And I said, 'This is my last, I'm resigning . . . I've turned over a page, and I'm not going to turn it back. . . . She said, 'Won't you even teach at the studio anymore?' And I said, 'No.'"

.   .   .

Depending upon who was asked discreetly, sotto voce, Martha Graham's rupture with Louis Horst was impetuous . . . or strategic; cruel . . . or inevitable; or, the rationalization least likely to incur her retributive wrath, simply: *Martha's way*. "She never stands still. She is a changing person," veteran dancer Yuriko recalled. "Whether a manager, a dancer, an artistic advisor, or a lover, few survived those harsh partings." After a six-year hiatus, Horst and Graham would reconcile, at her instigation; but in the heat of the moment, she headed elsewhere and outward, setting forth with Hawkins to their "potent land," New Mexico, on a second visit to her friend, the painter Cady Wells, at his Jacoma estancia overlooking the Nambe River in the Pojoaque Valley between the mountains of Sangre de Cristo and Jemez.

Shocking everyone they knew, on September 7, 1948, at the height of the fall harvest fiesta, in the foyer of the First Presbyterian Church of Santa Fe, Erick Hawkins and Martha Graham were married. "I was frightened that day," she told her husband, "but of what I cannot say." The lady did protest too much. One taproot into her anxiety was the prospect of succumbing to Hawkins's stubborn wish, in their pillow talk the morning after the ceremony, that now at last the "loose ends and dangling . . . [and] strangeness [would be] over"; and Aphrodite/Graham would cease to insulate her beautiful, neurotic Adonis/Hawkins from the weeping goddesses in her New York entourage, instead commanding them to sing of his resurrection and return.

Another fear was chronology: On the marriage license, Hawkins wrote his age, correctly, as thirty-nine; Graham listed hers as forty-six, eight years less than her true age. And there was the conflicted attitude about her bourgeois upbringing, as Graham revealed after she arrived in Santa Barbara, alone, following her stay at Jacoma. Feted at El Mirasol, her mother's residential hotel, she complained about but nonetheless graciously accepted wedding gifts and talismans offered "in the eyes of all the world" given at a tea reception by Mrs. Duffy's "ladies . . . in quite a flutter over it all"; and affected surprise, scarcely veiled by delight, when a boy new to the staff at the front desk loudly paged "*Mrs. Hawkins!*"

31

Eye of Anguish

Cordelia—adult—not naïve or stupid—[but] integrated . . . her understanding and awareness . . . her tragic acceptance—patience— (perhaps seeing it from another plane).

—MARTHA GRAHAM, notes for *Lear*, August/September 1948

In the back of his lovingly restored adobe, Cady Wells had built a Japanese garden bordered by cottonwood and fruit trees where wild titmouse, bunting, and sparrows peeped and bustled. Seated at a low wooden bench by the reflecting pool, sipping herbal tea after her morning exercise routine, contemplating the roofs of the San Ildefonso Pueblo in the near distance and the Barrancas cliffs beyond, Martha Graham began journal notes toward *Lear*, the mystery-dance she had first broached to Erick Hawkins five years earlier. Her plan was to try it out on a three-month tour starting at the end of January.

Graham did not intend to dance in *Lear*. She took pains to describe the piece as a gift, a starring vehicle for her husband. She was the Goneril in her own three-sistered family; however, in her choreographic musings, Graham identifies intimately and often with Lear's youngest daughter, Cordelia, whose faithful love lifts the King, her adored father, to wisdom when her death breaks his heart. Graham saw Cordelia as a "tragic actor not [a] pathetic victim." She joined the dancer's parade of goddesses descended from bright-eyed warrior-virgin Athena, the intelligent, father-born, childless daughter of Zeus. Lear's madnesses—the tempest in his psyche, the convulsion upon the heath—pervade the drama of the royal sufferer in league with Shakespeare's lunatics, lovers, and poets. Graham's other fixations in the dance are the characters' sacred garments and lack thereof: Lear's undone buttons and childlike bare-headedness except for a crown of

With Cady Wells in his garden, Taos, New Mexico, fall 1948.

weeds; and wretched "bare, forked" Edgar's improvised ragged disguise of near-nakedness.

Working rapidly, once the foundation is laid down in broad strokes, Graham intersperses flashes of movement to set the *Lear* narrative into an episodic structure. One sign that Hawkins will be the (thus-far-unnamed) principal dancer alludes to "Lear's—career—record of mistake & consequences of mistake," and his "express[ion of] truth in [the] wrong way," in contrast to Cordelia's smart, sentient "dance [of] her observation of Lear & his acts."

In medias res, the King appears desperate and alone against a bare, "luminous" tree, anachronistically Beckett-like. Graham then introduces, emerging from beneath Lear's cloak, the "3 sisters in [a] tube of transparent material (like Lamentation)." Cordelia escapes from Goneril and Regan to weave a "ceremonial . . . passionate" saraband "dance of dedication," the love of a child for a parent, "neither more nor less," as in the play's opening scene, when the father interrogates and tests the three daughters.

Cordelia exits; Lear must initiate his despairing "errand" to seek her out. "Two men enter," the "Fool as Chorus," to goad and lead the King, and Edgar/Poor Tom, the Philosopher, to help navigate the maze of chaos. "Demonic joy?" Graham asks herself, when the evil sisters degenerate into a pair of "voracious animals"—bloodthirsty maenads—fighting over Edgar's bastard brother, Edmund.

After the haven of Pojoaque, Graham fine-tuned the *Lear* scenario in Santa Barbara, and returned to New York, having decided upon a composer. Vincent Perischetti was born in Philadelphia in 1915. His parents enrolled the prodigy at the age of six in the Combs Broad Street Conservatory of Music. By eighteen, Vincent had performed on the radio as a pianist for the Matinee Musical Club Orchestra, played double bass for the All Philadelphia High School Orchestra, and been appointed organist for the Arch Street Presbyterian Church. Following a bachelor of music degree in composition at Combs, he became head of theory and composition there.

At this juncture in an accelerating career, Persichetti came into contact with Martha Graham. He delighted in *Every Soul Is a Circus*, with a score by his conservatory teacher and fellow Philadelphian Paul Nordoff, finding the piece "humorous, lighthearted and satiric . . . very beautiful," and became "a serious fan." His first musical attempt for Graham, in 1939, "a little prelude kind of dance . . . wild and unharnessed . . . maybe four or five minutes," did not meet her standards, but the two remained in touch. Persichetti, "the musical omnivore," reached eclectically across the spectrum of his art, creating sonatas, chamber and choral works, ensemble pieces for wind band, and—important to Graham—setting poems in the American idiom by Walt Whitman, E. E. Cummings, and Wallace Stevens.

In November 1948, Graham telephoned Persichetti, recently hired to the Juilliard School faculty, and invited him to a meeting in her book-strewn apartment, where he spoke with passion about the act of creation, that "in all the arts [it should] say more about less. And that kind of got [to Graham] . . . She's a concentrated gal," he recalled. "And she took notes," and "something clicked," and she said—" 'I have planted something in my mind and I'll be in touch with you later.' "

She sent Persichetti the edited, typed ideas from her notebook for the "choreographic poem," to "kind of warm [him] up," beginning, "The subject of the dance is anguish of a soul bound upon a 'wheel of fire' . . . This is not a dance version of the play King Lear with the words omitted. Rather, it is the play as myth . . . The storm [in the play] makes me think," Graham continued, "of the old mariners advice in time of typhoon. To try to reach the [storm's] center, because there is a place of quiet . . . in other words of utter awareness to look upon the reality of danger, the truth of the conflict . . . to face the horror of its ultimate and true shape." *Lear* was a convergence of poetic sensibilities: In 1944, Persichetti had set T. S. Eliot's "The Hollow Men" to trumpet and string orchestra; and Graham, since the thirties, had admired "Burnt Norton," the first section of Eliot's epic *Four Quartets.*

At the still point of the turning world. Neither flesh nor fleshless;
    Neither from nor towards; at the still point, there the dance is,
But neither arrest nor movement.
And do not call it fixity,
Where past and future are gathered. Neither movement
        from nor towards,
Neither ascent nor decline. Except for the point, the still
        point,
There would be no dance, and there is only the dance.

Advancing the prospectus for "the purgatorial history of King Lear" to a section headed "Action," Graham told Persichetti she was going for "a swift opening . . . as if we were catapulted into" the drama on the heath; she wanted "a sense of tragic shock rather than development" so that the audience would have to come to terms with a "man really alone before his gods." After a segment memorializing the "poignant . . . Final Union Between Lear and Cordelia . . . as an inseparable part of himself," the dance came in at twenty-one minutes, but she hoped, in the spirit of Ezra Pound's "poetry = condensation," to achieve "economy . . . to cut it down to exactly twenty minutes in time."

Choreographic outline in hand, six weeks later, the composer came back with a score for wind quintet, piano, and timpani that ran from ferocious to tranquil. *Lear's Dance of Challenge,* playing out, according to Persichetti's marginalia, in "rain and night with shafts of light," has a fluttery, "all-over" feeling. A sparkling, pointillist triangle hovers over heraldic trumpet blares. The French horn holds down the bottom registers in a minor key, foreshadowing trouble. Lear witnesses the "Dance of Three Daughters," Persichetti notes, in real time as well as "in moments of remembrance." The conflict

Erick Hawkins as King Lear in *Eye of Anguish*, 1949. (Photograph by Philippe Halsman)

carries on between trumpet and horn, two hounds of hell with menacing interruptions and unexpected crescendos; around their barking heads, the clarinet buzzes, a bothersome fly.

"Cordelia's Dance of Serenity," sultry swoops and echoes building and receding, represents "everything that Lear loves," and segues into the King's "Dance of Grief," the "lowest and most tragic point so far," and the show-piece for Erick Hawkins. No continuous eyewitness accounts or filmed documentation exist; we imagine muscular high steps, martial paces, and skulking. In tune with the King's darkening disposition, choppy piano and muted Valkyrie horn calls from faraway mountains penetrate fog and clouds. "The Fool and the Philosopher" (Edgar) arrives on the scene, to "a morris dance and gigues, in mock processional," with stately flute overtones. Counter voices diverge and come together, tentative piano moving into the lead.

Lear's "Mock Trial," Persichetti writes, "the refinement of evil and rapaciousness of the two elder daughters" sans Cordelia, is announced by an imperious bassoon and a seamless transition into kettle drum dominance. Harmony is drowned by effortful arguments between high and low dissonance. "Lear's real madness—when he 'snaps,' " is inflamed in the "Ensnarement" section, the net of circumstances enveloping the King as he tries to shove away encroachments, fortissimo piano rumbling, drummed thunder receding.

Cordelia's "Dance of Grief," announced "with flute descent," begins with balletic, jazzy trilling slowed to a halt by unaccompanied piano. A still, small voice cries in the wilderness for a few measures before horns leap in. With the "hopeful, calm, triumphally simple" "Final Union between Lear and Cordelia," the piece dies down. There is a sapping of energy, silences more frequent. A flute clambers in search of a resting place, but succumbs, announcing there is nowhere else to go except a recessional dirge, step by step to darkness and quietude.

.   .   .

In act IV, scene 3 of *King Lear*, the Doctor/Gentleman, attempting to calm Cordelia's tearful apprehensions about her father's well-being, reassures her that the King's torturous wanderings in the wilderness, "our foster-nurse of nature," will have had a palliative effect upon his frayed nerves, diminishing his "ungovern'd rage" and closing "the eye of anguish." Taking that cue, Martha Graham changed the title of the dance in the brochure announcing the January–April 1949 tour of Martha Graham and Dance Company sponsored by the Consolidated Concerts Corporation. *Lear* no longer, it was now called *The Eye of Anguish—The Purgatorial History of King Lear*, starring Erick Hawkins, with Natanya Neumann as Cordelia, Helen McGehee as Goneril, and Joan Skinner as Regan, "to be seen on the road before New York" among the familiar repertory of *Dark Meadow*, *Every Soul Is a Circus*, *Deaths and Entrances*, and others.

After a five-year stretch from conception, to composition, to performance, Graham's drive to revise (and repackage) her new choreographic offering at the last feasible minute culminated with an assertion calling into question the original impetus for *The Eye of Anguish* as a "gift" created for Hawkins. Now, Graham wanted the public to know, she had boldly "bypassed the Bard." Delving deeper than Shakespeare's source, Geoffrey of Monmouth's pseudohistorical twelfth-century *History of the Kings of Britain*, Graham preferred the example of the "harsh . . . more archaic . . . Gaelic

High King Laoghaire" of Tara, who personified the fatal flaw of "pride of power [and] vanity," and "was untrusting—doubt[ing] the love and fealty of those near him."

"In modern terms," Graham noted brusquely, on the brink of the tour, turning away from Lear's redemptive epiphany, "it is the tragedy of anyone who has lost his integrity—and lost himself."

On tour, Erick Hawkins, the public-facing performer, did not reveal any awareness of Graham's negative shift in perspective toward the originating play. Hinterland critics praised his "fine power . . . which has both dynamic smoothness and Herculean violence, focusing the effects sought." In private, Hawkins continued to recycle nagging problems, still lacking "the recognition I so deeply desire," feeling "the conflict . . . that I have an almost unexpressed, deeply-buried-in-the-unconscious desire to be superior as a dancer," and the frustration at not being able to "embody knowledge and present it on the stage."

During a decade with and against Martha Graham, body to body, centrifugally and centripetally, Erick Hawkins had lived, danced—and survived— way stations along the Hero's Journey mapped by their friend Joseph Campbell: hearing and obeying the "call to adventure"; coming to know, excruciatingly, the meaning of "self-achieved submission"; diving inward, fearlessly, to "be born again"; standing up, tender breastbone lifted to the monumental "threshold guardian" of Art; assuming Oedipus's mission to "confront the mystagogue"; in the breaths of dance, inhaling the *Eros* life wish and exhaling the *Thanatos* death wish; and sanctifying "marriage with the Queen Goddess," thereby ceding to "M's" transcendent power to remake him into "the incarnate god of her created world."

The one role Hawkins had not managed to experience was the Hero's triumphant Return from his Journey, despite embodying and traveling with King Lear. The company's tour concluded, "[n]ow I need the ritual," he confided to his journal, "whereby I can . . . make and dance the most exciting, rewarding, understanding, powerful, productive pieces that any man is able to do today."

. . .

Hawkins's despair broke to the surface during rehearsals for the January 1950 *Eye of Anguish* New York premiere. Out of town, he was able to channel his demons into the role; but in the home studio, it seemed to Vincent Per-

Eye of Anguish ensemble (left to right), Robert Cohan (Fool), Pearl Lang (Cordelia), Bertram Ross (Edgar/"Poor Tom"), Natanya Neumann (Regan), Stuart Hodes (Edmund), and Helen McGehee (Goneril), ca. 1950. (Photograph by Cris Alexander)

sichetti, on the sidelines, Hawkins could not capture "the spirit of the move- ment . . . and he wasn't getting it technically either . . . [He was] not being up to being a big person . . . [not] capable of doing that part at that time under those conditions . . . [There was] something false about" Hawkins's manner, Persichetti recalled regretfully, "just something not honest." Dur- ing one-on-one run-throughs with the angelic Pearl Lang stepping in as Cordelia, there was "a certain graciousness" to Graham's low-key demeanor, cradling a cup of tea while she walked about the studio in ankle-length black dress and black tights. She showed "a lot of joy" coaching Lang and the other dancers, "but there wasn't with the main character [Hawkins] . . . There were stops and . . . yelling," and no attempt, on either side, to moder- ate the emotional climate, regardless of who else was in the room.

"Sighing, holding their heads . . . and at times ignoring" the couple, none of the assembled company dared speak, beyond vague, murmured asides about problems in the relationship. *Eye of Anguish* could no longer be sustained as a work planted in the husband's body by the wife. The gift withdrawn by the giver, the choreographer recoiled the rope of the life preserver, leaving her man-dancer to swim or sink. If Graham had conflated unquenchable love for her father with Cordelia's worship of Lear, to what ambiguous netherworld ("purgatorial history") was Hawkins exiled?

Eye of Anguish opened at the 46th Street Theatre on Sunday evening, January 22, with Pearl Lang as Cordelia, Judith Yanus and Yuriko as Goneril and Regan, and Stuart Hodes and Bertram Ross as Edmund and Edgar. "Tonight for the first time ever I see my name in electric marquee," Hawkins wrote, "Martha Graham and Dance Company with Erick Hawkins."

The one-week sold-out run was highly anticipated. Graham had not appeared on Broadway for nearly two years. To begin the show, she roared back with a vengeance in a "superb performance" of *Errand into the Maze*. "Miss Graham and Stuart Hodes," her sensation du jour, succeeding Mark Ryder, "made a stunning contest out of this personalization of the myth of the Minotaur and the labyrinth . . . She makes of it a genuine emotional adventure," John Martin rhapsodized. "It may well have been the evening's high point." The audience agreed, with a standing ovation, responding in equal fashion to *Appalachian Spring*, "Miss Graham again in full command," joined by another robust, new, fresh-faced company member, twenty-five-year-old Robert Cohan, as the "Preacher."

Eye of Anguish, relegated by Martin to "novelty" status, did not come across as well. Perturbed that "Miss Graham herself does not appear in it," the critic depicted the piece as "a kind of frantic fantasia on themes from 'King Lear,' violent in movement and mood, attempting to give the external story development and the inner madness of Lear at the same time. In this it does not altogether succeed. It is inclined to be literary (read up on your 'King Lear') and dramatically static for all its technical strenuousness and tearing about."

All was assuredly not lost, Martin concluded. "The outstanding performance is that of Pearl Lang, always a lovely dancer, as Cordelia. Yuriko as Regan and Bertram Ross as Edgar are also excellent."

The coup de grâce was swift: "Erick Hawkins fairly knocks himself out as Lear, but not to any great effect."

32

The Choice

The intellect of man is forced to choose / Perfection of the life, or of the work.

—w. b. yeats, from *The Choice*, 1933

We are going to have a rightly extensive, financially and artistically successful tour of Europe at the right time next spring.

—erick hawkins, Notebook, September 12, 1949

S ince the war's end, Erick Hawkins had been trying to convince Martha Graham to take the company abroad. She had not been to Europe since the summer of 1922, for the Denishawn sojourn in London, and had no interest in returning. She did not accept the proving-ground ethos in the American dance world that performing overseas was a required building block for one's reputation at home. She did not relish the logistical burdens of such a voyage, diverting her precious energy from choreography. She was conflicted about sacrificing her edgy autonomy were she to become entangled in the strings attached to "this money raising business." She acknowledged the salutary effect of Lincoln Kirstein's patronage upon the talents of George Balanchine; while, in the same breath, rebuffing a deep-pocketed and sophisticated new ally, Bethsabée de Rothschild.

Born in London in 1914, Bethsabée was the youngest child of Baron Edouard Alphonse de Rothschild, director of the French banking empire, and his wife, Germaine Halphen. She was raised at the sprawling neo-Renaissance-style Château de Ferrières in the Île-de-France region, and the Talleyrand Palace on the rue Saint-Florentin in Paris. Her upbringing was cultured and practical. At home, she was surrounded by art masterpieces and antiques acquired by her grandfather, and encouraged to take a degree in biology at the Sorbonne. In 1940, the family fled to America. Bethsabée studied biochemistry at Columbia University and, during World War II, worked in the office of the France Libre/Free French movement in New York, enlisted in the occupying forces for the Battle of Normandy, and moved to Paris to serve as liaison between the French and American military.

Following the war, de Rothschild returned to New York. Joking that she was on her way to a dentist's appointment when she entered the wrong door at 66 Fifth Avenue, on a whim, she signed up for dance classes with Martha Graham. Older than the other students, possessed of low-key elegance and refined bearing, she caught the teacher's vigilant eye. They soon became confidantes. In 1948, de Rothschild married Donald Bloomingdale, scion of the department store family and attaché to the United States Embassy in Paris, and resumed a conspiratorial correspondence with Erick Hawkins about a Graham Company visit. The Committee of the American Festival in Paris guaranteed to the State Department that "only a small amount of money would be needed" in subvention for a Graham season, because "Mrs. David [sic] Bloomingdale (the youngest daughter of Baron Edouard de Rothschild) has donated a substantial part and is personally attempting to raise the remainder."

Teamed up with Hawkins, convinced of Graham's greatness and determined to help, de Rothschild overcame the dancer's reluctance. Secretary of State Dean Acheson notified the American Ambassador to France, David Bruce, that the "Manager of the Martha Graham dance troupe"—her personal secretary, Craig Barton, along with the company manager for the tour, LeRoy Leatherman—would be "arriving in Paris April 13, [1950]," to discuss preliminary arrangements. John Martin made it official in the *Times* that the Queen of American modern dance was "joining the trek," deciding "to make a European *tournée,*" with an opening engagement of two weeks beginning June 27 at the Théâtre des Champs-Élysées, presenting "a surprisingly large repertoire of fifteen pieces," that "will be a strong diet for Europe . . . which has not seen any of Miss Graham's work so far, or, indeed, much modern dance of anybody's creation since before the war. It will be extremely interesting for us here at home, who have watched Miss Graham grow up, as it were," Martin opined, "to note the foreign reactions." Replacing Louis Horst as the company music director would be Ted Dale, conductor of the popular, long-running *Carnation [Milk] Contented Hour,* airing Sunday evenings on CBS Radio.

. . .

Begun in New York and completed in Paris, Bethsabée de Rothschild had written *La danse artistique aux USA—Tendances modernes* (*Artistic Dance in America—Modern Trends*), inspired by her association with Martha Graham, Doris Humphrey, and May O'Donnell. The study was published on February 15, 1949, in an edition of two thousand copies by Editions Elzevir, associates of the storied Elsevier, Dutch printers since the seventeenth century in Leyden and the Low Countries. It was a labor of love and, the author believed, a corrective to French stereotypes of American dance limited to "le jazz . . . le jitterbug . . . le 'swing'" and "les girls" high-kicking at Radio City Music Hall.

"Idolized, detested, often misunderstood, constantly talked-about, Martha Graham will one day be judged as equal in importance to Isadora Duncan," de Rothschild begins, introducing Graham's early career in Denishawn, her "vibrant combination of extreme temperament and incisive, meticulous technique. Thus did she ripen as an artist." Graham's ambition intensified when she reached New York, "the great, anonymous, gargantuan city, a revelation" where, determined to "divest herself of sweetness and exoticism," she labored in obscurity into the early hours of the morning, committed to the long journey and "guided by her instincts." Explaining Graham's artistic intentions to educate uninitiated French readers, de Rothschild emphasizes that Graham pushed "against the accepted tastes of the times . . . her accentuated gestures in stark contrast to the graceful 'line' of ballet."

A diligent chronicler, the author tracks Graham's important dances from the mid-twenties through the late forties, summarizing plots, deconstructing scenarios, and interpreting some—by no means all—abstractions. De Rothschild is effective when speculating about her friend's nuanced personality and "layered intellect," *pensée fouillée,* and how they bear upon her technique: "How do I evoke this strange woman," she affectionately wonders, "so secretive, so simple, simultaneously down to earth and haughty? Her expression, not happy by nature, fascinates, passing in an instant from impenetrable coldness to sweet smile. She is of unprepossessing height, with brown eyes, and long black hair, pinned up among society, loosed to her shoulders in the studio. She is impeccably groomed and fashionable, never ostentatious. Her disposition comes across as calm, yet firm. In dance apparel, she shies from *déshabille,* preferring long, flowing dresses she designs and tailors herself."

"Martha Graham's daily life seems simple on the surface," de Rothschild writes. "She is devoted to her work, above all else—however, she harbors tremendous anxiety, waging a constant war of nerves against herself, a war crammed with hallucinations, attempts, doubts, deflations, crises of the soul and manic triumphs. Graham says her work is her only child; when she speaks of the dance, one sees the 'real' Martha Graham, made whole . . . She seeks communion: with the interior lives of others near to her, and with the universe; and in every mythic or created persona, where she looks for the communal element of sacrifice . . . She projects energy"—"whether standing utterly still, walking, or dancing. . . . Her entire being trembles with constrained passion. Even her neck and outstretched hand seem to breathe."

Graham's dance compositions, de Rothschild observes, do not "conclude"; they "arrive . . . A dance's gestures do not deliver the final note; they come up short, against the start of another breath, on the brink of the next instant, as if asking, And now . . . ? rather than declaring, There it is. I've said it all."

Anticipating the Paris season, de Rothschild recalls the words of Leopold Stokowski, who had named Graham his "Chosen One" for the premiere of *The Rite of Spring* in America, saying, "Here before us is a dancer with such astonishing force and power that her message transcends the earth-bound, touching the planets."

·   ·   ·

The company was booked into the Plaza Athénée. Graham, staying with de Rothschild and Bloomingdale at their mansion on the Avenue Foch, gave a revealing interview to de Rothschild's colleague, Pierre Tugal, *conservateur* of the Paris Archives Internationales de la Danse and a founder of L'Association de la Presse Chorégraphique. Tugal was well prepared. He had read *La danse artistique* in manuscript; and written the preface, lauding the book as "wise, comprehensive and unbiased." Graham began the conversation by confirming John Martin's statement that "to the American public our dance form is familiar," whereas, in Paris, "there are those who are enthusiastic, those who are puzzled and those who are antagonistic. There is never apathy."

When Tugal inquired "where [she] found thematic material for [her] ballets," Graham took gentle umbrage: "I do not use 'ballet' for my dances. I know it is an old and honored term; I do not use it only to avoid the possible confusion of the term 'ballet' as indicating a style, rather than a work as such." Rather than refer to a dance genre, Graham preferred to go to the

With Bethsabée de Rothschild (center) and François Schapira having tea, Tel Aviv, 1964.
(Photograph by Arik Dichne)

level of inhabiting a specific piece, executed by a specific dancer, at an inner, *present* time, incited by "some fundamental instant of life [that] may send a dancer into the realm of sheer movement for a theme . . . [M]any areas of experience as are part of the heart's experience," Graham elaborated, can potentially serve as material for a work, necessitating "behavior which cannot be expressed in other than dance terms . . . [T]he theme of a dance must not be perceived intellectually; the gesture inventions must be experienced within the body. The truth must need to be released through body speech."

Tugal pressed further: "What is the basis for your technique?" She replied, "My technique is an attempt to prepare the body by formal and impersonal means to become a dancer's instrument; strong, subtle, fully-conscious, free as only discipline can make it . . . [The body]," Graham added provocatively, "must be prepared for the ordeal of expressiveness."

Going forward, Tugal wondered, "What tendencies [for the contemporary dance] should we hope for?" Graham delivered an aperçu into her future standards: "An incorruptible integrity in the practice of an ancient and honorable art. A jealousy for the honor of the Dance, that it may be always a deeply meaningful and expressive art, rather than a superficial entertainment. An openness to exploration in adult and expressive uses of movement."

Last but not least, in the vocabulary of modernism, Martha Graham said she wanted to see "[a] willingness to use the deep and highly-organized twentieth-century being in the Dance."

. . .

For weeks preceding the trip, Hawkins had been warning his fretful and vulnerable partner, suffering from arthritis and "strained tendons in her legs," that the Paris repertory was too crowded; for example, he said, presenting fifty minutes of *Letter to the World* was ill-advised, because the quirky particulars of Emily Dickinson's epigrammatic-poetic language would fall on deaf ears. He was sick with worry that Graham "was tired . . . doing too much . . . working too God-damned hard." She waved off his pleas—"Don't push me . . . I cannot think about that now."

The June 27 opening was a gala affair. David Bruce shared the center box with Eleanor Roosevelt, an admirer of *American Document,* presented, at her request, in the first half of the program, with *Frontier* and *Appalachian Spring.* This onslaught of Americana was followed by *Every Soul Is a Circus,* placed after the intermission in hopes of providing comic relief. But what transpired in the Arenic World was sudden and tragic. During their vaudevillian duet toward the end, Hawkins took Graham into a lift they had executed countless times and, as he set her down, she "winced" when her left foot touched the ground, and danced through the pain, determined to complete the piece.

Graham wrote in *Blood Memory* through a blurry lens, "I can still remember the exact moment in Paris when my injury came. Erick and I were center stage; I was doing a simple *plié* and my knee went." In the dressing room, a doctor diagnosed that Graham had torn a cartilage. She forced a smile receiving admirers during the champagne reception. Sinister whispers followed, "stories that [Hawkins], some kind of monster," had "hauled [Graham] around" during *Circus,* and, worse, dropped her intentionally.

The next night, she hobbled in the wings, leaning on a cane, muttering angrily while the troupe presented *Diversion of Angels,* then an attempt at *Eye of Anguish,* and Hawkins's *Stephen Acrobat.* Pearl Lang stepped into *El Penitente* as Mary. "At the end of the evening," *Le Figaro* reported, epitomizing the response of the French critical establishment to the unfamiliar Graham mode, "one could not stand any more symbolism and metaphysics." The première danseuse could not dance. The Paris season was canceled. Expenses paid by de Rothschild, the dancers remained at the hotel while

Martha Graham and Erick Hawkins arriving in London, July 1950.
(Photograph by Mary Evans)

Graham tried, futilely, to rest; sought further medical advice; and vetoed suggestions of surgery.

The time came to move on to London and fulfill the next tour commitment. In the Piccadilly Theatre studio, rehearsals were raw, desultory, and frustrating. Graham favored her knee. No one in the company dared speak up, except Hawkins. The course of action was clear to him. On July 17, sharing a cab from the hotel to rehearsal, he told Graham, " 'It will be foolish to not do this well' . . . and so, out of concern for her, [he] was cancelling the [opening] show" and the three-week season as well. She "turned on [him]" and exploded with incendiary anger—it was finished between them—once more. Her remembrance again was cloudy: "Erick left me," she wrote. "He divided our money, left a note, and was gone." In reality, Graham departed immediately, flying to the States with de Rothschild, who had accompanied the troupe to London. Hawkins caught a less expensive flight home with the company the following week.

·   ·   ·

A month of silence followed.

Alone and lonely in New York, Hawkins was first to try to compose a letter, contorted, like Oedipus, "at a crossroads," resolving to be "honest and complete," forthright as possible, and avoid casting blame. He began with a memory from the days after Harvard graduation, when he attended a lecture by Raymond Duncan, elder brother of Isadora. The takeaway was that "love was not something in the mind"; the "physical proximity" that came with living with someone, Duncan said, determined one's love for that person. Since Hawkins "wanted to be with [Graham] more than anyone else," there was the proof: he had loved her from the beginning.

When he was introduced to Graham's June course in 1938, he went on to recall, she was "just an impersonal force" from whom he hoped to find out "what it meant to be an artist." Over the years, it became apparent he had set the bar too high. Yes, Hawkins was able to learn from Graham; but she was an insurmountable role model, and "I would have to be second to you in everything." That realization planted the seed of competition, which Hawkins dreaded, leading to guilt, which he reviled, because guilt inhibited the motivation to make his own solos so as to no longer be perceived as an "adjunct" partner dependent upon Graham to "carry" every dance. He duly acknowledged the progress in his choreography; but, even so, Hawkins could never summon up the self-confidence to accept the quiet approbation of those who actually preferred his dances to hers.

At forty-two, reflecting "only with the eyes of anguish" upon what they both referred to as the "accident" in Paris, Hawkins needed to accept that Graham had made "the greater contribution as dancer and choreographer . . . to the extension of technique." He was stalemated by the circular logic that to accept her preeminence he would have to carve out some way to define success for himself. A return to teaching could be the key, Hawkins told Graham, a time-tested realm within which to coexist at the school without "mixing [her] up." He loved mentoring the young people in his perennially popular October-through-May Saturday classes, outside the pressures of performance.

It took him a week of fits and starts to concede that he might as well stop typing and mail all twenty-seven pages on August 27, although "[i]t seems paltry and tame and doesn't read at all like what I feel." Perfection of the life, or of the work? "Maybe . . . if a man and woman are different enough," Hawkins wondered ruefully, "they shouldn't try to have a professional life together and a marriage . . . because the necessities for honesty and health in the two different relationships (professional and personal) aren't of the same nature and don't coincide."

One gleam of certainty lingered behind the clouds. "For all my confusion," Hawkins wrote to Graham, "I do have a healthy love for you and am troubled that it is so difficult to find a way to let the love flow as the deepest core of my being would like for it to."

.   .   .

Martha Graham was quick to respond. She had sought solace at Cady Wells's, praying to the Virgin of Guadeloupe icon hanging on the guest bedroom wall; then in late August went to her mother's. Revisiting the trauma of Paris, she wrote Hawkins on September 3, "I have heard that there is a kind of shock which can be very deep reaching" and "can produce a state of clarity." Graham had therefore taken a step toward "arriv[ing] at some condition of truth" by shedding her fear of entering analysis, accepting Hawkins's recommendation to reach out for help and advice to one of his therapists, analytical psychologist Frances Gillespy Wickes, a New York practitioner who had studied with William James and Josiah Royce, and trained under C. G. Jung. Hawkins predicted there would be a spiritual fit with Graham, because Wickes had encouraged Jung to visit the Taos Pueblo, where meeting "the people who live on the roof of the world" exercised a lifelong influence upon him.

Graham's truth-driven language was tempered by her conditional voice. "By what seemed and perhaps was rejection on my part," she wrote haltingly to her lover, "I may have contributed to your disturbance and it may have taken [away] the strength which you needed to put into the flowering of your own life." Despite this admission, and the insistence that she did not seek his pity, Graham could not help but reference "giv[ing Hawkins] the freedom [she] spoke of before." She defined his freedom as being hers to delegate; only Hawkins "can know what that may mean." She confessed to resenting "the great gap between" them in age, saying she overcompensated with efforts "to be young and glamorous" and make herself into "a kind of goddess with the fetish of [her] power" to achieve "the changelessness [she] wanted . . . I was an instrument of God," Graham stretched, to metaphoric heights, "I wanted to be the Deathless One."

The hard landing of the *Circus* "accident" and the forced rehabilitation while she lay in the sun lifting leg weights left Graham with too many hours to recycle "the jealous things" and "self-love" and "egocentrism" she had shown toward Hawkins. Again: Where and when did work begin and life end? Time and distance made her speculate whether the accretion of her possibly unintentional disparagements over the years had contributed to Hawkins's "trouble" with his dance-making: "I loved you as far as I knew how [but] now I see that it was not a very wonderful love for you to have." She parsed their partnership, weighing, on one hand, the peaceful sublimity of her role as "wife," the way that "when I am in union with you all fear left me," against, on the other, the dangers of her success and dominance as "the dancer, [when she] was perhaps more likely to be right, at least for myself, than you were," but stopped short of admitting that her canonical fame halted his aspirations.

Graham expressed gratitude for Hawkins's perseverance in growing the school, and praised his gifts as a teacher and affection for the youth. While he must feel no obligation, she said, tactfully, to contribute to the concert repertory for the coming season, it would be ideal were he able "to bring richness to the students" by resuming classes for ages ten to nineteen, especially for the young men who, thanks to Hawkins's bold example, were "assuming an equally important role in the contemporary dance . . . a new meaning, use, technique and expression created here, in this land."

There was no hint they would never see each other again.

"In spite of our troubles," Graham told Hawkins, the dance-love they made onstage was tangible, and "there was great rareness in what we had and great beauty" . . . "something real existing between us, something as alive and important as a real child with a life and power of its own."

*   *   *

Mid-autumn, solitary in his East Seventeenth Street apartment, Hawkins confided to distant friends that while "unsettled and unhappy in one way, in another I have concentrated and go inside and that is wonderful. . . . For the first time in years I have done nothing the last few weeks except think about myself and my own dances." Ideas stirred, wanting to be born, "so I shall try this winter to see what I have in me to dance."

Graham, likewise, tasted the allure of action: "What has been called my technique is ready for new strength and new experimentation," she declared. "That does not invalidate it or mean it is not of use. It is, very much so. But contemporary dance must remain contemporary and it must progress."

33

Coda

Transparence is the highest, most liberating value in art—and in criticism—today. Transparence means experiencing the luminousness of the thing in itself, of things being what they are.

—SUSAN SONTAG, *Against Interpretation*, 1964

I t is impossible to abandon Martha Graham.

Rather, bidding au revoir, the story comes full circle, to rest upon technique, agreeing with Walter Sorell's wise assessment, in 1951, that "Isadora's method . . . was soul minus technique, while Martha is technique plus soul." Martha Graham's contraction-coiled body was her proving ground. The *happening* of the work, wordless "art-speech [which] is the only truth," was brought into being by movement presence during the action of performance that only succeeded, Graham stipulated, if the spectator was not merely seeing, but attending, opening up, to dancers' gestures regardless of what "meaning" might be implied or "narrative" followed.

"Technique," Graham said, "prepares your body to speak in dance."

Another modernist giant speaks to this point via psychologist and composer Louis Danz's analogy: "Picasso's line is like Martha Graham's dancing. Martha Graham dances the path of feeling as it flows through her body. It flows through her body before it comes out." Technique turns abstract flow into manifest forms, segueing one plastique moment of a dance in time and space to the next . . . and the next.

The progression was institutionalized in the 1950–1951 manifesto of the Martha Graham School of Contemporary Dance, "developed parallel to and inseparable from Martha Graham's discoveries, technical inventions, and development in contemporary dance movement. . . . In this exciting art development of our time, historical necessity has combined dance, dancer, choreographer, teacher, and discoverer." That same season, Graham's became an integrated touring dance company when she added Mary Hinkson, and her college roommate, Matt Turney, to the ranks.

.   .   .

"After 1950," Erick Hawkins wrote, "I started to find my way," variations upon the theme that, following the Paris and London debacle, he began to emerge as "my own man . . . doing my own thing" . . . "pursuing my own vision" . . . "A man needs to work *freely* so that is what I [was] trying to do." A moth shedding a cocoon, Hawkins distinguished his approach to dance-making from Graham's in the way modern movement analysts Rudolf von Laban and Irmgard Bartenieff separated *free* flow from *bound* flow— Hawkins's liquid, "ever moving, ever active, quick shifts of weight, joyous" vs. Graham's controlled, "strained . . . tight, held-in . . . 'codified.'" Critic Alan Kriegsman, who followed Hawkins's oeuvre for the dancer's mature

In *Judith,* accompanied by the Louisville Symphony Orchestra, Robert Whitney conducting, January 4, 1950. The piece premiered in New York City at the end of December 1950. (Photograph by Lin Caufield)

career, admired that "easeful flow . . . in its primal strength and simplicity of utterance, its imperviousness to the winds of fashion, its classical economy and its timelessness . . . and its distillation of mood into bold, spare, strikingly sculpted and unabashedly heroic imagery."

On Hawkins's side, as well as Graham's, claimed liberation was curtailed by the other's absence. One moment, Hawkins convinced himself it was spiritually healthier that he rarely saw Graham; at other times, of an evening, he would notice how radiant she looked across the room at a party, or how magnificently she danced in *Judith,* her first solo since the Paris "accident." Performing at Carnegie Hall in January 1951, with a score by William Schuman, Graham reshaped the tale of the Assyrian general Holofernes's seduction and decapitation by the heroic Jewish widow into a self-referential, timely depiction of a courageous woman who "casts off the garments of mourning symbolic of her isolation, and puts on garments of gladness symbolic of her femininity" . . . "She must emerge and fight and in so doing she depersonalizes herself and becomes a symbol of woman rather than a woman."

Hawkins watched spellbound from the audience and came backstage to congratulate Graham, who cycled through being touched by and recoiling from his attentions: "Please do not write to me unless it is completely necessary," she admonished, reversing three months later with "I hope you will feel free to write to me or talk with me if you wish."

Hawkins insisted upon live music for his dances, and was seeking to hire "an accompanist who was also a composer." He had been introduced to twenty-year-old Lucia Dlugoszewski by Grete Sultan, her piano teacher at the 92nd Street Y. In January 1952, Dlugoszewski created an experimental score for Hawkins's dance, "Openings of the (Eye)," "a metaphor of important ideas of the spirit put into sensuous form" and a deliberate riposte to *Eye of Anguish.* The dancer and the multifaceted musician, who textured her work with "the poetry of everyday sounds" generated by handmade instruments, were secretly married in the late 1950s and remained inseparable collaborators.

Twenty-five years later, the couple were guests at the home of Sali Ann Kriegsman, dance consultant at the Smithsonian Institution and the author of *Dance in America: The Bennington Years,* and her husband, Alan "Mike" Kriegsman, the Pulitzer Prize–winning dance critic for the *Washington Post.* After dinner, Sali Ann pulled from a shelf in her study a special issue of

Martha Graham at Mills College Greek Theatre, summer 1939.
(Photograph by Thomas Bouchard)

Dance Perspectives magazine, "Days of Divine Indiscipline," memories of the Bennington School of the Dance with an essay by John Martin prefacing a portfolio of powerful black-and-white photographs from the "faithful Leica" of Thomas Bouchard. Hawkins, seated in an armchair, eager to peruse the journal, eventually arrived at the section featuring Martha Graham, with the heading, "part sex, part pride, part terror and all frenzy."

Among several portraits of the artist was a vignette from *Primitive Mysteries,* her "great, inspired landmark in human art," showing Graham, the Blessed Virgin, caught in stillness, right hand in a contraction, surrounded by arching acolytes; then she came leaping in a black ankle-length gown and layers of chiffon through a sequence of *Studies for an Unfinished Dance.* A few pages further, in Bouchard's inspired perspective from above, she turned and crouched en plein air, dressed in scoop-necked white linen, ropes of hair unbound, ascending the sun-bleached pavement stones in the Mills College Greek Theatre. Lingering upon this graphic image, Erick Hawkins burst into tears, exclaiming, "Such fresh passion!"

. . .

Returned to health through power of will—adhering to the spirit of Schopenhauer encountered long ago—and a creative rebirth after diverging from Erick Hawkins, Martha Graham faced forty years of immersive exploration among archetypes, mythology, romance, the feminine mystique, Americana, and satire, spanning from the cosmic to the intimate, revealing riches in concert dances beyond the boundaries of this book: *St. Joan/Seraphic Dialogue, Canticle for Innocent Comedians,* the epic *Clytemnestra, Embattled Garden, Acrobats of God, Episodes, Secular Games, Cortege of Eagles, Lucifer, Acts of Light, The Rite of Spring,* and *Maple Leaf Rag.*

A long denouement of global ambassadorship—tours through continental Europe, the UK, Asia, the Middle East, and the Far East—was punctured by the inevitable reckoning, thwarted physicality. The time arrived when Graham could not stand front and center in new works, nor could she perform convincingly in vintage dances she had made for herself as the central figure. With a contentious, approach-avoidance response to pleas that her signature repertory must be restored for a new generation of audiences, she gradually relinquished classic roles to others.

Confiding in the spring of 1962 to Kenneth Tynan, Graham said that she had, once upon a time, "wanted children," but likely suffered from a congenital endocrine dysfunction and was warned by her doctors that the risky remedial "operation [would be] difficult and dangerous."

Her recalcitrant body exacted a painful cost. Graham's final appearance onstage in the role of the nun, Heloise, lover of Abelard, led to an embittered depression in the late 1960s. Once heavenly *ekstasis* degenerated into reclusive purgatory, a "circular desert" of chronic alcoholism, debilitation, and hospitalization. Plagued by the solitude she once cherished, Graham suffered bouts of anger and loneliness, making insomniac middle-of-the-night phone calls when she needed to talk to someone—anyone.

"In renewed contact with Martha Graham's choreography after several years' hiatus," Alan Kriegsman wrote, "one frequently sensed those powerful, strange, brilliant and disturbing elements that make it manifestly a work of genius. But," even he, a stalwart believer, conceded, "genius can engender its own kind of tedium, and through much of the evening the same work [*Acts of Light,* 1981] seemed leaden, immobile and uninvolving. How much of this response may be ascribed to contradictions inherent in Graham's art, and how much to the personal sensibilities of an observer—myself—who has never completely fathomed the Graham mystique—remains moot."

Her final years were a surreal cauldron of retrospective gala tributes and honorary degrees, lifetime and industry awards, nights at Studio 54 and days at the East Sixty-Third Street studio, where, refusing to use a cane or wear glasses, perfectly groomed and accessorized, seated in a director's chair, arthritic hands hidden within elbow-length suede gloves, Graham valiantly continued to give classes.

After Martha Graham's death at ninety-six, on April 1, 1991, her ashes were scattered from the Sangre de Cristo Mountains in New Mexico.

.   .   .

Ralph Waldo Emerson said, "Institutions are the lengthened shadows of individuals." In the dance world, past and present works are passed along to responsible others for stewardship, codification, re-presentation and renewal. Humphrey, Limón, O'Donnell, Sokolow, Taylor, Cunningham, Ailey, Bill T. Jones, Pam Tanowitz, Camille A. Brown, and Mark Morris come, informally, to mind as foundational and contemporary dance-makers with organized, realistic sensibilities about the coming lives of their work.

At the other side of the stage, fists against hips, feet planted to the ground, a colossus astride her tradition-indebted and anarchic field, stands the living spirit of Martha Graham and her defiant legacy of mystery, captured by Miguel de Unamuno in *The Tragic Sense of Life,* seventeen years before Graham stalked around front and center in *Heretic,* as "the sin of heresy, the sin of thinking for ourselves."

An unrefined, essential gem sits at the questioning heart of Martha Graham's works, be they integral unto themselves, consecutive, or collective, demanding to be honored during all manner of presentation and perpetuation, from floor exercises during Company class, when blood-pulse warms the dancers as they discover the technique anew; to the occurrence of three seamless run-throughs within one hour in the cavernous eleventh-floor Graham Studio on Bethune Street; to reimagining a "lost" dance predicated upon a series of still photographs, a few handwritten lines from a letter, and the fragment of a score; to a vintage masterpiece staged under the tutelage of a regisseur who learned it directly from "Martha," thrust toward reawakening by young bodies, the vessels through which her art flows into the light of the current day.

Graham's defiant twirl in *Letter to the World,* 1940.
"Lightly stepped a yellow star / To its lofty place—"
(Photograph by Barbara Morgan)

Acknowledgments

The range and scope of these acknowledgments reflect the labor required to enter the courageous mind of Martha Graham, an omnivorous genius who spared no time for arbitrary distinctions between "personal" and "professional," taking on the entire knowable world as material for her body of work.

Janet Eilber, artistic director of the Martha Graham Center of Contemporary Dance, was the erudite Sherpa by my side during my trek up the jagged peaks and through the dense valleys of modern dance. Janet's dedicated constancy never faltered. Denise Vale, senior artistic associate of the Martha Graham Company, lit the flame for my inspiration and graciously allowed me to bear witness at many company rehearsals. LaRue Allen, executive director at Graham, assisted by Arnie Apostol, opened many crucial and timely doors; as did my cordial interlocutor, impeccable provenance detective, and amenable dance vocabulary coach, Oliver Tobin, director of Martha Graham Resources, preceded in his gatekeeping role by Krissy Tate and Suzy Upton.

I am grateful to the Graham "family" of dancers, past and present, for hospitality, coffee shop chats, and interviews: Tadej Brdnik, Terese Capucilli, Robert Cohan, Katherine Crockett, Ellen Graff, Diane Gray, Linda Hodes, Stuart Hodes, Susan Kikuchi, Lone Kjaer Larsen, Virginie Mecene, Peter Sparling, Marnie Thomas, Blakeley White-McGuire, Xin Ying, and Yuriko.

The curators and staff in libraries, archives, and special collections across the country and around the world have made it their inexhaustible mission to identify, align, and make sense of Martha Graham's scattered evidence in all shapes and genres, assisting me with the ephemeralities of modern dance history—grainy videos; truncated reel-to-reel films; sections of tape-recorded interviews drowned out by traffic noise; incomplete paper trails, undated correspondence, and indecipherable notebook scrawls.

I begin where all researchers on the performing arts must start, the Jerome Robbins Dance Division, at my alma mater, the New York Public Library. In my encyclopedic home away from home, I sat for hours in blessed, unhurried solitude with the *real thing.* I thank curator extraordinaire Linda Murray for her impeccable intellectual cheerleading and perspicacity, and her entire staff, particularly Jennifer Eberhardt, Nailah Holmes, Tanisha Jones, Phillip Karg, Cassie Mey, and Arlene Yu; as well as former curators Jan Schmidt, Danielle Castronovo, and Susan Kraft. John Calhoun of the NYPL Billy Rose Theatre Collection and Tom Lisanti, manager, Permissions Services, and his diligent staff lent helping hands.

Before, during, and after my marathon sessions in the Library of Congress, I relied upon the scholarship, institutional memory, passionate sleuthing, friendly humor, and telephone-centric prowess of Libby Smigel, dance curator and archivist of the Music Division. Libby's willing staff, especially Robert Lipartito, were there to *serve* (as Libby put it) when I needed them. Karen Fishman, research center supervisor, Motion Picture, Broadcasting, and Recorded Sound Division, was a valued resource; as was Elizabeth Aldrich, retired dance curator.

As evident in the preceding pages, Martha Graham left traces far and wide of her sleepless cultural curiosity. As I followed in her barefoot steps, I turned to a multitude of specialists for access and guidance: Hannah Abelbeck, curator, and Catie Carl, digital imaging archivist, Palace of the Governors Photo Archives, New Mexico History Museum; Sara Azam and Natalia Sciarini, Beinecke Rare Book and Manuscript Library, Yale University; Teresa Barnett, head, UCLA Library Center for Oral History Research; Melissa Watterworth Batt, archivist, literary collections and rare books, Archives and Special Collections, and Betsy Pittman, university archivist, University of Connecticut Library; Erin Beasley, National Portrait Gallery, Smithsonian Institution; Andre Bernard, vice president and secretary, John Simon Guggenheim Memorial Foundation; Richard J. Behles, historical librarian, Health Sciences and Human Services Library, University of Maryland; Janine Biunno, archivist, the Isamu Noguchi Foundation and Garden Museum, and Heidi Coleman, former archivist; Marisa Bourgoin, head, Reference Services, Archives of American Art; Joseph Cantrell, Reference Services, Santa Barbara Central Library; Virginia A. Hunt, associate university archivist for Collection Development and Records Management Services, Juliana

Kuipers, senior collection development curator/archivist, and Robin Carlaw, researcher, Harvard University Archives, Pusey Library, and Dale Stinchcomb, curatorial assistant, Harvard Theatre Collection, Houghton Library; David Coppen, special collections librarian and archivist, Eastman School of Music; David Day, curator, International Harp Archives, Brigham Young University; Anne Daye, director of education and research, Dolmetsch Historical Dance Society, Bedford, England; Amber Dushman, senior archivist, American Medical Association; Nancy Nagler Engelken, director, Perry-Mansfield Performing Arts Camp, and Karolynn Lestrud and Dagny McKinley; Daniel Entin, Director, the Roerich Museum; Nancy Friedland, Dance Specialist, Butler Library, Columbia University; Sarah Gilmor, reference librarian, History Colorado; Thomas Gladysz, president, Louise Brooks Society; David R. Grinnell, reference and access Archivist, University of Pittsburgh Library System; Genie Guerard, curator/manuscripts librarian, UCLA Library Special Collections; Tara Hart, archives manager, and Monica Crozier, assistant, Frances Mulhall Achilles Library and Archives, Whitney Museum of American Art; Shelley Hayreh, archivist, Avery Architectural and Fine Arts Library, Columbia University; Alice Helpern, director of programs, Dance Notation Bureau; Sharon Keinath Henning, Santa Barbara High School Alumni Association; Lesley Herzberg, curator, Hancock Shaker Village; Bonnie Oda Homsey, Los Angeles Dance Foundation and Michio Ito Foundation; Rob Hudson and Kathleen Sabogal, Carnegie Hall Archives; Mary Huelsbeck, assistant director, Wisconsin Center for Film and Theater Research, University of Wisconsin–Madison; Judith Lin Hunt, dean emeritus, Sprague Library, Montclair State University; Sherri Jackson, Bridgeman Images; Rebecca Jewett, coordinator of public services and operations, Thompson Special Collections, Ohio State University Library, and Tara Krieder and Orville W. Martin, staff members; Christian Kelleher, archivist, Nettie Lee Benson Latin American Collection, the University of Texas Libraries; Marie Kroger, Art Institute of Chicago Archives; Erin Lawrimore, university archivist, University Libraries, the University of North Carolina at Greensboro; Lauren Lean, digital asset coordinator, George Eastman Museum; Sharon Lehner, director of archives, Brooklyn Academy of Music; Leonda Levchuk, National Museum of the American Indian; Rachel McElroy, Society of Dance History Scholars; Kristan McKinsey, museum curator, Peoria Riverfront Museum, Peoria, Illinois; David McKnight, director, Rare Book and Manuscript Library, Kislak Center for Special Collections, Van Pelt–Dietrich Libraries, University of Pennsylvania; Ruthann B.

McTyre, director, Andrew W. Mellon Foundation Music Library; and Jonathan Manton, music librarian for Access Services, Gilmore Music Library, Yale University; Jeffrey Monseau, college archivist, Archives and Special Collections, Springfield College; Nils Morgan, Barbara and Willard Morgan Archive; Cindy Abel Morris, archivist, Center for Southwest Research and Special Collections, University of New Mexico Libraries; Jim Moske, managing archivist, Metropolitan Museum of Art; Joanne B. Mulcahy, Center for Documentary Studies, Duke University; Timothy D. Murray, head, Special Collections, University of Delaware Library; Chris Mustazza, co-director, PennSound Archives, University of Pennsylvania; Tim Noakes, head of public services, Stanford University Library Special Collections; David Olson, archivist, and the staff of the Columbia University Center for Oral History, Butler Library; Shannon O'Neill and Martha Tenney, Barnard College Archives and Special Collections; Norton Owen, director of preservation, Jacob's Pillow Dance Festival; Michael Pahn, head of archives and digitization, and Nathan Sowry, reference archivist, Smithsonian Institution, National Museum of the American Indian, Cultural Resources Division; Meg Partridge, director, Imogen Cunningham Trust; Michael Redmon, director of research, Santa Barbara Historical Museum, Gledhill Library, and Chris Ervin, Roy Regester, and Martha Hassenflug, research volunteers; Elizabeth Ellis Reilly, curator, Photographic Archives, University of Louisville; Nancy Reynolds, director of research, the George Balanchine Foundation; Andrea Roberts, Artistic Coordinator, the School of Toronto Dance Theatre; Oliver Halsman Rosenberg and Steve Rossi, Philippe Halsman Studio and Halsman Archive; Joel Rosencranz, Conner Rosencranz Gallery, New York City; Safron Rossi and Barbara Vilander, OPUS Archives and Research Center, Pacifica Graduate Institute; Margaret Schlankey, head of reference services, Dolph Briscoe Center for American History, University of Texas at Austin; Bernhard Schneider, director, Mozarteum Summer Academy, Salzburg; Linda Seckelson, senior reader services librarian, the Museum Libraries, and Sarah Szeliga, assistant visual resources manager, the Onassis Library for Hellenic and Roman Art, Department of Greek and Roman Art, the Metropolitan Museum of Art; Ruth Shrigley, principal curator, Collections Access, Manchester Art Gallery; James Stack, Special Collections Division, University of Washington Libraries; Gail Stavitsky, chief curator, Montclair Art Museum; Erik Stolarski, archivist, and Laura Dirado, National Museum of Dance, Saratoga Springs, New York; Laura Streett, archivist, Vassar College; Joe Struble, archivist, George Eastman House, and Jesse Peers, Eastman Legacy Collection; Jennifer Tobias and Elisabeth Thomas, Museum of Modern Art Library and Archives; Guy Webb, Montecito Historical Archives; Heinz-Jurgen Winkler, research assistant, Fondation Hindemith/Hindemith Institut Frankfurt; Matthew Wittman, curator, Harvard Theatre Collection, and Melanie Wisner, accessioning archivist, Houghton Library, Harvard University; Jennifer T. Yang, Harry Ransom Humanities Research Center, University of Texas at Austin; Faith Yoman, New Mexico State Library; and Margaret Zoller, reference services, Archives of American Art.

An intrepid volunteer army of fellow biographers, scholars, and estate family members were with me in spirit and encouragement. Affectionate memory first alights upon the departed and much-missed Don McDonagh and Leslie Getz, who shared their Morningside Heights home cooking, dance history book collection, personal papers, and NYPL archives. The day we met, Don signed his pioneering 1973 study of Martha Graham for me, and the paperback became my Bible. I extend retrospective thanks to Gary A. Anderson, professor of theology, University of Notre Dame; Deirdre Bair; Henrietta Bannerman, London Contemporary Dance School; David F. Beatty, Samuel Barber Trust; Thais Barry; Avis Berman; Gabriel Boyers, Schubertiade Music, Inc.; Sam K. Bryan, International Film Foundation; Marc Bryan-Brown, Estate of Paul Tanqueray; Greg Castillo, Department of Architecture, College of Environmental Design, University of California, Berkeley; Margareta Ingrid Christian, Department of Germanic Studies, University of Chicago; Joan Chodorow; Robert S. Cohen; Daniel L'Engle Davis; Mary V. Dearborn; Laura Dolp, Cali School of Music, Montclair State University; Katherine Duke, Erick Hawkins Dance Company; Anderson Ferrell; Norma Sue Fisher-Stitt, Dance Department, York University; Lisa Fusillo, Department of Dance, the University of Georgia; Joyce Greenberg; Ralph Hale, MD, American Congress of Obstetricians and Gynecologists; Penelope Hanstein, Cornaro professor emerita, Texas Woman's University; Anne Heller; Pilar and Scott Kennedy; Peter Jaszi, professor of law emeritus, Washington College of Law, American University; Rhona Richman Kinneally, editor, *Canadian Journal of Irish Studies*; Reiko Sunami Kopelson; Sali Ann Kriegsman; Kimerer LaMothe; Nancy Lassalle; Vincent Lenti, Eastman School of Music; Gail Levin; Mimi Muray Levitt, Nickolas Muray Photo Archives; Joshua R. Lynes; J. D. McClatchy; Malcolm McCormick; Elizabeth McPherson, director of dance, Montclair State University; David Martin, Martin-Zambito Fine Art, Seattle, Washington;

Edward Marx, University of Kochi; Ross Melnick, Department of Film and Media Studies, University of California, Santa Barbara; Lisa Miles; Allen Neville; Patricia O'Toole; Nell Irvin Painter; Thomas J. Parente; Marc Plate; Vicki Quade; Dennis Roberts; Carl Rollyson; Joel Sachs; Mary Ann Santos Newhall, University of New Mexico; Yoko Sato, Tokyo University of Agriculture and Technology; Stacy Schiff; Maxine Sheets-Johnstone; Scott Simmon, Department of English, University of California, Davis; Jeffrey S. Smith, Department of Cultural Geography, Kansas State University; Janet Mansfield Soares; Christel Stalpaert, professor of performance studies, University of Ghent; James Steichen, Stanford University; Travis Suazo, former executive director, Indian Pueblo Cultural Center; Amanda Vaill; Casey Villard; Tappan Wilder; Laura Pettibone Wright; and Charles Humphrey Woodford.

At Montclair State University, the undergraduate dance majors in my Danceaturgy Writing Workshop were eagerly chatting, smiling, coffees in hand, ready and waiting for me outside the seminar room when I arrived for our Friday 8:30 a.m. sessions. They taught me far more than I ever taught them. I also thank my former Department of Theatre and Dance colleagues and Creative Research Center contributors, beginning with emeritus dean of the College of the Arts, Geoffrey Newman, and emerita director of dance, Lori Katterhenry; dean Daniel Gurskis and his cordial administrative staff; professors Jennifer Chin, Kathleen Kelley, Nancy Lushington, Jessie DiMauro Marks, Debra Otte, Linda Roberts, Erhard Rom, Diann Sichel, Maxine Steinman; and, in Peak Performances/Arts and Cultural Programming, special thanks to Carrie Urbanic and Jedediah Wheeler.

I am grateful for family and friends—Andrew Baldwin, Barney Baldwin, Daniel Baldwin, Deborah Plutzik Briggs, Tony Cartwright, Colleen Marie Cavanagh, Karen Davidov, Maxine Davidowitz, Lola B. Fahrer, Roberta Friedman, Ron Gordon, John Haworth, Michael Lyden, Mark Morril, Henry Myerberg, Olga Okaty, Jonathan Plutzik, Bob Reiss, Paul Russo, M.D., and his team, Kenneth Spooner, and Daniel White.

Ali Shaw and her Indigo Editing colleagues, with a special thank-you to Jennifer Zaczek Kepler, have my enduring gratitude, accompanied by multiple sighs of relief, for wrestling my old-school manuscript into twenty-first-century format.

My editor at Knopf, Victoria Wilson, honed in upon what needed clarity in my discourse when it became discursive, astonishing me with her keen eye and oracular gifts. From the day, early on, when Vicky reminded me that Martha Graham's narrative must *take the reader in hand,* she was the uncanny, knowing voice of perspective. Her assistant, Marc Jaffee, never lost his sense of kindly bemusement. For their irrepressible energy, I also thank Penelope Belnap in publicity and Matthew Sciarappa in marketing.

My agent, Andy McNicol, at William Morris Endeavor, was far more than a vigilant advocate for my work as an author. Even when we did not see each other for stretches of time over many years, I felt her supportive, upbeat, and agile *presence.* An attendant and empathic ear, Andy cheered me on when the going (. . . often) got rough. Her assistants, Clio Seraphim and Brooke Drabkin, were ebullient readers and honest critics. Alex Kane of WME generously stepped in to help in the last lap of the journey.

And finally, as I sit here, in my third-floor study, the door closed and another day dawning, I thank my wife, Roberta, for a lifetime of love.

N.B., Autumn 2022

Notes

ABBREVIATIONS USED IN THE NOTES

AAA	Archives of American Art at the Smithsonian Institution
AS	Arnold Schoenberg
CORC	Charles Olson Research Collection
D&C	*Democrat & Chronicle*
DB	Dorothy Bird
EH	Erick Hawkins
EHC	Erick Hawkins Collection, Music Division, Library of Congress
GS	Gertrude Shurr
HNAI	*Handbook of North American Indians*
JM	John Martin
JMA	John Murray Anderson
JRDD	Jerome Robbins Dance Division of the New York Public Library
LB	Louise Brooks
LKP	Lincoln Kirstein Papers, Jerome Robbins Dance Division, New York Public Library
LH	Louis Horst
LHCM	Louis Horst Collection of Music, New York Public Library
LOC	Library of Congress
MG	Martha Graham
MGC	Martha Graham Collection
MGLA	Martha Graham Legacy Archive, Music Division, Library of Congress
MGR	Martha Graham Resources
NYPL	The New York Public Library
O&G	*Olive and Gold*
RM	Rouben Mamoulian
TS	Ted Shawn
TSC	Ted Shawn Collection, Jacob's Pillow Dance Festival Archives
WCW	William Carlos Williams
WPA	Workers of the Writers' Program of the Works Progress Administration in the Commonwealth of Pennsylvania

INTRODUCTION

xi For me, growing up in the Manhattan neighborhood: See B. Morgan, *Sixteen Dances*, cover and p. 125.

xii "It takes about ten years": MG, "How I Became a Dancer."

xiv "In the United States": Schmuhl, *Indecent Liberties*, 7.

xiv "Make it new": Pound, "How I Began," 211.

xiv "each venture": Eliot, *Four Quartets*, part V.

xv "In this infancy": Frank, *Our America*, 10.

xv "the modern dance is": Stodelle, *The First Frontier*, 57.

xv "We dancers, too": Ibid., 62.

xv "I don't think she thought": Catton, "The Great 20th Century Dance Companies."

xvi "every act of creation": McGehee, "An Opportunity Lost," 71.

xvi Jennie Graham saved: Lask, "First Lady of the Dance"; Leatherman, *Martha Graham*, 33; *People*, "Martha Graham."

xvi "was not a friend": Brooks, "A Bold Step Forward," 452.

xvi "I don't want people": The Ernestine Stodelle–Louis Horst Collections at the Newberry Library in Chicago contain no MG material. There is no correspondence to or from MG in the Doris Humphrey Papers at the NYPL or in the Doris Humphrey Archive at Goucher College Library. Among the Sophia Smith Collection, the NYPL, and the Library of Congress, less than a dozen letters survive from the four-decade "passionate friendship" of MG and Katharine "Kit" Cornell. When Sali Ann Kriegsman was compiling her history of the Bennington School of the Dance in the late 1970s, MG did not wish to speak with her; nor would MG consent in 1978 to a Columbia University Oral History interview about the Bennington years.

xvi In the Music Division: MG, notebooks, boxes 274–275, MGC. See also Barretto, "The Role of Martha Graham's Notebooks," 53–67; and N. W. Ross, *Notebooks of Martha Graham*, a compilation of unedited transcripts with no commentary, clarification of attributions, or scholarly apparatus.

xvi "We were friendly": Author's notes from Yuriko Kikuchi's talk at the Martha Graham School, July 12, 2014; Dunning, "The Graham Company."

xvi "What they did privately": Robert Cohan, interview with author, Westbeth Studios, New York City, May 28, 2014. John Martin, hired in 1927 as the first full-time dance critic for the *New York Times,* did much to interpret and advance Martha Graham's work for decades, proposed writing her biography in 1964, but never did, insisting, "We weren't *that* kind of close."

xvi "approachable to the earnest": Genzlinger, "Marion Horosko."

xvi "against any dramatization": Kisselgoff, "Martha Graham Dies at 96."

xvi She allowed him one: Don McDonagh's only interview with MG was on October 19, 1968. MG, interview by Don McDonagh, October 19, 1968, NYPL, Performing Arts Research Collection, JRDD, *MGZTL 4-2566.

xvii Agnes de Mille: See "Early Drafts and Papers Related to *Martha: The Life and Work of Martha Graham*," 196-?–1991, JRDD, *MGZMD 80; on the compositional difficulties of *Martha*, see McDonagh, "Martha Graham: Fiction and Fact."

xvii The book that dance critic Marcia Siegel: Phillips, "Martha Graham's Gilded Cage."

xvii "Marthology": Siegel, "Marthology."

xvii "Looking at the past": MG, "I Am a Dancer," *Routledge Dance Studies Reader*, 99.

xvii "Martha was her work": McGehee, review of *Martha: The Life and Work of Martha Graham.*

xvii "Off stage she was really": Sophie Maslow, interview by Janet Eilber, April 9 and 10, 2001, MGLA.

xvii "But on stage, performing": Ibid.

xvii "the only justification": N. W. Ross, *Notebooks of Martha Graham,* 269.

1: PITTSBURGH

3 "the soft chain of hills": WPA, *Story of Old Allegheny City,* 1–2, 45.

3 "the obligatory extra white shirt": Weber and Stearns, introduction to *The Spencers of Amberson Avenue,* xiv, xx; Parton, "Pittsburg," 36.

4 "on tightly-adjacent plots": McLaughlin and Uhl, *Nomination Form,* § 8; Miles, *Resurrecting Allegheny City,* 168.

4 This enclave of two-: McLaughlin and Uhl, *Nomination Form,* § 7 and USGS Pittsburgh, Pennsylvania, West Quadrant Map; Smith and Swetnam, *Guidebook to Historic Western Pennsylvania,* 27; Miles, *Resurrecting Allegheny City,* 168.

4 Today the area is designated: *Historic Pittsburgh Map Index,* 1901, Volume 1—Allegheny City: Wards 1–8, 12, and 13, Plate 5; Google Map of Brighton Place and environs courtesy David Grinnell, University of Pittsburgh Library; David Grinnell and author on walking tour and site visit of North Side; David Grinnell to author, May 13–15, 2014; Lisa A. Miles to author, October 19, 2013.

5 Named after her Irish: de Mille, *Martha,* 16; Laura Streett (Vassar College archivist) to author, February 24, 2014; Stodelle, *Deep Song,* 5.

5 paternal grandmother: Contrary to Graham's assertion in *Blood Memory,* p.25, that her paternal grandmother attended Vassar, this was not the case. Newburgh, NY, is near Poughkeepsie, which may have been the source for the confusion.

5 Martha's sister: McDonagh, *Martha Graham,* 8–9; Stodelle, *Deep Song,* 6; MG, *Blood Memory,* 27.

6 The who's who: *Biographical Review,* XXIV, *Containing Life Sketches of Leading Citizens of Pittsburgh and Vicinity, Pennsylvania, 1897,* Boston: Biographical Review Publishing Company, 444–45; Cushing, *History of Allegheny County.*

6 After attending the University of Pennsylvania: *Biographical Review,* 445; Rooney and Peterson, *Allegheny City,* 53.

6 "I call your attention": "Miss Dorothea Lynde Dix," obituary in Harper et al., *Annual Report of the Managers of the Western Pennsylvania Hospital for 1887,* 12–14.

7 Dr. Graham spent ten years: *Biographical Review,* 445; *Twelfth United States Census, 1990,* prepared by the Census Office, courtesy of University of Pittsburgh Library and Archives; Weber and Stearns, introduction to *The Spencers of Amberson Avenue,* xx; Stodelle, *Deep Song,* 5; McDonagh, *Martha Graham,* 8–9.

7 Martha Graham's father: Secondhand accounts of Martha Graham's fourteen years growing up in Allegheny can be found in Terry, *Frontiers of Dance,* 3–14; McDonagh, *Martha Graham,* 6–13; Stodelle, *Deep Song,* 1–7; de Mille, *Martha,* 16–19; and Leatherman, *Portrait of the Lady,* 33.

7 "My whole life": MG, interview by Don McDonagh, October 19, 1968, JRDD.

7 "I think I was my father's favorite": MG, *Blood Memory,* 41.

7 "A bit Olympian": McDonagh, *Martha Graham*, 10.

7 stern and demanding: Coleman, "Martha Graham Still Leaps Forward."

8 "Pure water": MG, *Blood Memory*, 18–19.

8 In the second episode: MG, *Notebooks*, 269, 270; MG, *Blood Memory*, 20; MG to Don McDonagh, NYPL interview, October 19, 1968; and Stodelle, 267n2, "Graham, reporting her father's words in conversation with the author."

8 Over the years: Dee Reynolds, "A Technique for Power," 9. "Far from being direct expression, Graham's strategy was a very deliberate construction and staging of emotional effects."

9 "You must abandon": C. Salas, *The Life & the Work*, 42n3.

9 At the turn of the century: McDonagh, *Martha Graham*, 9; *Allegheny City Census*, June 5, 1900, Schedule No. 1, Sheet No. 7528, entries for 1531 Fremont Street; Weber and Stearns, introduction to *The Spencers of Amberson Avenue*, xxvi–xxix; MG, *Blood Memory*, 21–23.

9 In the second-floor nursery: MG, *Blood Memory*, 32, 34, 35; Stodelle, *Deep Song*, 6, 267n10; MG, "Piano Lessons," informal talk to Juilliard students, late 1951, JRDD; Tennyson, *The Lady of Shalott*; MG recalls "reading everything . . ." as a child, in her interview by Don McDonagh, October 19, 1968, JRDD.

9 "choreographing": Dunning, "Lessons Learned in Youth."

9 "witches, wee folk": Genzlinger, "Marion Horosko."

10 "robed in snowy white": Udall, "Between Dream and Shadow," 35.

10 Weekdays, Martha and Mary: David Grinnell, email to author, August 11, 2014; WPA, *Story of Old Allegheny*, 144–45.

10 "Each and every Sunday": MG, *Blood Memory*, 38.

10 "smoothed out": Stodelle, *Deep Song*, 3; WPA, *Story of Old Allegheny*, 87

10 "If ever there": Bobinski, *Carnegie Libraries*, 32, 77.

11 Three blocks farther south: David Grinnell, email to author, February 25, 2014; Mayer, "North Side"; MG, *Blood Memory*, 38–39; Terry, *Frontiers of Dance*, 9; McDonagh, *Martha Graham*, 11.

11 Daily life was not all study: Access to American Medical Association Digital Archives courtesy Amber Dushman (senior archivist) via email to author, February 24, 2014.

11 "[sat] on a green": MG, *Blood Memory*, 33–34.

11 Punch and Judy: Paulding, "Scotland Loves 'The Goddess.'"

11 At the end of April 1906: Stodelle, *Deep Song*, 6, 267n, interview with "Auntie Re" Beers.

12 "My brother died": MG, interview by Walter Terry, Dance Laboratory series, Young Men's–Young Women's Hebrew Association, November 16, 1952, JRDD, *MGZTL 4-2113.

12 "health seeker movement": Baur, "The Health Seeker in the Westward Movement," 102; Stodelle, *Deep Song*, 6; de Mille, *Martha*, 18.

12 "the pleasantest of all": Nordhoff, *California*, 111, 113.

2: SANTA BARBARA

13 The rolling, clacketing: *Major Railroads in the U.S., 1900 Map*: National Park Service, *Teaching with Historic Places Site*, http://www.nps.gov/nr/twhp.

13 "When I would stand": MG, *Blood Memory*, 42–44.

13 Santa Barbara in 1908: de Mille, *Martha*, 19; Stodelle, *Deep Song*, 9.

14 "carrying a shaded candle": MG, *Blood Memory*, 50–51. Details on location and architectural features of the Graham home courtesy of Chris Ervin, archivist, Santa Barbara Historical Museum.

14 Queen of the Missions: Ibid., 49.

14 "loose-fitting garments": O'Hara, "Poor Clares," n.p.

14 "the Graham Girls": "Martha Graham's Visit Home Curtailed," *Santa Barbara News-Press*, September 14, 1947.

15 A favorite spot near home: Roy Regester (Santa Barbara Historical Museum), email to author, September 15, 2014.

15 "charge[d] across": Stodelle, *Deep Song*, 7, 9.

15 In August 1909, Martha was enrolled: McDonagh, *Martha Graham*, 13–14; Stodelle, *Deep Song*, 8–13; Jennie Graham [Mrs. Homer N. Duffey], interview by Verne Linderman, *Santa Barbara News-Press*, September 29, 1946; Klein, "Martha Graham."

15 "part wild": MG, *Blood Memory*, 51.

15 "I was anything but": "Martha Graham Honored on Return to Santa Barbara," *Santa Barbara News-Press*, November 3, 1966.

15 "Dr. and Mrs. Graham": Blanche Mukherjee (daughter of Mary Dewing) to Michael Redmon, July 25, 1995, p. 2, Gledhill Library Archives, Santa Barbara Historical Museum.

16 "Just Girls!": Santa Barbara High School, *O&G*, 1910–1911, n.p.

16 One spring Saturday afternoon: Stodelle, *Deep Song*, 10; Schlundt, *Professional Appearances*, 15–16.

17 "frigid beauty": Hardy, review of *Divine Dancer*, 63.

17 "the life-cycle of Egypt's rise and fall": Ruth St. Denis, quoted in TS, *Pioneer and Prophet*, 2:11; "Mason Opera House Brilliantly Opened," *Los Angeles Herald*, June 19, 1903.

18 For *Five East Indian Dances*: MG, interview by Walter Terry, "The Early Years," 1973, disc 1, JRDD; Shelton, *Divine Dancer*, 56ff.; Terry, *Frontiers of Dance*, 17–23; Terry, *Ted Shawn*, 43; Conner and Gillis-Kruman, *The Early Moderns*, chap. 2; Sherman and Schlundt, "Who's St. Denis?," 309; Stodelle, *Deep Song*, 11; TS, *Pioneer and Prophet*, 1: 33–43.

18 "I knew at that moment": MG, *Blood Memory*, 56, 63; Shelton, *Divine Dancer*, 184.

18 "Geisha Girl": "Martha Graham Honored on Return to Santa Barbara," *Santa Barbara News-Press*, November 3, 1966.

19 "extraordinary firebrand": Kendall, *Where She Danced*, 159.

19 "red-haired and Irish": Salpeter, "Martha Graham," 46.

19 "the first of many such conferences": Reed, "Modern Dance Exponent."

19 "I wore my long hair": MG, *Blood Memory*, 59.

20 Madame Schuman-Henk: The visiting diva in Martha's story, "Music and the Maid," was modeled after a famous contralto of the time, Ernestine Schumann-Heink (1861–1936).

20 Indeed, ever since: de Mille, *Martha*, 23; Klein, "Martha Graham."

20 The quandary of Ruth's uniqueness: MG, "Music and the Maid," *O&G*, December 1911.

20 "The Soul Call": by MG, *O&G*, June 1913, n.p.

20   "with her band": Review of *Dido and Aeneas*, *O&G*, December 1911, 43–44; Vergil, *Dido* (Miller's numbering), 1.1.

21   "There was something": Stodelle, *Deep Song*, xix, 12–13.

21   "the importance of": *O&G*, December 1913, masthead and pp. 44, 48, 57.

21   "handsome and popular": Blanche Mukherjee to Michael Redmon, July 25, 1995; "Exquisite Fantasy of Rhapsodic Love," unsigned review of *Prunella* at the Little Theatre, *New York Times*, October 27, 1913; Jennie Graham, interview by Verne Linderman, *Santa Barbara News-Press*, September 29, 1946.

22   "timid, yet loving": "*Prunella* Cast of Characters," *O&G*, Spring 1913, 15.

22   "some very original": *O&G*, *THE PLAY* [Review of *Prunella*], April 1913.

22   "the most artistic": Kendall, *Where She Danced*, 159.

22   "The interpretation": *Santa Barbara Morning Press*, April 6, 1913; Osborne/Newton anecdote: Blanche Mukherjee to Michael Redmon, July 25, 1995.

22   "the star . . . achiev[ing]": Senior portraits and profiles, *O&G*, Spring 1913, 49.

3: RUTH ST. DENIS AND TED SHAWN—THE DENISHAWN DANCERS

23   One thing Martha was *not*: Stodelle, *Deep Song*, 15.

23   "the great tragedy": MG, *Blood Memory*, 60.

23   "Miss Martha Graham, daughter of": Courtesy of Betsy Green, author of *Santa Barbara Way Back When*, posted October 5, 2014, http://www.edhat.com/site/tidbit.cfm?nid=141651.

23   "the belief that art": McDonagh, *Martha Graham*, 19.

23   "held him in high": Introduction, Finding Aid to the Robert McLean Cumnock Papers, Northwestern University Archives Repository, Evanston, IL, http://findingaids.library.northwestern.edu/catalog/inu-ead-nua-archon-691.

23   Mrs. Grigg put admiration: *Los Angeles Times* advertisement, April 8, 1902.

23   She created and taught: *Los Angeles Herald* advertisement, March 25, 1910, 6.

24   "Interpretative Readings": *Los Angeles Herald*, October 20, 1907.

24   Outside the literary-performance arena: Terry, *Frontiers of Dance*, 26.

24   These texts were leavened: Shelton, *Divine Dancer*, 1–12; Schlundt, "The Renaissance of Ruth St. Denis," 454; Sherman and Schlundt, "Who's St. Denis?," 308; Preston, *Modernism's Mythic Pose*, 4, 5, 58, 84–85.

24   "To each *spiritual* function": Sparshott, *A Measured Pace*, 147.

25   "[*poses*] *plastiques*": Shelton, *Divine Dancer*, 13–16; Macintosh, *The Ancient Dancer in the Modern World*, 6–7: "Not only can Modernist theatrical aesthetics be ultimately traceable to this longstanding fascination with the ancient moving statue, it could also be argued that Modern Dance itself stems from this same source."

25   Watching Stebbins: Spector, *Rhythm and Life*, 116; Ruyter, *Reformers and Visionaries*, 58.

25   "I glimpsed for": Ruyter, *Reformers and Visionaries*, 59–63.

25   "A talented girl is": Ruyter, *Reformers and Visionaries*, 59–63; Shelton, *Divine Dancer*, 103–104.

25   Having relocated with: Sherman and Schlundt, "Who's St. Denis?," 308, 312.

25   *tableaux vivants*: Paz, "Tableau Vivant."

25   Ruthie's twenties continued: Ruyter, *Reformers and Visionaries*, 60–63.

25   "incongruous juxtapositions": Sherman and Schlundt, "Who's St. Denis?," 314.

26 Mary Baker Eddy's advocacy: Hardy, review of *Divine Dancer*, 63.

26 "an unconventional female": *Zaza*—unsigned review in *Moving Picture World*, October 16, 1915.

26 "[m]y destiny as": Shelton, *Divine Dancer*, 46–47.

26 The hiatus: Ruyter, *Reformers and Visionaries*, 64–65, 71; Sherman and Schlundt, "Who's St. Denis?," 311; Schlundt, *Professional Appearances*, 11–15. For a "chronological list of solos . . . divided into the religious and the secular," see Sherman and Schlundt, "Who's St. Denis?," 328–29. For example, St. Denis designated *Radha* [1906] as "religious," whereas she listed *Egypta* [1910] in the "secular" column.

26 "sought the stamp": Shelton, *Divine Dancer*, 91.

27 Thanks to Harris's deep pockets: Schlundt, *Professional Appearances*, 15–16.

27 ". . . always the glamour": TS, *One Thousand and One Night Stands*, 25; TS, *Pioneer and Prophet*, 1:93.

27 "to keep the wolf": TS, *Pioneer and Prophet*, 1:18.

27 "command performances": Schlundt, "Vaudeville and Society Dates," 17–18.

27 "whose outer robes": "Ruth St. Denis Applauded/Dancer Exhibits Her Art in Pictorial Hindu and Japanese Plays," *New York Times*, March 12, 1913.

28 "reputable male dancer": Shelton, *Divine Dancer*, 111–12.

28 Martha Graham's first choreographic mentor: TS, "Biographical Sketch" (unpublished manuscript, ca. 1920), pp. 1, 2, 6, 8, box 193, Jacob's Pillow Dance Festival Archives, TSC; TS, *One Thousand and One Night Stands*, 11–13.

28 "good, but not exceptionally doting": Terry, *Ted Shawn*, 11.

29 "*men* don't dance": Terry, *Ted Shawn*, 131.

29 In March 1911: TS, *One Thousand and One Night Stands*, 12; TS, "Biographical Sketch," 1, 2; TS, *Record of Professional Life of Ted Shawn* (written ca. 1929), p. [1], box 192, TSC. Shawn divided the first two pages of the document into four columns: "Year; Activities; Personal Solo Dances Created; and Duets, Ballets and Trios, Ensembles."

29 As a consequence: TS, *One Thousand and One Night Stands*, 13: "Cupid did not triumph over Terpsichore"; TS, "Biographical Sketch," 2, 6, 8.

29 "To make money to further [his] art side": TS, three-page typewritten letter to the editor of *Dance Observer*, May 24, 1961, box 194, Jacob's Pillow Dance Festival Archives, TSC.

29 standard-bearer for the American pageantry movement: See Catherine Parsons Smith, "Of Pageantry and Politics," 115ff.

30 "one of the largest": TS, *One Thousand and One Night Stands*, 14.

30 In the spring of 1913: "Denishawn Dance Film," 1915?–1917, streaming video file, 12 min., JRDD, *MGZSIDF 1724.

31 In the new year, 1914: Hering, "Steps That Took a Master to the Top"; Schlundt, *Professional Appearances*, 18–19; Sherman, "The American Indian Imagery," 368.

31 As soon as the entourage: TS, *One Thousand and One Night Stands*, 19–24.

31 "triune ideal": Carman, *The Making of Personality*, viii, ix, 145, 217, 228.

31 In the February 1914 issue: Ellis, "The Philosophy of Dancing," 197, 198, 200, 203, 205, 207.

31 "Our Bible has been written": TS, *The Dancer's Bible*, "An appreciation of Havelock Ellis's [best-selling book] 'The Dance of Life,' [1923] by Ted Shawn, the foremost American man dancer" [author dates the essay to 1924: "two years ago it was my great privilege to meet and talk with Havelock Ellis in London"], three-page typescript with

TS holograph edits, Jacob's Pillow Collection, box 192, TSC. See also Alter, "Havelock Ellis's Essay," 27–35; and Sparshott, "On the Question," 6–7, on Ellis's theory of the union of architecture and dance.

32   "hurried with [the Havelock Ellis article]": TS, *The Dancer's Bible*, p. [1].

32   "most understanding soul": Shelton, *Divine Dancer*, 120.

32   "lessons in her own spiritual approach": TS, letter to *Dance Observer*, May 24, 1961.

33   The next morning: Murphy, *The People Have Never Stopped Dancing*, 112.

33   Shawn needed a mentor: TS, *One Thousand and One Night Stands*, 25–27, 41–44; Shelton, *Divine Dancer*, 121–23; Schlundt, *Professional Appearances*, 19–21.

33   The tour culminated: TS, *Pioneer and Prophet*, 2:iii, 19.

33   "[t]he art of the dance": TS, *Pioneer and Prophet*, cited in Elizabeth Poindexter, Texas Woman's University doctoral dissertation, "Ted Shawn: His Personal Life," 1963, p. 162, 163. Ted Shawn: "I, personally, am deeply grateful to [Elizabeth Poindexter] for having got down into permanent record so complete and so factual a record of my life and career."

33   The Ruth St. Denis School of Dancing: Poindexter, "Ted Shawn," 163, 167; Terry, *Frontiers of Dance*, 67; Or, *Body and Mind*, 203–5; Patton, *Bhagavad Gita*, 57.

34   "admitting of freedom": TS, "Biographical Sketch," 4.

34   the lotus position: For silent footage of the yoga-movement class en plein air, and glimpses of the girls frolicking in the swimming pool, see NYPL [Denishawn Dance Film].

34   A "normal course": Cohen-Straytner, "The Franchising of Denishawn," 2.

34   one of the violinists: Soares, *Louis Horst*, 18–19.

34   "Hessian stogie roller": LH interview, 1952, cassette 1, JRDD, *MGZTC 3-1239; LH, interview by Jeanette Schlottman Roosevelt, 1959–1960, cassette 1, JRDD, *MGZTC 3-2261.

34   "like an old Brahms": Madden, *You Call Me Louis*, 83.

35   Martha Graham's first dedicated accompanist: Soares, *Louis Horst*, 5–17; Dalbritton, *To Bear Witness*, 15.

35   Louis grew up: For the highlights of Louis Horst's early life, from 1884 to 1915, I am indebted to Soares's biography, *Louis Horst: Musician in a Dancer's World*, published in 1992 and out of print.

36   "priestess with a twinkle": Lloyd, *The Borzoi Book of Modern Dance*, 25.

36   "kind of crooning": Sears, "Louis Horst," 95.

36   Horst agreed: LH interview with Jeanette Schlottman Roosevelt, 1952, cassette 1, JRDD.

37   "no bigger than a living room": Sears, "Louis Horst: A Centennial Compendium," 97.

37   Seated in readiness: Stodelle, review of *Louis Horst*, 1,365.

37   "Louie": the name by which Horst would always affectionately be known in the dance world.

37   "Dance for me": Stodelle, *Deep Song*, 19–21, 268n.

37   "she has a special quality": Soares, *Louis Horst*, 23, 213n.

37   St. Denis took Shawn: Sherman, *Drama of Denishawn Dance*, 23; TS, *Reminiscences: From Childhood to the Dissolution of Denishawn*, 1969, disc 10, JRDD, *MGZTL 4-69.

38   Graham had one year: Or, "Body and Mind," 203–5.

38   Meeting privately: "Denishawn Dance Film," JRDD; Poindexter, "Ted Shawn," 165–67; Bachmann, *Dalcroze Today*, 19; TS, *Reminiscences*, discs 10 and 12, JRDD, *MGZTL

4-69; TS, interview by Don McDonagh, November 3, 1967, discs 1 and 2, JRDD, *MGZTL 4-2532.

38 "the great doelike": de Mille, *Dance to the Piper*, 146, 152.

38 "You have a long row to hoe": Poindexter, "Ted Shawn," 164.

38 The proprietary "papa": TS, *Reminiscences*, disc 10, JRDD; Robert Cohan, interview with author, Westbeth, New York City, May 28, 2014.

38 "like a lit lamp": Patton, *The Bhagavad Gita*, 75.

39 "not only a dancer": TS, *Pioneer and Prophet*, 1: 52.

39 "that has scarcely": Carol Hyman, "UC Berkeley's Greek Theatre Turns 100 Years Old This Month," press release, September 11, 2003, http://www.berkeley.edu/news/media /releases/2003/09/11_greek.shtml.

39 "tall athletic forms": Franklin, *Étant Donné*, 172–73.

39 For *Egypt*: JRDD, Dance Clipping File, *MGZB, "*EARLY PERFORMANCES OF MARTHA GRAHAM* . . . taken from clippings in the Denishawn scrapbooks"; "Ted gave me my first chance," MG, interview by Don McDonagh, October 19, 1968, part 1, JRDD, *MGZTL 4-2556.

39 The pharaoh: TS, *Pioneer and Prophet*, 1: 71–74; Dreier, *Shawn: The Dancer*, 78.

40 "a promising young reader": Personals, *Santa Barbara Morning Press*, October 1, 1916.

40 the Peppers: Myrick, *Montecito and Santa Barbara*, 1:179, 230–31; Myrick, *Montecito and Santa Barbara*, 2:439; Kendall, *Where She Danced*, 162.

40 "the artistic feature": Roy Regester to author, November 6, 2013.

40 Following graduation: Promotional brochure written by TS [ca. 1918], box 192, Jacob's Pillow Archive, TSC; Kendall, *Where She Danced*, 164.

41 "in a tweedy suit and toque": Lloyd, *The Borzoi Book of Modern Dance*, 33.

41 "perfectly-proportioned": Stodelle, "Steel and Velvet."

41 "there was no such thing": Doris Humphrey lecture, Juilliard School of Music, New York City, November 7, 1956, JRDD, *MGZTL 4-2267.

41 As a child: Humphrey, *The Art of Making Dances*, 9.

42 "music visualizations": Cohen, *Doris Humphrey*, 36; Sherman, *Drama of Denishawn Dance*, 47. See also *Variety*, May 16, 1919, for reference to Denishawn as the "dancing university."

42 "artist pupil": TS, "Biographical Sketch," 6.

42 "came to life": TS, *Reminiscences*, disc 10, JRDD; Stodelle, *Deep Song*, 26, 269n.

42 It would be another: Martha Graham Music Collection, box 194, folder 11; Sherman, *Drama of Denishawn Dance*, 23–24.

42 During the week: TS, *Reminiscences*, disc 10, JRDD.

43 "Ted found": Shelton, *Divine Dancer*, 156–57; TS, *One Thousand and One Night Stands*, 72.

4: HORST

44 "Better twenty minutes": "Rare Artistic Triumph Seen at Empire—Denishawn Dancers Scale New Heights," *Saskatoon Daily Star*, January 5, 1920.

44 Based upon: Synopsis of *Julnar the Sea-Born and Her Son King Badr Basim of Persia*, http://www.wollamshram.ca/1001/Vol_7/tale153.htm.

44 The sumptuous spectacle: TS, *One Thousand and One Night Stands*, 91–92.

45 "express[ing] the finer": St. Denis quoted in eight-page typescript compilation by TS of critics' comments, Jan.–Dec. 1920, pp. 2-a, 3-a, 6-a, box 192, Jacob's Pillow, TSC.

45 In Gotham: "Motion Picture Notes," *New York Times*, January 2, 1921; Melnick, *American Showman*, 81–180; Singer, "Vaudeville in Los Angeles," 103–13.

45 Roxy and his: Melnick, *American Showman*, 181, 183.

46 "the story of": "War as Rupert Hughes Sees It—A Novel That Deals with a Little-Known Phase of the Great Conflict," *New York Times Book Review*, May 18, 1919.

46 Roxy told Shawn: TS, *Reminiscences*, disc 10, JRDD; see also TS, interview by Don McDonagh, November 3, 1967, disc 2, JRDD, *MGZTL 4-2532: "She did do the Rothafel job."

46 Martha Graham's performance: January 4, 1920, *Los Angeles Times* advertisement.

46 "atmospheric prelude": "Drama" review, *Los Angeles Times*, January 5, 1920, courtesy of Ross Melnick to author.

46 "La Danse du Feu": Sommer, "Loie Fuller's Art," 395; Sperling, "Loïe Fuller (1862–1928)."

46 Whatever magic: Charles Weidman, who joined the Denishawn dancers in summer 1920, told Don McDonagh in a conversation on June 29, 1971, that "Roxy was very fond of Martha in those days." JRDD, *MGZTL 4-2534.

46 *When the Clouds Roll By*: Weidman also agreed with Shawn's assessment of MG. In a December 7, 1966, interview, CW told Marian Horosko that his first impression of "Martha . . . [was that she] had tremendous *fire* and a freer style."

46 "pure cultures": TS, interview by Don McDonagh, November 3, 1967, disc 2, JRDD, *MGZTL 4-2532.

46 "the special preparatory": Ouspensky, *Tertium Organum*, chap. 21, 215, 217–18.

46 "The literal reproduction": Murphy, *The People Have Never Stopped Dancing*, 111.

47 "with her gift": Kendall, *Where She Danced*, 168; Delpar, *The Enormous Vogue of Things Mexican*, 8–10.

47 "the vogue of things Mexican": Sherman, "The American Indian Imagery," 369.

47 With the desire: Homer Grunn to TS, April 1, 1924, box 192, Jacob's Pillow, TSC; De Huff and Grunn, *From Desert & Pueblo*, introductory note.

47 "champion Indian dance": Murphy, *The People Have Never Stopped Dancing*, 111–12.

47 "strong, close-to-the-ground": TS in Tacoma, Washington, *Ledger*, September 12, 1920.

47 "An authority on": Kendall, *Where She Danced*, 167.

47 For sets: Terry, *Frontiers of Dance*, 35.

47 "We talk about": Delpar, *Enormous Vogue*, 130.

47 The curtain rises: Sherman, *Drama of Denishawn Dance*, 59–63; mise-en-scène from Dreier, *Shawn: The Dancer*, 71.

47 Tending to the plants: TS, interview by Don McDonagh, November 3, 1967, disc 2, JRDD, *MGZTL 4-2532; *Martha Graham in Xochitl*, [dated 1919], 1920, White Studio photograph, Library of Congress, MGC.

48 "consists of flat-footed": Sherman, *Drama of Denishawn Dance*, 59–63.

49 "impressive stateliness": Sherman, *Drama of Denishawn Dance*, 62–64.

49 "a Charles Ray character": Lloyd, *The Borzoi Book of Modern Dance*, 34.

49 "just a skinny": Charles Weidman, interview by Marian Horosko, December 7, 1966, JRDD, *MGZTL 4-901, disc no. 3; "à terre": Weidman, interview by Don McDonagh, June 29, 1971, JRDD, *MGZTL 4-2535.

49 *Xochitl* headed: "Martha Graham in Vaudeville," Dance Collection Danse, 2006,

http://www.dcd.ca/exhibitions/vancouver/graham.html; TS, *Record of Professional Life of Ted Shawn*, p. 2, Jacob's Pillow, TSC, "Xochitl—1920."

49 "simply has intuitions": Salpeter, "Martha Graham," 63.

50 "Since that evening": TS compendium of press clips from Tacoma and Santa Barbara newspapers: September 12, October 2, and October 26, 1920, pp. 1-a, 2-a, box 192, Jacob's Pillow, TSC.

50 Basking in the financial: TS, *Record of Professional Life of Ted Shawn*, 1921, p. 2, TSC; Schlundt, *Professional Appearances*, 38–39.

50 In Shawn's *Church*: TS, *Autobiographical Sketch*, 7–8, Jacob's Pillow Collection; Ellis, "The Philosophy of Dancing."

50 she accompanied: Terry, *Frontiers of Dance*, 103–4; Sherman, *Drama of Denishawn Dance*, 64–66.

50 Graham made her debut: Kisselgoff, review of an evening of re-creations of "Denishawn/Graham Solos"; Jane Sherman, typescript notes for "Serenata Morisca," [February] 1986, personal collection of Terese Capucilli.

51 During the rape scene: "She beat me and cut my lip! She really *fought!*" TS, interview by Don McDonagh, September 7, 1971, JRDD.

52 "a quality of": *Omaha World-Herald*, October 25, 1921.

52 On the train: Stodelle, *Deep Song*, 36; "That's when all the things started with Martha and me," LH, interview by Jeanette Schlottmann Roosevelt, "recorded between 1959 and December 1960," JRDD, *MGZTC 3-2261; Shelton, *Divine Dancer*, 157.

52 "even Martha needed": Charles Weidman, interview by Don McDonagh, June 29, 1971, JRDD.

52 "frustrations": Charles Weidman, interview by Marian Horosko, December 7, 1966, JRDD.

52 "He became my lover": Soares, *Louis Horst*, 33.

52 The University of Texas: Finding Aid, Texas Archival Resources Online, Genaro García Papers, Benson Latin American Collection, University of Texas at Austin, http://www .lib.utexas.edu/taro/utlac/00021/lac-00021.html.

52 "poring over these": TS, *Reminiscences*, disc 10, JRDD.

52 The encyclopedic collection: Delpar, *The Enormous Vogue of Things Mexican*, 8; "Old Building at Texas U. Will Be Razed," *San Antonio News*, August 13, 1936.

53 "a Mexican *Rigoletto* in dances": "Ted Shawn Gives Novelty," *New York Times*, December 3, 1921.

53 "the internationally-known": TS, *One Hundred and One Night Stands*, 101.

53 From the packed: Charles Weidman, interview by Don McDonagh, June 29, 1971, JRDD; Schlundt, *Professional Appearances*, 40–53.

53 "smartest department stores": TS, *Reminiscences*, January 29, 1969, disc 11, JRDD.

53 "guilt-ridden": Soares, *Louis Horst*, 36.

54 "unmarried": TS, *Reminiscences*, disc 11, JRDD.

54 "The Dance of the Apsarases": Sherman, *Drama of Denishawn Dance*, 76–77.

54 Watching from: Charles Weidman, interview by Marian Horosko, December 7, 1966, JRDD.

54 "The one man": TS, *One Thousand and One Night Stands*, 106.

54 "to touch the garment": TS, *Reminiscences*, discs 11 and 12, JRDD.

55 "mature man": Terry, *Ted Shawn*, 107.

55 "there seem": Havelock Ellis to TS, "30 May/22," box 192, Jacob's Pillow Archives, TSC.

55 *The Intermediate Sex*: Shawn said in *Reminiscences*, NYPL disc 12, that Carpenter was "the finest theorist of homosexuality that I have ever read in my life."

55 Traveling in America: Tóibín, "Urning," 14–16; "Selected Extracts from *Towards Democracy*," Edward Carpenter Archive, http://www.edwardcarpenter.net/ectd1.htm.

55 "it is my constant": Teck, *Making Music for Modern Dance*, 38.

55 Martha Graham's offstage: TS, *Reminiscences*, discs 11 and 12, JRDD; TS, interview by Don McDonagh, September 7, 1971, JRDD; Terry, *Ted Shawn*, 106, 111.

56 During a weeklong: LH, interview by Jeanette Schlottman Roosevelt, 1959–1960, cassettes 2 and 3, JRDD.

56 They saw a collection: "Tanagra Figurines," Heilbrunn Timeline of Art History, Metropolitan Museum of Art, October 2004, https://www.metmuseum.org/toah/hd/tafg/hd_tafg.htm.

56 The statuettes: Herbert, "Terracotta Figurines at Bowdoin College," 99.

5: SCHOPENHAUER AND NIETZSCHE

57 Between the publications: Schlaes, "The Myth of Gatsby's Suffering Middle Class."

57 The moment was: Malnig, "Athena Meets Venus," 38–51; see also MacLean, "Too Much Freedom in Modern Dancing? NO!," 34–35, 63–64.

57 This brainchild: "Macfadden Dead; Health Cultist, 87," *New York Times*, October 13, 1955.

57 As an outgrowth: *Dance Lovers Magazine*, JRDD, vol. 1, no. 1, November 1923.

57 "liberated": Malnig, "Athena Meets Venus," 51.

57 "uplifted . . . the general tone": "Dancing Masters Move for Uplift," *New York Times*, August 24, 1920.

58 "the frantic jazzers": "Conspiracy of Silence Against Jazz . . . Least Said Soonest Mended," *New York Times*, September 21, 1919. This article contains the first mention of "modern dance" in *New York Times*.

58 "I'm sick of seeing": O'Leary, "More Ado About the Flapper."

58 The chorus girl: Latham, "The Right to Bare," 459, 462, 468–71.

58 "dance into the limelight": Fitzgerald, "Echoes of the Jazz Age," 460–61.

58 "by 1923 . . . [when]": Jenkins, "Women of a Certain Era."

58 "the extreme adolescence": Horyn, "Channeling the Flapper Girl."

58 "with splintery pine": TS, Reminiscences, NYPL, JRDD, disc 12; *Denishawn Announcement of Courses for Summer, 1922*; Paris, *Louise Brooks*, 33–34.

58 Five feet two: Service, "The Wichita Wow," 20–21, 62; Moriarty, *The Chaperone*, 24, 105–12.

58 "cropped just below": Zeitz, *Flapper*, 249.

59 "high-spirited wisp": Paris, *Louise Brooks*, 5, 22–31.

59 Since toddlerhood: Zeitz, *Flapper*, 248–50; Curtwright, "Raised in Wichita."

59 Ted Shawn was impressed: Thomas Gladysz, email to author, December 6, 2016; Terry, *Ted Shawn*, 109–11.

59 "Together, we saw": Service, "The Wichita Wow," 20–21, 62; Curtwright, "Raised in Wichita."

60 "very flirty in the hotels": Zeitz, *Flapper*, 251, quoting a fellow Denishawn dancer.

60 "That tour of the road": Service, "The Wichita Wow," 62.

60 The company: TS, *Reminiscences*, disc 12, JRDD.

60 "I identified": MG, *Blood Memory*, 79–81.

60 "learned to act": "Louise Brooks, 78, Rebel Star Who Didn't Shine in Hollywood," *Chicago Tribune*, August 10, 1985.

60 "compact, with her strong": Thomas Gladysz, quoting LB, email to author, December 6, 2016.

60 "expressive of": MG, notebook for *Dark Meadow*, 1946, p. 176.

60 "slipped one": Stodelle, *Deep Song*, 37.

60 Seven years later: Moriarty, *The Chaperone*, 56–57; photograph by Thomas Gladysz, Louise Brooks Society website, http://louisebrookssociety.blogspot.com/2012/06/louise -brooks-schopenhauer.html—Accessed June 20, 2012: "Rose Brooks [Louise's niece] shows off Louise Brooks' own well-worn copy of the essays of Schopenhauer."

60 "It was surprising": Roberts, "The Fervid Art of Martha Graham," 13, 63.

61 "*The world is my idea*": Schopenhauer, *Essays and Aphorisms*, 9–25, 31, 215–16.

61 Self-knowledge: Wicks, *Schopenhauer*, 57, 62.

61 She read: Schopenhauer, *Essays and Aphorisms*, 158–59, 164.

61 Citations from: Soares, *Louis Horst*, 33–34, 43, 81; de Mille, *Martha*, 439, entry 52.

61 In addition to: LaMothe, *Nietzsche's Dancers*, 58, 59, 91, 93; LaMothe, emails to author, July 14–15, 2012.

62 "My style is": Ellis, "The Art of Dancing."

62 "If you work": MG, Juilliard Composers Forum, March 25, 1952, Juilliard JMedia Archive, http://jmedia.juilliard.edu/digital/collection/p16995coll3/id/10913/; "[Graham's] work patterns were shown in the rehearsal regime she followed herself and imposed on others . . . We never had a holiday—Christmas day, maybe," Robert Cohan, "Reminiscences and Reflections at Eighty," n.p.

62 "*physiological* influence": Dolson, "The Influence of Schopenhauer," 241–46; Nietzsche, *Schopenhauer as Educator*, 1–16.

63 It was written in 1870–1871: Soares, *Louis Horst*, 126; Graham's readings aloud from Nietzsche corroborated by Horst's studio assistant, Nina Fonaroff, video interview with Janet Eilber, London, January 3, 2001.

63 In this symphonic book: LaMothe, *Nietzsche's Dancers*, 24–26.

63 "the first great culture": Michael Tanner, introduction to Nietzsche, *Beyond Good and Evil*, 9.

63 "floating . . . [upon]": Nietzsche, *Birth of Tragedy*, 38.

6: KANDINSKY AND ISADORA DUNCAN

64 "Sometimes . . . there is": Fitzgerald, "Echoes of the Jazz Age," 465.

64 Ruth St. Denis, with: Schlundt, *Professional Appearances*, 41; TS, *One Thousand and One Night Stands*, 116–17.

64 Graham quit the company: Martha Graham's name is nowhere to be found in Humphrey's *Autobiography*.

64 The tour program: Jordan, "Ted Shawn's Music Visualizations," 33–34.

64 "frothy as": Sherman, *Drama of Denishawn Dance*, 78–79.

65 After Pottsville: TS, *One Thousand and One Night Stands*, 122.

65 Barely settled: *Exhibition of Paintings from the Collection of the Late Arthur Jerome*

Eddy from September 19 to October 22, 1922, ex. cat. courtesy Marie Kroeger, Ryerson Archives, Art Institute of Chicago, to author, July 5, 2012. Eddy, the lawyer, pioneer art collector, and Chicago native, born 1859, died in New York City in the summer of 1920.

65   "One of our stops": MG, *Blood Memory,* 98.

65   "'I will make'": MG, *Blood Memory,* 98. MG made a series of tapes in 1971 that eventually fed into the text of this 1991 memoir. See Phillips, "Martha Graham's Gilded Cage," 71; Kisselgoff, "Martha Graham Dies at 96"; Marie Kroeger, email to author, July 5, 2012: "[The Eddy collection] is the only exhibition at the AIC [Art Institute of Chicago] which contained works by Kandinsky (ex. cat. #26–45) in the early 1920s. The Art Institute did not own any Kandinsky works until much later."

65   One of twenty: *Improvisation No.30*—Röthel, Kandinsky, and Benjamin, *Kandinsky, Catalogue Raisonné of the Oil-Paintings,* vol. 1, 1900–1915, n.p.

66   "(This was not painted": Eddy, exhibition catalogue, Art Institute of Chicago, 1922.

66   The note paraphrased: Eddy, *Cubists and Post-Impressionism,* 124–26.

67   "infusing painting": Jill Lloyd, curator, *Vasily Kandinsky: From Blaue Reiter to the Bauhaus, 1910–1925,* Neue Galerie, New York, October 3, 2013–February 10, 2014.

67   "Dancing is a little": MG, "The Medium of Dance," lecture, March 15, 1952, JRDD, *MGZTL 4-2594.

67   "vital forces": M. Johnson, *The Body in the Mind,* 83.

67   "The designation": Kandinsky, Lindsay, and Vergo, *Complete Writings,* 402–3.

67   "The truth": Ibid., 404–5.

67   "not purely illustrative": *Klänge,* in Kandinsky, Lindsay, and Vergo, *Complete Writings,* 291–92, 298–99: "He initially conceived of the album *Sounds* as a 'musical' publication . . . He also uses frequent repetition to divorce words from their meaning."

68   "[T]he juxtaposition": Kandinsky, Lindsay, and Vergo, *Complete Writings,* 193–94.

69   "There is no dancing": E. Moore, "St. Denis and Isadora Duncan Will Dance Here This Week."

69   "stylistic and gorgeous": Rosenfeld, "Ruth St. Denis and Ted Shawn Appear in Group of Dances."

69   "plastic possibilities": E. Moore, "Denishawns Give Needed Touch to American Dancing."

69   "[F]or the complete": Hackett, "Ruth St. Denis and Dancers at Orchestra Hall."

69   "customary unrigid": E. Moore, "St. Denis and Isadora Duncan."

69   "no longer a young": H. T. Parker, *Motion Arrested,* 66–73, excerpts from his *Boston Evening Transcript* reviews, October 21 and 23, 1922, "Sculptural Isadora," and "Isadora Incontinent."

70   "philistine": Joan Acocella, introduction to Duncan, *My Life,* xv.

70   "never saw Isadora": MG, interview by Don McDonagh, October 19, 1968, JRDD, *MGZTL 4-2566.

70   expatriate in Nice: See Nancy Chalfa Ruyter, *Reformers and Visionaries,* p.33: "[Duncan] performed in the United States only occasionally throughout her life: between 1895 and 1899, at the beginning of her career; and in short visits in 1908, 1911, 1915, 1916, 1917, and 1922."

70   Graham did recall: Lloyd, *The Borzoi Book of Modern Dance,* 48–49.

70   "the famous barefoot": Mason Opera House playbills, Special Collections and Archives, University of California, Irvine. According to his *Professional Career Chronology,* Horst was in Los Angeles from January 8 to 16, 1918, but he does not mention Duncan.

70 "as an isolated phenomenon": Stodelle, *Deep Song*, 41.

70 "didn't particularly like": LH, interview by Jeanette Schlottman Roosevelt, 1959–1960, cassette 3, JRDD, *MGZTC 3-2261.

71 "had learned": Kendall, *Where She Danced*, 175.

71 "[a]fter [Duncan]": Acocella, introduction to Duncan, *My Life*, xvii.

71 "Isadora Duncan may": Eilber, "Shape Shapes Meaning," 2.

71 "the greatest individual": MG, "Platform for the American Dance."

71 "talented loners": R. Smith, "Native Talents, Shrugging at Europe."

71 "It is so intensely": MG, interview by Don McDonagh, October 19, 1968, JRDD.

71 Duncan began: Preston, *Modernism's Mythic Pose*, 165.

71 "ravished my being": Star, "What Friedrich Nietzsche Did to America," 3.

71 "sacred home": LaMothe, *Nietzsche's Dancers*, 121.

71 Graham, going: Janet Eilber, email to author, December 16, 2014.

71 "First come": Sparshott, *Off the Ground*, 76.

72 "hard and disciplined": Salpeter, "Martha Graham," 62.

72 "an enemy": Duncan, *My Life*, 164.

72 "multiple one-ness": Preston, *Modernism's Mythic Pose*, 167. On the distinctions between central and distal initiation of motion, see Moore and Yamamoto, *Beyond Words*, 138–39; and Hart-Johnson, "On Structure in Martha Graham Technique," 196, on MG's need to emancipate herself from the "ballet box."

72 "Strangely enough": MG, "Seeking an American Art of the Dance," 249.

72 "emulative struggle": Grafton, Most, and Settis, *The Classical Tradition*, 472.

72 "conspicuously-accomplished and gifted": *Baltimore News*, January 21, 1923.

72 "gifts second only": *Raleigh News & Observer*, February 21, 1923.

72 "the most interesting": *St. Paul Pioneer Press*, March 19, 1923.

72 "jewel in its setting": TS, *Reminiscences*, January 29–30, 1969, disc 12, JRDD, *MGZTL 4-69.

72 "With tigerlike strides": Sherman, *Drama of Denishawn Dance*, 24, and her typescript "Serenata Morisca" notes for Terese Capucilli, [February] 1986; MG Video Archives, Martha Graham Resources, No. 1326; and Capucilli's *SM* performance at Teatro Municipale, Reggio Emilia, Italy, July 1986, JRDD, *MGZIA 4-1236.

73 "Where have you": TS, *Reminiscences*, January 29–30, 1969, disc 12, JRDD.

73 "*Comme ça*": Sikov, *Dark Victory*, 26; JMA, *Out without My Rubbers*, 1–3; "Who Is John Murray Anderson?" *New York Times*, April 25, 1920.

73 Under the aegis: "Performance in Aid of French Fund," *New York Times*, May 14, 1917.

73 Anderson's moderne: Kendall, *Where She Danced*, 178–79.

73 "street artists and musicians": Hischak, *Off-Broadway Musicals Since 1919*, 4–7.

73 Over the next three years: JMA, *Out without My Rubbers*, 61–79.

74 With the funds willed: Sherman, "Martha and Doris in Denishawn," 187; MG, interview by Don McDonagh, October 19, 1968, JRDD: "I *had* to [join GVF]! To make money!"

74 "I *need* to take": TS, *Reminiscences*, January 29–30, 1969, disc 3, JRDD.

74 "would not seek": Madden, *You Call Me Louis*, 41.

74 "I can't quite realize": An emotional MG letter [ca. April 22, 1923, or later] discovered in the Jacob's Pillow TSC and published in Sherman and Owen, "Graham's Debt to Shawn," 42–43.

74 "the time had come": Terry, *Ted Shawn*, 113.

74 To keep limber: *"Mariarden": A Summer Night's Dream*, documentary produced by Andrea Melville (New Hampshire Public Television, 1991), item no. 204, Jacob's Pillow Moving Image Collection.

74 "[y]oga sitting": ca. 1990 on-screen *"Mariarden"* interview with Lucy Pettingill Currier Steinert, a student of MG in summer 1923.

74 "big fight": Soares, *Louis Horst*, 39–40; and TS's recorded responses to questions provided by Don McDonagh, September 7, 1971, JRDD, *MGZTL 4-2533.

75 "skits, travesties": Stodelle, *Deep Song*, 43.

76 "classy *poesie*": Kendall, *Where She Danced*, 178–79, 182.

76 "lavish serial entertainment": *New York Times*, September 21, 1923.

76 "took a flying leap": JMA, *Out without My Rubbers*, 81.

76 "pouted and purred": "A Tragic Fall from Grace," *Daily Mail*, November 12, 2006.

76 Brother and sister: JMA, *Out without My Rubbers*, 81.

76 "two [shows]-a-day": Cullen, *Vaudeville, Old & New*, 450.

77 "the art spot": McDonagh, *Martha Graham*, 41.

77 "panting under": MG to Nickolas Muray, sent while on tour with *Kama*, headed "Boston," n.d. [ca. 1924], microfilm reels 4392–93, Nickolas Muray Papers, AAA.

77 "divine dissatisfaction": de Mille, *Dance to the Piper*, 335.

77 "might as well still": MG, *Blood Memory*, 92.

77 The second (1923–1924): Schlundt, *Professional Appearances*, 45–53.

77 "all over the country": Madden, *You Call Me Louis*, 41. LH quotations in Madden are taken from "Audiotaped and transcribed interviews by Jeanette S[chlottman] Roosevelt, New York City," as per Madden, *Sources*, 165.

77 "Who Are America's Favorite Dancers?": *Dance Lovers Magazine*, August 1925.

78 "in every important city": Denishawn concert program, Town Hall, New York City, April 16, 1923.

78 "as a logical development": TS, *Denishawn Announcement of Courses for Summer 1925*.

78 "In going to the Orient": *Denishawn Magazine* 1, no. 4 (Summer 1925), n.p., Jacob's Pillow Archives, TSC—courtesy of Norton Owen.

78 "innate sense of tempo": LH interview, [May 16] 1958, JRDD, *MGZTC 3-2115.

78 "moderato, but": Madden, *You Call Me Louis*, 96.

78 "dance-playing": LH, "The Musician Comments," 7–8.

78 "accompanying of singers": Twenty-five years later, Horst reiterated that: "[T]o gain its independence, dance has to exist . . . as a primary art, [not] as a handmaiden [i.e., to music]"—LH, "1952," JRDD, *MGZTC-3 1239.

79 "trance-dances": Shelton, *Divine Dancer*, 182–83.

79 "These have been": LH, interview by Jeanette Schlottman Roosevelt, 1959–1960, cassette 3, JRDD, *MGZTC 3-2261; Soares, *Louis Horst*, 42–44; Fonaroff, "Louis Horst," 4.

7: THE EASTMAN SCHOOL

80 "I left [the Follies]": MG, *Blood Memory*, 103.

80 "It takes about": Remarks in acceptance of the Aspen Award on July 30, 1965, published in the *Saturday Review*, August 28, 1965. MG revisits this observation, first made in 1936, throughout her career; see, for example, Armitage, *Martha Graham*, 98.

80 Mamoulian had seen: LH, "Chronology of Professional Career," entries for 1923, JRDD, *MGYP-Res. (Horst)

80 Declaring his belief: "Eastman School to Add Dance Faculty—New Department to Open in Autumn Under Mamoulian," *D&C*, July 4, 1925.

80 "the supremacy": RM, *Rochester Times Union*, November 28, 1923.

81 "the adaptation": "A Broader Education," editorial, *D&C*, July 6, 1925.

81 "Pupils will": *D&C*, July 25, 1925.

81 "these twin arts": *D&C*, July 25, 1925.

81 "intelligent and exciting!": RM, interview by Don McDonagh, February 4, 1972, JRDD, *MGZTL 4-2560.

81 In July: "John M. Anderson to Build Theatre—His Park Avenue in East 58th Street Building to House also Robert Milton School of Theatre," *New York Times*, July 8, 1925.

81 "a dilapidated collection": JMA, *Out without My Rubbers*, 105–7.

82 "from every form": Anderson-Milton School advertisement, *Dance Magazine*, September 1925.

82 "character and interpretative": JMA, *Out without My Rubbers*, 105–7.

82 "Miss Martha Graham, formerly": "Eastman School of Dance Acquires [*sic*] Martha Graham," *D&C*, August 2, 1925.

82 "[t]he word 'ballet' ": Lenti, *For the Enrichment of Community Life*, 142.

82 "the motion pictures": "No such films have survived at the Eastman School of Music." David P. Coppen (special collections librarian and archivist, Sibley Music Library, Eastman School of Music), email to author, June 21, 2014.

82 "acting": Horgan, "The Start of a Career."

82 "to recognize anew": Lenti, *For the Enrichment of Community Life*, 143.

83 "revive the ideal": "Eastman School of Dance Revives Ideal of Greeks," *D&C*, July 25, 1925.

83 As she crossed: Lloyd, *The Borzoi Book of Modern Dance*, 49–50.

83 "that glory [she]": MG, recalling her early days at the Eastman School, to Don McDonagh, October 19, 1968, JRDD, *MGZTL 4-2566.

83 "exquisite": MG autographed letter signed (ALS) to Stewart Sabin, September 25, 1926, LOC, MGC, ML95.G785. For "the unity of Venus unfolded in the trinity of the Graces," I am grateful to Wind, *Pagan Mysteries in the Renaissance*, 192.

83 "the floor work": Horosko, *Martha Graham*, 7–8.

83 "The first day Martha": Tracy, *Goddess*, 3–5.

84 Thelma Biracree: Thelma Biracree, interview by Don McDonagh, August 15, 1972, JRDD, *MGZTL 4-2544. For an analysis of Graham's stillness, spiraling, and floor work, see Lepczyk, "Martha Graham's Movement Invention," 48, 50, 52.

85 In Vienna: LH interview, 1952, cassettes 1 and 2, JRDD, *MGZTC 3-1239.

85 "a pull he": LH interview, 1958, cassette 1, JRDD, *MGZTC 3-2115.

85 "linear . . . undulations": LH interview, 1958, cassette 1, JRDD, *MGZTC 3-2115.

85 "germinal *idea*": LH interview, 1952, JRDD, *MGZTC 3-1239.

85 "a perfect blending": Pease, "Louis Horst," 83.

85 Nor did Professor Stöhr's: Kempny, *Das Mädchen*, n.p.

86 "dry and pedagogical": Soares, *Louis Horst*, 47.

86 The explosion of: Ibid., 46–51; Madden, *You Call Me Louis*, 44–48.

86 "peak years": G. Jackson, "Dance and the City," 465.

86   He attended: LH, "Chronology of Professional Career," entries for 1925, JRDD.

86   Aimless and depressed: "Harvest Dirge, Vienna, August 2, 1925," JPB 83-60, series 1, item f. 68, LHCM.

86   "I *had* to have that contact": LH interview, 1958, cassette 1, JRDD, *MGZTC 3-2115.

86   her "fortress": Madden, *You Call Me Louis*, 52.

86   Louis Horst, the bibliophile: "Louis brought back pictures of Wigman and Palucca from Vienna . . . We never saw them dance, but we saw the pictures," Gertrude Schurr (MG's student at Anderson-Milton School in fall 1925), interview by Agnes de Mille, January 24, 1984, cassette 1, JRDD, *MGZTC 3-1637; Madden, *You Call Me Louis*, 51.

87   After a flirtation: Newhall, *Mary Wigman*, 7–33; Spector, *Rhythm and Life*, 116–21.

87   "admirable tenacity": Wigman, "Rudolf von Laban on His Birthday," 90–91; Bradley, *Rudolf Laban*, 9–20.

87   "hard, bitter and hungry": Kendall, *Where She Danced*, 202.

87   In the pages of Rudolf: Delius, *Mary Wigman*, photographic plates 13, 19, 22, 27, and 36.

87   "acknowledging the pull": M. Odom, "Mary Wigman," 82, 87, 92.

88   "The shape of the": Sorell, *Mary Wigman Book*, 81–86.

88   "Among my first students": Jack Anderson, "Who Was Gret Palucca?"

88   "Gret Palucca . . . seemed": Sorell, *Mary Wigman Book*, 65.

88   Wigman was dark: Funkenstein, "Engendering Abstraction," 389–92.

88   "merry confusion": Jack Anderson, "Who Was Gret Palucca?"

88   "easy mingling": Funkenstein, "Engendering Abstraction," 389–92.

88   In *Painting, Photography, Film*: Kuhlmann, *Charlotte Rudolph*, 9, 86, and photographic plates dated 1924–25.

88   "Complete mastery": Kandinsky, Lindsay, and Vergo, *Complete Writings*, 519–32, 558, 619. Although Kandinsky's essay and subsequent book were published in 1926, according to Kuhlmann's chronology of Rudolph's professional career, she began photographing Palucca in June 1924; Rudolph's photographs for "Dance Curves" and Kandinsky's accompanying drawings are dated 1925. See Kuhlmann, *Charlotte Rudolph*, 86; and Funkenstein, "Engendering Abstraction," 395–400.

89   "would work up": Madden, *You Call Me Louis*, 52.

89   "Complete every": Helpern, *Technique of Martha Graham*, 9. Helpern notes that "Eastman dancers remember key phrases from Graham's classes."

89   "Gradually, I was able": Lloyd, *The Borzoi Book of Modern Dance*, 49–50.

89   "period of searching": Kendall, *Where She Danced*, 209.

89   In his teens: John Simon Guggenheim Memorial Foundation website of Fellowship winners (1930), https://web.archive.org/web/20060219192017/http://www.gf.org/30fellow.html.

89   "very early in": Teck, *Music for the Dance*, 30–32.

90   "the term *Gebrauchsmusik*": Ibid., 28.

90   To liven up: Horgan, *A Certain Climate*, 217–18; Otto Leuning Papers, box 81, folder 2, Music Division, NYPL.

90   "improve the visual": RM, interview by Don McDonagh, February 4, 1972, JRDD, *MGZTL 4-2560.

90   "an indication of": "New Dance Offering on Eastman Program Wins Strong Praise," *D&C*, October 26, 1925.

90   Two weeks later: Thelma Biracree, interview by Don McDonagh, August 15, 1972, JRDD, *MGZTL 4-2544.

91   "sole arranger": Lenti, *For the Enrichment of Community Life*, 145.

91   "are robed in": *D&C*, "Debussy in Dance," January 16, 1926.

91   "I feel so strongly": Schippers, *Reflections of John Joseph Martin*, 102.

91   "That was the start": Madden, *You Call Me Louis*, 53.

91   Al Jones and: McDonagh, *Martha Graham*, 48.

91   "the audience hankering": Frances Steloff, interview by Don McDonagh, January 24, 1973, JRDD, *MGZTL 4-2564.

92   "Oriental teachings": Steloff interview, January 24, 1973; Mitgang, "Frances Steloff Is Dead at 101."

92   "the concert was a great": K. Morgan, "Frances Steloff and the Gotham Book Mart," 762.

92   "I went down to Orchard": MG, interview by Don McDonagh, October 19, 1968, JRDD, *MGZTL 4-2566.

92   Graham sat on the floor: Debra Otte to author, March 3, 2015.

92   "spring musings": "The Gossip Shop," *Bookman* 63, no. 4 (June 1926): 512. See also Betty Macdonald, in Tracy, *Goddess*, 7: "Martha always did our costumes. She pinned them on us, and we had to sew them together."

92   "large and distinguished": McDonagh, *Martha Graham*, 50; "New York Hails Martha Graham as Fine Dancer—Metropolitan Audience Also Applauds Eastman School Pupils," *D&C*, April 20, 1926.

93   "many aristocrats": "The Blessed Damozel Comes Down from Rochester," *Dance Magazine*, July 1926.

93   The Kinneys: "New York Hails Martha Graham," *D&C*, April 20, 1926.

93   "the future history of the art": Troy and Kinney, *The Dance*, 358.

93   "three soft childish": "The Blessed Damozel," *Dance Magazine*, July 1926.

93   "curving . . . sculptural": Jowitt, "A Conversation with Bessie Schonberg," 39.

95   "made eloquent": "Dance Artists in Program of Varied Appeal—Martha Graham of Eastman School and Assistants Warmly Applauded," *D&C*, May 29, 1926.

95   "You know my intense": Delage, "Ravel and Chabrier," 546.

95   "Harvest Dirge": Alfred Kreymborg, "Harvest Dirge," in *Poetry: A Magazine of Verse, 1912–22*, ed. Harriet Monroe (New York: Bartleby.com, 2011), http://www.bartleby.com /300/956.html.

95   The second song, "Toys": Arthur Symons, "Toys," http://www.poemhunter.com/poem /toys-13/.

95   "*Du bout de la pensée*": Preston, *Modernism's Mythic Pose*, 86; Erik Satie, *Le Site du Compositeur*, http://www.erik-satie.com/tag/gnossienne/.

95   Horst and Graham had: "Music Visualization: Excerpts," *Gnossienne* choreography by TS, danced by Ralph Farrington, performed November 6, 1976, videocassette, 5 min., JRDD, *MGZIC 9-355.

95   The story of *Gnossiennes*: Grafton, Most, and Settis, *The Classical Tradition*, 503–4.

95   The dances were in tribute: Scully, *The Earth, the Temple, and the Gods*, 9–12. See Cristensen, Hammer, and Warburton, *The Handbook of Religions*, 109–13, for iconography of the Great Goddess, Pótnia.

96   In "Frieze": Fitton, "Three Mycenaean Terracottas," 24–25.

96 "prized for their naturalness": "Greek Art: Fourth Century B.C.," guide to Gallery 158, Metropolitan Museum of Art, http://www.metmuseum.org/collections/galleries/greek -and-roman/158.

96 "a series of statue-poses . . . handful of dirt": Preston, "Posing Modernism," 224.

96 "abstraction and essence": Kisselgoff, "Martha Graham Offers World Premiere."

96 "in which she stood": Selden, *The Dancer's Quest*, 93.

96 The loosely hanging: MG, outdoor performance, undated silent film, Martha Graham Resources, *MGDC_0196; see also "Solos," videorecording, 20 min., for Takako Asakawa's restaging of MG's solo during the Terzo Festival del Balletto at the Teatro Municipale, Reggio Emilia, Italy, July 1986, JRDD, *MGZIA 4-1236.

96 The fan was inspired: "New Museum Wing to Open Tomorrow," *New York Times*, April 4, 1926.

96 "a girl in a blue": Richter, "New Accessions in the Classical Department," 80–82.

97 already rich collection: Richter, "Miscellaneous Accessions in the Classical Department," 284. I am grateful to Sarah Szeliga, assistant visual resources manager in the Onassis Library for Hellenic and Roman Art, the Metropolitan Museum of Art, for drawing my attention to these important essays by Gisela Richter.

97 "of heavy gold cloth": *Dance Magazine*, August 1926.

97 "lovely draped batik": "The Blessed Damozel," *Dance Magazine*, July 1926.

97 "fey-like girls": [Fashion Editor], *Bookman*, June 1926, 512.

97 "so frolicsome": "The Blessed Damozel," *Dance Magazine*, July 1926.

97 "a series of pictures": "New York Hails Martha Graham as Fine Dancer," *D&C*, April 20, 1926.

97 "It is my hope": "The Leading Question—'Why Is a Fat Lady?' Martha Graham, Premier Danseuse, Gives the Answer," *New York Telegram*, April 19, 1926.

98 "[T]he groupings": MG describing her vision for the film to Lydia Barton, in *Stage & Screen,* February 1926, "The Flute of Krishna (Ballet Choreographed by Martha Graham)," http://lcweb2.loc.gov/diglib/ihas/loc.natlib.ihas.200182444/default.html.

98 According to the Hindu: Scott Simmon, *Note* for *The Flute of Krishna* in *Treasures of American Film Archives: 50 Preserved Films*, 299; Shapiro, "Martha Graham at the Eastman School."

98 "The Denishawn influence": Helpern, *Technique of Martha Graham*, 9–10.

98 "Rochester has seen": "Dance Artists in Program of Varied Appeal—Martha Graham of Eastman School and Assistants Warmly Applauded," *D&C*, May 29, 1926.

99 Graham's Queen: Alceste (Alkestis) would resurface in MG's oeuvre in the spring of 1960 with music by Vivian Fine; see *The Alcestis of Euripides*, Introductory Note, by Dudley Fitts, 143–45, *Four Greek Plays*, 1936.

99 "One cannot hope": Kemp, "Blessed Damozel of the Concert Stage."

99 Springtime at Eastman: Thelma Biracree, interview by Don McDonagh, August 15, 1972, part 2, JRDD, *MGZTL 4-2544; repertory checklist "compiled from Eastman Theatre Programs, 1925–1926," by professor John Mueller, University of Rochester, as addendum to Shapiro, "Martha Graham at the Eastman School."

99 Rouben Mamoulian resigned: "Rouben Mamoulian to Direct Here," *New York Times*, June 7, 1926; "Rouben Mamoulian, Broadway Director, Is Dead," *New York Times*, December 6, 1987.

99 "it was only a question": Horgan, *A Certain Climate*, 219–20.

99 On June 26, after *Ave Maria:* Lenti, *For the Enrichment of Community Life*, 147–49.
100 "turned, walked out": MG, *Blood Memory*, 108.

8: FROM MARIARDEN TO JOHN MARTIN

101 "It is a far cry from": M. Moore, *A Marianne Moore Reader*, 12–13.
101 "on a gray day": Gottlieb, *Reading Dance*, 47.
102 "a Roman candle": Unsigned review of *Terrible Honesty: Mongrel Manhattan in the 1920s*, by Ann Douglas, *Publishers Weekly*, January 2, 1995.
102 "the immediate excitement": B. Gage, review of *Supreme City.*
102 She would complain: On Graham's "self-criticism," see Bannerman, "Thoroughly Modern Martha," 32.
102 "a kind of 'inside' flu": ALS from MG to Evelyn Sabin, January 4 and June [n.d.] 1927, Carnegie Hall Archives.
102 "With modern art": LH citing MG to Ester E. Pease, LH interview, 1958, JRDD, *MGZTC 3-2115.
102 "nervous, sharp": Koritz, *Culture Makers*, 100.
102 "alluring stage set": Duvert, "Georgia O'Keeffe's *Radiator Building*," 2, 14; see also Williams, *Politics of Modernism*, 37–48. On the "ways [in which] urban areas and dance patterns affect each other," see Judith Lynne Hanna, "The Urban Ecosystem of Dance," in *To Dance Is Human*, 198.
102 Following a weekend: *Mariarden* concert program, August 20 and 21, 1926, box 308, MGC; Anderson-Milton School autumn 1926 semester announcement, *New York Times*, September 15, 1926.
103 "small, odd beauty": Sikov, *Dark Victory*, 26–29.
103 "It must be simple": Kemp, "Blessed Damozel of the Concert Stage."
103 "was all tension": Bette Davis was a student of Martha Graham at the Anderson-Milton School from October 24, 1927, to January 31, 1928.
103 To help pay: Background history of the Carnegie Hall Studios, and itemized roster of representative tenants from 1926 onward, provided to author by Rob Hudson and Kathleen Sabogal, Carnegie Hall Archives, August 7 and 29, 2013.
104 Louis Horst found: "Carnegie Hall's Music Colony Stays," *New York Times*, February 8, 1925.
104 The advertisement: MG's ad in the *New York Times*, October 17, 1926, and landlord's typescript "List of Vacancies/Season 1926–1927," provided to author by Rob Hudson and Kathleen Sabogal, Carnegie Hall Archives.
104 "who have to work": Roberts, "The Fervid Art of Martha Graham."
104 Floor work: Soares, *Louis Horst*, 63, 217n22.
104 "friendly and informal": Kemp, "Blessed Damozel of the Concert Stage."
105 "she made one think": Ibid. Janet Eilber (artistic director, Martha Graham Center of Contemporary Dance), email to author, August 2, 2013, notes: "I'm sure her ease at sitting in that position—her natural open hips and low center of gravity (short legs, long torso)—added to her development of the sitting floor exercises that are the basis of her technique!"
105 "I don't want to do": Kemp, "Blessed Damozel of the Concert Stage."

105 Familiar themes: Program for "Dance Recital by Martha Graham with Louis Horst, piano, Klaw Theatre, West 45th Street, Sunday evening, November 28 [1926] at 8:30 o'clock," Martha Graham Collection, LOC.

105 "looked like a Botticelli painting": Tracy, *Goddess*, 8.

105 "her marvelous": Robert Bell, "Echoes of the New York Stage."

105 A new offering: "Martha Graham Dances," *New York Times*, November 29, 1926, in an unbylined article of one perfunctory paragraph, refers to "an evening of interpretative dances to prevailingly modern music."

105 "fervent lamentation": Straus, "World Premiere of 'Baal Shem' by Bloch in Orchestral Transcription Is Heard": "Originally the suite, which was written twenty years ago, was composed for violin with piano support."

105 "spontaneity is not": Kemp, "Blessed Damozel of the Concert Stage."

106 "It is the Jewish soul": Bloch, *Ernest Bloch*, 61.

106 "Geordie": Kisselgoff, "Geordie Graham, 88, a Dancer with Denishawn Company, Dies."

106 Another voice: Program for "Guild Theatre, West 42nd Street, Sunday evening, February 27th [1927], Martha Graham," MGC.

106 "as a cow yields": Ralph T. H. Griffith, trans., Hymn XCII, "Dawn," in *The Rig Veda*, 1896, http://www.sacred-texts.com/hin/rigveda/rv01092.htm.

106 "In measure while": Symons, "Javanese Dancers," 148.

107 "instant conversion": McPherson, *Contributions of Martha Hill*, 17–23.

107 "pruned her teaching": Coleman, "Martha Graham Still Leaps Forward." Hill and Schonberg danced with Graham from 1919 to 1931.

107 "[S]he is one": Bell, "Echoes of the New York Stage."

107 "Several months ago": Editorial, "American Art and Foreign Fetishes," *Dance Magazine*, June 1927; "St. Mark's Church Gives Dance Ritual for Isadora Duncan," *New York Times*, October 17, 1927.

108 "young American composer": Duncan, *My Life*, 339–43.

108 "the theatre of": Isaacs, "The Great World Theatre," 565–70.

109 "emphasis on dance": Conner, *Spreading the Gospel of Modern Dance*, 88–90.

109 "flaunting the word": Gilder, *Theatre Arts Anthology*, xiii.

109 "a forum": R. Miller, "George Beiswanger and Dance Criticism," 50.

109 "effective and very": "In Modern Art the Form's the Thing," unsigned review of *A Primer of Modern Art* by Sheldon Cheney, *New York Times*, May 4, 1924.

109 "The rhythm of mere": Cheney, *A Primer of Modern Art*, 56.

109 "modern art is more": LH refers to *A Primer on Modern Art* as one of the several "books that influenced Martha and me." It remained in print until 1958. LH interview, 1952, cassettes 2 and 3, JRDD, *MGZTC 3-1239.

109 After *A Primer of Modern Art*: Edith J. R. Isaacs Papers, Wisconsin Center for Film and Theater Research; Sidney M. Shalett, "Theatre Arts through the Years," *New York Times*, January 19, 1941.

110 "range of taste": Gilder, *Theatre Arts Anthology*, xvi.

110 "spiritual mother": Lewis Myer Isaacs (son of Lewis Montefiore Isaacs and Edith Isaacs), interview by Agnes de Mille, 198-?, JRDD, *MGZTC 3-1624.

110 "outraged . . . as if possessed": GS, interview by Agnes de Mille, recorded May 25, 198-?, cassette 2, JRDD, *MGZTC 3-1637.

110 "finding essences": Schippers, *Reflections of John Joseph Martin*, 105.

110 At the Little Theatre: Arthur Honegger, *Sept Pièces pour Piano*, Paris: Les Editions de la Sirène, 1921, series 2, item f. 91, LHCM, JPB 83-60.

110 "to [the] mad music": *Dance Magazine*, December 1927; program for "Martha Graham assisted by Louis Horst at the Piano, the Little Theatre, New York, Sunday evening, October 16th, 1927," MGC.

111 Born in Bridgeport: Introduction to Lucile Marsh Papers, JRDD, *MGZMD 210; Conner, *Spreading the Gospel of Modern Dance*, 97–98.

111 "Martha Graham needs": Lucile Marsh, *New York World*, October 16 and 17, 1927.

111 At the *Herald Tribune*: Conner, *Spreading the Gospel of Modern Dance*, 100.

111 "I had to judge": Mary Watkins Cushing, interview by Walter Terry, August 10, 1974, JRDD, *MGZTL 4-816.

111 What she "really thought": MW review of MG concert at the Little Theatre, *New York Herald Tribune*, October 17, 1927.

112 " 'got' more and more": Dunning, "Critic's Notebook."

113 Martin was born: Schippers, *Reflections of John Joseph Martin*, 1–70; Conner, *Spreading the Gospel of Modern Dance*, 98–99; Morris, "Modernism's Role in the Theory of John Martin and Edwin Denby," 169–70.

113 He studied classics: Charles Weidman, interview by Don McDonagh, June 28, 1971, disc 2, JRDD, *MGZTL 4-2534.

113 "degraded by having": Mott, *A History of American Magazines, 1865–1885*, 198.

113 "Well, fifteen dollars": Schippers, *Reflections of John Joseph Martin*, 60.

113 He perceived her: Excerpts from JM articles in the *New York Times*, February 13, February 19, March 18, and April 23, 1928.

114 "As new waves": Beiswanger, *Three Essays in Dance Aesthetics*, 12.

114 "[T]he passion of": "The Dance: One Artist—Martha Graham's Unique Gift and Steady Development," March 10, 1929.

9: NEIGHBORHOOD PLAYHOUSE

115 The Denishawn Company: Schlundt, *Professional Appearances*, 54–61.

115 "The minute they": Pease, "Louis Horst," 21.

115 "The Shawns": Cohen, *Doris Humphrey*, 73.

115 "soul-wrecking": Charles Weidman, interview by Don McDonagh, June 29, 1971, JRDD, *MGZTL 4-2535.

115 "a hot-house flower": Cohen, *Doris Humphrey*, 73.

115 "it's just wonderful": "Denishawn Dancer on Leave," *Variety*, October 2, 1927.

115 "tired of darling": Cohen, *Doris Humphrey*, 73–75.

116 "Martyr Martha": King, *Transformations*, 51.

116 "The modern artist": V. Stewart, *Modern Dance*, 70.

116 "Doris feeling her": Shelton, *Divine Dancer*, 219–20.

116 Humphrey's dance program: "Dance Novelty Given by Doris Humphrey," *New York Times*, April 16, 1928.

116 "Through the wild": Siegel, *Days on Earth*, 65–69.

116 "The Banshee": Videotaped performance at the Sylvia and Danny Kaye Playhouse, New York City, May 28, 1993, with Rebecca Gotterer as The Banshee, JRDD, *MGZDIF 2780.

116 "rose from his stool": Cizmic, "Embodied Experimentalism and Henry Cowell's *The Banshee*," 452, 458n10.

117 "a shaft of light": Stodelle, "Steel and Velvet."

117 "the result of": LH, "Discussion of the Musical Selections of a Young Dancer."

117 "was the first original": Stodelle, *The First Frontier*, 12.

117 In other highlights: Redfield, review of *La Musique*, 136–37.

117 "handling a chiffon drapery": "Nickolas Muray Looks at the Dance: Martha Graham," *Dance Magazine*, July 1928.

117 "modernistic lyricism": Ibid.

117 Graham wearing a: MG sat for many clothed and unclothed portraits "professionally and just for the fun of it" by the Hungarian celebrity photographer Nickolas Muray, who admired her as an "inexhaustible creature . . . sweet, mobile, like an Indian goddess . . ." Nickolas Muray Papers, Archives of American Art, microfilm reels 4392–93.

117 "new vigor and animation": "Final Graham Recital: Dancer's Program Last Night Proves Most Interesting of All," *New York Times*, April 23, 1928; provenance for *Immigrant*, series 2, items f. 245 and f. 246, JPB 83-60, LHC.

117 "Bavarian wood carvings": "Nickolas Muray Looks at the Dance: Martha Graham," *Dance Magazine*, July 1928.

117 "one felt the surgings": "Martha Graham Dance Program Wins Applause—New Numbers Are Warmly Received by Eager Crowd at the Little Theatre," *New York Herald Tribune*, April 23, 1928.

117 "she looked": Charles Weidman, interview by Don McDonagh, June 29, 1971, JRDD, *MGZTL 4-2534. One thinks of precedents: Alfred Stieglitz's 1907 photograph *Steerage*; and Sergei Eisenstein's 1925 *Strike*, his self-described "first proletarian film . . . in revolutionary form."

118 Two excerpts: Leo Ornstein citations, biography, discography, and *Poems of 1917* audio files on website by his son, Severo, and grandson, David, http://www.poonhill.com/.

118 The score: Crane's poem "The Dance" was first published in the *Dial Magazine*, New York City, 1927; Crane, *Complete Poems & Selected Letters*, 751.

118 "repercussive ferocity": "Modern Music Given" [recital by Leo Ornstein of *Poems of 1917* at Steinway Hall], *New York Times*, March 17, 1930.

118 "nunlike figure": "Martha Graham Dance Program Wins Applause," *New York Herald Tribune*, April 23, 1928.

118 "[her] open mouth": de Mille, *Martha*, 88.

118 "I've had a year": Cohen, *Doris Humphrey*, 83.

118 "[The concert group]": "A Letter from Doris to a Prospective Member of the Group," October 31, 1929, http://www.dorishumphrey.org/a-letter-from-doris/; see also King, *Transformations*, 48–49.

118 "chanting passages": "Symphonic Festival," *New York Times*, April 1, 1928; "Plans of Musicians," *New York Times*, April 15, 1928.

119 The towering: Davidson, *Between Sittings*, 238: "I had never before designed any stage sets . . . I attended the first performance and it was thrilling to see the full-scale realization . . ."

119 "Martha and Charles": TS, *Reminiscences*, January 30, 1969, disc 12, JRDD, *MGZTL 4-69.

119 The serious: Danza, "The Neighborhood Playhouse," 13n14, cites the scholarship of

Linda J. Tomko and Melanie Neldo Blood on the tradition of American modern dance at the Neighborhood Playhouse.

119 The sisters followed: Crowley, *The Neighborhood Playhouse*, 4–5.

119 In 1907: "Festival Theatre for the East Side—Neighborhood Playhouse Soon to Open to Carry on Settlement Dramatic Work," *New York Times*, January 25, 1915.

119 "respond[ing] in a natural": Danza, "The Neighborhood Playhouse," 5–9.

119 Alice focused upon: "Organizational History" section, Neighborhood Playhouse scenarios, 1914–1934, JRDD, *MGZMD 104.

119 In 1920, Alice: "Endowed Theatre Is to Close Soon," *New York Times*, April 11, 1927.

119 Over the next half dozen years: Alice Lewisohn Crowley gift, ca. 1916–1931, Billy Rose Theatre Division, NYPL, *T-VIM 2010-056; "The Story of the Neighborhood Playhouse," *New York Times*, December 20, 1925.

120 "theme of the brotherhood": S. Young, "Forward and Backward," 316.

121 "its strange effect": Paul Rosenfeld, *Modern Music Magazine*, November–December 1940, 30.

121 By 1925, the Neighborhood: "The Story of the Neighborhood Playhouse," *New York Times*, December 20, 1925; Danza, "The Neighborhood Playhouse," 5, 6.

121 "spent in fulfillment": *Variety*, April 13, 1927; "Endowed Theatre Is to Close Soon," *New York Times*, April 11, 1927; C. Gray, "The Drama Queen of the Lower East Side."

121 "We found our lives": Lewisohn, "Essence of the Mohammedan East."

121 "wild dissonances": Peter Laki, "Ernest Bloch, *Israel* Symphony," written for the concert *Forged from Fire* performed May 30, 2014, at Carnegie Hall, http://americansymphony.org/ernest-bloch-israel-symphony/.

121 "the modern stage": JM, "The Dance as 'Theatre.'"

121 "these orchestral dramas": Crowley, *The Neighborhood Playhouse*, 240.

122 "gesture built on": Irene Lewisohn, "Drama and the Unseen Currents," *Progressive Education Quarterly*, n.p., New York, January 1931.

122 "an extremely busy": JM, "The Dance: A New Synthesis."

122 "third [annual] experiment": Atkinson, "Dance and Music in Dramatic Form."

122 "all-but-forgotten": Kisselgoff, "All-But-Forgotten Pioneer."

122 "oval-faced": O. Holmes, ed., *Motion Arrested*, 258.

122 In 1928, Ito: "The Dance: A Much-Heralded Artist," *New York Times*, November 4, 1928.

122 The eldest: Carruthers, "Translation of Fifteen Pages," 32–33; Cowell, "History of Michio Ito," 1; Prevots, *Dancing in the Sun*, 179.

123 "did I see total art": K. Porter, "As an Oriental Looks at Art"; Prevots, *Dancing in the Sun*, 179–80.

123 "five miles out": Carruthers, "Translation of Fifteen Pages," 33: "I remember Margaret [*sic*] Wigman, who later became famous as the producer of *Neuer Tanz*, was also in my class . . ."

123 "a nest of artists": Carruthers, "Translation of Fifteen Pages," 36.

123 "at a time when": Ashton, *Noguchi: East and West*, 24.

123 "pining for hieroglyphs": Fenollosa and Pound, *The Chinese Written Character*, 2–3, 11–14.

124 "perfect and lonely": Longenbach, "The Odd Couple—Pound and Yeats Together."

124 "power of Noh": Fleischer, *Embodied Texts*, 180.

124　"I am very fond": Pound, *Selected Letters*, 63.

124　"My play is made": Yeats, *Essays and Introductions*, 224.

124　" 'Please help me' ": Carruthers, "Translation of Fifteen Pages," 39.

124　"resemble, but": Cowell and Shimazaki, "East and West in the Work of Michio Ito," 13.

124　"Use no superfluous": "A Few Don'ts [*sic*] by an Imagiste," *Poetry Magazine*, March 1913.

124　"renovated poetry": Lavery, "Ernest Fenollosa," 132.

125　"as though walking": Koner, *Solitary Song*, 27. Koner danced with Ito in the 1920s.

125　"Mr. Itow's genius": Yeats, *Essays and Introductions*, 224, 236.

125　"no studied lighting": Ibid.

125　"half-Greek": Carruthers, "Translation of Fifteen Pages," 35. For the genesis of the play, see Schmitt, "Intimations of Immortality," 501–10.

126　Ito accepted: K. Porter, "As an Oriental Looks at Art," 35, 61.

126　After a few variety shows: "Japanese Drama Admirably Staged," *New York Times*, November 14, 1916; Kisselgoff, "All-But-Forgotten Pioneer"; "Japanese Seen in Greenwich Village in 'At the Hawk's Well,' " *New York Times*, July 11, 1918.

126　"short, abrupt motions": Parker, "Roshanara and Ito."

126　"Every one has his own": "Michio Itow's [*sic*] School" brochure, p. 2, courtesy Bonnie Oda Homsey (Michio Ito Foundation), by gift of David Pacun.

126　"to develop in my": K. Porter, "As an Oriental Looks at Art," 62.

126　"I am a sculptor": M. Gray, "Eastern Art Spiritual, Western Art Material."

126　"kata, or set forms": Cowell and Shimazaki, "East and West in the Work of Michio Ito," 14.

126　"these . . . were more expressive": Caldwell, *Michio Ito*, 29.

127　"gratifyingly lack[ing]": Kisselgoff, "Dance: Michio Ito Salute."

127　"always said the Oriental body": Chin, "Japanese Dancers in America."

127　"playground scupper": Crowley, *The Neighborhood Playhouse*, 245–46; "Rita Morgenthau, Social Worker, 84," *New York Times*, April 9, 1964.

127　"Colloquial subjects": LH interview, 1952, cassettes 2 and 3, JRDD, *MGZTC 3-1239.

127　"The moderns go to": LH and Russell, *Modern Dance Forms*, 52.

128　"when almost all": LH interview, 1952, cassette 3, JRDD, *MGZTC 3-1239.

128　"reflecting the life": Sears, "Louis Horst," 79–82; Dain, *The New York Public Library*, 265.

128　"miniature etudes": LH, *Pre-Classic Dance Forms*, v–vii and chapters 1–8.

128　"[and] the uneven rhythms": LH and Russell, *Modern Dance Forms*, 44.

128　"Any great art": Kemp, "Blessed Damozel of the Concert Stage," 19.

128　"[w]e were seated": GS, interview by Theresa Bowers, June 13 and June 30, 1978, JRDD, *MGZMT 5-697.

128　"short, stocky": Sears, "Louis Horst," 80.

128　"Martha was an actress": GS, interview by Agnes de Mille, June 27, [198-?], cassette 3, JRDD, *MGZTC 3-1637.

129　"could see that": GS, interview by Theresa Bowers, June 13 and June 30, 1978, JRDD, *MGZMT 5-697.

129　"Nobody could": GS, interview by Don McDonagh, December 8, 1972, disc 2, JRDD, *MGZTL 4-2542.

129　"re-educating the body": GS to her Master Class at University of Arizona, April 1988, quoting MG, ca. 1929–1930, videotape courtesy Nancy Lushington.

129 "[h]er pliés": GS, interview by Don McDonagh, December 8, 1972, disc 2, JRDD, *MGZTL 4-2542.

129 "let the whole breath out": GS, interview by Agnes de Mille, June 27, [198-?], cassette 3, JRDD, *MGZTC 3-1637.

130 "I never went": Coleman, "Martha Graham Still Leaps Forward."

130 "every table of": LaMothe, *Nietzsche's Dancers*, 8, 78–79.

131 "credo was": Jowitt, "A Conversation with Bessie Schonberg," 41.

131 "seek[ing] for beauty": [*Martha Graham*], by Mary F. Watkins, *Dance Magazine*, April 1929.

131 "arresting, even aggressive": Kendall, *Where She Danced*, 206.

131 "as if she dared": Stodelle, *Deep Song*, 51.

131 "reek[ing] with": JM, *America Dancing*, 193.

131 "lyrical calm": JM, "Martha Graham's Recital."

131 "wore her hair": de Mille, *Martha*, 88.

131 "or the monkish": [*Martha Graham*], by Mary F. Watkins, *Dance Magazine,* May 1929.

131 "childishly frank": JM, "Martha Graham's Recital."

131 "[with] pathos": [*Martha Graham]*, by Mary F. Watkins, *Dance Magazine*, May 1929.

131 "[t]he interesting question": JM, "The Dance: One Artist."

10: *HERETIC*

132 Martha Graham exhibited: Program for "Martha Graham Assisted by Dance Group— Louis Horst—Pianist," April 14, 1929, box 308, folder no. 27, Library of Congress, MGC.

133 "Couched exclusively": JM, "Recital a Triumph for Martha Graham."

133 "[T]inged with": *"Au Pardon de Rumengol,"* by Jacques Tchamkerten, *Grove Music Online*, article 48883.

133 "Fantasia Apocalypta": "Fantasia Apocalypta," by Albrecht Riethmüller; see *Grove Music Online,* article 23279; and Hermann Reutter, Composer Brochure, Schott Music, www.schott-music.com, Mainz, accessed June, 2015.

133 "contain extraordinary": JM, "Recital a Triumph for Martha Graham."

133 "purported to project": [*Martha Graham, assisted by her Dance Group*], by Mary F. Watkins, *Dance Magazine*, July 1929.

134 "[O]ne moving figure": JM, *America Dancing*, 194.

134 "puckish": *New York Herald Tribune*, April 15, 1929.

134 This second section: "Yulian Krein and Huit Préludes," essay by Galina Grigor'yeva, *Grove Music Online*, article 53459; LHCM, Series 1, item f. 114.

134 "dividing line": GS, interview by Agnes de Mille, January 24, 1984, reel 1, JRDD, *MGZTC 3-1867.

134 It was arranged: "Thedore Botrel, Composer of 1,000 Songs," *New York Times*, January 11, 1922.

134 "Economy of instrumentation": LH, "Discussion of the Musical Selections of a Young Dancer."

134 "These ten measures": Ibid.

135 "the apt use": Kandinsky, *Concerning the Spiritual in Art*, 34.

135   The piece begins: *Heretic,* Fox Movietone News videorecording, 1931, JRDD, *MGZIC 9-1550; Kisselgoff, "Revival of Martha Graham's '*Heretic.*'"

135   "tight-knit semi-circle": McPherson, *Contributions of Martha Hill,* 24.

135   "querie[s] and argue[s]": Jowitt, "Martha Graham, 1894–1991," 2.

135   "in stiff-necked": [*Martha Graham*], by Mary F. Watkins, *Dance Magazine,* July 1929.

135   "stubborn thump": McDonagh, *Martha Graham,* 66.

135   "black phalanx": Selden, *The Dancer's Quest,* 93.

135   "the tiniest ripple": Dunning, "'*Heretic,*' Early Work of Martha Graham."

136   kinesthetic empathy: See Beiswanger, "Doing and Viewing Dances," in *Three Essays in Dance Aesthetics,* 12, 13n9. Beiswanger candidly confesses to "physical discomfort" when first seeing Martha Graham perform, because he had to emancipate himself from the "perceptual insistence . . . that dance movement *rise from* rather than *dig into* the floor" (italics mine). On concision in modern poetry, see Donald Hall, *Marianne Moore: The Cage and the Animal* (New York: Pegasus, 1970).

136   "in a state": Schippers, *Reflections of John Joseph Martin,* 197.

136   "There is no beauty": LH interview, 1952, JRDD, *MGZTC 3-1239.

136   "I felt at the time": MG, *Blood Memory,* 114.

136   In archaic Greek: *The Oxford Dictionary of the Christian Church,* 3rd ed. (2009), s.v. "heretic."

136   "like a rider": Lampert, *Nietzsche's Task,* 217.

137   "to be a heretic": Arlen Shelley, "'For love of an idea': Jane Ellen Harrison, Heretic and Humanist," *Women's History Review,* 5:2, p.171.

137   "the fleeting": L. Sante, "In Baudelaire's Dream Brothel," *New York Review of Books,* March 21, 2013, 22.

137   "any 'modernity'": Prettejohn, *The Modernity of Ancient Sculpture,* 176–77.

137   "the age-old tragedy": Selden, *The Dancer's Quest,* 93, 94.

137   Composer Dane Rudhyar: "Dane Rudhyar," by Carol J. Oja, *Grove Music Online,* article 24082.

137   "the second act": Rudhyar, "The Birth of the American Dance Ritual."

137   "Tone . . . a living entity": Oja, "Dane Rudhyar's Vision of American Dissonance," 131–37.

138   "Martha Graham is": Rudhyar, "The Birth of the American Dance Ritual."

11: DANCE REPERTORY THEATRE AND *LAMENTATION*

139   "mutual independence": JM, "The Dance: A Unique Theatre Project."

139   "theatrically outrageous": Jack Anderson, "A Champion of Racial Justice."

139   "swept across": JM, "The Dance: Tamiris' Art."

139   "What more can I learn": McPherson, "Helen Tamiris," 1.

140   "she presented": "Tamiris in 'Dance Moods,'" *New York Times,* October 10, 1927.

140   "evenly-flowing": JM, "Tamiris, Dancer, Scores," *New York Times,* January 30, 1928.

140   "[t]he dance of today": Foulkes, *Modern Bodies,* 14–16.

141   "vivacious": King, *Transformations,* 52.

141   "the tail": LH interview, 1958, JRDD, *MGZTC 3-2115.

141   "their lonely": King, *Transformations,* 52.

141   "uniting so that": JM, "The Dance: A Unique Theatre Project."

141 "In spite of": Cohen, *Doris Humphrey*, 90.

141 Maxine Elliott's Theatre: JM, "The Dance: A Week of Unique Programs."

141 "In these dances": Manning, *Modern Dance, Negro Dance*, 2.

141 Huge arcs: Dr. Thais Barry (former Tamiris dancer), in conversation with the author, Montclair State University Dance Studio, and 92nd Street Y, New York City, January–May 2010.

141 "Cheers of enthusiasm": JM, "New Dance Theatre Scores a Success."

142 "(with its frank": JM, "Tamiris in Dance Recital," January 11, 1930.

142 "Nature moves": Main, *Directing the Dance Legacy of Doris Humphrey*, 55.

142 "that I think the ensemble": Conner, *Spreading the Gospel of Modern Dance*, 92.

142 In contrast: "Water Study," reconstructed by Silvana Cardell and William Robinson, Georgian Court University Dance Department, with score consultant Peter Bertini, video, 8:24, October 28, 2011, https://vimeo.com/31275334.

142 "in the absence": Humphrey, *The Art of Making Dances*, 142.

142 "clear, transparent": Selden, *The Dancer's Quest*, 75–76.

143 "his own brand": King, *Transformations*, 54–55.

143 "(Chaplinesque": M. Gage, "A Study in American Modernism," 231.

143 Weidman presented: King, *Transformations*, 53. The Rudhyar Archival Project, http://khaldea.com/rudhyar/listofworks.shtml, describes the provenance of *Salutation*.

144 Her dignity: See 1956 lecture at Juilliard (she died two years later), JRDD, *MGZTL 4-2267, where Humphrey tells the students that "Collaboration is the key to success."

144 "Doris Humphrey and Charles": Parker, "New Ways of the Dance."

144 "behind the wings": Shelton, "Looking for Martha," 102.

144 Among them: McDonagh, *Martha Graham*, 314.

144 "the transcendent": JM, "New Dance Theatre Scores a Success."

144 "inevitable and indispensable": [*Martha Graham, assisted by her Dance Group*], by Mary F. Watkins, *Dance Magazine*, April 1930.

144 "that had [a] hysterical": Watkins, "Martha Graham Presents Repertory Dance Program."

144 "this dancer's tense": Ibid.

145 "a neurotic, grim": Ibid.

146 "a work designed": Mary F. Watkins, *Dance Magazine*, April 1930.

146 "sheer heaping up": Selden, *The Dancer's Quest*, 94.

146 "[w]hat I may add": Martha Graham's "program notes for *Harlequinade* in B. Morgan, *Sixteen Dances*, 14 (with facing-page photographs), 58–59.

146 "new slow movement": *The Uncovered Ruggles,* album notes–essay by pianist Donald Berman for his *Premiere recordings of unpublished sketches, transcriptions, and realizations*, New World Records, 80629-2, May 31, 2005.

146 "What are those": *Portals*, by W. Whitman, in *Leaves of Grass*, "Songs of Parting," 381.

146 Graham had seen the piece: Gaume, "Ruth Crawford," 79–80; Tick, *Ruth Crawford Seeger*, 112.

146 "ice cream and": Tick, *Ruth Crawford Seeger*, 112.

146 "[w]hen we got together": Soares, *Louis Horst*, 86.

147 "Miss Graham's first adventure": JM, "Martha Graham Gives Dance without Music."

147 "moved through the design": [*Martha Graham, assisted by her Dance Group*], by Mary F. Watkins, *Dance Magazine*, April 1930.

147 "Alas for my face": Euripides, *The Trojan Women*, 41–42.

147   *Lamentation,* Martha Graham's: *Lamentation,* a motion picture study of MG, produced by the Harmon Foundation with Simon and Herta Moselsio, filmed at Bennington College, 1943, videorecording, 10 min., JRDD, *MGZIA 4-5971.

147   "reared up": MG coaching Joyce Herring and Maxine Sherman in *Lamentation* [April–May 1986], Martha Graham Resources, cat. number MGDC 0860.

149   "not the sorrow": B. Morgan, *Sixteen Dances,* 14.

149   "[w]hen I [first]": Typed transcript by Mary Shaw of interview between MG and Mr. and Mrs. Simon Moselsio, September 8, 1942, 2:00–3:00 p.m., Bennington, VT, reel 141, Simon Moselsio Papers, AAA.

149   "We tend in real life": LH interview, 1952, reels 3 and 4, JRDD, *MGZTC 3-1239.

149   "And she mourned": de Mille, *Martha,* 90.

150   "[I was sitting] against": MG, *Blood Memory,* 122.

150   "*Contrition* was important": Armitage, *Martha Graham,* 113.

150   "Sculpture and the dance": MG, interview with Simon and Herta Moselsio, September 8, 1942, pp. 3–4, Simon Moselsio Papers.

150   "unattached to a man": Neumann, *The Origins and History of Consciousness,* 48–54, 84, 101.

150   embodies earth's spirit: Terra-cotta seated goddess at the Metropolitan Museum—[M. E. C.], unsigned article, "[Recent] Classical Accessions: VI. Greek Terracottas," *Metropolitan Museum of Art Bulletin* 17, no. 5 (May 1922): 113.

150   "Wellspring of": Burkert, *Ancient Mystery Cults,* 2.

151   "cry for all cries": See Alexiou, *The Ritual Lament,* 61, 112–13, 133–37. I am grateful to Casey Dué, introduction to *The Captive Woman's Lament in Greek Tragedy,* for her scholarship on the *ephebes,* and for directing me to Alexiou's work.

151   "Why does tragedy exist?": Euripides, *Grief Lessons* (Carson), 7, 94.

151   "accompanying herself": Loraux, *The Mourning Voice,* 12, 38–39.

151   "smouldering Ilium": Euripides, *The Trojan Women,* 42.

151   "suppliants, mothers": Aeschylus, *Seven Against Thebes,* 26.

151   However, in the world: Caraveli-Chaves, "Bridge between Worlds," 129–44.

151   "(delight in dancing)": "Terpsikhore," The Theoi Project, http://www.theoi.com /Ouranios/MousaTerpsikhore.html.

151   "lull her beloved": Alexiou, *The Ritual Lament,* 57; Steiner, *The Death of Tragedy,* 3.

152   "We forget what": Steiner, *The Death of Tragedy,* 3.

152   "indelible images": Terry, *Frontiers of Dance,* 76–77.

152   tonsillitis: Mellow, *Walker Evans,* 102–8, 583n.

152   "the only authentic": Mary F. Watkins, review of Dance Repertory Theatre, *The Dance Magazine,* April 1930.

152   "a new band of liberators": JM, *New York Times,* January 19, February 16, and June 1, 1930.

153   "What is 'modernism'": "Bennett School to Present Annual Drama Festival," *Millbrook Round Table,* May 7, 1937; Margaret Gage and Euripides, "Inventory of Photographs of Dance Productions," Bancroft Library, University of California at Berkeley, *BANC PIC 19xx.070—PIC; program for "Martha Graham and Dance Group at the Bennett School, March 29, 1930," box 309, folder 33, Library of Congress, MGC.

153   "'Modernism' in the American": M. Gage, "A Study in American Modernism."

12: INTRODUCING: ISAMU NOGUCHI

154 "I'm curious about": Interview with Isamu Noguchi by Paul Cummings at the artist's studio in Long Island City, New York, November 7–December 26, 1973, AAA.

154 Two bronzes of his friend: Coleman, *Isamu Noguchi Catalogue Raisonné*.

154 Sterner's gallery: The original Sterner Gallery ex. cat. says *fifteen* heads; Nancy Grove, in her National Portrait Gallery essay "What Is This Face?" says *seventeen* heads.

154 The works were mounted: Wolf, *On Becoming an Artist*, 53–55.

154 "He has illuminating": E. A. J., "Work by Six Japanese Artists," *New York Times*, February 9, 1930.

155 "poet of the Flowery Kingdom": Harrington, "America as a Fountain of Youth to the Japanese."

155 "girl that stepped": Marx, *Leonie Gilmour*, 248. For this and other details on Noguchi's early childhood and upbringing in Japan, and the beginnings of his career in America, I am indebted to Dr. Marx's scholarship.

155 At thirteen: Finding Aid Introduction, Rumely Manuscripts, Lilly Library Manuscript Collections, Indiana University, Bloomington.

156 At eighteen: Ashton, *Noguchi: East and West*, 12–15; Grove, *Isamu Noguchi Portrait Sculpture*, 2–3; Duus, *The Life of Isamu Noguchi*, 96–97, 103–5; Wolf, "Artistic Beginnings," 11–17; Levy, "Isamu Noguchi," 2.

156 "You have the real stuff": Duus, *The Life of Isamu Noguchi*, 104.

156 Wanting to make connections: "Most probably Noguchi sought out the dancer . . ." Ashton, *Noguchi: East and West*, 24; "He [Ito] had a studio in the John Murray Anderson building . . . and so did Martha Graham. I think I met Martha Graham there . . ." Noguchi, interview by Paul Cummings, 1973, AAA.

156 "evolving her new": Stodelle, *Deep Song*, 153.

156 "inception of modern dance": Noguchi, *A Sculptor's World*, 23. Ito, Noguchi, Ailes Gilmour, and Graham report *Rashomon*-like versions of how and when Noguchi and Graham met. I have chosen the most likely scenario.

157 "American dealer": Mann, "The Brouhaha," 6.

157 "Out of the limitations": Grove, *Isamu Noguchi Portrait Sculpture*, 6.

157 "Transfixed by": Schewender, "Following the Leader."

157 "The interpretation of the": Noguchi "Guggenheim Proposal" Narrative, Collection of the Archives of the Isamu Noguchi Foundation and Garden Museum.

157 "acquir[ing] proficiency": Wolf, *On Becoming an Artist*, 22.

158 The day following: Baldwin, *Man Ray*, 118.

158 "private jungle": Levy, "Isamu Noguchi," 3.

159 "every inch": Prettejohn, *The Modernity of Ancient Sculpture*, 211.

159 "hang around": Noguchi, interview by Paul Cummings, 1973, AAA.

159 "communication was through": Schewender, "Following the Leader."

159 "dress and finish marble": Wolf, *On Becoming an Artist*, 27.

159 "a different girl": Ibid., 38.

159 After several months: Noguchi, interview by Paul Cummings, 1973, AAA; see also Riddle, *The Paris Abstractions*.

159 "surpassingly good": Duus, *The Life of Isamu Noguchi*, 11–12.

159 "Making heads": Noguchi, interview by Paul Cummings, 1973, AAA; Noguchi, *A Sculptor's World*, 19.

160 "living scholarship": Horosko, *Martha Graham*, 8–10; MG seminar at the Asia Society, May 19, 1988, JRDD, *MGZTL 4-1240.

161 Here were portrait heads: Grove and Botnick, *The Sculpture of Isamu Noguchi*, 8–13.

161 "too serious": MG, "From Collaboration, a Strange Beauty Emerged."

161 He was the Japanese American: Ashton, *Noguchi: East and West*, 16.

161 "We [artists] breathe": Noguchi, *A Sculptor's World*, 123.

161 Graham's recurrent inner: Ibid., 29.

161 "shape shapes meaning": Janet Eilber quoting MG in conversation with author, June 7, 2012.

161 "projections of the imagination": Noguchi, *A Sculptor's World*, 123.

161 When Marie Sterner's show: Coburn, "Water Colors and Sculptures Now Exhibited at Harvard Square Gallery."

162 On April 16, 1930: Duus, *The Life of Isamu Noguchi*, 129.

162 "Tell Martha": Noguchi to Ailes Gilmour, December 28, 1930, Archives of the Isamu Noguchi Foundation and Garden Museum.

13: LEAGUE OF COMPOSERS AND *THE RITE OF SPRING* IN AMERICA

163 "The centre": McBride, "American Expatriates in Paris."

163 finding new expression: This chapter is an expanded version of a talk presented by the author, "Defining Modern Dance: Martha Graham and *The Rite of Spring* in America," at the Society of Dance History Scholars' *Le Sacre at 100* Conference, York College, Toronto, April 20, 2013.

163 "The day of the unknown": Metzer, "The League of Composers," 45–46.

163 "by 'the musical youngsters'": Bauer and Reis, "Twenty-Five Years," 1–2.

164 "enough energy": Daniel, *Stokowski*, 246.

164 In her teens: Oda, "Women Patrons and Crusaders," 244–49.

165 "that had been used": Reis, *Composers, Conductors, and Critics*, 33.

165 "told the musical story": Bauer and Reis, "Twenty-Five Years," 6.

165 "unmitigated tonal asperity": Ibid., 1–4.

165 "that he was willing": Copland and Perlis, *Copland: 1900 through 1942*, 117–20.

166 "Some of us will": Downes, "Old and Modern Revolutionaries."

166 "this intensely-loyal": Copland, "Claire Reis," 386–88.

166 "I know all": Reis, *Composers, Conductors, and Critics*, 86–91; van den Toorn, *Stravinsky*, 82, 293–94; Daniel, *Stokowski*, 246–49; Downes, "Composers League in Unique Program."

167 "has [continued to make]": Daniel, *Stokowski*, 253.

167 Most hands-on: See van den Toorn, *Stravinsky and The Rite of Spring*, 44–56. A further-rewritten full-scale re-orchestration of the "Danse Sacrale" was published in 1943 when Stravinsky was living in Los Angeles; Nadia Boulanger assisted the composer.

167 revised first edition: R. Fink, "*The Rite of Spring* and the Forging of a Modernist Performing Style," 304–5, 318, and 358n2.

167 In an account: A. Ross, *The Rest Is Noise*, 97.

167 "vision . . . from": Daniel, *Stokowski*, 251–52, referencing Stravinsky's 1935–36 autobiography, *Chroniques de ma vie*.

167 "secret night games": Craft, "100 Years On," 2.

167 "metrical tug-of-war": van den Toorn and McGinness, *Stravinsky and the Russian Period*, 205.

168 "the earliest documentation": R. Fink, "*The Rite of Spring* and the Forging of a Modernist Performing Style," 334.

168 From the solitary opening: Taruskin, "Stravinsky and Us," 261.

168 "slashed the fabric": Grondines, "*The Rite of Spring*: Sacrificing Continuity," 1.

168 "Adolescents/Adolescentes": *Les adolescentes* is a feminine noun in French; "young girls" is a more accurate translation than "adolescents."

169 Despite his background: Doering, *The Great Orchestrator*, 4–8.

169 "Why, Mrs. Reis": Reis, *Composers, Conductors, and Critics*, 92–93.

169 "I am frankly": Typescript memorandum from Stokowski to Judson, dated September 23, 1929, in McCarthy, "1929 Philadelphia Orchestra Radio Broadcast of *The Rite of Spring*."

169 "The amazing thing": Review of the Philadelphia Orchestra's radio broadcast, *Musical Leader*, November 14, 1929, in McCarthy, "1929 Philadelphia Orchestra Radio Broadcast of *The Rite of Spring*."

170 Mrs. Reis's next move: Hodson, "Nijinsky's Choreographic Method," 7–15.

170 "Slavophil": Archer, "Nicholas Roerich and His Theatrical Designs," 5.

170 "(with each swing": Selivanova, *World of Roerich*, 26.

170 "the old *byliny*": Garafola, "The Enigma of Nicholas Roerich," 407.

170 "chooses a certain": Berman, "Painting in the Key of Color."

170 "the intensity": "Bonhams Offers Two Masterpieces of American Landscapes by Russian Painter in $14 Million Sale," *Art Daily*, November 20, 2011, http://www.artdaily .com.

170 The sacred dances: Berg, *Le sacre du printemps*, 82.

171 "to the creative efforts": Letter from Nicholas Roerich to Herbert Hoover, September 30, 1929, reference no. 203941, Nicholas Roerich Museum Archive.

171 "Great and young": Paelian, *Nicholas Roerich*, 47.

171 "to give the effect": Master Institute architect Harvey Wiley Corbett, interviewed in "West Side Hotel Has Art Museum," *New York Times*, September 15, 1929.

171 "confused but challenged": Reis, *Composers, Conductors, and Critics*, 96.

171 "eternal novelty": Paelian, *Nicholas Roerich*, 109.

171 In December 1920: Reis, *Composers, Conductors, and Critics*, 96–97.

172 "entertainment manufactory": John Martin, "The Dance: A Ballet Master Is Imported—Leonid Massine of the Diaghileff School Will Aid in Staging Presentations Here," *New York Times*, December 20, 1928.

172 "Ye Portals": Melnick, *American Showman*, 275–77.

172 "vaudevillian, razzle-dazzle": García-Márquez, *Massine: A Biography*, 174.

172 "asked [Massine]": Reis, *Composers, Conductors, and Critics*, 96–97.

173 "stupendous Danse Sacrale": Leopold Stokowski, "Producing Stravinsky's Ballet," *New York Times*, March 23, 1930.

173 "power to portray": Armitage, *Martha Graham*, 35.

173 "Graham is unique": Leopold Stokowski, in Armitage, *Martha Graham*, frontispiece.

173 "[i]t was Stokowski": Jowitt, "A Conversation with Bessie Schonberg," 52.

173 Stokowski told Massine: "Stokowski . . . imposed Graham on [Massine] in the title role." McDonagh, "Martha Graham: Fiction and Fact," 351.

173 Martha Graham was "the ideal choice": JM, "The Dance: Two Festivals."

174   "I was chosen": MG to Oliver Daniel, April 19, 1977, transcript, p. 5, Oliver Daniel Research Collection, Kislak Center, University of Pennsylvania Libraries.

174   "Recently returned": "Work on the Composers' Benefit," *New York Times*, February 9, 1930.

175   "a major drama": AS, *Style and Idea*, 104.

175   "gazes": A. Shawn, *Arnold Schoenberg's Journey*, 60–62, 68.

175   "We must be conscious": Auner, "Heart and Brain in Music," 118.

175   "independent progress": Ibid., 68; see AS, *Style and Idea*, 253–55: "The world of feelings is quite inseparable from the world of the intellect."

175   "a perfect gem": Schiff, "Schoenberg's Cool Eye for the Erotic."

175   "unrest or imbalance": AS, *The Musical Idea*, 62, 281; "Arnold Schoenberg (1874–1951): *Die glückliche Hand* (full)," the Simon Joly Chorus and the Philharmonia Orchestra, video, 21:16, July 17, 2013, https://www.youtube.com/watch?v=3zBirxta_iQ.

176   "can never perish": AS, *Style and Idea*, 123.

176   "nothing about the music": AS to Emil Hertzka [ca. September–October] 1913, in AS, *Sämtliche Werke*, 271.

176   "gestures, colors": AS, "Breslau Lecture," 106.

176   "It's not going to beat me": Reis, *Composers, Conductors, and Critics*, 95, 100.

176   "close friend ever since": Ibid.

176   "jutting forms": Biersdorfer, "Setting the Stage with Shadows."

176   "A good scene design": Macgowan, "Robert Edmond Jones," 137.

177   Philadelphia Grand Opera Company: On November 24, 1931, at the Metropolitan Opera House, Stokowski and Levin, Jones, and the Philadelphia Grand Opera Company rejoined forces to present the American premiere of *Wozzeck*, by Schoenberg's pupil Alban Berg, starring Ivan Ivantzoff in the title role.

177   MARTHA GRAHAM—headlined: King, *Transformations*, 58.

177   At Graham's insistence: *Choreocronicle*, compiled by Leighton Kerner and Andrew Wentink, addendum to McDonagh, *Martha Graham*, 312–14.

177   "when she did move": King, *Transformations*, 60.

177   "Miss *Grah*-ham": Jowitt, "A Conversation with Bessie Schonberg," 54.

177   "tug of war": Reis, *Composers, Conductors, and Critics*, 97.

178   "(I think the part": King, *Transformations*, 60.

178   "Did *Mr. Stokowski*": Soares, *Louis Horst*, 87.

178   "Oh, but I was angry . . . !": de Mille, *Dance to the Piper*, 152.

178   "You must dance": Reis, *Composers, Conductors, and Critics*, 98.

178   "eternal garment": Public lecture by Nicholas Roerich, with exhibition of his costumes, at the Wanamaker Auditorium, March 25, 1930.

178   "These are not costumes": Jane Pritchard, "Treasures from the *Sacre du Printemps*," lecture at Society of Dance History Scholars, *Le Sacre* at 100 Conference, Toronto, April 20, 2013.

178   Graham, the Fire Dancer: Roerich was not in New York City for the premiere of *The Rite of Spring*; he departed in early April for a research trip to the Western Himalayas.

178   "hissingly difficult": McDonagh, "Martha Graham: Fiction and Fact," 351.

178   "[a]s rehearsals progressed": Massine, *My Life in Ballet*, 178–79.

179   "I'm sorry to disappoint": García-Márquez, *Massine*, 211.

179   "watching carefully": Matthews, "China's Stage Idol Comes to Broadway."

179 "To have a body": Merleau-Ponty, *The Visible and the Invisible*, 189.

179 "lost in the crowd": Watkins, "The Dance's Part."

179 "almost onto the apron": Jowitt, "A Conversation with Bessie Schonberg," 54.

179 "a kind of pitched-forward": Berg, *Le sacre du printemps*, 85.

179 "opening up like a concertina": Norton, *Léonide Massine*, 87.

180 "couldn't take [her]": Jowitt, "A Conversation with Bessie Schonberg," 54.

180 Anna Sokolow believed: García-Márquez, *Massine*, 210.

180 "attitude and power": Lily Mehlman's reminiscences at the MG Seminar at the Asia Society, May 19, 1988, disc 3, JRDD, *MGZMT 4-1240.

181 "fully extended things": Jowitt, "A Conversation with Bessie Schonberg," 55.

181 Before the crowd: Downes, "Stokowski Gives Contrasting Music"; JM, "The Dance: A Novel Experiment"; Daniel, *Stokowski*, 257.

181 "theatre of synthesis": Samuel Chotzinoff, "Music," review of the April 22, 1930, *Rite of Spring* performance in New York City, *New York World*, April 23, 1930.

181 "dance of propitiation": Watkins, "The Dance's Part."

181 "mistress of the mentality": O. Holmes, *Motion Arrested*, 176.

181 "It was a performance": [John Martin], "Dancing by Massine Rich in Invention," *New York Times*, April 24, 1930.

181 "Somehow or another": Daniel, *Stokowski*, 257.

14: NORTHWEST TO SOUTHWEST

182 "Static in character": Concert program, June 2, 1930, *Martha Graham in Recital*.

182 "glove-silk shawl": Bell-Kanner, *Frontiers*, 17.

182 "The art [of dance]": Soares, *Louis Horst*, 88.

182 "of whom, it was": E. Armstrong, "Art of Martha Graham Evokes Great Ovation."

183 "every minute": Hays, "Dancer Wins Big Audience with New Art."

183 Raised in Spokane: Andrews and Caldbick, "Cornish College of the Arts."

183 "there were dressing": DB, *Bird's Eye View*, 15.

183 "little whirlwind": MG, "A Tribute [to Miss Cornish]," in Cornish, *Miss Aunt Nellie*, 270.

183 "historical, folk": Cornish, *Miss Aunt Nellie*, 205–6.

183 "called the dance students": Bell-Kanner, *Frontiers*, 10–11.

184 The poised, diminutive: In an interview with Walter Terry in 1973, when she was nearly eighty, MG told him she warned her dancers, "Don't come near me if you haven't washed your hair within the last day." MG, interview by Walter Terry, "The Early Years, 1973," JRDD, *MGZTL 4-807.

184 "I want you to": Anecdotal reminiscences from MG's summer 1930 classes at the Cornish School are drawn from these memories and reflections by Dorothy Bird, Graham's student, and a member of her company from 1930 to 1937: "Martha Graham's Early Technique and Dances: The 1930s," panel discussion moderated by Deborah Jowitt, October 1, 1994, in "Martha Graham," ed. Alice Helpern, special issue, *Choreography and Dance* 2 (1999): 7–13; DB, *Bird's Eye View*, 15–38, 47–57; MG Seminar at the Asia Society, May 19, 1988, disc 1, JRDD, *MGZMT 4-1240; Horosko, *Martha Graham*, 27–29, including DB's edited remarks from the Asia Society event; Dorothy Bird re-

creating Graham technique of the 1930s, assisted by dancer/demonstrator Sharon Neverson, videorecording, March 9, 1986, filmed at the Dickerson Arts Studio, New York City, JRDD, *MGZIA 4-4510, and color-corrected rendition, Collection of the Library of Congress Motion Picture, Television and Recorded Sound Division.

186   "What a pitiful sorrow": Dué, *The Captive Woman's Lament,* 1.

187   Hailing from Eleusis: R. P. Martin, *Myths of the Ancient Greeks,* 246–53.

187   "the wisdom-bringing": MG, *Notebooks,* 10.

187   "led by seven": Aeschylus, *Seven Against Thebes* (Hecht and Bacon), 3–15.

187   "he and Martha Graham": Cornish, *Miss Aunt Nellie,* 206–7.

187   "a semi-chorus of mourning": See Aeschylus, *Seven Against Thebes* (Hecht and Bacon), 20, 25.

187   "entr'acte/Dance Interludes": *Seven Against Thebes,* Concert Program, July 29, 30, 31, 1930, Cornish Theatre.

188   "down in the U.S.A.": DB, *Bird's Eye View,* 14.

189   "it dawned on": DB, *Bird's Eye View,* 96; "wayward child . . . second mother"—Joyce Greenberg, email and phone conversation with NB, May 24, 2020.

189   "depicted events": Haigh, *The Attic Theatre,* 284, 289.

189   "face-front face": DB, *Bird's Eye View,* 47–58. Eighteen-year-old Dorothy Bird's journal provides the only extant descriptions of Martha Graham's "Dance Interludes" for *Seven Against Thebes.*

189   *iakkhe*: Loraux, *The Mourning Voice,* 73.

190   "rose up high": DB, *Bird's Eye View,* 47–58.

190   "in a most uneven": Kitto, "The Greek Chorus," 2, 3. "I use the word 'dance,'" Kitto points out (p. 1.), "in the Greek sense, meaning any ordered physical movement."

190   "breathless . . . golden": MG letters to Mark Tobey from Santa Barbara, Thursday and Sunday, n.d. [August 1930], University of Washington Libraries.

190   "ultramodern": Sachs, *Henry Cowell,* 210.

191   He envisioned a thirteen-minute: Instrumentation for *Synchrony,* in William Lichtenwanger, *The Music of Henry Cowell: A Descriptive Catalogue,* item L.464.

191   To emphasize: *"Synchrony,"* Michael Tilson Thomas conducting the San Francisco Orchestra, video, 13:38, February 21, 2015, https://www.youtube.com/watch?v=LBlCQbAAk7g.

191   "musical values": Sachs, *Henry Cowell,* 211.

192   "Just as in a": L. E. Miller, "Henry Cowell and Modern Dance," 3 and 22n7.

192   Cowell completed *Synchrony*: Lichtenwanger, *Music of Henry Cowell,* item L.464; Cowell, *Synchrony* piano reduction, dated 1930, reproduced from holograph, JRDD, Music—*MYD-Amer.

192   "murky timbre": Judith Tick, concert program note, *American Modernism Seen and Heard,* Carnegie Hall, December 20, 1992.

192   There were no hard: L. E. Miller, "Henry Cowell and Modern Dance: The Genesis of Elastic Form," *Appendix A,* 20.

192   "sound-companion": Luening, "Henry Cowell, a Dancer's Musician," 10–11.

192   "We have lived upon": A. Ortiz, *HNAI,* 9:1. Grateful acknowledgment to Travis L. Suazo, former executive director, Indian Pueblo Cultural Center, Albuquerque, NM, for his review and critique of my descriptions of Martha Graham's sojourns at the Pueblos of the Southwest in the summers of 1930–1932.

192 From Santa Barbara: LH journal entry of their itinerary in Soares, *Louis Horst*, 89; Fred Eggan, "Pueblos: Introduction," in A. Ortiz, *HNAI*, 9:225, fig. 1.

192 "full-blooded": Murphy, *The People Have Never Stopped Dancing*, 111–16.

193 "white adobe houses": Adams, "How Native Dance Changed American Ballet," 15, 20.

193 "for two dancers": ALS, Homer Grunn to TS, April 1, 1924, box 192, Jacob's Pillow, TSC.

193 "the Indians of": TS, *The American Ballet*, 20.

193 religious duty: Kealiinohomoku, review of "Lessons from the Dancing Ground to the Studio," 33.

193 "[d]ancing and building": Ellis, *The Dance of Life*, chap. 2, "The Art of Dancing," p. 1.

193 "[m]ovement is, so to speak": Laban, *The Language of Movement*, 5; in Salter, *Entangled*, 373n8.

193 "where men and animals": Fergusson, *Dancing Gods*, 51.

194 "conform[s] to the": Anella, "Learning from the Pueblos," 35–36.

194 One of the warnings: *Please Follow These Rules of Etiquette When Visiting Our Pueblos* (Albuquerque, NM: Indian Pueblo Cultural Center), brochure courtesy Travis L. Suazo.

194 "Tribal communities do not": Ibid.; see also Evans and Evans, *American Indian Dance Steps*, 7, 8. "Some Pueblos prohibit photography at all times . . . Tribal dances are religious ceremonies. It is a privilege to witness a ceremony."—Indian Pueblo Cultural Center.

194 mantas: Valentina Litvinoff, comments to the editor, *Dance Research Journal* 7, no. 1 (1974–1975): 49.

194 "musically-accented": Littlebird, "Sacred Movement," 3–5, 9–10.

194 "clatter of": Sweet, *Dances of the Tewa Pueblo Indians*, 1.

194 "I observed that the": Jung, *Psychology of the Unconscious*, 1925 edition, part II, chap. 7. See *Collected Works*, vol. 5, paragraph 480.

194 "cleaving to earth": D. H. Lawrence, "The Dance of the Sprouting Corn," 453.

194 "seek, find": Sweet, *Dances of the Tewa Pueblo Indians*, 8, 10.

195 *okhua:* Ibid.

195 "a pale, uneven": D. H. Lawrence, "The Dance of the Sprouting Corn," 447.

195 Graham and Horst reached: John J. Bodine, "Taos Pueblo," in A. Ortiz, *HNAI*, 9: 266.

195 Across the plaza: Sweet, *Dances of the Tewa Pueblo Indians*, 7; Bodine, "Taos Pueblo," in A. Ortiz, *HNAI*, 9: 257, fig. 2.

196 "kept watch over": J. S. Smith, "Los Hermanos Penitentes," 70, 73.

196 "throughout the tumultuous": Eiselt, "*La Morada de Nuestra Señora de Guadalupe*," 1.

196 (alabados): Torrez, "Penitente Brotherhood in New Mexico."

196 *carreta del muerto*: Henderson, *Brothers of Light*, 43.

196 morada: J. S. Smith, "Los Hermanos Penitentes," 76–78; and JSS email to author, November 30, 2015.

196 "at the symbolic heart": J. S. Smith, "Penitente Moradas," 5–6.

197 *Las Tinieblas*: Torrez, "Penitente Brotherhood in New Mexico."

197 "reflects many": MG, typewritten program notes, *El Penitente*, Martha Graham Resources.

197 "I have never taken": Robertson, "Martha Graham Dances with the Future."

15: KNOW THE LAND

198 "So the answer": Sayler, *Revolt in the Arts*, 255.

198 "If there is in our country": Pagani, "Re-discovering Oliver M. Sayler," 4.

199 "the fierce white light": Brock, "Our Theatre, Past and Present." See also Anne Bogart, in conversation with Kristin Linklater, moderated by David Diamond, *American Theatre* magazine, January 2001, 105: "I think Martha Graham is the most important theatre person of the century . . . I play a game in my head sometimes: 'What would have happened if the Moscow Art Theatre never came to the U.S. in 1922 and '23?' I think, 'Maybe Martha Graham would have been our entire theatre!'"

199 "prodigious erudition": Brock, "The Battle of the Arts in the Machine Age."

199 "knows the theatre": JM, "The Dance: American Art."

199 "(frankly a magazine": *USA* 1, no. 1 (Spring 1930): 5.

199 "there is now a concerted": JM, "The Modern Dance in America," 48–49. On the birth and brief life of *USA*, see Payne, "Negotiating Photographic Modernism in *USA*," 1–6. The magazine ceased publication after three issues.

199 Sayler set the stage: Sayler, *Revolt in the Arts*, 91–96.

200 "Ted Shawn [had] beckoned": Ibid., 92.

200 "[w]e need never borrow": TS, *The American Ballet*, 26.

200 Martha Graham's affection: Kisselgoff, "'Dark Meadow': From Graham, via Jung, a Journey through an Erotic Landscape"; MG, "Seeking an American Art of the Dance," 249–55.

200 "cradling an art": MG, "Seeking an American Art of the Dance," 249.

200 "when a painting is finished": Dewey, *Art as Experience*, 111.

200 "gradually assuming": MG, "Seeking an American Art of the Dance," 250.

201 "[after] coming to Europe": Duncan, *The Art of the Dance*, 48.

201 "*in* this country": MG, "Seeking an American Art of the Dance," 250–52 (italics mine).

201 "To arrive at": Ibid., 253.

201 Graham cites just: Ibid., 254.

201 Toward the end: Ibid.; see also Ted Shawn, *The American Ballet*, 15: "The obvious themes which first come to mind when one thinks of American art production of any kind are the Indian and the Negro."

201 "spirit of place": MG, "Seeking an American Art of the Dance," 255.

202 "'Form!' was Louis Horst's": Stodelle, *The First Frontier*, 8.

202 After the Southwestern journey: LH, "Chronology of Professional Career," 1901–1962, JRDD, *MGYB-Res. (Horst)

202 "lessons based on": LH and Russell, *Modern Dance Forms*, 144.

203 "the pianistic saint": Soares, "Foreword," to Horst, *Pre-Classic Dance Forms*, vii.

203 The Modern Dance Forms: LH and Russell, *Modern Dance Forms*, 29–51; Pease, "Louis Horst," 130.

203 The next section: LH and Russell, *Modern Dance Forms*, 52–88.

203 "[w]e can never throw": LH interview, 1952, JRDD, *MGZTC 3-1239.

203 "[t]he surest way": Dalbotten, *To Bear Witness*, 68. See also Heinzelman, *Make It New*, 133.

204 "look elsewhere": Louppe, *Poetics of Contemporary Dance*, 166–67.

204 In the chapter: LH and Russell, *Modern Dance Forms*, 89–126; Pease, "Louis Horst," 131–32.

16: *PRIMITIVE MYSTERIES*

206 "The whole flowering": de Mille, *Dance to the Piper*, 145.

206 "spoiled egocentric": Ibid., 9.

206 Agnes and her younger sister: Ibid., chap. 1–11.

207 "character sketch": Ibid., 108.

207 One piece, "'49": "David Guion: 'Cowboy Composer,'" http://thompsonian.info /Guion-Prairie-Echoes-CD-liner-notes.pdf.

207 "satire of the": JM, *America Dancing*, 266; Edgar Degas, *The Little Fourteen-Year-Old Dancer*, 1922, bronze sculpture, The Met Breuer, New York, http://www.metmuseum .org/art/collection/search/196439; Vincent, "Edgar Degas (1834–1917)."

207 "the wax statuette": de Mille, *Dance to the Piper*, 108, 111.

207 "a young dancer fresh": Limón, *An Unfinished Memoir*, 32.

207 "dance-pantomimed": "Mozart Operetta Is Gayly Revived—Melodies Fresh as in 1775," *New York Times*, January 19, 1927.

207 "more or less familiar": [John Martin], "Two Dance Recitals," *New York Times*, January 23, 1928.

208 Another Ballets Russes émigré: de Mille to Ruth Page, July 23, 1927, Ruth Page Collection, 1918–1970, JRDD.

208 While the dance company: de Mille, *Dance to the Piper*, 123.

209 "Trying to reinforce": Ibid., 122–24.

209 Continuing his paternalism: Soares, *Louis Horst*, 245.

209 "natural gift for": Limón, *An Unfinished Memoir*, 17, 23.

209 "a picnic scene": King, *Transformations*, 83.

209 "the unresponsive swain": JM, *America Dancing*, 268.

209 "graphic portrait": JM, "Agnes de Mille Gives Fine Dance Program."

209 "a street kid from": Easton, *No Intermissions*, 74.

210 "with two ballet slippers": de Mille, *Dance to the Piper*, 132.

210 "light, undemanding": Siegel, "Modern Dance Before Bennington," 7.

210 "a comedienne": Barker, "Agnes de Mille," 113.

210 "an overdressed nouveau-riche": Easton, *No Intermissions*, 86. The Rontgen and Waldteufel scores are catalogued in LHCM, JPB 83-60.

210 "[B]y turns Amazon": Limón, *An Unfinished Memoir*, 32.

210 "her body rigid": Manning, *Modern Dance, Negro Dance*, 12.

210 "I am told that it": Chris Morrison, program notes, *Passacaglia for Piano*, https://www .allmusic.com/composition/passacaglia-for-piano-mc0002362661.

211 "this superb creature": Limón, *An Unfinished Memoir*, 31–32.

211 "Modern architecture": King, *Transformations*, 84, 87.

211 "pantherine grace": Owen, "José Limón."

212 "Mr. Weidman has broken": JM, "Weidman Makes Hit in a New Dance." See also Weir, *Decadence and the Making of Modernism*, 151–53.

212 "delectable": Lloyd, *The Borzoi Book of Modern Dance*, 90–91.

212   "who looked like a young goddess": "Letitia Ide, 84, Dies; A José Limón Dancer," *New York Times*, August 31, 1993.

212   "To watch": Lloyd, *The Borzoi Book of Modern Dance*, 90–91.

212   "Doris Humphrey is more impersonal": "The Birth of the American Dance-Ritual," *Carmelite*, July 31, 1929.

213   "leapt across the studio": Limón, *An Unfinished Memoir*, 16–17.

213   "notoriously unintellectual": Humphrey, *The Art of Making Dances*, 17–19.

213   "the [natural] life": Siegel, *Days on Earth*, 134.

213   "fall and recovery": Cohen, *Doris Humphrey*, 119.

213   Humphrey considered *Dances*: JM, "New Group Compositions by Doris Humphrey," *New York Times*, February 2, 1931.

213   "beat[ing] on exposed": King, *Transformations*, 83–84.

213   "solo of flowering": Limón, *An Unfinished Memoir*, 31.

213   "a tiny mincing": Lloyd, *The Borzoi Book of Modern Dance*, 93, 199.

213   Humphrey's other new work: Patterson, *The Shaker Spiritual*, introduction; see also Patterson, historical compilation of Shaker sources, http://www.folkstreams.net/context, 220.

214   "Come, life, Shaker life": Text and background, Alan Lomax Catalogue FSNA 37, http://www.folklorist.org/song/Come,_Life,_Shaker_Life; see also "Shaker Dancing," video, 13:22, July 26, 2016, https://www.youtube.com/watch?v=HydDrF7ALuM.

214   "Did we, as the 'original'": Stodelle, "Flesh and Spirit at War."

214   "sang in gift": Patterson, *The Shaker Spiritual*.

214   "Down the center": Stodelle, "Flesh and Spirit at War"; "American Dance Festival," *The Shakers* filmed at Connecticut College in August 1955, DVD, 59 min., JRDD, *MGZIDVD 5-7073.

215   "There was a center figure": Humphrey, *The Art of Making Dances*, 92, 129. See also Leslie Main, *Directing the Dance Legacy of Doris Humphrey*, 129–30.

215   "compulsions": S. Jones, *Literature, Modernism, and Dance*, 57–58.

215   "in silence": Andrews, "Dance in Shaker Ritual," 5, 9.

215   "three-sided square": Main, *Directing the Dance Legacy of Doris Humphrey*, 151.

216   "the wheeling of ranks": Andrews, "Dance in Shaker Ritual," 9.

216   "My life!": Main, *Directing the Dance Legacy of Doris Humphrey*, 131.

216   "It hath been": Narrative description of *Dance of the Chosen/The Shakers* compiled from Ernestine Stodelle's 1931 recollections; "American Dance Festival" DVD, JRDD; "International Festival for Modern Dance," José Limón Dance Company performance, 1984, videorecording, 35 min., JRDD, *MGZIDVD 5-865; and *The Doris Humphrey Legacy: The Shakers*, Dance Horizons DVD, 1997, 2008.

216   "I have seen few things": Stark Young, *New Republic*, December 23, 1931.

216   Martha Graham's newborn: The score for *Primitive Mysteries* is dated by Horst, "NYC, January 1931."

216   "the dance comes *first*!": Soares, *Louis Horst*, 93–94.

216   "Martha Todd . . . because": McPherson, *Contributions of Martha Hill*, 24.

216   "rhythmic patterns": Teck, *Making Music for Modern Dance*, 52.

217   "You must not fit": MG, quoted by DB, in "Dancing with Doris Humphrey," sound recording, February 1985, JRDD, *MGZTC 3-919.

217   Ever the mischievous: Gertrude Shurr, interview by Agnes de Mille, June 27, 1984, JRDD, *MGZTC 3-1637.

217 "hints of Gregorian chants": DB, *Bird's Eye View*, 79.

217 "welded . . . tone": Teck, *Making Music for Modern Dance*, 52.

217 "Martha didn't like": Sophie Maslow, interview by Janet Eilber, April 9 and 10, 2001, MGLA.

217 "Miss Graham would not": Limón, *An Unfinished Memoir*, 32, 60.

218 "needed a lot of quietness": Tobias, "A Conversation with May O'Donnell," 77, 80–81. O'Donnell danced in *Primitive Mysteries* when she joined the Graham dance group in 1932.

218 "he stimulated Martha": Ibid.

218 "the Indian rituals": Carter, "Reissue of *Martha Graham: Sixteen Dances in Photographs*," 42.

218 "ever told [her] what": Jowitt, "A Conversation with Bessie Schonberg," 47.

218 "Martha didn't say": "Martha Graham's Early Technique and Dances: The 1930s," panel discussion moderated by Deborah Jowitt, October 1, 1994, in "Martha Graham," ed. Alice Helpern, special issue, *Choreography and Dance* 2 (1999): 15; Maslow repeated this observation in her interview with Janet Eilber, April 9 and 10, 2001, MGLA.

218 "embodying in dance": Bennington College concert program for "Martha Graham and Dance Group, Monday evening, March 13, 1933."

218 "The work is *echt* Graham": Kisselgoff, "Martha Graham—Still Charting 'the Graph of the Heart.'" Marcia Siegel had referred in 1971 to "*echt-Graham* of the earliest vintage," *At the Vanishing Point*, 184.

219 "elongated throat": MG, quoted by DB, February 1985, JRDD, *MGZTC 3-919.

219 "See how Ailes presses": Marx, *Leonie Gilmour*, 356.

219 "deep stretch": Helpern, *Technique of Martha Graham*, 12.

219 "strength on the back leg": MG, quoted by DB, February 1985, JRDD, *MGZTC 3-919.

219 "a step, a pause": Ibid.

219 "Martha's mood [was]": Stodelle, *Deep Song*, 84.

219 "she had developed": DB, *Bird's Eye View*, 78.

219 "anxious [and] unsure": GS, interview by Don McDonagh, December 8, 1972, JRDD.

220 "Her nerves shattered": de Mille, *Martha*, 181.

220 "dressed in silence": GS, Louis Horst Centennial Tribute, *Ballet Review* 12, 81.

220 "[E]ach member of the": Armitage, *Martha Graham*, 61.

220 From the opening instant: Descriptions of *Primitive Mysteries* herewith and below are based upon rehearsals in New York City for a month before the August 16, 1964, Louis Horst Memorial Concert performances at Connecticut College School of the Dance, videorecording filmed and produced by Dwight Godwin, JRDD, *MGZHB 8-88, starring Yuriko (Amemiya) as the Virgin, and reconstructed from memory ("nothing was written down") by Sophie Maslow, assisted by Jane Dudley, Anna Sokolow, Helen Priest Rogers, and DB, with MG's "comments at the very end . . . she did not set foot into the studio . . ." (Diane Gray, telephone conversation with author, February 16, 2016, and email to author, February 18, 2016); and the June 13, 1977, rehearsal starring Janet Eilber and filmed by W. W. Films, Inc., JRDD, *MGZIC 9-1379 at the Lunt-Fontanne Theatre in New York City, restaged by Sophie Maslow, assisted by Yuriko and by Takako Akasawa, with MG's comments and corrections "at the conclusion of the rehearsals . . . the finish line" (Janet Eilber, interview with author, January 5, 2016). The size of the ensemble for *Primitive Mysteries* has varied over the decades. The premiere, in

February 1931, featured a chorus of twelve in addition to Graham; a performance nine months later, on November 22, 1932, was composed of a group of sixteen women with MG; in the 1977 version, there were fourteen dancers in addition to Eilber; as there were in the 1984 restaging by Susan Sentler in the Bonnie Bird Theatre at the London Laban Institute.

220 "phalanx": Kendall, *Where She Danced*, 210.

220 "the sacred color": Warner, *Alone of All Her Sex*, 273.

220 "players": Janet Eilber, interview with author, January 5, 2016.

220 "ritual of adoration": Stodelle, *Deep Song*, 75.

221 "like carved stone figures": DB, *Bird's Eye View*, 79.

221 "catch her": "Dorothy Bird Recreating Graham Technique of the 1930s," Dickerson Performing Arts Studio, March 9, 1986, 2 videocassettes, 123 min., JRDD, *MGZIA 4-4510.

221 "benign[ly] calm": Nancy Goldner, June 4, 1977, in Gottlieb, *Reading Dance*, 746.

222 "Handmaidens": Kendall, *Where She Danced*, 211.

222 "knuckles bulging": Nancy Goldner, June 4, 1977, in Gottlieb, *Reading Dance*, 745.

222 "closing the eyes": K. Armstrong, *A Short History of Myth*, 109.

222 "stomping like bison": Janet Eilber, interview with author, January 5, 2016. "More than any other animal, the bison is emblematic of the American frontier." Ketcham, "The Bison Roundup the Government Wants to Hide."

222 "flintlike, the movement": Selden, *The Dancer's Quest*, 95.

222 "pitched-forward": Berg, "The Rite of Spring," 85. Berg connects the "bison leaps" in part two of *Primitive Mysteries* with the style of the "Danse Sacrale" surrounding MG as the Chosen (Sacrificial) Virgin in Massine's 1930 production of *The Rite of Spring*.

222 "the suspended bodies": Bonnie Oda Homsey, email to author, February 16, 2015.

222 "experience of a great rhythm": Burkert, *Ancient Mystery Cults*, 114.

222 "brooding": Kendall, *Where She Danced*, 211.

223 ("Disciple"): Janet Eilber, interview with author, January 5, 2016.

223 "concluding obeisance": McDonagh, *Martha Graham*, 80.

223 "spread and shining": Lloyd, *The Borzoi Book of Modern Dance*, 53.

223 "hands meeting": Stodelle, *Deep Song*, 77.

223 "celestial dance": Syson Carter, "Celestial Dance," 15.

223 "throng of exulting angels": Warner, *Alone of All Her Sex*, 11 [Plate VIII], 95.

223 In addition to *Primitive Mysteries*: *Baccanale* [*sic*] scores, box 193, folders 2–6, Library of Congress, MGC.

223 "Dionysiac": JM, "Martha Graham Acclaimed in Dance."

223 "wildly abandoned": DB, *Bird's Eye View*, 81.

223 "moments of such": Watkins, "Work of Martha Graham Excels."

223 *Bacchanale* was Riegger's: Spackman, "Wallingford Riegger and the Modern Dance," 438, 442.

223 "fit such design": Ibid., 438, 442.

224 After the spectacle: On Villa-Lobos as one of LH's favorite composers, see for example, V-L's *Três Poemas Indígenas*—among catalogue items F 278–292 in *Guide to the Louis Horst Collection of Music*, NYPL Music Division, JPB 83-60.

224 "first idea [for a dance]": Young, "*Dolorosa* at Clark University," *New Republic*.

224 "the house burst": JM, "The Dance: Miss Graham—To a Performer . . ."

225 "the new formations": Sears, "Louis Horst," 81.

225 "Of this composition": S. Young, "Miss Graham and Mademoiselle."

225 "is, in our opinion": Watkins, "Work of Martha Graham Excels."

225 "the dancer's quest": Selden, *The Dancer's Quest*, 96–98.

226 "that it has suspended": JM, "The Dance: Vital Issues."

226 "in common with": JM, ibid.

226 "and the public": Siegel, "Modern Dance Before Bennington," 8.

17: "WE WILL NEVER UNDERSTAND ONE ANOTHER"

227 "What was to come": Allen, *Only Yesterday,* chapter 14, "Aftermath, 1930–31," 297.

227 "Martha, let me work": de Mille, *Dance to the Piper*, 160.

227 "the great romantic": de Mille, "The New Ballerina," 426–29.

228 "[a] knowledge of": Ibid., 429.

228 "an . . . artist on": Ibid., 431–32.

228 "some aspects of": "Composers' League Gives a Concert," *New York Times*, January 5, 1931.

229 "strange, hard beauty": JM, "Brilliant Dancing by Martha Graham."

229 "utterly astonished": Copland and Perlis, *Copland: 1900 through 1942*, 183.

229 "gleaming, streamlined": Flint, "Modernity Rules New School of Social Research," *Art News* 29, no. 16, January 17, 1931.

229 "panoply of pre-Depression": Vogel, "Thomas Hart Benton Masterwork Goes to Met."

230 Weekday evenings: New School Special Collections Digital Archive, http://digitalarchives .library.newschool.edu/index.php; "What Is Going on This Week," *New York Times*, March 8, 1931.

230 "a truly organic American": Neil Levine, introduction to Wright, *Modern Architecture*, xxviii, xxxvii.

230 The performing arts enjoyed: Griffey, Kornhauser, Herdrich, "Thomas Hart Benton's *America Today*," 6; DB, *Bird's Eye View*, 82–83.

230 "Dance Forms and": Catalogue description of JM's course, from "folk" through "modernism," New School Special Collections Digital Archive.

230 "move on a breath": DB, *Bird's Eye View*, 83.

230 "a proper stage": McDonough, *Martha Graham*, 82–83.

230 "clad in sweaters": Fokine, "A Sad Art," 28. Grateful acknowledgment to Norton Owen, curator, Jacob's Pillow Dance Festival Archives, for drawing my attention to this article.

231 To Fokine: Fokine, "A Sad Art," 29; King, *Transformations*, 80–81.

231 "a fanatical prophetess": Fokine, "A Sad Art," 29; King, *Transformations*, 81.

231 "It seems, sir": Fokine, "A Sad Art," 29, 63; King, *Transformations*, 81.

232 "young dancer": Fokine, "A Sad Art," 63, 64.

232 "Mr. Fokine": King, *Transformations*, 81.

232 "admits [into what]": Preston-Dunlop, *Dance Words*, 229, 375, 533.

232 "a triumph of misunderstanding": Barnes, "Dance: Martha Graham, Fokine and History."

233 A childless, unmarried: Ierulli, "A Community of Women?," 221.

233 "refuses to put": Perloff, "Tragedy Today," 830.

233 "never / will I": Sophocles, *Electra* (Carson), 110.

233 "to wars in [her] melancholy soul": Ierulli, "A Community of Women?," 228.

233 "one of the foremost": *Electra* concert program, May 25–June 1, 1931, Lydia Mendelssohn Theatre, University of Michigan, Ann Arbor, pp. 2–3.

233 "iron-willed women": Kaufman, "Blanche Yurka, Actress, Dead."

233 "Blanche Yurka plunges": *Electra* concert program, May 25–June 1, 1931, Lydia Mendelssohn Theatre, University of Michigan, Ann Arbor, pp. 2–3.

234 "All Chorus speeches": J. T. Sheppard, 1927 *Electra* typescript manuscript, Version 1,
Blanche Yurka Papers, Performing Arts Research Special Collections, NYPL, *Theatre
NCOF+12-2157.

234 "citizenesses": Loraux, *The Mourning Voice*, 21–23, 32–35.

234 As "the Dancer" in *Electra*: Scores for MG's three *Electra* solos, Louis Horst Papers,
Music, JPB 83-60, box 4, series 1, folder 93, LHCM. On the first page of the *Lamentation* section, Horst has written, "Much of the material in this composition was
incorporated in 'Dance for Furies,' Tragic Patterns, No. 3" [December 1932–May
1933].

234 "the Greek tongue": Woolf, "On Not Knowing Greek," 12, 16.

234 "extra-illustration": HTP cited by JM, "Miss Yurka as Electra," *New York Times*,
May 24, 1931.

234 "the peculiar stylizations": *Theatre Guild Magazine*, Spring 1931, n.p.

235 "Isadorable": "'Electra' to Open Jan. 8," *New York Times*, December 21, 1931.

235 "she didn't know": de Mille, *Martha*, 334.

235 "add to the educational": "History of the Fellowship," John Simon Guggenheim
Memorial Foundation, http://www.gf.org/about/history/.

235 "which part of the fingertip": P. R. W. Jackson, *The Last Guru*, 185.

236 "the artistic power": Owens, *Carlos Salzedo*, ii, 36–37.

236 "please give [him]": Henry Allen Moe to MG, May 2, 1931, courtesy J. S. Guggenheim
Memorial Foundation Archives.

236 Cunningham's affinity: Richard Lorenz, "Imogen Cunningham: *American*, 1886–
1976," Joseph Bellows Gallery, 1992, http://www.josephbellows.com/artists/imogen
-cunningham/bio/.

237 "the [day] was hot": Daly, "Inspiration Compounded."

237 Cunningham used her trusty Graflex: Imogen Cunningham Trust, https://www
.imogencunningham.com/.

237 "the leading exponent": [no byline] Caption accompanying photographs of MG by
Imogen Cunningham and Edward Steichen, *Vanity Fair*, December 1, 1931.

239 "suspected the choreographer's": Daly, "Inspiration Compounded."

239 "Cycles are circles": Kammen, *A Time to Every Purpose*, 106.

239 Sixty miles west: Soares, *Louis Horst*, 99–100.

239 Unlike kivas: Velma Garcia-Mason, "Acoma," in A. Ortiz, *HNAI*, 9:450–66.

240 "where the feet": Florence Hawley Ellis, "Laguna," in A. Ortiz, *HNAI*, 9:438–49.

240 "four stratified worlds": E. A. Hoebel, "Zia," in A. Ortiz, *HNAI*, 9:407–17.

240 "the highlanders": Joe S. Sando, "Jemez," in A. Ortiz, *HNAI*, 9:418–29; "History of the
Pueblo of Jemez," Pueblo of Jemez Welcome Center, http://www.jemezpueblo.com
/History.aspx; Charles H. Lange, "Santo Domingo," in A. Ortiz, *HNAI*, 9:379–89.

240 "bead upon": A. Ortiz, *HNAI*, 9:3.

240 "village of the": A. Ortiz, "San Juan," in *HNAI*, 9:278–95.

240 "'listen to the women'": Sweet, *Dances of the Tewa Pueblo Indians*.

241   "The Village Under": Nancy S. Arnon and W. W. Hill, "Santa Clara," in A. Ortiz, *HNAI*, 9:296–307; Naranjo, "Thoughts on Migration by Santa Clara Pueblo," 249; Sandra A. Edelman, "San Ildefonso," in A. Ortiz, *HNAI*, 9:308–16; Sweet, *Dances of the Tewa Pueblo Indians*.

241   "small jumps": Sandra A. Edelman and Alfonso Ortiz, "Tesuque," in A. Ortiz, *HNAI*, 9:330–35; Treib, *Sanctuaries of Spanish New Mexico*, 122–27.

241   Disillusioned with the crowded: Richardson, review of *Mary Austin and the American West*; Temple, "Mary Austin and the Challenges of Capturing Western American Rhythms," 403–6.

241   "little whorls of success": Pearce, *Mary Hunter Austin*, 46.

241   "beloved house": Kopecky, "Mary Austin's Crossing Boundaries," 28.

242   "If the desert were a woman": Austin, *Stories from the Country of Lost Borders*, 160.

242   "Sick for the color": A. Fink, *I-Mary*, 176, 226.

243   "Imagine a woman": P. Richardson, review of *Mary Austin and the American West*.

243   "worked within a shell": A. Fink, *I-Mary*, 240.

243   in the May 1925 *Theatre Arts Monthly*: Soares, *Louis Horst*, 88.

243   "lost in the never-never land": Luhan, "A Bridge between Cultures," 299–301.

243   "What is the familiar": Austin, *The American Rhythm*, 5.

243   "find [this rhythm]": Ibid., 9.

243   "stumbled": Ibid., 15.

243   "what the Indian describes": Mary Austin, *The American Rhythm*, addenda for the second edition, 1930, 67ff., sections 20–21.

243   "the 'purr' of": Walker, "Southwest as a Centre of a New Civilization."

244   "The natural rhythm": Austin, *The American Rhythm*, 38.

244   In September, Horst and Graham: "To Begin Courses Monday—Neighborhood Playhouse School Will Teach Drama and Dance," *New York Times*, September 30, 1931.

244   a few blocks uptown: Horosko, *Martha Graham*, 35.

244   "only official representative": V. Stewart, *Modern Dance*, 107.

244   Petite, doll-like, and witty: Louise Sunshine and Charles Perrier, *Overview to the Collection*, Hanya Holm Papers, JRDD, (S)*MGZMD 136.

244   "wide, china blue": Lloyd, *The Borzoi Book of Modern Dance*, 160.

244   "from the inside out": Newhall, *Mary Wigman*, 135–39.

244   "Today's girl": Sorell, *The Mary Wigman Book*, 104.

245   "To me, dancing is": Sorell, *Hanya Holm*, 36.

245   "as hard to describe": Partsch-Bergsohn, *Modern Dance in Germany and the United States*, 80.

245   "the dark vistas": V. Stewart, *Modern Dance*, 81.

245   "with this awakening": Ibid., 83.

245   "Mary Wigman *is* the German dance": JM, "The Dance: Mary Wigman's Art."

246   "Teutonic Amazon": S. Hurok, in Gottlieb, *Reading Dance*, 130–31.

246   "that great pioneer": Ibid.

246   "little enthusiasm": McDonagh, *Martha Graham*, 86.

246   "left to others": "An Interview with Martha Graham," *American Arts Monthly*, September, 1936, 17.

246   "in the method": JM, "The Dance: Artist and Influence."

246   "There may be pictures here": C. Gray, "Streetscapes: *Rebels on Eighth Street* Redux."

246 "marking the end": Jewell, "American Art Comes of Age."

246 "Our chief concern": Force and More, *Whitney Museum and Its Collection*, p. [10].

246 "sun-washed former stable": "A Sculptor's Sanctuary Opens Its Doors," *Wall Street Journal*, May 12, 2016.

246 "a haven for native talent": "From the Beginning—How the Idea of the Whitney Museum Has Developed," *New York Times*, November 15, 1931.

247 "old brick walls": "Whitney Museum to Be Opened Today," *New York Times*, November 17, 1931.

247 Strolling through Shaker furniture: Typewritten and hand-annotated checklist, "Opening exhibition—Part 1 of the permanent collection—painting and sculpture"— Courtesy of the Frances Mulhall Achilles Library and Archives, Whitney Museum of American Art.

247 Among this starry constellation: Noguchi, *A Sculptor's World*, exhibition catalogue item 12.

247 After a year and a half abroad: Grove, *Isamu Noguchi Portrait*, 10–11; Levy, "Isamu Noguchi," 4, 5.

247 "returned to the excitements": Noguchi, *A Sculptor's World*, 21.

247 "I believe that the 'quality' ": J. Richardson, *The Life of Picasso*, 144.

248 "It was one of": Coolsma, "Aaron Copland's *Piano Variations*," 38.

248 "to develop organically": Ibid., 41.

248 "Strike each note": "Hamelin Plays Copland—Piano Variations Audio + Sheet Music," played by Marc-André Hamelin, video, 11:19, July 30, 2011, https://www.youtube .com/watch?v=i1-vIw_M-Qg; Aaron Copland, *Piano Variations* holograph score, box 193, folder 11, MGC Music Inventory. For a schematic chart of the *Variations*, noting "expressive markings, dynamics, structure" and "transitions," see Coolsma, "Aaron Copland's *Piano Variations*," appendix A.

249 "written in sand": JM, "Martha Graham, Dancer, Is Cheered."

249 "sometimes fine and astonishing": S. Young, "Town Melange," *New Republic*, December 23, 1931, 163, review of *Dithyrambics* and *Primitive Mysteries*.

249 "irritated to the point": Armitage, *Martha Graham*, 24–26.

249 "the force of": Duberman, *The Worlds of Lincoln Kirstein*, 129.

249 "[*Variations*] was very": Jowitt, "A Conversation with Bessie Schonberg," 49–50.

249 "series of back-falls": de Mille, *Martha*, 184.

249 In the Graham lexicon: MG, quoted in "Martha Graham [at the New School]," *Dance Observer* 1, no. 8.

249 "Martha perform the astonishing feat": de Mille, *Martha*, 184.

249 "a series of ecstatic": B. Morgan, *Sixteen Dances*, 160.

249 "wits had been blitzed": Dugdale, *Greek Theatre in Context*, 2.

250 "the resurrection": Harrison, *Prolegomena to the Study of Greek Religion*, 436–38.

250 "There is a certain essence": Levin and Tick, *Aaron Copland's America*, 146.

18: FROM *CEREMONIALS* TO RADIO CITY MUSIC HALL

251 "Leading dancers are said": "Dance Recitals Show Biz Leap, Tho Yanks Lag," *Variety*, March 8, 1932.

251 And Martha Graham was: McDonagh, *Martha Graham*, 87–88, 316.

251 Born and raised: Barbanel, "Lehman Engel, 71, Conductor of Broadway Musicals, Dead."

252 "the high priestess": Engel, *This Bright Day*, 55–57.

252 "Noisy Sunshine": Soares, *Louis Horst*, 100.

252 "the stillness of": Engel, *This Bright Day*, 56–58.

252 "from the contemporary": Engel, "Music for the Dance," 4, 5.

252 "decided that the girls'": Engel, *This Bright Day*, 57.

252 "into her little": de Mille, *Dance to the Piper*, 155–58.

253 "the performance was jittery": Engel, *This Bright Day*, 57.

253 splintery wood stage: Bell-Kanner and Bird, *Frontiers*, 49.

253 "newcomer with such": JM, "Martha Graham Gives New Dances."

253 "simplicity and inevitability": JM, "Brilliant Dancing by Martha Graham."

253 In mid-winter: A. Hawkins, *Modern Dance in Higher Education*, 12–14; "Define Dance Ideals at First Symposium," *Barnard Bulletin* 36, no. 31 (March 1, 1932): 1, 3.

254 "take dance . . . from": McPherson, *Contributions of Martha Hill*, 35–36.

254 "grave, stripped": Parker, "Revelation to Bostonians of Martha Graham."

254 "dancer as creator": MG, "The Dance in America," 5–7; JM, "The Dance: An American Art."

255 "from a cognizance": MG, "The Dance in America," 7.

255 Following his hometown companion: Joshi, "Samuel Loveman: Shelley in Brooklyn," 41–64.

255 "darling Babylon": Crane, *Complete Poems & Selected Letters*, 662.

255 "band of brothers": *Dance Observer*, masthead statement, "Editorial Board," 1, no. 1 (February 1934).

255 "advocate sheet": Soares, *Louis Horst*, 116.

255 At noon on April 27, 1932: Gorman, "Hart Crane and the Machine Age."

255 "O *Appalachian Spring*!": Crane, *Complete Poems & Selected Letters*, 46–48.

255 "to attempt a mystical": Hall, "Hart Crane in Mexico," 135–38.

256 "ran the neighboring": Crane, *Complete Poems & Selected Letters*, 46–48.

256 "blank verse tragedy": Ibid., 666–67.

256 Martha Graham's application: MG and Henry Allan Moe, correspondence, February 19–March 15, 1932, including letter of appointment, February 26, 1932. Courtesy J. S. Guggenheim Foundation Archives.

256 "It is hardly a surprise": [John Martin], "In New York Galleries," *New York Times*, March 20, 1932.

256 "long, narrow, gray-walled": Washer, "Martha Graham Sees 'Divine Rhythm.'" Grateful acknowledgment to Don McDonagh for directing me to this article.

257 Many American artists: Delpar, *The Enormous Vogue of Things Mexican*, 55–90.

257 "not only the main roads": Oles, *South of the Border*, 3.

257 Despite awareness: MG, letter to Gertrude Shurr, n.d.: "One eats, one sleeps, one does not read."

257 "place of the dead": Baldwin, *Legends of the Plumed Serpent*, 44–53.

257 "the place where men": Ibid., 23–29.

257 The visitors paused: "Martha's First [*sic*] Guggenheim Mexico," box 5, folder 121, GS Papers, JRDD.

259 During a cocktail: MG letter [paraphrased] to Henry Allan Moe, August 6, 1932; LH, "Chronology of Professional Career," 1901–1962, JRDD, *MGYB-Res. (Horst)

259 "colorful, densely-scored": Schweitzer, "Bard Festival Salutes Carlos Chávez."

259 "chaotic reimagining": "To Give Mexican Ballet—Philadelphia Orchestra Will Offer Premiere of Chavez Work," *New York Times*, January 18, 1932.

259 Louis Horst, settled: Perry-Mansfield anecdotal information provided to the author by Nancy Nagler Engelken, Karolynn Lestrud, and Dagny McKinley, December 15, 2016.

260 Martha Graham, back: "Mary Austin Entertains at Tea for Famous Dancer," *Santa Fe New Mexican*, August 6, 1932.

260 The purpose of: In 2009, the Tribal Council of Santo Domingo revised its name to the original, traditional *Kewa*.

260 On the east bank: Charles H. Lange, "Santo Domingo Pueblo," in A. Ortiz, *HNAI*, 9:379–85.

260 "the crawling brown waters": Duffus, "A Dying Race Sits in Solemn Council."

261 Martha Graham and Mary: Composite descriptions of the Great Corn Dance— Henderson, "The Dance-Rituals of the Pueblo Indians"; Austin, *The American Rhythm*; Ferguson, *Dancing Gods*; Scully, *Pueblo*; Schultheis, "The Corn Dance"; Fussell, "A Timeless Pueblo Ritual"; Roediger, *Ceremonial Costumes of the Pueblo Indians*.

261 "The weights of the legs": Litvinoff, "Lessons from the Dancing Ground to the Studio."

262 "In any art you see a vision": "Dancer Gives Impressions—Martha Graham in Recital in Clark Fine Arts Course," *Worcester Gazette*, November 2, 1932.

262 May's journey to East Ninth Street: Horosko, *May O'Donnell*.

262 "back falls": Ibid., 4, 10–11, 13.

262 "sneaking off": Tobias, "A Conversation with May O'Donnell," 69, 71, 73; see also May O'Donnell, interview by documentary producer Stan Swan, November 4, 1999, box 2, MGLA, *ML31.G73.

262 "She watched us": Tobias, "A Conversation with May O'Donnell," 79.

263 "the exotic, dark-haired": DB, *Bird's Eye View*, 93.

263 "white skirts with solid red": Bell-Kanner and Bonnie Bird, *Frontiers*, 33.

263 Another premiere: Box 12/7, no. 182, LOC, EHC.

263 "Sometimes a baritone voice": JM, "Martha Graham in 3 New Dances."

263 "Consider these four": Engel, "The Dance: A Critical Review."

263 "Martha move . . . quickly": Bell-Kanner, *Frontiers*, 33.

263 "certain reiterations": S. Young, "Miss Graham and Mademoiselle."

263 "supreme art": Chávez, *Musical Thought*, 72, 84.

264 "has to concentrate": Ibid., 29, 30.

264 "a knowledge of our history": Cowell, *American Composers on American Music*, 167.

264 "fertilizing force": "Mexican Composers—Carlos Chavez Discusses the Creative Work of His Countrymen," *New York Times*, January 26, 1936. The definitive overview of Chávez is *Carlos Chávez and His World*, edited by Leonora Saavedra. LS notes via email to author, May 30, 2016: "I don't think [*Prelude*] could be an original composition for Graham because Chávez was so very busy that year, but rather that she used a piano piece he had already composed . . . I am thinking in particular of the *Seven Piano Pieces* (1923–1930)."

264 "her theory of dancing": "M. Graham Appears in Dance Recital on November 21," *Carolinian*, November 23, 1932.

264 "dark-haired . . . graceful creature": "Fine Arts Committee Brings Famed Dancer," *Times* (Lynchburg, VA), November 24, 1932.

265 Katharine Cornell's first sight: McDonagh, *Martha Graham*, 92.

265 Posed by Edward Steichen: A. Whitman, "Katharine Cornell Is Dead at 81"; "Ethereal Kit," *Vanity Fair*, March 1930; Atkinson, "Elizabeth the Poet."

265 "languorous": Unsigned review of *The Green Hat*, by Alan Dale, *Buffalo Courier*, September 20, 1925.

265 "mov[ing] across the stage": Luhan, "On the Career and Character of Katharine Cornell," 40.

265 "from lusty to romantic": Atkinson, "Elizabeth the Poet."

265 "If you're too accustomed": Katharine Cornell, cover story, *Time*, 20, no. 26 (December 26, 1932).

266 André Obey derived: Greer, "Let's Forget the Rape, Shall We?"; Van Gelder, "A Still-Resonant Tale of Power and Violation."

266 "surrounded by the women": Obey, *The Rape of Lucrece*, typescript, NYPL, JRDD—Theatre, NCOF.

266 "poetry in action": Butler, "The Stage This Quarter."

266 "the greatest theatrical adventure": Koolhaas, *Delirious New York*, 208.

266 "pageant of the entire theatre": "First Radio City Show Is Announced," *New York Times*, November 22, 1932.

266 "Miss Martha Graham he": JM, "The Dance: Big Projects."

267 "almost every bigwig": "Radio City Premieres," *Variety*, January 4, 1933.

267 "The Sixth Ave L": Sullivan, "Broadway."

267 "to supply a city": "Radio City Scale," *Variety*, November 22, 1932.

267 "We all watched him": Partsch-Bergsohn, *Modern Dance in Germany and the United States*, 58, 78.

268 "(Quack! Quack!": "Radio City Premiere," *Variety*, January 3, 1933.

19: THE AMERICAN RHYTHM

269 "We ran backward": DB, *Bird's Eye View*, 94.

269 "extraordinarily fine": JM, "The Dance: The First Experiment at Radio City."

269 "this uncompromising Cenobite": Watkins, "With the Dancers."

269 "It was a positive": Sullivan, "Broadway."

270 "no descriptive matter": "Music Hall (Show)," *Variety*, January 3, 1933.

270 Salaries for the: "Radio City's Red Upset," *Variety*, January 10, 1933.

270 "expelled . . . on the toe": Watkins, "With the Dancers."

270 Vaudeville's: C. Stein, *American Vaudeville*, 364–66.

270 "gurgling death rattle": Melnick, *American Showman*, 366, 368–69.

270 "Never again will": Addington, "End of Vaudeville" (part 1), *Theatre Arts Magazine*.

270 Martha Graham disappeared: JM, "The Dance: The First Experiment at Radio City."

271 "I remember Martha Graham telling me": Udall, *Dance and American Art*, 50. The statue was reinstalled and remains on view.

271 In Louis Horst's home library: LH's personal copy of William Hone, *Ancient Mysteries Described*, LHCM.

272 "innocent persecuted heroines": Stavsky, "Medieval French Miracle Plays," 116.

272 "to bring fresh": Atkinson, "Six Medieval Miracle Plays."

273 "single women [to]": Frederickson and Webb, *Singular Women*, 156, 161.

273   Graham responded to: "Medieval Miracle Plays," *New York Times*, February 5, 1933; Mantle, "A Sunday Evening for the Book."

273   "terribly stirring": MG to Dorothy Elmhirst, August 17, 1931.

273   "sparse, pure, admirable": S. Young, "Moments of Miracle."

273   "magenta, vermillion and puce": *Vogue*, April 1, 1933.

273   "wearing a sovereign crown": *Six Miracle Plays* concert program, Library of Congress, MGC.

273   "laying her cheek": S. Young, "Moments of Miracle."

273   "danced drama": Nye, " 'Choreography' Is Narrative," 56.

273   "This is the perfect medium": Atkinson, "Six Medieval Miracle Plays."

273   "Miss Graham is, in every fiber": Watkins, "With the Dancers."

274   "Martha Graham threw away": Engel, "Six Mystery Plays."

274   "the new archaism": *Plastic Redirections in Twentieth Century Painting*, by James Johnson Sweeney, *New York Times Book Review*, August 26, 1934.

274   "the foremost American": "Exponent of Modern Dance Comes to College to Give Recital," *Banner* (Bennington, VT), March 9, 1933.

274   "[a] dance dramatizing": Program note by MG, Martha Graham and Dance Group at Bennington College, March 13, 1933.

275   "a most stimulating address": Alexander, "Association News," 37.

275   "typically American rhythm": "American Dancer Is Evolving a Typically American Rhythm—Martha Graham Insistent on Producing a Dance Free from Importation," *Union and Republican*, April 30, 1933.

275   "Those who seek": Campbell, *Goddesses*, 101–2.

275   With Luigi Cancellieri: Grateful acknowledgment to Laura Dawn Armstrong, DMA, and Jonathan Manton (associate director for special collections, Gilmore Music Library, Yale University) for confirming that "Hindemith did not compose a work for solo clarinet," emails to author, June 23, 2016.

275   "Play this piece ferociously": Hindemith, *Piano Works*, vol. 1, by Hans Petermandl, notes translated by Keith Anderson. Rendition and explicatory notes available at Naxos Records, www.naxos.com.

276   "feet barely moving": DB, *Bird's Eye View*, 94–95.

276   Graham made the costume: B. Morgan, *Sixteen Dances*, 39–41.

276   "one particular length": DB, *Bird's Eye View*, 94–95.

277   "rest-impulses": Lehman Engel, "Details of Contemporary Collaboration," *Dance Observer*, February 1934.

277   pelvic thrusts: Kisselgoff, "Powerful Images of Martha Graham's Art." Further to the deep meaning of "ecstasy," see Heide Göttner Abendroth, "Nine Principles of a Matriarchal Aesthetic," in Ecker, *Feminist Aesthetics*, 90.

277   "intellect, emotion and": Peter Sparling, in conversation with author, New York City, July 15, 2013.

277   The concert ended: Examination and analysis of LH's score for *Tragic Patterns* by Robert S. Cohen, for NB, June 29, 2016, JRDD.

277   "wild white women-worshipers": Harrison, *Prolegomena to the Study of Greek Religion*, 395; see also chapter 8, "The Maenads," 388–401. Graham read Harrison's book in 1922 and it remained on her dancers' required reading list for decades.

277   "divinely-veiled": Wind, *Pagan Mysteries in the Renaissance*, 14.

277   "paraded against a startling": Watkins, "With the Dancers."

277   The young votaries: Lardinois, review of *Choruses of Young Women in Ancient Greece*.

278   "marvelously supple": "Martha Graham and Her Group," *New York Post*, May 5, 1933.

278   "absorbed silence": JM, "The Dance: The Art of Miss Graham."

278   "mystical and almost": Nietzsche, *The Birth of Tragedy*, 6.

278   "the friend who": Ibid., 111–12.

278   "In Elizabethan verse": Pearce, "An Unposted Letter to the Editors."

20: AIRBORNE

279   In a whirlwind: A. Ortiz, *HNAI*, 9:551; "Hopi Indians Dance for Theodore Roosevelt at Walpi, Arizona, 1913," video, 4:05, https://www.loc.gov/item/mp76281109/.

279   "Behold! The Men": Charles Francis Saunders, *The Indians of the Terraced Houses*, 203–19.

279   "atavism [and] grotesque": JM, "Martha Graham Hailed in Recital."

279   "[w]henever [Martha Graham]": JM, "The Dance: Martha Graham's Art."

280   "To the American dancer": V. Stewart, *Modern Dance*, 53–58.

280   Louis Horst captured: B. Morgan, *Sixteen Dances*, 42–43; JM, "The Dance: Miss Graham"; Kisselgoff, " 'Celebration' Revived after 50 Years"; Dunning, "Graham's 'Celebration,' from 1934"; "Celebration—LaGuardia High School Graduation—Class of 2013," staged by Oliver Tobin, video, 6:50, June 25, 2013, https://www.youtube.com/watch?v=NQ62nEJ8ojI.

280   "low- and mid-body": Marie Marchowski, interview by Laura Caplan, January 11 and February 1, 1979, JRDD, *MGZMT 3-460.

280   "real *American* tempos": Ethel Butler, interviewed by Elizabeth Kendall, January 12, 1977, JRDD, *MGZMT 3-426.

281   Since the publication: "Archibald MacLeish Is Dead; Poet and Playwright Was 89," *New York Times*, April 21, 1982.

281   "A special speech": Shapiro, *Essay on Rime*, 51.

281   "the conflict of": Diary entry, November 24, 1933, box 4, Lincoln Kirstein Papers, JRDD, (S)*MGZMD 123.

281   "she was crazy": Riley, "A Near Myth."

281   "represent the emotions": Atkinson, "The Play: MacLeish's 'Panic.' "

282   "excoriation of early": Ex. cat., item 8, *Modern American Dance*, photographs by B. Morgan, Museum of Modern Art, New York, March 28–April 29, 1945.

282   "its background the world": B. Morgan, *Sixteen Dances*, 15, 54–57.

282   "like the burning lightning": Shearer, *Without Wings*, 13.

282   The stage was set: *Frontier* description is derived from four iterations in the JRDD: *MGZIA 4-5534, 1937, filmed by Julien Bryan and Jules Bucher, danced by Martha Graham. Julien Bryan's wife was Marian Knighton, founder of the Dance Program at Sarah Lawrence College. *MGZHB 4-40, 1964, filmed by Dwight Godwin, danced by Ethel Winter; *MGZHB 4-1481, 1975, filmed by Amram Nowak, danced by Janet Eilber, and explicated by JE in conversation with the author, September 18, 2017; and *MGZIA 4-1223, 1985, filmed by Ken Tabachnik, danced by Peggy Lyman.

283   "curious intimacy": MG, "From Collaboration, a Strange Beauty Emerged."

283   "like cables looping off": Stodelle, *Deep Song*, 96–97.

283   "It's not the rope": Wolf, *On Becoming an Artist*, 80.

283   "long sets of bourrées": Bannerman, "Is Dance a Language?" 76. "Martha told us we were not tied to the barre in technique. [She said] [y]ou are constantly using space in different ways, going out, exploring . . ." Ethel Butler, interviewed by Elizabeth Kendall, January 12, 1977, JRDD.

284   "That girl, who was": "Martha Graham—Frontier," MG, introducing the 1975 rendition of *Frontier*, video, 6:34, accessed July 24, 2016, https://www.youtube.com/watch?v=wX—wIO82FY.

284   "In every country": MG, program note, *Panorama*, Bennington Vermont State Armory, August 14 and 15, 1935.

284   "endeavors to present": Ibid.

284   "source material . . . books": S. A. Kriegsman, *Modern Dance in America*, 131–32.

284   "[t]he purpose of design": Lauterer, "A Document for the Modern Dance," 137–42.

285   "The theatre planning problem": Lauterer, "Theatre Planning: A Symposium," 5.

285   "space language": MG, "This Modern Dance."

285   "completely re-creat[ing]": McDonagh, *Martha Graham*, 109.

285   "pongee skirts": Soares, *Martha Hill*, 70.

285   "it seems, bits": JM, "The Dance: A New Work"; JM, "Vermont Dancers at Bennington"; JM, "The Dance: Panorama."

285   "recalling the days": Bohm, "Festival Ends Dance Session at Bennington."

285   "built on the theme": H.G., "Martha Graham and Dance Group," *Dance Observer*, April 1936.

285   "notes of bravado": McCausland, "Definite Change in Graham's Art."

285   "not Miss Graham's finest": JM, UCLA Dance Department seminar, October 1967, JRDD.

285   "by the time": JM, "Vermont Dancers at Bennington."

285   Unwilling to suppress: McDonagh, *Martha Graham*, 110.

286   "You have never": JM, UCLA Dance Department seminar, October 12 and 17, 1967, JRDD, *MGZTC 3-2209.

286   The piece was: "Panorama: Excerpts," filmed at Bennington College, August 1935, videorecording, ca. 5:30, JRDD, *MGZIA 4-3793; "Panorama," Kim Jones's restaging at UNC Charlotte, video, 10:16, September 6, 2015, https://www.youtube.com/watch?v=fdcsM6i5_uw; Montclair State University Dance Division presentation at *Graham Deconstructed*, February 10, 2016, at the Graham Company Studio, 55 Bethune Street, NYC.

286   Edna Ocko: Garafola, "Writing on the Left."

286   "The most delicate moments": EO on MG in the July 1935 issue of *New Theatre*, cited in Irving Ignatin, "'Revolutionary' Dance Forms," *New Theatre*, December 1935.

286   Another proponent: Platt, "Elizabeth McCausland."

286   "new departures, spiritual": McCausland, "Definite Change in Graham's Art."

286   In 1933, after: "Indian Dances Parallel Cycle of the Seasons," *Republican*, September 1933.

287   "The ideal of the dance": McCausland, "American Dancer Is Evolving a Typically American Rhythm," *Republican*, April 30, 1933.

287   Impressed with the piece: MG notes to Elizabeth McCausland, 1934 and 1942, and *Dance, 1933–38*, box 26, folders 21–22, Elizabeth McCausland Papers, processed by Jennifer Meehan and Judy Ng, AAA.

287 "definite change": McCausland, "Definite Change in Graham's Art."

287 "I would find it impossible": "German Invitation Refused by Dancer," *New York Times*, March 13, 1936.

287 After Cleveland: JM, "The Dance Goes on Tour."

288 "She is given to cold": Excerpted from reviews of MG recitals in the *San Francisco Examiner*, *San Francisco Call-Bulletin*, *San Francisco News*, and the *Monterey Peninsula Herald*, March 30 and 31, 1936.

288 "occasional momentary bewilderment": Frankenstein, "Miss Graham Presents Dance Recital."

288 "powerful, matriarchal": S. A. Kriegsman, *Modern Dance in America*, 53–62.

288 "witty and caustic": Lloyd, "Student Impressions."

289 "Martha Graham is here": Shearer, *Without Wings*, 151.

289 Keeping a low profile: "Ballet Caravan to Dance at Bennington," *Bennington Banner*, July 6, 1936.

289 "That high green hill": Lloyd, "On with the Dance."

289 A group of: James Steichen, telephone conversation with author, July 27, 2017.

289 "dominantly interested in": Kirstein, *Blast at Ballet*, 198–202.

289 "heckling": Steichen, "The American Ballet's Caravan," 74.

289 "*rapprochement*": Partsch-Bergsohn, *Modern Dance in Germany and the United States*, 84.

289 "ferret out choreography": Soares, *Martha Hill*, 84.

289 "divinity [with] Praxitelian": "The Choreography of Lew Christensen," Lew Christensen Trust, 2001, http://www.lewchristensen.org.

289 "a satire on life": John Alan Haughton, "Music Notes," *Baltimore Sun*, April 5, 1942.

290 The third part of the program: McPherson, *Contributions of Martha Hill*, 84–86.

290 "The audience kindly": S. A. Kriegsman, *Modern Dance in America*, 58.

290 "when Bennington applauded": Garafola, "Lincoln Kirstein," 21.

290 "American ballet dancers": Steichen, "The American Ballet's Caravan," 87.

290 "Everyone was extremely": Duberman, *The Worlds of Lincoln Kirstein*, 319, 658n2.

290 "kids": Steichen, "The American Ballet's Caravan," 85.

290 "powerfully-sinewed": A. M. Kriegsman, "Erick Hawkins, the Modern Man."

290 "Nervous as a kitten": EH, interview by Don McDonagh, July 19, 1971, part 1, discs 1 and 2, JRDD, *MGZTL 4-2551.

21: ERICK HAWKINS AND LINCOLN KIRSTEIN

291 He cherished memories: EH, interview by Don McDonagh, July 19, 1971, JRDD; EH, interview by Billie Mahoney, from the public access cable TV series *Dance On*, taped June 7, 1981, in New York City, videodisc, 28 min., JRDD, *MGZIDVD 5-5651; EH, interview by Agnes de Mille, January 6, 1983, JRDD, *MGZTC 3-1618.

291 Frederick was a serious youngster: EH, interview by Beverly Brown, July 26 and 31, 1990, JRDD, *MGZTC 3-1879; EH Miscellaneous Early Notebooks, 1925 and ff. (unprocessed), temp. boxes 6–8, Music Division, Library of Congress.

292 "one most compelling": EH Harvard University application for admission (1926); EH, interviews by Billie Mahoney, June 7, 1981, and Beverly Brown, July 26 and 31, 1990, JRDD.

292 "unsurpassed in her": EH Early Notebooks, Erick Hawkins Collection, LOC.

292 Bearing an ever-present: EH, interview by Billie Mahoney, June 7, 1981, JRDD; Harvard University, Faculty of Arts & Sciences, Office of the Registrar, Record Card for Frederick Hawkins, UAIII 15.75.12, courtesy of Harvard University Archives.

292 "The Greeks probably": EH Notebooks, entry for September 22, 1928, EHC.

293 "I must have *no*": EH Notebooks, [spring] 1928, EHC.

293 He immersed himself: EH, interview by Don McDonagh, July 19, 1971, JRDD.

293 A perfect storm: EH application to "Committee on Scholarships and Other Aids to Undergraduates," March 28, 1928, and leave of absence "Petition to the Administrative Board of Harvard College," February 8, 1929, Harvard University Archives.

293 "dark-eyed, free-limbed": Page, *Page by Page*, 186–91.

293 Accompanist Louis Horst: A. M. Kriegsman, "Erick Hawkins."

293 "great sweeps of": JM, "The Dance: Kreutzberg."

293 "beautiful hands": O. Holmes, *Motion Arrested*, 207.

293 "That's what *I'm* going to do!": EH, interview by Billie Mahoney, June 7, 1981, JRDD.

293 He left Cambridge: EH handwritten "Employment Record" [February 1929–June 1933], Harvard University Archives.

293 Existentially mindful: EH Notebooks, entries April 20–August 11, 1929, EHC.

294 Things were going: EH request for and extension of leave of absence, September 9 and October 8, 1929, Harvard University Archives.

294 Seeing Harald Kreutzberg: EH, interview by Don McDonagh, July 19, 1971, part 1, discs 1 and 2, JRDD, *MGZTL 4-2551. Hawkins told McDonagh that seeing *Primitive Mysteries* was "one of the great experiences of [his] life"; Franko, *Martha Graham*, 29.

294 "ecstatic . . . deep physical": EH, interview by Don McDonagh, July 19, 1971, part 1, discs 1 and 2, JRDD, *MGZTL 4-2551.

294 In his final semesters: McDonagh, *The Complete Guide to Modern Dance*, 131–34; Edwin Strawbridge Clipping File, JRDD, *MGZ; JM, "The Dance: Men Emerge."

294 "a time when": EH, interview by Lee Edward Stern, *Speaking of Dance*, WNYC, November 13, 1981, JRDD, *MGZTC 3-1349.

295 "a finely-muscled": O. Holmes, ed., *Motion Arrested*, 200–213.

295 "I am studying": EH, "Vocational Plans and Interests," May 21, 1933, Harvard University Archives.

295 "A boy called Erick": Lincoln Kirstein Papers, Diary, May 26, 1933–January 24, 1934, box 4, folder 21 (S), *MGZMD 123

295 Although they were: Duberman, *The Worlds of Lincoln Kirstein*, 3–28.

295 "infected with": Nancy Reynolds, editor, quoting Kirstein, *Ballet: Bias and Belief*, 3.

296 Harvard proved fertile ground: For Kirstein's beginnings at Harvard, see Lincoln Kirstein, "Published Writings" (Chronologies, 1907–1926 and 1927–1936), https://www.lincolnkirstein.org/Chronology.html; L. Garafola, "Company Man," 4.

296 "bull session": Edward M. M. Warburg, interview by Sharon Zane, February 11, 1991, p. 2, Museum of Modern Art Oral History Program, MoMA Archives, New York; "Edward M. M. Warburg Strives to Give Life Meaning Through Art," *Jewish Telegraph Association Archives*, November 19, 1933.

296 "all the lorgnetted ladies": Edward M. M. Warburg, interview by Ellen M. Scholle, October, 1989, p. 23, William E. Wiener Oral History Library of the American Jewish Committee, NYPL.

297 "snarling": Edward M. M. Warburg, interview by Paul Cummings, May 13, 1971, AAA.

297 "The real basis": Warburg, interview by Sharon Zane, February 11, 1991, Museum of Modern Art Oral History Program, MoMA Archives, New York.

297 On summer vacation: Duberman, *The Worlds of Lincoln Kirstein*, 64–66.

297 *Le Fils Prodigue*: Kirstein, *Dance*, 318.

297 "Gestures flowed smoothly": Ibid.

297 "isolated genius": Duberman, *The Worlds of Lincoln Kirstein*, 64–66.

297 "idea of ballet": Garafola, "Lincoln Kirstein: More Resources."

297 "It was better than": Kirstein, "Kreutzberg; Wigman; *Pas d'Aciers;* The Future."

297 "was not a success": Kirstein, *Dance*, 318. Kirstein further critiqued MG's performance as the Chosen Maiden in "Prejudice Purely," *New Republic*, April 11, 1934.

298 "carnal indispensibles": Duberman, *The Worlds of Lincoln Kirstein*, 93.

298 "finally realized": Ibid., 125–26.

298 "the little sprig": Mason, *I Remember Balanchine*, 86.

298 Kirstein found: Anecdotes drawn from diary entries for June 2–July 16, and August 9, 1933, LKP, JRDD; Kirstein, *Dance*, 325.

298 "My pen burns": Mason, *I Remember Balanchine*, 115–19.

299 "There's only one": Edward M. M. Warburg, interview by Paul Cummings, May 13, 1971, AAA.

299 On September 1, 1933: EH, interview by Lee Edward Stern, *Speaking of Dance*, WNYC, November 13, 1981, JRDD; EH Notebooks, 1928–1940, temp. box 8, folders 6–8, EHC.

300 "with at least": Kirstein diary entries August 28–October 24, 1933, LKP.

300 "[y]ou couldn't just": EH, interview by Billie Mahoney, June 7, 1981, JRDD.

300 "I wanted to be with": EH, interview by Don McDonagh, July 19, 1971, JRDD.

300 "instruction will be given": JM, "The Dance: The American Ballet." On October 4, 1933, LK noted in his diary that, over lunch, an effusive John Martin assured him the School of American Ballet would be "swamped" with applicants.

22: INTERLUDE—*CHRONICLE*

301 "You do not realize": MG, *A Dancer's World*, 1957, Peter Glushanok, director; Nathan Kroll, producer. Remastered 2007. The Criterion Collection, DVD No. 46.

301 "it was not until": Armitage, *Martha Graham*, 37.

301 "She choreographed a lot": DB, *Bird's Eye View*, 110.

301 "She would just improvise": Jane Dudley, interview by Don McDonagh, March 3, 1972, part 1, JRDD, *MGZTL 4-2528; Jane Dudley, interview by David Sears, December 30, 1982, JRDD, *MGZTC 5-1531; Jane Dudley, interview by Janet Eilber, January 5, 2001, Martha Graham Resources.

301 "Martha kept experimenting": Marie Marchowski, interview by Laura Caplan, January 11, 1979, JRDD, *MGZTCO 3-460.

302 "you were supposed": Marie Marchowski, interview by Laura Caplan, February 1, 1979, JRDD, *MGZTCO 3-460.

302 "based upon the advent": JM, "The Dance: Experiment."

302 "does not attempt": Graff, *Stepping Left*, 117, 217n64.

302 "*Chronicle* traces the ugly": B. Morgan, *Sixteen Dances*, 160.

302 In "Spectre—1914": *Chronicle—Spectre—1914*, "Steps in the Street," and *Prelude to Action* in performance (*Masque* and *Tragic Holiday—In Memoriam,* originally part of

Dances Before Catastrophe and *Dances After Catastrophe,* were subsequently excised from parts I and II of *Chronicle).* Descriptions of this piece are derived from: 35 mm silent film by Julien Bryan and Jules Bucher, 1937; still photography by Robert Fraser, Guild Theatre, NYC, December 19, 1937; 16 mm silent film by Ann Barzel, Auditorium Theatre, Chicago, April 7, 1938; and archival video, Martha Graham Dance Company at the Joyce Theatre, New York City, February, 2015, starring PeiJu Chien-Pott [in the Graham role] and Carrie Ellmore-Tallitsch [in the O'Donnell role], courtesy of Oliver Tobin, director, Martha Graham Resources. Also, Barry Fischer, Ed.D. (with David Sanders), *Reconstruction of* "Steps in the Street," at NYU Education Theater, September 20, 1985, starring Alice Gill, streaming video, JRDD, *MGZIDF 1384, choreography refined by Yuriko, approved by Martha Graham, and premiered October 8, 1989, at City Center, starring Laura Jimenez; Barry Fischer, interview with the author, February 6, 2008; and author observations of Denise Vale, senior artistic associate of Martha Graham Company, conducting rehearsals for "Steps in the Street," at Memorial Auditorium, Montclair State University, January 2008.

304 "as if you are making": Jane Dudley, interview by David Sears, December 30, 1982, JRDD.

304 "a madhouse": Bell-Kanner, *Frontiers,* 90.

305 "aspiring, if not much else": G.G., "Martha Graham Offers New Opus," *New York Post,* December 21, 1936.

305 "with sorrow that": "Martha Graham and Group," *Dance Magazine,* February 1937.

305 "the suite . . . would": Bohm, "Suite Features Martha Graham Dance Program."

305 "abounds in striking": JM, "Martha Graham in Dance Recital," *New York Times,* December 21, 1936.

305 "It seems to me her courage": Denby, *Dance Writings,* 41–43. Denby, regretfully, did not return for the December 27 version: "I wish I had seen it again to clarify my own impression."

305 "rehearsed furiously": Bell-Kanner, *Frontiers,* 90.

305 "to the bone": "Martha Graham Recital," *New York Herald Tribune,* December 28, 1936.

305 "serious, intellectual": JM, "Miss Enters Gives Recital of Dances," *New York Times,* December 28, 1936.

305 "breathing life and passion": JM, "The Dance: Miss Graham," *New York Times,* January 3, 1937.

23: *AMERICAN DOCUMENT*

307 "unwilling to desert": MG, "The Future of the Dance."

307 "You could see the transitions": Horosko, *May O'Donnell,* 29.

308 "boasts a fine base": Evan, "Her Chosen Theme," 17–18. See also Bannerman, "An Overview of the Development of Martha Graham's Movement System," 17: "[Graham] has often denied any strong political stance, claiming that she is interested 'in human rights, not politics.'"

308 There, O'Donnell met: Tobias, "A Conversation with May O'Donnell," 87.

308 "folklorish": Ray Green, interview by Don McDonagh, July 14, 1993, JRDD, *MGZTL 4-2525.

308 The original title: Ray Green piano score *Of Pioneer Women*, datelined "San Francisco Aug 12, '37," box 84, May O'Donnell and Ray Green Papers, JRDD, *MGZMD 299.

309 "looking out over": Beaman and O'Donnell, "Looking Back," 97.

309 During *American Lyric*: "*In the American Grain* was her source for *American Document*"—Jane Dudley, interview by Don McDonagh, March 3, 1972, JRDD; Jane Dudley, interview by Janet Eilber, January 5, 2001, JRDD.

309 "sought to re-name": WCW, *In the American Grain*, [v].

309 Graham's friend in "constant devotion": WCW to Barbara Morgan, May 6, 1944, courtesy of Nils Morgan; WCW, *The Selected Letters*, 171.

309 Graham, in turn asked Williams: MG to Jack Anderson, prior to the premiere of the "new *American Document*" at City Center, in "Words of Beauty and Terror Inform a Graham Classic," *New York Times*, October 1, 1989.

309 "fiendish . . . ruthless concentration": Teresa Bowers, "Reminiscences of Ray Green, oral history, [March 11] 1979," transcript, Columbia Center for Oral History, Bennington Summer School of the Dance Project.

309 "beats": Sophie Maslow, interview by Janet Eilber, April 9 and 10, 2001, MGLA.

310 "a good rehearsal": Diary entries for March 5, April 24, May 9, and June 14, 1934, LKP.

310 "to have Balanchine's": EH Notebooks, July 5, July 28, August 8, 1935, EHC.

310 "You must continue": Steichen, "The American Ballet's Caravan," 77, 86.

310 "As soon as I have a fair": EH Notebooks, June 16 and 23, 1936, EHC.

310 "designed to exhibit": JM, "Caravan Dancers in Three Ballets."

310 "a young American": S. A. Kriegsman, *Modern Dance in America*, 58.

311 "care-free session": G.G., "Music by McBride Heard in Concert—Member of the Bennington College Faculty Appears on WPA Program," *New York Times*, April 22, 1937: "When Mr. McBride calls a piece of music for piano and oboe a 'Workout' he means just that."

311 ("Bravo, Erick!"): EH quoting Balanchine, in conversation with Agnes de Mille, January 6, 1983, JRDD.

311 "is the best of Caravan": EH Notebooks, November 28, 1937, EHC.

311 "That's the piece of choreography": Mason, *I Remember Balanchine*, 138–39.

311 "good-humored inventiveness": Denby, *Dance Writings*, 46–48. For the components of *Show Piece*, see "Robert McBride," American Composers Alliance, https://composers .com/robert-mcbride.

311 "passionate in [their] allegiance": Nina Fonaroff, interview by Elizabeth Kendall, April 27 and 28, 1976, JRDD, *MGZTL 4-397. See also Jane Dudley, interview by David Sears, December 30, 1982, JRDD: "We felt that [Graham] was 'it,' and we were the best in the world."

311 Anita Alvarez, Thelma Babitz: S. A. Kriegsman, *Modern Dance in America*, 191.

311 "sick of arabesques": EH, interview by Billie Mahoney, June 7, 1981, JRDD.

311 "feeling [his] way": EH, interview by Don McDonagh, July 19, 1971, JRDD.

311 "less-stringent than ballet": Dunning, "Muriel Stuart, 90."

312 "radio-like waves": EH, interview by Don McDonagh, July 19, 1971, JRDD.

312 He sat on the floor: S. A. Kriegsman, *Modern Dance in America*, 260.

312 "dreamed up": Ibid., 194.

312 "cutting entire movements": Fonaroff to Kendall, April 27 and 28, 1976, JRDD, *MGZTL 4-397.

313   "announced . . . out of the blue": Soares, *Louis Horst*, 140.

313   "took 'our Martha' from us": Dudley to Sears, December 30, 1982, JRDD.

313   "posturing": Marie Marchowsky, interview by Laura Caplan, January 11 and February 1, 1979, JRDD.

313   "in some ways it was easier": Tobias, "A Conversation with May O'Donnell," 81–83.

313   "full of beans": EH, interview by Don McDonagh, July 19, 1971, JRDD.

313   "We called him 'the torso' ": Soares, *Louis Horst*, 140.

313   "euphoric": Bell-Kanner, *Frontiers*, 107–8.

313   "flirtatiously": Ray Green, interview by Don McDonagh, July 14, 1993, JRDD.

313   "common knowledge": Soares, *Martha Hill*, 110.

314   "When we worked together": Barbara Brooks Morgan, interview by Theresa Bowers, December 17, 1978, Columbia Center for Oral History, Bennington Summer School of the Dance Project.

315   "My first glimpse": Campbell, "Betwixt the Cup and the Lip," 30.

315   "net and channel": Hering, "Barbara Morgan," 43.

315   Ray Green's score does survive: Ray Green's holograph one-page draft outlines for *American Document*, box 72, folders 2–3, O'Donnell-Green Papers, JRDD; Ray Green, interview by Don McDonagh, July 14, 1993, JRDD; confirming loss of cassette: Norton Owen and Janet Eilber, emails to author, July 25, 2017.

315   The accompanying *Dance Libretto*: MG, "Dance Libretto: *American Document*," 565–74.

316   "naturally intimidated": Francis Fergusson to Theresa Bowers and Nancy Goldner, February 12, 1979, Columbia Center for Oral History, Bennington Summer School of the Dance Project.

316   On moving picture film: Bennington, JRDD, *MGZHB 4-1439 [photographer undetermined] and Chicago, JRDD, *MGZIC 9-2790 [Ann Barzel].

316   "The dance is supposed": "Graham Interprets Democracy," MG speaking to Marcia Minor, *The Daily Worker*, October 7, 1938. I am also indebted to Maureen Needham Costonis's essay "Martha Graham's American Document" in *American Music* 9, no. 3 (Autumn 1991), and to Franko, *Martha Graham in Love and War*, 20–44.

316   "Ladies and Gentlemen, good evening": MG, "Dance Libretto: *American Document*," 566. All *AD* citations and stage directions below are taken from this version.

316   With these words from center stage: "Stage Manager—This play is called 'Our Town.' It was written by Thornton Wilder; produced and directed by A . . . In it you will see Miss C . . . ; Miss D . . . ; Miss E . . . and many others. The name of the town is Grover's Corners, New Hampshire . . . The day is May 7, 1901. The time is just before dawn." Wilder, *Our Town*, 5.

317   "a troupe of erect peacocks": Kirstein, "Martha Graham at Bennington," 230–31.

318   "forceful, direct, undecorated": JM, "Martha Graham Offers New Dance."

318   "the soul, the Psyche": Butler, " 'American Document' Re-Viewed."

318   "tender gesture": E. Hawkins, *The Body Is a Clear Place*, xi.

318   "unmoved mover": Campbell, *The Hero with a Thousand Faces*, 109.

319   "in contrapuntal rows": Graff, *Stepping Left*, 128.

319   "glimpse of 1938": Dana, "Martha Graham's 'American Document' at Carnegie."

319   "*That government of the people*": McCausland, "Martha Graham Finds New Accent."

319   "[Erick Hawkins's]": Kirstein, "Martha Graham at Bennington," 1938.

320   "What does she wish": Kirstein, "Prejudice Purely."

320   "blind to [her] aesthetic": Kirstein, "The Dance: Some American Dancers."

320   "to create her 'own system'": Kirstein, *Blast at Ballet*, 1938, in Nancy Reynolds, ed., *Ballet: Bias and Belief*, 249.

321   "an instinctive, clean": Kirstein, *Blast at Ballet*, 248–49.

321   "By communication [it] is": MG, "This Modern Dance," 270–72.

322   "knew that 'document'": Campbell, *The Ecstasy of Being*, 198.

24: *EVERY SOUL IS A CIRCUS*

323   "the depths of man's": MG, "This Modern Dance."

324   "smitten with adoration": Jean Erdman, interview by Don McDonagh, October 4, 1993, JRDD, *MGZTD 4-2567.

324   "Dionysos-dance": Campbell, "Betwixt the Cup and the Lip."

324   "Buddhist-Taoist": Wilhelm, *The Secret of the Golden Flower*, xiv–xvi.

324   "Martha called up Joe": Jean Erdman, interview by Don McDonagh, October 4, 1973, JRDD, *MGZTD 4-2567.

324   "it wasn't so much": Campbell, "Symbolism and the Dance," 52–53.

324   "make [him] dance well": MG to EH, EHC, temp. box 3, folder 1, letters dated ca. 1938–1940.

325   Accompanied by Mercier: Bell-Kanner, *Frontiers*, 106; interview with Merce Cunningham, *Dance in Video*, vol. II (1999), MacNeil-Lehrer Productions, https://search.alexanderstreet.com/preview/work/bibliographic_entity%7Cvideo_work%7C2362952.

325   "lean and muscular": Potter, "Merce Cunningham."

325   "outdoors under": McPherson, *Bennington School*, 141.

325   "She knew she could not": Bell-Kanner, *Frontiers*, 119.

325   Vachel Lindsay's epic: Lindsay, "Every Soul Is a Circus," 1–10.

325   "Direct, steady-gazed": Granger, "Monroe, Lindsay and Masters."

325   "Open Door": Poetry Foundation, "Harriet Monroe, 1860–1936."

325   "a rousing description": Granger, "Monroe, Lindsay and Masters."

325   "of athletic exuberance": Poetry Foundation, "Vachel Lindsay, 1879–1931."

325   "a modern knight-errant": Ibid.

326   "For every soul": Lindsay, "Every Soul Is a Circus," 5.

326   "circus of life": *Every Soul Is a Circus*, program note, Holiday Dance Festival Gala Premiere, St. James Theatre, New York, December 27, 1939.

326   "the dark Art Institute": Lindsay, "Every Soul Is a Circus," 1–10.

326   "Miss Graham" as "greatest": [NIK], "Martha Graham and Group." *Picasso: Forty Years of His Art* was organized in collaboration with the Museum of Modern Art and traveled from New York City to the Art Institute of Chicago, https://www.artic.edu/press/press-releases/2/press-releases-from-1940.

326   "prophets old": Lindsay, "Every Soul Is a Circus," 1–10.

326   "the cultured, delicate": Ware and Lockard, *P. T. Barnum Presents Jenny Lind*, flyleaf and pp. 24, 29, 37, 41, 73, 81, 82, 115, and notes 184–185.

327   When Martha Graham's dance: B. Morgan, *Sixteen Dances*, 102–13; Terese Capucilli, in conversation with author, February 23, 2019; silent, handheld fragmentary excerpts from MGDC performance at Chicago Civic Theater, March 10, 1940, by Ann Barzel,

JRDD, *MGZHB 6-2116; vintage silent film of original version (starring Graham, Hawkins, and Cunningham), Martha Graham Resources, DVD 22; *Every Soul Is a Circus*, performed by members of the Martha Graham Dance Company, led by Terese Capucilli and Donlin Foreman, Teatro Municipale, Reggio Emilia, Italy, July 1986, videocassette (VHS), 31 min., JRDD, *MGZIA 4-1221.

327 "This is not the literal": MG, program note, *Every Soul Is a Circus*, December 27, 1939.

327 "delight in irony": Terese Capucilli, in conversation with author, February 24, 2019.

328 "release" into a "new feeling": B. Morgan, *Sixteen Dances*, 148.

328 "a more perfect": JM, "Martha Graham in Dance Festival."

328 "the Beatrice Lillie": Terry, "Martha Graham Dances in New Satirical Work."

328 "rewarded Graham with": Excerpts from reviews of *Every Soul Is a Circus* in the *New York Times, Dance Observer, Baton Rouge State Times, Los Angeles News, Chicago Dancer*, and *Chicago Tribune*, from December 28, 1939, to March 11, 1940.

328 "neo-Romantic": Colin Andrew Lee, *Paul Nordoff*, 4, 62–65.

328 It was by Philadelphia-born: Lee, *Paul Nordoff*, chapter six, essay on E. E. Cummings songs by Leslie De'Ath, 89–90; *Romeo and Juliet* holograph manuscript score by Paul Nordoff, NYPL, Performing Arts Research Collections, Music—JPB 84-184.

328 "actively lolling": Terry, "Martha Graham Dances in New Satirical Work."

328 "stands by": Martha Graham's instructions in the studio to Terese Capucilli and Donlin Foreman during rehearsal for the 1986 restaging, recalled by Terese Capucilli, in conversation with author, February 24, 2019.

328 Here comes Nelle Fisher: Tobias, "Martha."

329 "a little entrance": Jean Erdman, speaking with Alice Helpern and Erick Hawkins about "The Dance Theater Pieces of the 1940s," moderated by Francis Mason, at "Radical Graham," a symposium at the New School, October 1, 1984, *Choreography and Dance,* 35.

329 "faun-like" company: Cecil Smith, "Martha Graham Adds Charm to Vigor in Dance."

330 "jazz duet": Lee, *Paul Nordoff*, 64–65.

330 "a whole theatre": [RS], "Martha Graham and Group."

25: *DEATHS AND ENTRANCES*—TEN CHARACTERS IN SEARCH OF A DANCE

331 "In reality you": MG letter to EH, temp. box 3, EHC.

331 Erick Hawkins, a notebook: EH Notebooks, "May [*sic*] 1940 through April 1941," box 3, EHC. Notebook entry for this proposed dance dated "2-15-40" by EH, in upper right corner.

332 "throughout the performance": MG, *A Modern Dancer's Primer for Action*, in Frederick R. Rogers, *Dance*, 182.

332 "dilemmas": MG, program note, *Punch and the Judy*, Bennington College Theatre, August 10, 1941.

332 "stately elm": Trickey, "The Story Behind a Forgotten Symbol."

332 Again accompanied: Holograph planning notes for a performance at the YMHA Dance Theatre Kaufman Auditorium with pianist Ralph Gilbert, [dated "1941?–1942?"], box 3, EHC.

332 "whenever he is": EH, program note, *Yankee Blue Breeches*, February 1947, the Symposium on Contemporary Arts, Washington, DC.

332 "I wasn't brot": Holograph planning notes for a performance at the YMHA Dance Theatre Kaufman Auditorium with pianist Ralph Gilbert, [dated "1941?–1942?"], box 3, EHC.

333 "wryly astringent": A. M. Kriegsman, "Dance—Erick Hawkins."

333 "clearly the outsider": Kisselgoff, "Dance: Hawkins Revival."

333 "[t]his is a work of the imagination": Vachel Lindsay, *Land Be Bright* concert program note, March 14, 1942, Chicago Civic Opera House. Grateful thanks to Chris Mustazza, co-director of the PennSound Archive, University of Pennsylvania, for discovering the provenance of this excerpt from VL's *The Litany of Washington Street.*

333 "one of the great": Fauser, *Aaron Copland's Appalachian Spring*, 19–26, 119nn3–4.

333 "when the collaboration": Ibid., 25.

333 "drunk with": MG [at Bennington] to Edith Isaacs, August 26, 1942, box 1, folder 3, Wisconsin Center for Film and Theatre Research, Edith J. R. Isaacs Papers, *US Mss 47AN.

333 "shining shoes": EH handwritten notes for *Uncle Sam and His Best Girl*; EH Notebooks, entries dated April 9, 1942–June 22, 1942; "*Uncle Sam's Pride & Joy/His Best Girl/His Better Half*," February 21, 1944, temp. box 3, EHC.

335 "feel[ing] no time": MG to Edith J. R. Isaacs, August 26, 1942, EIP.

335 "redolent with ghosts": Hughes, "Why Those Subversive Brontë Sisters Still Hypnotise Us."

336 "the strange wild": MG to Edith J. R. Isaacs, August 26, 1942, EIP.

336 "the thing I am": McDonagh, *Martha Graham*, 162; McDonagh, *Complete Guide*, 81–83.

336 "a pre-view": MG, typewritten program note for Bennington College premiere, July 18, 1943, Martha Graham Resources; JM, "The Dance: Summer Affairs."

336 "On almost": Thomas, "Deaths and Entrances."

336 "Deliverance from": Tindall, *A Reader's Guide to Dylan Thomas*, 206.

336 "There are so many": MG to David Zellmer, summer, 1943, https://marthagraham.org /portfolio-items/deaths-and-entrances-1943/.

336 On that rainy: *Deaths and Entrances: Music,* recording of Hunter Johnson score, duration 31:24 [dea_1943], Martha Graham Resources; *Deaths and Entrances*, vintage 1943–1944 performance film (no sound), Martha Graham Resources, MGDC_2131, duration 23:54; *Deaths and Entrances* rehearsal film, choreography by MG, performed by members of the Martha Graham Dance Company, with Phyllis Gutelius, Janet Eilber, and Diane Gray as the three sisters, Lunt-Fontanne Theatre, New York City, June 13, 1977, reel-to-reel motion picture, duration 42:30, JRDD, *MGZHB 16-1737.

336 "abstracted for": Janet Eilber, email to author, October 6, 2018. Eilber played Jane Dudley's role, "the archetypal domineering sibling," in the June 1977 restaging of *Deaths and Entrances*, supervised by MG. See NYPL, JRDD, *MGZHB 16-1737.

337 "dreams of romance": MG program note, *Deaths and Entrances*, July 18, 1943, Bennington College.

337 "imagination kindled": Hewlett, "Imperfect Genius," 756–84.

337 "the work . . . uses": Lloyd, "What's in a Word?"

338 "packed . . . to": JM, "Graham Dancers Pack the House."

338 " 'The Dark Beloved' ": EH, interview by David Sears, May 27, 1983, JRDD, *MGZTCO 3-1551.

338 "more in the nature": R. Lawrence, "Martha Graham at the Crossroads."

338 "a huge curtained": McDonagh, *Complete Guide*, 82.

338 "the secret life": MG, program note, *Deaths and Entrances*, July 18, 1943, Bennington College.

338 "thronged with memories": Lloyd, "Such Stuff as Dreams Are Made On."

338 "flame burns": Beiswanger, "Moderns in Review."

339 "adolescently tender": Denby, "Martha Graham's New 'Deaths and Entrances.'"

339 "giv[ing] animation": Ibid.

339 "I am reading": MG to EH, August 5, 1943, EHC. In the letter, MG also refers to finding "the essay on Freud by Thomas Mann very fine and illuminating."

339 "the analytic revelation": Mann, *Freud, Goethe, Wagner*, 43.

340 "I wish I could": MG to EH, August 5, 1943, EHC.

26: INTERLUDE—*APPALACHIAN SPRING*

341 To aficionados: Descriptions of the choreography and music of *Appalachian Spring* are derived from (1) the original, 31:04, black-and-white digitized archival silent version, Martha Graham Resources, New York City, cited by Janet Eilber to the author on March 27, 2019, as having been filmed in the fall of 1944 at the Library of Congress; (2) the 1958 black-and-white sound, 32:00, studio version, *Martha Graham, Dance on Film* (Criterion Collection, 2007), DVD, with an essay by Joan Acocella in the accompanying booklet, Cat. No. CC1714D; and (3) MGDC at Montclair State University, *Appalachian Spring* 75th Anniversary Celebration, November 14–17, 2019, Alexander Kasser Theater.

341 "harmonic treatment": Thomson, "Two Ballets."

343 With Copland's: Sister R. Mildred Parker and others, *Early Shaker Spirituals*, produced by Daniel W. Patterson, recorded at the United Society of Shakers, Sabbathday Lake, Maine, 1963, Rounder Records 0078, 1996, compact disc.

344 "wedding sermon": Pasles, "Appalachian Spring—Martha's Ballet."

27: *DARK MEADOW*

346 "is concerned with": MG, program note, *Dark Meadow*, S. Hurok Presents Martha Graham and Dance Company, Plymouth Theatre, New York, January 21–February 2, 1946.

346 double quartet for strings and winds: *La Hija de Cólquide*, the State of Mexico Symphony Orchestra under the direction of Enrique Batiz, recorded June 1994, ASV, Ltd., CD DCA 1058.

346 "the Soul having": N. W. Ross, *Notebooks of Martha Graham*, 177, 182.

346 Here and now: Descriptions derived from the 1946 *Dark Meadow* black-and-white film with original cast, Martha Graham Resources (Note: This is the only extant vintage version); and *Dark Meadow* rehearsal, choreography by Martha Graham, with Peggy Lyman, David Hatch Walker, and Takako Akasawa, Brooklyn Academy of Music, May 14, 1975, 16 mm, 43:30, JRDD, *MGZHB 16-1485.

348 "Only twenty stenographic": Box 274, folders 1–11, MGC; box 275, folders 1–9, MGC. "The Dark Meadow of the Soul" notebook is in box 274, folder 8.

349 C. G. Jung's idea: N. W. Ross, *Notebooks of Martha Graham*, 167–206.

349 "irreducible to conscious": Capobianco, "Heidegger and Jung," citing C. G. Jung's 1897 lecture "Some Thoughts on Psychology," delivered while he was a medical student at the University of Basel.

349 Jean Erdman recalls: Jean Erdman, interview by Don McDonagh, October 4, 1973, JRDD, *MGZTD 4-2567.

349 "the proper stuff": N. W. Ross, *Notebooks of Martha Graham*, 167–206.

350 "she of the ground": Ibid.

352 "a goddess with": Smeds, "Graves, Bachofen and the Matriarchy Debate," 10.

353 "When you were in Dark": EH, interview by David Sears, April 23, 1982, JRDD, *MGZTL 4-1549.

353 "Erick Hawkins did": [RL], "Martha Graham and Dance Company."

353 More than three decades: EH, interview by David Sears, May 27, 1983, disc 2, JRDD, *MGZTL 4-1551. On the staying power of *Dark Meadow* from the 1940s to the present, see Stuart Hodes in conversation with Janet Eilber at the Martha Graham Studio, September 16, 2016, https://www.youtube.com/watch?v=GqxjDH7zVIw.

353 "understands [Hawkins] a little": MG to EH, dated "Sunday, 2/46" in ink by EH, upper left-hand corner, temp. box 3, EHC.

354 "Your statement worries": MG to EH, dated "3/46" in ink by EH, upper right-hand corner, temp. box 3, EHC.

354 "For there is": N. W. Ross, *Notebooks of Martha Graham*, 206.

28: SERPENT HEART

355 Martha Graham, poised: No vintage film of *Serpent Heart/Cave of the Heart* exists. Descriptions of the work are derived from two versions: (1) the 1965, 25:58, "VHS recorded copy of the filmed documentation" in "The Helen McGehee Library and Choreography Archive" with HMcG (Medea), Robert Cohan (Jason), Yuriko (the Princess), and Matt Turney (Chorus)," uploaded to YouTube on July 23, 2018; and (2) the 1984 18 min. performance acccompanied by a 63 min. rehearsal videorecording of *Cave of the Heart*, NYPL, JRDD, *MGZIA 4-1210, introduced by Martha Graham and "reconceived in part for taping" under her supervision; directed by Thomas Grimm; and produced with the assistance of Linda Hodes and Ron Protas; with Takako Asakawa (Medea), Donlin Foreman (Jason), Jacqulyn Buglisi (The Princess), and Jeanne Ruddy (Chorus). With gratitude to Linda Hodes for her illuminating telephone conversation, October 13, 2018. For SB's orchestration, see *Cave of the Heart (Medea)*, in *Music for Martha Graham: The Original Versions*, with the Atlantic Sinfonietta orchestra, conducted by Andrew Schenck, recorded March 15, 1990, Koch International Classics 3-7019-2 H1, 1990.

355 "her noble tininess": Seldes, "Martha Graham's Gift to Drama."

355 "Medea was more": MG introduction to *Cave of the Heart*, telecast by WNET/Thirteen, New York, on the *Great Performances: Dance in America* series, December 13, 1984, VHS, 93 min., JRDD, *MGZIA 4-1210.

355 "marble relief fragment": *Head of Medea*, AD 1st–2nd century stone sculpture, 16.5 x 14 x 5.1 cm, Rogers Fund, acquired in 1923, Metropolitan Museum of Art, New York, https://www.metmuseum.org/art/collection/search/251419.

356 In Euripides's primordial: Dillon, *Girls and Women in Classical Greek Religion*, 169–77; Euripides, *Medea and Other Plays*, xv–xx, 169–70.

356 "quick-tempered": Euripides, *Medea and Other Plays*, 2–38.

356 "unobserved . . . crouched": Apollonius of Rhodes, *Jason and Medea*, 11–49.

357 "(I have used": MG, typewritten early draft for *Daughter of Colchis*, July 7, 1942, pp. 1–5, item 507, Aaron Copland Collection, Library of Congress.

357 "should not be used": Ibid., 4, 7.

357 "poetic creatures": EH, interview by David Sears, April 23, 1982, JRDD, *MGZTL 4-1459.

357 "at times queenly": MG, typewritten early draft for *Daughter of Colchis*, July 7, 1942, pp. 5–6, item 507, Aaron Copland Collection, Library of Congress.

357 Despite these ongoing: Pollock, *Aaron Copland*, 391–94; see also Parker, "Carlos Chávez and the Ballet," 199–201, and Franko, *Martha Graham in Love and War*, 79.

358 Born in West Chester: Wittke, *Samuel Barber*; Henahan, "Samuel Barber, Composer, Dead."

359 Robert Horan: See "A Variety (Three Kinds) of Verse," Selden Rodman's critique in the *New York Times Book Review*, August 8, 1948, on the publication of Horan's first book, *A Beginning*, adjudicated by W. H. Auden as the winner of the forty-sixth Yale Younger Poets Prize.

359 "improvise . . . alone": Seldes, "Martha Graham's Gift to Drama," recalling an MG acting class at the Neighborhood Playhouse "while Martha was planning *Serpent Heart* for her company."

359 "It was a red-letter": Samuel Barber, interview by John Gruen, May 20, 1975, JRDD, *MGZTL 4-336.

359 "as soon as he": Heyman, *Samuel Barber*, 265, 547n39.

359 Martha Graham's gift: Ibid., 265; Jeff James, liner notes, 6, for *Music for Martha Graham: The Original Versions*, with the Atlantic Sinfonietta, conducted by Andrew Schenck, recorded March 15, 1990, Koch International Classics 3-7019-2 H1, 1990.

359 "complete freedom": Samuel Barber, interview by John Gruen, May 20, 1975, JRDD, *MGZTL 4-336.

360 "Pain and Wrath": Jeffers, *Medea*, 10.

360 "within the cave": Heyman, *Samuel Barber*, 266.

360 "one like Medea": *Serpent Heart* program, first performance, Columbia University, May 10, 1946.

361 "terrible fights": Samuel Barber, interview by John Gruen, May 20, 1975, JRDD, *MGZTL 4-336.

361 "A group of flat-topped": Gomez, "When Noguchi Took the Stage," 16.

362 "Like the swing": Jeff James, liner notes for *Music for Martha Graham*, 6.

362 On three pages: N. W. Ross, *Notebooks of Martha Graham*, 151, 162–64.

362 "music of mixed": Jeffers, *Medea*, 107.

363 "daring . . . profound": Terry, "The Dance."

363 "rich and powerful": H. Johnson, "Rhythm and Reason."

363 "danced magnificently": [RS], "Reviews of the Month."

363 "in high-voltage theatricality": Chujoy, "Martha Graham and Dance Company."

363 "heroic, but the emotional": Cecil Smith, "The Maze of the Heart."

29: THE "BREAK-UP"

364 "where [he] went": EH, private notebook, August–September 1946, temp. box 3, EHC, Library of Congress.

365 "it struck [Jung]": Campbell, *The Portable Jung*, xx–xxiii.

365 "By sacrifice": Jung, *Psychology of the Unconscious*, 263.

365 "this summer": EH, private notebook, August–September 1946, temp. box 3, EHC.

365 "a complete synthesis": Sears, "Erick Hawkins Speaks His Mind."

365 "I want to say": EH, private notebook, August–September 1946, temp. box 3, EHC.

366 "passion play": EH, program note to *John Brown*, [February] 1947, the Symposium on Contemporary Arts, Washington, DC.

366 "distilled and refined": Sears, "Erick Hawkins Speaks His Mind."

366 "severe but eloquent": American Composers Alliance, "Charles Mills."

366 "construction simultaneously": Anderson, "Erick Hawkins and 'God's Angry Man.'" Note: The October 1984 concert series at the Joyce Theatre in NYC celebrated Hawkins's fiftieth anniversary as a dancer.

367 "unquestionably sincere": JM, "Graham Dancers Offer a Novelty."

367 "Mr. Erick Hawkins": S. Young, "Martha Graham."

368 "I want to vivify": EH, private notebook, August 1946, temp. box 3, EHC.

368 "an innocent hardiness": Gordon Norton, *5 Essays*, 24.

368 framework tower: Philippe Halsman, *Erick Hawkins in "Stephen Acrobat," Isamu Noguchi Set Design*, 1946, photograph, Magnum Photos.

368 "[S]winging in": [HSC], "Martha Graham Season Presents Two New Works."

368 "the number of men": Martha Graham Dance School announcement brochure for Christmas Course, December 1945–January 1946, Martha Graham Clipping File, box 2, JRDD, *MGZRC 62.

368 "burst, like": Stuart Hodes, interview with author, New York City, April 12, 2015.

369 "had a good *suffer* today": Ibid.

369 "male Eve": Franko, *Martha Graham in Love and War*, 82.

369 "sepulchrally": HCS, "Martha Graham Season Presents Two New Works."

369 "ancestral spirits": Morton, "Sigmund Freud, Géza Róheim, and the Strehlows," 202–6.

369 "write out": EH, private notebook, [summer 1946], temp. box 3, EHC; EH refers to "The Strangler," in progress, as "the Oidipous dance."

369 "half lion": EH, program notes, *The Strangler*, American Dance Festival, Connecticut College School of the Dance, August 22, 1948.

369 ("realiz[ing] with": Jung, *Symbols of Transformation*, 4.

369 "Ahab": EH, program note, EH Dance Company at the University of Michigan Power Center for the Performing Arts, October 16, 1987.

369 "by May [1947]": EH, private notebook, summer 1946, temp. box 3, EHC.

369 "A Dance in Four": Olson, *The Fiery Hunt and Other Plays*, 1.

370 "If I can execute": EH to Charles Olson, notes for *The Fiery Hunt*, April 7, 1947, box 160, CORC.

370 "I am glad": EH, program note, EH Dance Company at the University of Michigan Power Center for the Performing Arts, October 16, 1987.

370 "paraphrasing or weaving": Boxes 39 and 160, spanning February 26, 1946, to April 11, 1948, CORC. Located by Melissa Watterworth Batt, archivist for Literary Collections and Rare Books, Archives, and Special Collections, University of Connecticut Library.

370 "the Whale": EH note to Charles Olson, April 8, 1947, box 160, CORC, partially cited in George Butterick's introduction to *The Fiery Hunt and Other Plays*, pp. xiii–xiv.

370 "tragic flaw": Boxes 39 and 160, spanning February 26, 1946, to April 11, 1948, CORC.

370 "struggle to maintain": *The Fiery Hunt: A Dance-Play*, typescript manuscript, carbon copy draft, pp. 3–29, Constance Walsh Collection, Theatre Collection, Performing Arts Research Collections, NYPL, RM 7762.

371 "disentanglement": EH, private notebook, summer 1946, temp. box 3, EHC.

371 "I hope you": MG to EH, dated "Monday" by MG and "August 1946," in pencil, by EH, temp. box 3, EHC.

371 "I think we still": EH to MG, September 8, [1946], temp. box 3, EHC.

371 "complete break": EH, private notebook, fall 1946, temp. box 3, EHC.

371 "get through": MG, two handwritten notes to EH, October 4, October 14, 1946, temp. box 3, EHC.

372 "the particular kind": Fromm, *Escape from Freedom*, 290.

372 "marriage in the real sense": MG, typescript letter to EH, October 21, 1946, EHC.

372 downplaying the Jason: Krokover, "The Dance."

372 "a daring": Cecil Smith, "The Maze of the Heart."

372 "As the tension": MG, with SB, program note, *Cave of the Heart*, February 27, 1947.

372 For the next evening's: EH, interview by David Sears, June 9, 1985, JRDD, *MGZTL 4-1553.

373 In her subversive: Kisselgoff, "Mark Ryder."

373 "frozen in frenzy": Dunn, "When a Love Poet Writes an Epic."

373 "There is the accomplishment": MG program note, and the author's performance observation notes, Martha Graham Dance Company, *Errand into the Maze*, starring Charlotte Landreau and Lloyd Mayor, Joyce Theatre, New York, April 14, 2019.

373 "heart at the instant": MG program note, *Night Journey*, Leslie L. Cleveland Auditorium of the Cambridge High and Latin School, May 3, 1947.

373 "son-husband": McDonagh, *Martha Graham*, 200.

373 "I want to find": EH, private notebook, April 20, 1947, EHC.

373 "Technically: An": EH, manuscript draft, "What Is Modern Dance?" June 18, 1947, EHC. For the final version of the speech, "The Rite in Theater," delivered on November 27, 1947, at the Hotel Piccadilly in New York City, see EH, *The Body Is a Clear Place*, 2–7.

374 "In order to understand": Hastings, "Martha Graham," [1947].

30: HORST REVISITED

375 "Theatre Dance Pieces": Program for the Symposium on Contemporary Arts, directed by Robert Richman, King-Smith School of Creative Arts, Washington, DC, n.d. [ca. spring 1947].

375 For the summer: American Dance Festival timeline, https://americandancefestival.org/wp-content/uploads/2014/06/7-ADF-Timeline.pdf; McPherson, *Bennington School*, 277–79.

376 "diatonic harmonies": Mabary, "Martinů's Contribution to Modern Dance."

376 "her wings": Isherwood, "Anne Meacham."

376 "a single figure": Bergan, "Versatile Character Actor."

376 After the first performance: McDonagh, *Martha Graham*, 326.

376 "Contest, the habit": Belitt, "The Habit of Angels," 33.

376 "Out of a group": Herridge, "Graham Work Needs Graham."

377 "All are aspects": MG, *Blood Memory*, 98–99.

377 "in an even shorter": Herridge, "Graham Work Needs Graham."

377 "[won] audiences": McDonagh, *Complete Guide*, 88–89.

377 "purely lyric": JM, "Martha Graham in 2nd 'Visionary.'"

377 "practically everything": Barnes, "Style and Beauty of 'Diversion of Angels.'"

378 "full of the enthusiasm": McDonagh, *Complete Guide*, 88–89.

378 "felt useless": Soares, *Louis Horst*, 170.

378 "cantankerous tirade": Soares, *Louis Horst*, 171.

378 "incidental . . . aborted": EH, interview by Don McDonagh, July 19, 1971, part 3, disc 2, JRDD, *MGZTL 4-2551.

378 "couldn't take it": Soares, *Louis Horst*, 172.

379 "She never stands": Ibid., 174.

379 "potent land": de Mille, *Martha Graham*, 283.

379 on a second visit: Udall, "Martha Graham and Cady Wells," 126; and in Lois Rudnick, ed., *Cady Wells and Southwestern Modernism*, 139.

379 "I was frightened": MG to EH, correspondence, headed "Saturday morning" by MG, [ca. mid-September 1948].

379 On the marriage license: McDonagh, *Martha Graham*, 210.

379 "in the eyes": MG to EH, correspondence, headed "Friday" by MG, [ca. third week of September 1948], and "Wednesday night," dated September 29, 1948, in pencil by EH, EHC.

31: *EYE OF ANGUISH*

380 "Cordelia—adult": N. W. Ross, *Notebooks of Martha Graham*, 56.

380 In the back: Ibid., 41, 47.

380 "tragic actor": Ibid., 47. Early jottings for *Eye of Anguish*, in N. W. Ross, *Notebooks of Martha Graham*, 46–58, were based upon Graham's close reading of three books published in 1948: *This Great Stage: Image and Structure in King Lear*, by Robert Bechtold Heilman; *The White Goddess*, by Robert Graves; and *A Notebook on William Shakespeare*, by Dame Edith Sitwell.

381 "Lear's—career": N. W. Ross, *Notebooks of Martha Graham*, 56, 59–60.

382 Born in Philadelphia in 1915: Biographical information from Vincent Persichetti Papers, 1901–1996, JRDD, JPB 30-77.

382 "humorous, lighthearted": Vincent Persichetti, interview by Kathy Matheson, November 29, 1976, JRDD, *MGZTO 5-436; Shackelford and Persichetti, "Conversation with Vincent Persichetti," 121.

382 "the musical omnivore": Mast, *Vincent Persichetti Works for Band*, liner notes.

382 "in all the arts": Vincent Persichetti, interview by Kathy Matheson, November 29, 1976, JRDD, *MGZTO 5-436.

382 "The subject of": MG's *Lear* notes to Vincent Persichetti, transcribed and cited in Dor-

othea Persichetti, *A Monograph: Vincent Persichetti's Music* (unpublished manuscript), box 103, folders 15–18, pp. 63–68, and box 104, folders 1–2, Vincent Persichetti Papers, JRDD, JPB 90-77.

383 "At the still point": T. S. Eliot, *Four Quartets*, 15.

383 "rain and night": VP annotations in MG narrative plan for the score of *King Lear*, cited in D. Persichetti, *Monograph*, 69–73; *King Lear, Opus 35* (1948), recorded by the Albemarle Ensemble, Nancy Garlick, director (flute, oboe, B-flat clarinet, bassoon, French horn in F, with piano and timpani), on *American Camerata Performs*, AmCam Recordings, ACR 10305CD.

385 "our foster-nurse": *King Lear*, iv.3.10–22. References are to act, line, and scene.

385 *Lear* no longer: Draft press release by Wehlan Morgan [pseudonym for Isadora Bennett, publicity agent for MG, 1939–1970]. "Martha Graham By-Passes the Bard," p. 1, box 1, folder 3, Martha Graham Dance Company records, 1944–1945, JRDD.

385 "to be seen": Isadora Bennett, draft MG Company timeline, 1939–1949, "Special to Miss Evelyn Bonner," p. 4, box 1, folder 3, Martha Graham Dance Company records, 1944–1955, JRDD, (S)*MGZMD 152; Martha Graham and Dance Company 1949 tour brochure, box 69, EHC, Library of Congress.

385 "by-passed": Wehlan Morgan [Isadora Bennett], "Martha Graham By-Passes the Bard," draft press release, box 1, folder 3, Martha Graham Dance Company records, JRDD, (S)*MGZMD 152.

386 "fine power": "Graham's 'Lear,'" *Dallas Morning News*, ca. March 1949.

386 "the recognition": EH, private notebook, April 9, 1949, temp. box 3, EHC.

386 "call to adventure": Campbell, *The Hero with a Thousand Faces*, 11–139.

386 "[n]ow I need": EH, private notebook, September 12, 1949, box 3, EHC.

386 "the spirit of": Vincent Persichetti, interview by Kathy Matheson, November 29, 1976, JRDD, *MGZTO 5-436.

387 "Sighing, holding": Ibid.

388 "Tonight for the first": EH, private notebook, n.d. [January 1950], box 3, EHC.

388 "superb performance": JM, "Martha Graham Scores."

32: THE CHOICE

389 She had not been: From internal evidence, MG to EH, dated Monday [August/ September? 1946], and EH to MG, dated Sunday, September 8 [1946], box 3, EHC, Library of Congress.

389 Born in London: Dunning, "Batsheva de Rothschild"; Eshel, "Bethsabée Rothschild, 1914–1999."

390 Following the war: Samorzik, "Pas de Deux."

390 "only a small": Lenart, "Rehearsing and Transforming Cultural Diplomacy."

390 "Manager of the": Ibid.

390 "joining the trek": JM, "The Dance: Afield."

391 "le jazz": de Rothschild, *La danse artistique aux USA*, 13.

391 "Idolized, detested": de Rothschild, *La danse artistique aux USA*, 37–50, 51–67 (translations from the French herewith and below by the author). Chapter 5, pp. 51–67, is devoted to *Martha Graham: Analyse des oeuvres et discussion* [*Analysis and discussion of her works*], from *Primitive Mysteries* to *Cave of the Heart*.

392 "wise, comprehensive": de Rothschild, *La danse artistique aux USA*, 12.

392 "to the American public": Tugal, "Martha Graham Is Interviewed."

394 "strained tendons": Freedman, *Martha Graham*, 117–18, 137–38.

394 "was tired": EH, interview by Don McDonagh, July 19, 1971, JRDD, *MGZTL 4-2551.

394 "Don't push me": Freedman, *Martha Graham*, 117–18, 137–38.

394 The June 27 opening: Lenart, "Rehearsing and Transforming Cultural Diplomacy."

394 "winced": EH, interview/question by Don McDonagh, July 19, 1971 ("How did [Martha] hurt her knee?"), part 3, disc 2, JRDD, *MGZTL 4-2551.

394 "I can still remember": MG, *Blood Memory*, 181.

394 "stories that [Hawkins]": EH, interview by Don McDonagh, November 17, 1972, part 1, JRDD, *MGZTL 4-2556.

394 "hauled [Graham] around": Jean Erdman, interview by Don McDonagh, October 4, 1973, JRDD, *MGZTD 4-2567.

394 The next night: EH, interview by Don McDonagh, November 17, 1972, part 1, JRDD, *MGZTL 4-2556.

394 "At the end": de Mille, *Martha*, 297.

394 "one could not": Ibid., 297.

395 The time came: *New York Times*, "Graham Injured, Show Off."

395 "'It will be foolish'": EH, interview by Don McDonagh, July 19, 1971, part 2, disc 1, JRDD, *MGZTL 4-2551.

395 "Erick left me": MG, *Blood Memory*, 185.

395 In reality, Graham: EH to Bill and Sallie R. Wagner, August 6, 1950, Sallie R. Wagner Collection, 1950–1992, Music Division, Library of Congress. Grateful thanks to Libby Smigel, dance archivist, for bringing this important correspondence to my attention.

396 "at a crossroads": EH to MG, "6 East 17th St./August 21 [1950]," completed and sent "August 27," Correspondence, temp. box 3, EHC.

397 "I have heard that": MG to EH, September 3, 1950, Correspondence, temp. box 3, EHC.

397 Graham had therefore taken: *New York Times*, "Frances G. Wickes."

397 "the people who": Bair, *Jung*, 337.

397 "By what seemed": MG to EH, September 3, 1950, Correspondence, temp. box 3, EHC.

398 "assuming an equally": "Information About Erick Hawkins' Saturday Courses for Young People in the Martha Graham School of Contemporary Dance," 1951–1952 brochure, EH Scrapbooks, box 69, EHC.

398 "In spite of": MG to EH, September 3, 1950, Correspondence, temp. box 3, EHC.

398 dance-love: Oliver Tobin (director, Martha Graham Resources), in conversation with the author, June 11, 2019.

398 "there was great": MG to EH, September 3, 1950, Correspondence, temp. box 3, EHC.

398 "something real existing": MG to EH, dated "Monday" [ca. October 1950], Correspondence, temp. box 3, EHC.

398 "unsettled and unhappy": EH to Sallie and Bill Wagner, November 15, 1950, Sallie R. Wagner Collection, Music Division, Library of Congress.

398 "What has been called": MG to EH, September 3, 1950, Correspondence, temp. box 3, EHC.

33: CODA

399   Rather, bidding au revoir: On the Greek origin of "our idea of form as spatial," see *Against Interpretation*, by Susan Sontag, p. 8n; for MG's "movement and communication" as "deeply entwined," I am grateful to Denise Vale, senior artistic associate, Martha Graham Dance Company, email to the author, November 2, 2018.

399   "Isadora's method": Sorell, *The Dance Has Many Faces*, 34.

399   "art-speech": D. H. Lawrence, "The Spirit of Place," 1.

399   "Technique": Preston-Dunlop, *Dance Words*, 162.

399   "Picasso's line": Apostolos-Cappadona, ". . . With a Book in Your Hands," 3.

399   "developed parallel": Martha Graham School of Contemporary Dance catalogue, 1950–1951, Martha Graham Clippings File, JRDD, italics are the author's.

400   "After 1950": EH, *The Body Is a Clear Place*, 97.

400   "my own man": EH, interview by Lee Edward Stern, *Speaking of Dance*, WNYC, November 13, 1981, JRDD, *MGZTC 3-1349.

400   "pursuing my own vision": Dubin, "The Hawkins Code."

400   "A man needs to": EH to Sallie and Bill Wagner, ca. mid-January 1951, EHC.

400   "strained . . . tight": EH, *The Body Is a Clear Place*, 123–24.

401   "easeful flow": A. M. Kriegsman, "The Height of Hawkins."

401   "casts off the garments": Sabin, "The Dance Concerto."

401   "She must emerge": MG to Sallie Wagner, January 23, 1951, Sallie R. Wagner Collection, 1950–1992, Music Division, Library of Congress. *Judith* premiered in January 1950, at Louisville, Kentucky, with the Louisville Orchestra; the New York City premiere was in December 1950/January 1951 with the New York Philharmonic.

401   "Please do not": MG to EH, March 21 and May 20, 1952, EHC.

401   "an accompanist": Dunning, "Carrying On in a Master's Steps."

401   "a metaphor": Dunning, "Erick Hawkins."

401   "the poetry of": Hal Rammel, liner notes for *Disparate Stairway Radical Other*, by Lucia Dlugoszewski, Composers Recordings Inc. 859, 2000, compact disc.

401   Twenty-five years: Anecdotal recollections of EH and Lucia Dlugoszewski at Sali Ann and Mike Kriegsman's home "in the early eighties," and excerpts from SAK's personal copy of *Dance Perspectives* (no. 12, Autumn 1961), Sali Ann Kriegsman, telephone conversations with the author, November 29, 2018, July 8, 2019, and June 25, 2020.

402   "faithful Leica": Soares, "Unearthing the Treasures."

402   "great, inspired": EH, interview by Lee Edward Stern, *Speaking of Dance*, WNYC, November 13, 1981, JRDD, *MGZTC 3-1349.

403   "Such fresh passion!": Sali Ann Kriegsman, telephone conversation with the author, November 29, 2018. Erick Hawkins died on November 23, 1994, in New York City.

403   "wanted children": Tynan, "Martha Graham," *The Observer* (London), August 18, 1963.

403   congenital endocrine dysfunction: Diagnosis of MG ailment, Ralph Hale, MD, American College of Obstetricians and Gynecologists, emails to the author, July 24, 2017, and ff.

403   "In renewed contact": Alan R. Kriegsman, "The Graham Vision: Dance as Sculpture; the Tedium of Genius," *Washington Post*, February 25, 1981.

404   "the sin of heresy": Unamuno, *Tragic Sense of Life*, 71–72.

Bibliography

Adamo, Mark. "Albemarle Ensemble Performs *King Lear.*" *Washington Post,* March 11, 1991.

Adams, James Ring. "'A Great Charge': How Native Dance Changed American Ballet." *National Museum of the American Indian Magazine* 13, no. 4 (Winter 2012): 14–20.

Adams, Doug, and Diane Apostolos-Cappadonna, eds. *Dance as Religious Studies.* Eugene, OR: Wipf and Stock, 2001.

Addington, Sarah. "End of Vaudeville" (part 1), *Theatre Arts Magazine,* June, 1932, 7.

Adorno, Theodor W. *The Culture Industry: Selected Essays on Mass Culture.* London: Routledge, 1991.

Aeschylus. *Seven Against Thebes.* Translated by Anthony Hecht and Helen H. Bacon. New York: Oxford University Press, 1973.

Ahlborn, Richard E. *The Penitente Moradas of Abiquiú.* Washington, DC: Smithsonian Institution Press, 1986.

Albright, Daniel. *Modernism and Music: An Anthology of Sources.* Chicago: University of Chicago Press, 2004.

———. *Untwisting the Serpent: Modernism in Music, Literature, and Other Arts.* Chicago: University of Chicago Press, 2000.

Alexander, Louis. "Association News." *Journal of Health and Physical Education* 4, no. 6 (June 1933): 36–39.

Alexiou, Margaret. *The Ritual Lament in Greek Tradition.* Cambridge: Cambridge University Press, 1974.

Allen, Frederick Lewis. *Only Yesterday: An Informal History of the Nineteen Twenties.* New York: Harper & Row, 1931.

Alter, Judith B. "Havelock Ellis's Essay 'The Art of Dancing': A Reconsideration." *Dance Research Journal* 24, no. 1 (Spring 1992): 27–36.

American Composers Alliance. "Charles Mills." https://composers.com/charles-mills.

Amort, Andrea. "Free Dance in Interwar Vienna." In *Interwar Vienna: Culture Between Tradition and Modernity,* edited by Deborah Holmes and Lisa Silverman, 117–42. Rochester, NY: Camden House, 2009.

Anderson, Donna K. *The Works of Charles T. Griffes: A Descriptive Catalogue.* Ann Arbor, MI: UMI Research Press, 1983.

Anderson, Jack. *Ballet & Modern Dance: A Concise History.* Princeton, NJ: Princeton Book Company, 1992.

———. "A Champion of Racial Justice When Little Prevailed." *New York Times,* August 27, 1995.

———. "Dance: Erick Hawkins and 'God's Angry Man.'" *New York Times,* October 16, 1984.

———. "Dance View: Who Was Gret Palucca? A Legend in Her Time." *New York Times,* August 15, 1993.

Anderson, John Murray. *Out Without My Rubbers: The Memoirs of John Murray Anderson, as Told to and Written by Hugh Abercrombie Anderson.* New York: Library Publishers, 1954.

Andrews, Edward D. "The Dance in Shaker Ritual." In *Chronicles of the American Dance from the Shakers to Martha Graham,* edited by Paul Magriel, Vol. 1, No. 4, New York: Dance Index, April 1942: 56–67.

Andrews, Mildred, and John Caldbick. "Cornish College of the Arts." HistoryLink.org Essay 596, November 12, 2014. http://www.historylink.org/File/596.

Anella, Tony. "Learning from the Pueblos." In *Pueblo Style and Regional Architecture,* edited by Nicholas C. Markovich, Wolfgang F. E. Preiser, and Fred G. Sturm, 31–45. New York: Van Nostrand Reinhold, 1990.

Apollonius of Rhodes. *Jason and Medea.* Translated by E. V. Rieu. London: Penguin Little Black Classics, 2015.

Apostolos-Cappadona, Diane. "'. . . With a Book in Your Hands': A Reflection on Imaging, Reading, Space, and Female Agency." *Religions* 10, no. 3 (March 2019): 178–91.

Appel, Alfred. *Jazz Modernism: From Ellington and Armstrong to Matisse and Joyce.* New York: Alfred A. Knopf, 2002.

Archer, Kenneth. "Nicholas Roerich and His Theatrical Designs: A Research Survey." *Dance Research Journal* 18, no. 2 (Winter 1986–1987): 3–6.

Armitage, Merle, ed. *Martha Graham: The Early Years.* New York: Da Capo Press, 1978.

Armstrong, Everhardt. "Art of Martha Graham Evokes Great Ovation." *Seattle Post-Intelligencer,* June 3, 1930.

Armstrong, Karen. *A Short History of Myth.* Edinburgh and New York: Canongate, 2005.

Arvey, Verna. *Choreographic Music: Music for the Dance.* New York: Dutton, 1941.

Ashton, Dore. *Noguchi: East and West.* New York: Alfred A. Knopf, 1992.

Atkinson, J. Brooks. "Dance and Music in Dramatic Form: Cleveland Symphony Orchestra a Part of Irene Lewisohn's Synthetic Entertainment." *New York Times,* February 21, 1930.

———. "Elizabeth the Poet: Katharine Cornell at Her Almost Forgotten Best as the Heroine in 'The Barretts of Wimpole Street.'" *New York Times,* February 22, 1931.

———. "The Play: MacLeish's 'Panic.'" *New York Times,* March 16, 1935.

———. "Six Medieval Miracle Plays Under Martha Graham's Direction—Costumes and Pantomines." *New York Times,* February 6, 1933.

Au, Susan. "Martha Graham." In *The Grove Dictionary of American Music,* 2nd edition, edited by Charles Hiroshi Garrett. New York: Oxford University Press, 2013.

Auner, Joseph. "'Heart and Brain in Music': The Genesis of Schoenberg's *Die glückliche Hand.*" In *Constructive Dissonance: Arnold Schoenberg and the Transformations of Twentieth-Century Culture,* 112–20, edited by Juliane Brand and Christopher Hailey. Berkeley: University of California Press, 1997.

Austin, Mary Hunter. *The American Rhythm: Studies and Reexpressions of Amerindian Songs.* New York: Harcourt, Brace and Company, 1923.

———. *The Land of Journeys' Ending.* New York: Century, 1924.

————. *Stories from the Country of Lost Borders*. Edited by Marjorie Pryse. New Brunswick, NJ: Rutgers University Press, 1987.

Bachelard, Gaston. *Air and Dreams: An Essay on the Imagination of Movement*. Translated by Edith R. Farrell and C. Frederick Farrell. Dallas: Dallas Institute, 1988.

Bachmann, Marie-Laure. *Dalcroze Today: An Education Through and into Music*. Translated by David Parlett. Oxford: Clarendon Press, 1991.

Bair, Deirdre. *Jung: A Biography*. Boston: Little, Brown, 2003.

Baldwin, Neil. "Defining Modern Dance: Martha Graham and *The Rite of Spring* in America." Paper presented at the Society of Dance History Scholars *Sacre* Celebration Conference, York College, Toronto, April 20, 2013.

————. *Legends of the Plumed Serpent: Biography of a Mexican God*. New York: Public Affairs, 1998.

————. *Man Ray: American Artist*. New York: Clarkson N. Potter, 1988.

Bannerman, Henrietta. "Is Dance a Language? Movement, Meaning and Communication." *Dance Research Journal* 32, no. 1 (May 2014): 65–80.

————. "An Overview of the Development of Martha Graham's Movement System (1926–1992)." *Dance Research Journal* 17, no. 2 (Winter 1999): 9–46.

————. "Thoroughly Modern Martha." *Dance Theatre Journal* 17, no. 2 (January 2001): 32–36.

Barbanel, Josh. "Lehman Engel, 71, Conductor of Broadway Musicals, Dead." *New York Times*, August 30, 1982.

Barretto, Nolini. "The Role of Martha Graham's Notebooks in Her Creative Process." In "Martha Graham," edited by Alice Helpern. Special issue, *Choreography and Dance* vol. 5, part 2 (1999): 112.

Barfield, Owen. *Poetic Diction: A Study in Meaning*. Middletown, CT: Wesleyan University Press, 1973.

Barker, Barbara. "Agnes de Mille, Liberated Expatriate, and the American Suite, 1938." *Dance Chronicle* 19, no. 2 (1996): 113–50.

Barnes, Clive. "Dance: Martha Graham, Fokine and History." *New York Times*, June 2, 1977.

————. "Dance: Graham Company Accents Style and Beauty of 'Diversion of Angels.'" *New York Times*, November 11, 1965.

Barthes, Roland. *Image Music Text*. New York: Hill & Wang, 1977.

Baudelaire, Charles. *The Painter of Modern Life and Other Essays*. Edited and translated by Jonathan Mayne. New York: Phaidon, 1964.

Bauer, Marion, and Claire R. Reis. "Twenty-Five Years with the League of Composers." *Musical Quarterly* 34, no. 1 (January 1948): 1–14.

Baur, John E. "The Health Seeker in the Westward Movement, 1830–1900." *Mississippi Valley Historical Review* 46, no. 1 (June 1959): 91–110.

Beaman, Patricia, and May O'Donnell. "Looking Back: An Interview with May O'Donnell." *Dance Research Journal* 34, no. 1 (Summer 2002): 90–97.

Beauvoir, Simone de. *The Second Sex*. Translated by Constance Borde and Sheila Malovany-Chevallier. New York: Vintage Books, 2011.

Becker, Gisela, ed. *Feminist Aesthetics*. Translated by Harriet Anderson. Boston: Beacon, 1985.

Beiswanger, George W. "Doing and Viewing Dances: A Perspective for the Practice of Criticism." Lecture delivered at the annual meeting of the American Society for Aesthetics, Fairfield, Connecticut. In *Dance Perspectives*, no. 55 (1973): 7–13.

————. "Moderns in Review." *Dance News*, January 1944: 3.

Beiswanger, George W., Wilfried A. Hofmann, and David Michael Levin. *Three Essays in Dance Aesthetics*. New York: Dance Perspectives Foundation, 1973.

Bel Geddes, Norman, et al. "Theatre Planning: A Symposium." *Educational Theatre Journal* 2, no. 1 (March 1950): 1–7.

Belitt, Ben. "The Habit of Angels." In *Wilderness Stair: Poems 1938–1954*. New York: Grove, 1955.

Bell, Catherine. *Ritual Theory, Ritual Practice*. New York: Oxford University Press, 2009.

Bell, Robert. "Echoes of the New York Stage." *Washington Post*, March 6, 1927.

Bell-Kanner, Karen. *Frontiers: The Life and Times of Bonnie Bird*. Amsterdam: Harwood Academic, 1998.

Berg, Shelley C. *Le sacre du printemps: Seven Productions from Nijinsky to Martha Graham*. Ann Arbor, MI: UMI Research Press, 1988.

Bergan, Ronald. "Joseph Wiseman Obituary: Versatile Character Actor Best Remembered on Screen as James Bond's Adversary Dr No." *Guardian*, October 20, 2009.

Berman, Greta. "Painting in the Key of Color: The Art of Nicholas Roerich." *Juilliard Journal*, May–August http://journal.juilliard.edu/journal/painting-key-color-art-nicholas-roerich.

Bernstein, Michael André. "Making Modernist Masterpieces." *Modernism/modernity* 5, no. 3 (September 1988): 1–17.

Biersdorfer, J. D. "Setting the Stage with Shadows." *New York Times*, May 22, 2009.

Bird, Dorothy. *Bird's Eye View: Dancing with Martha Graham and on Broadway*. With a foreword by Joyce Greenberg. Pittsburgh: University of Pittsburgh Press, 1997.

Bloch, Suzanne. *Ernest Bloch: Creative Spirit. A Program Resource Book*. New York: Jewish Music Council of the National Jewish Welfare Board, 1976.

Bloom, Harold. *The Anxiety of Influence: A Theory of Poetry*. 2nd ed. New York: Oxford University Press, 1997.

Blundell, Sue, and Margaret Williamson, eds. *The Sacred and the Feminine in Ancient Greece*. London: Routledge, 1998.

Bobinski, George S. *Carnegie Libraries: Their History and Impact on American Public Library Development*. Chicago: American Library Association, 1969.

Bodensteiner, Kirsten Amalie. "Criticism Refined: An Analysis of Selected Dance Criticism of Alan M. Kriegsman." Master's thesis, American University, 2000.

Bodkin, Maud. *Archetypal Patterns in Poetry: Psychological Studies of Imagination*. London: Oxford University Press, 1934.

Bohm, Jerome. "Festival Ends Dance Session at Bennington." *New York Herald Tribune*, August 18, 1935.

———. "Suite Features Martha Graham Dance Program." *New York Herald Tribune*, December 21, 1936.

Bolens, Guillemette. *The Style of Gestures: Embodiment and Cognition in Literary Narrative*. Baltimore: Johns Hopkins University Press, 2012.

Bradbury, Malcolm. "The Nonhomemade World: European and American Modernism." *American Quarterly* 39, no. 1 (Spring 1987): 27–36.

Bradley, Karen K. *Rudolf Laban*. London: Routledge, 2009.

Brayshaw, Teresa, and Noel Witts. *The Twentieth-Century Performance Reader*. 3rd ed. London: Routledge, 2014.

Brock, H. I. "The Battle of the Arts in the Machine Age." Review of *Revolt in the Arts*, by Oliver W. Sayler. *New York Times Book Review*, December 14, 1930: T2.

———. "Our Theatre, Past and Present: A Vagabond Profession Now Respectable Even in

This Country." Review of *Our American Theatre,* by Oliver W. Sayler. *New York Times Book Review,* December 23, 1923: 4.

Brooks, Lynn Matluck. "A Bold Step Forward: Genevieve Oswald and the Dance Collection of the New York Public Library." *Dance Chronicle* 34, no. 3 (2011): 447–86.

Brown, Jean Morrison, Naomi Mindlin, and Charles H. Woodford, eds. *The Vision of Modern Dance in the Words of Its Creators.* 2nd ed. Hightstown, NJ: Princeton Book Company, 1998.

Bruner, Jerome. "Life as Narrative." *Social Research* 71, no. 3 (Fall 2004): 691–710.

Burkert, Walter. *Ancient Mystery Cults.* Cambridge, MA: Harvard University Press, 1987.

Burnshaw, Stanley. *The Seamless Web: Language-Thinking, Culture-Knowledge, Art-Experience.* New York: George Braziller, 1970.

Butler, Gervaise. " 'American Document' Re-Viewed." *Dance Observer,* November 1938.

———. "The Stage This Quarter." *Trend,* April–June 1933.

Butterworth, Jo, and Liesbeth Wildschut. *Contemporary Choreography: A Critical Reader.* London: Routledge, 2009.

Caldwell, Helen. *Michio Ito: The Dancer and His Dances.* Berkeley: University of California Press, 1977.

Campbell, Joseph. "Betwixt the Cup and the Lip." *Dance Observer* 11, no. 3 (March 1944): 30–31.

———. *The Ecstasy of Being: Mythology and Dance.* Edited by Nancy Allison. Novato, CA: Joseph Campbell Foundation, New World Library, 2017.

———. *Goddesses: Mysteries of the Feminine Divine.* Edited by Safron Rossi. Novato, CA: Joseph Campbell Foundation, New World Library, 2013.

———. *The Hero with a Thousand Faces.* New York: Pantheon Books, 1949.

———. "The Jubilee of Content and Form." *Dance Observer* 12, no. 5 (May 1945): 52–53.

———. *The Mysteries: Papers from the Eranos Yearbooks.* Bollingen Series. Princeton, NJ: Princeton University Press, 1955.

———, ed. *The Portable Jung.* New York: Penguin Books, 1971.

———. "Symbolism and the Dance, Parts 1, 2 and 3." In *The Ecstasy of Being,* 27–51.

———. "Text, or Idea?" *Dance Observer* 11, no. 6 (June–July 1944): 66, 73.

Capobianco, Richard. "Heidegger and Jung: Dwelling Near the Source." *Review of Existential Psychology and Psychiatry* 21, nos. 1–3 (1993): 50–62.

Caraveli-Chaves, Anna. "Bridge between Worlds: The Greek Women's Lament as Communicative Event." *Journal of American Folklore* 93, no. 368 (April–June 1980): 129–57.

Carbone, Teresa, ed. *Youth and Beauty: Art of the American Twenties.* New York: Skira Rizzoli, 2011.

Carman, Bliss. *The Making of Personality.* Boston: L. C. Page, 1908.

Carruthers, Ian. "A Translation of Fifteen Pages of Ito Michio's *Autobiography 'Utsukushiku Naru Kyoshitsu.*' " *Canadian Journal of Irish Studies* 2, no. 1 (May 1976): 32–43.

Carter, Curtis. "Reissue of *Martha Graham: Sixteen Dances in Photographs.*" *Dance Dimensions* 8, nos. 1–2 (Spring 1981): 40–41.

Castillo, Greg. "Le Corbusier and the Skyscraper Primitives." *Architectural Theory Review* 18, no. 1 (August 2013): 8–29.

Catton, Pia. "The Great 20th Century Dance Companies Face an Existential Crisis." *Bloomberg Businessweek,* March 22, 2018. https://www.bloomberg.com/news/articles/2018-03-22/great-20th-century-dance-companies-face-an-existential-crisis.

Cawley, A. C., ed. *Everyman and Medieval Miracle Plays.* London: J. M. Dent, 1993.

Caws, Mary Ann, ed. *Manifesto: A Century of Isms*. Lincoln: University of Nebraska Press, 2001.

Chávez, Carlos. *Musical Thought*. Cambridge, MA: Harvard University Press, 1961.

Cheney, Sheldon. *A Primer of Modern Art*. New York: Horace Liveright, 1924.

Chin, Gwin. "Japanese Dancers in America: What Draws Them?" *New York Times,* December 2, 1979.

Chisholm, Hugh, ed. "Dix, Dorothea Lynde." In *Encyclopedia Britannica,* 346. Cambridge, UK: Cambridge University Press, 1911.

Chodorow, Joan. "The Body as Symbol: Dance/Movement in Analysis." *The Jung Page* (blog), October 27, 2013. http://www.jungpage.org/learn/articles/analytical-psychology/88-the -body-as-symbol-dancemovement-in-analysis.

Chujoy, Anatole. "Martha Graham and Dance Company." *Dance News,* June–August 1946. [Clipping, Library of Congress, n.p.]

Cizmic, Maria. "Embodied Experimentalism and Henry Cowell's *The Banshee*." *American Music* 28, no. 4 (Winter 2010): 436–58.

Clark, T. J. *Farewell to an Idea: Episodes from a History of Modernism*. New Haven, CT: Yale University Press, 1999.

Coburn, F. W. "Water Colors and Sculptures Now Exhibited at Harvard Square Gallery." *Boston Herald,* March 1, 1930.

Cohan, Robert. "Reminiscences and Reflections at Eighty." *Dance Research Journal* 22, no. 2 (Winter 2004): 101–38.

Cohen, Selma Jeanne. *Doris Humphrey: An Artist First*. Middletown, CT: Wesleyan University Press, 1972.

———. *The Modern Dance: Seven Statements of Belief*. Middletown, CT: Wesleyan University Press, 1969.

———. "A Prolegomenon to an Aesthetics of Dance." *Journal of Aesthetics and Art Criticism* 21, no. 1 (Autumn 1962): 19–26.

Cohen-Straytner, Barbara Naomi, and A. J. Pischi. "The Franchising of Denishawn." *Dance Data,* no. 4 (1979): 1–48.

Coleman, Emily. "Martha Graham Still Leaps Forward." *New York Times,* April 9, 1961.

Coleman, Heidi, et al., eds. *Isamu Noguchi Catalogue Raisonné*. New York: Isamu Noguchi Foundation, 2012 and ff.

Conner, Lynne. *Spreading the Gospel of Modern Dance: Newspaper Dance Criticism in the United States, 1850–1934*. Pittsburgh: University of Pittsburgh Press, 1997.

Conner, Lynne, and Susan Gillis-Kruman. *The Early Moderns*. Online tutorial, 1996. http:// www.pitt.edu/~gillis/dance/disp.html.

Coolsma, Nan. "Aaron Copland's *Piano Variations*: A Study in Character." *McMaster Music Analysis Colloquium* 4 (2005): 38–51.

Copeland, Roger, and Marshall Cohen, eds. *What Is Dance? Readings in Theory and Criticism*. New York: Oxford University Press, 1983.

Copland, Aaron. "Claire Reis (1889–1978)." *Musical Quarterly* 64, no. 3 (July 1978): 386–88.

Copland, Aaron, and Vivian Perlis. *Copland: 1900 through 1942*. New York: St. Martin's Press, 1999.

Corn, Wanda M. *The Great American Thing: Modern Art and National Identity, 1915–1935*. Berkeley: University of California Press, 1999.

Cornish, Nellie Centennial. *Miss Aunt Nellie: The Autobiography of Nellie C. Cornish*. Edited by Ellen Van Volkenburg Browne and Edward Nordhoff Beck. Seattle: University of Washington Press, 1964. [Includes "A Tribute from Martha Graham."]

Cowell, Henry, ed. *American Composers on American Music.* Stanford, CA: Stanford University Press, 1933.

———. Papers. Music Division, The New York Public Library for the Performing Arts. *Synchrony of Dance, Music, Light.* "Coreography" [*sic*] Martha Graham. 1930. JPB 00-03, box 39, folder 23, L464.

Cowell, Mary-Jean, ed. "History of Michio Ito" and "The Ito Technique and Gesture Sequences." In *Michio Ito Study Guide.* Salt Lake City: Repertory Dance Company, 2009. https://rdtutah.org/5299-2/.

Cowell, Mary-Jean, and Satoru Shimazaki. "East and West in the Work of Michio Ito." *Dance Research Journal* 26, no. 2 (Autumn 1994): 11–23.

Cowley, Malcolm. *Exile's Return: A Literary Odyssey of the 1920s.* New York: Penguin Books, 1994.

Craft, Robert. "100 Years On: Igor Stravinsky on *The Rite of Spring.*" *Times Literary Supplement,* June 19, 2013.

Crane, Hart. *Complete Poems & Selected Letters.* New York: Library of America, 2006.

———. *O My Land, My Friends: The Selected Letters of Hart Crane.* Edited by Langdon Hammer and Brom Weber. New York: Four Walls Eight Windows, 1997.

Christensen, Lisbeth Bredholt, Olav Hammer, and David A. Warburton, eds. *The Handbook of Religions in Ancient Europe.* London: Routledge, 2014.

Critchley, Simon. "A Tragic Honesty." Review of *Grief Lessons,* by Anne Carson. *Bookforum,* Summer 2014. https://www.bookforum.com/print/2102/a-tragic-honesty-13267.

Crowley, Alice Lewisohn. *The Neighborhood Playhouse: Leaves from a Theatre Scrapbook.* New York: Theatre Arts Books, 1959.

Csikszentmihalyi, Mihaly. *Flow: The Psychology of Optimal Experience.* New York: Harper Perennial, 1991.

Cullen, Frank. *Vaudeville, Old & New: An Encyclopedia of Variety Performers in America.* New York: Routledge, 2007.

Curtwright, Bob. "Raised in Wichita, Silent Screen Star Louise Brooks Dies." *Wichita Eagle-Beacon,* August 9, 1985.

Cushing, Thomas, et. al. *History of Allegheny County, Pennsylvania: Including Its Early Settlement and Progress to the Present Time.* Chicago: A. Warner, 1889.

Dahlhaus, Carl. *The Idea of Absolute Music.* Chicago: University of Chicago Press, 1989.

Dahlinger, Charles W. "Old Allegheny." *Western Pennsylvania Historical Magazine* 1, no. 4 (October 1918): 161–223.

Dain, Phyllis. *The New York Public Library: A History of Its Founding and Early Years.* New York: New York Public Library, 1972.

Dalbotten, Ted. *To Bear Witness.* Self-published, Xlibris, 2007.

Daly, Ann. *Critical Gestures: Writings on Dance and Culture.* Middletown, CT: Wesleyan University Press, 2002.

———. *Done into Dance: Isadora Duncan in America.* Middletown, CT: Wesleyan University Press, 2002.

———. "An Inspiration Compounded of Hands and Feet." *New York Times,* January 31, 1999.

———. "Isadora Duncan and the Distinction of Dance." In *Critical Gestures: Writings on Dance and Culture,* 246–62. Middletown, CT: Wesleyan University Press, 2002.

Dana, Margery. "Martha Graham's 'American Document' at Carnegie." *New York Daily Worker,* October 12, 1938.

Dance Heritage Coalition. *Beyond Memory: Preserving the Documents of Our Dance Heritage.* Pelham, New York, 1994.

Daniel, Clay. "Reconstructing Weidman: A Dancer's Perspective." *Dance Research Journal* 39, no. 2 (Winter 2007): 83–98.

Daniel, Oliver. "*The Rite of Spring* in America: Graham-Stokowski-Massine." *Ballet Review* 10, no. 2 (Summer 1982): 67–71.

———. *Stokowski: A Counterpoint of View.* New York: Dodd, Mead, 1982.

Danza, Cynthia. "The Neighborhood Playhouse." Landmarks Preservation Commission, Designation List No. 440 LP-2433, March 22, 2011. http://s-media.nyc.gov/agencies/lpc/lp/2433.pdf.

Davidson, Jo. *Between Sittings: An Informal Autobiography.* New York: Dial Press, 1951.

Daye, Anne. "Keeping Alive the Wonder: *Primitive Mysteries,* New York 1931 to London 2009." *Dance Chronicle,* no. 33 (2010): 82–112.

De Huff, Elizabeth Willis, and Homer Grunn. *From Desert & Pueblo: Five Authentic Navajo and Tewa Indian Songs.* Boston: Oliver Ditson, 1924.

Delius, Rudolf von. *Mary Wigman.* Dresden, Germany: Carl Reissner, 1925.

Delpar, Helen. *The Enormous Vogue of Things Mexican: Cultural Relations between the United States and Mexico, 1920–1935.* Tuscaloosa: University of Alabama Press, 1992.

Delage, Roger. "Ravel and Chabrier." *Musical Quarterly* 61, no. 4 (1975): 546–52.

De Mille, Agnes George. *Dance to the Piper.* Boston: Little, Brown, 1952.

———. *Leaps in the Dark: Art and the World.* Edited by Mindy Aloff. Tallahassee: University Press of Florida, 2011.

———. *Martha: The Life and Work of Martha Graham.* New York: Random House, 1991.

———. "The New Ballerina." *Theatre Arts Monthly,* 15, no. 5, May 1931, 426–36.

Dempster, Elizabeth. "Women Writing the Body: Let's Watch a Little How She Dances." *Writings on Dance,* no. 3 (Winter 1988): 223–29.

Denby, Edwin. *Dance Writings.* Edited by Robert Cornfield and William MacKay. New York: Alfred A. Knopf, 1986.

———. "Martha Graham's New 'Deaths and Entrances.'" *New York Herald Tribune,* January 16, 1944.

Derrida, Jacques. *Archive Fever: A Freudian Impression.* Translated by Eric Prenowitz. Chicago: University of Chicago Press, 1996.

Dewey, John. *Art as Experience.* New York: Minton, Balch, 1934.

Diamond, David. "Balancing Acts: Anne Bogart and Kristin Linklater Debate the Current Trends in American Actor-Training." *American Theatre,* January 2001. https://www.americantheatre.org/2001/01/01/balancing-acts/.

Dillon, Matthew. *Girls and Women in Classical Greek Religion.* London: Routledge, 2002.

Dissanayake, Ellen. *Homo Aestheticus: Where Art Comes from and Why.* New York: Free Press, 1992.

Doering, James M. *The Great Orchestrator: Arthur Judson and American Arts Management.* Urbana: University of Illinois Press, 2013.

Dolson, Grace Neal. "The Influence of Schopenhauer upon Friedrich Nietzsche." *Philosophical Review* 10, no. 3 (May 1901): 241–50.

Donne, John. *Deaths Duell, or, A Consolation to the Soule, Against the Dying Life, and Living*

Death of the Body. London, 1632. https://www.bl.uk/collection-items/deaths-duel-by-john
-donne.

Douglas, Ann. *Terrible Honesty: Mongrel Manhattan in the 1920s*. New York: Farrar, Straus and Giroux, 1996.

Downes, Olin. "Composers League in Unique Program: Give Monteverdi's 'Combat of Tancred and Clorinda' and Stravinsky's 'Les Noces.'" *New York Times*, April 26, 1929.

———. "Old and Modern Revolutionaries: League of Composers' Programs to Illustrate 'Radical' Tendencies of Yesterday and Today—Will Publish New Works." *New York Times*, May 29, 1927.

———. "Stokowski Gives Contrasting Music: Brilliant Audience Crowds the Metropolitan to Hear Philadelphia Orchestra." *New York Times*, April 23, 1930.

Dreier, Katherine S. *Shawn: The Dancer*. New York: A. S. Barnes, 1933.

Duberman, Martin. *The Worlds of Lincoln Kirstein*. New York: Alfred A. Knopf, 2007.

Dubin, Zan. "The Hawkins Code: Effortlessness Is Everything for the Famed Choreographer, Who Will Bring His New Dance About Navajo Myths to Orange County." *Los Angeles Times*, April 21, 1991.

Dué [Hackney], Casey. *The Captive Woman's Lament in Greek Tragedy*. Austin: University of Texas Press, 2006.

Duffus, R. L. "A Dying Race Sits in Solemn Council." *New York Times*, May 12, 1929.

Dugdale, Eric. *Greek Theatre in Context*. Cambridge: Cambridge University Press, 2008.

Dumenil, Lynn. *The Modern Temper: American Culture and Society in the 1920s*. New York: Hill & Wang, 1995.

Duncan, Isadora. *The Art of the Dance*. Edited by Sheldon Cheney. New York: Theatre Arts Books, 1928.

———. *My Life*. New York: Boni & Liveright, 1927. Reprinted with an introduction by Joan Acocella. New York: Liveright, 2013.

Dunn, Daisy. "When a Love Poet Writes an Epic: Catullus's 'Poem 64.'" *Los Angeles Review of Books*, August 22, 2018.

Dunning, Jennifer. "Carrying On in a Master's Steps—Erick Hawkins's Muse and Mate." *New York Times*, March 1, 1995.

———. "Rediscovering a Pioneer Dance Critic." *New York Times*, March 5, 1987.

———. "Batsheva de Rothschild, 84, a Patron of Graham." *New York Times*, April 22, 1999.

———. "Erick Hawkins—Celebrating the Body and the Spirit." *New York Times*, September 13, 1981.

———. "The Graham Company Faces Life Without Martha." *New York Times*, October 6, 1991.

———. "Graham's 'Celebration,' from 1934." *New York Times*, October 13, 1991.

———. "'Heretic,' Early Work of Martha Graham." *New York Times*, October 24, 1987.

———. "Lessons Learned in Youth Have Lasting Influence." *New York Times*, September 18, 1988.

———. "Muriel Stuart, 90, Dancer for Pavlova and Ballet Teacher." *New York Times*, January 30, 1991.

Duryea, Bill. "At Studio @620, a Reading of Poet Archibald MacLeish's Prescient 'Panic.'" *Tampa Bay Times*, August 18, 2012.

Duus, Masayo. *The Life of Isamu Noguchi: Life Without Borders*. Princeton, NJ: Princeton University Press, 2004.

Duvert, Elizabeth. "Georgia O'Keeffe's *Radiator Building*: Icon of Glamorous Gotham." *Places* 2, no. 2 (1984): 3–17.

Eagleton, Terry. *The Event of Literature*. New Haven, CT: Yale University Press, 2012.

Easton, Carol. *No Intermissions: The Life of Agnes de Mille*. New York: Little, Brown, 1996.

Ecker, Gisela, ed. *Feminist Aesthetics*. Translated by Harriet Anderson. Boston: Beacon, 1986.

Eddy, Arthur Jerome. *Cubists and Post-Impressionism*. Chicago: A. C. McClurg, 1919.

Edwards, Holly. *Noble Dreams, Wicked Pleasures: Orientalism in America, 1870–1930*. With essays by Brian T. Allen, Steven C. Caton, Zepnep Çelik, and Oleg Grabar. Princeton, NJ: Princeton University Press, 2000.

Eilber, Janet. "Shape Shapes Meaning: A Tale of Two Marthas: The Play's the Thing." www.danceinsider.com/f-2005/f0406_1.html. 2005.

Eiselt, B. Sunday. "*La Morada de Nuestra Señora de Guadalupe:* Archaeological Assessment and National Register Update, Research Design for Summer 2010 Field Work." Dallas, TX: Southern Methodist University, 2010.

Eliot, T. S. *Four Quartets*. New York: Harcourt, Brace, 1943.

———. "Tradition and the Individual Talent." In *The Sacred Wood: Essays on Poetry and Criticism*, 42–53. London: Methuen, 1920.

"Elizabeth McCausland, Critic and Idealist." *Archives of American Art Journal* 6, no. 2 (April 1966): 16–20.

Ellis, Havelock. *The Dance of Life*. New York: Houghton Mifflin, 1923.

———. "The Philosophy of Dancing." *Atlantic Monthly,* February 1914: 197–206.

Engel, Lehman. "The Dance: A Critical Review." *Trend* 2, no. 1 (April–June 1933): 30–31.

———. "Music for the Dance." *Dance Observer* 1, no. 1 (February 1934): 4, 8.

———. "Six Mystery Plays." *Trend*, April–June 1933.

———. *This Bright Day: An Autobiography*. New York: Macmillan, 1974.

Enstad, Nan. "The 'New Woman' Unframed: Painting Gender and Class in Consumer America." *American Quarterly* 47, no. 3 (September 1995): 548–55.

Enwezor, Okwui. "These Weary Territories: A Conversation with Matthew Barney." *Modern Painters,* April 2014: 64–73.

Erenberg, Lewis A. *Steppin' Out: New York Nightlife and the Transformation of American Culture, 1890–1930*. Westport, CT: Greenwood Press, 1981.

Eshel, Ruth. "Bethsabée Rothschild, 1914–1999." *The Shalvi/Hyman Encyclopedia of Jewish Women*. Jewish Women's Archive, February 27, 2009. https://jwa.org/encyclopedia/article/rothschild-bethsabee-de.

Espinosa, J. Manuel. "The Origin of the Penitentes of New Mexico: Separating Fact from Fiction." *Catholic Historical Review* 79, no. 3 (July 1993): 454–77.

Estey, Judy. "Adolph Bolm (1884–1951)." Dance Heritage Coalition, 2012.

Euripides. *Grief Lessons: Four Plays by Euripides*. Translated by Anne Carson. New York: New York Review Books, 2006.

———. *Medea and Other Plays*. Edited and translated by James Morwood. Oxford: Oxford University Press, 2009.

———. *Ten Plays*. Translated by Moses Hadas. New York: Bantam Classics, 1981.

———. *The Trojan Women and Other Plays*. Translated by James Morwood. Oxford: Oxford University Press, 2009.

Evan, Blanche. "Her Chosen Theme: A Modern Dancer's Credo." *New Masses,* July 20, 1938: 17.

Evans, Harold. *The American Century*. New York: Alfred A. Knopf, 2000.

Evans, Bessie, and May G. Evans. *American Indian Dance Steps.* New York: A. S. Barnes & Company, 1931.

Fancher, Gordon, and Gerald Myers, eds. *Philosophical Essays on Dance.* Brooklyn, NY: Dance Horizons, 1981.

Fang, Achilles. "Fenollosa and Pound." *Harvard Journal of Asiatic Studies* 20, nos. 1–2 (June 1957): 213–38.

Fauser, Annegret. *Aaron Copland's Appalachian Spring.* New York: Oxford University Press, 2017.

Feldman, Edmund Burke. *Varieties of Visual Experience.* Englewood Cliffs, NJ: Prentice Hall, 1967.

Fenollosa, Ernest, and Ezra Pound. *The Chinese Written Character as a Medium for Poetry.* Edited by Haun Saussy, Jonathan Stalling, and Lucas Klein. New York: Fordham University Press, 2008.

———. *"Noh," or, Accomplishment: A Study of the Classical Stage of Japan.* New York: Alfred A. Knopf, 1917.

Fergusson, Erna. *Dancing Gods: Indian Ceremonials of New Mexico and Arizona.* New York: Alfred A. Knopf, 1931.

Ferriss, Hugh. *The Metropolis of Tomorrow.* New York: Ives Washburn, 1929.

Fink, Augusta. *I-Mary: A Biography of Mary Austin.* Tucson: University of Arizona Press, 1983.

Fink, Robert. " 'Rigoroso (♪ = 126)': *The Rite of Spring* and the Forging of a Modernist Performing Style." *Journal of the American Musicological Society* 52, no. 2 (Summer 1999): 299–362.

Fitton, J. L. "Three Mycenaean Terracottas." *British Museum Magazine,* Summer 1996.

Fitts, Dudley, ed. *Four Greek Plays.* New York: Harcourt, Brace, 1960.

Fitzgerald, F. Scott. "Echoes of the Jazz Age." *Scribner's Magazine* 90, no. 5 (November 1931): 459–65.

Fleisher, Mary. *Embodied Texts: Symbolist Playwright-Dancer Collaborations.* Amsterdam: Rodopi, 2007.

Flusser, Vilém. *Gestures.* Translated by Nancy Ann Roth. Minneapolis: University of Minnesota Press, 2014.

Fokine, Michel. "A Sad Art." *Dance Magazine,* May 1931: 29.

Foley, Helene P., and Jean E. Howard. "Introduction: The Urgency of Tragedy Now." *PMLA* 129, no. 4 (October 2014): 617–33.

Fonaroff, Nina. "Louis Horst." *Dance Research Journal* 2, no. 2 (Summer 1984): 3–10.

Force, Juliana, and Hermon More, eds. *The Whitney Museum and Its Collection.* New York: Whitney Museum of American Art, 1931.

Forster, Kurt W. "Aby Warburg: His Study of Ritual and Art on Two Continents." Translated by David Britt. *October* 77 (Summer 1996): 5–24.

Foster, Susan Leigh. "Choreographing Your Move." In *Move: Choreographing You: Art and Dance Since the 1960s,* edited by Stephanie Rosenthal, 32–37. Cambridge, MA: MIT Press, 2011.

Foster, Hal, Rosalind Krauss, Yve-Alain Bois, Benjamin H. D. Buchloh, and David Joselit. *Art Since 1900.* Vol. 1, *1900–1944.* New York: Thames & Hudson, 2011.

Foulkes, Julia. *Modern Bodies: Dance and American Modernism from Martha Graham to Alvin Ailey.* Chapel Hill: University of North Carolina Press, 2002.

Fraleigh, Sondra Horton, and Penelope Hanstein, eds. *Researching Dance: Evolving Modes of Inquiry.* Pittsburgh: University of Pittsburgh Press, 1999.

Frank, Waldo. *Our America.* New York: Boni & Liveright, 1919.

Frankenstein, Alfred. "Miss Graham Presents Dance Recital." *San Francisco Chronicle,* March 31, 1936.

Franklin, Paul. *Étant Donné: Marcel Duchamp.* Paris: Association pour l'étude de Marcel Duchamp, 2009.

Franko, Mark. *Martha Graham in Love and War: The Life in the Work.* New York: Oxford University Press, 2012.

Frazer, James George. *The Golden Bough: A Study in Magic and Religion.* New York: Oxford University Press, 2009.

Frederickson, Kristen, and Sarah E. Webb, eds. *Singular Women: Writing the Artist.* Berkeley: University of California Press, 2003.

Freedman, Russell. *Martha Graham: A Dancer's Life.* New York: Clarion Books, 1998.

Friedman, Leslie. "Léonide Massine." In *American National Biography.* Oxford: Oxford University Press, 2010. https://doi.org/10.1093/anb/9780198606697.article.1802048.

Friedman, Susan Stanford. "Definitional Excursions: The Meanings of Modern/Modernity/Modernism." *Modernism/modernity* 8, no. 3 (September 2001): 493–513.

Fromm, Erich. *Escape from Freedom.* New York: Farrar & Rinehart, 1941.

Funkenstein, Susan Laikin. "Engendering Abstraction: Wassily Kandinsky, Gret Palucca, and 'Dance Curves.'" *Modernism/modernity* 14, no. 3 (September 2007): 389–406.

Fussell, Betty. "A Timeless Pueblo Ritual." *New York Times,* July 22, 1984.

Gaborik, Patricia. Review of *Embodied Texts: Symbolist Playwright-Dancer Collaborations,* by Mary Fleischer. *Dance Research Journal* 41, no. 1 (Summer 2009): 103–5.

Gage, Beverly. "The Roar of the Crowd." Review of *Supreme City: How Jazz Manhattan Gave Birth to Modern America,* by Donald L. Miller. *New York Times,* July 24, 2014.

Gage, Margaret. "A Study in American Modernism." *Theatre Arts Monthly,* March 1930: 229–32.

Garafola, Lynn. "Company Man." Review of *The Worlds of Lincoln Kirstein,* by Martin Duberman. *Nation,* June 21, 2007. https://www.thenation.com/article/archive/company-man-1/.

———. "The Enigma of Nicholas Roerich." *Dance Chronicle* 13, no. 3 (1990): 401–12.

———. "Lincoln Kirstein, Modern Dance, and the Left: The Genesis of an American Ballet." *Dance Research Journal* 23, no. 1 (Summer 2005): 18–35.

———. "Massine." In *Legacies of Twentieth-Century Dance.* Middletown, CT: Wesleyan University Press, 2005.

———. "Writing on the Left: The Remarkable Career of Edna Ocko." *Dance Research Journal* 34, no. 1 (Summer 2002): 53–61.

García-Márquez, Vicente. *Massine: A Biography.* New York: Alfred A. Knopf, 1995.

Gardner, Howard. *Creating Minds: An Anatomy of Creativity Seen Through the Lives of Freud, Einstein, Picasso, Stravinsky, Eliot, Graham, and Gandhi.* New York: Basic Books, 1993.

Gaume, Matilda. "Ruth Crawford: A Promising Young Composer in New York, 1929–30." *American Music* 5, no. 1 (Spring 1987): 74–84.

Genzlinger, Neil. "Marion Horosko, Dancer and Advocate for the Art, Dies at 92." *New York Times,* September 22, 2017.

Getz, Leslie. *Dancers and Choreographers: A Selected Bibliography.* Wakefield, RI: Asphodel Press, 1995.

Ghiselin, Brewster, ed. *The Creative Process: A Symposium.* New York: New American Library/Mentor, 1955.

Gibbs, Angelica. "The Absolute Frontier: Martha Graham's Mode of Dance." *New Yorker,*

December 27, 1947. https://www.newyorker.com/magazine/1947/12/27/the-absolute-frontier.

Gibson, Arrell Morgan. *The Santa Fe and Taos Colonies: Age of the Muses, 1900–1942.* Norman: University of Oklahoma Press, 1983.

Gilder, Rosamond, ed. "Foreword." In *Theatre Arts Anthology: A Record and a Prophecy.* New York: Theatre Arts Books, 1950.

Gillespie, Andrew Robbins. "A Conductor's Guide to Vincent Persichetti's King Lear." Master's thesis, Colorado State University, 2018.

Glennon, Lorraine, ed. *Our Times: The Illustrated History of the 20th Century.* Atlanta: Turner, 1995.

Goff, Barbara. "The Women of Thebes." *Classical Journal* 90, no. 4 (April–May 1995): 353–65.

Goldberg, Jonathan. "Dover Cliff and the Conditions of Representation: *King Lear* 4:6 in Perspective." *Poetics Today* 5, no. 3 (1984): 537–47.

Gomez, Edward M. "When Noguchi Took the Stage." *Dance Index* 8, no. 1 (Fall 2017). This essay is the sole text in the inaugural issue of the relaunched *Dance Index.*

Gordon Norton, M. L., ed. *5 Essays on the Dance of Erick Hawkins.* New York: Foundation for Modern Dance, 1973.

Gorman, Herbert. "Hart Crane and the Machine Age." Review of *The Collected Poems of Hart Crane. New York Times,* April 30, 1933.

Gottlieb, Robert, ed. *Reading Dance: A Gathering of Memoirs, Reportage, Criticism, Profiles, Interviews, and Some Uncategorizable Extras.* New York: Pantheon Books, 2008.

Graff, Ellen. *Stepping Left: Dance and Politics in New York City, 1928–1942.* Durham, NC: Duke University Press, 1997.

Grafton, Anthony, Glenn W. Most, and Salvatore Settis, eds. *The Classical Tradition.* Cambridge, MA: Belknap Press, 2010.

Graham, Martha. "The American Dance." In *Modern Dance,* edited by Virginia Stewart, 53–58. New York: Weyhe, 1935. Reprint, 1970.

———. *Blood Memory: An Autobiography.* New York: Doubleday, 1991.

———. "The Dance in America." *Trend* 1, no. 1 (March/April/May 1932): 5–7.

———. "Dance Libretto: *American Document.*" *Theatre Arts Monthly,* September 1942: 565–74.

———. Foreword. In *Dance Drawings of Martha Graham,* by Charlotte Trowbridge. New York: Dance Observer, 1945.

———. "From Collaboration, a Strange Beauty Emerged." *New York Times,* January 8, 1989.

———. "The Future of the Dance." *Dance* 6, no. 4 (April 1939): 9.

———. "How I Became a Dancer." *Saturday Review,* August 28, 1965.

———. "I Am a Dancer." In *Routledge Dance Studies Reader,* edited by Alexandra Carter, 95–100. London: Routledge, 1998.

———. "A Modern Dancer's Primer for Action." In *Dance: A Basic Educational Technique,* edited by Frederick Rand Rogers, 178–87. New York: Macmillan, 1941.

———. Notebooks. Martha Graham Collection. Library of Congress, Washington, DC.

———. "Platform for the American Dance." Martha Graham and Dance Group. In *Trend* March–April 1935; and reprinted in *Program* for her first national tour, New York, 1936.

———. "Seeking an American Art of the Dance." In *Revolt in the Arts,* edited by Oliver Saylor, 249–55. New York: Brentano's, 1930.

———. "This Modern Dance: Two Important American Viewpoints, Part I." *Dancing Times,* December 1938: 270–72.

Granger, Bill. "Monroe, Lindsay and Masters: A Formidable Alliance in Chicago's Turn-of-the-Century Renaissance." *Chicago Tribune,* June 16, 1996.

Graves, Robert. *The White Goddess: A Historical Grammar of Poetic Myth.* Amended and enlarged edition. New York: Vintage Books, 1958.

Gray, Christopher. "The Drama Queen of the Lower East Side." *New York Times,* December 23, 2010.

———. "Streetscapes: Rebels on Eighth Street Redux." *New York Times,* September 12, 1993.

Gray, Madeleine. "Eastern Art Spiritual, Western Art Material, Says Michio Itow." *Musical America,* December 8, 1917: 9.

Greenberg, Clement. "Modernist Painting." In *The Collected Essays and Criticism.* Vol. 4, *Modernism with a Vengeance, 1957–1969,* edited by John O'Brian, 85–93. Chicago: University of Chicago Press, 1993.

Greer, Germaine. "Let's Forget the Rape, Shall We?" *Guardian,* May 31, 2001.

Gregg, Melissa, and Gregory J. Seigworth, eds. *The Affect Theory Reader.* Durham, NC: Duke University Press, 2010.

Griffey, Randall R., Elizabeth Mankin Kornhauser, and Stephanie L. Herdrich. "Thomas Hart Benton's *America Today*." *Metropolitan Museum of Art Bulletin* 72, no. 3 (Winter 2015): 1, 4–48.

Grondines, Pierre. "*The Rite of Spring*: Sacrificing Continuity." *La Scena Musicale* 5, no. 6 (March 1, 2000). http://www.scena.org/lsm/sm5-6/RiteOfSpring-en.htm.

Grove, Nancy. *Isamu Noguchi Portrait Sculpture.* Washington, DC: Smithsonian Institution Press for the National Portrait Gallery, 1989.

Grove, Nancy, and Diane Botnick. *The Sculpture of Isamu Noguchi, 1924–1979: A Catalogue.* New York: Garland, 1980.

Gruskin, Nancy. "Designing Women: Writing About Eleanor Raymond." In *Singular Women: Writing the Artist,* edited by Kristen Frederickson and Sarah E. Webb. Berkeley: University of California Press, 2003.

Gur, Golan. "Arnold Schoenberg and the Ideology of Progress in Twentieth-Century Musical Thinking." *Journal for New Music and Culture,* no. 5 (2009): 1–11.

Habermas, Jürgen. "Modernity—An Incomplete Project." *New German Critique* 22 (Winter 1981): 3–15.

Hackett, Karleton. "Ruth St. Denis and Dancers at Orchestra Hall." *Chicago Evening Post,* October 24, 1922.

Haigh, Arthur Elam. *The Attic Theatre.* Oxford: Clarendon Press, 1889.

Hall, Susanne E. "Hart Crane in Mexico: The End of a New World Poetics." *Mosaic* 46, no. 1 (March 2013): 139–49.

Hamalainen, Soili. "The Meaning of Bodily Knowledge in a Creative Dance-Making Process." In *Ways of Knowing in Dance and Art,* edited by Leena Rouhiainen. Finland: Theatre Academy, 2007.

Hambourg, Maria Morris, and Christopher Phillips, eds. *The New Vision: Photography Between the World Wars.* Ford Motor Company Collection. New York: Metropolitan Museum of Art, 1989.

Hamilton, Edith. *The Greek Way.* New York: W. W. Norton, 1930.

Hanna, Judith Lynne. *To Dance Is Human: A Theory of Nonverbal Communication.* Chicago: University of Chicago Press, 1987.

Hardy, Camille. Review of *Divine Dancer,* by Suzanne Shelton. *Dance Research Journal* 14, no. 1/2 (1981–1982): 62–64.

Harper, John, Joseph Reed, et al. *Annual Reports of the Managers of the Western Pennsylvania Hospital for the Insane.* Pittsburgh: 1882, 1885, 1887.

Harrington, John W. "America as a Fountain of Youth to the Japanese." *New York Times,* January 18, 1920.

Harrison, Jane Ellen. *Prolegomena to the Study of Greek Religion.* 3rd ed. Cambridge: Cambridge University Press, 1922.

———. *Themis: A Study of the Social Origins of Greek Religion.* Cleveland: World Publishing, 1969. First published 1912.

Harss, Marina. "A Form of Order: On Paul Taylor." *Nation,* September 12, 2012. https://www.thenation.com/article/archive/form-order-paul-taylor/.

Hart-Johnson, Diana. "On Structure in Martha Graham Technique, with Comparisons to American Sign Language." *Journal for the Anthropological Study of Human Movement* 2, no. 4 (Autumn 1983): 196–210.

Hastings, Baird. "Martha Graham." *Dance Magazine,* 1947.

———. "Martha Graham: The High Priestess of Modern Dance." In *Choreographer and Composer: Theatrical Dance and Music in Western Culture.* Boston: Twayne Publishers, 1983.

Hausman, Carl R. "Maritain's Interpretation of Creativity in Art." *Journal of Aesthetics and Art Criticism* 19, no. 2 (Winter 1960): 215–19.

Haviland, Linda Caruso. "Repetition Island: Some Thoughts on Restaging, Reconstruction, Reenactment, Re-performance, Re-presentation, and Reconstruction in Dance." Pew Center for Arts and Heritage, November 14, 2013. https://www.pcah.us/post/repetition-island.

Hawkins, Alma. *Modern Dance in Higher Education.* New York: Bureau of Publications, Teachers College, Columbia University, 1954.

Hawkins, Erick. *The Body Is a Clear Place and Other Statements on Dance.* With a foreword by Alan Kriegsman. Princeton, NJ: Princeton Book Company, 1992.

Hays, Richard E. "Dancer Wins Big Audience with New Art." *Seattle Times,* June 3, 1930.

H. C. S. "Martha Graham Season Presents Two New Works." *Musical Digest,* April 1947.

H'Doubler, Margaret N. *Dance: A Creative Art Experience.* Madison: University of Wisconsin Press, 1985.

Heidegger, Martin. "The Origin of the Work of Art." In *Poetry, Language, Thought,* translated by Albert Hofstadter, 15–79. New York: Harper Perennial/Modern Thought, 2013. First published 1935.

Heinzelman, Kurt, ed. *Make It New: The Rise of Modernism.* Austin, TX: Harry Ransom Humanities Research Center, 2003.

Helpern, Alice, ed. "Martha Graham." A special issue of *Choreography and Dance: An International Journal,* vol. 5, part 2 (1999).

———. "The Stories of Two Birds." Review of *Frontiers,* by Karen Bell-Kanner, and *Bird's Eye View,* by Dorothy Bird and Joyce Greenberg. *Dance Chronicle* 23, no. 2 (2000): 201–7.

———. *The Technique of Martha Graham.* Dobbs Ferry, NY: Morgan & Morgan, 1994.

Henahan, Donal. "Samuel Barber, Composer, Dead; Twice Winner of the Pulitzer Prize." *New York Times,* January 24, 1981.

Henderson, Alice Corbin. *Brothers of Light: The Penitentes of the Southwest.* New York: Harcourt, Brace, 1937.

———. "The Dance-Rituals of the Pueblo Indians." *Theatre Arts Monthly* 7, no. 2 (April 1923).

Herbert, Kevin. "Terracotta Figurines at Bowdoin College." *Classical Journal* 55, no. 3 (December 1959): 98–111.

Hering, Doris. "Barbara Morgan—One of America's Great Photographers Reflects a Decade of Dance, 1935–1945." *Dance Magazine*, July 1971, 43–56.

———. "Steps That Took a Master to the Top: Ted Shawn Looks Back." Review of *One Thousand and One Night Stands*, by Ted Shawn. *New York Times Book Review*, October 23, 1960.

Herridge, Frances. "Graham Work Needs Graham." *New York Star*, August 17, 1948.

Hesiod. *Theogony* and *Works and Days*. Translated by M. L. West. Oxford: Oxford University Press, 2008.

Hewlett, Henry G. "Imperfect Genius: William Blake." *Contemporary Review* 28 (1876–1877): 759–84.

Heyman, Barbara B. *Samuel Barber: The Composer and His Music*. New York: Oxford University Press, 1992.

H.H. "More Mountains, More Mice." *Nation*, January 11, 1933.

Hischak, Thomas S. *Off-Broadway Musicals Since 1919: From Greenwich Village Follies to the Toxic Avenger*. Lanham, MD: Scarecrow Press, 2011.

Hitchcock, H. Wiley, and Stanley Sadie, eds. *The New Grove Dictionary of American Music*. 4 vols. New York: Macmillan, 1986.

Hodson, Millicent. "Nijinsky's Choreographic Method: Visual Sources from Roerich for *Le sacre du printemps*." *Dance Research Journal* 18, no. 2 (1986–1987): 7–15.

Hoffman, Tyler. "The Ordeal of Vachel Lindsay, or, the Cultural Politics of the Spoken Word." In *American Poetry in Performance: From Walt Whitman to Hip Hop*, 55–87. Ann Arbor: University of Michigan Press, 2013.

Holmes, Olive, ed. *Motion Arrested: Dance Reviews of H. T. Harper*. Middletown, CT: Wesleyan University Press, 1982.

Holmes, Richard. *Dr. Johnson & Mr. Savage*. New York: Pantheon Books, 1994.

Homans, Jennifer. *Apollo's Angels: A History of Ballet*. New York: Random House, 2010.

Homsey, Bonnie Oda, dir. *Michio Ito: Pioneering Dancer-Choreographer*. DVD. Los Angeles Dance Foundation, 2013.

Hone, William. *Ancient Mysteries Described: Especially the English Miracle Plays*. London: W. Hone, 1823.

Horkheimer, Max, and Theodor W. Adorno. *Dialectic of Enlightenment: Philosophical Fragments*. Stanford, CA: Stanford University Press, 2002.

Horyn, Cathy. "Channeling the Flapper Girl." *New York Times*, May 15, 2013.

Horgan, Paul. *A Certain Climate: Essays in History, Arts, and Letters*. Middletown, CT: Wesleyan University Press, 1988.

———. "Rouben Mamoulian: The Start of a Career." *Films in Review*, August–September 1973.

Horosko, Marian. *Martha Graham: The Evolution of Her Dance Theory and Training*. Gainesville: University Press of Florida, 2002.

———. *May O'Donnell: Modern Dance Pioneer*. Gainesville: University Press of Florida, 2005.

Horst, Louis. "Chronology of Professional Career." Kept from 1901 through 1962. Holograph, partly typescript, n.p. Jerome Robbins Dance Division, Special Collections, New York Public Library for the Performing Arts.

———. Collection of Music. Music Division, New York Public Library for the Performing Arts.

———. "Discussion of the Musical Selections of a Young Dancer." *Music Mart*, September 1929. n.p.

———. "The Musician Comments." *Denishawn Magazine* 1, no. 4 (Summer 1925). n.p.

———. *Pre-Classic Dance Forms*. Brooklyn, NY: Dance Horizons, 1968.

Horst, Louis, and Carroll Russell. *Modern Dance Forms in Relation to the Other Modern Arts*. Brooklyn, NY: Dance Horizons, 1961.

Hoydis, Julia. "Only the Dance Is Sure: Dance and Constructions of Gender in Modernist Poetry." *Gender Forum*, no. 36 (2011): 1–25.

Hughes, Sarah. "Why Those Subversive Brontë Sisters Still Hypnotise Us." *Guardian*, March 26, 2016.

Humphrey, Doris. *The Art of Making Dances*. Princeton, NJ: Dance Horizons, 1987.

Hunter, Gordon. *What America Read: Taste, Class, and the Novel, 1920–1960*. Chapel Hill: University of North Carolina Press, 2011.

Hutcheon, Linda, and Micheal Hutcheon. "Late Style(s): The Ageism of the Singular." *Occasion: Interdisciplinary Studies in the Humanities* 4 (May 31, 2012): 1–11.

Ierulli, Molly. "A Community of Women? The Protagonist and the Chorus in Sophocles' *Electra*." *Mètis: Anthropologie des mondes grecs anciens* 8, nos. 1–2 (1993).

Ignatin, Irving. " 'Revolutionary' Dance Forms." *New Theatre*, December 1935.

Isaacs, Edith J. R. "The Great World Theatre—Theatre of the Dance—The Dearth of Dance Criticism in America." In "The Dance and Some Dancers." Special issue, *Theatre Arts Monthly* 11, no. 8 (August 1927).

———. Papers, 1889–1957. Wisconsin Historical Society Archives/Wisconsin Center for Film & Theatre Research, University of Wisconsin–Madison. http://digital.library.wisc.edu/1711.dl/wiarchives.uw-whs-us0047an.

Isherwood, Charles. "Anne Meacham, 80, Actress on New York Stages and TV." *New York Times*, January 17, 2006.

Jackson, George. "Dance and the City." Review of *Interwar Vienna*, edited by Deborah Holmes and Lisa Silverman. *Dance Chronicle*, 33, no. 3 (2010): 465–79.

Jackson, Paul R. W. *The Last Guru: Robert Cohan's Life in Dance from Martha Graham to London Contemporary Dance Theatre*. Binsted, Hampshire, UK: Dance Books, 2013.

Jeffers, Robinson. *Medea, Freely Adapted from the Medea of Euripides*. New York: Random House, 1946.

Jenkins, Jessica Kerwin. "Women of a Certain Era." Review of *Flappers,* by Judith Mackrell, and *Careless People,* by Sarah Churchwell. *New York Times*, February 14, 2014.

Jewell, Edward Alden. "American Art Comes of Age." *New York Times*, November 22, 1931.

Johnson, Harriett. "Rhythm and Reason." *New York Post*, May 11, 1946.

Johnson, Mark. *The Body in the Mind: The Bodily Basis of Meaning, Imagination, and Reason*. Chicago: University of Chicago Press, 1987.

Johnson, Robert. "Sacred Scandals." *Dance Chronicle* 15, no. 2 (1992) : 227–36.

Jones, Jack. "Otto Rank: A Forgotten Heresy." *Commentary*, September 1960: 219–29.

Jones, Robert Edmond. *The Dramatic Imagination*. New York: Theatre Arts Books, 1941.

———. *Towards a New Theatre: The Lectures of Robert Edmond Jones*. Transcribed and edited by Delbert Unruh. New York: Limelight Editions, 1992.

Jones, Susan. *Literature, Modernism, and Dance*. Oxford: Oxford University Press, 2013.

Jordan, Stephanie. "Ted Shawn's Music Visualizations." *Dance Chronicle* 7, no. 1 (1984): 33–49.

Joshi, S. T. "Samuel Loveman: Shelley in Brooklyn." In *Emperors of Dreams: Some Notes on Weird Poetry*, 41–64. Sydney, Australia: P'rea Press, 2008.

Jowitt, Deborah. "A Conversation with Bessie Schönberg." *Ballet Review* 9, no. 1 (Spring 1981): 31–63.

———. "The Critical Burden of History." *Dance Research Journal* 32, no. 1 (Summer 2000): 131–37.

———. "In Memory: Martha Graham, 1894–1991." *Drama Review* 35, no. 4 (Winter 1991): 14–16.

———. *Time and the Dancing Image*. Berkeley: University of California Press, 1988.

Jung, C. G. *The Archetypes and the Collective Unconscious*. Vol. 9, Part I, *The Collected Works of C. G. Jung*. Translated by R. F. C. Hull. Bollingen Series. Princeton, NJ: Princeton University Press, 1968.

———. *Jung on Active Imagination*. Edited by Joan Chodorow. Princeton, NJ: Princeton University Press, 1997.

———. *Psychology of the Unconscious*. Translated by Beatrice M. Hinkle. New York: Dodd, Mead, 1925.

———. *The Spirit in Man, Art, and Literature*. Vol. 15, *The Collected Works of C. G. Jung*. Translated by R. F. C. Hull. Bollingen Series. Princeton, NJ: Princeton University Press, 1966.

———. *Symbols of Transformation*. Vol. 5, *The Collected Works of C. G. Jung*. Translated by R. F. C. Hull. Princeton, NJ: Princeton University Press, 1990.

Kallen, Horace M. *Culture and Democracy in the United States*. New York: Boni & Liveright, 1924.

Kammen, Michael. *A Time to Every Purpose: The Four Seasons in American Culture*. Chapel Hill: University of North Carolina Press, 2004.

Kandinsky, Wassily. *Concerning the Spiritual in Art*. New York: Dover, 1977.

———. *Kandinsky: Complete Writings on Art*. Edited by Kenneth C. Lindsay and Peter Vergo. New York: Da Capo Press, 1994.

Kant, Marion. "The Evolution of the Modern Movement: Some Recent German Dance Scholarship." *Dance Research Journal* 24, no. 1 (Summer 2006): 54–59.

Karoglou, Kiki. "Dangerous Beauty: Medusa in Classical Art." *Metropolitan Museum of Art Bulletin* 75, no. 3 (Winter 2018).

Kaufman, Michael T. "Blanche Yurka, Actress, Dead; Rose to Stardom in 'Wild Duck.' " *New York Times*, June 7, 1974.

Kazin, Alfred. *Starting Out in the Thirties*. Boston: Little, Brown, 1965.

Kealiinohomoku, Joann Wheeler. "The Non-Art of the Dance: An Essay." Presented at the annual meeting of the Congress on Research in Dance, Philadelphia, November 11–14, 1976. In *Journal for the Anthropological Study of Human Movement* 1, no. 1 (Spring 1980): 47–50.

———. Review of *Lessons from the Dancing Ground to the Studio*, by Valentina Litvinoff. *Dance Research Journal* 7, no. 1 (Autumn 1974–Winter 1975): 33–34.

Kemp, Frances McClernan. "Martha Graham: Blessed Damozel of the Concert Stage." *Dance Magazine*, March 1927: 19, 54.

Kempny, Hedy, and Arthur Schnitzler. *Das Mädchen mit den dreizehn Seelen (The Girl with Thirteen Souls)*. Edited by Heinz P. Adamek. Reinbek bei Hamburg, Germany: Rowohlt Verlag, 1984.

Kendall, Elizabeth. *Where She Danced*. New York: Alfred A. Knopf, 1979.

Kenner, Hugh. *A Homemade World: The American Modernist Writers*. London: Marion Boyars, 1977.

Kermode, Frank. *The Sense of an Ending.* New York: Oxford University Press, 1967.

Ketcham, Christopher. "The Bison Roundup the Government Wants to Hide." *New York Times,* February 15, 2016.

King, Eleanor. *Transformations: The Humphrey-Weidman Era.* Brooklyn, NY: Dance Horizons, 1978.

Kinney, Troy, and Margaret West Kinney. *The Dance: Its Place in Art and Life.* New York: Frederick A. Stokes, 1924.

Kirstein, Lincoln. *Ballet: Bias & Belief.* Brooklyn, NY: Dance Horizons, 1983.

———. *Blast at Ballet: A Corrective for American Audiences.* New York: Marstin Press, 1938.

———. *Dance: A Short History of Classic Theatrical Dancing.* Princeton, NJ: Princeton Book Co., 1987.

———. "The Dance: Some American Dancers." *Nation* (February 27, 1935): 258.

———. "Dance Chronicle: Kreutzberg; Wigman; *Pas d'Acier;* The Future." *Hound & Horn* 4, no. 4 (Summer 1931): 573–80.

———. "Martha Graham at Bennington." *Nation* (September 3, 1938): 230–31.

———. Papers. Jerome Robbins Dance Division, New York Public Library for the Performing Arts.

———. "Prejudice Purely." *New Republic,* April 11, 1934: 37–41.

Kisselgoff, Anna. "An All-But-Forgotten Pioneer of American Modern Dance." *New York Times,* February 26, 1978.

———. " 'Celebration' Revived After 50 Years." *New York Times,* October 18, 1987.

———. "Dance: Hawkins Revival of 'Trickster Coyote.' " *New York Times,* October 17, 1984.

———. "Dance: Martha Graham Offers World Premiere." *New York Times,* May 28, 1986.

———. "Dance: Michio Ito Salute." *New York Times,* October 4, 1979.

———. " 'Dark Meadow': From Graham, via Jung, a Journey Through an Erotic Landscape." *New York Times,* February 18, 1999.

———. "Geordie Graham, 88, a Dancer with Denishawn Company, Dies." *New York Times,* October 13, 1988.

———. "Mark Ryder, 85, Former Dancer in Martha Graham's Company, Is Dead." *New York Times,* July 21, 2006.

———. "Martha Graham Dies at 96: A Revolutionary in Dance." *New York Times,* April 2, 1991.

———. "Martha Graham Reflects on Her Art and a Life in Dance." *New York Times,* March 31, 1985.

———. "Martha Graham—Still Charting 'the Graph of the Heart.' " *New York Times,* May 15, 1977.

———. "Powerful Images of Martha Graham's Art." *New York Times,* November 23, 1980.

———. Review of an evening of re-creations of "Denishawn/Graham Solos." *New York Times,* June 15, 1986.

———. "Revival of Martha Graham's '*Heretic.*' " *New York Times,* May 31, 1986.

Kitto, H. D. F. "The Greek Chorus." *Educational Theatre Journal* 8, no. 1 (March 1956): 1–8.

Klein, Hilary Dole. "Martha Graham: A Legend in Santa Barbara's Time." *Santa Barbara News-Press,* July 27, 1985.

Kleinman, H. H. *The Religious Sonnets of Dylan Thomas: A Study in Imagery and Meaning.* Berkeley: University of California Press, 1963.

Knox, Bernard, ed. *The Norton Book of Classical Literature.* New York: W. W. Norton & Company, 1993.

Kolocotroni, Vassiliki, Jane Goldman, and Olga Taxidou, eds. *Modernism: An Anthology of Sources and Documents*. Chicago: University of Chicago Press, 1999.

Koner, Pauline. *Solitary Song: An Autobiography*. Durham, NC: Duke University Press, 1989.

Koolhaas, Rem. *Delirious New York: A Retroactive Manifesto for Manhattan*. New York: Oxford University Press, 1978.

Kopecký, Petr. "Mary Austin's Crossing Boundaries." *Ars Aeterna* 1, no. 1 (2009).

Koritz, Amy. *Culture Makers: Urban Performance and Literature in the 1920s*. Urbana: University of Illinois Press, 2008.

Kostka, Stefan, and Dorothy Payne. *Tonal Harmony, with an Introduction to Twentieth-Century Music*. 5th ed. New York: McGraw-Hill, 2004.

Kott, Jan. "King Lear, or Endgame." In *Shakespeare, Our Contemporary*, 127–68. New York: Doubleday Anchor Books, 1966.

Kraemer, Casper J., Jr. "A Greek Element in Egyptian Dancing." *American Journal of Archaeology* 35, no. 2 (April–June 1931): 125–38.

Kriegsman, Alan M. [Erick Hawkins] "Dance." *Washington Post*, September 20, 1985.

———. "Erick Hawkins, the Modern Man." *Washington Post*, November 25, 1994.

———. "The Graham Vision: Dance as Sculpture; the Tedium of Genius." *Washington Post*, February 25, 1981.

———. "The Height of Hawkins." *Washington Post*, February 27, 1991.

Kriegsman, Sali Ann. *Modern Dance in America: The Bennington Years*. Boston: G. K. Hall, 1981.

Krokover, Rosalyn. The Dance. *Musical Courier*, March 16, 1947.

Kubler, George. *The Shape of Time*. New Haven, CT: Yale University Press, 1962.

Kuhlmann, Christiane. *Charlotte Rudolph: Tanzfotografie, 1924–1939*. Göttingen, Germany: Steidl, 2004.

Laban, Rudolf. *The Language of Movement: A Guidebook to Choreutics*. Annotated and edited by Lisa Ullmann. New York: Plays, 1974.

LaMothe, Kimerer L. *Nietzsche's Dancers: Isadora Duncan, Martha Graham, and the Revaluation of Christian Values*. New York: Palgrave Macmillan, 2006.

Lampert, Laurence. *Nietzsche's Task: An Interpretation of* Beyond Good and Evil. New Haven, CT: Yale University Press, 2001.

Landi, Ann. "When Is an Artwork Finished?" *ARTnews*, February 24, 2014: 78.

Langer, Susanne K. *Feeling and Form: A Theory of Art*. New York: Charles Scribner's Sons, 1953.

———. *Philosophy in a New Key: A Study in the Symbolism of Reason, Rite, and Art*. Cambridge, MA: Harvard University Press, 1942.

Lardinois, André. Review of *Choruses of Young Women in Ancient Greece: Their Morphology, Religious Role, and Social Functions*, by Claude Calame. *Bryn Mawr Classical Review*, September 27, 1997. https://bmcr.brynmawr.edu/1997/1997.09.27/.

Lask, Thomas. Books of the Times. *New York Times*, "First Lady of the Dance." November 2, 1966.

Latham, Angela J. "The Right to Bare: Containing and Encoding American Women in Popular Entertainments of the 1920s." In "Historicizing Bodies." Special issue, *Theatre Journal* 49, no. 4 (December 1997): 455–73.

Lauterer, Arch. "Theatre Planning: A Symposium." *Educational Theatre Journal* 2 (March 1950): 1–7.

Lauterer, Arch. "A Document for the Modern Dance—Design for the Dance." *Magazine of Art* 31, no. 3 (March 1938).

Lavery, Joseph. "Ernest Fenollosa: Out of Time, Out of Place." *Journal of Modern Literature* 35, no. 2 (Winter 2012): 131–38.

Lawrence, D. H. "The Dance of the Sprouting Corn." *Theatre Arts Monthly* 8, no. 7 (July 1924): 447–57.

———. "The Hopi Snake Dance." *Theatre Arts Monthly* 8, no. 12 (December 1924): 836–60.

———. "The Spirit of Place." In *Studies in Classic American Literature*, chapter 1, 1–8. New York: Thomas Seltzer, Inc., 1923.

Lawrence, Robert. "Martha Graham at the Crossroads." *New York Herald Tribune*, April 18, 1943.

Lears, T. J. Jackson. *No Place of Grace: Antimodernism and the Transformation of American Culture, 1880–1920*. New York: Pantheon Books, 1981.

Leatherman, LeRoy. *Martha Graham: Portrait of the Lady as an Artist*. New York: Alfred A. Knopf, 1966.

Le Corbusier. *Towards a New Architecture*. Translated by Frederick Etchells. New York: Dover, 1986.

Lee, Colin Andrew. *Paul Nordoff: Composer & Music Therapist*. University Park, IL: Barcelona Publishers, 2014.

Lenart, Camelia. "Martha Graham and Bethsabée de Rothschild—An Artistic Friendship in the Service of Modern Dance," 111–22. In *Proceedings: Thirty-Fourth Annual Conference, Society of Dance History Scholars, June 23–26, 2011*. Toronto: York University and University of Toronto, 2011.

———. "Rehearsing and Transforming Cultural Diplomacy: Martha Graham's Tours to Europe During the Fifties." In *Proceedings: Thirty-Sixth Annual Conference, Norwegian University of Science and Technology, June 8–11, 2013*, 219–31. Riverside, CA: Society of Dance History Scholars, 2013.

Lenti, Vincent A. *For the Enrichment of Community Life: George Eastman and the Founding of the Eastman School of Music*. Rochester, NY: Meliora Press, 2004.

Leonard, Miriam. *Tragic Modernities*. Cambridge, MA: Harvard University Press, 2015.

Lepczyk, Billie. "Martha Graham's Movement Invention Viewed through Laban Analysis." In *Dance: Current Selected Research*, edited by Lynette Y. Overby and James H. Humphrey. Vol. 1. New York: AMS Press, 1989.

Lepecki, André, ed. *Dance: Documents of Contemporary Art*. Cambridge, MA: MIT Press, 2012.

Levin, Gail, ed. *Theresa Bernstein: A Century in Art*. Lincoln: University of Nebraska Press, 2013.

———. "Wassily Kandinsky and the American Literary Avant-Garde." *Criticism: A Quarterly for Literature and the Arts* 21, no. 4 (Fall 1979): 347–61.

Levin, Gail, and Marianne Lenz, eds. *Theme & Improvisation: Kandinsky & the American Avant-Garde, 1912–1950*. Boston: Little, Brown, 1992.

Levin, Gail, and Judith Tick. *Aaron Copland's America: A Cultural Perspective*. New York: Watson-Guptill, 2000.

Levine, Caroline. *Forms: Whole, Rhythm, Hierarchy, Network*. Princeton, NJ: Princeton University Press, 2017.

Levi-Strauss, Claude. *Anthropology & Myth: Lectures 1951–1982*. London: Basil Blackwell, 1987.

Levy, Julien. "Isamu Noguchi." *Creative Art: A Magazine of Fine and Applied Art* 12, no. 1 (January 1933): 29–35.

Lewis, Mark. "Is Modernity Our Antiquity?" *Afterall*, no. 14 (Autumn/Winter 2006): 109–17. http://www.afterall.org/journal/issue.14/modernity.our.antiquity.

Lewisohn, Irene. "Drama and the Unseen Currents." Pamphlet, ca. 1931. Jerome Robbins Dance Division, New York Public Library for the Performing Arts. (S) *MGZMD. Box 1, folder 17.

———. "Essence of the Mohammedan East." *New York Times*, April 13, 1924.

Lichtenwanger, William. *The Music of Henry Cowell: A Descriptive Catalogue.* Institute for Studies in American Music Monograph Series, no. 23. New York: Conservatory of Music, Brooklyn College, 1986.

Limón, José. *An Unfinished Memoir.* Edited by Lynn Garafola. Middletown, CT: Wesleyan University Press, 2001.

Lindsay, Vachel. "Every Soul Is a Circus." *Poetry* 33, no. 1 (October 1928): 1-10.

———. *The Litany of Washington Street.* New York: Macmillan, 1928.

Lindsay Levine, Victoria. "American Indian Musics, Past and Present." In *The Cambridge History of American Music*, edited by David Nicholls, 1–29. New York: Cambridge University Press, 1998.

Littlebird, Sarracina. "Sacred Movement: Dance as Prayer in the Pueblo Cultures of the American Southwest." Thesis, Barnard College Senior Seminar in Dance, 2008. https://dance.barnard.edu/sites/default/files/inline/sarracina_littlebird.pdf.

Litvinoff, Valentina. "Lessons from the Dancing Ground to the Studio: Implications of Pueblo Indian Dance for Modern Dance." *Journal of Aesthetics and Art Criticism* 32, no. 3 (Spring 1974): 397–407.

———. *The Use of Stanislavsky Within Modern Dance.* New York: American Dance Guild, 1972.

Lloyd, Margaret. *The Borzoi Book of Modern Dance.* Brooklyn, NY: Dance Horizons, 1949.

———. "On with the Dance—Bennington the Focus of This New Movement." *Christian Science Monitor*, November 10, 1936.

———. "Student Impressions—School of the Dance More Than Mere Classes." *Christian Science Monitor*, November 17, 1936.

———. "Such Stuff as Dreams Are Made On." *Christian Science Monitor*, January 15, 1944.

———. "What's in a Word?" *Christian Science Monitor*, August 7, 1943.

Loewenthal, Lillian. *The Search for Isadora: The Legend and Legacy of Isadora Duncan.* Princeton, NJ: Princeton Book Company, 1993.

Longenbach, James. "The Odd Couple—Pound and Yeats Together." *New York Times*, January 10, 1988.

Loraux, Nicole. *The Mourning Voice: An Essay on Greek Tragedy.* Translated by Elizabeth Trapnell Rawlings. Ithaca, NY: Cornell University Press, 2002.

Louppe, Laurence. *Poetics of Contemporary Dance.* Translated by Sally Gardner. Alton, Hampshire, UK: Dance Books, 2010.

Love, Paul. *Modern Dance Terminology.* Princeton, NJ: Princeton Book, 1952.

Luening, Otto. "Henry Cowell, a Dancer's Musician." *Dance Scope*, Spring 1966.

Luhan, Mabel Dodge. "A Bridge Between Cultures." *Theatre Arts Monthly* 9, no. 5 (May 1925): 297–301.

———. "On the Career and Character of Katharine Cornell—An Attempt to Estimate the Essential Qualities of an American Actress." *Vanity Fair*, July 1925, 40.

Luhrssen, David. *Mamoulian: Life on Stage and Screen.* Lexington: University Press of Kentucky, 2012.

Mabary, Judith. "Martinů's Contribution to Modern Dance in America." *Bohuslav Martinů Newsletter* 6, no. 1 (January–April 2006): 16–17.

Macgowan, Kenneth. "Robert Edmond Jones: A Tribute." *Educational Theatre Journal* 7, no. 2 (May 1955): 136–37.

Macintosh, Fiona, ed. *The Ancient Dancer in the Modern World.* Oxford: Oxford University Press, 2010.

MacLean, Nada. "Too Much Freedom in Modern Dancing? NO! [An Interview with] Thomas Sheehy, President, Chicago Association of Dancing Masters." *Dance Lovers Magazine*, September 1924.

Madden, Dorothy. *"You Call Me Louis, Not Mr. Horst."* Amsterdam: Harwood Academic, 1996.

Magriel, Paul, ed. *Chronicles of the American Dance: From the Shakers to Martha Graham.* New York: Da Capo Press, 1978.

Main, Lesley. *Directing the Dance Legacy of Doris Humphrey: The Creative Impulse of Reconstruction.* Madison: University of Wisconsin Press, 2012.

Malnig, Julie. "Athena Meets Venus: Visions of Women in Social Dance in the Teens and Early 1920s." *Dance Research Journal* 31, no. 2 (Autumn 1999): 34–62.

Mamoulian, Rouben. Papers. Manuscript Division, Library of Congress, Washington, DC.

Mann, Tamara. "The Brouhaha: When the Bird Became Art and Art Became Anything." *Spencer's Art Law Journal* 2, no. 2 (Fall 2011).

Mann, Thomas. *Freud, Goethe, Wagner.* New York: Alfred A. Knopf, 1937.

Manning, Susan. *Modern Dance, Negro Dance: Race in Motion.* Minneapolis: University of Minnesota Press, 2004.

Mantle, Burns. "A Sunday Evening for the Book." New York *Daily News,* February 6, 1933.

Mao, Douglas, and Rebecca L. Walkowitz. "The New Modernist Studies." *PMLA* 123, no. 3 (2008): 737–48.

Margolin, Indrani. "Bodyself: Linking Dance and Spirituality." *Dance, Movement & Spiritualities* 1, no. 1 (2014): 143–62.

Maritain, Jacques. *Creative Intuition in Art and Poetry.* The Andrew W. Mellon Lectures in the Fine Arts, National Gallery of Art, Washington. New York: Pantheon Books/Bollingen Foundation, 1953.

Martin, John. "Agnes de Mille Gives Fine Dance Program; Assisted by Charles Weidman." *New York Times,* February 18, 1929.

———. *America Dancing.* New York: Dodge, 1936.

———. "Brilliant Dancing by Martha Graham." *New York Times,* April 4, 1932.

———. "Caravan Dancers in Three Ballets." *New York Times,* February 19, 1938.

———. "The Dance: Afield." *New York Times,* April 30, 1950.

———. "The Dance: American Art. The Case for and Against the Development of National Forms." *New York Times,* November 16, 1930.

———. "The Dance: An American Art." *New York Times,* April 3, 1932.

———. "The Dance: A New Synthesis." *New York Times,* February 16, 1930.

———. "The Dance: A New Work." *New York Times,* August 11, 1935.

———. "The Dance: A Novel Experiment." *New York Times,* April 27, 1930.

———. "The Dance: Artist and Influence." *New York Times,* December 27, 1931.

———. "The Dance: Art Suffers for Lack of a Script." *New York Times,* December 4, 1932.

———. "The Dance as 'Theatre'; Music Afield; The Orchestral Dramas to Be Given This Week Have a Wide Significance." *New York Times*, April 28, 1928.

———. "The Dance: A Unique Theatre Project." *New York Times*, November 10, 1929.

———. "The Dance: A Week of Unique Programs; Three Groups Join Forces to Advance a Common Cause." *New York Times*, January 5, 1930.

———. "The Dance: Big Projects." *New York Times*, July 31, 1932.

———. "The Dance: Experiment." *New York Times*, December 20, 1936.

———. "The Dance Goes on Tour." *New York Times,* February 16, 1936.

———. "The Dance: Graham Again." *New York Times*, November 25, 1934.

———. "The Dance: Kreutzberg." *New York Times*, January 27, 1929.

———. "The Dance: Martha Graham's Art." *New York Times*, November 26, 1933.

———. "The Dance: Mary Wigman's Art." *New York Times*, August 3, 1930.

———. "The Dance: Men Emerge." *New York Times*, February 22, 1931.

———. "The Dance: Miss Graham; An Attempt to Explain Her Art and the Secret of Her Popularity." *New York Times*, March 4, 1934.

———. "The Dance: Miss Graham; Significant Redirection Is Seen in Her Latest Appearance." *New York Times,* January 3, 1937.

———. "The Dance: Miss Graham; To a Performer, Now High in Her Art, an Audience of Americans Pays Tribute." *New York Times*, February 8, 1931.

———. "The Dance: One Artist." *New York Times*, March 10, 1929.

———. "The Dance: Panorama." *New York Times*, September 1, 1935.

———. "The Dance: Summer Affairs." *New York Times*, July 18, 1943.

———. "The Dance: Tamiris' Art." *New York Times*, February 3, 1928.

———. "The Dance: The American Ballet." *New York Times*, October 22, 1933.

———. "The Dance: The Art of Miss Graham." *New York Times*, May 14, 1933.

———. "The Dance: The First Experiment at Radio City." *New York Times*, January 8, 1933.

———. "The Dance: Two Festivals." *New York Times*, February 9, 1930.

———. "The Dance: Vital Issues." *New York Times*, March 8, 1931.

———. "Days of Divine Indiscipline." With photographs by Thomas Bouchard. Special issue, *Dance Perspectives*, no. 12 (1961).

———. "Graham Dancers Offer a Novelty." *New York Times*, May 17, 1945.

———. "Graham Dancers Pack the House." *New York Times*, January 10, 1944.

———. *Introduction to the Dance.* New York: W. W. Norton, 1939.

———. "Martha Graham, Dancer, Is Cheered." *New York Times*, December 7, 1931.

———. "Martha Graham Acclaimed in Dance." *New York Times*, February 3, 1931.

———. "Martha Graham Gives Dance Without Music." *New York Times*, January 9, 1930.

———. "Martha Graham Gives New Dances." *New York Times*, February 29, 1932.

———. "Martha Graham Hailed in Recital." *New York Times*, November 20, 1933.

———. "Martha Graham in 2nd 'Visionary.'" *New York Times*, April 18, 1961.

———. "Martha Graham in 3 New Dances." *New York Times*, November 21, 1932.

———. "Martha Graham in Dance Festival." *New York Times*, December 28, 1939.

———. "Martha Graham Offers New Dance." *New York Times*, October 10, 1938.

———. "Martha Graham Scores in Recital; Receives Ovation After 2-Year Absence—Novelty, 'Eye of Anguish,' Presented." *New York Times*, January 23, 1950.

———. "Martha Graham's Recital; Program of New and Old Dances Provide Emotional Afternoon." *New York Times*, March 4, 1929.

———. "Miss Enters Gives Recital of Dances." *New York Times*, December 28, 1936.

———. *The Modern Dance*. New York: A. S. Barnes, 1933.

———. "The Modern Dance in America." *USA Magazine*, Spring 1930.

———. "New Dance Theatre Scores a Success; Program by Four Stars." *New York Times*, January 6, 1930.

———. "New Group Compositions by Doris Humphrey." *New York Times*, February 2, 1931.

———. "Premiere of Dance; 'Stephen Acrobat' First New Work of Graham Troupe." *New York Times*, February 27, 1947.

———. "Recital a Triumph for Martha Graham; Closes Season with Debut of Her Dance Group." *New York Times*, April 15, 1929.

———. "Vermont Dancers at Bennington." *New York Times*, August 16, 1935.

———. "Weidman Makes Hit in a New Dance." *New York Times*, February 8, 1931.

Martin, Richard P. *Myths of the Ancient Greeks*. New York: New American Library, 2003.

Marx, Edward. *Leonie Gilmour: When East Weds West*. New York: Botchan Books, 2013.

Mason, Francis. *I Remember Balanchine: Recollections of the Ballet Master by Those Who Knew Him*. New York: Doubleday, 1991.

Mast, Andrew. Liner notes. *Vincent Persichetti: Works for Band*. Illinois State University Wind Symphony, conducted by Stephen K. Steele. Albany Records 1253, 2011, compact disc.

Matthews, Herbert L. "China's Stage Idol Comes to Broadway." *New York Times*, February 16, 1930.

May, Ernest K. *The First American Tour of Mei Lan-fang*. New York: China Institute in America, 1930.

Mabary, Judith. "Martinů's Contribution to Modern Dance." *Bohuslav Martinů Newsletter* 6, no. 1 (January–April 2006).

Mayer, Frederick P. "North Side: A Day in Old Allegheny." *Pittsburgh Record*, June 1930.

McBride, Henry. Modern Art. "American Expatriates in Paris." *Dial*, April 1929, 353–55.

McCarthy, Jack. "1929 Philadelphia Orchestra Radio Broadcast of *The Rite of Spring*." PhilOrch (*Philadelphia Orchestra* blog), March 11, 2013. Accessed May 15, 2013. https://www .philorch.org/blog/stokowski-celebration/1929-philadelphia-orchestra-radio-broadcast -rite-spring#/.

———. "Leopold Stokowski, the Philadelphia Orchestra, and *The Rite of Spring*." PhilOrch (*Philadelphia Orchestra* blog), February 22, 2013. Accessed May 15, 2013. https://www .philorch.org/blog/stokowski-celebration/leopold-stokowski-philadelphia-orchestra-and -rite-spring#/.

McCausland, Elizabeth. "American Dancer Is Evolving a Typically American Rhythm." *Republican*, April 30, 1933.

———. "Definite Change in Graham's Art—Noted Dancer Seems to Be Finding New Functions for Genius." *Union*, March 1, 1936.

———. "Martha Graham Finds New Accent." *Union*, October 16, 1938.

McCormick, John. "Portrait: Francis Fergusson, 1904–1986." *American Scholar* 56, no. 4 (Autumn 1987): 557–64.

McCormick, Malcolm. *INDEX: John Martin, The Dance, The New York Times*. Chronological Compendium of all John Martin reviews of and articles about Martha Graham, 1927ff. (Given to the author by McCormick.)

McDonagh, Don. *The Complete Guide to Modern Dance*. New York: Popular Library, 1977.

———. *Martha Graham*. New York: Popular Library, 1973.

———. "Martha Graham: Fiction and Fact." *Dance Chronicle* 15, no. 3 (1992): 349–60.

———. *The Rise and Fall and Rise of Modern Dance.* New York: Outerbridge & Dienstfrey, 1970.

McGehee, Helen. "The New Martha Graham Technique." Lecture/demonstration presented at the Society of Writers and Critics of the Dance, Paris, March 31, 1950.

———. "An Opportunity Lost." Helpern, Alice, ed. Martha Graham. A Special Issue of *Choreography and Dance: An International Journal,* vol. 5, part 2 (1999): 69–79.

———. Review of *Martha: The Life and Work of Martha Graham,* by Agnes de Mille, and *The Technique of Martha Graham,* by Alice Helpern. *Dance Research Journal* 11, no. 1 (Spring 1993): 99–103.

———. *To Be a Dancer.* Edited by Alfonso Umaña. Lynchburg, VA: Editions Heraclita, 1989.

McHale, Brian. "What Was Postmodernism?" *Electronic Book Review,* December 20, 2007. http://www.electronicbookreview.com.

McLaughlin, Patricia, and Charles Uhl. National Register of Historic Places Inventory— Nomination Form: Old Allegheny Rows Historic District. Pennsylvania Historical and Museum Commission to US Department of the Interior, National Park Service. Washington, DC. http://www.dot7.state.pa.us/CRGIS_Attachments/SiteResource/H064370 _01H.pdf. Surveyed 1978. Listed on NRHP November 1, 1984.

McNamara, Donald, and Louise Brooks. "Lulu in Rochester: Self-Portrait of an Anti-Star." *Missouri Review* 6, no. 3 (Summer 1983): 63–82.

McPherson, Elizabeth. *The Bennington School of the Dance: A History in Writings and Interviews.* Jefferson, NC: McFarland, 2013.

———. *The Contributions of Martha Hill to American Dance and Dance Education, 1900–1995.* Lewiston, NY: Edwin Mellen Press, 2008.

———. "Helen Tamiris (1902–1966)." Dance Heritage Coalition, 2012. http://www .danceheritage.org/treasures/tamiris_essay_mcpherson.pdf.

Mead, Andrew. "Bodily Hearing: Physiological Metaphors and Musical Understanding." *Journal of Music Theory* 43, no. 1 (Spring 1999): 1–19.

Mellow, James R. *Walker Evans.* New York: Basic Books, 1999.

Melnick, Ross. *American Showman: Samuel "Roxy" Rothafel and the Birth of the Entertainment Industry, 1908–1935.* New York: Columbia University Press, 2012.

Mendini, Shauna Thelin. "Gertrude Shurr: Portrait of a Modern Dance Teacher." Master's thesis, University of Arizona, 1986.

Menger, Pierre-Michel. *The Economics of Creativity: Art and Achievement Under Uncertainty.* Cambridge, MA: Harvard University Press, 2014.

Merleau-Ponty, Maurice. *The Visible and the Invisible, Followed by Working Notes.* Evanston, IL: Northwestern University Press, 1968.

Metropolitan Museum of Art. *Guide to the Collections.* 4th ed. New York: Metropolitan Museum of Art, 1924.

Metzer, David. "The League of Composers: The Initial Years." *American Music* 15, no. 1 (Spring 1997): 45–69.

Miles, Lisa A. *Resurrecting Allegheny City: The Land, Structures, & People of Pittsburgh's North Side.* Pittsburgh: Lisa A. Miles, 2007.

Miller, Cristanne. "Marianne Moore and the Women Modernizing New York." *Modern Philology* 98, no. 2 (November 2000): 339–62.

Miller, James. *Measures of Wisdom: The Cosmic Dance in Classical and Christian Antiquity.* Toronto: University of Toronto Press, 1986.

Miller, Leta E. "Henry Cowell and Modern Dance: The Genesis of Elastic Form." *American Music* 20, no. 1 (Spring 2002): Appendix A.

Miller, Perry. *Errand into the Wilderness.* Cambridge, MA: Belknap Press, 1956.

Miller, Raphael F. "George Beiswanger and Dance Criticism." *Dance Chronicle* 16, no. 1 (1993): 45–71.

Mitgang, Herbert. "Frances Steloff Is Dead at 101; Founded the Gotham Book Mart." *New York Times*, April 16, 1989.

Moore, Edward. "Denishawns Give Needed Touch to American Dancing." *Chicago Daily Tribune*, October 24, 1922.

———. "St. Denis and Isadora Duncan Will Dance Here This Week." *Chicago Daily Tribune*, October 22, 1922.

Moore, Marianne. *A Marianne Moore Reader.* New York: Viking, 1972.

Moore, Carol-Lynne, and Kaoru Yamamoto. *Beyond Words: Movement Observation and Analysis.* London: Routledge, 2012.

Morgan, Barbara. *Martha Graham: Sixteen Dances in Photographs.* Dobbs Ferry, NY: Morgan & Morgan, 1941.

Morgan, Kathleen. "Frances Steloff and the Gotham Book Mart." Special issue, *Journal of Modern Literature* 4, no. 4 (April 1975): 737–48.

Moriarty, Laura. *The Chaperone.* A novel. New York: Riverhead Books, 2012.

Morris, Gay. "Modernism's Role in the Theory of John Martin and Edwin Denby." *Dance Research Journal* 22, no. 2 (Winter 2004): 168–84.

Morton, John. "Sigmund Freud, Géza Róheim, and the Strehlows." In *German Ethnography in Australia*, edited by Nicolas Peterson and Anna Kenny, 195–221. Acton: Australian National University Press, 2017.

Mott, Frank Luther. *A History of American Magazines.* Vol. 1, 1741–1850. Cambridge, MA: Belknap Press, 1938.

Mullin, Amy. Review of *Nietzsche's Dancers*, by Kimerer LaMothe. *Hypatia* 23, no. 3 (Summer 2008): 221–23.

Mumaw, Barton, and Jane Sherman. "Ted Shawn, Teacher and Choreographer." *Dance Chronicle* 4, no. 2 (1981): 91-112.

Mumford, Lewis. *Technics and Civilization.* New York: Harcourt Brace, 1934.

Muray, Nickolas. *Muray's Celebrity Portraits of the Twenties and Thirties.* New York: Dover, 1978.

Murphy, Jacqueline Shea. *The People Have Never Stopped Dancing: Native American Modern Dance Histories.* Minneapolis: University of Minnesota Press, 2007.

Myrick, David F. *Montecito and Santa Barbara.* Vol. 1, *From Farms to Estates.* Glendale, CA: Trans-Anglo Books, 1988.

———. *Montecito and Santa Barbara.* Vol. 2, *The Days of the Great Estates.* Glendale, CA: Trans-Anglo Books, 1991.

Nadal-Melsió, Sara. "Dancing Icons, or the Syncopation of the Unsayable: Graham's *Lamentation* and the Cult of the Mater Dolorosa." *Lectora*, no. 2 (1996): 83-91.

Nancy, Jean-Luc. *The Muses.* Translated by Peggy Kamuf. Stanford, CA: Stanford University Press, 1996.

Naranjo, Tessie. "Thoughts on Migration by Santa Clara Pueblo." *Journal of Anthropological Archaeology* 14, no. 2 (1995): 247–50.

Needham, Maureen. "Who Is Isadora?" *Dance Chronicle* 19, no. 3 (1996): 331–40.

Neumann, Erich. *The Origins and History of Consciousness.* Translated by R. F. C. Hull. Bollingen Series. Princeton, NJ: Princeton University Press, 1954.

Newhall, Mary Ann Santos. *Mary Wigman.* Performance Practitioners Series. London: Routledge, 2009.

New York Landmarks Preservation Commission. Designation List No. 114 LP-0995: Radio City Music Hall. March 28, 1978. http://s-media.nyc.gov/agencies/lpc/lp/0995.pdf.

New York Times. "Frances G. Wickes, 91, Author of Psychology Books, Is Dead." May 8, 1967.

———. "Graham Injured, Show Off." July 18, 1950.

Nicholas Roerich Museum. *Roerich Museum Catalogue.* 6th ed. New York: Roerich Museum, 1930.

Nietzsche, Friedrich. *Beyond Good and Evil: Prelude to a Philosophy of the Future.* New York: Penguin Books, 1990.

———. *The Birth of Tragedy: Out of the Spirit of Man.* New York: Penguin Books, 2003.

———. *The Gay Science: With a Prelude in Rhymes and an Appendix of Songs.* Translated by Walter Kaufmann. New York: Vintage Books, 1974.

———. *Schopenhauer as Educator.* Translated by James W. Hillesheim and Malcolm R. Simpson. Chicago: Regnery, 1965.

N. I. K. "Martha Graham and Group." Review of performance at Chicago Civic Theatre, March 10, 1940. *Chicago Dancer,* March 1940.

Nochlin, Linda. "Why Have There Been No Great Women Artists?" *ARTnews,* January 1971. Reprinted in Linda Nochlin, *Women, Art and Power and Other Essays,* 145-78. New York: Harper & Row, 1988.

Noguchi, Isamu. *A Sculptor's World.* New York: Harper & Row, 1968.

Noland, Carrie. *Agency and Embodiment: Performing Gestures/Producing Culture.* Cambridge, MA: Harvard University Press, 2009.

Nordhoff, Charles. *California: For Health, Pleasure, and Residence: A Book for Travellers and Settlers.* New York: Harper & Brothers, 1873.

North, Michael. "The Making of 'Make It New.'" In *Novelty: A History of the New.* Chicago: University of Chicago Press, 2013.

Northrop, F. S. C. *The Meeting of East and West.* New York: Collier/Macmillan, 1966. First published 1946 by Macmillan (New York).

Norton, Leslie. *Léonide Massine and the 20th Century Ballet.* Jefferson, NC: McFarland, 2004.

Nye, Edward. "'Choreography' Is Narrative: The Programmes of the Eighteenth-Century Ballet d'Action." *Dance Research Journal* 26, no. 1 (Summer 2008): 42–59.

Oates, Joyce Carol. "Inspiration and Obsession in Life and Literature." *New York Review of Books,* August 13, 2015, 80–85.

Obey, André. *Le viol de Lucrèce/The Rape of Lucrece.* Translated by Thornton Wilder. New York: Riverside Press, 1933.

Odom, Maggie. "Mary Wigman: The Early Years, 1913–1925." *Drama Review* 24, no. 4 (December 1980): 81-92.

Odom, Selma Landen. "What Is Dalcrozian?" *Dance Research Journal* 10, no. 2 (Autumn 1992): 121–31.

Oesterley, W. O. E. *The Sacred Dance: A Study in Comparative Folklore.* New York: Macmillan, 1923.

O'Hara, Edwin. "Poor Clares." In *The Catholic Encyclopedia.* Vol. 12. New York: Robert Appleton, 1911.

Oja, Carol J. "Dane Rudhyar's Vision of American Dissonance." *American Music* 17, no. 2 (Summer 1999): 129-45.

———. "Women Patrons and Crusaders for Modernist Music: New York in the 1920s." In *Cultivating Music in America: Women Patrons and Activists Since 1860*, edited by Ralph P. Locke and Cyrilla Barr, chap. 8. Berkeley: University of California Press, 1997.

O'Keeffe, Georgia. *Georgia O'Keeffe*. New York: Viking Studio Books, 1976.

O'Leary, Margaret. "More Ado About the Flapper." *New York Times*, April 16, 1922.

Oles, James. *South of the Border: Mexico in the American Imagination, 1914–1947*. With an essay by Karen Cordero Reiman. Translated by Marta Ferragut. Washington and London: Smithsonian Institution Press, 1993.

Olson, Charles. *The Fiery Hunt and Other Plays*. Bolinas, CA: Four Seasons Foundation, 1977.

———. Papers. Charles Olson Research Collection. Archives & Special Collections at the Thomas J. Dodd Research Center, University of Connecticut Libraries, Storrs, Connecticut.

Oppenheim, Lois. "The Shape of Process: Martha Graham's Journey into the Self." In *A Curious Intimacy: Art and Neuro-psychoanalysis*. London: Routledge, 2005.

Or, Eileen. "Body and Mind: The Yoga Roots of Martha Graham's 'Contraction' and 'Release.'" In *Proceedings of the Conference "Border Crossings: Dance and Boundaries in Society, Politics, Gender, Education, and Technology,"* 202–13. Ryerson Polytechnic University, Toronto, Ontario, Canada, May 1-15, 1995.

Ortiz, Alfonso, ed. *Handbook of North American Indians*. Vol. 9, *Southwest*. Washington, DC: Smithsonian Institution, 1979.

———, ed. *Handbook of North American Indians*. Vol. 10, *Southwest*. Washington, DC: Smithsonian Institution, 1983.

———. "Ritual Drama and the Pueblo World View." In *New Perspectives on the Pueblos*, 135–61. Albuquerque: University of New Mexico Press, 1984.

Ortiz, Lori. "The Resurrection of Loïe Fuller." Review of *The Resurrection of Loïe Fuller*, by Ann Cooper Albright, Loïe Fuller, and Rhonda K. Garelick. *PAJ: A Journal of Performance and Art* 30, no. 3 (September 2008): 117–20.

Ouspensky, P. D. *Tertium Organum: [The Third Canon of Thought]: A Key to the Enigmas of the World*. New York: Alfred A. Knopf, 1981.

Owen, Norton. *A Certain Place: The Jacob's Pillow Story*. Rev. ed. Becket, MA: Jacob's Pillow Dance Festival, 2002.

———. "José Limón." Dance Heritage Coalition, 2012. http://www.danceheritage.org /limon.html.

Owens, Dewey. *Carlos Salzedo: From Aeolian to Thunder*. Chicago: Lyon & Healy, 1992.

Paelian, Garabed. *Nicholas Roerich*. Sedona, AZ: Aquarian Educational Group, 1996.

Pagani, Maria Pia. "Re-discovering Oliver M. Sayler." *Mimesis Journal* 2 (2013): 162–67.

Page, Ruth. *Page by Page*. Edited by Andrew Mark Wentink. Brooklyn, NY: Dance Horizons, 1978.

Paglia, Camille. "Erich Neumann: Theorist of the Great Mother." *Arion* 13, no. 3 (Winter 2006): 1–14.

Pakes, Anna. "Dance's Mind-Body Problem." *Dance Research Journal* 24, no. 2 (Winter 2006): 87–104.

Palfy, Barbara. Review of *After the Dance: Documents of Ruth St. Denis and Ted Shawn*, by Susan Brady. *Dance Research Journal* 30, no. 1 (Spring 1998): 64–67.

Pallaro, Patrizia, ed. *Authentic Movement: Essays by Mary Starks Whitehouse, Janet Adler, and Joan Chodorow.* London: Jessica Kingsley, 1999.

Panero, James. "Martha Martha Martha." *New Criterion*, September 3, 2015. https://newcriterion.com/blogs/dispatch/martha-martha-martha.

Paris, Barry. *Louise Brooks: A Biography.* New York: Alfred A. Knopf, 1989.

Parke, John E. *Recollections of Seventy Years and Historical Gleanings of Allegheny, Pennsylvania.* Boston: Rand, Avery, 1886.

Parker, H. T. "The New Ways of the Dance, to Boston Eyes." *Boston Evening Transcript*, March 8, 1930.

———. "Revelation to Bostonians of Martha Graham." *Boston Evening Transcript*, April 9, 1932.

———. "Roshanara and Ito." *Boston Evening Transcript*, December 5, 1917.

Parker, Robert L. "Carlos Chávez and the Ballet: A Study in Persistence." *Dance Chronicle* 8, nos. 3–4 (1984–85): 179–210.

Parsons, Elsie Worthington Clews. *Taos Pueblo.* Menasha, WI: George Banta, 1936.

Parton, James. "Pittsburg." *Atlantic Monthly* 21, no. 23 (January 1868): 17–36.

Partsch-Bergsohn, Isa. *Modern Dance in Germany and the United States: Crosscurrents and Influences.* Chur, Switzerland: Harwood Academic, 1994.

Pasles, Chris. "'Appalachian Spring'—Martha's Ballet." *Los Angeles Times,* January 3, 1991.

Patterson, Daniel W. *The Shaker Spiritual.* Princeton, NJ: Princeton University Press, 1979.

Patton, Laurie L., trans. and ed. *The Bhagavad Gita.* New York: Penguin Classics, 2008.

Paul, Sherman. "Dancing the Man." Review of *The Fiery Hunt and Other Plays*, by Charles Olson. *Boundary2* 6, no. 2 (Winter 1978): 623–27.

Paulding, Litti. "Punch and Judy—Scotland Loves the Goddess." *Santa Barbara News-Press*, October 16, 1963.

Pavis, Patrice. *Dictionary of the Theatre: Terms, Concepts, and Analysis.* Toronto: University of Toronto Press, 1998.

Payne, Carol. "Negotiating Photographic Modernism in *USA: A Quarterly Magazine of the American Scene* (1930)." *Visual Resources* 23, no. 4 (December 2007): 337–51.

Paz, Danielle. "Tableau Vivant." *Chicago School of Media Theory* (blog), University of Chicago. https://lucian.uchicago.edu/blogs/mediatheory/keywords/tableau-vivant/.

Pearce, Thomas Matthews. *Mary Hunter Austin.* Boston: Twayne Publishers, 1966.

———. "An Unposted Letter to the Editors of 'The London Times Literary Supplement,' September 17, 1954." *News Bulletin of the Rocky Mountain Modern Language Association* 8, no. 1 (October 1954): 3–4.

Pease, Esther Elizabeth. "Louis Horst: His Theories on Modern Dance Composition." PhD diss., University of Michigan, 1953.

Penicka, Sarah. "Men of Faith: Stravinsky, Maritain and the Ideal Christian Artifex." In *Through a Glass Darkly: Reflections on the Sacred*, edited by Frances Di Lauro. Sydney, Australia: Sydney University Press, 2006.

People. "Martha Graham, the Revolutionary Mother of Modern Dance, Takes Her Final Leave of the Spotlight." April 15, 1991.

Perl, Jed. "Modernism in Art." In *The Classical Tradition*, edited by Anthony Grafton, Glenn W. Most, and Salvatore Settis, 594–98. Cambridge, MA: Belknap Press, 2010.

Perloff, Carey. "Tragedy Today." *PMLA* 129, no. 4 (2014): 830–33.

Phillips, Victoria. "Martha Graham's Gilded Cage: *Blood Memory—An Autobiography* (1991)." *Dance Research Journal* 45, no. 2 (August 2013): 63–84.

Picón, Carlos A., et al. *Art of the Classical World in the Metropolitan Museum of Art*. New York: Metropolitan Museum of Art; New Haven, CT: Yale University Press, 2007.

Platt, Susan. "Elizabeth McCausland: Art, Politics, and Sexuality." In *Women Artists and Modernism*, edited by Katy Deepwell, 83–96. Manchester, UK: Manchester University Press, 1998.

Poetry Foundation. "Harriet Monroe, 1860–1936." https://www.poetryfoundation.org/poets/harriet-monroe.

———. "Vachel Lindsay, 1879–1931." https://www.poetryfoundation.org/poets/vachel-lindsay.

Poindexter, Elizabeth. "Ted Shawn: His Personal Life, His Professional Career, and His Contributions to the Development of Dance in the United States of America from 1891 to 1963." PhD diss., Texas Woman's University, 1963.

Polcari, Stephen. "Martha Graham and Abstract Expressionism." *Smithsonian Studies in American Art* 4, no. 1 (Winter 1990): 2–28.

Pollack, Howard. *Aaron Copland: The Life and Work of an Uncommon Man*. New York: Henry Holt, 1999.

Porter, Keyes. "As an Oriental Looks at Art: Michio Itow [*sic*], Distinguished Japanese Dancer, Gives His Theories on Dancing and the Other Arts." *Dance Magazine*, January 1926, 33-62.

Porter, Roy. *Flesh in the Age of Reason: The Modern Foundations of Body and Soul*. New York: W. W. Norton, 2005.

Posnock, Ross. "American Idol: On Nietzsche in America." *Nation*, November 1, 2011, 33-35.

Potter, Michelle. "Merce Cunningham (1919–2009)." Dance Heritage Coalition, 2012. http://new.danceheritage.org/html/treasures/cunningham_essay_potter.pdf.

Pound, Ezra. "The Constant Preaching to the Mob." In *Literary Essays of Ezra Pound*, edited with an introduction by T. S. Eliot, 64-65. New York: New Directions, 1968.

———. "How I Began." In *Early Writings: Poems and Prose*, edited by Ira B. Nadel, 211-15. New York: Penguin Books, 2005.

———. "Patria Mia." In *Selected Prose, 1909–1965*, edited by William Cookson, 99-141. New York: New Directions, 1973.

———. *Personae: The Collected Shorter Poems*. New York: New Directions, 1949.

———. *Selected Letters of Ezra Pound, 1907–1941*. Edited by D. D. Paige. New York: New Directions, 1971.

Preston, Carrie J. "Introduction: Modernism and Dance." *Modernist Cultures* 9, no. 1 (2014): 1–6.

———. *Modernism's Mythic Pose: Gender, Genre, Solo Performance*. New York: Oxford University Press, 2011.

———. "Posing Modernism: Delsartism in Modern Dance and Silent Film." *Theatre Journal* 61, no. 2 (May 2009): 213–33.

Preston-Dunlop, Valerie, ed. *Dance Words*. Chur, Switzerland: Harwood Academic, 1995.

Prettejohn, Elizabeth. *The Modernity of Ancient Sculpture*. New York: I. B. Tauris, 2012.

Preucel, Robert, and Frank G. Matero. "Placemaking on the Northern Rio Grande: A View from Kuaua Pueblo." In *Archaeologies of Placemaking: Monuments, Memories, and Engagement in Native North America*, edited by Patricia E. Rubertone, chap. 4. Walnut Creek, CA: Left Coast Press, 2008. http://repository.upenn.edu/hp_papers?15.

Prevots, Naima. *Dancing in the Sun: Hollywood Choreographers, 1915–1937*. Ann Arbor, MI: UMI Research Press, 1987.

Rancière, Jacques. *Aisthesis: Scenes from the Aesthetic Regime of Art.* Translated by Zakir Paul. New York: Verso, 2013.

Rank, Otto. *Art and Artist: Creative Urge and Personality Development.* New York: W. W. Norton, 1989. First published 1932.

———. *The Myth of the Birth of the Hero and Other Writings.* Edited by Philip Freund. New York: Vintage Books, 1964. First published 1909 (parts 1 and 2) and 1922 (part 3).

Rasula, Jed. *History of a Shiver: The Sublime Impudence of Modernism.* New York: Oxford University Press, 2016.

Raymond, David. "The Eastman Connection." *Eastman Notes* 22, no. 1 (December 2003): 12–13.

Redfield, Robert. Review of *La Musique des Incas et ses Survivances,* by R. D'Harcourt and M. D'Harcourt. *American Journal of Sociology* 33, no. 1 (July 1927): 136–37.

Reed, Jane Carol. "Modern Dance Exponent Is Product of Local Schools." *Santa Barbara News-Press,* April 4, 1937.

Reis, Claire Raphael. *Composers, Conductors, and Critics.* New York: Oxford University Press, 1955.

Reynolds, Debbie. "Movie Prologues." *Matinee at the Bijou* (blog), January 2, 2009. http://matineeatthebijou.blogspot.com/2009/01/movie-prologues.html.

Reynolds, Dee. "A Technique for Power: Reconfiguring Economies of Energy in Martha Graham's Early Work." *Dance Research Journal* 20, no. 1 (Summer 2002): 3–32.

Reynolds, Nancy, and Malcolm McCormick. *No Fixed Points: Dance in the Twentieth Century.* New Haven, CT: Yale University Press, 2003.

Rich, Daniel Catton. *The Arthur Jerome Eddy Collection of Modern Paintings and Sculpture.* Chicago: Art Institute of Chicago, 1931. Exhibition catalogue.

Richardson, John. *A Life of Picasso: The Triumphant Years, 1917–1932.* New York: Alfred A. Knopf, 2010.

Richardson, Peter. Review of *Mary Austin and the American West,* by Susan Goodman and Carl Dawson. *Los Angeles Times Book Review,* January 25, 2009.

Richter, Gisela M. A. "Greek Terracottas: Recent Accessions." *Metropolitan Museum of Art Bulletin* 19, no. 5 (May 1924): 127–30.

———. *Handbook of the Classical Collection.* New York: Metropolitan Museum of Art, 1930.

———. "Miscellaneous Accessions in the Classical Department." *Metropolitan Museum of Art Bulletin* 21, no. 12 (December 1926): 282–86.

———. "New Accessions in the Classical Department." *Metropolitan Museum of Art Bulletin* 21, no. 3 (March 1926): 80–84.

———. "Recent Accessions of the Classical Department." *Metropolitan Museum of Art Bulletin* 15, no. 5 (May 1920): 107–9.

Riddle, Carl. *The Paris Abstractions.* Catalogue monograph for exhibition at the Isamu Noguchi Foundation and Garden Museum, New York, 2007.

Riley, Kathleen. "A Near Myth." Review of *Martha Graham in Love and War,* by Mark Franko. *Times Literary Supplement,* December 21, 2012.

Rilke, Rainer Maria. *Letters of Rainer Maria Rilke, 1892–1910.* Translated by Jane Bannard Greene and M. D. Herter Norton. New York: W. W. Norton, 1945.

R.L. "Martha Graham and Dance Company." *Dance Observer,* March 1946.

Roberts, W. Adolphe. "The Fervid Art of Martha Graham." *Dance Magazine,* August 1928, 13, 63.

Robertson, Nan. "Martha Graham Dances with the Future." *New York Times*, October 2, 1988.

Robin, William. "Asking Whether Copland's Abstruse Works Are the Exception or the Rule." *New York Times*, April 12, 2016.

Rodrigues, Chris, and Chris Garratt. *Introducing Modernism*. London: Icon Books, 2010.

Roediger, Virginia More. *Ceremonial Costumes of the Pueblo Indians: Their Evolution, Fabrication, and Significance in the Prayer Drama*. Berkeley: University of California Press, 1991.

Rogers, Frederick Rand, ed. *Dance: A Basic Educational Technique*. New York: Macmillan, 1941.

Rooney, Dan, and Carol Peterson. *Allegheny City: A History of Pittsburgh's North Side*. Pittsburgh: University of Pittsburgh Press, 2013.

Rosenfeld, Maurice. "Ruth St. Denis and Ted Shawn Appear in Group of Dances." *Chicago Daily News*, October 24, 1922.

Rosenfeld, Paul. "American Painting." *Dial*, December 1921, 649-70.

———. *Port of New York: Essays on Fourteen American Moderns*. New York: Harcourt Brace, 1924.

Ross, Alex. *The Rest Is Noise: Listening to the Twentieth Century*. New York: Farrar, Straus and Giroux, 2007.

Ross, Nancy Wilson, ed. *The Notebooks of Martha Graham*. New York: Harcourt Brace Jovanovich, 1973.

Röthel, Hans Konrad, Wassily Kandinsky, and Jean K. Benjamin. *Kandinsky, Catalogue Raisonné of the Oil-Paintings*. Vol. 1, *1900–1915*. Ithaca, NY: Cornell University Press, 1982.

Rothschild, Bethsabée de. *La danse artistique aux USA: Tendances modernes*. Paris: Editions Elzevir, 1949.

R.S. "Martha Graham and Group." *Dance Observer*, February 1940.

———. "Reviews of the Month." *Dance Observer,* June–July 1946.

Rudhyar, D. "The Birth of the American Dance Ritual." *Carmelite*, July 31, 1929, 1.

Rudnick, Lois P. " 'Under the Skin' of New Mexico: The Life, Times, and Art of Cady Wells." In *Cady Wells and Southwestern Modernism*, edited by Lois P. Rudnick, 15–93. Santa Fe: Museum of New Mexico Press, 2009.

Rudnick, Lois P., and MaLin Wilson-Powell, eds. *Mabel Dodge Luhan & Company: American Moderns and the West*. Santa Fe: Museum of New Mexico Press, Harwood Museum of Art/ University of New Mexico, 2016.

Ruyter, Nancy Lee Chalfa. "The Delsarte Heritage." *Dance Research Journal* 14, no. 1 (Summer 1996): 62–74.

———. *Reformers and Visionaries: The Americanization of the Art of Dance*. Brooklyn, NY: Dance Horizons, 1979.

Saavedra, Leonora, ed. *Carlos Chávez and His World*. Princeton, NJ: Princeton University Press, 2015.

Sabin, Robert. "The Dance Concerto: Martha Graham and William Schuman Create a New Form for the Theatre." *Dance Observer* 17, no. 2 (February 1950): 22–23.

———. "Louis Horst and the Modern Dance in America: Part 4—A Summing Up." *Dance Observer* 27, no. 4 (April 1953) 37–40.

Sachs, Joel. *Henry Cowell: A Man Made of Music*. New York: Oxford University Press, 2012.

Said, Edward W. *Beginnings: Intention and Method*. New York: Columbia University Press, 1985.

———. *On Late Style: Music and Literature Against the Grain.* New York: Vintage Books, 2007.

———. *Orientalism.* New York: Random House, 1978.

Salas, Elizabeth. *Soldaderas in the Mexican Military: Myth and History.* Austin: University of Texas Press, 1990.

Salpeter, Harry. "Martha Graham." *Mademoiselle* 4 (February 1937).

Salter, Chris. *Entangled: Technology and the Transformation of Performance.* Cambridge, MA: MIT Press, 2010.

Samorzik, Elad. "Pas de Deux." *Haaretz,* May 6, 2011. https://www.haaretz.com/1.5008940.

Sanders, Carla. "O Pioneers!" *Inland Living,* February–March 2011, 16.

Satterfield, Jay. "Merle Armitage: Accent on Taste." *Books at Iowa* 64, no. 1 (April 1996): 31–39.

Saunders, Charles Francis. *The Indians of the Terraced Houses.* New York: G. P. Putnam's Sons, 1912.

Sayler, Oliver M. *Revolt in the Arts: A Survey of the Creation, Distribution and Appreciation of Art in America.* New York: Brentano's, 1930.

Schewender, Martha. "Following the Leader, and Sometimes Moving Past." Review of *Survey of Paris Abstractions* at the Noguchi Museum. *New York Times,* July 27, 2007.

Schiff, David. "Music; Schoenberg's Cool Eye for the Erotic." *New York Times,* August 8, 1999.

Schippers, Donald J. *Reflections of John Joseph Martin.* Oral history transcript. Oral History Program, University of California, Los Angeles, 1967.

Schlaes, Amity. "The Myth of Gatsby's Suffering Middle Class." *New York Times,* June 1, 2013.

Schlundt, Christena L. *The Professional Appearances of Ruth St. Denis & Ted Shawn: A Chronology and an Index of Dances, 1906–1932.* New York: New York Public Library, 1962.

———. "The Renaissance of Ruth St. Denis." Review of *Divine Dancer: A Biography of Ruth St. Denis,* by Suzanne Shelton. *Dance Chronicle* 4, no. 4 (1981): 452–59.

Schmitt, Natalie Crohn. "Intimations of Immortality: W. B. Yeats's *At the Hawk's Well.*" *Theatre Journal* 31, no. 4 (December 1979): 510–10.

Schmuhl, Robert. *Indecent Liberties.* Notre Dame, IN: University of Notre Dame Press, 2000.

Schoenbach, Lisi. *Pragmatic Modernism.* New York: Oxford University Press, 2015.

Schoenberg, Arnold. "Breslow Lecture" [ca. 1928]. In *Arnold Schoenberg, Wassily Kandinsky: Letters, Pictures and Documents,* edited by Jelena Hahl-Koch. Translated by John C. Crawford. London: Faber and Faber, 1984.

———. *The Musical Idea and the Logic, Technique and Art of Its Presentation.* Edited and translated by Patricia Carpenter and Severine Neff. Bloomington: Indiana University Press, 2006.

———. *Sämtliche Werke.* Edited by Josef Rufer. Mainz, Germany: B. Schott's Söhne, 1966.

———. *Style and Idea: Selected Writings.* Edited by Leonard Stein. Translated by Leo Black. 16th ed. Berkeley: University of California Press, 1984.

Schopenhauer, Arthur. *Essays and Aphorisms.* Selected and translated by R. J. Hollingdale. New York: Penguin Books, 2004.

Schultheis, Robert. "The Corn Dance: Complex, Hypnotic." *New York Times,* July 11, 1976.

Schwartz, Hillel. "Torque: The New Kinaesthetic of the Twentieth Century." In *Zone 6: Incorporations,* edited by Jonathan Crary and Sanford Kwinter, 70-127. New York: Urzone, Inc., 1992.

Schweitzer, Vivien. Review: "Bard Festival Salutes Carlos Chávez." *New York Times*, August 10, 2015.

Schwendener, Martha. "Following the Leader, and Sometimes Moving Past." Review of *Survey of* Paris Abstraction at the Noguchi Museum. *New York Times,* July 27, 2007.

Scruton, Roger. *Beauty: A Very Short Introduction.* Oxford: Oxford University Press, 2011.

Scully, Vincent. *The Earth, the Temple, and the Gods: Greek Sacred Architecture.* New Haven, CT: Yale University Press, 1962.

————. "The Great Goddess." In *The Earth, the Temple, and the Gods: Greek Sacred Architecture* (rev. ed.), chap. 2. New York: Yale University Press, 1979.

————. *Pueblo: Mountain, Village, Dance.* New York: Viking, 1975.

Seaford, Richard. "In the Mirror of Dionysus." In *The Sacred and the Feminine in Ancient Greece*, edited by Sue Blundell and Margaret Williamson. London: Routledge, 1998.

Sears, David, ed. "Erik [*sic*] Hawkins Speaks His Mind on Dance." *New York Times*, October 7, 1984.

————, ed. "Louis Horst: A Centennial Compendium." *Ballet Review* 12, no. 2 (Summer 1984).

Segal, Charles. *Tragedy and Civilization: An Interpretation of Sophocles.* Norman: University of Oklahoma Press, 1999.

Seibert, Gary. "Breathing In & Out: Martha Graham, R.I.P." *Commonweal,* September 15, 1991, 516–18.

Selden, Elizabeth. *The Dancer's Quest: Essays on the Aesthetic of the Contemporary Dance.* Berkeley: University of California Press, 1935.

————. *Elements of the Free Dance.* New York: A. S. Barnes, 1930.

Seldes, Marian. "Martha Graham's Gift to Drama." *New York Times*, October 4, 1987.

Selivanova, Nina. *The World of Roerich.* New York: Corona Mundi, International Art Center, 1922.

Service, Faith. "The Wichita Wow—Motion Pictures Took Louise Brooks from the Stage to Make a Star of Her—She Herself Insists That Dancing Deserves All the Credit." *Dance Magazine*, March 1928, 20–21, 62.

Shackelford, Rudy, and Vincent Persichetti. "Conversation with Vincent Persichetti." *Perspectives of New Music* 20, nos. 1–2 (Autumn 1981–Summer 1982): 104–33.

Shakespeare, William. *King Lear.* Edited by Jonathan Bate and Eric Rasmussen. New York: Modern Library, 2009.

Shapiro, Joel. "Martha Graham at the Eastman School." *Dance Magazine*, July 1974, 55–57.

Shapiro, Karl. *Essay on Rime.* New York: Reynal & Hitchcock, 1945.

Shawn, Allen. *Arnold Schoenberg's Journey.* Cambridge, MA: Harvard University Press, 2003.

Shawn, Ted. *The American Ballet.* New York: Henry Holt, 1926.

————. *One Thousand and One Night Stands.* With Gray Poole. New York: Da Capo Press, 1979.

————. Papers. Jacob's Pillow Dance Festival Archives, Becket, MA.

————. *Ruth St. Denis: Pioneer and Prophet, Being a History of Her Cycle of Oriental Dances.* 2 vols. San Francisco: Printed for John Howell by John Henry Nash, 1920.

Shearer, Sybil. *Without Wings the Way Is Steep.* Vol. 1, *Within This Thicket.* Northbrook, IL: Morrison-Shearer Foundation, 2006.

Sheets-Johnstone, Maxine. "An Account of Recent Changes in Dance in the USA." *Leonardo* 11, no. 3 (Summer 1978): 197–201.

———. " 'Man Has Always Danced': Forays into the Origins of an Art Largely Forgotten by Philosophers." *Contemporary Aesthetics* 3 (2005).

———. *The Phenomenology of Dance.* Fiftieth Anniversary Edition. Philadelphia: Temple University Press, 2015.

Shelton, Suzanne. *Divine Dancer: A Biography of Ruth St. Denis.* Garden City, NY: Doubleday, 1981.

———. "Looking for Martha." Review of *Deep Song: The Dance Story of Martha Graham,* by Ernestine Stodelle. *Dance Chronicle* 8, nos. 1–2 (1985): 101–3.

Sherman, Jane. "The American Indian Imagery of Ted Shawn." *Dance Chronicle* 12, no. 3 (1989): 366–82.

———. *The Drama of Denishawn Dance.* Middletown, CT: Wesleyan University Press, 1979.

———. "Martha and Doris in Denishawn: A Closer Look." *Dance Chronicle* 17, no. 2 (1994): 179–93.

Sherman, Jane, and Norton Owen. "Martha Graham and Ted Shawn." *Dance Magazine,* July 1995.

Sherman, Jane, with Christena L. Schlundt. "Who's St. Denis? What Is She?" *Dance Chronicle* 10, no. 3 (1987): 305–29.

Shlaes, Amity. "The Myth of Gatsby's Suffering Middle Class." *New York Times,* June 1, 2013.

Siegel, Marcia B. *At the Vanishing Point: A Critic Looks at Dance.* New York: Saturday Review Press, 1972.

———. *Days on Earth: The Dance of Doris Humphrey.* Durham, NC: Duke University Press, 1993.

———. "Marthology." *Hudson Review* 46, no. 1 (Spring 1993): 183–88.

———. "Modern Dance Before Bennington: Sorting It All Out." *Dance Research Journal* 19, no. 1 (Summer 1987): 3–9.

Sikov, Ed. *Dark Victory: The Life of Bette Davis.* New York: Henry Holt, 2007.

Silverman, Debora L. "Biography, Brush, and Tools: Historicizing Subjectivity; the Case of Vincent Van Gogh and Paul Gauguin." In *The Life & the Work: Art and Biography,* edited by Charles G. Salas, 76–96. Los Angeles: Getty Research Institute, 2007.

Simmon, Scott. Note for *The Flute of Krishna.* In *Treasures of American Film Archives: 50 Preserved Films.* Washington, DC: National Film Preservation Foundation, 2000.

Singer, Stan. "Vaudeville in Los Angeles, 1910–1926: Theaters, Management, and the Orpheum." *Pacific Historical Review* 61, no. 1 (February 1992): 103–13.

Sklar, Deidre. "Five Premises for a Culturally Sensitive Approach to Dance." *DCA* [Dance Critics Association] *News,* Summer 1991, 4, 9.

Smeds, John. "Graves, Bachofen and the Matriarchy Debate." *Focus on Robert Graves and His Contemporaries* 1, no. 10 (1990): 1–17.

Smith, Catherine Parsons. "Of Pageantry and Politics." Review of *American Historical Pageantry,* by David Glassberg, and *American Pageantry,* by Naima Prevots. *American Quarterly* 44, no. 1 (March 1992): 115–22.

Smith, Cecil. "Martha Graham Adds Charm to Vigor in Dance." *Chicago Tribune,* March 11, 1940.

———. "The Maze of the Heart." *Theatre Arts,* May 1947.

Smith, Helene, and George Swetnam. *A Guidebook to Historic Western Pennsylvania.* Rev. ed. Pittsburgh: University of Pittsburgh Press, 1991.

Smith, Jeffrey S. "Los Hermanos Penitentes: An Illustrative Essay." *North American Geographer* 2, no. 1 (2000): 70–84.

————. "Penitente Moradas: A Vestige of the Nuevomexicano Cultural Landscape." *Material Culture* 47, no. 2 (Fall 2015): 23–40.

Smith, Roberta. "Native Talents, Shrugging at Europe." Review of *American Legends: Calder to O'Keeffe* at the Whitney Museum of American Art. *New York Times*, December 27, 2012.

Soares, Janet Mansfield. *Louis Horst: Musician in a Dancer's World.* Durham, NC: Duke University Press, 1992.

————. *Martha Hill & the Making of American Dance.* Middletown, CT: Wesleyan University Press, 2009.

————. "Unearthing the Treasures of Photographer Thomas Bouchard." *Dance Chronicle* 40, no. 3 (September–December 2017): 393–99.

Sommer, Sally R. "Loïe Fuller's Art of Music and Light." *Dance Chronicle* 4, no. 4 (1981): 389–401.

Sontag, Susan. *Against Interpretation And Other Essays.* New York: Farrar, Straus and Giroux, 1966.

————. "Dancer and the Dance." *London Review of Books* 9, no. 3 (February 1987): 9–10.

Sophocles. *Electra.* Translated by Anne Carson. Oxford: Oxford University Press, 2001.

Sorell, Walter, ed. *The Dance Has Many Faces.* 2nd ed. New York: Columbia University Press, 1966.

————. *Hanya Holm: The Biography of an Artist.* Middletown, CT: Wesleyan University Press, 1969.

————, ed. *The Mary Wigman Book: Her Writings Edited and Translated.* Middletown, CT: Wesleyan University Press, 1975.

Spackman, Stephen. "Wallingford Riegger and the Modern Dance." *Musical Quarterly* 71, no. 4 (1985): 437–67.

Sparshott, Francis. "Imagination: The Very Idea." *Journal of Aesthetics and Art Criticism* 48, no. 1 (Winter 1990): 1–8.

————. *A Measured Pace: Toward a Philosophical Understanding of the Arts of Dance.* Toronto: University of Toronto Press, 1995.

————. *Off the Ground: First Steps to a Philosophical Consideration of the Dance.* Princeton, NJ: Princeton University Press, 1988.

————. "On the Question: 'Why Do Philosophers Neglect the Aesthetics of the Dance?'" *Dance Research Journal* 15, no. 1 (Autumn 1982): 5–30.

Spector, Irwin. *Rhythm and Life: The Work of Emile Jaques-Dalcroze.* Dance and Music Series No. 3. Stuyvesant, NY: Pendragon Press, 1990.

Spencer, Ethel. *The Spencers of Amberson Avenue: A Turn-of-the-Century Memoir.* Edited by Michael P. Weber and Peter N. Stearns. Pittsburgh: University of Pittsburgh Press, 1983. Especially the introduction.

Sperling, Jody. "Loïe Fuller (1862–1928)." Dance Heritage Coalition, 2012. http://www .danceheritage.org/treasures/fuller_essay_sperling.pdf.

Stalpaert, Christel. "Staging Age and Aging in *The Rite of Spring*: Reconstruction or Critical Intervention?" *Aging Studies in Europe* 2 (2012): 53–74.

Star, Alexander. "What Friedrich Nietzsche Did to America." Review of *American Nietzsche* by Jennifer Ratner Rosenhagen. *New York Times Book Review*, January 15, 2012.

Stavsky, Jonathan. "Medieval French Miracle Plays: Seven Falsely Accused Women." *Medieval Feminist Forum* 48, no. 2 (2013): 115–17.

Steedman, Carolyn. *Dust: The Archive and Cultural History.* New Brunswick, NJ: Rutgers University Press, 2002.

Steichen, James. "The American Ballet's Caravan." *Dance Research Journal* 47, no. 1 (April 2015): 69–94.

Stein, Charles W., ed. *American Vaudeville: As Seen by Its Contemporaries.* New York: Alfred A. Knopf, 1984.

Stein, Gertrude. "Composition as Explanation." London: Hogarth Press, 1926.

———. *The Geographical History of America.* New York: Random House, 1936.

Steiner, George. *The Death of Tragedy.* New York: Alfred A. Knopf, 1961.

———. *Grammars of Creation.* New Haven, CT: Yale University Press, 2001.

———. *The Poetry of Thought: From Hellenism to Celan.* New York: New Directions, 2012.

Stewart, Dorothy Newkirk. *Handbook of Indian Dances: 1, New Mexico Pueblos.* Albuquerque: Museum of New Mexico, 1952.

Stewart, Virginia, ed. *Modern Dance.* Brooklyn, NY: Dance Horizons, 1970. First published 1935 by Weyhe (New York).

Stodelle, Ernestine. *Deep Song: The Dance Story of Martha Graham.* New York: Schirmer Books, 1984.

———. *The First Frontier: The Story of Louis Horst and the American Dance.* Photographs by Barbara Morgan. Cheshire, CT: Ernestine Stodelle, 1964.

———. "Flesh and Spirit at War." *New Haven Register*, March 23, 1975.

———. Review of *Louis Horst: Musician in a Dancer's World*, by Janet Mansfield Soares. *Music Library Association* 50, no. 4 (June 1994).

———. "Steel and Velvet: A Centennial Reminiscence." http://www.dorishumphrey.org /steel-velvet/.

Stolz, George. "How van Gogh Became van Gogh." *ARTnews*, May 1, 2013, 64–69.

Straus, Noel. "World Premiere of '*Baal Shem*' by Bloch in Orchestral Transcription Is Heard." *New York Times*, October 20, 1941.

Stravinsky, Igor, and Robert Craft. *Dialogues.* Berkeley: University of California Press, 1982.

Suisman, Doug. "The Next Page: Reviving the North Side's 'Lost City.'" *Pittsburgh Post-Gazette*, April 8, 2007.

Sullivan, Ed. "Broadway." New York *Daily News,* December 28, 1932.

Suzuki, D. T. *Essays in Zen Buddhism.* First Series. London: Luzac, 1927.

Sweet, Jill D. *Dances of the Tewa Pueblo Indians: Expressions of New Life.* Santa Fe, NM: School of Advanced Research Press, 2004.

Symons, Arthur. "Javanese Dancers." In *Poems of the Dance: An Anthology*, edited by Edward R. Dickson, 148. New York: Alfred A. Knopf, 1921.

Syson Carter, Françoise. "Celestial Dance: A Search for Perfection." *Dance Research Journal* 5, no. 2 (Autumn 1987): 3–17.

Tamiris, Helen. "Tamiris in Her Own Voice: Draft of an Autobiography." Transcribed, edited, and annotated by Daniel Nagrin. *Studies in Dance History* 1, no. 1 (Fall/Winter 1989): 1–64.

Taruskin, Richard. "A Myth of the Twentieth Century: *The Rite of Spring*, the Tradition of the New, and 'The Music Itself.'" *Modernism/modernity* 2, no. 1 (January 1995): 1–26.

———. "Stravinsky and Us." In *The Cambridge Companion to Stravinsky*, edited by Jonathan Cross, 260–84. Cambridge: Cambridge University Press, 2003.

Teck, Katherine. "Choreography: A Collaborative Effort." In *Ear Training for the Body: A Dancer's Guide to Music*, chap. 5. Pennington, NJ: Princeton Book, 1994.

———, ed. *Making Music for Modern Dance: Collaboration in the Formative Years of a New American Art.* New York: Oxford University Press, 2011.

————. *Music for the Dance: Reflections on a Collaborative Art.* New York: Greenwood Press, 1989.

Temple, Judy Nolte. "Mary Austin and the Challenges of Capturing Western American Rhythms." In *The Shade of the Saguaro: Essays on the Literary Cultures of the American Southwest*, edited by Gaetano Prampolini and Annamaria Pinazzi, 403–8. Florence, Italy: Firenze University Press, 2013.

Tennyson, Lord Alfred. *The Lady of Shalott.* With color illustrations by Howard Pyle. New York: Dodd, Mead, 1881.

Terry, Walter. "The Dance." *New York Herald Tribune,* May 11, 1946.

————. *Frontiers of Dance: The Life of Martha Graham.* New York: Thomas Y. Crowell, 1975.

————. "Martha Graham Dances in New Satirical Work." *New York Herald Tribune*, December 28, 1939.

————. *Ted Shawn, Father of American Dance.* New York: Dial Press, 1975.

Thomas, Dylan. "Deaths and Entrances." (Poem) *Horizon* 3, no. 13 (January 1941): 12–13.

Thomas, Penny. "Claire Reis: Advocate for Contemporary Music." PhD diss., University of Florida, 1991.

Thomson, Virgil. "Two Ballets." *New York Herald Tribune*, May 20, 1945.

Tichi, Cecelia. *Shifting Gears: Technology, Literature, Culture in Modernist America.* Chapel Hill: University of North Carolina Press, 1987.

Tick, Judith. "Henry Cowell's *Synchrony*." Written for the concert *American Modernism Seen and Heard: The Abstract and Geometric Tradition in Music and Painting, 1930–1975*, performed on December 20, 1992, at Carnegie Hall. http://americansymphony.org/henry -cowells-synchrony/.

————. *Ruth Crawford Seeger: A Composer's Search for American Music.* New York: Oxford University Press, 1997.

Tindall, William York. *A Reader's Guide to Dylan Thomas.* New York: Octagon Books, 1984.

Tobias, Tobi. "A Conversation with May O'Donnell." *Ballet Review* 9, no. 1 (Spring 1981): 64–81.

————. "Martha." Review of *Every Soul Is a Circus*, Joyce Theater and City Center, New York City. *Seeing Things* (blog), March 16, 2012. https://www.artsjournal.com/tobias/2012 /03/martha.html.

Todd, Ellen Wiley. *The "New Woman" Revised: Painting and Gender Politics on Fourteenth Street.* Rev. ed. Berkeley: University of California Press, 1993.

Toenjes, John. "The Evolution of Martha Graham's Collaborations with Composers of Music for the Modern Dance." *International Guild of Musicians in Dance Journal* 2 (1992).

Toepfer, Karl. *Empire of Ecstasy: Nudity and Movement in German Body Culture, 1910–1935.* Berkeley: University of California Press, 1997.

Tóibín, Colm. "Urning." Review of *Edward Carpenter: A Life of Liberty and Love*, by Sheila Rowbotham. *London Review of Books* 31, no. 2 (January 29, 2009).

Tommasini, Anthony. "Review: San Francisco Symphony at Carnegie Hall." *New York Times*, April 14, 2016.

Torrez, Robert J. "Penitente Brotherhood in New Mexico." Website of the Office of the State Historian, New Mexico. http://newmexicohistory.org/people/penitente-brotherhood-in -new-mexico.

Tracy, Robert. *Goddess: Martha Graham's Dancers Remember.* New York: Limelight Editions, 1997.

Treib, Marc. *Sanctuaries of Spanish New Mexico.* Berkeley: University of California Press, 1993.

Trickey, Erick. "The Story Behind a Forgotten Symbol of the American Revolution: The Liberty Tree." *Smithsonian Magazine*, May 19, 2016. https://www.smithsonianmag.com /history/story-behind-forgotten-symbol-american-revolution-liberty-tree-180959162/.

Trowbridge, Charlotte. *Dance Drawings of Martha Graham*. New York: Dance Observer, 1945.

Troxell, Mary. "Arthur Schopenhauer (1788–1860)." *Internet Encyclopedia of Philosophy*. http:// www.iep.utm.edu/schopenh/.

Tugal, Pierre. "Martha Graham Is Interviewed by Pierre Tugal." *Dancing Times*, October 1950, 21–22.

Turner, Victor. *From Ritual to Theatre: The Human Seriousness of Play*. New York: PAJ Publications, 1982.

Udall, Sharyn Rohlfsen. "Between Dream and Shadow: William Holman Hunt's 'Lady of Shalott.'" *Woman's Art Journal* 11, no. 1 (Spring–Summer 1990): 34–38.

———. *Dance and American Art: A Long Embrace*. Madison: University of Wisconsin Press, 2012.

———. "Martha Graham and Cady Wells: New American Rhythms." In *Cady Wells and Southwestern Modernism*, edited by Lois P. Rudnick, 122–36. Santa Fe: Museum of New Mexico Press, 2009.

Unamuno, Miguel de. *The Tragic Sense of Life in Men and Nations*. Translated by Anthony Kerrigan. Bollingen Series. Princeton, NJ: Princeton University Press, 1972. First published 1913.

Valéry, Paul. *Dance and the Soul*. Translated by Dorothy Bussy. London: John Lehmann, 1951. First published 1923 by Gallimard.

———. "Introduction to the Method of Leonardo da Vinci." In *Leonardo, Poe, Mallarmé*. London: Routledge & Kegan Paul, 1972. [Essay written 1894; revised 1930. Vol. 8 of the *Collected Works of Paul Valéry*.]

van den Toorn, Pieter C. *Stravinsky and* The Rite of Spring. Berkeley: University of California Press, 1987.

van den Toorn, Pieter C., and John McGinness, eds. *Stravinsky and the Russian Period: Sound and Legacy of a Musical Idiom*. Cambridge: Cambridge University Press, 2012.

Van Gelder, Lawrence. "A Still-Resonant Tale of Power and Violation." Review of Willow Cabin Theater Company's production of *Lucrece,* a play adopted from Shakespeare's *The Rape of Lucrece. New York Times*, May 26, 2000.

Van Praagh, Peggy, and Peter Brinson. *The Choreographic Art: An Outline of Its Principles and Craft*. New York: Alfred A. Knopf, 1963.

Van Vechten, Carl. *Martha Graham*. Lancaster, PA: All Kinds Blintzes Press, 2000.

Vergil. *Dido, the Phoenician Queen*. In *Two Dramatizations from Vergil*. Arranged and translated into English verse by Frank Justus Miller. Stage directions and music contributed by J. Raleigh Nelson. Chicago: University of Chicago Press, 1908.

Vincent, Clare. "Edgar Degas (1834–1917): Bronze Sculpture." In *Heilbrunn Timeline of Art History*. New York: Metropolitan Museum of Art, 2000–. Text available: http://www .metmuseum.org/toah/hd/dgsb/hd_dgsb.htm (October 2004).

Vogel, Carol. "Thomas Hart Benton Masterwork Goes to Met." *New York Times*, December 12, 2012.

Waddell, Helen. *The Wandering Scholars*. London: Constable, 1927.

Waley, Arthur. *The Noh Plays of Japan*. New York: Tuttle, 1921.

Walker, Waldo. "Southwest as a Centre of a New Civilization—Mary Austin, Novelist, Predicts a Great Race Development in the Desert Region Soon to Be Watered by the Colorado River." *New York Times*, October 19, 1924.

Wallace, Rob. *Improvisation and the Making of American Literary Modernism.* New York: Continuum Books, 2010.

Walls, David. "On the Naming of Appalachia." In *An Appalachian Symposium: Essays Written in Honor of Cratis D. Williams*, edited by J. W. Williamson. Boone, NC: Appalachian State University Press, 1977.

Warburg, Aby M. *Images from the Region of the Pueblo Indians of North America.* Translated by Michael P. Steinberg. Ithaca, NY: Cornell University Press, 1995.

Ware, Caroline F. *Greenwich Village, 1920–1930: A Comment on American Civilization in the Post-War Years.* Boston: Houghton Mifflin, 1935.

Ware, W. Porter, and Thaddeus C. Lockard, Jr. *P. T. Barnum Presents Jenny Lind: The American Tour of the Swedish Nightingale.* Baton Rouge: Louisiana State University Press, 1980.

Warner, Marina. *Alone of All Her Sex: The Myth and the Cult of the Virgin Mary.* New York: Alfred A. Knopf, 1976.

Washer, Ben. "Martha Graham Sees 'Divine Rhythm'—Awarded Guggenheim Fellowship to Continue Her Studies." *New York World-Telegram*, April 18, 1932.

Watkins, Mary F. "The Dance's Part in the Important Events Staged During Last Week at Metropolitan Opera House; Martha Graham Is Winner of New Laurels." *New York Herald Tribune*, April 27, 1930.

———. "Martha Graham Presents Repertory Dance Program." *New York Herald Tribune*, January 9, 1930.

———. "Six Dances Offered by Martha Graham in Season's Finale." *New York Herald Tribune*, May 5, 1933.

———. "With the Dancers." *New York Herald Tribune*, January 8, 1933.

———. "The Work of Martha Graham Excels in Recent Dance Repertory Season." *New York Herald Tribune*, February 22, 1931.

———. The World of the Dance. *New York Herald Tribune*, February 7, 1931.

Watson, Steven, and Catherine J. Morris, eds. *An Eye on the Modern Century: Selected Letters of Henry McBride.* New Haven, CT: Yale University Press, 2000.

Watters, Mary. "The Penitentes: A Folk-Observance." *Social Forces* 6, no. 2 (December 1927).

Weir, David. *Decadence and the Making of Modernism.* Amherst: University of Massachusetts Press, 1995.

Weir, Lucy. "Primitive Rituals, Contemporary Aftershocks: Evocations of the Orientalist 'Other' in Four Productions of *Le Sacre du printemps*." *AVANT* 4, no. 3 (December 2013): 111–43.

Welsford, Enid. *The Fool: His Social & Literary History.* Gloucester, MA: Peter Smith, 1966. First published 1935.

West, Martha Ullman. "Eugene Loring (1911–1982)." Dance Heritage Coalition, 2012. http://www.danceheritage.org/loring.html.

Weston, Jessie L. *From Ritual to Romance.* Edited by Robert A. Segal. Princeton, NJ: Princeton University Press, 1993. First published 1920.

White-McGuire, Blakeley. "Re-examining the Inevitable Rise." *Performance Research* 18, no. 4 (November 2013): 42–47.

Whitman, Alden. "Katharine Cornell Is Dead at 81." *New York Times*, June 10, 1974.

Whitman, Walt. *Leaves of Grass.* New York: New American Library, 1964. First published 1885.

Wicks, Robert L. *Schopenhauer's* The World as Will and Representation. *A Reader's Guide.* London: Continuum Books, 2011.

Wigman, Mary. "Rudolf von Laban on His Birthday." *Schrifttanz* 2, no. 4 (December 1929). Reprinted in *Schrifttanz: A View of German Dance in the Weimar Republic*, edited by Valerie Preston-Dunlop and Susanne Lahusen. London: Dance Books, 1990.

Wilder, Thornton. *Our Town: A Play in Three Acts.* New York: Harper & Row, 1938.

Wilhelm, Richard, trans. *The Secret of the Golden Flower: A Chinese Book of Life.* With a commentary by C. G. Jung. New York: Harcourt Brace Jovanovich, 1962. First published 1931.

Williams, Drid. *Anthropology and the Dance: Ten Lectures.* Urbana: University of Illinois Press, 2004.

Williams, Raymond. *Politics of Modernism: Against the New Conformists.* London: Verso, 2007.

Williams, William Carlos. "America, Whitman, and the Art of Poetry." *Poetry Journal* 8, no. 1 (November 1917): 27–36.

———. *The Autobiography of William Carlos Williams.* New York: Random House, 1948.

———. *In the American Grain.* New York: New Directions, 1956. First published 1925.

———. *The Selected Letters of William Carlos Williams.* New York: McDowell, Obolensky, 1957.

Wilson, Edmund. *Literary Essays and Reviews of the 1920s & 30s.* New York: Library of America, 2007.

Wind, Edgar. *Pagan Mysteries in the Renaissance.* London: Faber and Faber, 1958.

Winnicott, D. W. "The Capacity to Be Alone." *The International Journal of Psychoanalysis,* 39: 416–20.

Wittke, Paul. *Samuel Barber: An Improvisatory Portrait.* New York: G. Schirmer, 1994.

Wolf, Amy. *On Becoming an Artist: Isamu Noguchi and His Contemporaries, 1922–1960.* New York: Isamu Noguchi Foundation and Garden Museum, 2010.

Woolf, Virginia. "On Not Knowing Greek." In *The Common Reader.* New York: Harcourt Brace, 1925.

Workers of the Writers' Program of the Works Progress Administration in the Commonwealth of Pennsylvania. *Story of Old Allegheny City.* Pittsburgh: Allegheny Centennial Committee, 1941. Reprinted 1994 by the Allegheny City Society with support of the Buhl Foundation.

Wosien, Maria-Gabriele. *Sacred Dance: Encounter with the Gods.* Art and Imagination Series. London: Thames & Hudson, 1974.

Wright, Frank Lloyd. *Frank Lloyd Wright Collected Writings.* Vol. 1, *1894–1930.* Edited by Bruce Brooks Pfeiffer. New York: Rizzoli/Frank Lloyd Wright Foundation, 1992.

———. *Modern Architecture: Being the Kahn Lectures for 1930.* With a new introduction by Neil Levine. Princeton, NJ: Princeton University Press, 2008.

Yeats, William Butler. *Essays and Introductions.* New York: Scribner, 1968.

Yeoh, Francis. "The Choreographic Trust: Preserving Dance Legacies." *Dance Chronicle* 35, no. 2 (2012): 224–49.

Young, Julian. *Nietzsche's Philosophy of Art.* Cambridge: Cambridge University Press, 1994.

Young, Stark. "*Dolorosa* at Clark University." *New Republic,* Nov. 1, 1932.

———. "Forward and Backward." *New Republic* 30, no. 388 (May 10, 1922): 315–16.

———. "Martha Graham." *New Republic* 112, no. 23 (June 4, 1945): 790–91.

————. "Miss Graham and Mademoiselle." Review of *Primitive Mysteries* and other dances by Martha Graham. *New Republic*, December 14, 1932, 127–29.

————. "Moments of Miracle." *New Republic*, March 1, 1933, 71–73.

————. "Town Melange." Review of *Dithyrambics* and *Primitive Mysteries*, by Martha Graham. *New Republic*, December 23, 1931, 161–64.

Yu, Arlene. "So You Think You Can Find Dance: A Guide to Research." *New York Public Library* (blog), June 1, 2012. http://www.nypl.org/blog/2012/06/01/so-you-think-you-can-find-dance-guide-research.

Yurka, Blanche. *Bohemian Girl: Blanche Yurka's Theatrical Life*. Athens: Ohio University Press, 1970.

Zeitlin, Froma I. *Playing the Other: Gender and Society in Classical Greek Literature*. Chicago: University of Chicago Press, 1996.

Zeitz, Joshua. *Flapper: A Madcap Story of Sex, Style, Celebrity, and the Women Who Made America Modern*. New York: Crown, 2006.

Zilczer, Judith. "Beyond Genealogy: American Modernism in Retrospect." *American Art* 15, no. 1 (Spring 2001): 4–9.

Index

(Page references in *italics* refer to illustrations.)

Abbott, Berenice, 161, 287

Abbott, Keene, 52

abstraction: Brancusi and, 157; Crane's *The Bridge* and, 255–6; in Graham's oeuvre, 96, 116, 224, 249, 254, 287, 308, 336, 338, 377, 391, 399; Humphrey's move toward, 116; Kandinsky and, 65–8, *66*; Noguchi's stage sets and, 161; Schoenberg's *Die glückliche Hand* and, 175–6; Stebbins's *plastiques* from Greek and Egyptian themes and, 25

Acocella, Joan, 71

Acoma Pueblo, 239, *239*, 260

Adams, Ansel, 243

Adolescence (Prelude and Song), 131, 144, 153, 160, 275

Aeschylus, 234, 292; *Seven Against Thebes* by, 186–90, 193

Against Interpretation (Sontag), 399

Ailey, Alvin, 122, 404

Air on a Ground Bass, 144, 211

Alceste, 99, 105

Alexander, Cris, *360, 377, 387*

Allen, Frederick Lewis, 227

Alvarez, Anita, 311, 317

Americana, 140, 204–5, 307, 327, 333, 394

American Alliance for Health, Physical Education, Recreation, and Dance, 274–5

American Ballet Company, 230–1, 289, *299*, 310

American dance: Duncan's "I See America Dancing" and, 108; Graham's "Seeking an American Art of the Dance" and, 198, 200–1, 254; Graham's "The American Dance" and, 275, 288; Martin's "The Modern Dance in America" and, 199; relations with other modernities and, 204; rooted in its own time and place, 275; Sayler's *Revolt in the Arts* and, 199–200

"American Dance, The" (Graham), 275, 288

American Dance Festival, Connecticut College, 218; inaugural season of (1948), 375–9, *378*

American Document, *312*, 315–22, *317*, 323, 328, 331, 394; description of, 316–19; evolution and rehearsals of, 309, 311, *312*, 312–14, 316; Kirstein's praise for, 319–21; as watershed moment in Graham's metamorphosis of modern dance, 321

American Lyric—Dance of Assembly, 307–8, 309

American Provincials—Act of Piety; Act of Judgment, 282, 287, *315*

American Rhythm, The (Austin), 243–4, 278

Ancient Mysteries Described (Hone), 271

Anderson, John (critic), 234

Anderson, John Murray, 73–4, 75, *75*, 76, 77, 80, 81–2, 91, 107

Anderson, Maxwell, 376

Anderson—Milton School of Theatre and
  Dance, New York, 81–2, 89, 102–3, 104,
  107, 122, 133, 156
Angel of the Last Judgment, The, 293
Antheil, George, 141, 142, 165
Apollonius of Rhodes, 356
Appalachian Spring, 5, 12, 118, 229, 309, 333,
  341–5, *342, 344*, 354, 357, 367, 388, 394;
  Copland's score for, 229, 333, 341, 342,
  343; description of, 341–5; emotional
  tonalities of, 12; Noguchi's set for, 341–2;
  provenance of title for, 255; "Simple
  Gifts" lyrics and, 343–4
architecture, 230; created by human
  movements, 193; dance and, as the two
  primary and essential arts, 32; modern,
  affinity of modern dance and, xv, 211;
  pueblo, 193–4
Ariadne's tale, Graham's *Errand into the
  Maze* and, 373, 376, 388
Armstrong, Everhardt, 182–3
"Art as Communication" (Graham), 263–4
Arthur, Helen, 121, 141
Art Institute of Chicago, 65–8, 326
Asquith, Ruby, 289
Astaire, Fred and Adele, 101
Atheneos, Cleo, 212
Atkinson, Brooks, 273
Atlantic Monthly, 3, 31
At the Hawk's Well (Yeats), *125*, 125–6
Ausdruckstanz, 87, 244
Austin, Arthur Everett "Chick," Jr., 299,
  300
Austin, Mary Hunter, 197, 236, 241–4, *242*,
  257, 260, 261, 275, 278, 279
Aztec culture, 33, 47–8, *48*, 361

Babitz, Thelma, 311, 317
Bacchanale, 187, 223–4, 230, 301
Bach, J. S., 116, 133, 217
Bacon, Francis, 136
Balanchine, George, 211, 289, 295, 297, *298*,
  298–300, *299*, 310, 311, 389
Bales, William, 375
ballet: Fokine and Graham's New School
  sparring match and, 231–3; Graham's
  views on, 72, 129, 201, 231–2; Horst's

Pre-Classic Dance Forms course and,
  127–8, 202
Ballet Caravan, 289–90, 310–11, 314, *320*,
  356
Ballet Intime, 208–9, 237
Ballets 1933, Les, 298
Ballets Russes, 123, 133, 171–2, 206, 208, 230,
  295, 297
"Banshee, The," 116, 191
Barber, Samuel, xii, *358*, 358–60, 361, 362,
  372
Barnes, Clive, 232–3
Barnum, P. T., 326–7
Bartenieff, Irmgard, 288, 400
Bartók, Béla, 106, 203, 224, 263
Barzel, Ann, 316
Bassols, Narciso, 259
Bateson, F. W., 341
Baton, Rhené-Emmanuel, 133
Baudelaire, Charles, 95, 137, 255
Bauer, Marion Eugénie, 163
Bay, Anita, 177, 178
Becker, Helen. *See* Tamiris
Becque, Oscar, 253
Beerbohm, Max, 212
Beers, John (grandfather), 7, 9
Beers, Mary ("Auntie Re"), 5, 21
Beers, Mary (grandmother), 7, 9, 11, 12
Beiswanger, George, 113–14, 134, 328, 338
Belasco, David, 16, 26, 198, 206, 233
Bel Geddes, Norman, 163
Belitt, Ben, 313, 333, 373, 376
Bell, Robert, 107
Beltran-Masses, Federico, 97
Bennett, Julia, 64
Bennett School, Millbrook, N.Y., 153
Bennington College and School of the
  Dance, 202, 275, 282, 284, 288–90, 315,
  324, 325, 328, 331, 332, 335, 339, 366, 402;
  American Document developed at, 309,
  311, *312*, 312–14, 316; Ballet Caravan at,
  289–90, 310, 356; *Deaths and Entrances*
  developed at, 335–7; founding of dance
  program, 253–4; Graham's first recital
  at, 274
Benton, Thomas Hart, 229, 309
Bergamasco, Hugo, 132, 217, 263

Bernheim, Marcel, 97
Bernstein, Aline, 121
"Betty's Music Box," 64–5
Beyond Good and Evil (Nietzsche), 61–2, 136
Billy the Kid, 320
Biracree, Thelma ("Teddy"), 83, 84, *84*, 90, 91, 93, 97, 98, 99, 102
Bird, Bonnie, 187–8, 189, 263, 264, 280, 304, 325
Bird, Dorothy, 187, *188*, 188–9, 219, 263, 269, 276, 277, 280, 289, 301
Birth of Tragedy: Out of the Spirit of Music, The (Nietzsche), 61, 62–3, 71, 278
Blake, William, 147, 296, 320, 326, 337, 350
Blitzstein, Marc, 163, 166
Bloch, Ernest, 149–50, 165; Baal Shem Suite by, 105–6, 121; *Israel* by, 118–19, 121, 122
Blood Memory (Graham), xvii, 7, 60, 394
Bodkin, Maud, 349
Bohm, Jerome D., 305
Boleslavsky, Richard, 113, 316
Bolm, Adolph, 126, 208, 237
Borglum, Gutzon, 156
Boris, Ruthanna, 290
Botticelli, Sandro, 105; *Primavera, 94*, 213
Bouchard, Thomas, *402*, 402–3
Boulanger, Nadia, 165, 210, 212, 281, 308
Bowen, Dorothea, 50, 54
Brackette, Joseph, 343
Brahms, Johannes, 34, 94
Brancusi, Constantin, 65, 157, 158–9, 161, 204
Brentano's, 198
Bridge, The (Crane), 118, 152, 255–6
Briton, Virginia, 133
Brontë, Anne, Charlotte, and Emily, 335–7, 351
Brontë, Branwell, 337
Brooks, Louise, 58–60, *59*, 61, 64, 65, *76*
Brown, Camille A., 404
Brown, Joe E., 76
Brown, John, Hawkins's *John Brown* and, 353, 354, 366–8, 369, 375
Browning, Robert, 24, 95, 265
Budapest String Quartet, 228

Bulgakov, Leo, 118
Bulliet, C. J., 160
Bunsick, Hortense, 133, 177
Butler, Ethel, 280, 304, 311, 329, 337, *337*
Butler, John, 337, *337*
Byrd, Jane Carol, 19, 22

Calder, Alexander, 159, 285, 296
Campbell, Joseph, 275, 315, 321–2, 323–4, 335, 349, 386
Cancellieri, Luigi, 275
Cansino, Eduardo, Elisa, Volga, and Margarita, 76, 103
Carman, Bliss, 31
Carnegie, Andrew, 10, 103, 171
Carnegie Hall, New York, 70, 110, 115, 122, 146, 150, 159, 230, 401; Graham's classes at studio in, *104*, 104–5; offices, apartments, and studios built in, 103–4
Carpenter, Edward, 55
Carson, Anne, 151
Cartier, Jacques, 207
Cassius Longinus, 72
Catullus, *Poem 64, 372–3*
Caufield, Lin, *400*
Cave of the Heart, 360, 372
Celebration, 129, 280, 309
Ceremonials, 251–3, 254, 274
Chávez, Carlos, xii, 259, 263–4, 346, 357–8, 376; *Prelude* by (Graham's dance also known as *Salutation*), 263, 264, 274, 275, 462n
Cheney, Sheldon, 109–10, 203
Chicago Daily News, 69
Chicago Daily Tribune, 69
Chicago Evening Post, 59
Chopin, Frédéric, 51, 74, 291
Choreutics (Laban), 193
Choric Dance for an Antique Greek Tragedy, 266, 269–70
"Chorus of the Unemployed," 281
Chorus of Youth—Companions, 262–3
Christensen, Harold, 289
Christensen, Lew, 289, 290
Christian Science, 26, 36
Christian Science Monitor, 289
Chronicle, xiii, 224, 301–6, *303*, 317

Church Service in Dance, 50

Civic Repertory Theatre, New York, 103, 142

Civil War, 6, 209

Civil War Songs, 209

Clytemnestra, 235, 403

Coburn, Alvin Langdon, 28, *125*

Cohan, Robert, xvi, *377*, *387*, 388

Cole, Miriam, 342

Coleridge, Samuel Taylor, 350

Color Harmony, 116, 117

Columbiad, 331

Conductorless Symphony Orchestra, 146

Conkling, Harold, 99

Contrition, 105, 121, 149–50

Coolidge, Elizabeth Sprague, 208, 275, 333, *344*, 357

Copland, Aaron, xii, 163, *165*, 165–6, 204, 212, 255, 259, 281, 305, 366; *Appalachian Spring* and, 118, 229, 333, 341, 342, 343, 357; *Daughter of Colchis* scenario and, 357; *Olympus Americanus (A Twentieth-Century Ballet)* by, 210–11; *Piano Variations* by, 229, 247–50 (*see also Dithyrambic*); *Serpent Heart* and, 357

Coppicus, F. C., 236

Corbin Henderson, Alice, 197

Corn Dance, 239, 244, 259, *260*, 260–2, 266, 286–7

Cornejo, Francisco, 47

Cornell, Ezra, 10

Cornell, Grace, 187

Cornell, Katharine, 126, 264–6, *265*, 328, 376

"Corner in Spain, A," 91, 99

Cornish, Nellie Centennial, 183–4, *184*, 187, 190, 236

Cornish School, Seattle, 183–90, *184*, 219, 325; Graham's classes at, 184–6; *Seven Against Thebes* staged at, 186–90

Cowell, Henry, xii, xiii, 116–17, 137, 163, 190–2, *191*, 211, 230, 236, 259, 333

Crane, Hart, 118, 152, 198, *255*, 255–6, 281

Creston, Louise Gotto, 133, 177, 277

Crist, Bainbridge, 54

Cuadro Flamenco, 79

Cubists and Post-Impressionism (Eddy), 66

Cummings, E. E., xiv, 296, 328, 382

Cummings, Paul, 154

Cumnock School of Expression, Los Angeles, 22, 23–4, *37*, 38, 40

Cunningham, Imogen, *211*, 236–9, *238*

Cunningham, Merce, 353, 404; in *Appalachian Spring*, 342; in *Deaths and Entrances*, 337, *337*, 338, 339; in *Every Soul Is a Circus*, 326, 329; Graham's company joined by, 325, 326

Cup of Fury, The, 45–6, 266

Currier, Marie, 74, 102

Curtis, Edward S., 236

Curtis, Mina, 297–8

Curtis Institute of Music, Philadelphia, 177, 307, 358

Dada, 87, 285

Dahlinger, Charles W., 3

Dalcroze, Émile Jaques-, 38, 86, 87, 108, 113, 123, 244

Dale, Ted, 390

Damrosch, Frank, 85

"Dance in America, The" (Graham), 254–5

Dance: Its Place in Art and Life, The (Kinney), 93

Dance Libretto, 315–16

Dance Lovers Magazine (later *The Dance Magazine of the Stage and Screen*), 57, 77–8

Dance Magazine, 60–1, 202, 305, 323, 374

Dance Observer, 45, 202–3, 255, 287, 306, 335, 353, 374

Dance of Life, The (Ellis), 32, 193

Dance of the Chosen (retitled *The Shakers*), 213–16, *215*, 225

Dance of the City, 141, 142

Dance Perspectives, 402

Dance Repertory Theatre, 139, 141–53, 206, 209–26; de Mille and Leonard's debut week at, 209–10; first season of, 142–53; Graham's dances for, 144–52, 216–25 (*see also Lamentation*; *Primitive Mysteries*); Graham's praise for, 201; Humphrey's and Weidman's performances at, 142–4, *143*, 177, 211; Humphrey's dances for, 212–16, *215*; second season of, 209–25; suspension

of activities of, 225–6, 227; Tamiris's
dances for, 141–2, 210–11; Weidman's new
dances for, 211–12

Dance/Revolt, 62, 110, 111, 112, *112*, 130–1,
132

Dances for Women, 213

Dances of the Ages, The, 30

Dance Songs, 263, 276

danse artistique aux USA, La (de
Rothschild), 391–2

"Danse du Feu, La ", 46

Danse Languide, 93, *94*, 204

Danz, Louis, 399

Dark Meadow, 137, 200, 346–54, *347*, 358,
385; description of, 346–8; Empedocles's
Fragments and, 346; Graham's notebook
for, 348–52, 354; Graham's program note
for, 346

Daughter of Colchis scenario, 357–8, 359

Davidson, Jo, 119

Davis, Bette, 64, 103

Davis, Stuart, xv, 159, 204, 248

Deaths and Entrances, 335–9, *337*, 351, 354,
385; description of, 338–9; inspiration for,
335–6; provenance of title for, 336

Deaths Duell (Donne), 336

Debussy, Claude, xv, 42, 91, 93, 94, 105, 122,
137, 140

Deep Song, 192

Degas, Edgar, dancer statuette by, 207–8

de la Grange, Henry-Louis, 359

Dello Joio, Norman, 376, 378

Delsarte, François, 24–5, 31, 57, 71, 103, 150

de Mille, Agnes, xvii, 8, 149, 206–10, *208*,
227–8, 235, 249; Ballet Intime tour and,
208, 209; Dance Repertory Theatre
and, 206, 209–10, 225, 227; Graham
praised by, 228; Horst's work with, 209,
210; Leonard as partner for, 209–10;
"The New Ballerina" essay by, 227–8;
professional debut of, 207–8; Weidman
as partner for, 209

de Mille, Margaret, 206–7

Denby, Edwin, xviii, 305, 311, 338

Denishawn Company, xvi, 36–56, *59*,
77–9, 80, 91, 98, 112, 121, 137, 192, 236,
271, 391; Brooks's stint with, 58–60; *A*

Dance Pageant of Egypt, Greece and India
performed by, 39–40; founding of, 33,
34; global tour of, 78, 115; Graham's
departure from, 73–4; Graham's first
performance with, 40; Horst hired
by, 34, 36; Horst's departure from,
78–9, 85; Humphrey's audition for, 42;
Humphrey's departure from, 115–16;
London performances of, 54–6, 389;
Mayer tours and, 53–4, 60, 64–5, 68–9,
72–3, 77, 78; performing on vaudeville
theatre circuits, 43, 44, 46, 49–56, 60;
power struggles at, 43; quarters of, 40–1;
Xochitl performed by, 47–50, *48*, 51, 53,
54, 59, 65, 69, 70, 77, 174, 183

Denishawn Magazine, 78–9, 203

Denishawn School, Los Angeles, 78; classes
taught by Graham at, 42–3, 45; Graham's
audition at, 37–8; New York branch of,
53, 58, 103; quarters of, 40–1

Dennis, Ruth Emma ("Emma"), 24, 25, 26

de Remer, Dini, 132, 134

Dewey, John, 42, 164, 200

Dewing, Hazel, 15, 21

Diaghilev, Sergei, 126, 170, 171–2, 200, 251,
295, 297, 298

Dichne, Arik, *393*

Dickinson, Emily, 281; Graham's homage to
(*Letter to the World*), xi, 332, 335, 336, 354,
394, 405

Dido: The Phoenician Queen (Virgil), 20

Dithyrambic (to Copland's *Piano
Variations*), 229, 247–50, 254, 271, 276,
294

Diversion of Angels, 376–8, *377*, 394

Dlugoszewski, Lucia, 401–2

Dollar, William, 289

Dolorosa, 224

Donne, John, xiii, 336

Dorame, Anthony, 239

Downes, Olin, 113, 166

Dramatic Mirror, 113

Duchamp, Marcel, 65, 157

Dudley, Jane, 249, 262, 301, 311, 313, 319,
336, *337*, 375

Duffy, Homer N., 190

Dulac, Edmund, 92, 125

Duncan, Anna, 235
Duncan, Isadora, xiv, 57, 69–72, *70*, 82, 93, 96, 108, 113, 123, 127, 138, 161, 199, 201, 209, 251, 321, 374, 391, 399; "I See America Dancing" by, 108; Tamiris's studies with, 139–40
Duncan, Raymond, 396
Dyer, Carlos, 331

Eagle, Arnold, *337*, *342*
Eastman, George, 80, 82, 89, 99
Eastman Kodak Company, 98
Eastman School of Dance and Dramatic Action, Rochester, NY, 80–1, 82–4, *84*, 89–91, 92, 93, 97, 98–100, 121, 133
Eddy, Arthur Jerome, 65, 66, 67
Eddy, Mary Baker, 26, 36
Edwards, Jonathan, 318
Egypta, *17*, 27
Egyptian themes, 16–17, *17*, 18, 25, 26, 27, 27, 32, 39–40, 46, 65
Eilber, Janet, xv, 71
Eisner, Lotte, 60
Ekstasis (retitled *Ekstasie*), *276*, 276–7, 287
Elegiac, 275, 276
Elektra (Sophocles), 233–5, 278, 294
Eliot, T. S., xiv, 91, 296, 350, 383
Ellis, Henry Havelock, 31–2, 50, 54–5, 62, 193
Elwell, Herbert, 212
Emerson, Ralph Waldo, 24, 108, 171, 243, 319, 365, 366, 404
Emery, Irene, 177
Empedocles, *Fragments* by, 346
Engel, Lehman, 251–2, 253, 255, 263, 274, 276–7
Erdman, Jean, 315, 321–2, 323, 324, 329, 332, 349
Errand into the Maze, 373, 376, 388
Escape from Freedom (Fromm), 372
Euripides, 99, 147, 151, 153, 234; Medea story and, 355, 356
Evan, Blanche, 307–8
Evans, Walker, 152, 255, 298
Every Soul Is a Circus, 325–30, *329*, 331, 332, 333, 351, 367, 368, 382, 385, 394, 396; critical and public responses to, 327–8;

description of, 328–30; Lindsay's poem appropriated for, 325–7
expressionist dance, 66–7, 87–8, 112, 225
Eye of Anguish—The Purgatorial History of King Lear, 339, 380–8, *384*, *387*, 394, 401; Broadway run of, 388; Graham's conception of, 380–3; intended as gift for her husband, 380, 385, 388; Martin's review of, 388; Persichetti chosen to compose score for, 382; Persichetti's description of, 383–5; problems in Graham-Hawkins relationship surfacing during, 386–8; Shakespeare bypassed for his source, Geoffrey of Monmouth, for, 385–6; title chosen for, 385

Fairchild, Blair, 204
Falla, Manuel de, 97, 105, 120
Fenollosa, Ernest Francisco, 123, 124
Fergusson, Francis, 230, 316
Fiery Hunt, The, 369–71
Finkel, Constance, 98
Fisher, Nelle, 187, 328
Fitzgerald, F. Scott, xiv, 58, 64
Fitzgerald, Robert, 293, 369, 376
Flannery, Vaughn, 199
Flier, Frieda, 329
Florentine Madonna, A, 97
Flute of Krishna, The, 97, 98, 99
Fokine, Michel, 139, *231*, 251, 286, 290, 298; Graham's debate with, 230–3
Fonaroff, Nina, 311, 312, 314, 337, *337*, 342, *342*, *378*
Footlight Parade, 174
Force, Juliana, 246
Foster, Ruth, 366
Four Casual Developments, 192
Four Insincerities, 131, 144
Four Quartets (Eliot), xiv, 383
Fowlie, Wallace, 350
Fragilité, 117, 131
Fragments: Tragedy and Comedy, 117
Frampton, Eleanor, 49
Franck, César, 93, 95
Frank, Waldo, xv, 118, 230, 257
Frankenstein, Alfred, 288
Fraser, Robert, *282*, *303*

Freier Tanz (free dance), 86
Frenetic Rhythms: Three Dances of Possession,
 224, 279, 287, 301
Freud, Sigmund, 127, 204, 339, 365
From Desert and Pueblo (Grunn), 47
Fromm, Erich, 372
Frontier: American Perspective of the Plains,
 5, 247, *282*, 282–4, 286, 287, 308, 328,
 331, 394
Fruhauf, Aline, *45*, *173*
Fuller, Buckminster, 161–2, 226
Fuller, Loie, 25–6, 46, 321
"Future of the Dance, The" (Graham),
 323

Gage, Margaret, 153
García, Genaro, 52
Garden of Kama, The, 33, 77, 80, 122
Genthe, Arnold, *70*, *242*
Geoffrey of Monmouth, 385
Georgi, Yvonne, 293
German aesthetics and culture, 32, 93, 109,
 113, 200, 245
German expressionism, 109, 267
Gershwin, George, 140, 161, 198, 204
Gilbert, Ralph, 331, 332
Gilfond, Edythe, xii, 328, 346
Gilman, Lawrence, 111, 242
Gilmour, Ailes, 155, 156, 160, *160*, 162, 219,
 251, 263, 273, 277
Gilmour, Leonie, 155, 156
Glenn, John, 143
Gluck, C. W., 99, 105
glückliche Hand, Die, 174–7, 179
Glushanok, Peter, 341
Goebbels, Joseph, 287
Goetschius, Percy, 85, 223
Golden, Samuel L., 45
Goluth Studio, *180*
Goossens, Eugene, 97, 105, 228, 229
Gorham, Robert, 49, 64, 313
Gotham Book Mart, New York, 91–2
Gould, Norma, 29–30, 31
Graham, George Greenfield (father), 5, *6*,
 6–8, 11, 15, 17, 23, 74, 271, 352
Graham, Georgia ("Geordie") (sister), 5, 9,
 11, *12*, 14, 15, 77, 106, 216, 273, 337

Graham, Jane ("Jennie") Beers, later Mrs.
 Homer N. Duffy (mother), xvi, 5, *6*, 7,
 8, 11, 12, 14, 15, 16, 17, 190, 236, 239, 313,
 354, 379, 397
Graham, Martha: Allegheny City, Pa.,
 as childhood home of, 3–12, *4*; "The
 American Dance" by, 275, 288; ancestors
 of, 5, 6–7; "Art as Communication"
 by, 263–4; autonomy and detachment
 of, 15, 107; ballet as viewed by, 72, 129,
 201, 231–2; childhood of, 3–5, *4*, *5*, 7–16;
 "choreography before music" rule of,
 229, 252; contraction and release of, xii,
 xiii, 71, 89, 116, 129, 136, 160, 174, 186,
 200, 243–4, 362, 399; costuming and,
 92, 96, 98, 117, 150, 178, 252, 276–7;
 creative process of, 217–20, 224, 252–3,
 307, 323; "The Dance in America"
 by, 254–5; European tour of Dance
 Company (1950), 389, 390, 392, 394–5,
 395; first ensemble of men choreographed
 by, 99; on form in dancing, 201, 262;
 "The Future of the Dance" by, 323;
 on her technique, 393; histrionics and
 tantrums of, 110, 178–9, 262, 285–6,
 395, 403; on how to command the
 stage, 185–6; humor in dances of, 327–8;
 inner workings of body central to, 8–9,
 129, 243, 374; knee injury of (the Paris
 "accident"), 394–5, 396, 401; legacy of,
 404–5; on meaning and intention in
 dance, 136; "A Modern Dancer's Primer
 for Action" by, 332; movement symbols
 employed by, 308; New York debut of
 Concert Group, 91–7, 98; notebooks
 of, 348–52, 354, 362; private warm-up
 sessions of, 307; religious upbringing
 of, 11, 50; schooling of, 10, 15–16, 18–22,
 23–4, 38, 40; School of Contemporary
 Dance founded by, 5, 399–400; on
 sculpture's relationship to dance, 150;
 "Seeking an American Art of the Dance"
 by, 198, 200–1, 254; stories and poems
 written by, 16, 19–20; as teacher, xii–xiii,
 42, 72, 80–4, 89–90, 97–8, 103, 104–5,
 128–9, 136, 173, 184–6, 262–4. *See also
 specific dances, people, and topics*

Graham, Mary ("Mimi") (sister), 5, 9, 10,
  11, 12, *12*, 14, 15, 337
Graham, William Henry (brother), 6, 11–12,
  12, 23, 337
Granville-Barker, Harley, 21, 119
Great Sacrifice, The (Roerich), 170
Greek architecture, 194
Greek myths and themes, 25, 31, 32, 39,
  46, 63, 232, 271, 311; Ariadne's tale,
  Graham's *Errand into the Maze* and, 373,
  376, 388; dithyrambs and, 249–50 (*see
  also Dithyrambic*); Hawkins's *Stephen
  Acrobat* and, 368; Hawkins's *The Strangler*
  and, 369, 373, 376; *Heretic* and, 136–7;
  Maenads, *Tragic Patterns* and, *277*,
  277–8; Medea myth and, 355–6, 372 (*see
  also Serpent Heart/Cave of the Heart*);
  Minotaur and Labyrinth, 311, 368, 373,
  388; Oedipus, 187, 281, 369, 373, 376,
  386, 396; powerful female characters'
  lamentation and, 151; riddle of the
  Sphinx, 369, 376; terra-cotta female
  statues, 150–1 (*see also* Tanagra figurines);
  Trois Gnossiennes and, 95–6, 105, 150, 203
Green, Morrris, 91
Green, Ray Burns, 308–9, 312, 313, 315
Greenwich Village Follies, The, 73–7, *75*, *76*,
  80, 81, 82, 91, 122, 178, 200, 207, 236, 271
Greenwood, Marion, *104*
Grieg, Edvard, 116
Grigg, Mrs. Merrill Moore, 23–4
Gris, Juan, 247
Gruenberg, Louis, 142, 163, 165, 166, 204
Grunn, Homer, 47, 193
Guggenheim Foundation Fellowship,
  235–6, 256
Guion, David Wendel, 207
Gustafson, Ester, 82

Hackett, Karleton, 69
Halsman, Philippe, *347*, *367*, *384*
Hammond, Natalie Hays, *272*, 272–3
Hansen, Paul, *129*, *188*, *221*, *298*, *299*
Hanson, Howard, 100, 107
Hapgood, Norman, 198–9
Happy Hypocrite, 212
d'Harcourt, Raoul and Marguerite, 117

Hardenbergh, Henry J., 103
Hare, Will, 366
Hargrave, Roy, 220
Harker, James W., 333
Harlem Renaissance, 140–1
Harlequinade: Pessimist and Optimist, *145*,
  146, 243, 254
Harris, Henry Birkhardt, 16, 26–7
Harris, Natalie, 311
Harrison, Jane Ellen, 136–7, 349, 464n
Harsányi, Tibor, 133
Harvard Society of Contemporary Art, 161,
  296
Hastings, Baird, 374
Hawkins, Erick (born Frederick Hawkins),
  xii, xvi, 291–5, *292*, 299, 300, 309–14,
  325, 349, 355, 364–74, 378, 400–3; "Ahab"
  project and, 369–71; *American Document*
  and, *312*, 312–13, 317, *317*, 318–20, 321;
  Appalachian Spring and, 254, 342, *342*,
  344, 345, 354; ballet background of,
  309–10, 331–2; in Ballet Caravan, 290,
  320, 356; choreographic projects of, 324–5,
  332–4, 339, 353, 366–71; on classicism,
  375; *Dark Meadow* and, 346, *347*, 352,
  353; *Deaths and Entrances* and, 336, 337,
  337, 338–9; *Every Soul Is a Circus* and,
  328, *329*, 368; existential discontent of,
  364–6, 386, 396–7; Graham Company's
  1950 European tour and, 389, 390, 394,
  395, *395*; Graham's first encounters with,
  290, 301, 310, 312–13, 356; Graham's
  marriage to, 379; Graham's relationship
  with, 313–14, 324–5, 339–40, 353–4,
  365–6, 371–3, 375, 386–8, 395–8, 401, 403;
  Graham's ruptures with, 371–3, 375, 376,
  395–8; as Graham's student, 311–12, 324–5,
  396; Harvard education of, 292–3, 294–5,
  365; haunted, ambivalent dreams of,
  364–5; Horst's relationship with Graham
  disparaged by, 378; *John Brown* and, 353,
  354, 366–8, 369, 375; Jung read by, 324,
  365; as King Lear, 339, 380, 384, *384*, 385,
  386–8; Kirstein's praise and support for,
  310, 311, 319–20, 321; literary interests
  of, 291; Martin's critical assessments of,
  367, 388; *Night Journey* and, 373; physical

presence of, 290, 313; *Primer for Action* by, 331–2; at School of American Ballet, 300, 309–10, 311, 364, 368; *Serpent Heart and*, 361, 363; *Show Piece* and, 310–11; *Stephen Acrobat* and, *367*, 368–9, 375, 394; *The Strangler* and, 369, 373, 376; as teacher, 331, 366, 396, 398; "What Is Modern Dance?" speech given by, 373–4

Haworth Parsonage, Yorkshire, England, 335

Hawthorne, Nathaniel, 282

Hays, Richard E., 183

Hayworth, Rita, 76

Helpern, Alice, 98

Henderson, Robert, 233, 235

Heretic, *132*, 133, 134–5, 136–8, 144, 150, 160, *188*, 199, 224, 228, 230, 274, 282, 306, 404; Horst's ideal of music and, 134–5; origin of title of, 136–7

Herodiade, 354

Heroic Dance, 192

Herridge, Frances, 376–7

Hija de Cólquide, La, 357–8

Hill, Martha, 106–7, *107*, 131, 144, 216, 255, 267, 313–14; American Dance Festival and, 375; Bennington School of the Dance and, 253–4, 274, 275, 282, 289, 325

Hindemith, Paul, 90, 131, 133, 144, 228, 275

Hinkson, Mary, 400

Hinman, Mary Wood, 42

L'Histoire du Soldat, 166, 174, 177

Hodes, Stuart, 342, 345, *367*, 368–9, 375, *387*, 388

Holm, Hanya, 244–5, *245*, 246, 253, 262, 286, 288, 301, 306, 325

Hone, William, 271

Honegger, Arthur, 146, 182. *See also Dance/ Revolt*

Hopi, 47, 279, 369

Horan, Robert, 337, 359

Horgan, Paul, 90, 99

Horizon magazine, 336

Horizons, 285, 287

Horosko, Marian, xvi

Horst, Betty ("Bessie"), 36, 40, 52, 53, 56, 74, 78, 308, 314

Horst, Louis, xii, xvi, 34–6, 37, 38, 39, 40, 43, 44, 52, 54, 61, 64, 65, 67, 70, 77, 89–90, 94, 102, 105, 106, 110, 137, 153, 177, 182, *202*, 224, 230, 246, 271, 278, 288, 293, 305, 306, 311, 336, 379, 390; American Dance Festival and, *378*, 378–9; *American Document* and, 308, 313; Ballet Intime tour and, 208–9; *Celebration* and, 280, 309; *Ceremonials* and, 252–3; *Chorus of Youth—Companions* and, 262–3; Copland's *Piano Variations* and, 249; Cornish School and, 184; Dance Composition course taught by, 127–8; *Dance Observer* and, *45*, 202–3, 255, 287, 374; Dance Repertory Theatre and, 141, 144–7, 225; death of, xvi; de Mille's music and, 209, 210; departure from Denishawn, 78–9, 85; Fonaroff's affair with, 314; *Frontier* and, 283; Graham's 1928 Little Theatre recitals and, 117, 118; Graham's 1929 Booth Theatre recitals and, 130–5; Graham's estrangement from, 378–9; Graham's New York debut and, 91–5, 98; Graham's romantic relationship with, 52, 53, 55–6, 74, 85, 95, 378; "Harvest Dirge" setting by, 86, 95; *Heretic* and, 134–5, 136; Hindemith compositions and, 275; hired by St. Denis, 34, 36; *Lamentation* and (1930 solo), 147, 149; *Lamentation* and (second work so titled), 277–8; Modern Dance Forms class taught by, 202–5; "The Musician Comments" essay by, 78–9, 203; Neighborhood Playhouse School and, 127–8, 183, 202, 203, 244; Nietzsche's writings and, 209, 278; *Panorama* and, 284; Perry-Mansfield School and, 202, *202*, 259–60; Pre-Classic Dance Forms class taught by, 127–8, 202; *Primitive Mysteries* and, 216, 217, 218, 220, 222; on relationship of music to dance, 78–9, 85, 285; *Scène Javanaise* and, 86, 99; Tamiris's music and, 140, 141, 142; theory of dance and, 109, 127–8, 134–5, 201, 202, 204–5; *Tragic Patterns* and, 277–8; traveling in Mexico with Graham, 257–9, *258*; traveling through New Mexico's pueblos with Graham, 192, 195, 196, 218, 239–41, 260, 279; Vienna sojourn of, 79, 85–7, 95

Horton, Lester, 122

Hound & Horn, 296, 297, 298, 316

Howe, George, 199

Howland, Olin, 177

Humphrey, Doris, *41*, 41–2, 115–17, 128, 139, *143*, 153, 177, 191, 230, 246, 288, 301, 305, 325, 375, 391, 404; Dance Repertory Theatre and, 141, 142–4, 211, 212–16, *215*, 225; in Denishawn Company, 41–2, 43, 49, 53, 64, 77, 115–16; fall and recovery technique of, 116, 213; school opened by, 118; *The Shakers* (originally titled *Dance of the Chosen*) and, 213–16, *215*, 225

Hurok, Sol, 69, 244, 246, 354

Ide, Letitia, 212

Iliad (Homer), 150–1

Immediate Tragedy, 192

Immigrant, 117, 144, 182

Incas, music of, 117

India, stories and themes related to, 18, 25, 26, 33, 39, 46, 54, 77, 83, 98, 106

Indians (indigenous to the Americas), 31, 47, 119, 255–6; Austin's writings on, 242, 243–4; Chávez's thoughts on national style in music connected to, 264; Crane's and Graham's shared goal of connecting to, 255–6; Graham on what she learned from, 197; Shawn on dances of, 192–3; Shawn's thoughts on national style in dance rooted in, 192–3. *See also* primitives, primitive sources; Pueblo peoples, pueblos

In the American Grain (Williams), 280–1, 309

In Time of Armament, 332–3

Isaacs, Edith J. R., 109–10, *110*, 153, 236, 335, 336

Isaacs, Lewis Montefiore, 110

Israel (Bloch), 118–19, 121, 122

Ito, Michio, 77, 82, 118, 122–7, *125*, 133, 156, 158, 166, 184, 262; as Graham's dance partner, 122, 313; Noguchi's *Michio Ito* and, *157*

Ivantzoff, Ivan, 176–7, 448n

Ives, Charles, 325

Jackson, William Henry, *239*

Java, dances and themes related to, 40, 50, 86, 99, 106, 211

Jazz Age, 58, 64

Jemez Pueblo, 170, 240, 279

Jewell, Edward Alden, 154

Jocasta story, 187, 373

John Brown, 353, 354, 366–8, 369, 375

Johnson, Alvin, 229, 236

Johnson, Evangeline Love Brewster, 173

Johnson, Hazel, 375

Johnson, Hunter, 336

Johnson, James, 274

Jones, Al, 91

Jones, Bill T., 404

Jones, Robert Edmond ("Bobby"), 163, 176, 198, 264, 335

Joyce, James, 89, 91, 120, 183, 350, 359, 368

Judith, *400*, 401

Judson, Arthur, 115, 169

Julnar of the Sea, 44, 50

Jung, C. G., 194, 323, 324, 349, 351, 365, 370, 397

jungle gym, *367*, 368

"Just Girls!" (Graham), 16, 19

Kahn, Adelaide (Mrs. Otto H. Kahn), 163, 174

Kahn, Otto H., 166

Kales, Arthur, *30*

Kandinsky, Wassily, 65–8, 88–9, 135, 175, 293, 302; "Dance Curves: On the Dances of Palucca" by, 88–9; *Improvisation No. 30 (Cannons)* by, 65–7, *66*, 68, 146, 326; "Sehen/Seeing" by, 68; *Sounds* by, 67–8, 428n

Kendall, Elizabeth, 71

Kikuchi, Yuriko. *See* Yuriko

King, Eleanor, 177, 211, 212, 216, 306

King, Mary Perry, 31

King Lear. See Eye of Anguish—The Purgatorial History of King Lear

Kinney, Troy and Margaret West, 93

Kirstein, Lincoln, 147, 161, 295–300, *296*, 320, 326, 337, 350, 374, 389; *American Document* praised by, 319–21; Balanchine brought to America by, 298–300; Ballet

Caravan and, 289–90; at first skeptical of Graham, 249, 297, 321; at Harvard, 296–7; Hawkins praised and supported by, 310, 311, 319–20, 321; *Hound & Horn* and, 296, 297, 298, 316

Kisselgoff, Anna, 218

Kitto, H. D. F., 190

Knighton, Marian, 324

Kochno, Boris, 298

Kodály, Zoltán, 117, 147, 203, 228

Kolb, Harold, 99

Koussevitzky, Serge, 165

Krein, Yulian, 134

Krenek, Ernst, 145–6

Kreutzberg, Harald, 209, 267, 269–70, 293, 294, *294*, 295, 299

Kreymborg, Alfred, 86, 95

Kriegsman, Alan ("Mike"), 400–1, 403–4

Kriegsman, Sali Ann, 400–1

Kruger, Alma, 273

Laban, Rudolf von, 86, 87, 187, 193, 244, 287, 400

Laguna Pueblo, 239–40, 260

Lamentation, 147–52, *148*, 182, 254, 274, 276, 287, 348, 381; Horst's second work entitled, 277–8

Land Be Bright, 333

Land of Journeys' Ending, The (Austin), 241, 243

Lanfer, Helen, 338

Lang, Pearl, 337, *337*, 342, 346, 352, 377, *377*, 387, *387*, 388, 394

Laskey, Charles, 211

Laughlin, Alice Denniston, *272*, 272–3

Lauterer, Arch, 284–5, 314, 336

Lawrence, D. H., 324

Lawrence, Pauline, 118, 142, 214

Lawton, Dorothy, 128, 236

League of Composers, 163, 165–6, 169, 174, 228–9, 235, 259, 295, 305

Lear. See Eye of Anguish—The Purgatorial History of King Lear

Lederman, Minna, 305

Le Gallienne, Eva, 103, 108, 198

Leigh, Robert Devore, 253–4

Leonard, Warren, 209–10

LeSueur, Eugene, 143

Letter to the World, xi, 332, 335, 336, 354, 394, *405*

Lewisohn, Alice, 127

Lewisohn, Irene, 119, 121–2, 127, 128, 139, 158, 235, 236

Lewisohn Stadium, Bronx, New York, 78, 230

Leyssac, Paul, 273

Liberty Tree, 332

Limón, José, 118, 187, 210–11, *211*, 213, 217–18, 288, 375, 404

Lind, Jenny, 326–7

Lindsay, Vachel, 325–7, 333

Lloyd, Margaret, 289, 337

Lloyd, Norman, 192, 284, 288

Loring, Eugene, 289, 290, *320*

Louppe, Laurence, 204

Loveman, Samuel, 255

Lucrece (Obey), 264, *265*, 266

Luening, Otto, 89–90, 236, 311, 313

Luhan, Mabel Dodge, 197, 242, 243, 265

Lynes, George Platt, *296*, *320*

Lyon, Annabelle, 289

Macdonald, Betty, 83–4, *84*, 90, 91, 93, *94*, 97, 98, 99, 102, 105, 133

MacDowell, Edward, 41, 146

Macfadden, Bernarr, 57, 107–8

MacLeish, Archibald, 263, 281

Maeterlinck, Maurice, *Sister Beatrice* by, 90, 91

Maeterlinck, Paul, 90, 99

Making of Americans, The (Stein), xiv

"Malagueña," *51*

Maleingreau, Paul de, 204

Mamoulian, Rouben, 80–1, *81*, 82–3, 90, 92, 99, 107, 121, 176

Manchester, England, Tanagra figurines at City Art Gallery in, 56, 96

Mann, Thomas, 339

Manning, Katharine, 213

Marchowsky, Marie, *129*, 280, 301–2, 311, 313, 319

Mariarden theatrical camp, near Peterborough, N.H., 74, 102, 103, 110

"Marionette Show, The," 97, 105

Marrow, Macklin, 207

Marsh, Lucile, III, 113

Marsh, Reginald, 73, 204

Martin, John, 91, 112–14, 117, 122, 131, 133, 146, 149, 152–3, 173–4, 210, 212, 230, 232, 236, 249, 251–2, 254, 269, 279, 288, 300, 328, 402; on *Ceremonials*, 253; on *Chronicle*, 305; on Dance Repertory Theatre's first season, 152–3; on de Mille's professional debut, 207–8; on *Every Soul Is a Circus*, 328; on *Eye of Anguish*, 388; on Graham Company's 1950 European tour, 390, 392; Hawkins critiqued by, 367, 388; incremental evolution and education of, 113–14; on Massine's role at the Roxy Theatre, 172; "The Modern Dance in America" by, 199; on *Panorama*, 285–6, 305; on *The Rite of Spring*, 181; on viewer's experience of dance, 136; Wigman admired by, 244, 245–6

Martinů, Bohuslav, 376

Maslow, Sophie, xvii, 217, 218, 251, 262, 277, 280, 311, 313, 317, *317*, 319, 328–9, 336, *337*, 375

Massine, Léonide, 171–4, *173*, 174, 177–8, 179, 181, 185, 233, 297

Mathis, Paul, 64

Maugham, W. Somerset, 265

May, Betty, 50, 54, 64, 65

May Day, 209

Mayer, Daniel, 53

Mazia, Marjorie, 311, 329, 342, *342*, 346, 352

McAlmon, Robert, 158–9

McBride, Robert, 163, 311

McCausland, Elizabeth, 286–7

McDonagh, Don, xvi–xvii, 8, 378

McGann, Grace Chatfield-Taylor, 40, 50

McGehee, Helen, xvii, 342, 377, 385, *387*

McLaverty, James, 341

McWilliams, Carey, 243

Meacham, Anne, 376

Medea: *Daughter of Colchis* scenario and, 357, 359. *See also* Serpent Heart/Cave of the Heart

Mehlman, Lily, 177, 180–1, 277

Mei Lanfang, 179

Melville, Herman, Hawkins's "Ahab" project and, 369–71

Mendelssohn, Félix, 105

Menotti, Gian Carlo, 358, 359, 373

Mercati, Countess (née Marie Manice), 174

Mercier, Jean, 186–7, 189

Merleau-Ponty, Maurice, 179

Metropolitan Museum of Art, New York: Degas's statuette of ballet child at, 207; marble relief of Medea at, 355; Tanagra figurines at, 96–7; terra-cotta statue of seated female at, *150*, 150–1

Mexican history and themes, 52–3, 193, 361; Aztecs and, 33, 47–8, *48*, 361; music for Hawkins's *The Strangler* and, 376. *See also* Xochitl

Mexico, Graham's travels in, 256, 257–9, *258*

Milhaud, Darius, 131, 308

Miller, Bethene, 187

Miller, Kenneth Hayes, *Casual Meeting* by, *130*

Mills, Charles Borromeo, 366

Mills College, Oakland, Calif., 20, 202, *211*, 237, 325, *402*, 403

Milton, Robert, 81–2

Minneapolis–St. Paul *Pioneer Press*, 72

Minor, Marcia, 316

Minotaur and Labyrinth, myth of, 311, 368, 373, 388

Miracle Plays, 271–4, *272*

Mirror Before Me/Herodiade, 275

mobiles, experimentation with, 285

modern dance, 107–9, 116; communicating experience by means of *action* as reason for, 321; emphasis on dance as theatre art and, 108–9; evolution of dance criticism and, 108–14; Graham's exhortation to "Know the land" and, 198; Graham's "The Future of the Dance" and, 323; Hawkins's speech at 1947 National Theatre Conference and, 373–4; mid-1920s dance boom, 108; modern painting and sculpture and, 204, 226; "moving from the inside out" and, 116; for ranks of "overdomesticated" women, 97–8;

useful applications for (early 1920s),
57–8; "*What makes dance modern?*"
question and, 108–9

*Modern Dance Forms in Relation to the
Other Modern Arts* (Horst and Russell),
202–5

*Modern Dance Magazine: A New Spirit in
Art and Life* (*MDM*), 57

"Modern Dancer's Primer for Action, A"
(Graham), 332

modern dance teachers, 1932 symposium
of, 253–4

modernism, 182–3, 249, 254; archaism
combined with, in *Miracle Plays*, 273,
274; Baudelaire on role of Greek ideal
in, 137; Gage's "Study in American
Modernism" and, 153; Graham's
combination of primitive suggestion
and, 254–5; Horst's *Modern Dance Forms*
and, 202–5; link between avant-garde
practices and dance and, 204

Modern Music, 165, 305

Moe, Henry Allen, 236

Moholy-Nagy, László, 88

Mompou, Federico, 203

Monroe, Harriet, 113, 124, 325

Monteux, Pierre, 167, 308

Moore, Edward, 69

Moore, Marianne, xv, 101, 136

Morgan, Agnes, 121

Morgan, Ann, 141

Morgan, Barbara, xi, *145*, 146, *148, 215, 245,
276, 312*, 314, *314*, 315, *315, 315, 317, 329*

Morgenthau, Rita Wallach, 127, 236

Morosco, Oliver, 126

Morris, Mark, 404

Moscow Art Theatre, 80, 113, 118, 199,
452n

Moselsio, Simon, 150

Mozart, Wolfgang Amadeus, 207, 289

Mozarteum Society, 140, *294*, 295

Mozartiana, 310

Munson, Gorham B., 230

Muray, Nickolas, *48, 51*

"Music and the Maid" (Graham), 19–20

*Music for the Theatre: Suite in Five Parts
for Small Orchestra* (originally entitled

*Incidental Music for an Imaginary
Drama*), 165–6

Music Visualizations, 64

mystery plays, 272

myth: Jung's psychology of, 324. *See also*
Greek myths and themes

National Anthem, The, 58

National Theatre Conference (1947), 373–4

Naumburg, Margaret, 164

Navajo, 359

Negro sources, 201, 309; Tamiris's *Negro
Spirituals* and, 140, 141, 142, 210

Neighborhood Playhouse, New York,
119–21, *120*, 126, 132, 158, 235, 335

Neighborhood Playhouse School of
Theatre, New York, 127–9, 132, 160, 183,
187, 199, 202, 203, 244, 281, 316, 335, 376;
Graham's classes at, 128–9; Horst's Dance
Composition course at, 127–8

Neumann, Natanya, 346, 376–7, 385, *387*

New Masses, 307–8

New Mexico: Graham and Hawkins's
wedding in, 379; Graham and Horst's
travels in, 218, 239–41, 260–2, 279;
Graham's visit with Wells in, 379, 380,
381. *See also* Pueblo peoples, pueblos

New Republic, 120, 224, 287

New School for Social Research, New York,
190, 229–33; Graham's sparring match
with Fokine at, 230–3

Newton, John, 21

New York Herald Tribune, 111–12, 142, 305,
338

New York Post, 234, 305

New York Times, 27–8, 53, 76, 109, 166, 199,
256, 300, 375; Martin hired as first dance
columnist for, 112–14. *See also* Martin,
John

New York World, 111

New York *World-Telegram*, 256–7

Nietzsche, Friedrich, 32, 52, 61–3, 71, 130,
132, 136, 178, 201, 209, 278, 351

Night in Japan, A, 18

Night Journey, 373, 375

Nijinsky, Vaslav, 39, 171, 173, 235

Noces, Les, 166, 174

Noguchi, Isamu, xii, 154–62, *158*, 204, 226, 247, 296, 376; *Appalachian Spring* and, 341–2; Brancusi visited in his atelier by, 158–9; bronze portrait heads of Graham by, 154, *155*, 161; *Chronicle* and, 302, 304; *Dark Meadow* and, 346, 350, 352; *Frontier* and, 283; *Michio Ito* by, *157*; *Serpent Heart* and, 361; *Stephen Acrobat* and, *367*, 368
Noh plays, 123–5, 126, 156
Nolde, Emil, 87
Nordoff, Paul, 204, 328, 382
North, Alex, 307
Novikoff, Laurent, 77

Obey, André, 264, 266
Ocko, Edna, 286
O'Donnell, May, *129*, 218, 262–3, 277, 280, 303, 307, 308, 309, 311, 313, 318, 346, 352, 355, 372, 391, 404; in *Appalachian Spring*, 309, 342, *342*; Graham Company debut of, 262–3
Oedipus myth, 187, 281, 369, 373, 386, 396; Hawkins's *The Strangler* and, 369, 373, 376; MacLeish's *Panic* and, 281
Of Pioneer Women, 308–9
O'Keeffe, Georgia, 102, 286, 296
Olive and Gold, The, 15, 19, 21, 22
Olson, Charles, 369–71
Olympic Games (Berlin, 1936), 287
Olympus Americanus (*A Twentieth-Century Ballet*), 210–11
On the Genealogy of Morals (Nietzsche), 130
On the Spiritual in Art (Kandinsky), 68
Orientalia, 65
Ornstein, Leo, 118, 163, 182
Osgood, Beth, 378
Oswald, Genevieve, xvi
Ouspensky, P. D., 46

Page, Ruth, 208, 247, 295
Painter of Modern Life, The (Baudelaire), 137
Palucca, Gret, 87, 88–9, 432n
Panorama, 284–6, 301, 302, 305
Pantages vaudeville circuit, 43, 49, 50, 183
Park, Rosemary, 375
Parker, H. T, 126, 144, 181, 234, 254
Francis W. Parker School, Chicago, 41–2

Pas d'Acier, Le, 172, 295
Pavlova, Anna, 53, 77, 82, 188, 206, 208, 231, 251, 295, 311
Peck, Esther, 121
Peking Opera, 179
Penitente, El, 197, 243, 332, 371, 375, 394
Penitentes, 195–7, 243, 291
Perry–Mansfield Performing Arts School and Camp, Steamboat Springs, Colo., 202, *202*, 259–60
Persichetti, Vincent, 382–5, 386–8
Philadelphia Orchestra, 166–7, 168, 169, 175, 259
Physical Culture, 57
Picasso, Pablo, xvi, 65, 160, 204, 326, 399
Pitot, Genevieve, 210
Poems of 1917, 118
Poetics of Contemporary Dance (Louppe), 204
Poetry: A Magazine of Verse, 113, 124, 325
Point and Line to Plane (Kandinsky), 67
Portrait—After Beltran-Masses, 97
Portrait of the Artist as a Young Man (Joyce), 368
Possell, George, 106
Poulenc, Francis, 134, 144
Pound, Ezra, xiv, 91, 123–5, 296, 335, 383
Powell, Lillian, 44
Pre-Classic Dance Forms (Horst), 127–8, 202
Prendergast, Elizabeth ("Lizzie," or "Sizzie"), 9, 11, 12, 14, 21
Primer of Modern Art, A (Cheney), 109, 203
Primitive Mysteries, 133, 160, 187, 188, 216–23, *217*, 221, 228, 230, 234, 237, *238*, 253, 254, 265, 274, 280, 294, 317, 402; description of, 220–3; Horst's score for, 216, 217, 222; public response to, 224–5; rehearsals for, 217–20; source of, 218
primitives, primitive sources, 47, 201, 203–4, 249, 251, 271, 376; Graham's combination of modernist technique and, 254–5; Graham's travels in Mexico and, 256–7. *See also* Greek myths and themes; Indians; Pueblo peoples, pueblos
Prokofiev, Sergei, 131, 144, 172, 295
Prunella, or, Love in a Dutch Garden (Housman and Granville-Barker), 21–2

Pueblo peoples, pueblos, 170, 184, 192–7,
   195, 217, *239*, 239–41, 279, 286, 312,
   359, 380, 397; architecture of, 193–4;
   Ceremonials and, 251; Corn Dance of,
   239–40, 244, 259, *260*, 260–2, 266,
   286–7; Penitentes and, 195–7, 243, 291;
   Primitive Mysteries and, 217, 218, 220,
   221; seasonal cycles and rituals of, 239–41;
   Shawn's adaptation of Eagle Dance of,
   193
Punch and the Judy, 332, 336, 353, 354
Purcell, Henry, 144, 211
Puritans, Puritanism, 214, 275, 282, 284,
   309; *American Document* and, 309,
   318–19; Graham's ancestry and, 357

Rachmaninoff, Sergei, 97
Radha, 18, 26, 98
Radio City Music Hall, New York, 266–8,
   269–71, 278
Ravel, Maurice, 95, 97, 117, 144, 204, 211
Ray, Lillian, 133, 177, 277
Reese, Kitty, 133–4, 177, *180*
Reinhardt, Aurelia, 325
Reis, Arthur M., 165
Reis, Claire, 163–6, *164*, 169, 170, 171, 172,
   174, 176, 178, 235, 259
Reutter, Hermann, 133
Revolt in the Arts (Sayler), 198–200
Rhapsodics—Song—Interlude—Dance, 224
Ribaupierre, André de, 106
Richman, Robert, 366, 368
Richter, Gisela, 97
Riddle of the Sphinx, or Human Origins, The
   (Róheim), 369
Riebeselle, Henry, 99
Riegger, Wallingford, xiii, 163, 223–4, 236,
   263, 279, 288, 301
Rite of Spring, The (*Le Sacre du Printemps*),
   133, 137, 167–74, *173*, 177–81, 193, 343;
   description of score, 169; fundraising
   effort for, 174; Graham cast in, 173–4,
   392; Graham's performance in, 179–81,
   182, 185, 254, 271, 277, 297, 320; Massine's
   1930 staging of, 171–4, *173*, 177–8, 179,
   180, 181, 185; 1913 performances of, 167,
   169, 170, 171; radio broadcast of, 169;

recording of, 168; rehearsals for, 177–9;
   restaged on Graham's own company,
   181, 403; Roerich's designs for, 170, 171,
   178, 179; source material for, 167, 170;
   Stokowski-led concert version of, 166–7;
   Stravinsky's score for, 167–9, 263, 446n
Rivera, Diego, 216, 259
Rivoire, Mary, 133, 177, 219, 251, 277
Roberts, W. Adolphe, 60–1
Robinson, Leonard, 366
Roerich, Nicholas, 163, 167, 170–1, 173, *173*,
   178, 179
Rogers, Frederick Rand, 332
Rohde, Erwin, 62
Róheim, Géza, 369, 376
Rosen, Max, *164*
Rosenfeld, Maurice, 69
Rosenthal, Jean, xii, 346
Rosing, Vladimir, 80, 89, 99
Ross, Bertram, 342, *387*, 388
Ross, Robert, 98, 99
Rothafel, Samuel Lionel "Roxy," 45–6, 93,
   172, 174, 266–7, 269, 270, *270*, 271
Rothschild, Bethsabée de, 389–90, 391–2,
   393, 394–5
Royal Cansinos, 76, 103
Roxy Theatre, New York, 172
Rudhyar, Dane, 137–8, 143–4, 163, 211, 212,
   213
Rudolph, Charlotte, 88, 432n
Rudy, Ethel, 133, 177
Ruggles, Carl, 146, 163
Rumely, Edward A., 156, 158, 159
Ryder, Mark, 346, 373, 388

Sabin, Evelyn, 83, *84*, 90, 91, 93, *94*, 97, 98,
   99, 102, 105, 133
*Sacre du Printemps, Le. See Rite of Spring,
   The*
St. Denis, Ruth, *17*, 24–8, *28*, 32–4, 40,
   44–5, 49, 53, 57, 64, 65, 68–9, 71, 74,
   77–8, 79, 83, 93, 109, 251, 321, 366; "An
   Essay on the Future of the Dance," 24;
   Graham's audition for, 37–8; Graham's
   first vision of, 16–18, 25; Horst hired
   by, 34, 36; Humphrey's audition for, 42;
   Humphrey's break from, 115–16; "music

St. Denis, Ruth *(continued)*
 visualizations" of, 42, 51; Shawn's first
 performance for, 32–3; Shawn's first
 vision of, 29; Shawn's marriage to, 33, 43,
 54–5. *See also* Denishawn Company
Ruth St. Denis School of Dancing and Its
 Related Arts, Los Angeles, 33–4
Salem Shore, 354, 375
Salutation (Chávez's *Prelude*), 263, 264, 274,
 462n
"Salutation" (Honegger), 182
Salutation to the Depths, 143–4, 211
Salut au Monde, 120
Salvin, Paul, 73
Salzedo, Carlos, 163, 235–6
San Ildefonso Pueblo, 193, 241, 380
San Juan Pueblo, 240
Santa Barbara High School, 15–16, *16*,
 18–22, 23
Santa Barbara News-Press, 40, 49–50
Santa Clara Pueblo, 241, 279
Santa Fe Railroad, 31
Santo Domingo Pueblo, 192, 240, 244, *260*,
 260–1, 279, 286
Sarabande, 192
Sarah Lawrence College, dance program at,
 202, 323–4
Sargeant, William, 217
Sargeant, Winthrop, 106, 150, 255
Sarnoff, David, 169
Satie, Erik, 96, 105, 125, 144, 150, 203
Savelli, Rosina, *94*, 102, 105, 133
Sayler, Oliver M., 198–200
Scarlet Letter (Hawthorne), 282
scene design: experimentation with mobiles
 in, 285; Jones on, 176. *See also* Noguchi,
 Isamu
Scène Javanaise, 86, 99
Schapira, François, *393*
Schoenberg, Arnold, 174–7, 204, 248
Schonberg, Bessie, 107, 130–1, 144, 146, 173,
 177, 180, 181, 218, 249
School of American Ballet, New York, 289,
 300, 309–10, 311, 364, 368
Schopenhauer, Arthur, 52, 60–1, 62, 403
Schuman, William, xii, 401
Schuman-Henk, Madame, 20

Schumann, Robert, *41*, 54, 93–4, 96
Scott, Cyril, 99, 140
Scriabin, Alexander, 93, 95, 117, 131, 144, 204
Scully, Vincent, 259
Sears, David, 338, 375
Second Annual Festival of Contemporary
 Music, 359
Secret of the Golden Flower, The, 324
"Seeking an American Art of the Dance"
 (Graham), 198, 200–1, 254
Selden, Elizabeth, 137, 146, 153, 225
"Serenata Morisca," 42, 50–1, 64, 72–3, 77
Serpent Heart/Cave of the Heart, 355–63,
 372, 477n; ambivalent critical responses
 to, 362–3; Barber enlisted to compose
 score for, 358–9; composition process
 for, 359–60; *Daughter of Colchis* scenario
 and, 357–8, 359; Graham's histrionic
 power as Medea in, *360*, 361–2; Medea
 story's meaning for Graham and, 355–6;
 Noguchi's set for, 361; titling and retitling
 of, 360–1, 372
Sessions, Roger, 251, 366
Seven Against Thebes (Aeschylus), 186–90,
 193
Shakers, The (originally titled *Dance of the
 Chosen*), 213–16, *215*, 225
Shakespeare, William, 23, 153, 266, 380, 385.
 See also Eye of Anguish—The Purgatorial
 History of King Lear
Shapero, Lillian, 133, 177, *180*, 251, 277, 306
Shawn, Allen, 174
Shawn, Ted, 28–33, *30*, 44, 46–55, *51*, 57,
 60, 64, 65, 71, 77–8, 79, 93, 95, 107, 119,
 266, 313, 352; Ellis's meeting with, 54–5;
 Graham's audition and, 37–8; Graham's
 estrangement from, 74–5, 115; Graham's
 squabble with, 53; Graham's training
 supervised by, 38, 42–3; Humphrey's
 break from, 115–16; St. Denis first seen
 by, 29; St. Denis's marriage to, 33, 43,
 54–5; *Xochitl* and, 47–50, 51. *See also*
 Denishawn Company
Shearer, Sybil, 289
Shelly, Mary Josephine, 275, 289, 325
Show Piece—Ballet Workout in One Act,
 310–11

Shubert Organization, 225–6
Shurr, Gertrude, 128–9, *129*, 134, 144, 188, 225, 251, 262, 267, 277, 280, 306, 308, 311
Siegel, Marcia, xvii
Simonson, Lee, 295
Sister Beatrice (Maeterlinck), 90, 91
Skinner, Joan, 385
Slagle, Kathleen, *129*
Smith, Cecil, 372
Sokolova, Lydia, 174, 177
Sokolow, Anna, 144, 177, 180, 251, 263, 277, 280, 306, 307, 404
Sontag, Susan, 399
Sophocles, 281, 291; *Elektra* and, 233–5
Soudeikine, Serge, 166
"Soul Call, The" (Graham), 20
Spanish Civil War, 301, 302
Sparshott, Francis, 71–2
Spencer, Frances, 291
Sphinx, Hawkins's *The Strangler* and, 369, 376
Spring Round (Rondo), 310
Spring Song, 209
Stage Alliance, 272–4
Stanislavsky, Konstantin, 80, 113, 199
Stapp, Philip, 328
Stebbins, Genevieve, 25, 119
Steel and Stone, 211
Steerage, 117, 228
Stein, Gertrude, xiv, 91, 229, 248, 286
Steloff, Ida Frances, 91–2
Stephen Acrobat, *367*, 368–9, 375, 394
"Steps in the Street", xii–xiii
Sterner, Marie, 154, *155*, 161
Stevens, Gould, 177
Stevens, Houseley, Jr., 316, 317
Stevens, Wallace, 382
Stewart, J. A., 350
Stodelle, Ernestine Henoch, 8, 202, 214
Stöhr, Richard, 85–6
Stokowski, Leopold, 166–9, 179, 236, 257, 259, 267; *Die glückliche Hand* and, 174–6; *The Rite of Spring* and, 167–9, 171, 173, *173*, 178, 181, 392
Stolcer-Slavenski, Josip, 117, 144, 182
Strangler: A Rite of Passage, The, 369, 373, 376

Strauss, Johann, II, 210
Strauss, Richard, 9, 122
Stravinsky, Igor, 120, 142, 166–9, 175, 208; League of Composers' presentations of, 165, 166, 169, 174; *Les Noces* and, 166, 174; *The Rite of Spring* and, 167–9, 171, 174, 263, 446n
Strawbridge, Edwin, 294–5
Strike, 117, 199
Strumlauf, Helen, 177
Stuart, Muriel, 311, 368
Studies for an Unfinished Dance, 402
Studio Club, New York, 157, 246–7
Study in Lacquer, A, 97
Sullivan, Ed, 267, 269
Sunami, Soichi, *94*, *112*, *132*, 199
Sweeney, James Johnson, 274
Symons, Arthur, 95, 106
Synchrony of Dance—Music—Light, 191–2

Tagore, Rabindranath, 40
Talhoff, Albert, 244
Tamiris (Helen Becker), 139–42, *140*, 152, 153, 209, 210–11, 225, 306
Tanagra figurines, *55*, 56, 71, 96–7; Duncan's response to, 71, 96; Graham's "Tanagra" and, 96–7, 105, 117, 131, 144, 153, 182–3
Tanowitz, Pam, 404
Tanqueray, Paul, *208*
Tanzstücke/Five Dance Pieces, 275
Taos Pueblo, 143, 192, 194, 195, *195*, 196, 217, 243, *381*, 397
Tapper, Bertha Fiering, 118, 164
Taylor, Laurette, 58
Taylor, Paul, 404
Taylor, Peggy, 64
Tennyson, Alfred, Lord, 9–10, 24, 291
Terry, Walter, 12, 74, 111, 152, 290, 328
Tertium Organum (Ouspensky), 46
Theatre Arts Monthly, 108–10, 111, 139, 153, 199, 243, 336, 372; de Mille's "The New Ballerina" in, 227–8; Gage's "Study in American Modernism" in, 153
Theatre Guild, 99, 176
Theatre Guild Magazine, 234–5, 255
Thomas, Dylan, 336
Thomson, Virgil, 165, 298, 305

Thoreau, Henry David, 24, 366
Three Negro Spirituals, 141
Three Poems of the East, 106
Thus Spake Zarathustra (Nietzsche), 62, 71
Tobey, Mark, 190
Toch, Ernest, 146, 204
Toltec history. *See Xochitl*
Tragic Patterns, 277–8
Trend: A Quarterly of the Seven Arts, 254–5
Trickster Coyote, 333
Trois Gnossiennes, 95–6, 105, 150, 203
Trowbridge, Charlotte, 336
Tryout, 209
Tugal, Pierre, 392–4
Turney, Matt, 342, 400
Twilight of the Idols, The (Nietzsche), 62
Two Chants: Futility and Ecstatic Song, 146
Two Primitive Canticles (Ave and Salve), 224
Tyler, Parker, 368

Unamuno, Miguel de, 404
Uncle Sam and His Best Girl, 333–4
Urban, Joseph, 229, 230
USA: A Quarterly Magazine of the American Scene, 199

Vale, Denise, xiii
Valse/Choreographic Waltz, La, 211
Valses Nobles et Sentimentales, 95, 117, 204
Vanity Fair, 59, 207, 237, 265
Van Tuyl, Marian, 203
Van Vechten, Carl, *265*
Varèse, Edgard, 144, 259
Varèse, Louise, 163–4
Variety, 251, 270
Vaughan, Clifford, 116, 117
Verlaine, Paul, 93, 203, 255
Villa-Lobos, Heitor, 224
Vision of the Aissoua, The, 79
Vision of the Apocalypse, 133–4

Wagner, Richard, 69, 90, 201
Walker, John, III, 161, 296
Wallack, Hazel, 29
Walton, Blanche Wetherill, 146, 236
Wanderer, The, 335

Warburg, Edward M. M. ("Eddie"), 161, 289, 296–7, 299, 300
Washer, Ben, 256–7
Wasserstrom, Sylvia, 133, 177
Water Study, 142, 147
Watkins, Mary F., III–12, 113, 142, 145, 146, 152, 179, 181, 225, 236, 269, 273–4
Watson, Douglas, 346
Wayman, Agnes, 253
Weidman, Charles, 117, 118, 122, 139, 141, 152, 177, 190, 206, 246, 288, 306, 313, 325, 352; background and training of, 49; Dance Repertory Theatre and, 142–4, 206, 211–12; as de Mille's partner, 209; in Denishawn Company, 49, 50, 51, 52, 54, 64, 65, 77, 115; as Humphrey's partner, 116, 128, 142–4, *143*, 153, 211
Weisshaus, Imre, 263, 276
Wells, Cady, 379, 380, *381*, 397
Weston, Edward, 237, 257
Weston, Hope, 22
Weston, Jessie Laidlaw, 349
Whitman, Walt, xv, 47, 55, 108, 120, 136, 146, 171, 210, 281, 324, 382
Whitney, Gertrude Vanderbilt, 246–7
Whitney, Robert, *400*
Whitney Museum, New York, 246; Studio Club precursor of, 157, 246–7
Wickes, Frances Gillespy, 397
Wigman, Mary, *87*, 87–8, 123, 209, 244–6
Mary Wigman School, New York, 244–5, 253, 262, 288
Wilckens, Friedrich, 293
Wilde, Oscar, 73–4, 123, 212, 296
Wilder, Austin, 333
Wilder, Thornton, 264; *Our Town*, 316, 472n
Wilderness Stair: Diversion of Angels, 376–8, *377*, 394
Wilhelm, Richard, 324
Williams, William Carlos, 280–1, 307, 309
Will to Power, The (Nietzsche), 62
Windsperger, Lothar, 203
Winter, Ethel, 342, 346, 352, 375
Wiseman, Joseph, 376
Wolf-Ferrari, Ermanno, 99
Wood, Grant, 309

Woolf, Virginia, 234, 349–50
World as Will and Idea, The (Schopenhauer), 61, 62
World War I, xiv, 23, 40, 43, 66, 73, 87, 101, 102, 111, 123, 137, 170, 244
World War II, 273, 302, 319, 358, 368, 390
Wright, Frank Lloyd, xv, 122, 198, 230
Wuthering Heights (Brontë), 336

Xochitl, 47–50, *48*, 51, 53, 54, 59, 65, 69, 70, 77, 174, 183, 193

Yankee Blue Breeches, 332, 375
Yanus, Judith, 388
Yasgour, Rose, 177
Yeats, William Butler, 120, 124, 125–6, 389
Yesenin, Sergey, 70

Young, Stark, 120, 216, 224, 225, 249, 263, 367–8
Yuriko (Yuriko Kikuchi in full), xvi, 218, 286, 342, *342*, 346, 352, 355, 372, 379, 388
Yurka, Blanche, *233*, 233–4, 235, 264, 278, 294

Zellmer, David, 336, 346
Zemach, Nahum, 118
Zia Pueblo, 240, 279
Ziegfeld, Florenz, 73
Ziegfeld Follies, 36, 60, 65, 73, 115
Zoeller, Mabel, 95
Zola, Émile, 8–9
Zorach, William, *The Spirit of the Dance* by, *270*, 270–1

ILLUSTRATION CREDITS

Page

xi   Barbara and Willard Morgan photographs and papers, Library Special Collections, Charles E. Young Research Library, UCLA

4   *Historic Pittsburgh* Collection, Detre Library and Archives, Heinz History Center, University of Pittsburgh

5   Courtesy of Martha Graham Resources, a division of the Martha Graham Center of Contemporary Dance, Inc.

6   Martha Graham Collection, Music Division, Library of Congress, box 256, folder 24

12   Martha Graham Collection, Music Division, Library of Congress, box 254, folder 40

14   Courtesy Santa Barbara Historical Museum, Gledhill Library Archive, Santa Barbara, CA

16   Courtesy Santa Barbara High School Alumni Association, Santa Barbara, CA

17   George Grantham Bain Collection, Prints and Photographs Division, Library of Congress

28   Digital positive from original gelatin silver negative. The George Eastman Museum Collection; and courtesy of the Estate of Alvin Langdon Coburn, The Universal Order, Godalming, Surrey, UK

30   Jerome Robbins Dance Division, The New York Public Library for the Performing Arts

37   Courtesy of John Cross, personal collection. *Los Angeles Herald*, April 27, 1915

41   Jerome Robbins Dance Division, The New York Public Library for the Performing Arts

45   Jerome Robbins Dance Division, The New York Public Library for the Performing Arts

48   Courtesy of Martha Graham Resources, a division of the Martha Graham Center of Contemporary Dance, Inc.; and © Nickolas Muray Photo Archives

51   Jerome Robbins Dance Division, The New York Public Library for the Performing Arts; and © Nickolas Muray Photo Archives

55   Collection of the Louvre Museum, Paris. Courtesy Bridgeman Images

59   Courtesy Louise Brooks Society Collection

66   Arthur Jerome Eddy Memorial Collection, Art Institute of Chicago

70   Lantern slide made from a negative. Genthe Photograph Collection, Prints and Photographs Division, Library of Congress

75   Martha Graham Collection, Performing Arts Databases, Library of Congress

76   George Grantham Bain Collection, Prints and Photographs Division, Library of Congress

81   Courtesy MPTV Images, Van Nuys, CA

84   Martha Graham Collection, Music Division, Library of Congress, box 254, folder 30

87   Jerome Robbins Dance Division, The New York Public Library for the Performing Arts

94   (top) Martha Graham Collection, Music Division, Library of Congress, box 308, folder 12; and courtesy Reiko Sunami Kopelson

94   (bottom) Collection of the Uffizi Gallery

104   Courtesy of the Estate of Marion Greenwood

107   Courtesy of Fort Hays State University, Hays, KS; and Elizabeth McPherson

110   Photographer unknown

112   Courtesy of Martha Graham Resources, a division of the Martha Graham Center of Contemporary Dance, Inc.; and courtesy Reiki Sunami Kopelson

120   George Grantham Bain Collection, Prints and Photographs Division, Library of Congress

125   Gelatin silver print, printed later. The George Eastman Museum Collection; and courtesy of the Estate of Alvin Langdon Coburn, The Universal Order, Godalming, Surrey, UK

129   Courtesy of Martha Graham Resources, a division of the Martha Graham Center of Contemporary Dance, Inc.; and © Paul Hansen

130   Private collection. Photograph © Christie's Images/Bridgeman Images

132   Courtesy of Martha Graham Resources, a division of the Martha Graham Center of Contemporary Dance, Inc.; and courtesy Reiko Sunami Kopelson

140   *The New York Times,* April 7, 1929

143   Jerome Robbins Dance Division, The New York Public Library for the Performing Arts

145   (top and bottom) Barbara and Willard Morgan photographs and papers, Library Special Collections, Charles E. Young Research Library, UCLA

148   Barbara and Willard Morgan photographs and papers, Library Special Collections, Charles E. Young Research Library, UCLA

151   The Metropolitan Museum of Art, Fletcher Fund, 1934. Accession 34.11.1

155   © The Isamu Noguchi Foundation and Garden Museum, New York/Artists Rights Society [ARS]

155   © The Isamu Noguchi Foundation and Garden Museum, New York/Artists Rights Society [ARS]

157   © The Isamu Noguchi Foundation and Garden Museum, New York/Artists Rights Society [ARS]

158   © The Isamu Noguchi Foundation and Garden Museum, New York/Artists Rights Society [ARS]

160   © The Isamu Noguchi Foundation and Garden Museum, New York/Artists Rights Society [ARS]

164   Collection of Hilda Reis Bijur, from Carol J. Oja, *Women Patrons and Crusaders for Modernist Music,* p. 247, University of California E-Books Collection, 1982–2004

165   Music Division, The New York Public Library for the Performing Arts

173   "Top Notes," *New York Telegram,* April 5, 1930

180   Gelatin silver print. National Portrait Gallery, Smithsonian Institution, NPG 97.110

184   Cornish School Archives, University of Washington Library, Special Collections, Seattle, WA

188   Courtesy Casey Villard, personal collection; and © Paul Hansen

191   Henry Cowell Papers, Music Division, The New York Public Library

Note: The Martha Graham Dance Company Collection was acquired by the Jerome Robbins Dance Division of the New York Public Library in 2020. It is currently being processed, and, upon completion of that work, will be available to all members of the public free of charge. The Graham Company holds a digitized version of the entire collection, available for public access through Martha Graham Resources, and retains all intellectual property rights to the material.

The Isamu Noguchi Foundation and Garden Museum Archives. Excerpts from Isamu Nogu-chi Guggenheim Fellowship Application, MS_COR_316_001, January 1, 1927; and Nogu-chi ALS to Ailes Gilmour, MS_COR_404_011, December 28, 1930.

Oral History Archives at Columbia, Rare Book and Manuscript Library, Columbia Uni-versity in the City of New York. The Bennington Summer School of the Dance Project: Excerpts from Reminiscences of Ray Green (March 11, 1979); Barbara Brooks Morgan and Martha Hill (December 17, 1978); and Francis Fergusson (February 12, 1979). Excerpts from Reminiscences of Henry Cowell (1963, part 3, pp.102–109).

Harvard University Archives. Excerpts from Erick Hawkins college application and under-graduate records, ca. 1926–1933.

Center for Oral History Research, University of California, Los Angeles. John Joseph Mar-tin, interviewed by Donald J. Schippers, 1965. https://oralhistory.library.ucla.edu/catalog /21198-zz0008zn5z

Checklist for Opening Exhibition—Part 1 of the Permanent Collection (Painting and Sculp-ture), 1931, Box 1, Folder 1, Whitney Museum of American Art Exhibition Records, Main Branch Exhibition Records, Frances Mulhall Achilles Library and Archives, Whitney Museum of American Art, New York, N.Y.

A NOTE ON THE TYPE

This book was set in Adobe Garamond. Designed for the Adobe Corporation by Robert Slimbach, the fonts are based on types first cut by Claude Garamond (c. 1480–1561). Garamond was a pupil of Geoffroy Tory and is believed to have followed the Venetian models, although he introduced a number of important differences, and it is to him that we owe the letter we now know as "old style." He gave to his letters a certain elegance and feeling of movement that won their creator an immediate reputation and the patronage of Francis I of France.

Composed by North Market Street Graphics, Lancaster, Pennsylvania
Printed and bound by Berryville Graphics, Berryville, Virginia
Designed by Maggie Hinders